T0016600

ULTIMATE GUIDE SERIES

ULTIMATE BIBLE DICTIONARY

BRENTWOOD TENNESSEE

Ultimate Bible Dictionary

ISBN: 978-1-5359-3471-8

Formerly published as and updated from the *Holman QuickSource Guide to Understanding the Bible* (copyright © 2005).

Typesetting and design by 2/K DENMARK, Højbjerg, Denmark

Dewey Decimal Classification: 220.3 Subject Heading: BIBLE / DICTIONARIES

Printed in China
8 9 10 11 12 • 27 26 25 24 23
RRD

CONTENTS

Editorial Forward IV

A 1
B 39
C 65
D 92
E 106
F 133
G 151
H 175
I 208
J 225
K 257
L 265
M 283
N 314
O 331
PQ 339
R 378
S 397
T 436
UV 465
W 474
XYZ 490

Art Credits 504

EDITORIAL FOREWORD

Over two hundred years ago, Voltaire predicted that the Bible would pass from the scene within a generation and become just a historical relic. Yet as late as March 2004, Tom Brokaw reported on *NBC Nightly News* that 40 percent of Americans read the Bible once a day.

The staying power of the Bible is phenomenal. It's amazing that a collection of 66 books, written over a period of 1,500 years by 40 persons from 40 different generations, continues to be the best seller it is.

Mortimer Adler and Charles Van Doren claimed that in Western civilization the Bible has not only been the most widely read book but the most carefully read book. It has also been the most carefully preserved and transmitted book in history. Bernard Ramm wrote,

> Jews preserved it as no other manuscript has ever been preserved. With their massora . . . they kept tabs on every letter, syllable, word and paragraph. They had special classes of men within their culture whose sole duty was to preserve and transmit these documents with practically perfect fidelity—scribes, lawyers, massoretes. Who ever counted the letters and syllables and words of Plato or Aristotle? Cicero or Seneca? (Bernard Ramm, *Protestant Christian Evidences*, Chicago: Moody Press, 1957).

The Bible is a life-changing book. It is designed by its Author to transform both individuals and whole cultures—and it has. Even those who deny the Bible's divine authority and complete truthfulness benefit from living in a civilization whose most desirable qualities have been shaped by the Bible.

The same great care is called for in reading and understanding the Bible as has been exercised in its preservation and transmission. As we grow in our understanding of the background out of which the Bible comes, so we will grow in our comprehension of what the Bible says. To this end, Holman is pleased to make available this highly portable, pocket Bible dictionary that can slip into a pocket, briefcase, purse, or backpack. Worlds of information are available in other volumes. But for starters, for those who are looking for succinct background information in a handy format, *the Ultimate Bible Dictionary* will be a perfect tool.

Holman Bible Publishers

ULTIMATE BIBLE DICTIONARY

The Abana River (modern Barad River) flows through the country of Syria.

AARON Moses's brother; Israel's first high priest. His parents Amram and Jochebed were from the tribe of Levi, Israel's tribe of priests (Exod. 6:16-26). Miriam was his sister.

AARON'S ROD Aaron used a rod to demonstrate to the pharaoh that the God of the Hebrews was Lord. It became a snake when cast down (Exod. 7:8-13) and brought about the first three plagues (Exod. 7:19-20; 8:5-7,16-19). This rod was the same one used to strike the rocks at Horeb and Kadesh to bring forth water (Exod. 17:1-7; Num. 20:7-11).

ABANA or **ABANAH** (NASB) River in Syria. In his anger, Naaman wanted to wash here rather than in the dirty Jordan (2 Kgs. 5:12).

ABBA Aramaic word for "father" used by Jesus to speak of his own intimate relationship with God, a relationship that others can enter through faith.

ABEDNEGO In Dan. 1:7 the Babylonian name given to Azariah, one of the three Hebrew youths conscripted along with Daniel to serve in the king's court. God delivered them from the fiery furnace (Dan. 2:48–3:30).

ABEL Though best known as the name of the second son of Adam and Eve, the word *abel* also occurs frequently meaning "vanity, breath, or vapor." See *Ecclesiastes, Book of.* Perhaps as a personal name, Abel alludes to the shortness of life. Such was the case with Abel (Gen. 4:8). Having offered "by faith ... a better sacrifice than Cain" (Heb. 11:4 CSB), he was murdered by Cain. Why Abel's sacrifice as a keeper of flocks was better than Cain's, whose sacrifice came from harvested fruits, is not directly stated in Gen. 4:4.

ABIATHAR Personal name meaning "father of abundance." The son of Ahimelech and the eleventh high priest in succession from Aaron through the line of Eli. He survived the slaughter of the priests at Nob and fled to David, hiding in the cave of Adullam from King Saul (1 Sam. 22). Having escaped with the ephod, Abiathar became the high priest and chief counselor for David (1 Sam. 23:6-12; 30:7).

ABIB Month of the exodus deliverance from Egypt (Exod. 13:4) and thus of the Passover festival (Exod. 23:15; 34:18; Deut. 16:1).

ABIGAIL Personal name meaning "my father rejoiced." **1.** Wife of David after being wife of Nabal. She was praised for wisdom in contrast to Nabal, her arrogant and overbearing husband, who was a significant landowner and successful shepherd. **2.** Sister of David and the mother of Amasa (1 Chron. 2:16-17), married to Jether, an Ishmaelite (also called Ithra). Amasa, her son, was at one time the commander of the army rallied by rebellious Absalom against his father David (2 Sam. 17:25) and later commander of David's army (2 Sam. 19:13).

ABIHU Personal name meaning "my father is he." The second son of Aaron; one of Israel's first priests (Exod. 6:23; 28:1). He saw God along with Moses, Aaron, his brother, and 70 elders (Exod. 24:9-10). He and his brother Nadab offered "strange fire" before God (Lev. 10:1-22), resulting in judgment. God's fire consumed them.

ABILENE Small mountainous region ruled by the tetrarch Lysanias at the time that John the Baptist began his public ministry

(Luke 3:2-3). Abilene was located about 18 miles northwest of Damascus in the Anti-Lebanon mountain range. Its capital was Abila.

ABIMELECH Personal name meaning "my father is king." **1.** King of Gerar, who took Sarah for himself, thinking she was Abraham's sister rather than his wife (Gen. 20). He restored her to Abraham after a nighttime dream of God. **2.** Probably the same as 1., a king who disputed the ownership of a well at Beer-sheba with Abraham and then made a covenant of peace with him (Gen. 21:22-34). **3.** King of Philistines at Gerar related to or identical with 1. Isaac lived under his protection and fearfully passed Rebekah, his wife, off as his sister. Abimelech scolded Isaac and warned his people not to touch Rebekah. A dispute over water wells led to Isaac's leaving but finally to a treaty of peace (Gen. 26) at Beer-sheba. **4.** Son of Gideon, the judge of Israel (Judg. 8:31). **5.** Priest under David with Zadok (1 Chron. 18:16), but correct reading of text here is probably Ahimelech as in 2 Sam. 8:17. **6.** Person mentioned in title of Ps. 34, which apparently refers to 1 Sam. 21:10-15, where Achish is David's opponent. Abimelech may have been an official title for Philistine kings.

ABINADAB Personal name meaning "my father is generous." **1.** Resident of Kirjath-jearim whose house was the resting place of the ark of the covenant for 20 years after the Philistines returned it. His son Eleazar served as priest (1 Sam. 7:1-2). **2.** Son of Jesse passed over when David was selected as king (1 Sam. 16:8; 17:13). **3.** Son of King Saul killed by Philistines in battle of Mount Gilboa (1 Sam. 31:2). **4.** Solomon's official and son-in-law over Dor, the Mediterranean seaport below Mount Carmel, was the Son of Abinadab or Ben-abinadab (1 Kgs. 4:11).

ABIRAM Personal name meaning "my father is exalted." **1.** Leader of rebellion against Moses and Aaron, seeking priestly authority. He died when God caused the earth to open and swallow the rebels (Num. 16; 26:9-11). **2.** Son of Hiel sacrificed in foundation of rebuilt Jericho, fulfilling Joshua's warning (1 Kgs. 16:34).

ABISHAG Personal name meaning "my father strayed" or "is a wanderer." A young virgin or "maiden" (RSV) brought to David's bed in his last days to keep him warm (1 Kgs. 1:1-4). They had no sexual relations, but Solomon considered her David's wife when his brother Adonijah asked to marry her after David's death (1 Kgs. 2:17).

ABISHAI Personal name meaning "father exists." Son of David's sister Zeruiah and brother of Asahel and Joab, David's general. One of David's 30 elite warriors (1 Sam. 26:6; 1 Chron. 2:15-16).

ABISHALOM Personal name meaning "my father is peace." Another spelling for Absalom (1 Kgs. 15:2,10). See *Absalom*.

ABLUTIONS Ceremonial washings with water to make oneself pure before worship. The practice of ablutions is one background for NT baptism. The Hebrew term *rachats* is the everyday word for washing with water, rinsing, or bathing (Gen. 18:4; Exod. 2:5; Ruth 3:3). The Greek word *louein* is similar (Acts 9:37; 16:33; 2 Pet. 2:22).

ABNER Personal name meaning "father is a lamp." The chief military officer for King Saul and Saul's uncle (1 Sam. 14:50). At Saul's death, he supported Ish-bosheth, Saul's son (2 Sam. 2:8), until Ish-bosheth accused him of treason for taking one of Saul's concubines (2 Sam. 3:7-8). Abner transferred loyalty to David. Joab, David's general, went into a jealous rage when David welcomed Abner. Joab then killed Abner, who was buried in Hebron (2 Sam. 3). See 1 Sam. 17:55-58; 20:25; 26:5,14-15.

ABOMINATION, ABOMINATION OF DESOLATION That which is detestable to God and is particularly related to idolatry. "Abomination of desolation" is a special term in the book of Daniel and in these NT references: Matt. 24:15; Mark 13:14.

ABRAHAM Personal name meaning "father of a multitude." The first Hebrew patriarch, he became known as the prime example of faith. He was the son of Terah, a descendant of Noah's son Shem (Gen. 11:27). His childhood

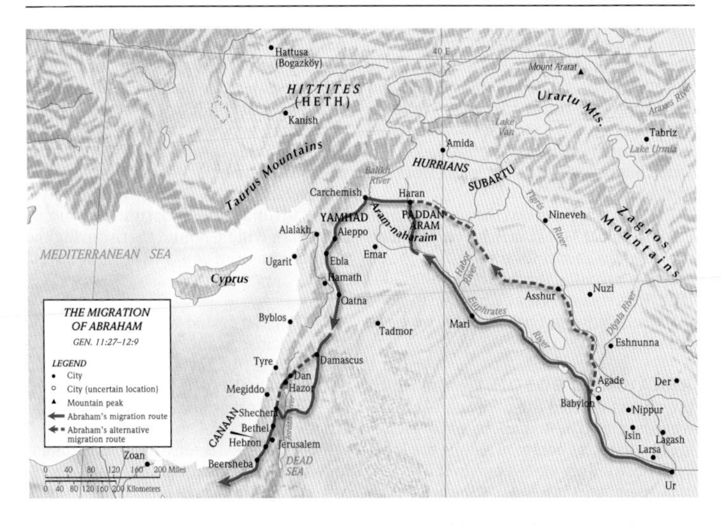

was spent in Ur of the Chaldees, a prominent Sumerian city. He was known at the beginning as "Abram" ("father is exalted"), but this was changed subsequently to "Abraham" ("father of a multitude," Gen. 17:5).

Terah, his father, moved to Haran with the family (Gen. 11:31) and after some years died there. God called Abram to migrate to Canaan, assuring him that he would father a vast nation. At different times he lived in Shechem, Bethel, Hebron, and Beer-sheba. His wife Sarai's beauty attracted the pharaoh when they moved to Egypt during a famine (Gen. 12:10), but God intervened to save her. The trouble arose partly because Abram had claimed her as his sister rather than his wife, and in fact she was his half sister (Gen. 20:12). After returning to Palestine, Abram received further covenantal assurances from God (Gen. 15). He decided he could produce offspring by taking Sarai's handmaid Hagar as a concubine. Though the union produced a son, Ishmael, he was not destined to become Abram's promised heir. Even after another covenantal assurance (Gen. 17:1-21) in which the rite of circumcision was made a covenantal sign, Abram and Sarai still questioned God's promise of an heir.

Then Sarai, whose name had been changed to Sarah ("princess"), had her long-promised son, Isaac ("laughter"), when Abraham was 100 years old. Ishmael's presence caused trouble in the family, and he was expelled with his mother Hagar to the wilderness of Paran. Abraham's faith and obedience were tested by God in Moriah when he was commanded to sacrifice Isaac. God provided an alternative sacrifice, however, saving the boy's life. As a reward for Abraham's faithfulness, God renewed the covenant promises of great blessing and the growth of a mighty nation to father and son.

Subsequently, Sarah died and was buried in the cave of Machpelah (Gen. 23:19), after which Abraham sought a bride for Isaac. A woman named Rebekah was obtained from Abraham's relatives in Mesopotamia, and Isaac married her (Gen. 24:67). In old age Abraham remarried and had further children, finally dying after 175 years. Abraham recognized God as the almighty Lord of all and the author of a covenant by which the Hebrews would become a mighty nation. God himself was known subsequently as the God of Abraham (Exod. 3:6). Through him God had revealed God's plan for human salvation (Exod. 2:24). The promises to Abraham became assurance for future generations (Exod. 32:13; 33:1). Abraham became known as "God's friend forever" (2 Chron. 20:7).

John the Baptist and Paul showed that descent from Abraham did not guarantee salvation (Matt. 3:9; Rom. 9). Indeed, foreigners would join Abraham in the kingdom (Matt. 8:11; cp. Luke 16:23-30). Jesus invited lost sons of Abraham to salvation (Luke 19:9). True children of Abraham do the works of Abraham (John 8:39).

For Paul, Abraham was the great example of faith (Rom. 4; Gal. 3). In Hebrews Abraham provided the model for tithing (Heb. 7) and played a prominent role in the roll call of faith (Heb. 11). James used Abraham to show that justification by faith is proved in works (James 2:21-24).

ABRAHAM'S BOSOM Place to which the angels carried the poor man Lazarus when he died. The Roman custom of reclining at meals was common among the Jews. Such positioning placed one in the bosom of the neighboring person. To be next to the host, that is to recline in the bosom of the host, was considered the highest honor. Lazarus was comforted after death by being given the place of closest fellowship with the father of the whole Hebrew nation (Luke 16:22-23). See *Heaven.*

ABRAM Personal name meaning "father is exalted." The name of Abraham ("father of a multitude") in Gen. 11:26–17:4. See *Abraham.*

ABSALOM Personal name meaning "father of peace." Third son of King David, who rebelled against his father and was murdered by Joab, David's commander (2 Sam. 3:3; 13–19). See *Abishalom.*

ABYSS Transliteration of Greek word *abussos,* literally meaning "without bottom." KJV translates "the deep" or "bottomless" pit. CSB, NASB, NIV, RSV use "abyss" to refer to the dark abode of the dead (Rom. 10:7). Abaddon rules the abyss (Rev. 9:11), from which will come the beast of the end time of Revelation (11:7). The beast of the abyss faces ultimate destruction (Rev. 17:8), and Satan will be bound there during the millennium (Rev. 20:1-3). See *Hades; Hell; Sheol.*

ACACIA Hardwood with a beautiful fine grain or close grain, which darkens as it ages. Insects find the taste of acacia wood distasteful, and its density makes it difficult for water or other decaying agents to penetrate.

Moses received the instructions for building the tabernacle on Mount Sinai (Exod. 25–35), in the Arabian Desert (Gal. 4:25) where acacia is among the larger of the few timber species to be found. Items constructed for the tabernacle of acacia (shittim) wood include: the ark of the covenant and its poles, the table of showbread and its poles, the brazen altar and its poles, the incense altar and its poles, and all the poles for the hanging of the curtains and the supports (Exod. 36:20,31,36; 37; 38).

ACCO or **ACCHO** (KJV) Place-name for famous Mediterranean seaport north of Mount Carmel. Territory was assigned to tribe of Asher, but they could not conquer it (Judg. 1:31). The Greeks renamed Acco, Ptolemaïs.

So-called Tomb of Absalom in the Kidron Valley in Jerusalem

Port of Acco from the south

ACCOUNTABILITY, AGE OF Age at which God holds children accountable for their sins. When persons come to this point, they face the inevitability of divine judgment if they fail to repent and believe the gospel.

ACCURSED Translation of Hebrew *cherem*, a technical term in warfare for items captured from the enemy and devoted to God. Paul used a technical Greek term, *anathema*, to call for persons to be put under a holy ban or be accursed (Rom. 9:3; 1 Cor. 12:3; Gal. 1:8-9; cp. 1 Cor. 16:22). Paul used the term in the sense of the Hebrew *cherem*. See *Anathema; Blessing and Cursing*.

ACCUSER Legal term describing a person who claims another is guilty of a crime or a moral offense. The Hebrew word for "accuser" is *Satan* (cp. Ps. 109:6 in various translations). See *Satan*.

ACELDAMA or **AKELDAMA** (KJV) Judas Iscariot purchased this field where he killed himself (Acts 1:19). The name is Aramaic and means "field of blood."

ACHAIA Roman province that consisted roughly of the southern half of ancient Greece, including the Peloponnesus. Major cities in Achaia included Sparta, Athens, and Corinth, which was the administrative center. Paul preached successfully in the province (Acts 18:27-28).

ACHAN or **ACHAR** (1 Chron. 2:7). In Josh. 7:1, a Judahite whose theft of a portion of the spoil from Jericho brought divine displeasure and military defeat on the Israelite army.

ACHBOR Personal name meaning "mouse." **1.** Father of king in Edom (Gen. 36:38). **2.** Man that King Josiah commissioned to ask God the meaning of the book of the law found in the temple (2 Kgs. 22:12-14). **3.** Father of Elnathan, whom Jehoiakim sent to bring back the prophet Uriah from Egypt in order to execute him (Jer. 26:22; cp. 36:12).

ACHISH Philistine personal name. **1.** King of Gath, a Philistine city, to whom David fled in fear of Saul (1 Sam. 21:10). **2.** King of Gath to whom Shimei went to retrieve his servants but in so doing violated his agreement with Solomon and lost his life (1 Kgs. 2:36-46).

ACHOR Place-name meaning "trouble, affliction," or "taboo." The valley in which Achan and his household were stoned to death (Josh. 7:24-26). Later it formed part of the border of Judah. It is the subject of prophetic promises in Isa. 65:10 and Hos. 2:15. See *Joshua*.

ACHSA or **ACHSAH** (CSB, NASB, RSV, TEV) or **ACSAH** (NIV) Personal name meaning "bangle" or "ankle ornament." Daughter of Caleb offered as wife to a man who conquered Kirjath-sepher (Josh. 15:16).

ACRE Translation of Hebrew *tsemed*, literally a "team" of oxen. As a measure of land, it refers to the land a team can plow in one day (1 Sam. 14:14; Isa. 5:10).

ACROSTIC Literary device by which each section of a literary work begins with the succeeding letter of the alphabet. The acrostic style helped people memorize the poem and expressed completeness of subject matter from A to Z.

ACTS OF THE APOSTLES Fifth book of the NT tracing growth of the early church. The most significant help in discovering the author of Acts is simply recognizing this book's relationship to the Gospel of Luke: both books begin with a greeting to a man named Theophilus ("friend of God"); Acts' greeting to Theophilus refers to a previous writing; the end of Luke intentionally overlaps with the beginning of Acts to provide continuity between the two volumes; and the author's writing style, vocabulary, and attention to specific themes remain constant throughout both books.

ADAM Place-name of city near Jordan River, where waters of Jordan heaped up so Israel could cross over to conquer the land (Josh. 3:16). Its location is probably Tel ed-Damieh near the Jabbok River.

ADAM AND EVE First man and woman created by God from whom all other people are descended. They introduced sin into human experience. In its most common occurrence, the word *'adam* refers to mankind in general. It has this use in Gen. 1:26-27, where it includes both male and female, those who were created in the image of God. It is also used in referring to a specific man where it occurs with the Hebrew definite article (Gen. 4:1).

In the NT, Adam is used as a proper name, clearly referring to our ancestral parents. Jesus's genealogy is traced back to Adam (Luke 3:38). However, the most important NT usage treats Jesus as a second Adam (1 Cor. 15:45), where the word is used as a symbol. Furthermore, Paul in a similar manner treats Adam as a type of Christ (Rom. 5:14). As the "first Adam" brought death into the world, the "second Adam" brought life and righteousness (Rom. 5:15-19).

ADAR Twelfth month of Jewish calendar after the exile, including parts of February and March. Time of Festival of Purim established in Esther (9:21).

ADMAH Place-name meaning "red soil." City connected with Sodom and Gomorrah as border of Canaanite territory (Gen. 10:19).

ADMINISTRATION Spiritual gift that God gives to some members to build up the church (1 Cor. 12:28 NASB, NIV, RSV; CSB "administrating"), called "governments" in KJV. The Greek word *kubernesis* occurs only here in the Greek NT. It describes the ability to lead or hold a position of leadership.

ADONIJAH Personal name meaning "Yah is Lord." **1.** Fourth son of David. His mother's name was Haggith (2 Sam. 3:4). **2.** Levite that Jehoshaphat sent to teach the people of Judah the book of the law (2 Chron. 8). **3.** Leader of the Jews after the exile who signed Nehemiah's covenant to obey God's law (Neh. 10:16).

ADONIKAM Personal name meaning "the Lord has arisen."

ADONIRAM Personal name meaning "the Lord is exalted." Officer in charge of the work gangs Solomon conscripted from Israel (1 Kgs. 4:6; 5:14).

ADONIS God of vegetation and fertility with Syrian name meaning "lord." Worshiped in Greece and Syria.

ADONI-ZEDEK Personal name meaning "the Lord is righteous" or "the god Zedek is lord." King of Jerusalem who gathered coalition of Canaanite kings to fight Gibeon after Joshua made a peace treaty with Gibeon (Josh. 10).

ADOPTION Legal process whereby one person receives another into his family and confers upon that person familial privileges and advantages. The "adopter" assumes parental responsibility for the "adoptee." The "adoptee" is thereby considered an actual child, becoming the beneficiary of all the rights, privileges, and responsibilities afforded to all the children of the family.

References to adoption in the OT are rare. Adoption is an action of the Father (Gal. 4:6; Rom. 8:15) and is based on the love of the Father (Eph. 1:5; 1 John 3:1). The basis of this activity of God is the atoning work of Jesus Christ (Gal. 3:26). Adoption involves peacemaking (Matt. 5:9) and compels the believer to become Christlike (1 John 3:2). As an expression of the familial relationship, God as Father disciplines his children (Heb. 12:5-11). Believers are to regard all those who have come to Christ by grace through faith as members of God's family (1 Tim. 5:1-2). See *Regeneration; Salvation.*

ADRAMYTTIUM or **ADRAMYTIAN** (NASB) Place-name of a seaport on the northwest coast of modern Turkey in the Roman province of Asia. Paul used a ship whose home port was Adramyttium to make the first leg of his journey from Caesarea to Italy to appeal his case to Caesar (Acts 27:2).

ADRIA or **ADRIATIC SEA** (NASB, NIV) During Paul's time, the designated body of water between Crete and Sicily where Paul's ship was battered by gale force winds and resultant high waves for 14 days as he sailed toward Rome to appeal his case to Caesar (Acts 27:27). Later the Adriatic Sea was extended to cover the waters between Greece and Italy.

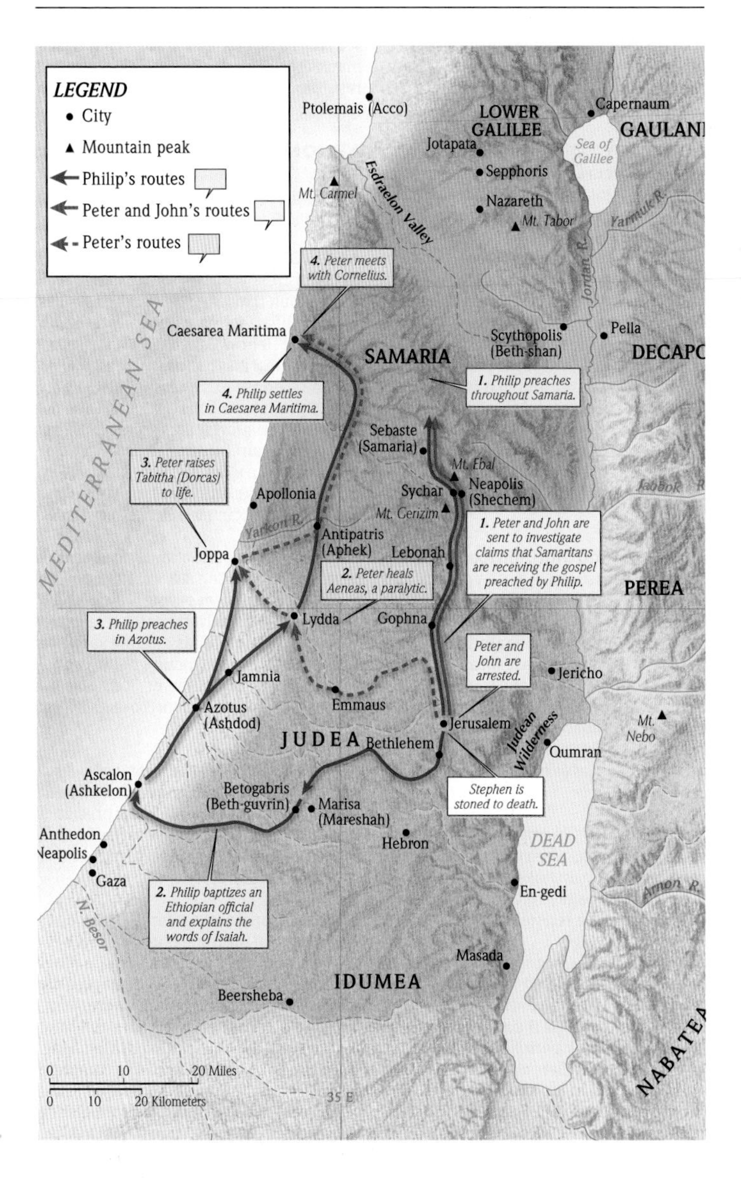

LEGEND
City
Mountain peak
Philip's routes
Peter and John's routes
Peter's routes
Ptolemais (Acco)
LOWER GALILEE
Capernaum
GAULANI
Sea of Galilee
Jotapata
Sepphoris
Nazareth
Mt. Tabor
Mt. Carmel
Esdraelon Valley
Yarmuk R.
Jordan R.
4. Peter meets with Cornelius.
MEDITERRANEAN SEA
Caesarea Maritima
SAMARIA
Scythopolis (Beth-shan)
Pella
DECAPO
1. Philip preaches throughout Samaria.
4. Philip settles in Caesarea Maritima.
Sebaste (Samaria)
Mt. Ebal
3. Peter raises Tabitha (Dorcas) to life.
Apollonia
Sychar
Neapolis (Shechem)
Jabbok R.
Mt. Gerizim
Yarkon R.
Antipatris (Aphek)
1. Peter and John are sent to investigate claims that Samaritans are receiving the gospel preached by Philip.
Joppa
Lebonah
2. Peter heals Aeneas, a paralytic.
PEREA
Lydda
Gophna
3. Philip preaches in Azotus.
Peter and John are arrested.
Jamnia
Jericho
Emmaus
Azotus (Ashdod)
Jerusalem
Judean Wilderness
Mt. Nebo
JUDEA
Bethlehem
Qumran
Ascalon (Ashkelon)
Betogabris (Beth-guvrin)
Marisa (Mareshah)
Stephen is stoned to death.
Anthedon
Neapolis
Hebron
DEAD SEA
Gaza
En-gedi
Arnon R.
2. Philip baptizes an Ethiopian official and explains the words of Isaiah.
N. Besor
Masada
IDUMEA
Beersheba
NABATEA
0 10 20 Miles
0 10 20 Kilometers
35 E

ADULLAM Place-name meaning "sealed-off place." City five miles south of Beth-shemesh in Judah, probably modern Tell esh-Sheikh Madkur.

ADULTERY Act of unfaithfulness in marriage that occurs when one of the marriage partners voluntarily engages in sexual intercourse with a person other than the marriage partner.

Israel's covenant law prohibited adultery (Exod. 20:14) and thereby made faithfulness to the marriage relationship central in the divine will for human relationships. Jesus's teachings expanded the OT law to address matters of the heart. Adultery has its origins within (Matt. 15:19), and lust is as much a violation of the law's intent as is illicit sexual intercourse (Matt. 5:27-28). Adulterers can be forgiven (John 8:3-11); and once sanctified through repentance, faith, and God's grace, they are included among God's people (1 Cor. 6:9-11).

ADVENT Word with Latin roots, meaning "coming." Christians of earlier generations spoke of "the advent of our Lord" and of "his second advent." The first phrase refers to God's becoming incarnate in Jesus of Nazareth. The latter phrase speaks of Jesus's second coming. In a second sense, "advent" designates a period before Christmas when Christians prepare for the celebration of Jesus's birth. This practice may have begun in some churches as early as the late fourth century.

ADVERSARY Enemy, either human or satanic. Psalmists often prayed for deliverance from adversaries (Pss. 38:20; 69:19; 71:13; 81:14; 109:29). The devil is the greatest adversary and must be resisted (1 Pet. 5:8-9).

ADVOCATE One who intercedes on behalf of another and is used to refer to Christ interceding with the Father on behalf of sinners. "Advocate" is the translation often given to the Greek *parakletos* in 1 John 2:1, a word found elsewhere only in John's Gospel as a title referring to the Holy Spirit, and there translated "Helper," "Comforter," "Counselor," or "Advocate" (John 14:16,26; 15:26; 16:7).

AENEAS Personal name of a paralyzed man Peter healed at Lydda (Acts 9:33-34), resulting in great evangelistic victories in the area.

AENON Place-name meaning "double spring." The location where John the Baptist was baptizing during the time that Jesus was baptizing in Judea (John 3:23).

AFFLICTION Condition of physical or mental distress. While the source and purpose of affliction may vary, the Bible describes the state of affliction with many terms. In the OT, the Hebrew language uses as many as 13 words that may be translated "affliction."

As a response to affliction, the believer should pray to the Lord (Ps. 25:18; Lam. 1:9; James 5:13); comfort others (James 1:27; Phil. 4:14); remain faithful through patient endurance (2 Cor. 6:4; 1 Tim. 4:5; James 1:2,12; 1 Pet. 4:13); cultivate an attitude of joy (James 1:2); and follow the example of Jesus Christ (1 Pet. 2:19-23).

The purpose of affliction is to show the power of Christ (2 Cor. 12:8-9). The discipline of affliction produces strong faith. The end of affliction is the salvation of God's people. Christ's affliction in his atoning sacrifice and the continued affliction of his people will end in the exaltation of God and consummation of his kingdom (Col. 1:24; 2 Tim. 2:10).

AGABUS Personal name meaning "locust." Prophet in the Jerusalem church who went to visit the church at Antioch and predicted a universal famine. His prophecy was fulfilled about 10 years later in the reign of Claudius Caesar (Acts 11:27-29).

AGAG Personal name meaning "fiery one." He was king of the Amalekites, a tribal people living in the Negev and in the Sinai Peninsula. The Amalekites had attacked the Israelites in the wilderness and were therefore cursed (Exod. 17:14). In 1 Sam. 15:8, Saul destroyed all the Amalekites but King Agag. Since the Lord had ordered the complete destruction of the Amalekites, Samuel, Saul's priest, rebuked Saul for his disobedience and reported God's rejection of Saul as king. Then Samuel himself executed Agag.

AGAGITE Apparently, the term means a descendant of Agag. Only Haman, the arch villain in the book of Esther, is called an Agagite (Esth. 3:1). Agagite is probably a synonym for Amalekite.

AGATE Translucent quartz with concentric bands. "Agate" translates three words in the Bible: a stone in the breast piece of judgment (Exod. 28:19; 39:12), the material in the pinnacles of Jerusalem (Isa. 54:12; Ezek. 27:16), and the third jewel in the foundation wall of the new Jerusalem (Rev. 21:19).

AGE TO COME The expression "age to come" or "coming age[s]" is found in the Apocrypha (2 Esdras 7:113; 8:52) and several times in the NT (Matt. 12:32; Mark 10:30; Luke 18:30; Eph. 1:21; 2:7; 1 Tim. 6:19; Heb. 6:5). It is usually either explicitly or implicitly considered in opposition to "this age" or "the present age" (Matt. 12:32; Luke 16:8; 20:34-35; 1 Cor. 2:6–8; 2 Cor. 4:4; Gal. 1:4; Eph. 1:21; 2:2; 1 Tim. 6:17; 2 Tim. 4:10; Titus 2:12). The expression "the end of the age" (Matt. 13:39,40,49; 24:3; 28:20) refers to the end of the present age and therefore relates to the age to come.

AGUE KJV translation of Hebrew word meaning "burning with fever." The Hebrew term appears in Lev. 26:16 and Deut. 28:22, KJV translating "fever" in the second passage.

AGUR Personal name meaning "hired hand." Author of at least part of Prov. 30.

AHAB Personal name meaning "father's brother." The seventh king of Israel's northern kingdom, married a foreigner, Jezebel, and incited God's anger more than any of Israel's previous kings. Ahab was the son and successor of Omri. His 22-year reign (874–853 BC), while enjoying some political and military success, was marred by spiritual compromise and failure (1 Kgs. 16:30).

AHASUERUS Hebrew spelling for Xerxes (NIV, TEV), the king in the book of Esther.

AHAVA River in Babylon and town located beside the river where Ezra assembled Jews to return to Jerusalem from exile (Ezra 8:15,21,31). Ahava was probably located near the city of Babylon, but the exact site is not known.

Ruins of Ahab's Palace.

AHAZ **1.** Evil king of Judah (735–715 BC). Ahaz, whose name means "he has grasped," was the son and successor of Jotham as king of Judah and the father of Hezekiah. Ahaz is characterized as an evil man who participated in the most monstrous of idolatrous practices (2 Kgs. 16:3). His 16-year reign was contemporary with the prophets Isaiah and Micah. **2.** A Benjaminite descended from Saul (1 Chron. 8:35-36; 9:42).

AHAZIAH Name of two OT kings, the king of Israel (850–840 BC) and the king of Judah (ca. 842). The name means "Yahweh has grasped."

AHIEZER Personal name meaning "my brother is help." **1.** Aide to Moses in the wilderness from the tribe of Dan (Num. 1:12; 2:25). **2.** Chief warrior who joined David at Ziklag.

AHIJAH Personal name rendered several ways in Hebrew and English meaning "my brother is Yahweh." **1.** Priest of the family of Eli in Shiloh (1 Sam. 14:3-4). **2.** Scribe of Solomon (1 Kgs. 4:3). **3.** Prophet from Shiloh who tore his clothes in 12 pieces and gave 10 to Jeroboam to signal God's decision to divide the kingdom after Solomon's death (1 Kgs. 11:29-39). **4.** Father of King Baasha of Israel from the tribe of Issachar (1 Kgs. 15:27). **5.** Son of Jerahmeel (1 Chron. 2:25). **6.** Son of Ehud in tribe of Benjamin, an official in Geba (1 Chron. 8:7). **7.** One of David's 30 military heroes whose home was Pelon (1 Chron. 11:36). **8.** Signer of Nehemiah's covenant to obey God's law (Neh. 10:26). **9.** The Hebrew text of 1 Chron. 26:20 says Ahijah, a Levite, had charge of temple treasuries under David (KJV, RSV).

AHIKAM Personal name meaning "my brother stood up." Son of Josiah's scribe Shaphan. He took the book of the law found in the temple to Huldah the prophetess to determine God's will (2 Kgs. 22:8-20).

AHILUD Personal name meaning "a brother is born." The father of Jehoshaphat, David's court recorder (2 Sam. 8:16), who retained the position under Solomon (1 Kgs. 4:3).

AHIMAAZ Personal name with uncertain meaning, "brother of anger" and "my brother is counselor" being suggestions. **1.** Saul's father-in-law (1 Sam. 14:50). **2.** Son of Zadok, one of David's priests (2 Sam. 15:27). He served as one of David's secret messengers from the court when Absalom rebelled and drove his father from Jerusalem (2 Sam. 15:36; 7:17). **3.** One of 12 officers over Solomon's provinces, he had charge of Naphtali. He married Solomon's daughter Basemath. He may be the same as 2, above, Zadok's son (1 Kgs. 4:15).

AHIMAN Personal name with uncertain meaning. **1.** One of the giants of Anak (Num. 13:22). Caleb drove him and his two brothers out of Hebron (cp. Judg. 1:10, where the tribe of Judah killed the three brothers). **2.** Levite and temple gatekeeper (1 Chron. 9:17).

AHINOAM Personal name meaning "my brother is gracious." **1.** King Saul's wife (1 Sam. 14:50). **2.** Wife of David; from Jezreel (1 Sam. 25:43), she lived with him under the Philistines at Gath (27:3).

AHIRA Personal name meaning "my brother is a friend." Leader of tribe of Naphtali under Moses (Num. 1:15) who presented the tribe's offerings at the dedication of the altar (7:78-83) and led them in the wilderness marches.

AHIRAM Personal name meaning "my brother is exalted." Son of Benjamin who gave his name to a clan (the Ahiramites) in that tribe (Num. 26:38).

AHISAMACH Personal name meaning "my brother has supported." Father of Oholiab, the artisan who helped Bezalel create the artwork of the wilderness tabernacle (Exod. 31:6; 35:34; 38:23).

AHISHAHAR Personal name meaning "brother of the dawn." A member of tribe of Benjamin (1 Chron. 7:10) but not listed in the genealogy of 1 Chron. 8.

AHISHAR Personal name meaning "my brother sang." Head of Solomon's palace staff (1 Kgs. 4:6).

AHITHOPHEL Personal name meaning "brother of folly" if it is not a scribal attempt to hide an original name including a Canaanite god such as Ahibaal. The name of David's counselor who joined Absalom's revolt against King David (2 Sam. 15:12).

AHITUB Personal name meaning "my brother is good." **1.** Priest, son of Phinehas and grandson of Eli, ministering in Shiloh (1 Sam. 14:3). He was Ahimelech's father (22:9). **2.** Father of Zadok, the high priest under David and Solomon (2 Sam. 8:17). The name occurs twice in the Chronicler's list of priests (1 Chron. 6:7-8,11-12,52; cp. 9:11). Ezra descended from Ahitub's line (Ezra 7:2).

AHLAB Place-name meaning "mountain forest" or "fertile." Probably located at Khirbet el-Macalib on the Mediterranean coast four miles above Tyre. The tribe of Asher could not conquer it (Judg. 1:31).

AHLAI Personal name meaning "a brother to me," perhaps an abbreviated form of Ahliya, "the brother is my god." Others interpret as interjection meaning "O would that." **1.** Member of clan of Jerahmeel (1 Chron. 2:31). Ahlai's father was Sheshan. **2.** Father of a valiant soldier of David (1 Chron. 11:41).

AHOAH Personal name of uncertain meaning. Grandson of Benjamin (1 Chron. 8:4), but lists in 2:25; 8:7; and evidence of early translations may point to Ahijah as the original name.

AHOHITE Clan name. In time of David and Solomon, military figures of this clan or place became military leaders (2 Sam. 23:9,28; 1 Chron. 11:12,29; 27:4).

AHUZZATH Personal name meaning "that grasped" or "property." Official who accompanied Abimelech, king of Philistines, to make covenant of peace with Isaac (Gen. 26:26).

AHZAI or **AHASAI** (KJV) Personal name meaning "property" or abbreviated form of Ahzaiah, "Yahweh has grasped." A priest after the return from exile (Neh. 11:13). Sometimes said to be the same as Jahzerah (1 Chron. 9:12).

AI Name means "the ruin" in Hebrew. According to the accounts of Genesis and Joshua, Ai is said to be east of Bethel (Gen. 12:8; Josh. 7:2). Bethel is very near Ai (Josh. 12:9). A mountain is said to separate Bethel and Ai (Gen. 12:8), and Ai is implied to be a small town (Josh. 7:3). Khirbet el-Maqatir (Ai) was an important military target to Joshua and the Israelites, because it guarded the approach to a strategic central crossroads to the central hill country—Bethel. The topography of the account in Joshua fits with this site, as does a dating of the conquest in the Late Bronze Age (ca. 1400 BC). Israel learned at Ai that they could not prevail without God. The sin of one man, Achan, affected the whole nation's conquest commission. Ai was originally in Ephraimite territory (1 Chron. 7:28) and was later occupied by Benjaminites (Neh. 11:31).

AIAH Personal name imitating the cry of a hawk, then meaning "hawk." **1.** Son of Zibeon among the clans of Edom descended from Esau (Gen. 36:24). **2.** Father of Rizpah, Saul's concubine (2 Sam. 3:7) and grandfather of Mephibosheth (2 Sam. 21:8).

AIJALON Also spelled "Ajalon." Place-name meaning "place of the deer." **1.** Town and nearby valley where moon stood still at Joshua's command (Josh. 10:12). **2.** Elon, a judge of the tribe of Zebulon, was buried in a northern Aijalon (Judg. 12:12), whose location may be at Tell et-Butmeh.

AIJELETH SHAHAR Musical direction in title of Ps. 22, literally "doe of the dawn."

AIN Place-name meaning "eye" or "water spring." Often used as first part of a place-name indicating the presence of a water source. English often used "En" as first part of such names. See *En-dor*, for example. **1.** Place on eastern border of Canaan (Num. 34:11). Location is uncertain. **2.** City of southern Judah (Josh. 15:32) belonging to Simeon (Josh. 19:7) but assigned as homestead for the Levites, who had no land allotted (Josh. 21:16).

AKHENATON Egyptian pharaoh (1370–1353 BC). Originally named Amenhotep IV, he made a radical religious switch from worshiping Amon to serving Aton, the sun disc. During his reign, he received the reports and requests from city-state rulers in Palestine that archaeologists call the Amarna letters. These show the lack of unity and harmony in Palestine that Joshua found when he entered to conquer Palestine.

AKKUB Personal name possibly meaning "protector" or "protected one." **1.** Descendant of Solomon in postexilic Judah about 420 BC (1 Chron. 3:24). **2.** Gatekeeper of the temple after the return from exile (1 Chron. 9:17; Ezra 2:42; Neh. 7:45; 11:19); he was a Levite (Neh. 12:25). **3.** Levite who helped Ezra teach the law to God's returned people (Neh. 8:7). He may have been related to 2, above. **4.** The head of another family of temple staff personnel (Ezra 2:45).

ALAMOTH Musical notation meaning literally "upon or according to young woman." This apparently signifies a tune for a high voice, a song for a soprano (1 Chron. 15:20; Ps. 46 title).

ALARM Signal given by shouting or playing an instrument. The Hebrew term (*teru' ah*) literally means a shout, but musical instruments were used as the trumpets of Num. 10:1-10. The alarm called the wilderness community to march (Num. 10:5-6). Later in Israel, the alarm called them to battle (10:9) and reminded them of God's presence with their armies (cp. 31:6). The alarm announcing the enemy coming in war brought shock, sadness, and fear (Jer. 4:19; Hos. 5:8). The greatest fear should come, however, when God sounds the alarm for his day (Joel 2:1).

ALDEBARAN Red star of first magnitude in the eye of Taurus; brightest star in Hyades; REB and KJV read Arcturus (Job 9:9; 38:32).

ALEMETH Place and personal name meaning "concealed" or "dark." **1.** City set aside for the Levites from Benjamin's allotment (1 Chron. 6:60). Known as Almon in Josh. 21:18. **2.** Grandson of Benjamin (1 Chron. 7:8). **3.** Descendant of Saul and Jonathan in tribe of Benjamin (1 Chron. 8:36).

ALEXANDER Five NT men: the son of Simon of Cyrene (Mark 15:21), a relative of Annas (Acts 4:6), a Jew of Ephesus (Acts 19:33), a false teacher (1 Tim. 1:19-20), and a coppersmith (2 Tim. 4:14).

ALEXANDER THE GREAT Succeeded his father as king of Macedonia and quickly conquered the Persian Empire. Alexander the Great (356–323 BC) was one of the greatest military leaders in history. His father was Phillip of Macedon, king of a region of Greece known as Macedonia.

While Alexander is never directly named in the Bible, the culture he brought to Palestine greatly affected the biblical world, especially during the time between the writing of the OT and NT. His empire is one element of the historical background of Daniel. See *Alexandria; Greece.*

ALEXANDRIA Capital of Egypt from 330 BC, founded by Alexander the Great as an outstanding Greek cultural and academic center.

Alexandria was designed to act as the principal port of Egypt located on the western edge of the Nile Delta. The Pharos lighthouse was visible for miles at a height of more than 400 feet and is remembered today as one of the Seven Wonders of the Ancient World.

The educated Jews of Alexandria contended with Stephen (Acts 6:9). Apollos, the great Christian orator, came from Alexandria (Acts 18:24), and Paul rode the ships of that port (Acts 27:6; 28:11). Although the Christians suffered persecution there, they produced a school with such notables as Clement and Origen in leadership. The school was noted for its allegorical approach to Scripture.

Lighthouse in the harbor at Alexandria.

ALGUM Rare wood that Solomon imported from Lebanon for the temple (2 Chron. 2:8). The exact type of wood is not known. First Kings 10:11-12 also refers to "almug" wood imported from Ophir (cp. 2 Chron. 9:10-11). The rare wood was used for gateways and for musical instruments.

ALIAH Personal name meaning "height." A leader of Edom (1 Chron. 1:51), known in Gen. 36:40 as Alvah.

ALIAN Personal name meaning "high one." Descendant of Esau and thus an Edomite (1 Chron. 1:40). Known in Gen. 36:23 as Alvan.

ALIEN Someone living in a society other than his or her own. Related terms are "foreigner," "stranger," and "sojourner." Israel had a special place for aliens because Israel began history in Egypt as aliens (Exod. 23:9). Special laws provided food and clothing for aliens (Deut. 24:19-20; 26:12). Aliens had rights in the courtroom (Deut. 24:17; 27:19). The ritual expectations of the alien are not always clear (Deut. 14:21; Lev. 17:15). God loves aliens (Deut. 10:19), and the alien could worship God and was supposed to keep the Sabbath (Exod. 23:12; Deut. 31:12). They could observe Passover just as any Israelite (Num. 9:14) and offer sacrifices (Lev. 17:8). They should obey sexual laws (Lev. 18:26).

ALLAMMELECH Place-name meaning "king's oak" or "royal holy tree." Border town of Asher (Josh. 19:26) whose specific location is not known.

ALLEGORY Literary device in which a story or narrative is used to convey truths about reality. The word "allegory" is taken from two Greek words: *alla* (other) and *agoreuo* (to proclaim). An allegory conveys something other than its literal meaning. Sometimes "allegory" is defined as an extended metaphor. Cicero viewed allegory as a continuous stream of metaphors.

ALLON Personal name meaning "oak." Leader of the tribe of Simeon (1 Chron. 4:37).

ALLONBACHUTH or **ALLONBACUTH** Place-name meaning "oak of weeping." Burial place near Bethel of Rebekah's nurse (Gen. 35:8).

ALLOTMENT OT concept of land allocation either by God or by lot. The allotment of the land of Canaan to the tribes of Israel is recorded in Num. 32 and Josh. 13–19. God directed the process through the lot of the priest (Josh. 14:1-2). The tribes of Reuben and Gad, along with half the tribe of Manasseh, requested land east of the Jordan (Num. 32:33). Ezekiel 48 also contains a version of the allotment of the land for the Jews after the exile, revised so that each tribe received an equal share.

ALMIGHTY Title of God, translation of Hebrew *El Shaddai*. The early Greek translation introduced "Almighty" as one of several translations. Recent study has tended to see "the Mountain One" as the most likely original meaning. The name was particularly related to Abraham and the patriarchs (Gen. 17:1; 28:3; 35:11; 49:25). Job is the only book to use *El Shaddai* extensively, 31 times in all. Paul used "Almighty" once at the end of a series of OT quotations to imitate OT style and to underline divine power to bring God's word to fulfillment. Revelation refers to God nine times as "Almighty," again giving a feeling of power to the vision of Revelation.

ALMODAD Personal name meaning "God is a friend." Grandson of Eber and ancestor of Arabian tribes (Gen. 10:25-26).

ALMON Place-name meaning "darkness" or "hidden" or "small road sign." City given to Levites from the tribe of Benjamin, called Alemeth in 1 Chron. 6:60. The site is probably modern Khirbet Almit.

ALMOND Large, nut-bearing tree and the nuts that it bears. Noted as the first tree to bloom (January) and for its pretty white or pink blossoms. Jacob used the almond (KJV, "hazel") as a breeding device to increase his herds (Gen. 30:37). He sent almonds as one of the best fruits of the land to satisfy the Egyptian ruler (Gen. 43:11). The bowls for the tabernacle had almond-shaped decorations (Exod. 25:33-34). Aaron's rod miraculously produced ripe almonds, showing that he and his tribe were the only chosen priests (Num. 17:8).

ALMON-DIBLATHAIM Place-name meaning "road sign of the two figs." A stopping place near the end of the wilderness wandering near Mount Nebo (Num. 33:46-47).

ALMS Gifts for the poor.

Old Testament Although the Hebrew language apparently had no technical term to refer to "alms" or "almsgiving," the practice of charitable giving, especially to the poor, became a very important belief and practice within Judaism.

New Testament The NT regards alms as an expression of a righteous life. The technical term for alms (Gk. *eleemosune*) occurs 13 times in the NT. This does not include Matt. 6:1, where the preferred reading is "righteousness" (NASB, NIV) instead of "alms" (KJV). By the first century AD, righteousness and alms were synonymous in Judaism. Although Jesus criticized acts of charity done for the notice of men (Matt. 6:2-3), he expected his disciples to perform such deeds (Matt. 6:4) and even commanded them (Luke 11:41; 12:33). Alms could refer to a gift donated to the needy (Acts 3:2-3,10) or to acts of charity in general (Acts 9:36; 10:2,4,31; 24:17).

ALOE Large tree grown in India and China, producing resin and oil used in making perfumes. Balaam used the beauty of the aloe tree to describe the beauty of Israel's camp as he blessed them (Num. 24:6). The aloe perfume gave aroma to the king's garment as he was married (Ps. 45:8). Aloe also perfumed the harlot's bed (Prov. 7:17). The beloved's garden includes aloe (Song 4:14). Nicodemus brought aloe with myrrh to perfume Jesus's body for burial (John 19:39).

ALOTH Place-name meaning "the height" if not read Bealoth (NASB, RSV), "feminine baals." Center of activity for Baana, one of Solomon's 12 district supervisors (1 Kgs. 4:16).

ALPHA AND OMEGA First and last letters of the Greek alphabet, used in Revelation to describe God or Christ (Rev. 1:8,17; 21:6; 22:13). "Alpha and omega" refers to God's sovereignty and eternal nature. God and Christ are "the first and the last, the beginning and the end" (Rev. 22:13 CSB).

ALPHAEUS or **ALPHEUS** Personal name. **1.** Father of apostle called James the Less to distinguish him from James, the son of Zebedee and brother of John (Matt. 10:3; Mark 3:18; Luke 6:15; Acts 1:13). **2.** Father of the apostle Levi (Mark 2:14). Comparison of Matt. 9:9 and Luke 5:27 would indicate Levi was also called Matthew.

ALTAR Structure used in worship as the place for presenting sacrifices to God or gods.

Old Testament The Hebrew word for altar that is used most frequently in the OT is formed from the verb for "slaughter" and means literally "slaughter place." Altars were used primarily as places of sacrifice, especially animal sacrifice. "Altar" is distinct from "temple." Whereas temple implies a building or roofed structure, altar implies an open structure.

New Testament The Greek word used for altar literally translates "place of sacrifice." New Testament references to altars concern proper worship (Matt. 5:23-24) and hypocrisy in worship (Matt. 23:18-20). The altar of incense described in the OT (Exod. 30:1-6) is mentioned in Luke 1:11. Several NT references to altars refer back to OT altar events (Rom. 11:3; James 2:21). In Revelation, John described a golden altar (Rev. 9:13) that, like the OT bronze altar, had horns.

While direct references to altar and the sacrifice of Jesus Christ are few in the NT (Heb. 13:10), the message that Jesus Christ is the ultimate sacrifice who effects reconciliation with God is the theme of the NT.

ALTASHHETH (NASB) or **AL-TASCHITH** (KJV). Word in psalm title (Pss. 57; 58; 59; 75), transliterated letter for letter from Hebrew to English by NASB and KJV, but translated "Do not destroy" by CSB, NIV, RSV. This may indicate the tune used to sing the psalm.

AMALEKITE Nomadic tribe of formidable people that first attacked the Israelites after the exodus at Rephidim. Descendants of Amalek, the grandson of Esau (Gen. 36:12), they inhabited the desolate wasteland of the northeast Sinai Peninsula and the Negev.

AMANUENSIS One employed to copy manuscripts or write from dictation. Romans 16:22 identifies Tertius as the one "who penned this epistle" (cp. Col. 4:18; 1 Pet. 5:12). See *Scribe.*

AMARIAH Personal name meaning "Yahweh has spoken." Popular name, especially among priests, after the exile. Brief biblical comments make it difficult to distinguish with certainty the number of separate individuals. **1.** Priest in the line of Aaron (1 Chron. 6:7,52; Ezra 7:3). **2.** Priest in the high priestly line after Solomon's day (1 Chron. 6:11). **3.** Priestly son of Hebron in Moses's line (1 Chron. 23:19; 24:23). **4.** Chief priest and highest judge of matters involving religious law under King Jehoshaphat (2 Chron. 19:11). **5.** Priest under Hezekiah responsible for distributing resources from Jerusalem temple to priests in priestly cities outside Jerusalem (2 Chron. 31:15). **6.** Man with foreign wife under Ezra (Ezra

10:42). **7.** Priest who sealed Nehemiah's covenant to obey the law (Neh. 10:3). **8.** Ancestor of a member of tribe of Judah living in Jerusalem during Nehemiah's time (Neh. 11:4). **9.** Priest who returned to Jerusalem from exile in Babylon with Zerubbabel (Neh. 12:2). **10.** Head of a course of priests in Judah after the exile (Neh. 12:13). **11.** Ancestor of Zephaniah, the prophet (Zeph. 1:1).

AMARNA, TELL EL Site approximately 200 miles south of Cairo, Egypt, where, in 1888, 300 clay tablets were found describing the period of history when the Israelites were in bondage in Egypt. Amarna is not mentioned by name in the Bible.

The so-called Amarna letters were written in Akkadian, the international language of that era. These letters were primarily diplomatic communications between Egypt and Egyptian-controlled territories, including Syria and Palestine. Rulers of small Palestinian city-states including Shechem, Jerusalem, and Megiddo complained of mistreatment by other rulers and asked for Egyptian aid. These letters evidence the political unrest, disunity, and instability of the period prior to or immediately following the Hebrew conquest. Reference to the *Habiru* of this time has intrigued senders, but no conclusive connection to the Hebrews is yet decisive.

AMASAI Personal name meaning "burden bearer." **1.** Levite in the line of Kohath (1 Chron. 6:25). **2.** Levite in the line of Kohath and of Heman the singer (1 Chron. 6:35), often identified with 1. **3.** The chief of David's captains, who received prophetic inspiration from the Spirit (1 Chron. 12:18). Note that he does not appear in 2 Sam. 23. **4.** Priest and musician who blew trumpets before the ark of God in David's time (1 Chron. 15:24). **5.** Levite, father of Mahath, who helped purify the temple under Hezekiah (2 Chron. 29:12).

AMASHAI or **AMASHSAI** (NASB, TEV) Personal name of priest after the exile (Neh. 11:13).

AMASIAH Personal name meaning "Yahweh has borne." One of the captains of Jehoshaphat (2 Chron. 17:16).

AMAZIAH Personal name meaning "Yahweh is mighty." **1.** A Simeonite (1 Chron. 4:34). **2.** A Levite and a descendant of Merari (1 Chron. 6:45). **3.** Priest at Bethel who sent Amos the prophet home, saying he did not have the right to prophesy against King Jeroboam II of Israel (789–746 BC) in the king's place of worship (Amos 7:10-17). **4.** Ninth king of Judah, the son of Joash and father of Uzziah (797–767 BC). He was 25 years old when he ascended the throne.

AMBASSADOR Representative of one royal court to another. Paul saw himself even in prison as an ambassador sent by the divine King to proclaim salvation through Christ to the world (Eph. 6:20; cp. 2 Cor. 5:20).

AMBER Yellowish or brownish translucent resin that takes a good polish. Also translated as gleaming bronze in RSV, but amber in NRSV, glowing metal in NASB and NIV, and bronze in TEV (Ezek. 1:4,27; 8:2).

AMEN Transliteration of Hebrew word signifying something as certain, sure and valid, truthful and faithful. It is sometimes translated "so be it." In the Gospels, Jesus used "amen" to affirm the truth of his own statements. English translations often use "verily," "truly," "I tell you the truth" to translate Jesus's "amen." He never said it at the end of a statement but always at the beginning. Jesus is called "the Amen" in Rev. 3:14, meaning that he himself is the reliable and true witness of God. Perhaps the writer had in mind Isa. 65:16 where the Hebrew says, "God of Amen."

AMETHYST Deep purple variety of stone of the aluminum oxide family. Used in the breastplate of the high priest (Exod. 28:19; 39:12) and the twelfth stone in the foundation wall of the new Jerusalem (Rev. 21:20).

AMI Personal name with uncertain meaning. A servant in the temple after the exile belonging to a group called "children of Solomon's servants" (Ezra 2:55-57). Ami is apparently called Amon in Neh. 7:59.

AMITTAI Personal name meaning "loyal," "true." Father of the prophet Jonah who lived in Gath-hepher (2 Kgs. 14:25).

AMMI Name meaning "my people" was given to Israel by Hosea in contrast to the name Lo-ammi (Hos. 1:9) meaning "not my people." The name Lo-ammi was given to the third child of Gomer, the wife of Hosea the prophet, to pronounce God's rejection of Israel. The name "Ammi" was the new name to be given the restored Israel in the day of redemption.

AMMIEL Personal name meaning "people of God" or "God is of my people," that is, God is my relative. **1.** Spy who represented the tribe of Dan whom Moses sent to spy out the promised land. He was one of 10 who brought a bad report and led people to refuse to enter the land (Num. 13:12). **2.** Father of Machir, in whose house Mephibosheth, son of Jonathan and grandson of Saul, lived after the death of his father and grandfather. The family lived in Lo-debar (2 Sam. 9:4; 17:27). **3.** Father of Bath-shua, David's wife (1 Chron. 3:5). Second Samuel 11:3 speaks of Bathsheba, daughter of Eliam. Many Bible students think these verses are talking about the same person, whose names have been slightly altered in the process of copying the manuscripts. **4.** Gatekeeper of the temple whom David appointed (1 Chron. 26:5).

AMMIHUD Personal name meaning "my people are splendid." **1.** Father of Elishama, who represented the tribe of Ephraim to help Moses during the wilderness wandering (Num. 1:10). He presented the tribe's offerings at the dedication of the altar (7:48) and led them in marching (10:22). He was Joshua's grandfather (1 Chron. 7:26). **2.** Father of Shemuel of the tribe of Simeon, who helped Moses, Eleazar, and Joshua allot the land to the tribes (Num. 34:20). **3.** Father of Pedahel of tribe of Naphtali, who helped allot the land (Num. 34:28). **4.** Father of King of Geshur to whom Absalom fled after he killed his brother Amnon (2 Sam. 13:37). **5.** Member of tribe of Judah who returned from exile (1 Chron. 9:4).

AMMINADAB Personal name meaning "my people give freely." **1.** Aaron's father-in-law (Exod. 6:23). Father of Nahshon, who led the tribe of Judah in the wilderness (Num. 1:7). Ancestor of David (Ruth 4:19) and Jesus (Matt. 1:4; Luke 3:33). **2.** Son of Kohath in genealogy of Levites (1 Chron. 6:22), but this may be copyist's change for Izhar (Exod. 6:18,21). **3.** Head of a family of Levites (1 Chron. 15:10). He helped carry the ark of the covenant to Jerusalem (1 Chron. 15:11-29).

AMMISHADDAI Father of Ahiezer, the leader of the tribe of Dan in the wilderness (Num. 1:12). The name Ammishaddai means "people of the Almighty."

AMMIZABAD Personal name meaning "my people give." Son of Benaiah, one of the captains of David's army (1 Chron. 27:6).

AMMON, AMMONITES Territory east of the Jordan roughly equivalent to the modern state of Jordan. The Ammonites were a Semitic people living northeast of the Dead Sea in the area surrounding Rabbah who often battled with the Israelites for possession of the fertile Gilead.

AMNON Personal name meaning "trustworthy, faithful." **1.** Firstborn son of King David (2 Sam. 3:2). He raped his half sister Tamar. Tamar's brother Absalom avenged this outrage by killing Amnon (2 Sam. 13). This incident marked the beginning of the decline of David's family following his adulterous relationship with Bathsheba and the murder of Uriah. See *David*. **2.** Member of the tribe of Judah (1 Chron. 4:20).

AMOK Personal name meaning "deep." A priestly family after the return from exile (Neh. 12:7,20).

AMON Personal name meaning "faithful." **1.** Governor of Samaria when Jehoshaphat was king of Judah, who followed orders from the king of Israel and put the prophet Micaiah in prison (1 Kgs. 22:26). **2.** King of Judah (642 BC) following his father Manasseh. He followed the infamous idolatry of his father and was killed in a palace revolt (2 Kgs. 21:19-23). The people of Judah, in turn, killed the rebels. Good King Josiah, Amon's son, succeeded to his throne. See Matt. 1:10. **3.** Ancestor of temple staff members after the exile (Neh. 7:59), called Ami in Ezra 2:57.

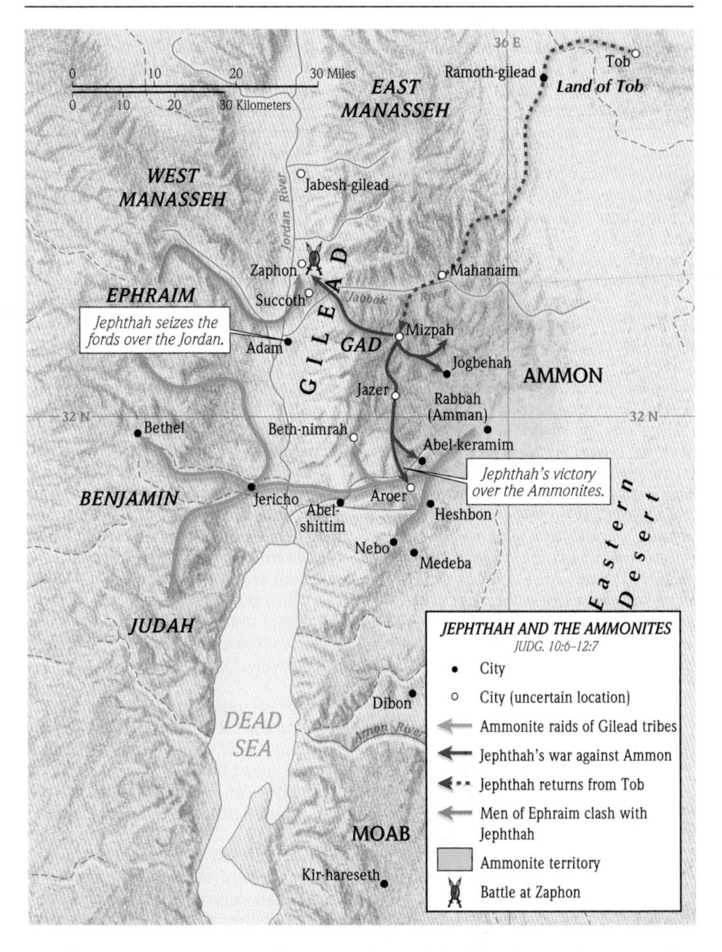

4. Egyptian god whose worship center at Thebes Jeremiah threatened with divine destruction (Jer. 46:25). KJV translates "the multitude of No."

AMORITES People who occupied part of the promised land and often fought Israel. Their history goes back before 2000 BC.

Abraham assisted Mamre the Amorite in recovering his land from four powerful kings (Gen. 14), but later the Amorites were a formidable obstacle to the Israelites' conquest and settlement of Canaan. They preferred living in the hills and valleys that flank both sides of the Jordan River. Sihon and Og, two Amorite kings, resisted the Israelites' march to Canaan as they approached east of the Jordan (Num. 21:21-35); but after the Israelite victory there, Gad, Reuben, and half of Manasseh settled in the conquered area.

AMOS Personal name meaning "burdened" or, more likely, "one who is supported [by God]." Prophet from Judah who ministered in Israel about 750 BC.

Amos was a layperson who disclaimed professional status as a prophet. He lived in a time of relative peace on the international political scene and when internally the political structures of both Israel and Judah were stable.

Morally, Israel and Judah were suffering under the corruption generated as a by-product of Canaanite and Tyrian Baalism, as well as infidelity to the Lord's covenant. Israelite society had experienced the inevitable decay that characterizes misdirected prosperity.

Exploitation of the poor occurred throughout the land (Amos 2:6; 3:10; 4:1; 5:11; 8:4-6). Justice was distorted. The dynamism of personal religious experience gave way to the superficiality of institutional religion as demonstrated in the conflict between Amos and Amaziah, the priest of Bethel (7:10-15).

Amos's opposition to those moral and religious evils led him to emphasize the primary theme of the book of Amos: "let justice roll down like waters, and righteousness like an everlasting stream" (5:24 RSV).

Amos was listed as an ancestor of Jesus (Luke 3:25), but it is not known specifically if it was this prophet.

Ruins of small building, probably dating from post-biblical times, at Tekoa, Israel, Amos's hometown.

AMOS, BOOK OF One of the 12 Minor Prophets of the OT. The book of Amos may be divided into three sections. Chapters 1 and 2 are a basic section, divided into subsections that begin with a common literary introduction (1:3,6,9,11,13; 2:1,4,6). The second section of the book consists of judgment oracles directed against Israel (3:1–6:14). The third section contains the visions of Amos (7–9), which may have been the earliest revelations through the prophet. The visions were central to his call experience. Aware of the awesome reality of human sin and divine judgment, these visions shaped his prophetic messages (7:1-3,4-6,7-9; 8:1-3; 9:1-4).

AMOZ Personal name meaning "strong." Father of the prophet Isaiah (2 Kgs. 19:2).

AMPHIPOLIS City near the Aegean Gulf between Thessalonica and Philippi. Paul and Silas passed through it on their way to Thessalonica on Paul's second missionary journey (Acts 17:1) as they traveled the famous Egnatian Way.

AMPLIAS or **AMPLIATUS** Christian convert in Rome to whom Paul sent greetings (Rom. 16:8). Amplias was a common name often given to slaves. Paul referred to this individual as "my dear friend in the Lord" (CSB), which may suggest a particularly warm and affectionate relationship between Amplias and the apostle. Modern translations spell the name "Ampliatus."

AMRAM Personal name meaning "exalted people." **1.** Father of Moses, Aaron, and Miriam and grandson of Levi (Exod. 6:18-20). **2.** One of the 12 sons of Bani who was guilty of marrying foreign women (Ezra 10:34). **3.** One of four sons of Dishon in 1 Chron. 1:41.

AMULETS NASB, RSV, CSB translation of rare Hebrew word for charms inscribed with oaths, which women wore to ward off evil (Isa. 3:20). NIV translates "charms"; KJV, "earrings."

AMZI Personal name meaning "my strong one," or an abbreviation for Amaziah. **1.** Member of temple singer family (1 Chron. 6:46). **2.** Ancestor of Adaiah, who helped build the second temple (Neh. 11:12).

ANAB Place-name meaning "grape." Joshua eliminated the Anakim from southern Judah including Hebron, Debir, and Anab (Josh.

11:21). Joshua allotted the mountain city to Judah (Josh. 15:50). Located at modern Khirbet Anab about 15 miles southwest of Hebron.

ANAH Personal name meaning "answer." **1.** Mother of Oholibamah, a wife of Esau (Gen. 36:2), and grandmother of Jeush, Jalam, and Korah (36:14). **2.** Son of Seir and brother of Zibeon (Gen. 36:20).

ANAHARATH Place-name meaning "gorge." City on border of Issachar (Josh. 19:19) located possibly at modern Tell el-Mukharkhash between Mount Tabor and the Jordan.

ANAIAH Personal name meaning "Yahweh answered." Ezra's assistant when Ezra read the Law to the postexilic community (Neh. 8:4). He or another man of the same name signed Nehemiah's covenant to obey God's law (Neh. 10:22).

ANAK, ANAKIM, ANAKITES (NIV) Personal and clan name meaning "long necked" or "strong necked." The ancestor named Anak had three children: Ahiman, Sheshai, Talmai (Num. 13:22). They lived in Hebron and the hill country (Josh. 11:21) before being destroyed by Joshua.

ANAMMELECH Personal name meaning "Anu is king." A god of the Sepharvites who occupied part of Israel after the northern kingdom was exiled in 721 BC. Worshipers sacrificed children to this god (2 Kgs. 17:31).

ANAMIM or **ANAMITES** (NIV) Tribe or nation called "son of Egypt" in Gen. 10:13. No further information is known about these people.

ANAN Personal name meaning "cloud." Signer of Nehemiah's covenant to obey God (Neh. 10:26).

ANANI Personal name meaning "cloudy" or "he heard me." Descendant of David's royal line living after the return from exile (1 Chron. 3:24).

ANANIAH Personal name meaning "Yahweh heard me." **1.** Grandfather of Azariah, who helped Nehemiah repair Jerusalem (Neh. 3:23). **2.** Village where tribe of Benjamin dwelt in time of Nehemiah (Neh. 11:32). It may be located at Bethany, east of Jerusalem.

ANANIAS Greek form of the Hebrew name Hananiah, which means "Yahweh has dealt graciously." **1.** Husband of Sapphira (Acts 5:1-6). They sold private property, the proceeds of which they were to give to the common fund of the early Jerusalem church (Acts 4:32-34). They did not give all the proceeds from the sale, as they claimed, and both were struck dead for having lied to the Holy Spirit (Acts 5:5,10). **2.** Disciple who lived in the city of Damascus (Acts 9:10-19). In response to a vision he received from the Lord, this Ananias visited Saul (Paul) three days after Saul had his Damascus road experience. Ananias laid his hands on Saul, after which Saul received both the Holy Spirit and his sight. Acts 9:18 may imply that Ananias was the one who baptized Saul. **3.** Jewish high priest from AD 47 to 58 (Acts 23:2; 24:1).

ANATH Personal name meaning "answer," or possibly the name of a Canaanite god. Father of Shamgar, a judge of Israel (Judg. 3:31).

ANATHEMA Greek translation of Hebrew *cherem*; booty taken in a holy war that must be thoroughly destroyed (Lev. 27:28; Deut. 20:10-18). The total destruction of this booty showed that it was being completely turned over to God. In the NT, anathema has two seemingly opposite meanings. It means "gifts dedicated to God" (Luke 21:5 CSB) as well as something cursed. Paul invoked such a curse on those who did not love the Lord (1 Cor. 16:22) as well as on one who preached another gospel other than the gospel of grace (Gal. 1:8-9). From these uses, anathema has come to mean "banned or excommunicated by a religious body." Paul said he was willing to become anathema, cursed and cut off from the Messiah, for the benefit of his Jewish brothers and sisters (Rom. 9:3 CSB).

ANATHOTH Personal and place-name. **1.** City assigned to the tribe of Benjamin, located about three miles northeast of

Jerusalem (Josh. 21:18). King Solomon sent Abiathar the priest there after removing him as high priest (1 Kgs. 2:26-27). It was also the home of Jeremiah the prophet, who may have been a priest in the rejected line of Abiathar (Jer. 1:1). **2.** The eighth of nine sons of Becher, the son of Benjamin (1 Chron. 7:8). **3.** A chief who was a family or clan leader, who along with 84 other priests, Levites, and leaders signed a covenant that the Israelites would obey the law of God given through Moses (Neh. 10:19).

ANCHOR Weight held on the end of a cable that when submerged in water holds a ship in place. Anchors were made of stone, iron, and lead during biblical times. "Anchor" is used in a figurative sense in Heb. 6:19 where the hope of the gospel is compared to "an anchor for the soul, firm and secure" (CSB)—that is, a spiritual support in times of trial.

ANCIENT OF DAYS Phrase used in Dan. 7:9,13,22 to describe the everlasting God. Ancient of days literally means "one advanced in (of) days" and may possibly mean "one who forwards time or rules over it."

ANDREW Disciple of John the Baptist who became one of Jesus's first disciples and led his own brother Simon to Jesus. Because of John the Baptist's witness concerning Jesus, Andrew followed Jesus to his overnight lodging and became one of his first disciples. Subsequently Andrew brought his brother Simon to Jesus (John 1:40-41). He was a fisherman by trade (Matt. 4:18). He questioned Jesus about his prophecy concerning the temple (Mark 13:3). Andrew brought the lad with his lunch to Jesus, leading to the feeding of the 5,000 (John 6:8). He and Philip brought some Greeks to see Jesus (John 12:22). He is mentioned for the last time in Acts 1:13. He is believed to have been killed on an x-shaped cross. See *Apostle; Disciple.*

ANDRONICUS Kinsman of Paul honored by the church. He had suffered in prison for his faith and had been a Christian longer than Paul (Rom. 16:7). Evidently he lived in Rome when Paul wrote Romans. He is referred to as an "apostle" in the broadest sense, meaning "messenger."

ANEM Place-name meaning "fountains." A city given the Levites from the territory of Issachar (1 Chron. 6:73). Joshua 21:29 lists the city as En-gannim.

ANER Personal and place-name. **1.** Ally of Abraham in the battle against the coalition of kings in Gen. 14. **2.** City from the tribe of Manasseh given to Levites (1 Chron. 6:70). In Josh. 21:25, the Levites' city is called Taanach. See *Taanach.*

ANGEL Created beings whose primary function is to serve and worship God. Though some interpret the "us" in Gen. 1:26 as inclusive of God and his angelic court, the Bible does not comment as to when they were created. Unlike God, they are not eternal or omniscient. The Hebrew word in the OT is *mal'ak*, and the NT Greek word is *angelos*. They both mean "messenger" and occasionally refer to human messengers.

ANIAM Personal name meaning "I am a people," "I am an uncle," or "mourning of the people." A member of the tribe of Manasseh (1 Chron. 7:19).

ANIM Place-name meaning "springs." City given tribe of Judah (Josh. 15:50). Located at modern Khirbet Ghuwein at-Tahta, 11 miles south of Hebron.

ANISE KJV translation of the Greek term more properly translated as "dill" in Matt. 23:23.

ANKLET Ornamental rings worn above the ankles; sometimes called "ankle bracelets." The KJV has "tinkling ornaments about their feet" (Isa. 3:18; cp. 3:16). Anklets were luxury items worn by the women of Jerusalem during the days of Isaiah.

ANNA Aged prophetess who recognized the Messiah when he was brought to the temple for dedication (Luke 2:36). Anna, whose name means "grace," was the daughter of Phanuel of the tribe of Asher. After seven years of marriage, she was widowed and became an attendant of the temple. She was 84 when she recognized the Messiah, thanked God for him, and proclaimed to all hope for the redemption of Jerusalem.

ANNAS Son of Seth; a priest at the time John the Baptist began his public preaching (Luke 3:2). Evidently Annas, whose name means "merciful," was appointed to the high priesthood about AD 6 by Quirinius, governor of Syria. Though he was deposed in AD 15 by Gratus, he continued to exercise considerable influence. When Jesus was arrested, he was taken before Annas (John 18:13). After Pentecost, Annas led other priests in questioning Peter and the other church leaders (Acts 4:6).

ANNUNCIATION In Christian historical tradition, the annunciation refers specifically to the announcement with which the angel Gabriel notified the virgin Mary of the miraculous conception of Christ within her (Luke 1:26-38; Joseph received a similar announcement in Matt. 1:20-25).

ANOINT, ANOINTED Procedure of rubbing or smearing a person or thing, usually with oil, for the purpose of healing, setting apart, or embalming. A person can anoint himself, be anointed, or anoint another person or thing. While olive oil is the most common element mentioned for use in anointing, oils produced from castor, bay, almond, myrtle, cyprus, cedar, walnut, and fish were also used. In Esth. 2:12, for example, the oil of myrrh is used as a cosmetic.

The Hebrew verb *mashach* (noun, *messiah*) and the Greek verb *chrio* (noun, *christos*) are translated "to anoint."

ANON Archaic word used in the KJV meaning "immediately."

ANTEDILUVIANS Meaning "before the deluge"; refers to those who lived before the flood described in Gen. 6–8.

ANTHOTHIJAH Descendant of Benjamin (1 Chron. 8:24). The name may represent connection with city of Anathoth.

ANTHROPOLOGY Biblical anthropology concerns the origin, essential nature, and destiny of human beings.

ANTHROPOMORPHISM Words which describe God as if he had human features.

ANTICHRIST Describes a particular individual or a group of people who oppose God and his purpose. In the NT, the only use of the term "antichrist" is in the Johannine Epistles. First John 2:18 speaks of the antichrist who is the great enemy of God and, in particular, antichrists who precede that great enemy. These antichrists were human teachers who had left the church. Such antichrists deny the incarnation (1 John 4:3) and Christ's deity (1 John 2:2). In 2 Thess. 2:1-12, the antichrist figure is armed with satanic power and is fused with Belial, a satanic being (2 Cor. 6:15). In this passage, the Roman government is viewed as restraining its power. In Revelation, the Roman Caesar is the evil force.

Contemporary Concerns Christians today have differing views of the antichrist figure. Dispensationalists look for a future Roman ruler who will appear during the tribulation and will rule over the earth. Those in the amillennialist school interpret the term symbolically.

ANTINOMIANISM False teaching that says since faith alone is necessary for salvation, one is free from the moral obligations of the law. The word "antinomianism" is not used in the Bible, but the idea is spoken of. Paul appears to have been accused of being an antinomian (Rom. 3:8; 6:1,15).

ANTIOCH Name of two NT cities.

One of the cities called Antioch was the third-largest city of the Roman Empire after Rome in Italy and Alexandria in Egypt. Because so many ancient cities were called by this name, it is often called Antioch on the Orontes River or Antioch of Syria. This was home to many Diaspora Jews (Jews living outside of Palestine and maintaining their religious faith among the Gentiles), and the place where believers, many of whom were Gentiles, were first called Christians.

Another city called Antioch was in Pisidia, Asia Minor, west of Iconium. Paul preached in a synagogue there on his first missionary journey (Acts 13:14) and was warmly received (13:42-44).

The Cilician Gates through the Taurus Mountains north of Antioch of Syria where Paul would have passed on his second missionary journey.

ANTIOCHUS Name of 13 rulers of Syria-Palestine headquartered in Antioch. They were part of the

Seleucid dynasty that inherited part of Alexander the Great's kingdom.

ANTIPAS Name of the son of Herod the Great and of a martyr in Revelation. **1.** Tetrarch of Galilee at the time John the Baptist and Jesus began their public ministries (Luke 3:1). **2.** According to tradition, the martyr of the church of Pergamum in Rev. 2:13 was roasted in a brazen bowl at Domitian's request.

ANTIPATRIS Place-name meaning "in place of father." City that Herod the Great built to honor his father Antipater in 9 BC. It was 40 miles from Jerusalem and 25 miles from Caesarea on the famous Via Maris, "way of the sea," international highway. Roman soldiers taking Paul from Jerusalem to Caesarea spent the night at Antipatris (Acts 23:31). It is located on the site of OT Aphek. See *Aphek*.

ANTONIA, TOWER OF Fortress near the temple built around AD 6 that served as a palace residence for King Herod, barracks for the Roman troops, a safe deposit for the robe of the high priest, and a central courtyard for public speaking. The tower of Antonia is not mentioned directly in the Bible.

ANUB Personal name meaning "grape" or "with a mustache." A member of the tribe of Judah (1 Chron. 4:8).

ANXIETY State of mind wherein one is concerned about something or someone. This state of mind may range from genuine concern (Phil. 2:20,28; 2 Cor. 11:28) to obsessions that originate from a distorted perspective of life (Matt. 6:25-34; Mark 4:19; Luke 12:22-31). Jesus did not prohibit genuine concern about food or shelter, but he did teach that we should keep things in their proper perspective. We should make God's kingdom our first priority; everything else will fall in line after we do that (Matt. 6:33).

APELLES A Christian in Rome whom Paul saluted as "approved in Christ" (Rom. 16:10), which may mean he had been tested by persecution and proved faithful.

APHEK Place-name meaning "bed of brook or river" or "fortress." **1.** City whose king Joshua defeated (Josh. 12:18), where Philistine armies formed to face Israel in days of Samuel (1 Sam. 4:1) resulting in Philistine victory and capture of Israel's ark of the covenant. **2.** Northern border city that Joshua did not conquer (Josh. 13:4). This may be modern Afqa, 15 miles east of ancient Byblos and 23 miles north of Beirut, Lebanon. **3.** City assigned to Asher (Josh. 19:30) but not conquered (Judg. 1:31). This may be modern Tell Kerdanah, three miles from Haifa and six miles southeast of Acco. **4.** City east of Jordan near the Sea of Galilee where Benhadad led Syria against Israel about 860 BC but met defeat as a prophet predicted for Israel (1 Kgs. 20:26-30).

APHEKAH City that Joshua assigned to the tribe of Judah (Josh. 15:53). Its location is unknown.

APHIAH Personal name meaning "forehead." An ancestor of King Saul from the tribe of Benjamin (1 Sam. 9:1).

APOCALYPTIC Occurs 18 times in the NT in the Greek noun form *apokalupsis* and 26 times in the verb form *apokalupto*. These Greek terms derive from the combination of the preposition *apo* and the verb *kalupto*, resulting in the definition "to uncover, unveil, or reveal." Such "uncovering" or "revelation" comes through visions or dreams and refers to the eschatological disclosure of secrets with reference to the last days. The use of the term "apocalyptic" is due to the opening word of Revelation, *apokalupsis*, meaning a revelation.

APOCRYPHA Jews did not stop writing for centuries between the OT and the NT. The intertestamental period was a time of much literary production. We designate these writings as Apocrypha and Pseudepigrapha. They did not attain canonical status, but some of them were cited by early Christians as almost on a level with the OT writings, and a few were copied in biblical manuscripts. Some NT authors were familiar with various noncanonical works, and the letter from Jude made specific reference to at least one of these books. They were ultimately preserved by the Christians rather than by the Jews.

APOCRYPHA, NEW TESTAMENT Collective term referring to a large body of religious writings dating back to the early Christian centuries that are similar in form to the NT (gospels, acts, epistles, and apocalypses) but were never included as a part of the canon of Scripture. The NT Apocrypha is significant for those who study church history.

APOLLONIA Place-name meaning "belonging to Apollo." Paul visited Apollonia on his second missionary journey, though the Bible reports no activity there (Acts 17:1). The city is in northern Greece or Macedonia on the international highway called Via Egnatia, 30 miles from Amphipolis and 38 miles from Thessalonica.

APOLLOS Alexandrian Jew who came to Ephesus following Paul's first visit and was taught Christian doctrine by Priscilla and Aquila. An educated man, Apollos handled the OT Scriptures with forcefulness. However, he was lacking in a full understanding of the way of God, so Priscilla and Aquila took him aside and instructed him (Acts 18:26). In 1 Cor. 4:6, Paul placed Apollos on the same level as himself. They both sought to defeat the arrogance and superiority that comes from being self-centered rather than Christ-centered. Because of Apollos's knowledge of the OT, Luther suggested that Apollos might well be the writer of the letter to the Hebrews.

APOLLYON Greek name meaning "destroyer" (Rev. 9:11).

APOSTASY Act of rebelling against, forsaking, abandoning, or falling away from what one has believed. The English word "apostasy" is derived from a Greek word (*apostasia*) that means "to stand away from." The Greek noun occurs twice in the NT (Acts 21:21; 2 Thess. 2:3), though it is not translated as "apostasy" in the KJV. A related noun is used for a divorce (Matt. 5:31; 19:7; Mark 10:4). The corresponding Greek verb occurs nine times.

Apostasy certainly is a biblical concept, but the implications of the teaching have been hotly debated. The debate has centered on the issue of apostasy and salvation. Based on the concept of God's sovereign grace, some hold that, though true believers may stray, they will never totally fall away. Others affirm that any who fall away were never really saved. Though they may have "believed" for a while, they never experienced regeneration. Still others argue that the biblical warnings against apostasy are real and that believers maintain the freedom, at least potentially, to reject God's salvation.

Persons worried about apostasy should recognize that conviction of sin in itself is evidence that one has not fallen away. Desire for salvation shows one does not have "an evil heart of unbelief."

APOSTLE In the NT, "apostle" has three broad uses. First, it referred to the Twelve whom Jesus chose to train for the task of carrying his message to the world. The second designation of apostle is a person authorized by a local congregation with the safe delivery of specific gifts for another Christian church (2 Cor. 8:23; Phil.2:25). The third sense of apostle is those whom Jesus Christ has sent. Paul refers to a number of people as apostles in this sense (Rom. 16:7; 1 Cor. 9:1,5; 12:28; Gal. 1:17-19). See *Disciple.*

APOSTOLIC COUNCIL Meeting in Jerusalem at which the apostles and elders of Jerusalem defended the right of Paul and Barnabas to preach the gospel to the Gentiles without forcing converts to obey the Jewish laws (Acts 15).

APOSTOLIC FATHERS Group of early church writers, some of whom knew the apostles. These writers were not grouped together or called the Apostolic Fathers until the late seventeenth century. That first collection, titled the Apostolic Fathers, included the works of Clement, Ignatius, Polycarp, Barnabas, and Hermas. Other works such as the Didache, Diognetus, and Papias often are included in recent collections. The documents (except for Diognetus and Papias) were written between approximately AD 96 and 156 but were not accepted as part of the NT canon, although Codex Sinaiticus (fourth century) included the Epistle of Barnabas and the Shepherd of Hermas, and Codex Alexandrinus (fifth century) included the two epistles of Clement.

APOTHECARY KJV translation of a word translated as "perfumer" in modern versions (Exod. 30:25,35; 37:29; 2 Chron. 16:14; Neh. 3:8; Eccles. 10:1).

APPAIM Personal name meaning "nostrils." Member of the clan of Jerahmeel of the tribe of Judah (1 Chron. 2:30-31).

APPHIA Christian woman Paul greeted as "beloved" while writing Philemon (v. 2). Early Christian tradition identified her as Philemon's wife, a claim that can be neither proved nor disproved.

APPI FORUM KJV translation of Acts 28:15 reference to Forum of Appius or Market of Appius. See *Forum.*

APPLE OF THE EYE English expression that refers to the pupil of the eye and therefore to something very precious. Three different Hebrew words or phrases are rendered as the apple of the eye.

APRON Translation of a Hebrew word in the OT otherwise translated as "girdle" (1 Sam. 18:4; 2 Sam. 18:11; 20:8; 1 Kgs. 2:5; Isa. 3:24). In Gen. 3:7, the fig leaves sewn together by Adam and Eve are called aprons to hide their nakedness. In the OT, the girdle was an inner garment wrapped around the waist. In the NT, the girdle was wrapped around the waist of the outer garment. In Acts 19:12, the aprons and handkerchiefs of Paul had healing powers.

AQABA, GULF OF TEV translation in 1 Kgs. 9:26 to indicate reference to the eastern arm of the Red Sea, below the Dead Sea. Its northern port city is Eloth (or Elath, NIV).

Pharaoh's Island in the Gulf of Aqaba.

AQUEDUCTS Troughs cut out of rock or soil, or pipes made of stone, leather, or bronze that were used from very early times in the Middle East to transport water from distant places into towns and cities.

AQUILA AND PRISCILLA Married couple who came from Italy to Corinth after the emperor Claudius ordered Jews expelled from Rome, became Christians, and assisted Paul in his ministry. They were tentmakers by trade (2 Tim. 4:19). They came into contact with Paul, who was a tentmaker, in Corinth (Acts 18:2). It is not clear whether they became Christians before or after meeting Paul, but they became workers in the gospel and accompanied Paul to Ephesus (Acts 18:19).

ARA Leader in tribe of Asher (1 Chron. 7:38).

ARAB Place-name meaning "ambush." **1.** City in the hill country of Judah near Hebron (Josh. 15:52). Usually identified with modern er-Rabiyeh. **2.** Member of the Semitic people of the Arabian Peninsula. See *Arabia.*

ARABAH Place-name meaning "dry, infertile area" and common Hebrew noun meaning desert with hot climate and sparse rainfall. Modern usage refers specifically to the rift area below the Dead Sea to the Gulf of Elath or Aqaba, a distance of 110 miles. This was a copper-mining region and was guarded by military fortresses. Control of the Arabah along with control of the Red Sea port on its southern end meant control of valuable trade routes and sea routes connecting to southern Arabia and eastern Africa (Deut. 2:8; 1 Kgs. 9:26-27).

ARABIA Asian peninsula lying between the Red Sea on the west and the Persian Gulf on the east incorporating more than 1.2 million square miles of territory.

Old Testament The Arabian Peninsula, together with the adjoining lands that were home to the biblical Arabs, includes all of present-day Saudi Arabia, the two Yemens (San'a' and Aden), Oman, the United Arab Emirates, Qatar, and Kuwait, as well as parts of Iraq, Syria, Jordan, and the Sinai Peninsula. The vast Arabian Peninsula was divided into two distinct economic and social regions. Most biblical references to Arab peoples or territory are to the northern and western parts of this whole but sometimes include both the northern and southern portions.

New Testament The NT references to Arabia are fewer and less complex. The territory of the Nabatean Arabs is probably intended in each instance. The Nabateans controlled what is today southern Jordan and the Negev of Israel; for a time they controlled as far north as Damascus. Arabs heard the gospel at Pentecost (Acts 2:11). Paul went to Arabia after his conversion (Gal. 1:17).

ARABIM NASB transliteration of name of a waterway mentioned in Isa. 15:7. Other translations include: "brook of the willows" (KJV); "Ravine of the Poplars" (NIV); "Valley of Willows" (TEV); "Wadi of the Willows" (NRSV, CSB). The water source indicated may be the Wadi el-Chesa at the southern end of the Dead Sea in Moab.

ARAD Two towns of significance to the OT. One town (Num. 21:1-3) is said to be destroyed during the time of Moses. Another was inhabited during the period of the monarchy. Both are located in the dry, semidesert region known as the Negev in the southern extreme of Judah's territory.

A man called Arad was one of six sons of Beriah the Benjaminite (1 Chron. 8:15-16), who was one of the major inhabitants of Aijalon.

ARAH Personal name meaning "ox" or "traveler." **1.** Clan of 775 people who returned to Jerusalem with Zerubbabel from Babylonian exile about 537 BC (Ezra 2:5). Nehemiah 7:10 gives the number as 652. **2.** Father of Schechaniah, father-in-law of Tobiah, who led opposition to Nehemiah (Neh. 6:18). May be identical with clan head of 1, above. **3.** Member of tribe of Asher (1 Chron. 7:39).

ARAM Personal, ethnic, and geographical name. **1.** Arameans. See *Aramean.* **2.** Original ancestor of Arameans, the son of Shem and grandson of Noah (Gen. 10:22-23). **3.** Grandson of Nahor, Abraham's brother (Gen. 22:21). **4.** Member of the tribe of Asher (1 Chron. 7:34).

ARAMAIC North Semitic language similar to Phoenician and Hebrew. It was the language of the Arameans whose presence in northwestern Mesopotamia is known from about 2000 BC.

Old Testament Parts of the OT were written in Aramaic: Ezra 4:8–6:18; 7:12-26; Dan. 2:4b–7:28; Jer. 10:11. Two words in Gen. 31:47, *Jegar-sahadutha* (heap of witness) are in Aramaic. A number of Aramaic words came into common Hebrew usage, and several passages in the Hebrew Bible show Aramaic influence.

New Testament The wide diffusion of Aramaic, along with its flexibility and adaptability, resulted in the emergence of various dialects. Jewish Palestinian Aramaic words and phrases occur in the NT, such as Abba (father) (Mark 14:36), *talitha koum* (maiden, arise; Mark 5:41), *lemá sabachtháni* (why have you abandoned me?; Mark 15:34 CSB).

ARAMEAN or **ARAMAEAN** People from a loose confederation of towns and settlements spread over what is now called Syria as well as in some parts of Babylon from which Jacob and Abraham came (Deut. 26:5).

ARAMITESS KJV translation in 1 Chron. 7:14 for an unnamed concubine from Aram, thus an Aramean or Syrian. She was mother of Machir, son of Manasseh.

ARAM-MAACAH Territory in Syria (1 Chron. 19:6), also called Syria-maachah, Maacah, Maachah. In 2 Sam. 10:6 only Aram-Zobah is named.

ARAM-NAHARAIM Country name meaning "Aram of the two rivers." Appears in the title of Ps. 60 in KJV. Transliterated from Hebrew also in Gen. 24:10; Deut. 23:4; Judg. 3:8; and 1 Chron. 19:6 by NIV. It refers to the land between the Tigris and Euphrates Rivers.

ARAM-ZOBAH Alternate name for the Aramean town and kingdom of Zobah found in the superscription of Ps. 60. See *Zobah*.

ARAN Personal name, perhaps meaning "ibex." A Horite descended from Seir (Gen. 36:28).

ARARAT Mountainous region in western Asia. **1.** Area where the ark came to rest after the flood (Gen. 8:4). **2.** Region where Sennacherib's sons fled for refuge after murdering their father (2 Kgs. 19:37). **3.** Jeremiah included Ararat in a prophetic call for a war league as judgment against Babylon (Jer. 51:27). The references in Kings and Isaiah are rendered "Armenia" in KJV, following the Septuagint tradition.

This mountain in modern Turkey may be part of the Mountains of Ararat where Noah's ark came to rest after the flood.

ARAUNAH Personal name of unknown meaning. A Jebusite whose threshing floor David purchased as a site for sacrifice, following the prophetic command of God, holding back a divine plague after David disobeyed by taking a census (2 Sam. 24:15-25). Second Chronicles 3:1 and 1 Chron. 21:15-30 refer to Araunah as Ornan.

ARBA Personal name meaning "four." Father of Anak for whom Kiriath-arba was named (Josh. 14:15; 15:13). The city became known as Hebron. Arba was the outstanding warrior among the Anakim. See *Anak, Anakim*.

ARBATHITE Resident of Beth-arabah (2 Sam. 23:31). See *Beth-arabah*.

ARBITE Native of Arab, a village in Judah near Hebron (Josh. 15:52), identified as modern er-Rabiyeh. One of David's 30 elite warriors was Paarai, an Arbite (2 Sam. 23:35).

ARCH KJV rendering of a Hebrew word in Ezek. 40:16-36. The KJV translates the word as "porch" elsewhere (e.g., 1 Kgs. 6:3; 7:12,19,21). Other versions translate the word as "porch" (NASB), "portico" (CSB), "galleries (NIV), "vestibule" and "walls" (RSV), and "entrance room" and "galleries" (TEV).

ARCHAEOLOGY AND BIBLICAL STUDY Archaeology is the study of the past based upon the recovery, examination, and explanation of the material remains of human life, thought, and activity, coordinated with available information concerning the ancient environment. Biblical archaeology, a discipline largely developing since 1800, searches for what can be learned about biblical events, characters, and teachings from sources outside the Bible. Dealing with what ancient civilizations left behind, its goal is to give a better understanding of the Bible itself. Though the idea that archaeology can prove the Bible is frowned on by many archaeologists, it has nevertheless confirmed biblical accounts in many cases. The main function of archaeology is illumination of past cultures. The great gulf in time, language, and culture between our day and biblical times makes knowledge of archaeological discoveries essential for thorough understanding of the Bible.

Step trench cut into the tel of Old Testament Jericho by archaeologists to uncover levels of destruction.

ARCHANGEL Chief or first angel. The English term "archangel" is a derivative of the Greek word *archangelos*, which occurs only twice in the NT (1 Thess. 4:16; Jude 9). Michael is the only named archangel.

ARCHELAUS Son and principal successor of Herod the Great (Matt. 2:22).

ARCHEVITES Group who joined Rehum the commander in writing a letter to King Artaxerxes of Persia protesting the rebuilding of Jerusalem under Zerubbabel's leadership about 537 BC. NASB, NIV, NRSV translate Archevites as people or men of Erech.

ARCHI, ARCHITE Unknown group of people who gave their name to a border point of the tribes of Ephraim and Benjamin (Josh. 16:2).

ARCHIPPUS Personal name meaning "first among horsemen." A Christian whom Paul greeted in Col. 4:17 and Philem. 2, entreating him to fulfill the ministry God gave him. Some have suggested he was the son of Philemon and Appia, but this can be neither proved nor disproved.

ARCTURUS Constellation of stars God created (Job 9:9; 38:32) of which exact identification was not clear to the earliest Bible translators and continues to be debated. Modern translations generally use "Bear" (NASB, NIV, NRSV, CSB). TEV uses "the Dipper." Some scholars prefer "the lion." Whatever the identification, the star points to the sovereign greatness of God beyond human understanding.

ARD, ARDITE Personal name meaning "hunchbacked." **1.** Son of Benjamin and grandson of Jacob (Gen. 46:21). **2.** Grandson and clan father of Benjamin (Num. 26:40). Apparently listed as Addar in 1 Chron. 8:3.

ARDON Son of Caleb (1 Chron. 2:18).

ARELI, ARELITES Son of Gad (Gen. 46:16) and original ancestor of the clan of Arelites (Num. 26:17).

AREOPAGITE Member of the highly respected Greek council that met on the Areopagus in Athens. See *Areopagus; Athens; Dionysius*.

AREOPAGUS Site of Paul's speech to the Epicurean and Stoic philosophers of Athens (Acts 17:19). It was a rocky hill about 370 feet high, not far from the Acropolis and the Agora (marketplace) in Athens, Greece. The word also was used to refer to the council that originally met on this hill. The name probably was derived from Ares, the Greek name for the god of war known to the Romans as Mars. See *Mars Hill.*

ARETAS Personal name meaning "moral excellence, power." The ruler of Damascus in NT times. He sought to arrest Paul after Paul's conversion (2 Cor. 11:32). The name Aretas was borne by several Arabian kings centered in Petra and Damascus. Aretas IV ruled from Petra (9 BC–AD 40) as a subject of Rome. Herod Antipas married his daughter, then divorced her to marry Herodias (Mark 6:17-18). Aretas joined with a Roman officer to defeat Herod's army in AD 36.

ARGOB Personal and geographical name meaning "mound of earth." **1.** Man who might have joined Pekah (2 Kgs. 15:25) in murdering Pekahiah, king of Israel (742–740 BC) or possibly was killed by Pekah. **2.** Territory in Bashan in the hill country east of the Jordan River. Argob was probably in the center of the fertile tableland and was famous for its strong cities (Deut. 3:4).

ARIDAI Persian personal name, perhaps meaning "delight of Hari" (a god). Son of Haman, the archenemy of Esther and the Jews. He died as the Jews reversed Haman's scheme and gained revenge (Esth. 9:9).

ARIDATHA Persian personal name, perhaps meaning "given by Hari" (a god). Brother of Aridai who shared his fate. See *Aridai.*

ARIEL Personal name meaning "God's lion." **1.** Jewish leader in captivity who acted as Ezra's messenger to the Levites to send people with Ezra to Jerusalem about 458 BC (Ezra 8:16). **2.** Code name for Jerusalem in Isa. 29.

ARIMATHEA City of Joseph, the disciple who claimed the body of Jesus following the crucifixion and in whose own new tomb the body was placed (Matt. 27:57). The location of Arimathea is not certainly known.

ARIOCH Personal, probably Hurrian, name meaning "servant of the moon god." **1.** King of Ellasar, who joined alliance against Sodom and Gomorrah (Gen. 14) but was eventually defeated by Abraham. **2.** Commander of bodyguard of King Nebuchadnezzar (Dan. 2:14-25).

ARISAI Persian personal name. Son of Haman (Esth. 9:9) who suffered his brothers' fate. See *Aridai.*

ARISTARCHUS Personal name, perhaps meaning "best ruler." Paul's companion caught by the followers of Artemis in Ephesus (Acts 19:29).

ARISTOBULUS Head of a Christian household in Rome whom Paul greeted (Rom. 16:10).

ARK Boat or water vessel and in particular one built by Noah under God's direction to save Noah, his family, and representatives of all animal life from the flood. The ark became both a symbol of a faith on the part of Noah and a symbol of grace on the part of God (Gen. 6:8,22).

ARK OF THE COVENANT Original container for the Ten Commandments and the central symbol of God's presence with

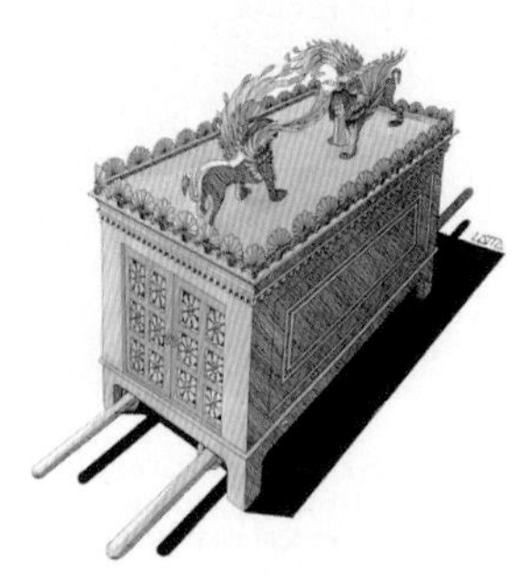

Reconstruction of the ark of the covenant drawn in the Egyptian style, reflecting the 400 years of bondage in Egypt.

the people of Israel. Hebrews 9:1-10 shows the ark was a part of the old order with external regulations waiting for the new day of Christ to come with a perfect sacrifice able to cleanse the human conscience. Revelation 11:19 shows the ark of the covenant will be part of the heavenly temple when it is revealed.

ARM Upper limb of the human body used to symbolize power and strength.

ARMAGEDDON Middle East site of the final battle between the forces of good and evil (Rev. 16:16). The word "Armageddon" appears once in Scripture and is not found in Hebrew literature.

ARMENIA KJV translation for land of Ararat (2 Kgs. 19:37). See *Ararat.*

ARMONI Personal name meaning "born in Armon." Son of Rizpah and Saul, whom David gave to the Gibeonites in revenge for Saul's earlier killing of Gibeonites (2 Sam. 21:7-9).

ARNAN Personal name meaning "quick." Person in messianic line of King David after the return from exile (1 Chron. 3:21).

ARNI Ancestor of Jesus in difficult text of Luke 3:33. NASB, NIV, CSB read Ram, correlating with list in 1 Chron. 2:10.

ARNON Place-name meaning "rushing river" or "river flooded with berries." River forming border of Moab and Amorites (Num. 21:13).

AROD or **ARODI** Personal name meaning "hump-backed." Arodi (Gen. 46:16) or Arod (Num. 26:17) was son of Gad and grandson of Jacob. He was the original ancestor of the Arodite clan.

AROER Place-name meaning "juniper." **1.** City on north rim of Arnon Gorge east of Dead Sea on southern boundary of territory Israel claimed east of the Jordan River (Josh. 13:9). **2.** City of the tribe of Gad (Josh. 13:25) near Rabbah, capital of the Ammonites. This may be the Aroer where Jephthah defeated the Ammonites (Judg. 11:33). **3.** Town in southern Judah about 12 miles southeast of Beersheba with whose leaders David divided the spoil of battle (1 Sam. 30:28). This is located at modern Khirbet Arara. The text of Josh. 15:22 may have originally read "Aroer." Two of David's captains hailed from Aroer (1 Chron. 11:44).

ARPACHSHAD or **ARPHAXAD** (NT) Third son of Shem, son of Noah, and ancestor of the Hebrew people (Gen. 10:22). He was born two years after the flood and was the grandfather of Eber.

ARPAD or **ARPHAD** City-state in northern Syria closely identified with Hamath.

ARTAXERXES Persian royal name meaning "kingdom of righteousness," belonging to four Persian rulers and forming a major piece of evidence in dating Ezra and Nehemiah. **1.** Son of Xerxes I, Artaxerxes I ruled Persia from 465 to 424 BC. He was called Longimanus or "long handed." **2.** Artaxerxes II ruled Persia 404–359 BC. Some Bible students identify him as the ruler under whom Ezra worked. **3.** Artaxerxes III ruled 358–337 BC. **4.** Name assumed by Arses, who ruled Persia 337–336 BC.

ARTEMAS Personal name probably shortened from Artemidoros, meaning "gift of Artemis." If this is the case, the parents worshipped the Greek goddess Artemis. Paul promised to send Artemas or Tychicus to Titus, so Titus could join Paul in Nicopolis (Titus 3:12). Artemas would apparently take over Titus's pastoral duties in Crete. Tradition says Artemas became bishop of Lystra.

ARTEMIS Name for the Greek goddess of the moon, the daughter of Zeus and Leto, whose worship was threatened by Paul's preaching of the gospel. Artemis was the goddess who watched over nature for both humans and animals. She was the patron deity of wild animals, protecting them from ruthless treatment and at the same time regulating the rules of hunting activities for humans. She was considered the great mother image and gave fertility to humankind. The most famous statue of Artemis was located in the city of Ephesus, the official "temple keeper" for Artemis. Artemis was the chief deity of Ephesus, and her temple was one of the Seven Wonders of the Ancient World. Diana was a Roman deity somewhat similar to the more popular Artemis.

ARUBBOTH City name meaning "smoke hole" or "chimney." One of Solomon's provincial officials made headquarters there and administered over Sochoh and the land of Hepher (1 Kgs. 4:10).

ARUMAH Place-name meaning "exalted" or "height." Abimelech, the judge, lived there while he fought to control Shechem (Judg. 9:41).

ARVAD, ARVADITE Place-name of unknown meaning and persons from that place. It provided sailors and soldiers for Tyre (Ezek. 27:8,11). It was probably the rocky island called Rouad today, off the coast of Syria. It is related to Canaan in the family of nations (Gen. 10:18).

ARZA Personal name meaning "wood worm" or "earthiness." Steward of the house of King Baasha (908–886 BC) in Tirzah. The king was drunk in Arza's house when Zimri killed Baasha (1 Kgs. 16:8-10).

ASA Personal name meaning "doctor" or "healing." **1.** Son and successor of Abijam as king of Judah (1 Kgs. 15:8). He reigned for 41 years (913–873 BC). A pious man, he instituted several reforms to remove foreign gods and foreign religious practices from the land, even removing his mother from political power (1 Kgs. 15:13). **2.** Levite who returned from the exile to Jerusalem. He was the head of a family in the villages of the Netophathites near Jerusalem (1 Chron. 9:16).

ASAHEL Personal name meaning "God acted" or "God made." **1.** David's nephew, brother of Joab and Abishai One of David's 30 elite warriors, known for his great speed as a runner.. He was killed in battle by Saul's commander, Abner (2 Sam 2:17-24). **2.** Levite during the reign of Jehoshaphat, Asa's son. Asahel was sent out along with several princes, other Levites, and priests to teach the people of Judah the book of the law of God (2 Chron. 17:8). **3.** A Levite under Hezekiah, the king of Judah following Ahaz. **4.** Father of Jonathan who along with Jahaziah opposed Ezra's direction for the men of Judah to separate themselves from the foreign wives they had married. Ezra indicated they had sinned in marrying foreign women (Ezra 10:15).

ASAHIAH or **ASAIAH** Personal name meaning "Yahweh made." **1.** Servant of King Josiah sent with others to Huldah, the prophet, to determine the meaning of the book of the law found in the temple about 624 BC. **2.** Leader of the tribe of Simeon who helped drive out the people of Ham from pastures of Gedor when Hezekiah was king of Judah (715–686 BC). **3.** Musical Levite in the line of Merari (1 Chron. 6:30). **4.** Leader of clans from Shiloh who returned from Babylonian exile about 537 BC (1 Chron. 9:5).

ASAPH Personal name meaning "he collected." **1.** Father of Joah, a court historian under King Hezekiah (715–686 BC) who in sadness reported the threats of Assyria to the king (2 Kgs. 18). **2.** Levite musician whom David appointed to serve in the tabernacle until the temple was completed (1 Chron. 6:39). Asaph was the father of the clan of temple musicians who served through the history of the temple.

ASAREL or **ASAREEL** (KJV) Personal name meaning "God has sworn" or "God rejoiced." A member of the tribe of Judah (1 Chron. 4:16).

ASARELAH KJV, NIV, NRSV, CSB spelling of Asharelah (NASB, RSV, TEV) in 1 Chron. 25:2. This appears to be a variant of Jesharelah or Jesarelah in 1 Chron. 25:14. The person is a descendant or son of Asaph among the temple singers.

ASCENSION Movement or departure from the lower to the higher with reference to spatial location. Both OT and NT record the events of human ascension in the lives of Enoch (Gen. 5:24), Elijah (2 Kgs. 2:1-2), and, most important, Jesus Christ (Acts 1:9). The ascension concluded the earthly ministry of Jesus, allowing eyewitnesses to see both the resurrected Christ on earth and the victorious, eternal Christ returning to heaven to minister at the right hand of the Father.

ASENATH Egyptian name meaning "belonging to Neith" (a goddess). Wife of Joseph and daughter of a priest in Egyptian temple at On or Heliopolis. Asenath was Pharaoh's present to Joseph (Gen. 41:45). She was mother of Ephraim and Manasseh (Gen. 41:50-51).

ASH KJV in Isa. 44:14. Some manuscripts of the Hebrew text have the word for cedar, which is very similar to the word found in the text translated by the KJV. Modern versions differ. The word is translated fir (NASB), pine (NIV), cedar (NRSV, REB), and laurel tree (TEV, CSB).

ASHAN Place-name meaning "smoke." City in western hills of the tribe of Judah (Josh. 15:42) given to the tribe of Simeon (Josh. 19:7). The Aaronic priests claimed Ashan as one of their cities (1 Chron. 6:59; called Ain in Josh. 21:16). Ashan was located at modern Khirbet Asan just northwest of Beer-sheba.

ASHBEL, ASHBELITES Personal name meaning "having a long upper lip." Son of Benjamin, grandson of Jacob, and original ancestor of the Ashbelite clan (Gen. 46:21).

ASHCHENAZ or **ASHKENAZ** Personal and national name given two spellings in KJV but spelled Ashkenaz in modern translations. A son of Gomer (Gen. 10:3) and original ancestor of people called kingdom of Ashkenaz (Jer. 51:27). Usually identified with Scythians.

ASHDOD One of five principal cities of the Philistines, where the Philistines defeated Israel and captured the ark of the covenant. Ashdod was 10 miles north of Ashkelon and about 2.5 miles east of the Mediterranean Sea on the Philistine plain.

ASHER or **ASER** (NT Gk.), **ASHERITES** Personal, place, and tribal name meaning "fortune," "happiness." **1.** Eighth son of Jacob, born of Zilpah, the concubine (Gen. 30:13). His four sons and one daughter began the tribe of Asher (Gen. 46:17). Jacob's blessing said Asher would have rich food that he would give a king (Gen. 49:20), perhaps suggesting a period when the tribe would serve a foreign king. **2.** The tribe of Asher numbered 53,400 in the wilderness (Num. 26:47), having grown from 41,500 (Num. 1:41). They formed part of the rear guard in the wilderness marches (Num. 10:25-28). Asher's territorial allotment was in Phoenicia in the far northwest reaching to Tyre and Sidon on the Mediterranean coast (Josh. 19:24-31). **3.** Apparently a border town in Manasseh (Josh. 17:7) but possibly a reference to the border joining the tribal territories of Manasseh and Asher.

ASHERAH, ASHERIM (pl.) or **ASHEROTH** (pl.) Fertility goddess, the mother of Baal, whose worship was concentrated in Syria and Canaan, and the wooden object that represented her. The KJV translated Asherah "grove" and the proper noun "Ashtaroth."

ASHES Often associated with sacrifices, mourning, and fasting. Grief, humiliation, and repentance were expressed by placing ashes on the head or by sitting in ashes. The use of ashes to express grief and repentance continued into the NT period. Their use in purification rites is contrasted with the cleansing brought by Christ's blood. They also represent the devastating effect of God's wrath on Sodom and Gomorrah (2 Pet. 2:6).

ASHHUR Modern translation spelling of Ashur (KJV, TEV). Personal name meaning "to be black," or "belonging to Ishara." Son of Hazron, born after his father's death (1 Chron. 2:24). His title, "Father of Tekoa," may indicate he founded the city later famous for native son Amos, the prophet.

ASHIMA Syrian god made and worshipped in Hamath (2 Kgs. 17:30). The Hebrew word *'asham* means "guilt." Hebrew writers may have deliberately written a word associated with guilt instead of the name of the god or goddess.

ASHKELON One of five principal cities of the Philistines (Pentapolis), located on the Mediterranean coast on the trade route Via Maris and designated for Judah in the conquest. Ashkelon was a Mediterranean coastal city 12 miles north of Gaza and 10 miles south of Ashdod. It was the only Philistine city directly on the seacoast. Its history extends into the Neolithic Period. The economic importance came from both its port and its location on the Via Maris.

ASHNAH Place-name. **1.** City in the valley of the tribe of Judah (Josh. 15:33), possibly modern Aslin. **2.** City in the valley or Shephelah of Judah (Josh. 15:43), possibly modern Idna, about eight miles northwest of Hebron.

ASHPENAZ Chief eunuch guarding the family of Nebuchadnezzar, king of Babylon (605–562 BC) (Dan. 1:3). He administered the diet and lifestyle of Daniel and his three friends, giving them new Babylonian names (Dan. 1:7). Daniel developed a close, loving relationship with him.

ASHTAROTH is the plural form of Ashtoreth, a Canaanite goddess of fertility, love, and war and the daughter of the god El and the goddess Asherah. **1.** OT uses the plural form, Ashtaroth, more than the singular form, Ashtoreth. The only references to Ashtoreth come in 1 Kgs. 11:5,33; 2 Kgs. 23:13. **2.** Egyptian documents dating from the eighteenth century BC onward refer to a city called Ashtartu or Ashtarot in the region of Bashan. Joshua 21:27 mentions a city with the name Be-eshterah in Bashan, while a man named Uzzia is called an Ashterathite (1 Chron. 11:44).

ASHURBANIPAL Assyria's last great king who is identified in Ezra 4:10 as the king of Assyria who captured Susa, Elam, and other nations and settled their citizens in Samaria.

ASHURITES or **ASHURI** (NIV) Apparently a tribe or clan over which Ish-bosheth, Saul's son, ruled (2 Sam. 2:9). CSB: Asher.

ASHVATH Personal name meaning "that which has been worked" (as iron). Descendant of Asher (1 Chron. 7:33).

ASIA The NT refers to a Roman province on the west of Asia Minor whose capital was Ephesus. The Roman province of Asia comprised generally the southwest portion of Anatolia. Its first capital was Pergamum, but the capital was later changed to Ephesus.

ASIA MINOR, CITIES OF Cities located on the Anatolian peninsula (modern-day Turkey). Cities of Asia Minor important to the NT accounts included Alexandria Troas, Assos, Ephesus, Miletus, Patara, Smyrna, Pergamum, Sardis, Thyatira, Philadelphia, Laodicea, Colossae, Attalia, Antioch, Iconium, Lystra, Derbe, and Tarsus. The cities figured prominently in the apostle Paul's missionary journeys, several of the churches receiving epistles. Among those listed are the Seven Cities of the Revelation.

ASIARCHS Somewhat general term for public patrons and leaders named by cities in the Roman province of Asia.

ASIEL Personal name meaning "God has made." A descendant of Simeon and clan leader who settled in Gedor in rich pasturelands (1 Chron. 4:35-40).

ASNAH Proper name possibly with Egyptian origins relating to the god Nah. One of the Nethanims or temple servants who returned to Jerusalem with Zerubbabel from exile about 537 BC (Ezra 2:50).

ASNAPPER KJV reading in Ezra 4:10. Modern translations read Osnappar (NASB, RSV) or Ashurbanipal (TEV, NIV, CSB).

ASP KJV translation for a dangerous, poisonous snake (Deut. 32:33; Job 20:14,16; Isa. 11:8; Rom. 3:13). Other translations use "serpent," "viper," or "cobra" at some or all of these places.

ASPATHA Persian personal name. Son of Haman killed by Jews (Esth. 9:10).

ASRIEL, ASRIELITES Personal name meaning "God has made happy." A son of Gilead and clan in the tribe of Manasseh (Num. 26:31). They received a land allotment (Josh. 17:2). In 1 Chron. 7:14, KJV spells it Ashriel.

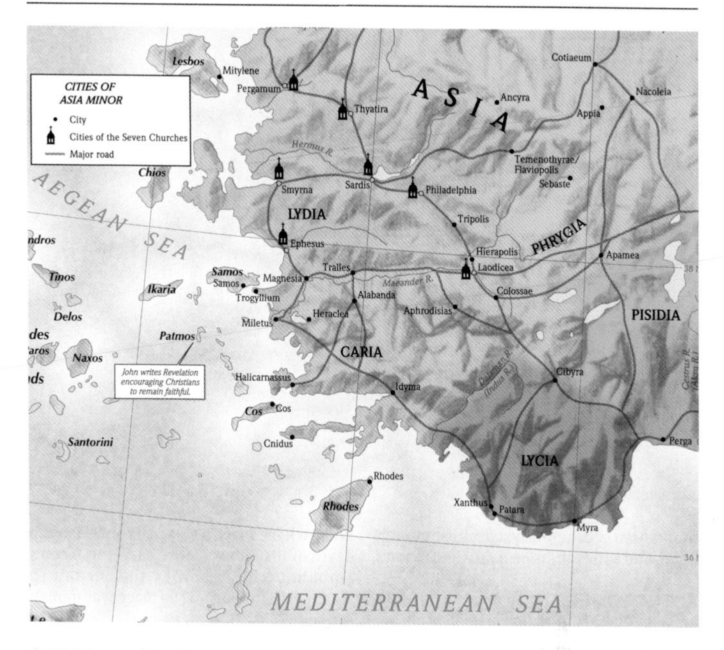

ASS "Beast of burden" and "wild animal" in KJV but translated "donkey" in most modern translations. Six different Hebrew words and two Greek words lie behind the English translations. This animal appears more than 120 times in the Bible.

ASSASSINS Organized Jewish group who attempted to win freedom from the Romans. The word in Greek is derived from the Latin term *Sicarii* and literally means "dagger men." In Acts 21:38, Paul was mistaken as a leader of 4,000 *Sicarii*. KJV calls them murderers; REB and TEV, terrorists; CSB, assassins.

ASSAYER One who tests ore for its silver and gold content. According to modern versions of Jer. 6:27, the calling of Jeremiah was to be an assayer of the people. He did not find them to be a precious metal.

ASSEMBLY Official gathering of the people of Israel and of the church.

ASSHUR, ASSHURIM, ASSHURITES (NIV) Personal and national name. **1.** Son of Shem and thus a Semite, as were the Hebrew people (Gen. 10:22). **2.** Unknown Arabian tribe (Gen. 25:3). This tribe may also be meant in Balaam's oracle (Num. 24:22-24), but a reference to Assyria is more likely. **3.** The nation Assyria and its inhabitants are generally meant by the Hebrew term *Asshur*. This is the likely meaning in Gen. 10:11; Ezek. 27:23; 32:22; Hos. 14:3. See *Assyria*.

ASSYRIA Nation in northern Mesopotamia in OT times that became a large empire during the period of the Israelite kings. Assyrian expansion into the region of Palestine (ca. 855–625 BC) had enormous impact on the Hebrew kingdoms of Israel and Judah.

History Assyria lay north of the region of Babylonia along the banks of the Tigris River (Gen. 2:14) in northern Mesopotamia. The name Assyria (Hb., *Ashshur*) is from Asshur, its first capital, founded about 2000 BC. The

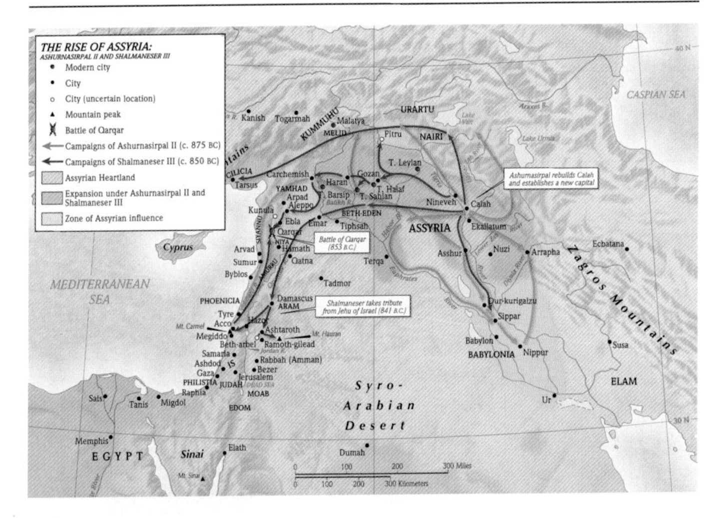

foundation of other Assyrian cities, notably Calah and Nineveh, appears in Gen. 10:11-12.

ASTROLOGER Person who "divided the heavens" (literal translation of Hebrew phrase, Isa. 47:13) to determine the future. Particularly the Babylonians developed sophisticated methods of reading the stars to determine proper times for action. The Bible does not seek to describe the skills, tactics, or methods of foreign personnel engaged in various practices to determine the opportune time. Rather the Bible mocks such practices and shows that God's word to the prophets and the wise of Israel far surpasses any foreign skills.

ASUPPIM KJV interpretation in 1 Chron. 26:15,17. Modern translations read "storehouses."

ASWAN NIV, TEV in Ezek. 29:10; 30:6 for Syene.

ASYNCRITUS Personal name meaning "incomparable." Roman Christian whom Paul greeted (Rom. 16:14).

ATAD Personal name meaning "thorn." Owner of threshing floor, or part of name of Bramble Threshing Floor, east of the Jordan River where Joseph stopped to mourn the death of his father before carrying Jacob's embalmed body across the Jordan to Machpelah for burial. The place was named Abel-mizraim (Gen. 50:10-11).

ATARAH Personal name meaning "crown" or "wreath." Second wife of Jerahmeel and mother of Onam (1 Chron. 2:26).

ATAROTH Place-name meaning "crowns." **1.** Town desired and built up by the tribe of Gad (Num. 32:3,34). **2.** Village on border of Benjamin and Ephraim (Josh. 16:2,7).

ATAROTH-ADDAR Place-name meaning "crowns of glory." A border town in Ephraim (Josh. 16:5), bordering Benjamin (Josh. 18:13), probably modern Khirbet Attara at the foot of Tell en-Nasbeh or possibly identical with Tell en-Nasbeh and thus with biblical Mizpah.

ATER Personal name meaning either "crippled" or "left-handed." Clan of which 98 returned from Babylonian exile with Zerubbabel about 537 BC (Ezra 2:16). They were temple gatekeepers (Ezra 2:42). The head of the clan signed Nehemiah's covenant to keep God's law (Neh. 10:17).

ATHACH Place-name meaning "attack." Town in southern Judah to which David sent spoils of victory while he fled Saul among the Philistines (1 Sam. 30:30). May be the same as Ether (Josh. 15:42), a small copying change causing the difference.

ATHAIAH Leader of tribe of Judah who lived in Jerusalem in the time of Nehemiah (Neh. 11:4).

ATHALIAH Personal name meaning "Yahweh has announced his exalted nature" or "Yahweh is righteous." **1.** Wife of Jehoram, king of Judah, and mother of Ahaziah, king of Judah. She was the daughter of Ahab and Jezebel of Israel (2 Kgs. 8:18) or of Omri, king of Israel (2 Kgs. 8:26). **2.** Son of Jeroham in the tribe of Benjamin (1 Chron. 8:26). **3.** Father of Jeshaiah, who led 70 men back to Jerusalem from exile with Ezra (Ezra 8:7).

ATHARIM Hebrew word of uncertain meaning. It names a roadway the king of Arad took to attack Israel under Moses. After an initial setback, Israel prayed and found victory under God (Num. 21:13). KJV translates "spies," following the Septuagint, the earliest Greek translation. Modern translations simply transliterate the Hebrew. The site may be Tamar, a few miles south of the Dead Sea.

ATHENS Capital of Attica, an ancient district of east central Greece, where Paul preached to the Greek philosophers (Acts 17:15-34).

The Parthenon on the Acropolis at Athens.

ATHLAI Personal name meaning "Yahweh is exalted." A man who agreed (Ezra 10:28) under Ezra's leadership to divorce his foreign wife and return to faithfulness to Yahweh.

ATONEMENT Biblical doctrine that God has reconciled sinners to himself through the sacrificial work of

Jesus Christ. The concept of atonement spans both Testaments, everywhere pointing to the death, burial, and resurrection of Jesus for the sins of the world. All are invited to find refuge in the atonement of Christ (Luke 14:16-17). The apostles plead with sinners to trust in the atoning work of Jesus (Acts 2:40; 2 Cor. 5:20). All human beings are not only invited but commanded to believe the gospel (Acts 17:30-31). This does not mean, however, that the objective accomplishment of the atonement brings about universal salvation. Jesus is himself the One who is the propitiation of God's wrath against the world (1 John 2:2). Those who are redeemed are saved from God's judgment because they are united to Christ through faith (Eph. 1:7). On the final day of judgment, those who are not "in Christ" will bear the eternal penalty for their own sins (2 Cor. 5:10) and for the dread transgression of rejecting God's provision in Christ (John 3:19; Heb. 10:29).

ATROTH (KJV) or **ATROTH-BETH-JOAB** Place-name meaning "crowns of the house of Joab." A "descendant" of Caleb and Hur (1 Chron. 2:54), the name apparently refers to a village near Bethlehem.

ATROTH-SHOPHAN Town built by the tribe of Gad of unknown location (Num. 32:35). Earliest translations spelled name various ways: Shophar, Shaphim, Shopham, Etroth Shophan.

ATTAI Personal name meaning "timely." **1.** Member of the clan of Jerahmeel in the tribe of Judah (1 Chron. 2:35-36). **2.** Warrior of the tribe of Gad who served David in the wilderness as he fled from Saul (1 Chron. 12:11). **3.** Son of Maachah (2 Chron. 11:20), the favorite and beloved wife of King Rehoboam of Judah (931–913 BC).

ATTALIA Seaport city on northern Mediterranean coast in Asia Minor where

Paul stopped briefly on first missionary journey (Acts 14:25). Modern Antalya continues as a small seaport with some ancient ruins.

AUGUSTAN COHORT Unit of the Roman army stationed in Syria from about AD 6. The cohort's place among the rest of the Roman army is indicated by the fact that it was named after the emperor. This special unit was given charge of Paul on his way to Rome (Acts 27:1). In Luke's eyes, this demonstrated the importance of Paul and, more important, the gospel that Paul preached.

AUGUSTUS Title meaning "reverend" that the Roman Senate gave to Emperor Octavian (31 BC–AD 14) in 27 BC. He ruled the Roman Empire, including Palestine, when Jesus was born and ordered the taxation that brought Joseph and Mary to Bethlehem (Luke 2:1). He was the adopted son of Julius Caesar.

AVA or **AVVA** People the Assyrians conquered and settled in Israel to replace the people they took into exile (2 Kgs. 17:24).

AVEN Hebrew noun meaning "wickedness," used in place-names to indicate Israel's understanding of the place as a site of idol worship. **1.** Referred to On or Heliopolis in Egypt (Ezek. 30:17). **2.** Referred to major worship centers of Israel such as Bethel and Dan (Hos. 10:8). **3.** Referred to a valley, perhaps one in place of popularly known names such as Beth-aven for Bethel (Josh. 7:2; 18:12).

AVENGER Person with the legal responsibility to protect the rights of an endangered relative. Avenger translates Hebrew *go'el*, which in its verbal form means to redeem. Redemption applies to repossessing things consecrated to God (Lev. 27:13-31) or to God's actions for his people (Exod. 6:6; Job 19:25; Ps. 103:4; Isa. 43:1). Ultimately God is the *go'el* (Isa. 41:14).

AVIM, AVIMS, AVITES, AVVIM, AVVITE **1.** People of whom nothing is known outside biblical sources. They lived on the Philistine coast before the Philistines invaded about 1200 BC (Deut. 2:23). **2.** City in the tribal territory of Benjamin (Josh. 18:23) about which nothing is known.

AVITH City name meaning "ruin." Capital city of Hadad, king of Edom, before Israel had a king (Gen. 36:35). Its location is unknown.

AWE, AWESOME Refers to an emotion combining honor, fear, and respect before someone of superior office or actions (Pss. 4:4; 33:8; 119:161 KJV) (Gen. 28:17; Deut. 7:21; Heb. 12:28 CSB). It most appropriately applies to God.

AWL Instrument or tool made of flint, bone, stone, or metal to bore holes. Biblical references refer to using the awl to pierce a servant's ear (Exod. 21:6; Deut. 15:17). Perhaps a ring or identification tag was placed in the hole. This marked the slave as a permanent slave, for life. Excavators in Palestine unearth many such boring tools.

AX, AX HEAD English translation of several Hebrew terms indicating cutting instruments used in normal small industry and in war.

AYYAH Place-name meaning "ruin." In the unclear Hebrew text of 1 Chron. 7:28, modern translations read Ayyah as a city on the border of Ephraim. Some identify this with Ai. Others follow a Greek text tradition that apparently read Gaza.

AZALIAH Personal name meaning "Yahweh has reserved." Father of Shaphan, Josiah's scribe (2 Kgs. 22:3). See *Shaphan*.

AZANIAH Personal name meaning "Yahweh listened." Father of a Levite who signed Nehemiah's covenant to obey God's law (Neh. 10:9).

AZARAEL (KJV, Neh. 12:36), **AZAREEL** (KJV) or **AZAREL** Personal name meaning "God helped." **1.** David's soldier at Ziklag, skilled with bow and arrow and able to sling stones with either hand (1 Chron. 12:6). **2.** Leader of a course of priests selected by lot under David (1 Chron. 25:18). **3.** Leader of the tribe of Dan under David (1 Chron. 27:22). **4.** Priest who had married a foreign wife under Ezra (Ezra 10:41). **5.** Father of Amashai, head of a priestly family who lived in Jerusalem under Nehemiah (Neh. 11:13).

6. Priest who played a musical instrument in time of Nehemiah (Neh. 12:36), probably the same as 5, above.

AZARIAH Personal name meaning "Yahweh has helped." **1.** Son and successor of Amaziah as king of Judah (792–740 BC). Also called Uzziah. See *Uzziah*. **2.** High priest under Solomon (1 Kgs. 4:2) listed as son of Zadok (1 Kgs. 4:2) or of Ahimaaz (1 Chron. 6:9), the son of Zadok (2 Sam. 15:27). If the latter is accurate, then son in 1 Kgs. 4:2 means descendant. **3.** Son of Nathan in charge of the system of obtaining provisions for the court from the 12 governmental provinces (1 Kgs. 4:5). He would have supervised the persons listed in 1 Kgs. 4:7-19. **4.** Great grandson of Judah (1 Chron. 2:8). **5.** Member of the clan of Jerahmeel in the tribe of Judah (1 Chron. 2:38-39). **6.** High priest, son of Johanan (1 Chron. 6:10). **7.** High priest, son of Hilkiah (1 Chron. 6:13-14) and father of Seraiah, who is listed as Ezra's father (Ezra 7:1). The list in Ezra is not complete. Apparently some generations have been omitted. **8.** Member of family of Kohath, the temple singers (1 Chron. 6:36). Apparently called Uzziah in 6:24. **9.** A priest, son of Hilkiah (1 Chron. 9:11) may be same as 7 above. **10.** Prophet, son of Oded, whose message gave King Asa (910–869 BC) courage to restore proper worship in Judah (2 Chron. 15:1-8). **11.** Two sons of Jehoshaphat, king of Judah (873–848 BC) according to 2 Chron. 21:2. Perhaps the boys had different mothers, each of whom gave the son the common name Azariah. **12.** Son of Jehoram, king of Judah (852–841) according to 2 Chron. 22:6, but the correct name is probably Ahaziah as in 2 Kgs. 8:29. Azariah represents a copyist's error in Chronicles. **13.** Two military commanders of 100 men who helped Jehoiada, the high priest, depose and murder Athaliah as queen of Judah and install Joash as king (835–796). **14.** High priest who led 80 priests to oppose King Uzziah of Judah (792–740 BC) when Uzziah tried to burn incense in the temple rather than let the priests. God struck Uzziah with a dreaded skin disease (2 Chron. 26:16-21). **15.** A leader of the tribe of Ephraim under Pekah, king of Israel (752–732 BC), who rescued captives Pekah had taken from Judah, cared for their physical needs, and returned them to Jericho (2 Chron. 28:5-15). **16.** Levite whose son Joel helped cleanse the temple under Hezekiah, king of Judah (715–686 BC) (2 Chron. 29:12-19). **17.** A Levite who helped cleanse the temple (2 Chron. 29:12-19). See 16, above. **18.** Chief priest under King Hezekiah who rejoiced with the king over the generous tithes and offerings of the people (2 Chron. 31:10-13). **19.** Son of Meraioth in the list of high priests and father of Amariah (Ezra 7:3). Since the list in Ezra is incomplete, this Azariah may be the same as 6, above. **20.** Helper of Nehemiah in rebuilding the wall of Jerusalem (Neh. 3:23). **21.** Man who returned from exile with Zerubbabel (Neh. 7:7) about 537 BC. He is called Seraiah in Ezra 2:2. **22.** Man who helped Ezra interpret the law to the people in Jerusalem (Neh. 8:7). **23.** Man who put his seal on Nehemiah's covenant to obey God's law (Neh. 10:2). **24.** A leader of Judah, possibly a priest, who marched with Nehemiah and others on the walls of Jerusalem to celebrate the completion of rebuilding the city defense walls (Neh. 12:33). He may be identical with any one or all of 20–23, above. **25.** Daniel's friend renamed Abednego by Persian officials. God delivered him from the fiery furnace (Dan. 1:7; 4:1-30). See *Abednego; Daniel*. **26.** Son of Hoshaiah and leader of Jewish people who tried to get Jeremiah to give them a word from God directing them to go to Egypt after the Babylonians destroyed Jerusalem. When Jeremiah said not to go, they accused him of lying (Jer. 42:1–43:7). Hebrew text reads Jezaniah in 42:1.

AZARIAHU Long form of Azariah used by NASB, NIV in 2 Chron. 21:2 to differentiate two men named Azariah. See *Azariah*.

AZAZ Personal name meaning "he is strong." A descendant of the tribe of Reuben (1 Chron. 5:8).

AZAZIAH Personal name meaning "Yahweh is strong." **1.** Levite David appointed to play the harp for the temple worship (1 Chron. 15:21). **2.** Father of leader of the tribe of Ephraim under David (1 Chron. 27:20). **3.** Overseer among the priests under Hezekiah (715–686 BC) (2 Chron. 31:13).

AZBUK Father of a Nehemiah who repaired Jerusalem under the leadership of Nehemiah, son of Hachaliah (Neh. 3:16).

AZEKAH Place-name meaning "cultivated ground." City where Joshua defeated southern coalition of kings led by Adoni-zedek of Jerusalem, as God cast hailstones from heaven on the fleeing armies. In the battle, Joshua commanded the sun and moon to stand still (Josh. 10:1-14).

AZEL Personal and place-name meaning "noble." **1.** Benjaminite descendant of Saul and father of six sons (1 Chron. 8:37-38). **2.** Unclear word in Hebrew text of Zech. 14:5 may be a place-name, perhaps near Jerusalem, or a preposition meaning "near to" or "beside" or a noun meaning "the side." Translations vary: "Azal" (KJV, NRSV, CSB), "the other side" (TEV), "Azel" (NASB, NIV), "the side of it" (RSV).

AZGAD Personal name meaning "Gad is strong." **1.** Clan of which 1,222 (Neh. 7:17 says 2,322) returned from exile in Babylon with Zerubbabel to Jerusalem in 537 BC (Ezra 2:12). One hundred ten more returned with Ezra about 458 BC (Ezra 8:12). **2.** Levite who signed the covenant Nehemiah made to keep God's law (Neh. 10:15).

AZIEL Short form of Jaaziel in 1 Chron. 15:20.

AZIZA Personal name meaning "strong one." Israelite who agreed under Ezra's leadership to divorce his foreign wife to help Israel remain true to God (Ezra 10:27).

AZMAVETH Personal and place-name meaning "strong as death" or "death is strong." **1.** Member of David's elite 30 military heroes (2 Sam. 23:31). He lived in Barhum or perhaps Baharum (NRSV). See *Baharum*. **2.** Descendant of Saul in from tribe of Benjamin (1 Chron. 8:36). **3.** Father of two of David's military leaders (1 Chron. 12:3), probably identical with 1 above. **4.** Treasurer of David's kingdom (1 Chron. 27:25). He, too, may be identical with 1 above. **5.** City probably the same as Beth-azmaveth. Forty-two men of the city returned to Jerusalem from exile in Babylon with Zerubbabel in 537 BC (Ezra 2:24). Levites on the temple staff as singers lived there. It apparently is near Jerusalem, perhaps modern Hizmeh, five miles northeast of Jerusalem (Neh. 12:29).

AZMON Place-name meaning "bones." Place on southern border of the promised land (Num. 34:4). Joshua assigned it to Judah (Josh. 15:4). It is located near Ain el-Quseimeh, about 60 miles south of Gaza. Some would identify it with Ezem.

AZNOTH-TABOR Place-name meaning "ears of Tabor." A border town of the tribe of Naphtali (Josh. 19:34). It may be modern Umm Jebeil near Mount Tabor.

AZOR Personal name of an ancestor of Jesus (Matt. 1:13-14).

AZRIEL Personal name meaning "God is my help." **1.** Head of a family of eastern part of the tribe of Manasseh (1 Chron. 5:24). **2.** Head of the tribe of Naphtali under David (1 Chron. 27:19). **3.** Father of royal officer commanded to arrest Baruch, Jeremiah's scribe (Jer. 36:26).

AZRIKAM Personal name meaning "my help stood up." **1.** Descendant of David after the exile (1 Chron. 3:23). **2.** Benjaminite descendant of Saul (1 Chron. 8:38). **3.** Father of a Levite who led in resettling Jerusalem after the exile (1 Chron. 9:14). **4.** Officer in charge of the palace for Ahaz, king of Judah. Zicri, a soldier in Israel's army, killed him when Israel attacked Judah about 741 BC (2 Chron. 28:7).

AZUBAH Personal name meaning "forsaken." **1.** Queen mother of Jehoshaphat (1 Kgs. 22:42), king of Judah (873–848 BC). **2.** First wife of Caleb, son of Hezron (1 Chron. 2:18-19).

AZZAN Personal name meaning "he has proved to be strong." Father of representative of the tribe of Issachar in assigning territorial lots to the tribes after God gave Israel the promised land (Num. 34:26).

AZZUR Personal name meaning "one who has been helped." **1.** Jewish leader who sealed Nehemiah's covenant to obey God's law (Neh. 10:17). **2.** Father of Hananiah, the prophet, in Jeremiah's days (Jer. 28:1). **3.** Father of Jaazaniah, Jewish leader in Jerusalem who plotted evil in Ezekiel's day (Ezek. 11:1).

Statuette of Baal, the Canaanite weather god, from Minet-el-Beida (fifteenth–fourteenth century BC)

BAAL Lord of Canaanite religion and seen in the thunderstorms, Baal was worshipped as the god who provided fertility. He proved a great temptation for Israel. "Baal" occurs in the OT as a noun meaning "lord, owner, possessor, or husband," as a proper noun referring to the supreme god of the Canaanites, and often as the name of a man.

BAALAH Place-name meaning "wife, lady," or "residence of Baal." **1.** City on the northern border of the tribe of Judah equated with Kirjath-jearim (Josh. 15:9-11). David kept the ark there before moving it to Jerusalem (1 Chron. 13:6). **2.** Town on southern border of Judah (Josh. 15:29) that may be the same as Balah (Josh. 19:3) and as Bilhah (1 Chron. 4:29). Occupied by the tribe of Simeon, its location is unknown. **3.** Mountain on Judah's northern border between Jabneel and Ekron. It may be the same as Mount Jearim.

BAALATH Place-name meaning "feminine Baal." City in original inheritance of the tribe of Dan (Josh. 19:44).

BAALATH-BEER Place-name meaning "the baal of the well" or "the lady of the well." A city in the tribal allotment of Simeon (Josh. 19:8), identified with Ramath of/in the south (KJV, CSB) or Ramah of the Negev (NASB, NIV, NRSV). It may be identical with Baal (1 Chron. 4:33) and/or with Bealoth (Josh. 15:24).

BAAL-BERITH In Judg. 8:33, a Canaanite deity whom the Israelites began to worship following the death of Gideon. The name means "lord of covenant," and the god's temple was located at Shechem.

BAALE (KJV), **BAALE-JUDAH** (NASB, NRSV, CSB) Place-name meaning "Baals of Judah" or "lords of Judah." Second Samuel 6:2 may be read as "from the lords of Judah" or as "went from Baale-judah."

BAAL-GAD Place-name meaning "Baal of Gad" or "lord of Gad." Town representing northern limit of Joshua's conquests (Josh. 11:17) in the Valley of Lebanon at the foot of Mount Hermon.

BAAL-HAMON Place-name meaning "lord of abundance." Location of Solomon's vineyard according to Song 8:11.

BAAL-HANAN Personal name meaning "Baal was gracious." **1.** King of Edom prior to any king ruling in Israel (Gen. 36:38). **2.** Official under David in charge of olive and sycamore trees growing in the Judean plain or Shephelah (1 Chron. 27:28).

BAAL-HAZOR Place-name meaning "Baal of Hazor." Village where David's son Absalom held a celebration of sheep shearing (2 Sam. 13:23).

BAAL-HERMON Place-name meaning "Baal of Hermon" or "lord of Hermon." It marked the Hivites' southern border and Manasseh's northern border (1 Chron. 5:23).

BAALI Form of address meaning "my lord," or "my Baal." Hosea used a play on words to look to a day when Israel would no longer worship Baal (Hos. 2:16).

BAALIM Hebrew plural of Baal.

BAALIS Personal name of king of Ammon who sent Ishmael to kill Geduliah, governor of Judah, immediately after Babylon captured Jerusalem and sent most of Judah's citizens into the exile (Jer. 40:14).

BAAL-MEON Place-name meaning "lord of the residence" or "Baal of the residence." City tribe of Reuben built east of Jordan (Num. 32:38), probably on the tribe's northern border.

BAAL-PEOR In Num. 25:3, a Moabite deity the Israelites worshipped when they had illicit sexual relations with Moabite women. The guilty Israelites were severely punished for this transgression, and the incident became a paradigm of sin and divine judgment for later generations of Israelites (Deut. 4:3; Ps. 106:28; Hos. 9:10).

BAAL-PERAZIM Place-name meaning "lord of the breakthroughs" or "Baal of the breaches." Place of David's initial victory over the Philistines after he became king of all Israel at Hebron, then captured and moved to Jerusalem (2 Sam. 5:20). The location is not known. It is probably identical with Mount Perazim (Isa. 28:21).

BAAL-SHALISHAH Place-name meaning "Baal of Shalishah" or "lord of Shalishah." Home of unnamed man who brought firstfruits to Elisha, who used them to feed a hundred men (2 Kgs. 4:42-44).

BAAL-TAMAR Place-name meaning "Baal of the palm tree" or "lord of the palm tree." Place where Israelites attacked and defeated the tribe of Benjamin for killing the concubine of a traveling Levite (Judg. 20:33). It must have been near Gibeah.

BAAL-ZEBUB Deity's name meaning "lord of the flies." In 2 Kgs. 1:2, a Philistine deity from which the Israelite king Ahaziah sought help after injuring himself in a fall. Jesus used the name Beelzebub in reference to the prince of demons (Matt. 10:25). Beelzebul/Beelzebub is clearly a variation of Baalzebub.

BAAL-ZEPHON Place-name meaning "lord of the north" or "Baal of the north." Place in Egypt near which Israel camped before the miracle of crossing the sea (Exod. 14:2,9). The exact location is not known.

BAANA or **BAANAH** Personal name of uncertain meaning. Some have suggested "son of grief" or "son of Anat." English spelling variations reflect similar Hebrew spelling variations. **1.** One of Solomon's district supervisors tasked with providing food one month a year for the court (1 Kgs. 4:12). **2.** Another district supervisor over Asher, the western slopes of Galilee in the north. His father, Hushai, may have been "David's personal adviser" (2 Sam. 15:37 CSB). **3.** Father of Zadok, who repaired walls of Jerusalem under Nehemiah (Neh. 3:4). **4.** A captain of Ish-bosheth's army after Saul died and Abner deserted to David and was killed by Joab. **5.** Father of Heleb, one of David's 30 heroes (2 Sam. 23:29). **6.** Man who returned with Zerubbabel from Babylonian captivity about 537 BC (Ezra 2:2). **7.** One who signed Nehemiah's covenant to obey God's law (Neh. 10:27).

BAARA Personal name meaning "burning" or a name intentionally changed from one honoring Baal. Wife of Shaharaim in the tribe of Benjamin (1 Chron. 8:8).

BAASEIAH Personal name of unknown meaning. A Levite ancestor of Asaph (1 Chron. 6:40).

BAASHA King of Israel who was at war against Asa, king of Judah (1 Kgs. 15:16). Baasha reigned over Israel for 24 years (908–886 BC).

BABBLER Derogatory term the Epicureans and Stoics used against Paul in Athens (Acts 17:18). The Greek word literally means "seed picker" and was used of birds (especially crows) that lived by picking up seeds.

BABEL Hebrew word meaning "confusion," derived from a root which means "to mix." It was the name given to the city built by the disobedient descendants of Noah so they would not be scattered over all the earth (Gen. 11:4,9). Babel is also the Hebrew word for Babylon. The tower and the city that were built were intended to be a monument of human pride, for they sought to "make a name" for themselves (Gen. 11:4).

BABYLON City-state in southern Mesopotamia during OT times that eventually became a large empire. During the reign of King Nebuchadnezzar II (605–562 BC), the Babylonians invaded the nation of Judah. Jerusalem fell in August 587 BC. The city was burned and the temple destroyed (Jer. 52:12-14). Many Judeans were taken to their exile in Babylonia (2 Kgs. 25:1-21; Jer. 52:1-30).

BACA Place-name meaning "balsam tree" or "weeping." Used for a valley in Ps. 84:6, reflecting a poetic play on words to describe a person forced to go through a time of weeping who found God and turned tears into a well, providing water.

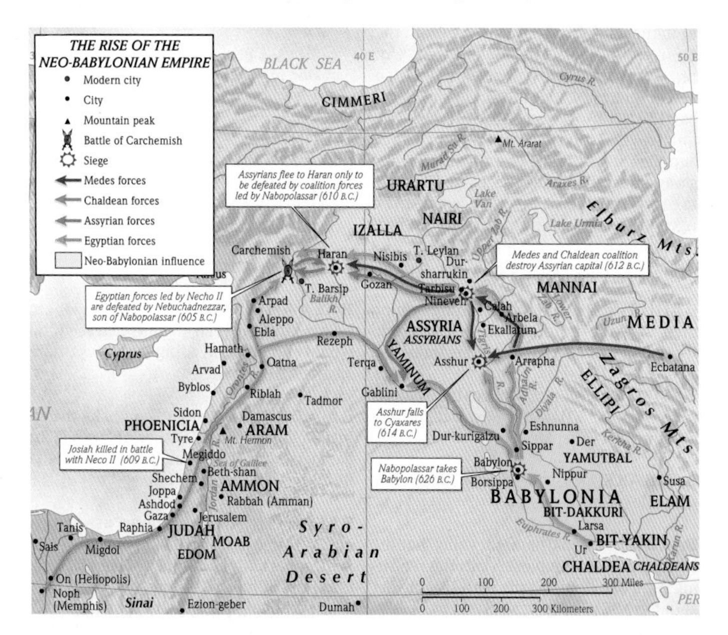

BACHRITE KJV spelling of Becherite (NASB, NRSV, CSB) or Bekerite (NIV) clan in Num. 26:35.

BACKSLIDING KJV term used by the prophets to describe Israel's faithlessness to God (Isa. 57:17 RSV; Jer. 3:14,22; 8:5; 31:22; 49:4; Hos. 11:7; 14:4). In these passages it is clear that Israel had broken faith with God by serving other gods and by living immoral lives. CSB often uses the word "faithless."

BADGER SKINS KJV translation of the skin used to cover the tabernacle (Exod. 26:14; 36:19; 39:34), the ark, and other sacred objects (Num. 4:6-14). The leather was also used for shoes (Ezek. 16:10). CSB: fine leather.

BAG Flexible container that may be closed for holding, storing, or carrying something. **1.** Large bags in which large amounts of money could be carried (2 Kgs. 5:23; Isa. 3:22; KJV, "crisping pins"). **2.** Small bag (purse) used to carry a merchant's weights (Deut. 25:13; Prov. 16:11; Mic. 6:11) or smaller sums of money (Prov. 1:14; Isa. 46:6). **3.** Cloth tied up in a bundle is translated as "bag" (Job 14:17; Prov. 7:20; Hag. 1:6) or "bundle" (Gen. 42:35; 1 Sam. 25:29; Song 1:13). **4.** The shepherd's bag (KJV "scrip" or "vessel"). Used by shepherds and travelers to carry one or more days' supplies, it was made of animal skins and slung across the shoulder. **5.** Large sack used to carry grain (Gen. 42:25,27,35; Josh. 9:4; Lev. 11:32). **6.** KJV translates *glossokomon* as "bag" in John 12:6; 13:29. The *glossokomon* was actually a money-box. CSB: money-bag.

BAHURIM Place-name meaning "young men." Village on road from Jerusalem to Jericho in tribal territory of Benjamin.

BAJITH (KJV, Isa. 15:2) Modern translations read "temple." KJV interprets as name of a Moabite worship place.

BAKBAKKAR Levite living in Judah after the exile (1 Chron. 9:15).

BAKBUK Personal name meaning "bottle." Levite who was a temple servant after returning from Babylonian exile with Zerubbabel about 537 BC (Ezra 2:51; Neh. 7:53).

BAKBUKIAH Personal name meaning "Yahweh's bottle." Leader among the Levites in Jerusalem after the exile (Neh. 11:17; 12:9,25).

BAKERS' STREET Jerusalem street known as "bakers' street" where most, if not all, the bakeries of the city were located. Zedekiah promised Jeremiah, whom he had imprisoned, that he would have food for as long as bread was available on bakers' street (Jer. 37:21).

The village baker prepares dough for baking in the stone oven his left.

BAKING OT speaks most often of the baking of bread and cakes, which were the main part of the meal for Hebrews and Canaanites alike (Gen. 19:3; Exod. 12:39; Lev. 26:26; 1 Kgs. 17:12-13; Isa. 44:15). The bread of the presence (Lev. 24:5) and other offerings (Lev. 2:4-6) were also baked.

BALAAM Non-Israelite prophet whom Balak, king of Moab, promised a fee if he would curse the invading Israelites (Num. 22:21-30; 2 Pet. 2:16).

BALADAN Akkadian personal name meaning "God gave a son." Father of Merodach-baladan, king of Babylon (722–711; 705–703 BC). See *Merodach-baladan.*

BALAH Place-name meaning "used, worn out." City in tribal territory of Simeon (Josh. 19:3), apparently the same as Baalah (Josh. 15:29) and Bilhah (1 Chron. 4:29). Location in southwest Judah is unknown.

BALAK In Num. 22:2, the king of Moab who sent for Balaam the prophet to pronounce a curse on the Israelites. Balaam, however, spoke no curse, and Balak was denied a military victory over Israel.

BALANCES Used to measure weights early in the development of civilization. Balances were well known to the Hebrews and in common use in the OT (Lev. 19:36; Job 6:2; Hos. 12:7).

BALLAD SINGERS Refers to the makers and repeaters of proverbs (Num. 21:27). KJV "they that speak in proverbs" gives that sense.

BALM Aromatic resin or gum widely used in the ancient Near East for cosmetic and medical purposes.

BALM OF GILEAD Substance known in the ancient world for its medical properties. Exported from Gilead to Egypt and Phoenicia (Gen. 37:25; Jer. 8:22; 46:11; Ezek. 27:17). See *Balm*; *Gilead*.

BALSAM Translation of two Hebrew words. *Baka'* is translated as "balsam trees" in the modern versions (2 Sam. 5:23-24; 1 Chron. 14:14-15; CSB, NASB, NIV, NRSV, TEV).

BAMAH Hebrew noun meaning "back, high place." Word is used frequently to describe places of worship, usually false worship of Yahweh containing Canaanite elements.

BAMOTH Place-name and common noun meaning "high places." A place in Moab where Israel stayed during the wilderness wanderings (Num. 21:19-20). Some would equate it with Bamoth-baal.

BAMOTH-BAAL Place-name meaning "high places of Baal." Mesha, king of Moab about 830 BC, mentioned it in the Moabite stone. Numbers 22:41 speaks of Bamoth or high places of Baal near the Arnon River. There Balak and Balaam could see all Israel. Joshua 13:17 lists it as a city Moses gave the tribe of Reuben. It may be modern Gebel Atarus.

BANI Personal name meaning "built." **1.** Man from the tribe of Gad in David's special 30 warriors (2 Sam. 23:36). **2.** Levite descended from Merari (1 Chron. 6:46). **3.** Ancestor of Uthai of the tribe of Judah who was among the first Israelites to return to Palestine from Babylonian exile about 537 BC (1 Chron. 9:4). **4.** Original ancestor of 642 clansmen who returned from Babylonian exile with Zerubbabel about 537 BC (Ezra 2:10). **5.** Father of Rehum, a Levite who helped Nehemiah repair the wall of Jerusalem (Neh. 3:17).

BANNER Sign carried to give a group a rallying point. A banner was usually a flag or a carved figure of an animal, bird, or reptile. It may have been molded from bronze, as was the serpent in Num. 21:8-9. Each tribe of Israel may have had some such animal figures as their standard or banner.

BANQUET Elaborate meal, sometimes called a "feast." In the OT and NT, banquets and feasts are prominent in sealing friendships, celebrating victories, and for other joyous occasions (Dan. 5:1; Luke 15:22-24). The idea of hospitality ran deep in the thought of those in the Near East (Gen. 18:1-8; Luke 11:5-8). In Revelation, the final victory day is described in terms of a "marriage feast of the Lamb" of God (Rev. 19:9 CSB).

BAPTISM The Christian rite of initiation practiced by almost all who profess to embrace the Christian faith. In the NT era, persons professing Christ were immersed in water as a public confession of their faith in Jesus, the Savior. This was accomplished in direct obedience to the explicit mandate of the Lord (Matt. 28:16-20).

BAPTISM FOR THE DEAD The only biblical mention of this is 1 Cor. 15:29. Paul refers to something being practiced without commenting on it. He does not commend, condone, or condemn it.

BAR Aramaic translation of the Hebrew word *ben*. Both words mean "son of."

BARABBAS Name means "son of the father." A murderer and insurrectionist held in Roman custody at the time of the trial of Jesus (Mark 15:15). All four Gospels record that when Pilate offered to release Jesus or Barabbas, the crowd demanded the release of Barabbas. Pilate gave in to the demand, ordered Jesus crucified, and set Barabbas free.

BARACHEL Personal name meaning "God blessed." Father of Job's friend Elihu (Job 32:2).

BARAK Son of Abinoam whom the prophetess Deborah summoned to assume military leadership of the Israelites in a campaign against Canaanite forces under the command of Sisera (Judg. 4:6).

BARBARIAN Originally referred to stammering, stuttering, or any form of unintelligible sounds. Even the repeated syllable "bar-bar" mimics this. The term "barbarian" came to be synonymous with "foreigner," one who did not speak Greek or one who was not a Greek.

BARHUMITE Used in 2 Sam. 23:31; variant Hebrew spelling for Baharumite (1 Chron. 11:33), used to describe one of David's 30 elite warriors.

BAR-JESUS Jewish magician and false prophet at Paphos (Acts 13:6). Paul the apostle denounced him, and he was struck blind. In Acts 13:8 he is called Elymas.

BAR-JONA Surname of Simon Peter (Matt. 16:17). The meaning is "son of John."

BAR-KOKHBA Means "son of the star" and was the title given by Jewish rebels to Simeon bar Kosevah, the leader of their revolt in AD 132–135. The title designated him as the Messiah (Num. 24:17). The revolt erupted because the Roman emperor Hadrian had begun to rebuild Jerusalem as a pagan city with plans to replace the ruined Jewish temple with one dedicated to Jupiter.

BARKOS Aramaic name possibly meaning "son of (god) Kos." The original ancestor of a clan of Nethinim or temple employees who returned to Jerusalem from exile in Babylon with Zerubbabel about 537 BC (Ezra 2:53).

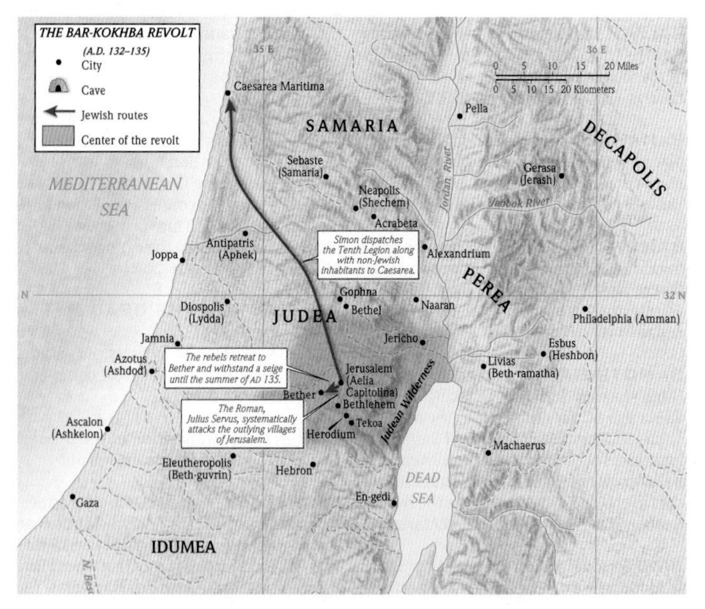

BARLEY Grain for which Palestine was known (Deut. 8:8). Barley was the food of the poor (Lev. 23:22) as well as feed for horses, mules, and donkeys (1 Kgs. 4:28).

BARLEY HARVEST Began in late April or early May and preceded the wheat harvest by about two weeks (Exod. 9:31-32). At the beginning of the barley harvest (Ruth 2:23), the first fruits were offered as a consecration of the harvest (Lev. 23:10).

BARN Storage place for seed (Hag. 2:19; CSB, granary) or grain (Matt. 13:30). Equivalent to modern granaries or silos.

BARNABAS Name probably means "son of prophecy" or one who prophesies or preaches ("son of exhortation," Acts 4:36). Barnabas was a Levite and native of the island of Cyprus; named Joseph (Joses) before the disciples called him Barnabas. The church chose Barnabas to go to Syrian Antioch to investigate the unrestricted preaching to the Gentiles there. He became the leader of the work and secured Saul (Paul) as his assistant. On Paul's "first missionary journey," Barnabas seems to have been the leader (chaps. 13–14). He and Paul agreed to go on another missionary journey but separated over whether to take John Mark with them again (15:36-41).

BARREL KJV translation found in 1 Kgs. 17:12-16; 18:33. Modern versions translate the same word as "jar." Jars were used for carrying water and storing flour.

BARREN, BARRENNESS Term used to describe a woman who is unable to give birth to children: Sarai (Gen. 11:30), Rebekah (Gen. 25:21), Rachel (Gen. 29:31), Manoah's wife (Judg. 13:2), Hannah (1 Sam. 1:5), and Elizabeth (Luke 1:7,36). Barrenness was considered a curse from God (Gen. 16:2; 20:18; 1 Sam. 1:5).

BARSABAS or **BARSABBAS** Personal name meaning "son of the Sabbath." **1.** Name given Joseph Justus, candidate not elected when church chose replacement for Judas, the traitor (Acts 1:23). **2.** Last name of Judas, whom the Jerusalem church chose to go with Paul and Silas to Antioch after the Jerusalem council (Acts 15:22).

BARTHOLOMEW One of the 12 apostles (Mark 3:18). The name Bartholomew means "son of Talmai." Many believe Bartholomew and Nathanael are identical.

BARTIMAEUS or **BARTIMEUS** (KJV) Blind beggar near Jericho who cried to Jesus for mercy despite efforts to silence him. Jesus said that his persistent faith had made him whole. Able to see, he followed Jesus (Mark 10:46-52).

BARUCH Son of Neriah who served as Jeremiah's scribe and friend.

BARZILLAI Personal name meaning "made of iron." **1.** Man from Gilead east of the Jordan who met David at Mahanaim as he fled from Absalom. Barzillai and others gave needed supplies for David's company (2 Sam. 17:27-29). **2.** Father of Adriel whose sons David delivered to the Gibeonites for execution in payment for Saul's inhumane slaying of Gibeonites (2 Sam. 21:8). This Barzillai could be the same as 1, above. **3.** Priestly clan whose ancestor had married the daughter of 1, above, and taken his name.

BASEMATH Personal name meaning "balsam." **1.** Hittite woman whom Esau married, grieving his parents, Isaac and Rebekah (Gen. 26:34-35; 27:46). **2.** Daughter of Solomon who married Ahimaaz, district supervisor providing supplies for the royal court from Naphtali (1 Kgs. 4:15).

BASHAN Northernmost region of Palestine east of the Jordan River. Though its precise extent cannot be determined with certainty, it was generally east of the Sea of Galilee.

BASIN (KJV, "bason") Used interchangeably with "bowl" to refer to various sizes of wide hollow bowls, cups, and dishes used for domestic or more formal purposes (John 13:5). The most common material used to make such instruments was pottery. However, basins were also made of brass (Exod. 27:3), silver (Num. 7:13), and gold (2 Chron. 4:8).

BASKET Five kinds of baskets are mentioned in the OT. The NT uses two words for basket. The smaller basket is referred to in the story of the feeding of the 5,000 (Matt. 14:20). The larger basket is mentioned in the feeding of the 4,000 (Matt. 15:37). The apostle Paul also used the larger basket as a means of escape over the wall of Damascus (Acts 9:25).

BASTARD Illegitimate child, but not necessarily a child born out of wedlock. The term could refer to offspring of an incestuous union or of a marriage that was prohibited (Lev. 18:6-20; 20:11-20). Illegitimate children were not permitted to enter the assembly of the Lord (Deut. 23:2). According to Hebrews, those who do not have the discipline of the Lord are illegitimate children (12:8). Also translated as "a mongrel people" (Zech. 9:6 CSB, NRSV).

BAT The Hebrew word translated "bat" is the generic name for many species of this mammal found in Palestine (Isa. 2:20). Although the bat is listed among unclean birds in the Bible (Lev. 11:19; Deut. 14:18), it belongs to the mammals because it nurses its young.

BATH Liquid measure roughly equivalent to 5.5 gallons (US). It was used to measure the molten sea in the temple (1 Kgs. 7:26,38) as well as oil and wine (2 Chron. 2:10; Ezra 7:22; Isa. 5:10; Ezek. 45:11,14). The bath was one-tenth of a homer.

BATHING Biblical languages make no distinction between washing and bathing primarily because the dry climate of the Middle East prohibited bathing except on special occasions or where there was an available source of water (John 9:7). Therefore, where "bathe" occurs in the biblical text, partial bathing is usually intended. However, two notable exceptions are that of Pharaoh's daughter in the Nile (Exod. 2:5) and that of Bathsheba on her rooftop (2 Sam. 11:2).

BATH-RABBIM Place-name meaning "daughter of many." A gate of Heshbon, which was near pools of fish. Song of Songs 7:4 uses its beauty as comparison for the beauty of the beloved woman's eyes. See *Heshbon*.

BATHSHEBA Daughter of Eliam and wife of Uriah the Hittite (2 Sam. 11:3). She was a beautiful woman with whom David the king had an adulterous relationship (2 Sam. 11:4). When David learned that she had become pregnant as a result, he embarked on a course of duplicity that led finally to the violent death of Uriah. David then took Bathsheba as his wife. She was the mother of Solomon and played an important role in ensuring that he be made king (1 Kgs. 1:11–2:19).

BATHSHUA Personal name meaning "daughter of nobility." **1.** Canaanite wife of Judah and mother of Er, Onan, and Shelah (1 Chron. 2:3 NASB, TEV, NRSV, CSB). KJV, NIV read "daughter of Shua." Genesis 38:2 says her name was Shua, while Gen. 38:12 calls her daughter of Shua or Bath-shua. **2.** Name for Bathsheba in 1 Chron. 3:5.

BATTALION RSV translation of one-tenth of a Roman legion, about 600 men (Mark 15:16). KJV translates "band"; CSB uses "whole company."

BAVAI or **BAVVAI** (NASB, TEV, RSV) Government official in Keilah who helped Nehemiah rebuild wall of Jerusalem (Neh. 3:18). CSB, NRSV, NIV read Binnui on basis of Neh. 3:24 and other textual evidence.

BAY KJV translation of a term referring to horses in Zech. 6:3,7. KJV took the term as referring to the color of the horses. The earliest translators had trouble with the word, as do modern versions. Recent interpreters take the Hebrew word as referring to the strength of the horses (CSB, NIV, NASB), though NRSV reads "gray" in verse 3 and "steeds" in verse 7, while REB omits the word in verse 3 and emends the text in verse 7.

BAY TREE KJV translation in Ps. 37:35. The Hebrew word (*'ezrach*) means "native" or "indigenous."

BAZAAR Section of a street given over to merchants. Ben-hadad of Damascus gave Ahab permission to set up bazaars in Damascus as Ben-hadad's father had done in Samaria (1 Kgs. 20:34). CSB: marketplaces.

BAZLITH or **BAZLUTH** Personal name meaning "in the shadow" or "onions." Original ancestor of a clan of temple employees who returned from exile in Babylon with Zerubbabel in 537 BC (Neh. 7:54). Name is spelled Bazluth in Ezra 2:52, which NIV reads in Neh. 7:54.

BDELLIUM Translation of *bedolach*, a word of uncertain meaning. It has been identified as a gum or resin, pearl, or stone. Genesis 2:12 mentions bdellium, gold, and onyx as products of Havilah. Numbers 11:7 likens manna to bdellium in appearance.

BEADS RSV translation of a term for articles of gold jewelry (Num. 31:50). The exact identification of these objects is uncertain. They are variously identified as tablets (KJV), armlets, pendants (REB, NRSV), necklaces (CSB, TEV, NIV, NASB), and breastplates.

BEALIAH Personal name meaning "Yahweh is Lord." Literally, "Yahweh is baal." Soldier who joined David at Ziklag while he fled from Saul and served the Philistines (1 Chron. 12:5).

BEALOTH Place-name meaning "female Baals" or "ladies." **1.** Town on southern border of tribal territory of Judah (Josh. 15:24). This may be the same as Baalath-beer (19:8). **2.** Region along with Asher making up a district to supply food for Solomon's court (1 Kgs. 4:16). KJV, NIV read "in Aloth."

BEANS Leguminous plant (*Faba vulgaris*) grown in the ancient world as food. Beans mentioned in 2 Sam. 17:28 and Ezek. 4:9 were the horse or broad bean.

BEAR Large, heavy mammal with long, thick, shaggy hair. It eats insects, fruit, and flesh. The bear of the Bible has been identified with a high degree of certainty as the Syrian bear. They may grow as high as six feet and weigh as much as 500 pounds.

BEARD Hair growing on a man's face often excluding the mustache. Ancient Hebrews are often depicted in ancient Near Eastern art with full, rounded beards. This is in contrast to Romans and Egyptians who preferred clean-shaven faces.

BEAST Daniel and Revelation use beasts of various sorts in their symbolism. The OT used "beast" as a symbol for an enemy, and the writers of Daniel and Revelation may have built on that (Ps. 74:19; Jer. 12:9). Daniel saw four great beasts who represented four great kings arise out of the sea (Dan. 7:2-14). These four beasts would threaten God's kingdom, but God's people would prevail over them (Dan. 7:18).

The book of Revelation speaks of two beasts. The first beast arises out of the sea (Rev. 13:1), is seven headed, and derives its authority from the dragon (Rev. 12:3; 13:4). This beast has several of the characteristics of the four beasts of Dan. 7. The second beast arises out of the earth (Rev. 13:11). It serves the first beast by seeking devotees for it and is referred to as the "false prophet" (Rev. 16:13; 19:20; 20:10). Both the beast and the false prophet persecute the church but are finally judged by Christ (Rev. 19:20; 2 Thess. 2:6-12).

Mount of Beatitudes as viewed from the Sea of Galilee

BEATITUDES Aphorisms so designated because they begin with the expression "blessed is" or "happy is" (Hb. *'ashre*; Gk.

makarios; Lat. *beatus*). The most widely known and extensive collection of such blessings introduces Jesus's Sermon on the Mount (Matt. 5:3-12; cp. Luke 6:20-26).

BEAUTIFUL GATE Scene of the healing of a lame man by Peter and John (Acts 3:2,10). Neither the OT nor other Jewish sources mention a "Beautiful Gate."

BEBAI Babylonian personal name meaning "child." **1.** Original ancestor of 623 clansmen (628 in Neh. 7:16) who returned with Zerubbabel from exile in Babylon about 537 BC (Ezra 2:11). **2.** Signer of Nehemiah's covenant to obey God's law (Neh. 10:15).

BECHER or **BEKER** (NIV) **1.** Personal name meaning "firstborn" or "young male camel." Son of Benjamin and grandson of Jacob (Gen. 46:21). He had nine sons (1 Chron. 7:8). **2.** Original ancestor of a clan in the tribe of Ephraim (Num. 26:35). First Chronicles 7:20 spells the name "Bered."

BECHORATH or **BECORATH** Personal name meaning "firstborn." Ancestor of King Saul (1 Sam. 9:1).

BEDAD Personal name meaning "scatter" or "be alone." Father of Hadad, king of Edom (Gen. 36:35).

BEDAN Personal name of uncertain meaning. **1.** Listed as a judge in 1 Sam. 12:11. **2.** Descendant of Machir and Manasseh (1 Chron. 7:17).

BEDEIAH Personal name meaning "Yahweh alone" or "branch of Yahweh." Man with foreign wife who divorced her under Ezra's leadership to prevent tempting Israel with foreign gods (Ezra 10:35).

BEELIADA Personal name meaning "Baal knows" or "the Lord knows." Son of David born in Jerusalem (1 Chron. 14:7). In 2 Sam. 5:16, the Baal part of the name is replaced with "El," a Hebrew word for God, becoming "Eliada."

BEELZEBUB (KJV, NIV) or **BEELZEBUL** (NASB, TEV, NRSV, CSB) Name for Satan in NT, spelled differently in Greek manuscripts. The term is based on Hebrew Baal-zebub, "lord of the flies."

BEER Place-name meaning "well." **1.** One of the camps of the Israelites during the wilderness wandering (Num. 21:16). **2.** Jotham fled to Beer when he feared his brother Abimelech would kill him (Judg. 9:21). This may be modern Bireh.

BEERA Personal name meaning "a well." A descendant of the tribe of Asher (1 Chron. 7:37).

BEERAH Personal name meaning "a well." A leader of the tribe of Reuben taken captive by Tiglath-pileser, king of Assyria, about 732 BC (1 Chron. 5:6).

BEER-ELIM Place-name meaning "well of the rams, the heroes, the terebinths, or the mighty trees." Place involved in mourning according to Isaiah's lament over Moab (Isa. 15:8).

BEERI Personal name meaning "well." **1.** Hittite father of the woman Esau married, grieving his parents, Isaac and Rebekah (Gen. 26:34-35; 27:46). **2.** Father of Hosea, the prophet (Hos. 1:1).

BEER-LAHAI-ROI Place-name meaning "well of the Living One who sees me." After Sarai had Abram put Hagar out of the house, an angel appeared to Hagar announcing the birth of a son. Hagar interpreted this as a vision of the living God and named the well where she was Beer-lahai-roi (Gen. 16:14).

BEEROTH Place-name meaning "wells." **1.** Wells of the sons of Jaakan, where Israel camped in the wilderness (Num. 33:31; Deut. 10:6); Beeroth Bene-jaakan. **2.** City of the Gibeonites to which Joshua and his army came to defend the Gibeonites after making a covenant with them (Josh. 9:17).

BEER-SHEBA Beer-sheba and its surrounding area factors significantly in the OT from the earliest sojourns of the patriarchs (Gen. 21; 22; 26) to the return of the Hebrew exiles with Nehemiah (Neh. 11:27,30). Since it was an important crossroad to Egypt in the geographic center of the dry, semidesert region known as the Negev, Beer-sheba also served as the administrative center of the region.

Tel Beer-sheba well

BEESHTERAH Place-name meaning "in Ashtaroth." Place east of the Jordan, from territory of the tribe of Manasseh, set aside for the Levites (Josh. 21:27).

BEHEMOTH Large beast known for its enormous strength and toughness. Described in detail in Job 40:15-24, this animal has been variously identified as an elephant, a hippopotamus, and a water buffalo, with the hippopotamus the most likely.

BEKA or **BEKAH** Equal to a half shekel. The amount contributed by each Israelite male for the use of the temple (Exod. 38:26).

BEL Name of Babylonian god, originally as city patron of Nippur, but then as a second name for the high god Marduk of Babylon. Jeremiah prophesied shame coming on Bel (Jer. 50:2). Bel would have to spit out the nations he had swallowed up (Jer. 51:44). An apocryphal book is called Bel and the Dragon.

BELA or **BELAH** Personal and place-name meaning "he swallowed." **1.** Name for Zoar. Its king joined coalition to fight off attacks from eastern kings (Gen. 14:2). See *Zoar*. **2.** King of Edom who ruled in city of Dinhabah before Israel had a king (Gen. 36:32). **3.** Son of Benjamin and grandson of Jacob (Gen. 46:21); the original ancestor of the clan of Belaites (Num. 26:38; 1 Chron. 7:7). **4.** Descendant of Reuben (1 Chron. 5:8).

BELIAL Transliteration of a Hebrew common noun meaning "useless" or "worthless." It is a term of derision (Deut. 13:13). In the NT the word occurs one time (2 Cor. 6:15), where Paul the apostle declared the mutual irreconcilability of Christ and Belial, who thus appears to be equated with Satan.

BELL Golden object fastened to the garments of the high priest that served as a signal or warning of the high priest's movements (Exod. 28:33-35; 39:25-26).

BELLOWS Instrument that blows air on a fire, making it burn hotter. The term is used only in Jer. 6:29.

BELOVED DISCIPLE Expression used to refer to a disciple for whom Jesus had deep feelings. Church tradition and interpretation of biblical evidence appear to point to John.

BELSHAZZAR Name meaning "Bel's prince." Babylonian king whose drunken feast was interrupted by the mysterious appearance of the fingers of a human hand that wrote a cryptic message on the palace wall (Dan. 5:1).

BELTESHAZZAR Babylonian name meaning "protect the king's life." Name given to Daniel by the prince of eunuchs under Nebuchadnezzar, king of Babylon (Dan. 1:7).

BEN Hebrew noun meaning "son of." A Levite who became head of a clan of temple porters under David (1 Chron. 15:18 NASB, KJV).

BEN-ABINADAB Personal name meaning "son of Abinadab." The district supervisor over Dor in charge of provisions for Solomon's court one month a year. He married Solomon's daughter Taphath (1 Kgs. 4:11). KJV reads "son of Abinadab."

BENAIAH Personal name meaning "Yahweh has built." **1.** Captain of David's professional soldiers (2 Sam. 8:18; 20:23), known for heroic feats such as disarming an Egyptian and killing him with his own sword as well as killing a lion in the snow (2 Sam. 23:20-23). **2.** A Pirathonite who is listed among the 30 elite warriors of David (2 Sam. 23:30). **3.** In 1 Chron. 4:36, a Simeonite prince who was involved in a defeat of the Amalekites. **4.** In 1 Chron. 15:18, a Levitical musician involved in the procession when the ark of the covenant was brought to Jerusalem. **5.** In 1 Chron. 15:24, a priest who sounded a trumpet when the ark was brought to Jerusalem. **6.** In 2 Chron. 20:14, an Asaphite, the grandfather of Jahaziel. **7.** In 2 Chron. 31:13, one of the overseers who assisted in the collection of contributions in the house of the Lord during the reign of Hezekiah. **8.** In Ezek. 11:1, the father of Pelatiah. **9.** In Ezra 10, the name of four Israelite men who put away their foreign wives.

BEN-AMMI Personal name meaning "son of my people." Son of Lot and his younger daughter after his two daughters despaired of marriage and tricked their father after getting him drunk (Gen. 19:38). Ben-ammi was the original ancestor of the Ammonites.

BEN-DEKER Personal name meaning "son of Deker" or "son of bored through." Solomon's district supervisor in charge of supplying the royal court for one month a year (1 Kgs. 4:9).

BENE-BERAK Place-name meaning "sons of Barak" or "sons of lightning." City of the tribe of Dan (Josh. 19:45).

BENEDICTION Prayer for God's blessing or an affirmation that God's blessing is at hand. The most famous is the priestly benediction (or Aaronic blessing) in Num. 6:24-25. Most NT Epistles close with benedictions.

BENEDICTUS Latin word meaning "blessed." The first word in Latin of Zechariah's/Zacharias's psalm of praise in Luke 1:68-79 and thus the title of the canticle.

BENE-JAAKAN Place-name meaning "sons of Jaakan." Same as Beeroth Bene-jaakan.

BEN-GEBER Personal name meaning "son of Geber" or "son of a hero." Solomon's district supervisor in the towns northeast of the Jordan River around Ramoth-gilead (1 Kgs. 4:13). He provided supplies for the royal court one month a year. KJV reads "son of Geber."

BEN-HADAD Personal name or royal title meaning "son of (the god) Hadad." References to Israel's interaction with Damascus and other city-states in Syria show the power of the kings of Damascus.

BEN-HAIL Personal name meaning "son of strength." Official under King Jehoshaphat of Judah (873–848 BC), who sent him to help teach God's law in the cities of Judah (2 Chron. 17:7).

BEN-HANAN Personal name meaning "son of the gracious one." Son of Shimon in lineage of Judah (1 Chron. 4:20).

BEN-HESED Personal name meaning "son of mercy." Solomon's district supervisor over the Mediterranean coastal region between Aphek on the south and Hepher. He supplied the royal court one month a year (1 Kgs. 4:10).

BEN-HINNOM Place-name meaning "son of Hinnom." A valley south of Jerusalem serving as northern border of the tribe of Judah (Josh. 15:8) and southern boundary of Benjamin (Josh. 18:16). Pagan child sacrifices occurred here, even by some kings of Judah (Ahaz, 2 Chron. 28:3; Manasseh, 2 Chron. 33:6).

BEN-HUR Personal name meaning "son of a camel" or "son of Horus." Solomon's district supervisor over Mount Ephraim in charge of supplying the royal court one month a year (1 Kgs. 4:8).

BENINU Personal name meaning "our son." A Levite who sealed the covenant Nehemiah made to obey God's law (Neh. 10:13).

BENJAMIN Personal name meaning "son of the right hand" or "son of the south." The second son Rachel bore to Jacob (Gen. 35:17-18). He became the forefather of the tribe of

Benjamin. The tribe of Benjamin occupied the smallest territory of all the tribes. Yet it played a significant role in the Hebraic history. Saul, Israel's first king, was a Benjaminite. In the NT, the apostle Paul proudly proclaimed his heritage in the tribe of Benjamin (Rom. 11:1; Phil. 3:5).

BENJAMIN GATE Jerusalem gate (Jer. 37:13; 38:7). Identified by some with Nehemiah's Sheep Gate or with the Muster Gate, it could indicate a gate that led to tribal territory of Benjamin.

BENO Proper name meaning "his son." A Levite under David (1 Chron. 24:26-27).

BEN-ONI Personal name meaning "son of my sorrow."

BEN-ZOHETH Personal name meaning "son of Zoheth." Son of Ishi in the tribe of Judah (1 Chron. 4:20).

BEON Place-name of uncertain meaning. Probably a copyist's change from original Meon (Num. 32:3), a short form of Beth-meon or Beth-baal-meon.

BEOR Proper name meaning "burning." **1.** Father of Bela, king of Edom centered in Dinhabah, in the time of the patriarchs (Gen. 36:32). **2.** Father of prophet Balaam (Num. 22:5).

BERA Personal name, perhaps meaning "with evil" or "victory." King of Sodom in days of Abraham and Lot (Gen. 14:2). He joined coalition of local kings against a group of invading eastern kings.

BERACAH or **BERACHAH** (KJV) Personal name meaning "blessing." **1.** Skilled soldier able to use right or left hand with slingshot and with bow and arrows. He joined David's band in Ziklag, when David fled from Saul and joined the Philistines (1 Chron. 12:3). **2.** Valley where King Jehoshaphat of Judah (873–848 BC) and his people blessed God after God provided miraculous victory over Ammon, Moab, and Edom (2 Chron. 20:26).

BERAIAH Personal name meaning "Yahweh created." A Benjaminite (1 Chron. 8:21).

BEREA Place-name meaning "place of many waters." City in Macedonia to which Paul escaped after the Jews of Thessalonica rioted (Acts 17:10).

BERECHIAH Personal name meaning "Yahweh blessed." **1.** Descendant of David, after Jews returned from exile in Babylon (1 Chron. 3:20). **2.** Father of Asaph (1 Chron. 6:39). **3.** Leader of the Levites after the return from exile who lived around the city of Netophah (1 Chron. 9:16). **4.** Levite in charge of the ark when David moved it to Jerusalem (1 Chron. 15:23). He could be identical with 2, above. **5.** Leader of the tribe of Ephraim who rescued prisoners of war that Pekah, king of Israel (752–732 BC), had taken from Ahaz, king of Judah (735–715 BC) (2 Chron. 28:12). **6.** Father of Meshullam, who repaired the wall with Nehemiah (Neh. 3:4). His family was tied in marriage to Tobiah, Nehemiah's enemy (Neh. 6:17-19). **7.** Father of the prophet Zechariah (Zech. 1:1; Matt. 23:35).

BERED Personal name meaning "cool." **1.** Place used to locate Beer-lahai-roi (Gen. 16:14), but a place that cannot be located today. **2.** Son of Ephraim (1 Chron. 7:20). Numbers 26:35 spells the name Becher.

BERIAH Personal name meaning "Yahweh created." **1.** Son of Asher and grandson of Jacob (Gen. 46:17). He thus became original ancestor of the clan of Beriites (Num. 26:44). **2.** Son of Ephraim born after his sons Ezer and Elead died in battle against Gath (1 Chron. 7:20-25). **3.** Clan leader of the tribe of Benjamin in the area of Ajalon. He helped drive out the inhabitants of Gath (1 Chron. 8:13). **4.** Levite under King David (1 Chron. 23:10).

BERITH Hebrew word meaning "covenant."

BERNICE Name meaning "gift." Companion of Herod Agrippa II (Acts 25:13). She was the daughter of Herod Agrippa I, born probably about AD 28.

BERODACH-BALADAN King of Babylon who wrote Hezekiah, king of Judah (2 Kgs. 20:12). Parallel passage in Isa. 39:1 reads

Merodach-baladan, so most Bible students think Berodach resulted from a copyist's change in the text (cp. NIV, TEV, NRSV).

BEROTHAH Place-name meaning "wells." Northern border town in Ezekiel's vision of a restored promised land (Ezek. 47:16). It may be located east of the Jordan River about seven miles south of Baalbeck at Bereiten.

BEROTHAI Place-name meaning "wells." City in Syria from which David took brass as tribute after he defeated King Hadadezer (2 Sam. 8:8).

BEROTHITE Person from Beeroth (1 Chron. 11:39).

BERYL Light green precious stone closely related to emeralds and aquamarines. Mentioned in OT and in Revelation.

BESAI Personal name of unknown meaning. A clan of temple employees who returned from exile in Babylon with Zerubbabel about 537 BC (Ezra 2:49).

BESODEIAH Personal name meaning "in Yahweh's counsel." Father of Meshullam, who helped Nehemiah repair the gate of Jerusalem (Neh. 3:6).

BESOM Broom made of twigs (KJV, Isa. 14:23).

BESOR Place-name, perhaps meaning "wadi of the good news." Brook where David left 200 weary soldiers while he and the remaining 400 pursued the Amalekites after they had burned Ziklag and captured David's wives (1 Sam. 30:9-10).

BESTIALITY Sexual intercourse between a human and an animal, punishable by death in OT legal codes (Exod. 22:19; Lev. 18:23; 20:15-16; Deut. 27:21). Israel's neighbors practiced bestiality in fertility worship and worship of animal gods.

BETAH Place-name meaning "security." City from which King David took brass after defeating King Hadadezer (2 Sam. 8:8). First Chronicles 18:8 lists Betah as Tibhath. NIV reads Tebah in 2 Sam. 8:8.

BETEN Place-name meaning "womb." Border town of tribe of Asher (Josh 19:25). It may be located at Khirbet Abtun, 11 miles south of Acco.

BETH-ABARA Place-name meaning "house of crossing." KJV reading for Bethany in John 1:28 following some Greek manuscripts.

BETH-ANATH Place-name meaning "house of Anath." A fortified city in the territory of the tribe of Naphtali (Josh. 19:38).

BETH-ANOTH Place-name meaning "house of Anath" or "house of being heard." A city of Judah (Josh. 15:59), a temple to the Canaanite goddess Anath may have been here.

BETHANY Known primarily in the Gospels as the home of Mary, Martha, and Lazarus. Ancient Bethany occupied an important place in the life of Jesus. Jesus often stayed in Bethany at the home of his closest friends as he ministered in Jerusalem. Located on the Mount of Olives' eastern slope, Bethany sat "less than two miles" (John 11:18 CSB) southeast of Jerusalem.

View of the ancient city of Bethany, the hometown of Mary, Martha, and Lazarus

BETH-ARABAH Place-name meaning "house of the desert." A border town of the tribe of Judah (Josh. 15:6,61) also claimed as a city of Benjamin (Josh. 18:22). It may be modern Ain el-Gharbah southeast of Jericho.

BETH-ARBEL Place-name meaning "house of Arbel." Site of infamous battle that Hosea could use as an example of what would happen to Israel (Hos. 10:14). The battle is unknown to us.

BETH-ASHBEA Place of unknown location in Judah known for clans of linen workers, thus giving evidence of craft guilds in Israel (1 Chron. 4:21).

BETH-AVEN Place-name meaning "house of deception" or "of idolatry." **1.** City near Ai east of Bethel (Josh. 7:2). It formed a border of Benjaminite territory (Josh. 18:12) and was west of Michmash (1 Sam. 13:5). Saul defeated the Philistines here after God used his son Jonathan to start the victory (1 Sam. 14:23). **2.** Hosea used the term as a description of Bethel. Instead of a house of God, Bethel had become a house of deception and idolatry (Hos. 4:15).

BETH-AZMAVETH Place-name meaning "house of the strength of death." Hometown of 42 people who returned to Palestine with Zerubbabel from exile in Babylon about 537 BC (Neh. 7:28).

BETH-BAAL-MEON Place-name meaning "house of Baal's residence." City allotted to the tribe of Reuben (Josh. 13:17).

BETH-BIREI or **BETH-BIRI** Place-name meaning "house of my creation." Town allotted to the tribe of Simeon (1 Chron. 4:31). It is apparently the same as Lebaoth (Josh. 15:32) and Beth-lebaoth (Josh. 19:6).

BETH-CAR Place-name meaning "house of sheep." Final site of battle where God thundered from heaven to defeat the Philistines for Samuel (1 Sam. 7:11).

BETH-DAGON Place-name meaning "house of Dagon." Apparently the name indicates a worship place of Philistine god Dagon. **1.** Town in the tribal territory of Judah (Josh. 15:41). It is probably modern Khirbet Dajun on the road connecting Ramallah and Joppa. **2.** Town in Asher (Josh. 19:27) without certain present location.

BETH-DIBLATHAIM Place-name meaning "house of the two fig cakes." Town in Moab on which Jeremiah prophesied judgment (Jer. 48:22).

BETH-EDEN Place-name meaning "house of bliss." Amos announced God's threat to take the royal house out of Beth-eden or the "house of Eden" (KJV) (Amos 1:5).

BETH-EKED Place-name meaning "house of shearing" (KJV, "shearing house"). Place where Jehu, after slaughtering all members of King Ahab's house in Jezreel, met representatives from King Ahaziah of Judah and killed them (2 Kgs. 10:12-14).

BETHEL Name meaning "house of God." **1.** Bethel was important in the OT for both geographic and religious reasons. Because of its abundant springs, the area was fertile and attractive to settlements as early as 3200 BC and first supported a city around the time of Abraham. **2.** Another city variously spelled Bethul (Josh. 19:4), Bethuel (1 Chron. 4:30), and Bethel (1 Sam. 30:27). This may be modern Khirbet el Qaryatein north of Arad. **3.** Bethel was apparently the name of a West Semitic god. Many scholars find reference to this deity in Jer. 48:13. Others would find the mention of the deity in other passages (especially Gen. 31:13; Amos 5:5). See *El-Bethel.*

BETHELITE Resident of Bethel (1 Kgs. 16:34).

BETH-EMEK Place-name meaning "house of the valley." A border town in the tribal territory of Asher (Josh. 19:27). Located at modern Tel Mimas, about 6.5 miles northeast of Acco.

BETHER Place-name meaning "division." A mountain range used as an emotional image in Song 2:17. NIV reads "rugged hills"; CSB, divided mountains.

BETHESDA Name of a pool in Jerusalem where Jesus healed a man who had been sick for 38 years (John 5:2). The name, appropriately, means "house of mercy." Most ancient manuscripts identify Bethesda as the place of the pool. Some ancient manuscripts name it Bethzatha or Bethsaida.

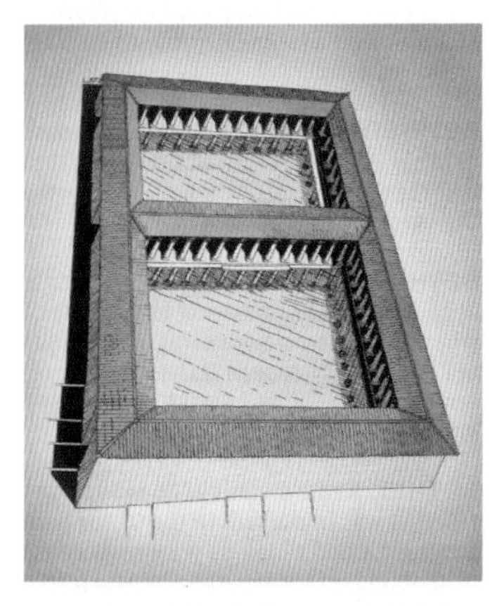

The Pool of Bethesda at Jerusalem, a spring-fed pool near the Sheep Gate where the sick used to come to receive healing. Jesus healed a man there who had been stricken with an unidentified infirmity for 38 years.

BETH-EZEL Proper name meaning "house of the leader" or "house at the side." City Micah used in a wordplay to announce judgment on Judah about 701 BC (Mic. 1:11).

BETH-GADER City founded by or controlled by descendants of Hareph, a descendant of Caleb (1 Chron. 2:51).

BETH-GAMUL Place-name meaning "house of retaliation." City in Moab on which Jeremiah announced judgment (Jer. 48:23). Its location was modern Khirbet el-Jemeil about seven miles east of Dibon.

BETH-GILGAL Place-name meaning "house of the wheel or circle." A village of Levitical singers near Jerusalem whose occupants participated in the dedication of the newly built city wall under Nehemiah (Neh. 12:29).

BETH-HACCEREM or **BETH-HACCHEREM** Place-name meaning "house of the vineyard." City used to signal that enemies approached from the north (Jer. 6:1).

BETH-HAGGAN Place-name (CSB, NIV, TEV, NRSV) or common noun (KJV, NASB) meaning "house of the garden." King Ahaziah of Judah (841 BC) fled there from Jehu, but Jehu finally caught up and killed him (2 Kgs. 9:27). It is probably modern Jenin, southeast of Tanaach.

BETH-HARAM Place-name meaning "house of the exalted one" or "house of height" (KJV, Betharam). A city Moses allotted to the tribe of Gad (Josh. 13:27). It is probably Tell er-Rameh though others suggest Tell Iktanu. It is probably the same as Beth-haran.

BETH-HARAN Place-name meaning "house of height." Town east of the Jordan that the tribe of Gad strengthened after Moses gave it to them (Num. 32:36). It is probably the same as Beth-haram.

BETH-HOGLAH Place-name meaning "house of the partridge." Border city between tribes of Judah and Benjamin (Josh. 15:6; 18:19,21). It is probably modern Ain Hajlah, four miles southeast of Jericho.

BETH-HORON Place-name of uncertain meaning. An important road here dominates the path to the Shephelah, the plain between the Judean hills and the Mediterranean coast. Joshua used the road to chase the coalition of southern kings led by the king of Jerusalem (Josh. 10:10).

BETH-JESHIMOTH or **BETH-JESIMOTH** (KJV) Place-name meaning "house of deserts." A town in Moab where Israel camped just before Moses died and Joshua led them across the Jordan (Num. 33:49).

BETH-LE-APHRAH Place-name meaning "place of dust." Town Micah used in a wordplay to announce judgment on Judah. The house of dust would roll in dust, a ritual expressing grief and mourning (Mic. 1:10).

BETH-LEBAOTH Place-name meaning "house of lionesses." City in Simeon's territorial allotment (Josh. 19:6).

BETHLEHEM Place-name meaning "house of bread," "house of fighting," or "house of (god) Lahamu." **1.** Approximately five miles southwest of Jerusalem just off the major road from Jerusalem to the Negev lies the modern Arabic village Bethlehem. The book of Ruth takes place in the region of Bethlehem. This story leads to the events that gave major importance to the village as the home and place of the anointing of David (1 Sam. 16:1-13; 17:12,15). The relationship of Bethlehem to Christ has ensured its place in Christian history. Micah 5:2 was understood to indicate that the Messiah, like David, would be born in Bethlehem not Jerusalem. **2.** Town in the territory of Zebulun, about seven miles northwest of Nazareth (Josh. 19:15), which was the burial site of Ibzan (Judg. 12:10), in modern Beit Lahm. **3.** Personal name, as in 1 Chron. 2:51,54.

BETHLEHEM-EPHRATAH (KJV) or **BETHLEHEM-EPHRATHAH** (CSB, NASB, NIV, NRSV) Place-name used by Mic. 5:2 to designate birthplace of new David who would come from Bethlehem, David's birthplace, and of the clan of Ephratah, that of Jesse, David's father (1 Sam. 17:12).

BETH-MAACAH (CSB, NASB, NRSV) or **BETH-MAACHAH** (KJV) Place-name meaning "house of Maacah" or "house of pressure." Usually appears as Abel Beth-Maacah/Maakah (always so in NIV). Beth-Maacah apparently appears as final stop on Sheba's trip through Israel to gain support against David (2 Sam. 20:14).

BETH-MARCABOTH Place-name meaning "house of chariots." City allotted to the tribe of Simeon (Josh. 19:5). Its location is uncertain.

BETH-MEON Place-name meaning "house of residence." City in Moab on which Jeremiah pronounced judgment (Jer. 48:23). Apparently the same as Beth-baal-meon and Baal-meon.

BETH-MILLO Place-name meaning "house of fullness." **1.** Part of Shechem or a fortress guarding Shechem, where the citizens of Shechem proclaimed Abimelech king (Judg. 9:6,20). **2.** Fortification in Jerusalem where two of his servants killed King Joash (835–796 BC; 2 Kgs. 12:19-20). It is also called "Millo."

BETH-NIMRAH Place-name meaning "house of the panther." City east of the Jordan that the tribe of Gad rebuilt after Moses allotted it to them (Num. 32:36). It provided good grazing land (Num. 32:3). It is located at either Tell Nimrin or nearby at Tell el-Bleibil, about 10 miles northeast of the mouth of the Jordan.

BETH-PAZZEZ Place-name meaning "house of scattering." Town in tribal allotment of Issachar (Josh. 19:22).

BETH-PELET Place-name meaning "house of deliverance." Southern town in tribal allotment of Judah (Josh. 15:27). After the return from exile in Babylon, the Jews lived there (Neh. 11:26). KJV spellings are Beth-palet and Beth-phelet.

BETH-PEOR Place-name meaning "house of Peor." A temple for the god Peor or Baal Peor probably stood there. Town in whose valley Israel camped as Moses delivered the sermons of the book of Deuteronomy (Deut. 3:29).

BETHPHAGE Place-name meaning "house of unripe figs." A small village located on the Mount of Olives near Bethany on or near the road between Jerusalem and Jericho (Matt. 21:1; Mark 11:1; Luke 19:29). Bethphage was where Jesus gave instruction to two disciples to find the colt on which he would ride into Jerusalem for his triumphal entry.

BETH-REHOB Place-name meaning "house of the market." Town near where the tribe of Dan rebuilt Laish and renamed it Dan (Judg. 18:28).

BETHSAIDA Place-name meaning "house of fish." The home of Andrew, Peter, and Philip (John 1:44; 12:21), located on the northeast side of the Sea of Galilee.

BETH-SHAN, BETHSHAN, or **BETHSHEAN** Place-name meaning "house of quiet." Beth-shean stood at the crossroads of the Jezreel and Jordan Valleys, commanding the routes north-south along the Jordan and east-west from Gilead to the Mediterranean Sea. Biblical references to Beth-shean relate to the period from Joshua until the United Monarchy. The city is listed among the allocations of the tribe of Manasseh, though the city was within the territory of Issachar (Josh. 17:11).

Beth-shan

BETH-SHEMESH Place-name meaning "house of the sun." Beth-shemesh is a name applied to four different cities in the OT. The name probably derives from a place where the Semitic god Shemesh (Shamash) was worshipped. **1.** Beth-shemesh of Issachar was situated on the tribal border with Naphtali between Mount Tabor and the Jordan River (Josh. 19:22). **2.** Beth-shemesh of Naphtali was probably located in central upper Galilee because of its association with Beth-anath (Josh. 19:38; Judg. 1:33). This Canaanite town remained independent and unconquered until the time of David. **3.** Beth-shemesh of Egypt is to be identified with Heliopolis (five miles northeast of Cairo) according to the Septuagint or early Greek translation (Jer. 43:13). **4.** Beth-shemesh of Dan is located on the south tribal border with Judah (Josh. 15:10; 19:41) overlooking the Sorek Valley about 24 miles west of Jerusalem.

BETH-SHITTAH Place-name meaning "house of Acacia." Battle scene when Gideon and his 300 men defeated the Midianites (Judg. 7:22).

BETH-TAPPUAH Place-name meaning "house of apples." Town assigned to the tribe of Judah in Judean hills (Josh. 15:53).

BETH-TOGARMAH Place-name meaning "house of Togarmah," who is listed in the Table of Nations (Gen. 10:3) as a son of Gomer and great grandson of Noah. Beth-togarmah (Ezek. 27:14; 38:6) is a city mentioned (as Togarmah) in Assyrian and Hittite texts. It was north of Carchemish on an Assyrian trade route.

BETHUEL or **BETHUL** Place-name and personal name meaning "house of God." **1.** Nephew of Abraham and son of Nahor (Gen. 22:22). His daughter Rebekah married Isaac (Gen. 24:15,67). **2.** Town where the children of Shimei lived (1 Chron. 4:30).

BETHZATHA TEV, NSRV reading of place-name in John 5:2 based on different Greek manuscripts than those followed by other translators; CSB: Bethesda.

BETH-ZUR Place-name meaning "house of the rock." **1.** City allotted to the tribe of Judah (Josh. 15:58). Rehoboam, Solomon's son and successor as king of Judah (931–913 BC), built it up as a defense city (2 Chron. 11:7) in view of the threat of Shishak of Egypt (2 Chron. 12:2). **2.** Son of Maon in line of Caleb (1 Chron. 2:45), apparently indicating the clan that settled the city.

BETONIM Place-name meaning "pistachios." A border town in tribal allotment of Gad (Josh. 13:26).

BETROTHAL Act of engagement for marriage, in Bible times as binding as marriage.

The biblical terms "betrothal" and "espousal" are almost synonymous with marriage and as binding.

BEULAH Symbolic name meaning "married," used in reference to Jerusalem (Isa. 62:4 KJV).

BEYOND THE JORDAN Often used to describe the territory on the east side of the Jordan River (also referred to as the Transjordan). Five times the phrase describes the territory on the west side of the Jordan (Gen. 50:10-11; Deut. 3:20,25; 11:30).

BEYOND THE RIVER Refers to the Euphrates River in Mesopotamia. From the perspective of those living in Palestine, "beyond the river" meant on the east side of the Euphrates. The expression is often used when speaking of the ancestral home of the patriarchs (Josh. 24:3,14-15; KJV has "on the other side of the flood").

BEZAI Contraction of Bezaleel. **1.** Clan of 323 (Ezra 2:17) who returned from Babylonian exile with Zerubbabel about 537 BC. **2.** Man who signed Nehemiah's covenant to obey God's law (Neh. 10:18).

BEZALEEL or **BEZALEL** Personal name meaning "in the shadow of God." **1.** Son of Uri, a member of the tribe of Judah (Exod. 31:2) and great grandson of Caleb (1 Chron. 2:20). He and another man, the Danite Aholiab, were skilled craftsmen who were responsible for making the tabernacle, its furnishings, and trappings. His skill derived from his being filled with the Spirit of God. Most modern translations render the names of these men Bezalel and Oholiab. **2.** Man who followed Ezra's leadership and divorced his foreign wife (Ezra 10:30).

BEZEK Place-name meaning "lightning." Place where Judah and Simeon defeated Canaanites who were led by Adoni-bezek (literally "lord of Bezek") (Judg. 1:4).

BEZER Place-name meaning "inaccessible." A city of refuge in tribal territory of Reuben (Deut. 4:43; Josh. 20:8), set aside as a city for the Levites (Josh. 21:36).

BIBLE, FORMATION AND CANON "Bible" derives from the Greek word for "books" and refers to the OT and NT. The 39 OT books and 27 NT books form the canon of Holy Scripture. "Canon" originally meant "reed" and came to signify a ruler or measuring stick. In this sense, the Bible is the rule or standard of authority for Christians. The concept of canon and process of canonization refer to when the books gained the status of "Holy Scripture," authoritative standards for faith and practice.

BICHRI Personal name meaning "firstborn" or clan name "of the clan of Becher." Father of Sheba, who led revolt against David after Absalom's revolt (2 Sam. 20:1).

BIDKAR Officer of Jehu who took body of Joram, king of Israel (852–841 BC), and threw it on Naboth's land after Jehu murdered the king (2 Kgs. 9:25). Bidkar and Jehu had originally served as chariot officers for Ahab, Joram's father.

BIGTHA Persian personal name possibly meaning "gift of God." A eunuch who served King Ahasuerus of Persia and took the king's command to Queen Vashti to come to a party (Esth. 1:10).

BIGTHAN May be identical with Bigtha. He plotted with Teresh, another of the king's eunuchs, to assassinate King Ahasuerus of Persia (Esth. 2:21). Mordecai foiled the plot, thus setting up the king's need to honor Mordecai at Haman's expense (Esth. 6:1-12).

BIGVAI Persian name meaning "god" or "fortune." **1.** Leader with Zerubbabel of exiles who returned from Babylon about 537 BC (Ezra 2:2). **2.** One who sealed Nehemiah's covenant to obey God's law (Neh. 10:16).

BILDAD Proper name meaning "the Lord loved." One of the three friends of Job (Job 2:11). He is identified as a Shuhite, perhaps a member of a group of nomadic Arameans.

BILEAM City given to Levites from tribal territory of western Manasseh. It is often identified with Ibleam. Joshua 21:25, a parallel passage, reads "Gath-rimmon."

BILGAH Personal name meaning "brightness." **1.** Original ancestor of one of the divisions of priesthood (1 Chron. 24:14). **2.** Priest who returned from exile with Zerubbabel about 537 BC (Neh. 12:5).

BILGAI Priest who sealed Nehemiah's covenant to obey God's law (Neh. 10:8).

BILHAH Personal name meaning "unworried." The handmaid of Rachel (Gen. 29:29). When Rachel failed to bear children to her husband Jacob, Bilhah became his concubine at Rachel's instigation. Bilhah became the mother of Dan and Naphtali (Gen. 29:29; 30:4-8).

BILHAN Personal name, perhaps meaning "afraid" or "foolish." **1.** Descendant of Seir or Edom (Gen. 36:27). **2.** Descendant of Benjamin (1 Chron. 7:10).

BILSHAN Akkadian personal name meaning "their lord." Leader of returning exiles with Zerubbabel from Babylon about 537 BC (Ezra 2:2).

BIMHAL Descendant of tribe of Asher (1 Chron. 7:33).

BINEA Descendant of the tribe of Benjamin (1 Chron. 8:37) and of King Saul (1 Chron. 9:43).

BINNUI Personal name meaning "built." **1.** Father of Noadiah, Levite who assured the temple treasures Ezra brought back from exile were correctly inventoried (Ezra 8:33). **2.** Two men who divorced foreign wives when Ezra sought to remove temptation to idolatry and purify the community (Ezra 10:30,38). **3.** Man who helped Nehemiah repair the wall of Jerusalem (Neh. 3:24). **4.** Clan leader of 648 members who returned with Zerubbabel from Babylon about 537 BC (Neh. 7:15; Ezra 2:10 spells it "Bani" with 642 people). **5.** Levite who sealed Nehemiah's covenant to obey God's law (Neh. 10:9). Could be same as any of the above. He came up with Zerubbabel from Babylonian exile (Neh. 12:8).

BIRDS The Bible contains approximately 300 references to birds, scattered from Genesis to Revelation. The Hebrew people's keen awareness of bird life is reflected in the different Hebrew and Greek names used for birds in general or for specific birds. Although bird names are difficult to translate, many birds of the Bible can be identified from the descriptions of them given in the Scriptures.

Some of the specific birds mentioned are cock (rooster), dove (turtledove), eagle, ostrich, pigeon, quail, raven, sparrow, and vulture. See other individual bird names in the alphabetical dictionary listing.

Birds of abomination The birds of abomination are in the list of 20 birds not to be consumed by Israelites (Lev. 11:13-19). The reason for the exclusion of these birds is unclear. Some have suggested that the birds were prohibited because they were associated with the worship of idols. Others have suggested that they were excluded because they ate flesh that contained blood or because they had contact with corpses—both of which would make one ritually unclean (Lev. 7:26; 17:13-14; 21:1-4,11; 22:4; Num. 5:2-3; 6:6-11).

BIRSHA Personal name with uncertain meaning, traditionally, "ugly." King of Gomorrah who joined coalition of Dead Sea area kings against an eastern group of invading kings (Gen. 14:2).

BIRTHRIGHT Special privileges that belonged to the firstborn male child in a family. Prominent among those privileges was a double portion of the estate as an inheritance. If a man had two sons, his estate would be divided into three portions, and the older son would receive two. If there were three sons, the estate would be divided into four portions, and the oldest son would receive two. The oldest son also normally received the father's major blessing.

BIRTH STOOL Object upon which a woman sat during labor (Exod. 1:16 NASB, NKJV). The birth stool may have been of Egyptian origin. The same Hebrew word (*'obnayim*) is also translated as "potter's wheel" (Jer. 18:3).

BIRZAITH or **BIRZAVITH** (KJV) Descendant of Asher (1 Chron. 7:31).

BISHLAM Personal name or common name meaning "in peace." A representative of the

Persian government in Palestine who complained about building activities (Ezra 4:7) of the returned Jews to Artaxerxes, king of Persia (464–423 BC).

BISHOP Term that comes from the Greek noun *episkopos*, which occurs five times in the NT (Acts 20:28; Phil. 1:1; 1 Tim. 3:2; Titus 1:7; 1 Pet. 2:25). "Overseer" (CSB) more accurately identifies the function of the office-holder than does the term "bishop."

BIT Metal bar fastened to the muzzle end of the horse's bridle. The bit and bridle were used figuratively in the Bible to refer to different forms of control (James 1:26; 3:2; 2 Kgs. 19:28; Isa. 37:29).

BITHIA (NASB) or **BITHIAH** Personal name meaning "daughter of Yahweh" or Egyptian common noun meaning "queen." Daughter of an Egyptian pharaoh whom Mered, a descendant of Judah, married (1 Chron. 4:17 NASB, RSV; 4:18 CSB, KJV, NIV).

BITHYNIA District in northern Asia Minor that Paul's missionary company desired to enter with the gospel (Acts 16:7). The Holy Spirit prevented them from doing so and directed them instead to Macedonia.

BITTER HERBS Eaten with the Passover meal (Exod. 12:8; Num. 9:11), the herbs were interpreted as symbolizing the bitter experiences of the Israelites' slavery in Egypt.

BITTERN KJV translation for an animal of desolation mentioned three times (Isa. 14:23; 34:11; Zeph. 2:14). The name "bittern" is applied to any number of small or medium-sized herons with a characteristic booming cry. CSB: heron.

BITTER WATER A woman suspected of adultery was given bitter water to drink (Num. 5:11-31). If she was innocent, she would not be harmed and would conceive children as a blessing. If she was guilty, her "womb would shrivel" and her "body swell" (CSB).

BITUMEN (NRSV, RSV, ESV) Mineral pitch or asphalt (KJV has "slime"; NASB, NIV, "tar pits") found in solid black lumps in the Cretaceous limestone on the west bank of the Dead Sea (Gen. 14:10).

BIZIOTHIAH or **BIZJOTHJAH** (KJV) Place-name meaning "scorns of Yahweh." Southern town in tribal allotment of Judah (Josh. 15:28).

BIZTHA Persian personal name of uncertain meaning. One of seven eunuchs who served King Ahasuerus in matters relating to his wives (Esth. 1:10).

BLAINS KJV word for sores or boils in Exod. 9:9-10.

BLASPHEMY Transliteration of a Greek word meaning literally "to speak harm." In the biblical context, blasphemy is an attitude of disrespect that finds expression in an act directed against the character of God.

Old Testament Blasphemy draws its Christian definition through the background of the OT. Leviticus 24:14-16 guides the Hebrew definition of blasphemy. The offense is designated as a capital crime, and the offender is to be stoned by the community.

New Testament The NT broadens the concept of blasphemy to include actions against Christ and the church as the body of Christ. Jesus himself was regarded by the Jewish leaders as a blasphemer (Mark 2:7). The unity of Christ and the church is recognized in the fact that persecutions against Christians are labeled as blasphemous acts (1 Tim. 1:13; 1 Pet. 4:4; Rev. 2:9). It is also important that Christians avoid conduct that might give an occasion for blasphemy, especially in the area of attitude and speech (Eph. 4:31; Col. 3:8; 1 Tim. 6:4; Titus 3:2).

The sin of blasphemy is a sin that can be forgiven. However, there is a sin of blasphemy against the Holy Spirit that cannot be forgiven (Matt. 12:32; Mark 3:29; Luke 12:10). This is a state of hardness in which one consciously and willfully resists God's saving power and grace.

BLEMISH Condition that disqualifies an animal as a sacrifice (Lev. 22:17-25) or a man from priestly service (Lev. 21:17-24). In the NT, Christ is the perfect sacrifice (without blemish, Heb. 9:14; 1 Pet. 1:19) intended to sanctify the church and remove all its blemishes (Eph. 5:27). The children of God are commanded to live lives without blemishes (Phil. 2:15; 2 Pet. 3:14).

BLESSING AND CURSING To "bless" meant to fill with benefits, either as an end in itself or to make the object blessed a source of further blessing for others. God is most often at least the understood agent of blessing in this sense. In another sense, the word could mean to "praise," as if filling the object of blessing with honor and good words. Thus individuals might bless God (Exod. 18:10; Ruth 4:14; Pss. 68:19; 103:1), while God also could bless men and women (Gen. 12:2-3; Num. 23:20; 1 Chron. 4:10; Ps. 109:28; Isa. 61:9). Persons might also bless one another (Gen. 27:33; Deut. 7:14; 1 Sam. 25:33), or they might bless things (Deut. 28:4; 1 Sam. 25:33; Prov. 5:18).

In the NT, "blessed" often translates *makarios*, meaning "blessed, fortunate, happy." It occurs 50 times in the NT, most familiarly in the "beatitudes" in Jesus's Sermon on the Mount (Matt. 5:3-11).

The concept of cursing was clearly more prevalent in the OT. Depending on who is speaking, one who "curses" is either predicting, praying, or causing great trouble for someone. As belonging to God and his people meant blessing, being cursed often meant separation from God and the community of faith. It thus involved the experience of insecurity and disaster.

In the NT, the act of "cursing" sometimes means to wish misfortune on someone (Luke 6:28; Rom. 12:14; James 3:9-10). The concept of the "curse" is also applied to those who are outside God's blessings, which are by his grace (Matt. 25:41). They are therefore under divine condemnation, the "curse of the law" because of sin (John 7:49; Gal. 3:10,13; 1 Cor. 16:22). Especially serious is the situation of those who reject or actively oppose the work of God (Gal. 1:8-9; 2 Pet. 2:14; Rev. 16:9,11,21).

BLINDNESS Physical blindness in the biblical period was very common. The suffering of the blind person was made worse by the common belief that the affliction was due to sin (John 9:1-3). Jesus frequently healed blind persons (Matt. 9:27-31; 12:22; 20:30-34; Mark 10:46-52; John 9:1-7).

The Bible addresses spiritual blindness as the great human problem. Peter listed the qualities a person must have to have spiritual sight. Without these, a person is blind (2 Pet. 1:5-9).

BLOOD Blood is intimately associated with physical life. The Hebrews of OT times were prohibited from eating blood. Even when the OT speaks of animal sacrifice and atonement, the sacredness of life is emphasized (Lev. 17:11).

Blood of Christ—Meaning and Effects The term "blood of Christ" designates in the NT the atoning death of Christ. Atonement refers to the basis and process by which estranged people become at one with God (atonement = at-one-ment). When we identify with Jesus, we are no longer at odds with God. In the language of sacrifice we have "propitiation" (removal of sins, Rom. 3:25 CSB); we are "sprinkled with the blood of Jesus Christ" (1 Pet. 1:1-2 CSB); redeemed "with the precious blood of Christ, like that of an unblemished and spotless lamb" (1 Pet. 1:19 CSB); "blood of Jesus his Son cleanses us from all sin" (1 John 1:7 CSB); blood that will "cleanse our consciences" (Heb. 9:14 CSB); and "blood of the everlasting covenant" (Heb. 13:20 CSB).

BLOODGUILT Guilt usually incurred through bloodshed.

BLUE Hebrew word translated "blue" (*tekeleth*), also translated as "purple" (Ezek. 23:6) and "violet" (Jer. 10:9). Blue was considered inferior to royal purple but was still a very popular color. Blue was used in the tabernacle (Exod. 25:4; 26:1,4; Num. 4:6-7,9; 15:38), in the temple (2 Chron. 2:7,14; 3:14), and in the clothing of the priests (Exod. 28:5-6,8,15; 39:1).

BOANERGES Name meaning "sons of thunder," given by Jesus to James and John, the sons of Zebedee (Mark 3:17).

BOAZ Personal name, perhaps meaning "lively." **1.** Hero of the book of Ruth; a wealthy relative of Naomi's husband. **2.** The left or north pillar Solomon set up in the temple (1 Kgs. 7:21).

BOCHERU Personal name meaning "firstborn." Descendant of Benjaminite King Saul (1 Chron. 8:38).

BOCHIM Place-name meaning "weepers." Place where angel of God announced judgment on Israel at beginning of the period of the judges because they had not destroyed pagan altars but had made covenant treaties with the native inhabitants. Thus the people cried and named the place Bochim (Judg. 2:1-5).

BOHAN Place-name and personal name meaning "thumb" or "big toe." A place on the northern border of the tribal allotment of Judah called the "stone of Bohan," "the son of Reuben" (Josh. 15:6). This was the southern border of the tribe of Benjamin (Josh. 18:17).

BOLLED KJV translation (Exod. 9:31) of a term that means "having bolls"—that is, having seedpods.

BOND Translation of several Hebrew and Greek words with the meanings of "obligation," "dependence," or "restraint." Used literally to speak of the bonds of prisoners or slaves (Judg. 15:14; 1 Kgs. 14:10; Ps. 107:14; 116:16; Luke 8:29; Philem. 13). Used figuratively to speak of the bonds of wickedness or sin.

BOOK OF LIFE Heavenly record (Luke 10:20; Heb. 12:23) written by God before the foundation of the world (Rev. 13:8; 17:8) containing the names of those who are destined because of God's grace and their faithfulness to participate in God's heavenly kingdom. The OT refers to a record kept by God of those who are a part of his people (Exod. 32:32; Isa. 4:3; Dan. 12:1; Mal. 3:16).

BOOK(S) Term which often refers to a scroll. A document written on parchment or papyrus and then rolled up. The "book" may be a letter (1 Kgs. 21:8) or a longer literary effort (Dan. 9:2).

BOR-ASHAN Place-name meaning "well of smoke" or "pit of smoke." Place in most manuscripts of 1 Sam. 30:30; others read Chor-ashan (KJV). A town of the tribe of Judah to whom David gave part of his spoils of victory. It is usually equated with Asham, the town of Judah in which Simeon lived (Josh. 15:42; 19:7).

BOTTLE Word used often in the KJV to translate several Hebrew and Greek words. Modern versions often translate these words as "skin" or "wineskin." Although glass and glass bottles were known in ancient times, ancient "bottles" were almost always made of animal skins since they were easier to carry than earthenware vessels.

BOTTOMLESS PIT Literal translation of the Greek in Rev. 9:1-2,11; 11:7; 17:8; 20:1,3. It represented the home of evil, death, and destruction stored up until the sovereign God allowed them temporary power on earth.

BOWELS Translation used in modern versions to refer to intestines and other entrails (Acts 1:18). In the KJV, "bowels" is also used to refer to the sexual reproductive system (2 Sam. 16:11; Ps. 71:6) and, figuratively, to strong emotions (Job 30:27), especially love (Song 5:4) and compassion (Col. 3:12). Both Hebrew and Greek picture the entrails as the center of human emotions and excitement.

BOX TREE KJV, REB, and NASB translation in Isa. 41:19; 60:13. The Hebrew word means "to be straight" and apparently refers to the tall, majestic cypress trees. Such wonders of nature reflect the greatness of the Creator (Isa. 41:20).

BOZEZ Place-name, perhaps meaning "white." A sharp rock marking a passage in the Wadi Suwenit near Michmash through which Jonathan and his armor bearer went to fight the Philistines (1 Sam. 14:4).

BOZRAH Place-name meaning "inaccessible." **1.** Ancestral home of Jobab, a king in Edom in the patriarchal period (Gen. 36:33). **2.** City of Moab Jeremiah condemned (Jer. 48:24). It may be equated with Bezer.

BRACELET Ornamental band of metal or glass worn around the wrist (as distinct from an armlet worn around the upper arm). Bracelets were common in the ancient Near East and were worn by both women and men.

Serpentine bracelet

BRAMBLE Shrub (*Lycium Europaeum*) with sharp spines and runners usually forming a tangled mass of vegetation (Judg. 9:8-15; Luke 6:44). It had beautiful, attractive flowers, but its thorns were troublesome to animal flocks.

BRASS Any copper alloy was called "brass" by the KJV translators. Brass is the alloy of copper and zinc, a combination unknown in the ancient Near East.

BREAD Frequency of mention is just one indication that bread (not vegetables and certainly not meat) was the basic food of most people (except nomads and the wealthy) in Bible times. A course meal was ground from wheat (Gen. 30:14) or barley (John 6:9,13). In addition to being used as a staple food, bread was used as an offering to God (Lev. 2:4-10). It was used in the tabernacle and temple to symbolize the presence of God (Exod. 25:23-30; Lev. 24:5-9). Bread was also used in the OT to symbolize such things as an enemy to be consumed (Num. 14:9, KJV, RSV), the unity of a group (1 Kgs. 18:19), hospitality (Gen. 19:3), and wisdom (Prov. 9:5).

BREAD OF THE PRESENCE Also "bread of the faces." In Exod. 25:30, the Lord's instructions concerning the paraphernalia of worship include a provision that bread be kept always on a table set before the holy of holies. This bread was called the "Bread of the Presence" (CSB) or "showbread/shewbread." It consisted of 12 loaves of presumably unleavened bread, and it was replaced each Sabbath.

BREASTPIECE OF THE HIGH PRIEST Piece of elaborate embroidery about nine inches square worn by the high priest upon his breast. It was set with 12 stones with the name of one of the 12 tribes of Israel engraved on each stone.

BREASTPLATE Piece of defensive armor. Paul used the military breastplate as an illustration of Christian virtues. Ephesians 6:14 reflects Isa. 59:17, symbolizing the breastplate as righteousness. Faith and love are symbolized in 1 Thess. 5:8. Breastplates were also strong symbols of evil (Rev. 9:9,17).

BRICK Building material of clay, molded into rectangular-shaped blocks while moist and hardened by the sun or fire, used to construct walls or pavement. The tower of Babel (Gen. 11:3), made of bricks, had mortar of slime, a tarlike substance. Later the descendants of Joseph, as slaves of the pharaoh in Egypt, built storehouse cities of brick in Pithom and Ramses. Both straw-made bricks and bricks of pure clay have been found there. When David conquered the Ammonites,

Mud-clay bricks in the ruins of the city of Ur

he required that they make bricks (2 Sam. 12:31). Isaiah (65:3) condemned Israel for their paganlike practice of offering incense on altars of brick.

BRIDE Biblical writers have little to say about weddings or brides. They occasionally mention means by which brides were obtained (Gen. 24:4; 29:15-19). Ezekiel 16:8-14 describes the bride, her attire, and the wedding ceremony. The Song of Songs is a collection of love poems in which the bride describes her love for her bridegroom. In the NT, the bride imagery is used often of the church and her relationship to Christ. The bride belongs to Christ, who is the Bridegroom (John 3:29; Rev. 21).

BRIER Translation of various Hebrew words referring to thorny plants. Used metaphorically of the enemies of Israel (Ezek. 28:24) and of land that is worthless (Isa. 5:6; 7:23-25; 55:13; cp. Mic. 7:4).

BRIMSTONE Combustible form of sulfur. Used as a means of divine retribution (Gen. 19:24; Deut. 29:23; Job 18:15; Ps. 11:6; Isa. 30:33; 34:9; Ezek. 38:22; Luke 17:29; Rev. 14:10; 19:20; 20:10; 21:8). It lies on the shore of the Dead Sea and can burst into flame when earthquakes release hot gases from the earth's interior.

BRONZE SERPENT Moses made a bronze serpent and set it on a pole in the middle of the Israelite camp (Num. 21). God had told Moses to do this so the Israelites bitten by serpents could express their faith by looking at it and be healed. Jesus made the final mention of this symbol in John 3:14. There, in his conversation with Nicodemus, Jesus compared his own purpose with that of the bronze serpent. The serpent, lifted up in the wilderness, had been God's chosen way to provide physical healing. Jesus, lifted up on the cross, is God's chosen means of providing spiritual healing for all afflicted by sin. Whoever believes in Jesus "will not perish but have eternal life" (John 3:16 CSB).

BROOCH Class of jewelry brought by both men and women as offerings (Exod. 35:22). The Hebrew term denotes a golden pin (KJV has "bracelets"; REB, "clasp"; TEV, "decorative pins"). At a later time, brooches were bow shaped and made of bronze or iron. Some recent interpreters think "nose rings" were meant.

BROOM TREE Bush that often grows large enough to provide shade (1 Kgs. 19:4-5). Its foliage and roots were often used as fuel (Job 30:4; Ps. 120:4).

BROTHERS In the OT, "brother" usually refers to the blood relationship of siblings (Exod. 4:14; Judg. 9:5). The term "brother" is also used in the OT to signify kinsmen, allies, fellow countrymen. This shift of focus from blood to spiritual kinship is found in the teachings of Jesus when he designated as brothers "those who hear and do the word of God" (Luke 8:21 CSB). The fledgling Christian community continued this emphasis on brother as expressing a spiritual relationship. In most of the NT passages, "brothers" is used to designate the entire Christian community (male and female).

BROTHERS, JESUS'S Jesus's Nazareth critics listed them in Mark 6:3 as James, Joses, Judas, and Simon. Their names appear again in the parallel passage of Matt. 13:55, except Joseph is used as the alternate spelling of Joses.

BUCKLER (KJV) Small rounded shield that was carried in the hand or worn on the arm. Larger shields were also used that covered the entire body. Modern translations: shield.

BUKKI Personal name shortened from Bukkiah, meaning "Yahweh proved" or "Yahweh has emptied." **1.** Representative of the tribe of Dan on commission to distribute the promised land among the tribes (Num. 34:22). **2.** High priestly descendant of Aaron (1 Chron. 6:5,51) and ancestor of Ezra (Ezra 7:4).

BUKKIAH Son of Herman, among David-appointed temple musicians (1 Chron. 25:4). He or a person of same name headed the sixth course of musicians (1 Chron. 25:13).

BUL Name of eighth month or parts of October and November meaning "harvest month." Solomon finished building the temple in this month (1 Kgs. 6:38).

BULL The bull was the symbol of great productivity in the ancient world and was a sign of great strength. Moses portrayed the future strength of Joseph with the term *shor* (Deut. 33:17). The king of Assyria boasted of his great strength with the term *abbir* (Isa. 10:13). The most frequent use of the bull in the OT was as a sacrificial animal.

BULRUSH In Exod. 2:3, the material used to make the basket in which the infant Moses was placed to protect him from the edict of Pharaoh requiring that every male Hebrew child be drowned. A kind of reed plant. CSB: papyrus.

BUNNI Personal name meaning "built." Levite leader of worship service confessing Israel's sin in days of Ezra (Neh. 9:4). A man of same name, probably same man, signed Nehemiah's covenant to obey God's law (Neh. 10:15). His son Hasabiah was a Levite living in Jerusalem in Nehemiah's time (Neh. 11:15).

BURIAL Partly because of the warm climate of Palestine and partly because the corpse was considered ritually impure, the Hebrews buried their dead as soon as possible and usually within 24 hours of death (Deut. 21:23). To allow a body to decay or be desecrated above the ground was highly dishonorable (1 Kgs. 14:10-14; 2 Kgs. 9:34-37), and any corpse found by the wayside was required to be buried (2 Sam. 21:10-14).

BUTLER Translation of a Hebrew word that literally means "one who gives drink." The butler was an officer of the royal court who had charge of wines and other beverages. The butler was a trusted member of the royal court as this person helped prevent the poisoning of the king. The term that is translated "butler" (KJV, Gen. 40:1-23; 41:9) is also translated "cupbearer" (see also 1 Kgs. 10:5; 2 Chron. 9:4; Neh. 1:11).

BUZ Place and personal name meaning "scorn." **1.** Son of Nahor, brother of Abraham (Gen. 22:21). **2.** A member of the tribe of Gad (1 Chron. 5:14). **3.** A land in eastern Arabia (Jer. 25:23) that Jeremiah condemned.

BUZI Personal name meaning "scorn." Priest and father of Ezekiel, the prophet and priest (Ezek. 1:3).

BUZZARD Unclean bird, not suitable for food. Listed in the NASB and NLT in Lev. 11:13; Deut. 14:12 with the birds of abomination. Revelation 18:2 (NLT) has "filthy buzzards" nesting in the fallen Babylon.

BYWORD (KJV) Object of ridicule and scorn among other peoples. Used to speak of the fate of faithless Israel (Deut. 28:37; 1 Kgs. 9:7; 2 Chron. 7:20; Job 17:6; 30:9; Ps. 44:14).

Byzantine street at Caesarea Maritima with two colossal statues, one possibly of the emperor Hadrian

CABBON Place-name of uncertain meaning. Town in tribal allotment of Judah (Josh. 15:40).

CABIN KJV translation of Hebrew word appearing only in Jer. 37:16 and meaning vault, cellar, or prison cell (cistern, NRSV).

CABUL Place-name meaning "fettered" or "braided." **1.** Town on northeast border of Asher (Josh. 19:27). May be located at modern Kabul, nine miles southeast of Acco. **2.** Region of cities in Galilee Solomon gave Hiram, king of Tyre, as payment for materials and services in building the temple and the palace.

CAESAR Family name of Julius Caesar assumed as a title by the emperors who followed him.

CAESAREA Located on the Mediterranean Sea 23 miles south of Mount Carmel is the city of Caesarea, known also as Caesarea-on-the-Sea (Maritima). Herod determined to build a fine port facility and support it by a new city. The harbor, which he named Sebastos (Latin, Augustus), was a magnificently engineered project. After Archelaus was removed in AD 6, Caesarea became the capital of the province of Judea and served as the official home of the procurators.

CAESAREA PHILIPPI About 1,150 feet above sea level, Caesarea Philippi is located on a triangular plain in the upper Jordan Valley along the southwestern slopes of Mount Hermon. Caesarea Philippi seems to have been a religious center from its earliest days. The Canaanite god Baal-gad, the god of good fortune, was worshipped here in OT times. Later, in the Greek period, a shrine in the cave was dedicated to the god Pan. Near here Jesus asked his disciples the famous question about his identity. Peter, acting as the group's spokesman, replied with his famous statement that Jesus is the Christ.

CAIAPHAS Personal name meaning "rock" or "depression." High priest at the time of the trial and crucifixion of Jesus (Matt. 26:3). He was the son-in-law of Annas and a leader in the plot to arrest and execute Jesus.

CAIN Personal name meaning "acquisition." The firstborn son of Adam and Eve (Gen. 4:1). Cain was a farmer, and his brother Abel was a shepherd. When the two men each brought an offering to the Lord, Abel's was accepted, but Cain's was not. Subsequently, Cain murdered Abel his brother.

CAINAN Personal name of unknown meaning. **1.** Ancestor of Noah (Gen. 5:10-14), sometimes seen as a variant spelling of Cain (Gen. 4:17). **2.** Descendant of Noah listed in the Septuagint Greek translation of Gen. 11:12 (but not in Hebrew). Luke used this early Greek translation of the OT and included Cainan in Christ's ancestors (Luke 3:36).

CALAH Assyrian place-name. City that Nimrod built along with Nineveh and Rehoboth (Gen. 10:8-12).

CALAMUS Ingredient of holy anointing oil (Exod. 30:23). It was a good-smelling spice made from an imported reed. It is also translated "fragrant cane" (CSB, NIV, NASB) or "aromatic cane" (NRSV).

CALCOL Personal name of uncertain meaning. Wise man who served as comparison for Solomon's unsurpassed wisdom (1 Kgs. 4:31). First Chronicles 2:6 makes him a grandson of Judah, the son of Jacob.

CALEB, CALEBITE Personal and clan name meaning "dog." Caleb, the son of Jephunneh, was one of the 12 spies sent by Moses to scout out the territory of Canaan (Num. 13:6). A descendant of Judah, he was one of only two who brought back a positive report (Num. 13:30). Because of his steadfast loyalty to the Lord, God rewarded him by letting him survive the years of wilderness wandering and giving him the region of Hebron as his portion in the promised land. At age 85, Caleb conquered Hebron (Josh. 14).

CALENDAR OT mentions days, months, and years, the basic elements of a calendar. It was in the post-biblical rabbinical period that the written treatise on Jewish traditions, *Rosh Hashanah*, a part of the Mishna, organized the biblical data into the detailed calendrical system that the Jews observe today.

CALF Young of the cow or other closely related animals. Calves were fattened in stalls to provide veal on special occasions (Gen. 18:7-8; 1 Sam. 28:24; Luke 15:23,27,30). Calves were also used in sacrificial settings (Lev. 9:2-3; Jer. 34:18; cp. Gen. 15:9-10, heifer). A calf symbolized the bullish Gentile armies (Ps. 68:30) and Egyptian mercenary soldiers (Jer. 46:21). The feet of one of the cherubim described by Ezekiel looked like those of a calf (Ezek. 1:7). One of the four creatures around the throne resembled a calf (Rev. 4:7 KJV; most translations read "ox").

CALKERS, CALKING (KJV) Those who place some substance like bitumen into the seams of a ship's planking to make it watertight (Ezek. 27:9,27).

CALNEH, CALNO Place-name of uncertain meaning. **1.** A part of the kingdom of Nimrod in Babylonia (Gen. 10:10). **2.** City in Syria under Israel's control in the days of Amos and Isaiah (ca. 740 BC).

CALVARY English name for the place where Jesus was crucified (Luke 23:33), derived from the Latin *Calvaria*, which is the Vulgate's

Gordon's Calvary is one of two sites considered to be the possible location of Jesus's crucifixion.

translation of the Greek *Kranion*, "skull." The other three Gospels (Matt. 27:33; Mark 15:22; John 19:17) refer also to the Semitic name "Golgotha," meaning "skull" or "head."

CALVES, GOLDEN Representation of young bulls used to symbolize the god's presence in the worship place. As Moses was on Mount Sinai, Aaron formed a golden calf to use in a "feast to Yahweh" (Exod. 32:4-5). Similarly, Jeroboam placed calves in Dan and Bethel for the northern kingdom to use in its worship of Yahweh (1 Kgs. 12:28) so the people would not have to go to Jerusalem, the southern capital, to worship. In both instances the calves represent the gods who brought Israel up from Egypt. Thus the sin of the calves is not worshiping the wrong god but worshiping the true God in the wrong way through images (Ps. 106:19-20).

CAMEL Large hump-backed mammal of Asia and Africa used for desert travel to bear burdens or passengers. Recent discoveries show it was domesticated before 2000 BC.

Old Testament The camel, called the "ship of the desert," is adapted for desert travel with padded feet, a muscular body, and a hump of fat to sustain life on long journeys. A young camel can walk 100 miles in a day. Wealth was measured by many things, including camels (Gen. 24:35; Job 1:3).

New Testament A proverb picturing things impossible to accomplish was quoted by Jesus (Mark 10:25) when he said it is easier for a camel to pass through the eye of a needle (Matt. 19:24) than for a rich man to enter heaven.

CAMEL'S HAIR Very coarse material was woven from the hair of a camel's back and hump. A finer material was woven from the hair taken from underneath the animal. John the Baptist wore coarse camel's hair (Mark 1:6). Jesus contrasted John's cloak to the "soft raiment" (KJV) of the members of the king's court (Matt. 11:8). Wearing a hairy mantle was the mark of a prophet (Zech. 13:4; cp. 2 Kgs. 1:8).

CAMP, ENCAMPMENT Temporary settlement for nomadic and military people. Hence the frequent reference to "the camp" or "the camp of Israel" (Exod. 14:1,9; 16:13). Leviticus and Deuteronomy contain laws regulating life "in the camp."

CAMPHIRE KJV spelling of "camphor," Song 1:14; 4:13. Most modern versions read "henna."

CANA Place-name meaning "the nest." In John 2:1, the town was the scene of a wedding during which Jesus changed water into wine. In Cana an unnamed nobleman sought out Jesus to ask him to heal his son in Capernaum (John 4:46). Cana was also the home of Nathanael, one of the apostles (John 21:2).

CANAAN Territory between the Mediterranean Sea and the Jordan River reaching from the brook of Egypt to the area around Ugarit in Syria or to the Euphrates. This represents descriptions in Near Eastern documents and in the OT. Canaan meant different things at different times. Numbers 13:29 limits Canaanites to those who "live by the sea and along the Jordan" (CSB; cp. Josh. 11:3). Israel was aware of the larger "promised land" of Canaan (Gen. 15:18; Exod. 23:20; Num. 13:17-21; Deut. 1:7; 1 Kgs. 4:21), but Israel's basic land reached only from "Dan to Beer-sheba" (2 Sam. 24:2-8,15; 1 Kgs. 4:25). At times, Israel included land east of the Jordan (2 Sam. 24:5-6). Other times the land of Gilead was contrasted to the land of Canaan (Josh. 22:9). After the conquest, Israel knew "a great deal of the land remains to be possessed" (Josh. 13:1 CSB). Canaan thus extended beyond the normal borders of Israel yet did not include land east of the Jordan. At times, the land of Canaanites and the land of Amorites are identical. Whatever the land was called, it exercised extraordinary influence as the land bridge between Mesopotamia and Egypt and between the Mediterranean and the Red Sea.

CANALS Translation of a Hebrew word that refers to the branches of the Nile River (Exod. 7:19; 8:5; Isa. 19:6). The KJV uses "rivers."

CANDACE In Acts 8:27, the queen of Ethiopia whose servant became a believer in Christ and was baptized by Philip. It is generally

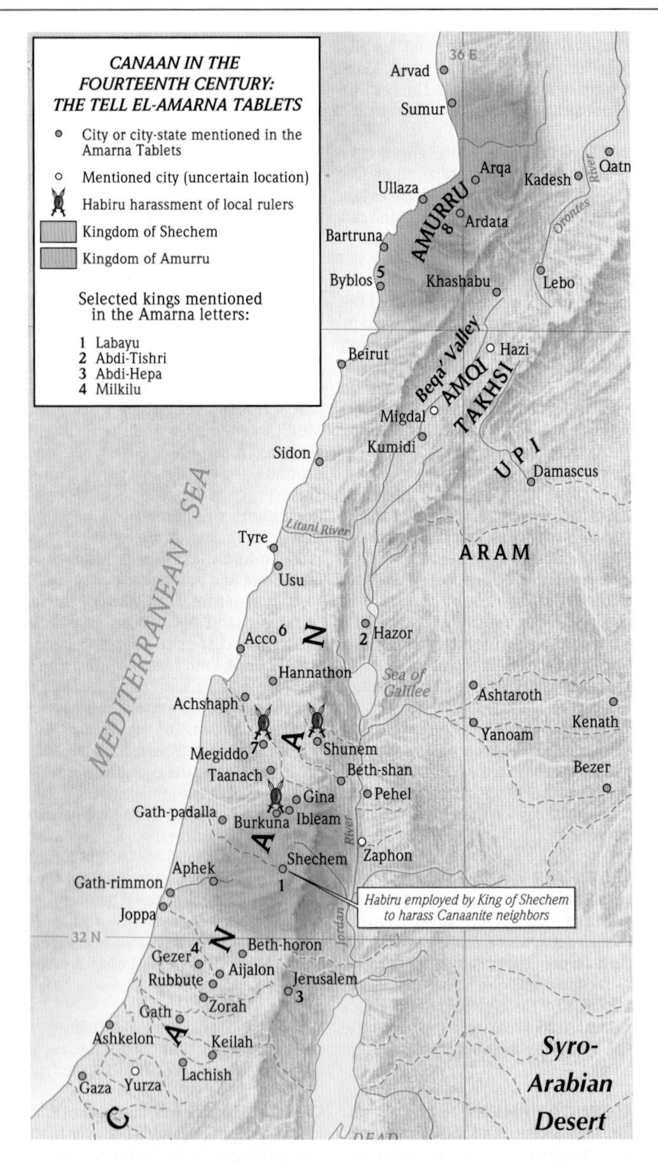
CANAAN IN THE FOURTEENTH CENTURY: THE TELL EL-AMARNA TABLETS
City or city-state mentioned in the Amarna Tablets
Mentioned city (uncertain location)
Habiru harassment of local rulers
Kingdom of Shechem
Kingdom of Amurru
Selected kings mentioned in the Amarna letters:
1 Labayu
2 Abdi-Tishri
3 Abdi-Hepa
4 Milkilu
Arvad
Sumur
Arqa
Kadesh
Qatn
Ullaza
AMURRU
Ardata
Bartruna
Byblos
Khashabu
Lebo
Orontes
River
Beirut
Hazi
Beqa' Valley
AMQI
TAKHSI
Migdal
Kumidi
Sidon
UPI
Damascus
MEDITERRANEAN SEA
Litani River
Tyre
Usu
ARAM
Acco
Hazor
Hannathon
Sea of Galilee
Ashtaroth
Achshaph
Kenath
Yanoam
Megiddo
Shunem
Taanach
Beth-shan
Bezer
Gina
Pehel
Gath-padalla
Burkuna
Ibleam
Zaphon
Shechem
Aphek
Gath-rimmon
Joppa
Habiru employed by King of Shechem to harass Canaanite neighbors
Jordan
32 N
36 E
Beth-horon
Gezer
Aijalon
Rubbute
Jerusalem
Zorah
Gath
Ashkelon
Keilah
Lachish
Gaza
Yurza
CANAAN
Syro-Arabian Desert

agreed that Candace was a title rather than a proper name, though its meaning is uncertain. The title was used by several queens of Ethiopia.

CANDLE, CANDLESTICK (KJV) Candles as we know them were not in use in biblical times. The reference is to "lamp" or "lampstand."

CANKER KJV translation in 2 Tim. 2:17 and James 5:3. In general, "canker" may refer to any source of corruption or debasement. In 2 Tim. 2:17, the reference is to gangrene, which is the local death of soft tissues due to loss of blood supply—a condition that can spread from infected to uninfected tissue. In James 5:3, the reference is to rust.

CANKERWORM KJV translation in Joel 1:4; 2:25; Nah. 3:15-16. The Hebrew refers to a type of locust. See *Insects; Locust.*

CANNEH Northern Syrian city that traded with Tyre and gained Ezekiel's mention in condemning Tyre (Ezek. 27:23). It may be variant spelling of Calneh or a city called Kannu in Assyrian documents.

CAPERNAUM Meaning "village of Nahum." Capernaum, located on the northwest shore of the Sea of Galilee about 2.5 miles west of the entrance of the Jordan River, was chosen as the base of operations by Jesus when he began his ministry.

CAPHTOR Original home of the Philistines (Amos 9:7). In Jer. 47:4 and in Deut. 2:23, its inhabitants are called Caphtorim (cp. Gen. 10:14). Though several places have at times been proposed for its location, current scholarship is generally agreed that Caphtor is the island of Crete.

CAPITAL PUNISHMENT Capital punishment, or the death penalty, refers to the

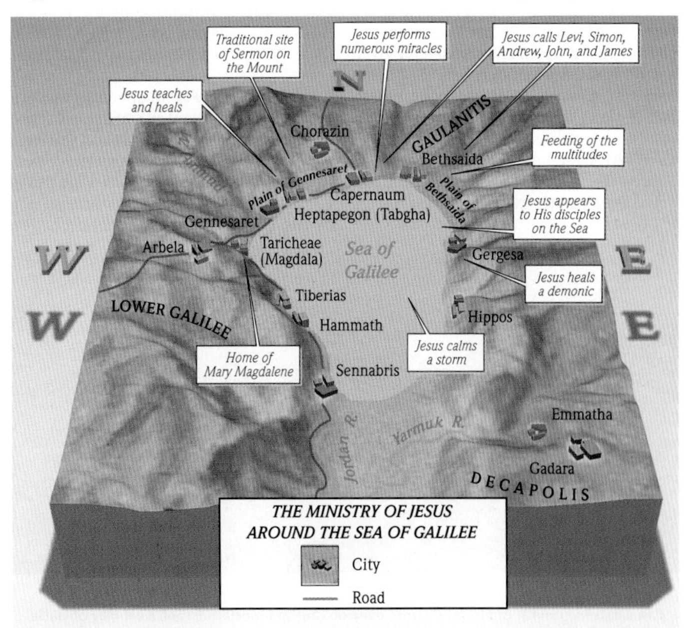

THE MINISTRY OF JESUS AROUND THE SEA OF GALILEE

execution by the state of those guilty of certain crimes. Though some have opposed capital punishment for ideological and practical reasons, it is important to note that God mandated its use. This divine mandate occurs first immediately after the Noahic flood. God instructed Noah and his sons, "Whoever sheds human blood, by humans his blood will be shed" (Gen. 9:6 CSB). Capital punishment is reserved for the state, not the individual. There is no place for personal revenge in administration of this punishment (Rom. 12:19).

CAPPADOCIA Roman province in Asia Minor mentioned twice in the NT: Acts 2:9; 1 Pet. 1:1. Although the extent of Cappadocia varied through the centuries depending on the currently dominant empire, it lay south of Pontus and stretched about 300 miles from Galatia eastward toward Armenia, with Cilicia and the Taurus Mountains to the south. From Acts 2:9, we know that Jews from Cappadocia were in Jerusalem when Peter preached at Pentecost. Those converted to Christianity that day must have given a good witness when they returned home because in 1 Pet. 1:1 believers there are mentioned along with others in Pontus.

CAPTAIN English translation of several Hebrew words usually referring to an officer or leader; variously translated, often applied to Christ.

CAPTAIN OF THE TEMPLE Officer second in authority only to the high priest. Pashhur ("chief official in the temple of the Lord," Jer. 20:1 CSB) and Seraiah ("chief official of God's temple," Neh. 11:11 CSB) held this office in the OT times. In Acts, it appears that one of the main functions of this officer was to keep order in the temple (Acts 4:1; 5:24,26). The plural (Luke 22:4,52) may refer to officers under the command of the captain of the temple.

CAPTIVITY Term used for Israel's exile in Babylon between 597 and 538 BC.

CARBUNCLE Precious stone used in the priest's breastpiece (Exod. 28:17 KJV) and part of the king of Tyre's apparel in the garden of Eden according to Ezekiel's ironic description (Ezek. 28:13). Equation with a stone used today is difficult if not impossible.

CARCAS Persian name meaning "hawk." One of the seven eunuchs under King Ahasuerus of Persia commanded to bring Queen Vashti to the king's party (Esth. 1:10).

CARCHEMISH Fort of Chemosh; modern Jerablus. An important city on the great bend of the Euphrates River. It was on the west bank of the river, at an important river crossing point on the international trade route. Carchemish lies mostly on the Turkish side of the modern Turkish-Syrian border.

The western summit of Mount Carmel overlooking the modern Israeli port city of Haifa.

Carchemish was the site of a strategic battle in 605 BC when Nebuchadnezzar defeated Egypt's Pharaoh Neco II.

This victory gave Babylon authority over all of western Asia within the next few years; for this reason it ranks as one of the most decisive battles of all time.

CARMEL Place-name meaning "park, fruitful field." **1.** Village in the tribal territory assigned to Judah (Josh. 15:55). King Saul set up a monument there after he defeated the Amalekites (1 Sam. 15:12). **2.** The towering mountain (1 Kgs. 18:19) where Elijah confronted the prophets of Baal. The mountain is near the Mediterranean coast between the Plain of Acco to the north and the Plain of Sharon to the south. It reaches a maximum elevation of about 1,750 feet.

CARMI Personal name meaning "my vineyard." **1.** Son of Reuben (Gen. 46:9) and thus original ancestor of a clan in the tribe of Reuben (Num. 26:6). **2.** Father of Achan (Josh. 7:1). **3.** Son of Judah (1 Chron. 4:1).

CARNAL Anything related to the fleshly or worldly appetites and desires rather than to the godly and spiritual desires. People walk either in the flesh or in the Spirit, leading to death or to life. The carnal person is hostile to God, unable to please God (Rom. 8:1-11).

CARPENTER Trade or skill lifted to a high position of honor by Jesus (Mark 6:3).

CARPUS Personal name meaning "fruit." A Christian friend with whom Paul left his cloak in Troas. He asked Timothy to retrieve it for him (2 Tim. 4:13).

CARSHENA Wise counselor of King Ahasuerus of Persia to whom the king turned for advice on how to deal with his disobedient wife Vashti (Esth. 1:14).

CASIPHIA Place-name meaning "silversmith." Place in Babylon where Levites settled in exile (Ezra 8:17) and from which Ezra summoned Levites to return with him to Jerusalem. The place is unknown outside this passage.

CASLUH, CASLUHIM, CASLUHITES Clan name of "sons of Mizraim (or Egypt)" and "father" of the Philistines as named in the Table of Nations (Gen. 10:14).

CASSIA Bark of an oriental tree (*Cinnamomum cassia Blume*) related to cinnamon. One of the ingredients used to make anointing oil (Exod. 30:24), it was acquired through trade with Tyre (Ezek. 27:19) and was desired for its aromatic qualities (Ps. 45:8). One of Job's daughters was named Keziah (Job 42:14), a name that means "cassia."

CASTAWAY KJV translation of Greek *adokimos*, referring to battle testing of soldiers, qualifications for office, or testing of metals to make sure they are genuine. Paul used his own example of personal discipline to ensure that his preaching proved true in life as a call to others to do the same (1 Cor. 9:27). He did not want to be cast away as impure metal or disqualified as an unworthy soldier or candidate.

CASTLE KJV translation for six Hebrew words and one Greek word. NASB uses "castle" only for one Hebrew term in 2 Kgs. 15:25 and Prov. 18:19. RSV uses "castle" in Prov. 18:19 and also for a different Hebrew term in Neh. 7:2. CSB and NIV do not use "castle."

CASTOR AND POLLUX Greek deities, the twin sons of Zeus, represented by the astral sign of Gemini. In Acts 28:11, Castor and Pollux were the sign or figurehead of the ship that carried Paul from Malta toward Rome.

CATERPILLAR Worm-like larvae of butterflies and moths. The term appears in different English versions to translate various Hebrew words. CSB uses the word in Ps. 78:46.

CATHOLIC EPISTLES NT letters not attributed to Paul and written to a more general or unidentifiable audience: James; 1 and 2 Peter; 1, 2, and 3 John; Jude. The title is from tradition.

CATTLE Domesticated quadrupeds used as livestock. In the Bible, the term commonly refers to all domesticated animals. English translations use "cattle" for at least 13 different Hebrew words and six Greek words referring to animals.

CAUDA or **CLAUDA** Small island whose name is variously spelled in the Greek manuscripts. Paul sailed by the island on his way to Malta and ultimately to Rome (Acts 27:16).

CAUL Part of the liver that appears to be left over or forms an appendage to the liver, according to KJV. Other translations refer to the "lobe" (CSB, NASB), "covering" (NIV), or "appendage" (NRSV) of the liver (Exod. 29:13).

CAVES In the Bible, caves were often used as burial places. Abraham bought the cave of Machpelah as a tomb for Sarah (Gen. 23:11-16,19). Lazarus was buried in a cave (John 11:38). David used the cave of Adullam for refuge (1 Sam. 22:1), as did five Canaanite kings at Makkedah (Josh. 10:16).

CEDAR Tree grown especially in Lebanon and valued as building material (probably *Cedrus libani*). Cedar played a still-unknown role in the purification rites of Israel (Lev. 14:4; Num. 19:6). Kings used cedar for royal buildings (2 Sam. 5:11; 1 Kgs. 5:6; 6:9–7:12). Cedar signified royal power and wealth (1 Kgs. 10:27). Still, the majestic cedars could not stand before God's powerful presence (Ps. 29:5). The cedars owed their existence to God, who had planted them (Ps. 104:16).

One of the cedars of Lebanon

CEDRON (KJV, John 18:1) See *Kidron Valley*.

CELIBACY Abstention by vow from marriage. The practice of abstaining from marriage may be alluded to twice in the NT. Jesus said that some have made themselves eunuchs for the sake of the kingdom and that those who were able to do likewise should do so (Matt. 19:12). This statement has traditionally been understood as a reference to celibacy. Paul counseled the single to remain so (1 Cor. 7:8). Both Jesus (Mark 10:2-12) and Paul (1 Cor. 7:9,28,36-39; 9:5), however, affirmed the goodness of the married state. One NT passage goes so far as to characterize the prohibition of marriage as demonic (1 Tim. 4:1-3).

CENCHREA or **CENCHREAE** Eastern port city of Corinth. Phoebe served in the church there (Rom. 16:1), and Paul had his head shaved there when he took a vow (Acts 18:18).

CENSER Vessel used for offering incense before the Lord (Lev. 10:1). Nadab and Abihu used it improperly and so brought God's destruction. It probably was also used for carrying live coals employed in connection with worship in the tabernacle or the temple, each priest having one (cp. Num. 16:17-18).

CENSUS Enumeration of a population for the purpose of taxation or for the determination of manpower of war.

CENTURION Officer in the Roman army, nominally in command of 100 soldiers. They were usually career soldiers, and they formed the real backbone of the Roman military force. Centurions in the NT appear in a generally favorable light.

CHAFF Husk and other materials separated from the kernel of grain during the threshing or winnowing process. It blew away in the wind (Hos. 13:3) or was burned up as worthless (Isa. 5:24; Luke 3:17).

CHALCEDONY Transliteration of Greek name of precious stone in Rev. 21:19.

CHALCOL (KJV, 1 Kgs. 4:31). See *Calcol*.

CHALDEA Refers either to a geographical locality (Chaldea) or to the people who lived there (Chaldeans). Chaldea was situated in central and southeastern Mesopotamia—the land between the lower stretches of the Tigris and Euphrates Rivers. Today Chaldea lies in the country of Iraq, very close to its border with Iran, and touching upon the head of the Persian Gulf.

CHALDEES Another expression for Chaldeans.

CHALKSTONE Soft stone easily crushed, used for comparison to the destruction of altar stones (Isa. 27:9).

CHAMBER English translation of at least seven Hebrew words referring to a portion of a house or building.

CHAMBERING KJV translation of a Greek word in Rom. 13:13 rendered as "debauchery" or "sexual promiscuity" in modern versions. CSB: sexual impurity.

CHAMBERLAIN High military or political official whose title is related to Hebrew term meaning "castrated" or "eunuch" but actually may be derived from an Akkadian term for royal official.

CHAMELEON Unclean animal that moves on the ground (Lev. 11:30), usually identified as the *Chamaeleo calyptratus*. A Hebrew word with the same spelling but perhaps with different historical derivation occurs in Lev. 11:18 and Deut. 14:16, where it is apparently the barn owl, *Tyto alba*.

CHAMOIS Small antelope (*rupicapra*) that stands about two feet high and is found in mountainous regions. Translated as "mountain sheep" in modern versions (Deut. 14:5).

CHAMPAIGN Open, unenclosed land or plain (Deut. 11:30 KJV).

CHAMPION Hebrew phrase in 1 Sam. 17:4,23 is literally "the man of the space between"—that is, the man (like Goliath) who fights a single opponent in the space between two armies. The Hebrew word translated "champion" in 1 Sam. 17:51 is a different word meaning "mighty one, warrior."

CHANCELLOR Title of a royal official of the Persian government living in Samaria and helping administer the Persian province after Persia gained control of the region (Ezra 4:8-9,17).

CHAPITER KJV translation of Hebrew architectural term meaning a capital made to stand on top of a pillar (1 Kgs. 7:16) or the base on which the capital is placed.

CHAPMAN Old English word for trader (2 Chron. 9:14 KJV).

CHARGER(S) **1.** Large flat serving dish (Num. 7:13-85; Matt. 14:8,11 KJV). **2.** Horses used in battle to charge or attack (Nah. 2:3 NRSV; cp. TEV, REB based on early Greek translations; cp. Isa. 31:1,3; Jer. 8:6; Rev. 6:2).

CHARIOTS Two-wheeled land vehicles made of wood and strips of leather and usually drawn by horses. Egyptian chariots are the first mentioned in the Bible (Gen. 41:43; 46:29; 50:9). The iron chariots of the Philistines were fortified with plates of metal that made them militarily stronger than those of the Israelites (Judg. 1:19; 4:3,13-17; 1 Sam. 13:5-7). Chariots were used in prophetic imagery (Rev. 9:9; 18:13) and for transportation of the Ethiopian eunuch (Acts 8:26-38).

CHARITY KJV translation of Greek *agape*, a pure form of love. NASB uses "charity" to translate Greek *ekdidomai*, "to give out" in relation to helping the poor (Luke 11:41; 12:33; Acts 9:36).

CHARRAN Greek and KJV spelling of Haran (Acts 7:2,4).

CHASTE Holy purity demanded of God's people with special reference to sexual purity.

CHASTEN or **CHASTISEMENT** Refers to an act of punishment intended to instruct and change behavior.

CHEBAR River/canal in Babylon where Ezekiel had visions (Ezek. 1:1; 3:15; 10:15; 43:3). This is probably to be identified with the nar Kabari, a channel of the Euphrates River southeast of Babylon.

CHEDOR-LAOMER King of Elam who joined a coalition of kings against kings of Sodom and Gomorrah, leading to Abraham's involvement and victory (Gen. 14:1).

CHEESE Dairy product forming a basic part of the diet. The three occurrences of cheese in English translations reflect three different Hebrew expressions. Job 10:10 refers to cheese; 1 Sam. 17:18 speaks literally of a "slice of milk"; and 2 Sam. 17:29 uses a word usually interpreted as meaning "curds of the herd."

CHELAL Personal name of a man with foreign wife in the postexilic community (Ezra 10:30).

CHELLUH Personal name of a man with a foreign wife in postexilic community (Ezra 10:35).

CHELUB **1.** Descendant of the tribe of Judah (1 Chron. 4:11), probably to be identified with Caleb, the hero of the spy narrative of Num. 13–14. See *Caleb, Calebite*. **2.** Father of Ezri, overseer of workers on David's farms (1 Chron. 27:26).

CHELUBAI Hebrew variant of Caleb, the hero of the spy narratives (Num. 13–14).

CHEMOSH Divine name meaning "subdue." Deity the Moabites worshipped (Num. 21:29).

CHENAANAH **1.** Personal name meaning "tradeswoman." Father of the false prophet Zedekiah (1 Kgs. 22:11). See *Zedekiah*. **2.** Member of the tribe of Benjamin (1 Chron. 7:10).

CHENANI Personal name meaning "one born in the month of Kanunu." A Levite who led Israelites in a prayer of renewal and praise (Neh. 9:4).

CHENANIAH Personal name meaning "Yahweh empowers." **1.** Chief of the Levites under David who instructed people in singing and played a leading role in bringing the ark back to Jerusalem (1 Chron. 15:22,27). **2.** Levite whose family had charge of business outside the temple, including work as officials and judges (1 Chron. 26:29).

CHEPHAR-AMMONI Place-name meaning "open village of the Ammonites." A village in the tribal territory of Benjamin (Josh. 18:24).

CHEPHIRAH Place-name meaning "queen of the lions." It is located at Khirbet Kefire about four miles west of Gibeon (Josh. 9:17;18:26).

CHERAN Descendant of Seir (or Edom) listed in Gen. 36:26.

CHERETHITES, CHERETHIM People who lived south of or with the Philistines (1 Sam. 30:14). They were probably related to or paid soldiers for the Philistines. Crete may have been their original home. David used some of these soldiers as personal bodyguards (2 Sam. 8:18). Ezekiel pronounced judgment on them (Ezek. 25:16), as did Zephaniah (Zeph. 2:5).

CHERITH Place-name meaning "cutting" or "ditch." A wadi or brook east of the Jordan River, the modern Wadi Qilt south of Jericho. Elijah pronounced God's judgment to Ahab, king of Israel, in the form of a two-year drought and then found God's protection at the brook of Cherith, where he had water to drink (1 Kgs. 17:3). When Cherith finally went dry, Elijah found refuge with the widow of Zarephath.

CHERUB Man who left Tel-melah in Babylonian exile to go to Jerusalem with Zerubbabel about 537 BC. He could not provide a family list to prove he was an Israelite (Ezra 2:59).

CHERUB or **CHERUBIM** Class of winged angels. The Hebrew *cherub* (plural, *cherubim*) is of uncertain derivation. In the OT, it is the name of a class of winged angels who functioned primarily as guards (Gen. 3:24) or attendants (Ezek. 10:3-22). The only NT reference to cherubim is in a description of the furnishings of the holy of holies (Heb. 9:5).

CHESALON Place-name meaning "on the hip." Village on eastern border of the territory of the tribe of Judah (Josh. 15:10). It is equated with Mount Jearim and is modern Kesla, about 10 miles west of Jerusalem.

CHESED Personal name meaning "one of the Chaldeans." Son of Nahor, the brother of Abraham (Gen. 22:22). His name may indicate he was the original ancestor of the Chaldeans.

CHESIL Place-name meaning "foolish." A city of the tribe of Judah (Josh. 15:30).

CHESTNUT KJV translation for plane tree in Gen. 30:37. It apparently refers to the smooth-barked *Platanus orientalis*.

CHESULLOTH Place-name meaning "on the hips." A border town of the tribe of Issachar (Josh. 19:18), probably the same as the border town of Zebulun called Chisloth-tabor in Josh. 19:12. It is the modern Iksal, four miles south of Nazareth.

CHEZIB Place-name meaning "deceiving." Birthplace of Shelah, son of Judah and Shuah, a Canaanite (Gen. 38:5).

CHICKEN Nesting, brooding bird. Both tame and wild chickens were known in Bible times. Jesus compares his care for Jerusalem to the care of a mother hen for her nestlings (Matt. 23:37; Luke 13:34).

CHIDON Personal name meaning "crescent sword." First Chronicles 13:9 reads "Chidon" for "Nacon" in 2 Sam. 6:6. Chidon could be a place-name in the text.

CHIEF English translation of at least 13 different Hebrew words designating a leader in political, military, religious, or economic affairs.

CHILDREN (SONS) OF GOD In the OT, "sons of God" can refer to spirit beings (Job 1:6; 38:7; Ps. 89:6-7) but more often refers to persons who stand in covenant relationship with God.

CHILEAB Personal name meaning "everything of the Father." David's second son (2 Sam. 3:3) born to Abigail.

CHILION Personal name meaning "sickly." One of the two sons of Elimelech and Naomi (Ruth 1:2). With his parents, he immigrated to Moab, where he married a Moabite woman named Orpah. He died in Moab.

CHILMAD Place-name meaning "marketplace." A trading partner of Tyre according to Hebrew text of Ezek. 27:23.

CHIMHAM Personal name meaning " paleface." **1.** Apparently the son of Barzillai, the patron of David when he fled to Mahanaim east of the Jordan before Absalom (2 Sam. 19:37). **2.** Village near Bethlehem (Jer. 41:17).

CHINNERETH Place-name meaning "harp-shaped." **1.** Sea or lake otherwise called the Sea of Galilee, Lake of Gennesaret, or Sea of Tiberias. **2.** City on the western edge of the Sea of Chinnereth, also called Chinneroth (Josh. 11:2), though this could be a reference to the Sea.

CHIOS Island with city of same name. Paul stopped here while returning from third missionary journey (Acts 20:15). The Greek poet Homer supposedly came from Chios. It lies in the Aegean Sea five miles off the coast of Asia Minor. It is now called Scio.

CHISEL English term CSB and NIV use to translate several Hebrew expressions for working with wood and stone.

CHISLEU or **CHISLEV** Name of the ninth month of the Jewish calendar after the exile, apparently borrowed from the Babylonian name Kisliwu (Neh.1:1; Zech. 7:1).

CHISLON Personal name meaning "clumsy." Father of Elidad, who represented the tribe of Benjamin on the commission that divided the land for Israel (Num. 34:21).

CHLOE Personal name meaning "verdant." A woman whose household members informed Paul of dissension within the church at Corinth (1 Cor. 1:11). Where she lived and how her people learned of the situation in Corinth are not known.

CHOINIX Dry measure used to measure grain and was equivalent to about a quart, or a daily ration for one person (Rev. 6:6).

CHORAZIN One of the cities Jesus censured because of the unbelief of its inhabitants (Matt. 11:21). It was located in Galilee.

CHOSEN PEOPLE Israel as the elect of God. See *Election*.

CHRIST, CHRISTOLOGY "Christ" is English for the Greek *Christos*, "anointed one." The Hebrew word is *Mashiach*, Messiah. Christology is a compound of the Greek words *Christos* and *logos* (word, speech). Christology is the study of the person (who he is) and work (what he did/does) of Jesus Christ, the Son of God.

CHRISTIAN Greek word *Christianos* originally applied to the slaves belonging to a great household. It came to denote the adherents of an individual or party. A Christian is an adherent of Christ. The word is used three times in the NT (Acts 11:26; 26:28; 1 Pet. 4:16 CSB). Agrippa responded to Paul's witness, "Are you going to persuade me to become a Christian so easily?" (Acts 26:28 CSB).

CHRISTMAS Of the major Christian festivals, Christmas is the most recent in origin. The name, a contraction of the term "Christ's mass," did not come into use until the Middle Ages.

In the early part of the fourth century, Christians in Rome began to celebrate the birth of Christ. The practice spread widely and rapidly, so that most parts of the Christian world observed the new festival by the end of the century.

No evidence remains about the exact date of the birth of Christ. The December 25 date was chosen as much for practical reasons as for theological ones. Throughout the Roman Empire, various festivals were held in conjunction with the winter solstice. In Rome, the Feast of the Unconquerable Sun celebrated the beginning of the return of the sun. When Christianity became the religion of the empire, the church either had to suppress the festivals or transform them. The winter solstice seemed an appropriate time to celebrate Christ's birth. Thus the festival of the sun became a festival of the Son, the Light of the world.

CHRONICLES, BOOKS OF First and Second Chronicles are the first and second books of a four-book series that includes Ezra and Nehemiah. These four books provide a scribal (priestly) history of Israel from the time of Adam (1 Chron. 1:1) to the rebuilding of the house of God and the walls of Jerusalem and the restoration of the people in the worship of God according to the law of Moses (Neh. 13:31). Special focus is on the fortunes of God's house in Jerusalem upon which God has set his name forever (2 Chron. 7:16).

The principal purpose of 1 and 2 Chronicles is to show God's control of history to fulfill his desire to dwell among his people in a perfect relationship of holiness in which God is God and the redeemed are his people.

A second purpose is to show God's choice of a person and a people to build his house. The person is the Son of David—the Messiah. Solomon built the temple in Jerusalem, but the Son who is building and shall build to completion God's true house and the Son whose reign God will establish forever is the Lord Jesus Christ (1 Chron. 17:12; Luke 1:31-33; Acts 15:14-16).

A third purpose is to show the necessity to come to God by way of the altar of sacrifice as ministered by the Levitical priesthood. God in his merciful forgiveness of David revealed the place of the altar of sacrifice to be in Jerusalem at the threshing floor of Ornan (Araunah) (1 Chron. 21:18–22:1). There David erected the altar and later, Solomon built the temple according to God's directions. But, most important, there the Son of God, our great High Priest, sacrificed himself on the cross in our stead to bring his people into the glorious presence of God (Heb. 2:17; 5:1-10).

A fourth purpose of Chronicles is to encourage God's people to work together with God and with one another to build God's house.

CHRYSOLITE Mineral from which the seventh stone of the foundation of the New Jerusalem is made (Rev. 21:20).

CHRYSOPRASE Mineral forming the tenth stone of the foundation of the New Jerusalem (Rev. 21:20).

CHUB KJV transliteration of Hebrew name of a people in Ezek. 30:5.

CHURCH In the NT, the Greek word *ekklesia* refers to (1) any assembly, local bodies of believers, or (2) the universal body of all believers.

The Church as Body of Christ The church is not merely a sectarian religious society. Jesus speaks of personally building this new community on the confession of his lordship (Matt. 16:18-19). The apostles recognized the birth of the church at Pentecost as the work of Jesus himself.

The description of the church as the body of Christ designates Jesus's rule over the community. As the exalted Son of David, he exercises sovereignty by his Spirit and by his Word. The body of Christ does not only refer to the universal church, but applies to each local congregation of believers. The fact that the church is the body of Christ necessarily entails that individual members belong to Christ. As such, each church must be composed of a regenerate membership, those giving evidence of faith in Jesus Christ.

The Church as Covenant Community The NT refers to the church as "the pillar and foundation of the truth" (1 Tim. 3:15 CSB). From the beginning, the church was to serve as a confessional body, holding to the truth of Christ as revealed by the prophets and apostles he had chosen (Eph. 2:20).

The Church and the World The Bible presents the church as sharply distinct from the world. The church is to be composed of regenerate believers called out of a world hostile to the gospel of Christ. As such, the church is called to confront the world with the reality of coming judgment and the gospel of redemption through Christ.

The Church's Commission The multinational, multiethnic character of the NT church testifies not only to the universality of the gospel message (Rom. 10:11-12) and to the personal reconciliation accomplished at the cross (Eph. 2:14-16), but also to the global extent of the coming reign of Christ (Ps. 2:8). Thus, obedience to the Great Commission (Matt. 28:16-20) is not simply a function of the church, but is essential to her identity as the people of God.

Similarly, worship is not incidental. Because God has assembled a people "to the praise of his glorious grace" (Eph. 1:6 CSB), worship is necessary to the corporate life of the church.

CHUSHAN-RISHATHAIM KJV spelling of Cushan-rishathaim, Mesopotamian king who oppressed Israel until he was defeated by Othniel the son of Kenaz (Judg. 3:8).

CHUZA Personal name meaning "seer." The steward of Herod Antipas (Luke 8:3). He was the husband of Joanna, one of the women who provided material support for Jesus.

CILICIA Geographical area and/or Roman province in southeastern Asia Minor. The region was home to some of the people who

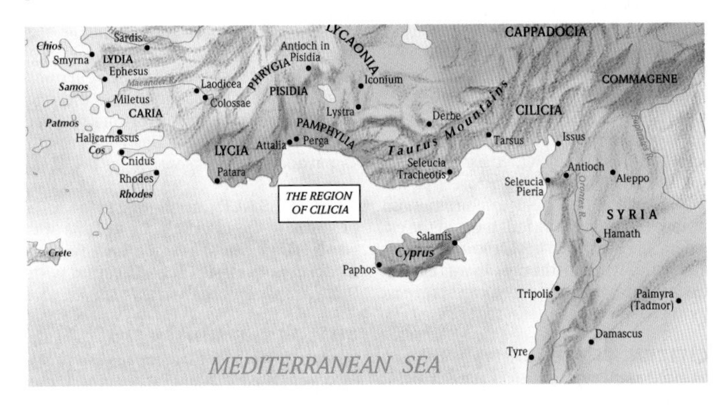

THE REGION OF CILICIA

opposed Stephen (Acts 6:9). It was located on the coast of the Mediterranean Sea in the southeast part of Asia Minor. One of its important cities was Tarsus, the birthplace of Paul the apostle (Acts 21:39; 22:3). By the time of the Council of Jerusalem (Acts 15), Christianity had already penetrated Cilicia. Paul passed through the region during the course of his missionary travels (Acts 15:41; 27:5; Gal. 1:21).

CINNAMON Spice used in making fragrant oils. Such oil was used to anoint the wilderness tent of meeting (Exod. 30:23).

CIRCUMCISION Act of removing the foreskin of the male genital. In ancient Israel, this act was ritually performed on the eighth day after birth upon children of natives, servants, and aliens (Gen. 17:12-14; Lev. 12:3). Circumcision was carried out by the father initially, using a flint knife (cp. Josh. 5:3). Later specialists were employed among the Jewish people.

Circumcision and Christianity Controversy arose in the early church (Acts 15:1-12) as to whether Gentile converts needed to be circumcised. First-century AD Jews disdained the uncircumcised. The leadership of the apostle Paul in the Jerusalem Council was crucial in the settlement of the dispute: circumcision was not essential to Christian faith and fellowship. Circumcision of the heart via repentance and faith were the only requirements (Rom. 4:9-12; Gal. 2:15-21).

CISTERN Translation of a Hebrew term that means "hole," "pit," or more often "well." The difference between "cistern" and "well" often is not apparent.

CITIES OF REFUGE Safe place to flee for a person who had accidentally killed another. The city provided asylum to the fugitive by sheltering and protecting him until a trial could be held to determine guilt or innocence. If, in the judgment of the city elders, the death had occurred accidentally and without intent, the person was allowed to stay there without fear of harm or revenge by the relatives of the deceased (Josh. 20:2-6).

CITIZEN, CITIZENSHIP Officially recognized status in a political state bringing certain rights and responsibilities as defined by the state. Paul raised the issue of citizenship by appealing to his right as a Roman citizen (Acts 16:37; 22:26-28).

CITY OF DAVID Most ancient part of Jerusalem. In the OT, the phrase "the city of David" refers to Jerusalem. The name was given to the fortified city of the Jebusites after David captured it (2 Sam. 5:6-10). Its original reference may have been only to the southeastern hill and the Jebusites' military fortress there. In Luke 2:4,11, the reference is to Bethlehem, the birthplace of David (John 7:42).

A view of the excavations of the city of David led by Kathleen Kenyon.

CITY OF MOAB Where Balak went to meet Balaam (Num. 22:36). Some identify the city as Ar.

CITY OF PALM TREES Probably to be identified with a site near Jericho where the Kenites lived (Judg. 1:16; see Deut. 34:3; Judg. 3:13; 2 Chron. 28:15). Jericho itself lay in ruins from the time of the conquest until the time of Ahab. Some identify the region with Zoar on the south side of the Dead Sea or with Tamar about 20 miles south of the Dead Sea.

CITY OF SALT City allotted to the tribe of Judah "in the desert" (Josh. 15:62). Its precise location is not known. Archaeological finds do not support identification with Qumran that some have tried to make.

CITY OF THE SUN (CSB, NRSV) Usually taken as a reference to Heliopolis (Isa. 19:18). Also translated "city of destruction."

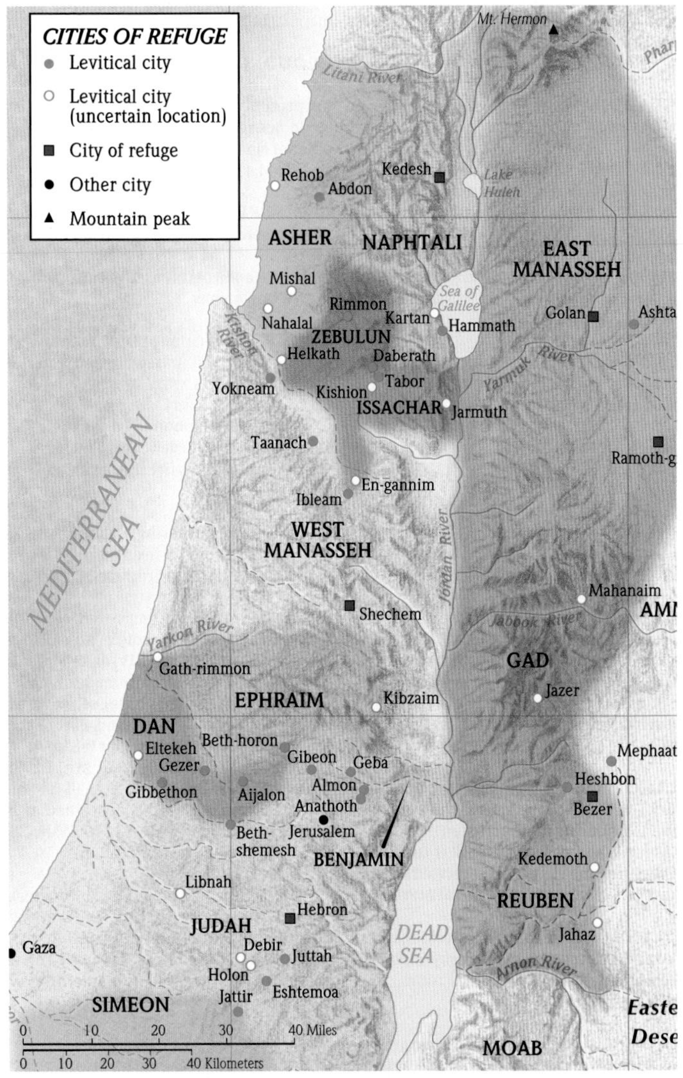
CITIES OF REFUGE
Levitical city
Levitical city (uncertain location)
City of refuge
Other city
Mountain peak
Mt. Hermon
Litani River
Rehob
Abdon
Kedesh
Lake Huleh
ASHER
NAPHTALI
EAST MANASSEH
Mishal
Sea of Galilee
Rimmon
Kishon River
Nahalal
Kartan
Hammath
Golan
ZEBULUN
Helkath
Daberath
Yarmuk River
Tabor
Yokneam
Kishion
ISSACHAR
Jarmuth
MEDITERRANEAN SEA
Taanach
En-gannim
Ibleam
WEST MANASSEH
Jordan River
Mahanaim
Shechem
Jabbok River
Yarkon River
Gath-rimmon
GAD
EPHRAIM
Kibzaim
Jazer
DAN
Eltekeh
Beth-horon
Gezer
Gibeon
Geba
Mephaat
Gibbethon
Aijalon
Almon
Heshbon
Anathoth
Bezer
Beth-shemesh
Jerusalem
BENJAMIN
Kedemoth
Libnah
REUBEN
Hebron
JUDAH
DEAD SEA
Jahaz
Gaza
Debir
Juttah
Arnon River
Holon
Eshtemoa
Jattir
SIMEON
0 10 20 30 40 Miles
0 10 20 30 40 Kilometers
MOAB

CITY OF WATERS City in Ammon, probably to be identified with part or all of Rabbah, the capital. Joab captured it for David (2 Sam. 12:27).

CLAUDIA Woman who sent greetings to Timothy (2 Tim. 4:21).

CLAUDIUS 1. Roman emperor from AD 41 to 54. He made Judea a Roman province in AD 44. He expelled Jews from Rome in about AD 49 (Acts 18:2), probably due to conflict between Jews and Christians in Rome. **2.** Roman army captain who protected Paul from Jews who wanted to assassinate him (Acts 23:26-27).

CLAY Basic building and artistic material consisting of various types of dirt or sand combined with water to form a material that could be molded into bricks for building, sculptures, pottery, toys, or writing tablets.

CLEMENT Fellow worker in the gospel with Paul (Phil. 4:3). He was apparently a member of the church at Philippi. No other information about him is available.

CLEOPAS Follower of Jesus, who with a companion was traveling toward the village of Emmaus on the day of Christ's resurrection (Luke 24:13-25). A person whom they did not recognize joined them. Later, they discovered that the stranger was Jesus himself.

CLEOPHAS (KJV, John 19:25) or **CLOPAS** Relative of one of the Marys who were near the cross during the crucifixion (John 19:25). "Mary, who [was] of Clopas" is the literal Greek text and has been interpreted to mean that Clopas was the husband of Mary.

CLOSET Private room in a dwelling where Jesus encouraged people to pray (Matt. 6:6). A biblical closet is an actual room, not a storage place.

CLOTH, CLOTHING Biblical and archaeological sources concur that the earliest clothing resources were the hides of wild animals (Gen. 3:21). The Bible contains little information, however, about the process of manufacturing clothes from vegetable fibers.

CLOUD, PILLAR OF Means by which God led Israel through the wilderness with his presence and still hid himself so they could not see his face. By day, Israel saw a pillar of cloud; by night, they saw a pillar of fire (Exod. 13:21-22).

CLOUT KJV translation in Jer. 38:11-12 for Hebrew word meaning "tattered clothes, rags."

CLUB Weapon of war used in close combat to strike an enemy.

CNIDUS Place-name of city in southwest Turkey. Paul's ship passed by here on the way to Rome (Acts 27:7).

COAL Charred wood used for fuel. The altar of sacrifice burned coals (Lev. 16:12), as did the blacksmith's fire (Isa. 44:12) and the baker's (Isa. 44:19).

COAST Land bordering a major body of water and used by KJV in an obsolete sense of territories, borders, frontiers.

COAT OF MAIL Protective device worn from the neck to the girdle. Also called a brigandine (Jer. 46:4; 51:3 KJV) or habergeon (2 Chron. 26:14 KJV). Usually made of leather, though it may at times have been covered with metal scales of some kind. Part of the usual equipment of the soldier (1 Sam. 17:5; 2 Chron. 26:14; Neh. 4:16; Jer. 46:4; 51:3). David refused to wear Saul's coat of mail (1 Sam. 17:38). Leviathan's skin is described as a double coat of mail (Job 41:13 NRSV, NASB following early Greek translation).

COCK Strutting, crowing bird (rooster), *Zarzir motnayim* (Prov. 30:31). The crowing of the cock is probably the most well-known bird sound in the Bible. All of the NT references to the cock (except the mention of "cockcrow" in Mark 13:35) relate to Peter's denial of Christ.

COCKATRICE KJV translation of legendary serpent and poisonous snakes (Isa. 11:8; 14:29; 59:5; Jer. 8:17).

COCKLE Plant whose name derives from Hebrew word for "stink." It appears in Scripture only at Job 31:40. CSB: stinkweed.

COFFER Old English word for box in 1 Sam. 6:8,11,15 (KJV).

COHORT Roman military unit with capacity of 1,000 men; 10 cohorts formed a legion.

COLHOZEH Personal name meaning "he sees everything" or "everyone a seer." Father whose son Shallun was ruler of part of Mizpah and who helped Nehemiah repair Jerusalem's gates (Neh. 3:15).

COLLEGE KJV translation (2 Kgs. 22:14) of Hebrew word meaning "repetition, copy, second," referring to the second district or division of Jerusalem (cp. Zeph. 1:10).

COLONY Only Philippi is described as a colony of Rome (Acts 16:12), though many cities mentioned in the NT were considered as such. The functioning of the local governments of Roman colonies is seen in Acts 16:12-40.

COLORS Writers of biblical literature reflected little or nothing of an abstract sense of color. Nevertheless, they made frequent references to a select group of colors when their purposes in writing so demanded it.

References to Colors Moving beyond color in the abstract sense, one does find frequent references to certain objects that have color designations. When reference is made to a particular color or colors, it is likely made for one of two basic reasons. First, a writer may wish to use color in a descriptive sense to help identify an object or clarify some aspect about that object. A second reason for color designations in the Bible involves a more specialized usage. At times a writer may use color in a symbolic sense to convey theological truth about the subject of his writing. Color designations have general symbolic significance. For instance, white may be symbolic of purity or joy; black may symbolize judgment or decay; red may symbolize sin or lifeblood; and purple may be symbolic of luxury and elegance. Color symbolism became for the writers of apocalyptic literature (Daniel, Revelation) an appropriate tool for expressing various truths in hidden language. In their writings, one may find white representative of conquest or victory, black representative of famine or pestilence, red representative of wartime bloodshed, paleness (literally "greenish-gray") representative of death, and purple representative of royalty.

COLOSSIANS, LETTER TO THE Letter from Paul to the church at Colossae. It is one of the Prison Epistles (along with Ephesians, Philemon, and Philippians). Traditional date and place of writing are AD 61 or 62 and Rome. The letter itself does not name the place where Paul was imprisoned, and Caesarea and Ephesus have been suggested as alternatives to Rome. If written from Ephesus, the time of writing would be in the mid-50's; if from Caesarea, the late 50's.

The City of Colossae Colossae was located in the southwest corner of Asia Minor in what was then the Roman province of Asia. Hierapolis and Laodicea were situated only a few miles away. All three were in the Lycus River Valley. A main road from Ephesus to the east ran through the region.

The Primary Purpose of Colossians Paul sought to correct false teachings that were troubling the church. These false teachings

The Lycus River valley as seen from Colossae

apparently involved the legalistic observance of "traditions," circumcision, and various dietary and festival laws (2:8,11,16,21; 3:11). The worship of angels and lesser spirits was encouraged by the false teachers (2:8,18). Asceticism, the deprivation or harsh treatment of one's "evil" fleshly body, was promoted (2:20-23). The false teachers claimed to possess special insight (perhaps special revelations) that made them (rather than the apostles or the Scriptures) the ultimate source of truth (2:18-19).

To correct these false teachings, Paul describes the grandeur of the preeminent Christ (1:15-20). Though the precise meaning of some words and phrases is uncertain, there is no doubt as to Paul's intent. He meant to present Jesus as fully God incarnate (1:15,19), as supreme Lord over all creation (1:15-17), as supreme Lord of the church (1:18), and as the only Source of reconciliation (1:20).

COLT Young of various riding animals. **1.** Young camels (Gen. 32:15), noted by the Hebrew term for "sons." **2.** Young donkeys (Gen. 49:11), also "son" in Hebrew (cp. Judg. 10:4; 12:14, where Hebrew is "donkeys"). The NT uses the reference in Zech. 9:9 as a prediction of Jesus's triumphal entry into Jerusalem (Matt. 21; Mark 11; Luke 19; John 12:15).

COMFORTER Commonly used translation of the Greek word *paracletos*. The compound noun refers to "one called alongside." John's Gospel features five passages in which this word details the work and ministry of the Comforter for believers. CSB in John: "Counselor."

COMPASSION Meaning "to feel passion with someone" or "to enter sympathetically into one's sorrow and pain."

CONANIAH Personal name meaning "Yahweh has established." **1.** Levite in charge of collecting temple offerings under King Hezekiah (2 Chron. 31:12). **2.** Perhaps the grandson of 1, above. He and other Levites contributed 5,000 sheep and goats and 500 bulls for Josiah's Passover offering (2 Chron. 35:9).

CONCISION Archaic English noun meaning "a cutting off." KJV uses "concision" in Phil. 3:2 to describe Paul's opponents who insisted on circumcision as necessary for right relationship with God (Phil. 3:2).

CONCUBINE A wife of lower status than a primary wife. Taking of concubines dates back at least to the patriarchal period. Although the taking of concubines was not totally prohibited, monogamous marriage was more common and seems to be the biblical ideal (Gen. 2:24; Mark 10:6-9).

CONCUPISCENCE KJV translation of Greek *epithumia*, "desire, lust." The Greeks used the term to mean excitement about something in a neutral sense and then in an evil sense of wrongly valuing earthly things.

CONDEMN Act of pronouncing someone guilty after weighing the evidence. The word appears first in the context of a court of law (Exod. 22:9) where a judge hears a charge against a thief and condemns the culprit. NT usage of "condemn" is unique in its reference to the final judgment, especially in John 3:17-19. A similar teaching appears in John 5:24. Paul felt that avoiding that final condemnation was a reason for accepting the Lord's chastening in this life (1 Cor. 11:32).

CONDUIT Water channel or aqueduct in or near Jerusalem channeling water into the city (2 Kgs. 18:17; 20:20; Isa. 7:3).

CONEY Wild hare—*Procavia syriaca*, also called *Hyrax syriacus*. Resembled a rabbit in size and color. The badger of Exod. 23:5; 26:14 has been identified by some scholars as the Syrian coney.

CONFESSION Admission, declaration, or acknowledgment that is a significant element in the worship of God in both OT and NT. The majority of the occurrences of the term can be divided into two primary responses to God: the confession of sin and the confession of faith.

Confession of Sin Numerous OT passages stress the importance of the confession of sin within the experience of worship. Likewise, in the NT, confession of sin is an aspect of both individual and corporate worship.

Confession of Faith Closely related to the confession of sin in the OT is the confession of faith, that is, the acknowledgment of and commitment to God. In 1 Kgs. 8:33,35 (as well as 2 Chron. 6:24,26) acknowledgment of the name of God results in forgiveness of sins. Such acknowledgment came to be standardized in the confessional formula known as the Shema (Deut. 6:4-5).

Such declaration of commitment to God, or particularly to Christ, is also found in the NT. One's public acknowledgment of Jesus is the basis for Jesus's own acknowledgment of that believer to God (Matt. 10:32; Luke 12:8; cp. Rev. 3:5).

CONGREGATION Assembled people of God.

CONGREGATION, MOUNT OF Mountain considered by Israel's neighbors to stand in the far north and serve as a meeting place of the gods (Isa. 14:13). CSB: "the mount of the gods' assembly."

CONQUEST OF CANAAN The book of Joshua and the first chapter of the book of Judges describe the conquest of Canaan, which resulted in Israel's settlement in the land of promise.

CONSCIENCE Human capacity to reflect upon the degree to which one's behavior has conformed to moral norms. For the believer, these norms should be those established by God. The word does not occur in the OT, although clearly there are times when the concept is present (seven times in CSB). In the NT, two-thirds of the occurrences of the term are in Paul's writings.

CONSECRATION Persons or things being separated to or belonging to God. They are holy or sacred. They are set apart for the service of God. The Hebrew *qadesh* and Greek *hagiazo* are translated by several different English words: holy, consecrate, hallow, sanctify, dedicate.

CONSUMMATION End of history and the fulfillment of God's kingdom promises. The term comes from Dan. 9:27 speaking of the complete destruction God had decreed on the prince who threatened God's sanctuary.

CONVERSION Turning or returning of a person to God, a crucial biblical and theological concept. The word itself is relatively rare in Scripture.

CONVICTION Sense of guilt and shame leading to repentance.

COPPER Reddish metal that can be shaped easily by hammering and can be polished to a shining finish. While gold was probably the first metal humans used, the oldest tools and utensils recovered by archaeologists in Bible lands are of copper, usually combined with some alloy.

COR Large liquid and dry measure of unknown quantity.

CORAL Calcareous or horny skeletal deposit produced by anthozoan polyps, found exclusively in the Mediterranean and Adriatic Seas (*Corallium rubrum*). Coral was among the goods of trade between Israel and Edom (Ezek. 27:16).

CORBAN Gift particularly designated for the Lord, and so forbidden for any other use (Mark 7:11). Jesus referred to some persons who mistakenly and deliberately avoided giving needed care to their parents by declaring as "corban" any money or goods that could otherwise be used to provide such care. Thus what began as a religious act of offering eventually functioned as a curse, denying benefit to one's own parents.

CORIANDER SEED Herb (*Coriandrum sativum*) of the carrot family with aromatic fruits used much as poppy, caraway, or sesame seeds are today. The manna of the wilderness period was like coriander seed either in appearance (Exod. 16:31) or taste (Num. 11:7).

CORINTH One of four prominent centers in the NT account of the early church, the other three being Jerusalem, Antioch of

Syria, and Ephesus. Paul's first extended ministry in one city was at Corinth. On his first visit to Corinth, he remained for at least 18 months (Acts 18:1-18). Paul's three longest letters are associated with Corinth. First and Second Corinthians were written to Corinth, and Romans was written in Corinth. Prominent Christian leaders associated with Corinth include Aquila, Priscilla, Silas, Timothy, Apollos, and Titus.

Corinth as Paul found it was a cosmopolitan city composed of people from varying cultural backgrounds. Being near the site of the Isthmian Games held every two years, the Corinthians enjoyed both the pleasures of these games and the wealth that the visitors brought to the city. While their ships were being carried across the isthmus, sailors came to the city to spend their money on the pleasures of Corinth. Even in an age of sexual immorality, Corinth was known for its licentious lifestyle.

CORINTHIANS, FIRST LETTER TO THE First Corinthians is a practical letter where Paul dealt with problems concerning the church as a whole and also with personal problems.

Paul wrote 1 Corinthians to give instruction and admonition that would lead to the solving of the many problems in the congregation. Some of these problems may have arisen out of a "super spiritualist" group that had been influenced by incipient gnostic teachings. All of the problems in chapters 1–14 were grounded in egocentric or self-centered attitudes in contrast to self-denying, Christ-centered attitudes. Chapter 15 concerning the resurrection may reflect sincere misconceptions on the part of the Corinthians.

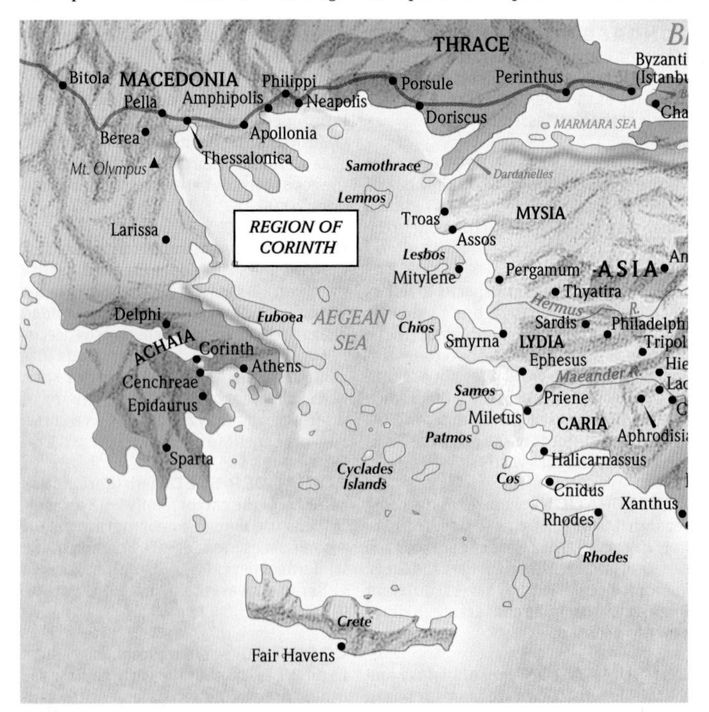

CORINTHIANS, SECOND LETTER TO THE Paul wrote 2 Corinthians to deal with problems within the church and to defend apostolic ministry in general and his apostleship in particular. In so doing, Paul revealed much about himself, his apostleship, and his apostolic ministry. Second Corinthians is relevant for today in its teachings concerning ministers and their ministries. Among these teachings are the following: (1) God was in Christ reconciling the world to himself and has given to us a ministry of reconciliation. (2) True ministry in Christ's name involves both suffering and victory. (3) Serving Christ means ministering in his name to the total needs of persons. (4) Leaders in ministry need support and trust from those to whom they minister.

CORMORANT Large seafowl (*Phalacrocorax carbo carbo*) listed among the unclean birds (Lev. 11:17; Deut. 14:17). Other translators call it a Fisher-owl (REB).

CORN General term used by the translators of the KJV for any grain.

CORNELIUS Centurion in the Roman army who lived at Caesarea (Acts 10:1). His conversion marked the beginning of the church's missionary activity among Gentiles.

CORNER BUTTRESS (CSB, NASB, 2 Chron. 26:9) See *Turning of the Wall*.

CORNER GATE Gate of Jerusalem in the northwest corner of the city not far from the Ephraim Gate (2 Kgs. 14:13; 2 Chron. 25:23). It is not mentioned in Nehemiah's restoration of Jerusalem.

CORNERSTONE Stone laid at the corner to bind two walls together and to strengthen them. Used symbolically as a symbol of strength and prominence in the Bible.

CORNET KJV for several different kinds of musical instruments. See *Music, Instruments, Dancing*.

CORNFLOOR KJV for threshing floor in Hos. 9:1.

COS Island and its chief city between Miletus and Rhodes where Paul landed briefly on his return voyage after his third missionary journey (Acts 21:1). It was a center for education, trade, wine, purple dye, and ointment. Hippocrates founded a school of medicine there. It is modern Kos.

COSAM Personal name meaning "diviner." Ancestor of Jesus (Luke 3:28).

COULTER KJV word for both mattock and plowshare.

COUNCIL OF JERUSALEM Name given to the meeting described in Acts 15:6-22. The purpose of the council was to determine the terms on which Gentile converts to Christianity would be received into the church.

COUNSELOR One who analyzes a situation and gives advice to one who has responsibility for making a decision. Israelite kings seem to have employed counselors on a regular basis (2 Sam. 16:23; 1 Kgs. 12:6-14; Isa. 1:26; 3:3; Mic. 4:9). God is often regarded as a counselor (Pss. 16:7; 73:24) as is his Messiah (Isa. 9:6; 11:2) and the Holy Spirit (John 14:16,26; 15:26; 16:7).

COUNTENANCE One's face as an indication of mood, emotion, or character (Gen. 4:5-6; Prov. 15:13; Eccles. 7:3; Mark 10:22). To speak of God lifting up his countenance upon one is a way of speaking about being in God's presence (Ps. 21:6; Num. 6:26).

COUNTERVAIL Old English word meaning "to equal," "be commensurate with," "compensate for" in Esther 7:4.

COURIERS Members of the royal guard who carried messages throughout the kingdom (2 Chron. 30:6,10; Esth. 3:13,15; 8:10,14).

COURT OF THE GUARD or **COURT OF THE PRISON** Open court in the Jerusalem palace reserved for the detention of prisoners during the day of Jeremiah (Jer. 32:8,12; 33:1; 37:21; 38:6,13,28; 39:14-15 KJV). Translated in the modern versions as "court of the guard."

COUSIN At times the KJV uses "cousin" when a distant relative is referred to (Mark 6:4; Luke 1:36,58; 2:44; 14:12). The same Greek word in all these passages means relatives, kin, or countryman.

COVENANT Oath-bound promise whereby one party solemnly pledges to bless or serve another party in some specified way. Sometimes the keeping of the promise depends upon the meeting of certain conditions by the party to whom the promise is made. On other occasions, the promise is made unilaterally and unconditionally. The covenant concept is a central, unifying theme of Scripture, establishing and defining God's relationship to humans in all ages.

COVET, COVETOUS Inordinate desire to possess what belongs to another, usually tangible things. While the Hebrew word for "covet" can also be translated "to desire," in the tenth commandment it means an ungoverned and selfish desire that threatens the basic rights of others.

COW Designates domestic bovine animals, especially the female.

COZBI Personal name meaning "my falsehood." A Midianite woman who was slain by Phinehas after being brought into the tent of an Israelite man named Zimri (Num. 25:15). When both she and Zimri were executed, a plague that was sweeping through the Israelite camp was stopped.

COZEBA Place-name meaning "deceptive." Home of descendants of Judah (1 Chron. 4:22). Its location is uncertain.

CRACKNEL Old English word for a hard brittle biscuit (1 Kgs. 14:3 KJV).

CRANE KJV translation of the Hebrew word in Isa. 38:14; Jer. 8:7. Some modern translations read "swift" (NIV, NASB, REB) or "dove" (REB).

CREATION The Bible's teaching on the creation of the universe is a central theme that runs from Genesis to Revelation. God is eternal and transcendent, creation is not (Gen. 1:1). Everything owes its creaturely existence (Isa. 44:24; 45:12; Ps. 33:6; Rev. 4:11) to the work of the Father, Son, and Holy Spirit (cp. Gen. 1:1; John 1:1; Gen. 1:2), with Christ as the preeminent agent of creation (John 1:10; Col. 1:16). Biblical teaching implies that God created the world out of nothing (Heb. 11:3). Unlike God, any created thing can be shaken; only what God desires will continue to exist (Heb. 1:3; 12:27; Col. 1:17).

In spite of its present subjection to ethical and material corruption, God's creation still bears the original impress of its complete goodness (Gen. 1:31; 1 Tim. 4:4). The human race alone enjoys the privilege of bearing God's image (Gen. 1:27—all subsequent people, though not directly created as were Adam and Eve, are regarded as God's special handiwork; Ps. 89:47; cp. Ps. 102:18). Divine purpose (Col. 1:16) and design (e.g., the marking of time by the movements of the heavenly bodies in Gen. 1:14) pervade creation. The creation speaks of the glory of God in bold contrast with man (Pss. 8; 19:1-4).

CREATURE Something having life, either animal or human. The phrase used in the Hebrew Bible *nephesh chayah* is translated by "creature," "living [thing, soul]," and "beast."

CRESCENS Personal name meaning "growing." Christian worker with Paul who had gone to Galatia when 2 Timothy was written (2 Tim. 4:10).

CRETANS, CRETES, CRETIANS Citizens of Crete.

CRETE Long, narrow, mountainous island south of mainland Greece, running 170 miles east-west but never more than about 35 miles wide.

Paul made his voyage to Rome as a prisoner on a Roman grain ship. The voyage followed the route south of Crete, which gave partial shelter from the northwest winds and avoided the peril of the lee shore on the north coast, while still involving the need to beat against largely adverse winds.

The only other references to Crete in the NT are in Paul's epistle to Titus. Paul had left Titus in Crete to exercise pastoral supervision over the churches there (Titus 1:5). The char-

A harbor on Crete through which Paul likely passed on his journey from Caesarea Maritima to Rome

acter of the people is described in a quotation from a prophet of their own: "Cretans are always liars, evil beasts, lazy gluttons" (Titus 1:12 CSB), words attributed to the Cretan seer Epimenides, who was also credited with having advised the Athenians to set up altars to unknown gods (cp. Acts 17:23).

CRIB Feeding trough for the ox (Prov. 14:4) or the ass (Isa. 1:3; cp. Job 39:9) and probably for any number of other domesticated animals.

CRICKET Hebrew term often translated "cricket" (Lev. 11:22) is difficult to identify, probably a locust or grasshopper.

CRIMSON The same Hebrew words translated as "crimson" are also translated "scarlet" ("red" comes from a root word from which the Hebrew word for "blood" comes and designates a different color). Crimson or scarlet thread (Gen. 38:28,30), cord (Josh. 2:18,21), and cloth (Lev. 14:4; Num. 4:8; 2 Sam. 1:24; 2 Chron. 2:7,14; 3:14; Prov. 31:21; Jer. 4:30; Nah. 2:3) are mentioned in the Bible. Crimson or scarlet along with purple were considered royal colors (Matt. 27:28; Rev. 17:3-4; 18:11-12,16). Isaiah used scarlet as the imagery to describe sins (Isa. 1:18).

CRISPING PIN KJV translation in Isa. 3:22. A crisping pin was used for curling the hair. Modern versions translate the word "handbag" or "purse" (CSB) or "flounced skirt" (REB).

CRISPUS Personal name meaning "curly." Leader of synagogue in Corinth (Acts 18:8) and one of few whom Paul personally baptized (1 Cor. 1:14). Church tradition says he became bishop of Aegina.

CROSS, CRUCIFIXION Method the Romans used to execute Jesus Christ. The most painful and degrading form of capital punishment in the ancient world, the cross became the means by which Jesus became the atoning sacrifice for the sins of all humankind. It also became a symbol for the sacrifice of self in discipleship (Rom. 12:1) and for the death of self to the world (Mark 8:34).

For Paul the "word of the cross" (1 Cor. 1:18 CSB, NASB) is the heart of the gospel, and the preaching of the cross is the soul of the church's mission. "Christ crucified" (1 Cor. 1:23; cp. 2:2; Gal. 3:1) is more than the basis of our salvation; the cross was the central event in history, the one moment that demonstrated God's control of and involvement in human history.

Jesus himself established the primary figurative interpretation of the cross as a call to complete surrender to God. He used it five times as a symbol of true discipleship in terms of self-denial, taking up one's cross, and following Jesus (Mark 8:34; 10:38; Matt. 16:24; Luke 9:23; 14:27).

Closely connected to this is Paul's symbol of the crucified life. Conversion means the individual "no longer live(s)" but is replaced by Christ and faith in him (Gal. 2:20). Self-centered desires are nailed to the cross (Gal. 5:24), and worldly interests are dead (Gal. 6:14). The Christian paradox is that death is the path to life.

CROWN Special headdress worn by royalty and other persons of high merit and honor. While most references to "crown" in the OT point to the actual headdress, in the NT it usually has a figurative significance. Paul envisioned "a crown of righteousness" for himself and others (2 Tim. 4:8), and James anticipated "the crown of life" (James 1:12).

In the book of Revelation, crowns are both realistic and figurative. The 24 elders seated around God's throne were wearing gold crowns (4:4); as they worshipped, they "cast their crowns before the throne" (4:10 CSB). Later a seven-headed dragon appeared wearing a crown on each head (12:3), but opposing all the evil forces was the "Son of Man" wearing a golden crown (14:14). In each case the crown symbolized power, either good or evil.

CROWN OF THORNS Crown made by the Roman soldiers to mock Jesus, the "King of the Jews" (Matt. 27:29; Mark 15:18; John 19:3; not mentioned in Luke). The identification of the plant used to plait this crown is unknown. Jesus used the imagery of "thorns" in his teaching in a negative sense (Matt. 7:16; Mark 4:7,18; Heb. 6:8).

CRUCIBLE Melting pot or "fining pot" (KJV), probably made of pottery, used in the refining of silver. The crucible is used in the Bible as a figure for testing of people (Prov. 17:3; 27:21).

CRUSE Elongated pottery vessel about six inches tall used for holding liquids such as oil (1 Kgs. 17:12,14,16) or water (1 Kgs. 19:6).

CRYSTAL Nearly transparent quartz that may be colorless or slightly tinged. "Crystal" is the modern translation of several Hebrew and Greek words used to describe something valuable (Job 28:17), a clear sky (Ezek. 1:22), a calm sea or river (Rev. 4:6; 22:1), or the radiance of the new Jerusalem (Rev. 21:11).

CUBIT Unit of measure. It was reckoned as the distance from a person's elbow to the tip of the middle finger, approximately 18 inches.

CUCKOW KJV for an unclean bird (Lev. 11:16; Deut. 14:15); also spelled "cuckoo." Since the bird in question is grouped with carrion-eating or predatory birds, the cuckoo would seem to be eliminated from the diet since it eats only insects. Modern versions read "sea gull."

CUMIN, CUMMIN Herb of the carrot family (*Cuminum cyminum* L.) mentioned with dill. Used in Bible times to season foods. Isaiah portrayed the planting and threshing of cumin (Isa. 28:25,27). Jesus faulted the Pharisees for giving attention to small things like tithing mint, dill, and cumin while ignoring the weightier matters of the law (Matt. 23:23; Luke 11:42).

CUNEIFORM Most widely used system of writing in the ancient Near East until it was supplanted by alphabetic scripts like Aramaic. The word "cuneiform" is derived from the Latin *cuneus*, "wedge" and is used to refer to characters composed of wedges. The system of writing was originated apparently by the Sumerians before 3000 BC.

CUP Drinking vessel made of pottery or various metals such as gold, silver, or bronze. In the Bible the word "cup" frequently is used in a figurative sense. The contents of the cup are accentuated, since symbolically God serves the drink. Thus the cup might represent blessings or prosperity for a righteous person (Pss. 16:5; 23:5; 116:13). Likewise, it portrayed the totality of divine judgment on the wicked (Pss. 11:6; 75:8; Isa. 51:17,22; Jer. 25:15; 49:12; 51:7; Ezek. 23:31-34; Rev. 14:10; 16:19; 17:4; 18:6). Jesus voluntarily drank the cup of suffering (Matt. 20:22; 26:39,42; Mark 10:38; 14:36; Luke 22:42; John 18:11). For Jesus, that cup was his death and everything that it involved. The cup had a prominent place in the liturgy of the Jewish Passover meal, and so, subsequently, in the Lord's Supper. In the Christian ordinance, the cup is a symbolic reminder of the atoning death of Jesus (Matt. 26:27-28; Mark 14:23-24; Luke 22:20; 1 Cor. 11:25-26).

CURSE See *Blessing and Cursing*.

CUSH 1. Member of the tribe of Benjamin about whom the psalmist sang (Ps. 7:1). Nothing else is known of him. **2.** Son of Ham and grandson of Noah (Gen. 10:8). In the Table of Nations he is seen as the original ancestor of inhabitants of the land of Cush. **3.** Nation situated south of Egypt with differing boundaries and perhaps including differing dark-skinned tribes (Jer. 13:23) at different periods of history. The Hebrew word *Cush* has been traditionally translated "Ethiopia."

CUSHAN Tent-dwelling people that Habakkuk saw experiencing God's wrath (Hab. 3:7).

CUSHAN-RISHATHAIM Personal name meaning "dark one of double evil." King of Aram Naharaim to whom Yahweh gave Israel in the early period of the Judges (Judg. 3:8).

CUSHI Personal name meaning "Cushite." **1.** Father of the prophet Zephaniah (Zeph. 1:1). **2.** Ancestor of a royal official under King Jehoiakim (Jer. 36:14).

CUSHITE Citizen or inhabitant of Cush. The Hebrew word is the same as the proper name Cushi. God has concern for and control over them just as he does for his own people (Amos 9:7). **1.** Unnamed Cushite served as Joab's messenger to bring the news of Absalom's death to David (2 Sam. 18:21-32). **2.** Eunuch under King Zedekiah who helped Jeremiah escape from a cistern into which the king had had him thrown (Jer. 38:6-12; 39:16).

CUSTODIAN Wealthy Greek and Roman families often had a slave who attended boys under the age of about 16. The major responsibilities of the custodian were to escort the boys to and from school and to attend to their behavior. The pedagogue or custodian had responsibility to discipline or punish the boy. Once the boys reached manhood, they no longer needed the services of the custodian. Often the young man rewarded the custodian by granting him freedom. Paul spoke of the law as the custodian of God's people until Christ came (Gal. 3:23-26). The law cannot save; but it can bring us to the point where we could have faith in Christ by showing us our unrighteousness (Gal. 3:19; cp. Rom. 7:7-12). Of course, the law was not nullified by Christ's death or by our becoming Christians. We are still expected to live according to the moral principles found in the law (Rom. 7:12,16; cp. Matt. 5:17-48).

CUTH, CUTHAH Place-names with two spellings in Hebrew and English. Cuthah was the center of worship of Nergal, god of death in Mesopotamia. Residents of the city were exiled by the Assyrians to live in Israel (2 Kgs. 17:24). Once settled, they made an idol to worship Nergal (2 Kgs. 17:30), thus aggravating the tendency to worship Yahweh of Israel along with other gods. Cuth was located at Tell Ibrahim, about 18 miles northeast of Babylon.

CYPRIAN Citizen or resident of Cyprus. See *Cyprus*.

CYPRUS Large island in the eastern Mediterranean Sea mentioned most prominently in Acts. In the OT, scattered references refer to the island as Kittim ("Chittim," Isa. 23:1; Jer. 2:10), although in some passages the term has a wider scope and includes lands other than Cyprus lying west of Palestine (Dan. 11:30).

Cyprus is first mentioned in the NT as the birthplace of Joseph surnamed Barnabas, a Hellenistic Jewish convert who later accom-

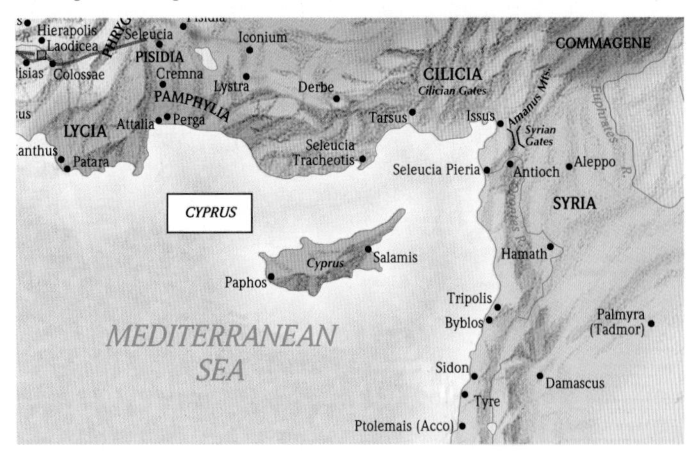

panied Paul (Acts 4:36-37). As a result of the persecution associated with the martyrdom of Stephen in Jerusalem, Jewish Christians journeyed to Cyprus and preached the gospel to the Jewish community on the island (Acts 11:19-20). In AD 46 or 47, Paul undertook his first missionary journey accompanied by Barnabas and John Mark (Acts 13). Arriving at Salamis on the eastern side of Cyprus, the group crossed the island to Paphos, preaching the new faith.

CYRENE Home of a certain Simon who was compelled to carry Jesus's cross to the place of crucifixion (Matt. 27:32). Located in northern Africa, it was the capital city of the Roman district of Cyrenaica during the NT era. Cyrenaica and Crete formed one province. Simon of Cyrene may have belonged to the rather large population of Greek-speaking Jews who resided in the city during the first part of the first century AD.

CYRENIAN Citizen and/or resident of Cyrene.

CYRENIUS Roman official mentioned in Luke 2:2 as the governor of Syria when the birth of Jesus took place. Some translations of the NT use the name Cyrenius, an Anglicized form of his Greek name, while others use the Latin form Quirinius.

CYRUS Third king of Anshan, Cyrus (the Great) assumed the throne about 559 BC. According to the best histories, Cyrus was reared by a shepherd after his grandfather, Astyages, king of Media, ordered that he be killed. Apparently, Astyages had dreamed that Cyrus would one day succeed him as king before the reigning monarch's death. The officer charged with the execution instead carried the boy into the hills to the shepherds.

As an adult, Cyrus organized the Persians into an army and revolted against his grandfather and father (Cambyses I). He defeated them and claimed their throne.

Cyrus's military exploits have become legendary. However, he is best remembered for his policies of peace. His famous decree in 539 BC (2 Chron. 36:22-23; Ezra 1:1-4) set free the captives Babylon had taken during its harsh rule. Among these prisoners were the Jews taken from Jerusalem in 586 BC. They were allowed to return to rebuild the temple and city. Along with this freedom, Cyrus restored the valuable treasures of the temple taken during the exile. Since the Jews

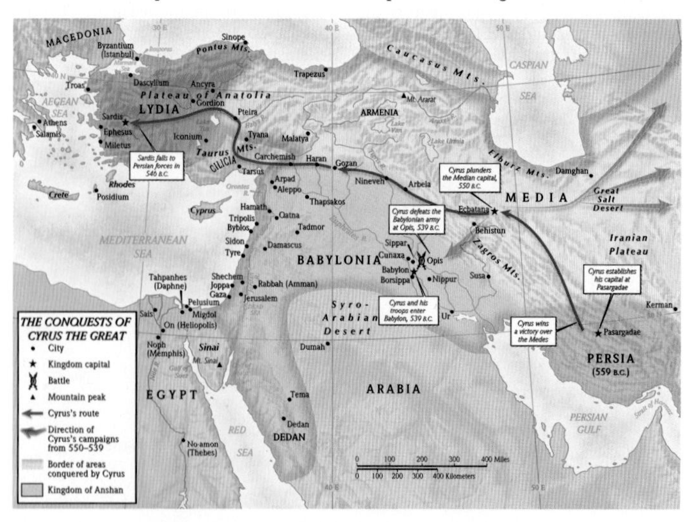

had done well in Babylon financially, many of them did not want to return to the wastes of Judah. From these people Cyrus exacted a tax to help pay for the trip for those who did wish to rebuild Jerusalem.

An astute politician, Cyrus made it a practice to publicly worship the gods of each kingdom he conquered. In so doing, he won the hearts of his subjects and kept down revolt. He is referred to as Yahweh's shepherd and anointed (Isa. 44:28–45:6) because of his kindness to the Jews and worship of Yahweh.

His last years are obscure. Cyrus was killed while fighting a frontier war with the nomadic Massagetae people. His tomb is in Pasargadae (modern Murghab).

Wall of the New Testament period in Damascus from which Paul might have escaped to begin his ministry

DABBASHETH or **DABBESHETH** Place-name meaning "hump." A border town of the tribe of Zebulun (Josh. 19:11). It is modern Tell esh-Shammam northwest of Jokneam.

DABERATH or **DABAREH** (KJV, Josh. 21:28). Place-name meaning "pasture." Border city of Zebulun near Mount Tabor (Josh. 19:12). In Josh. 21:28, it is a city given the Levites from the territory of Issachar. It is modern Daburiyeh at the northwest foot of Mount Tabor.

DAGGER KJV translation for the short, double-edged weapon of Ehud, the judge (Judg. 3:16-22). Other translations use "sword." Ehud's weapon was one cubit in length (18–22 inches), enabling him to conceal it under his cloak.

DAGON Name of a god meaning "little fish" or "dear." Dagon is a god associated with the Philistines. After the Philistines subdued Samson, they credited the victory to Dagon (Judg. 16:23). However, when Samson collapsed Dagon's temple upon himself and the Philistines, he proved the superiority of Israel's God. Likewise, the overthrow of the idol of Dagon before the ark of the covenant demonstrated God's predominance (1 Sam. 5:1-7). Nevertheless, the Philistines later displayed the head of Saul as a trophy in the temple of Dagon (1 Chron. 10:10).

DALMANUTHA Place to which Jesus and his disciples came following the feeding of the 4,000 (Mark 8:10). Its location is not known. The parallel reference in Matt. 15:39 suggests it was in the area of Magdala.

DALMATIA Place-name referring to the southern part of Illyricum, north of Greece and across the Adriatic Sea from Italy. At the writing of 2 Timothy, Titus had left Paul to go to Dalmatia (2 Tim. 4:10). Paul had preached in Illyricum (Rom. 15:19).

DALPHON Personal name apparently derived from Persian word perhaps meaning "sleepless." One of 10 sons of Haman, chief enemy of Mordecai and Esther. The sons were killed when the Jews protected themselves against the Persian attack (Esth. 9:7).

DAMARIS Personal name meaning "heifer." An Athenian woman who became a Christian following Paul's sermon at the Areopagus, the highest court in Athens (Acts 17:34).

DAMASCUS Capital of important city-state in Syria with close historical ties to Israel. Apparently Damascus has been occupied continuously for a longer period of time than any other city in the world and can claim to be the world's oldest city. Its geographical location enabled Damascus to become a dominant trading and transportation center. Standing 2,300 feet above sea level, it lay northeast of Mount Hermon and about 60 miles east of Sidon, the Mediterranean port city. Both major international highways—the Via Maris and the King's Highway—ran through Damascus.

In the Bible Abraham chased invading kings north of Damascus to recover Lot, who had been taken captive (Gen. 14:15). Abraham's servant Eliezer apparently came from Damascus (Gen. 15:2). When Ahaz went to

Damascus to pay tribute to Tiglath-pileser, he liked the altar he saw there and had a copy made for the Jerusalem temple (2 Kgs. 16:10-16). By the first century AD, Jews had migrated to Damascus and had establish synagogues there. Saul went to Damascus to determine if any Christian believers were attached to the synagogues there so that he might persecute them (Acts 9). Thus the Damascus road became the sight of Saul's conversion experience and Damascus the sight of his introduction to the church. He had to escape from Damascus in a basket to begin his ministry (2 Cor. 11:32-33). Damascus gained importance, eventually becoming a Roman colony.

DAN Personal name meaning "judge." First son born to Jacob by Rachel's maid Bilhah (Gen. 30:6). He was the original ancestor of the tribe of Dan. When the Israelites entered Canaan, the tribe of Dan received land on the western coast. They could not fully gain control of the territory, especially after the Philistines settled in the area. The last chapters of Judges show Samson of the tribe of Dan fighting the Philistines. Eventually, Dan migrated to the north and was able to take a city called Laish. They renamed the city Dan and settled in the area around it. The biblical city of Dan is often mentioned in the description of the land of Israel, namely "from Dan to Beer-sheba" (Judg. 20:1).

DANCING Essential part of Jewish life in Bible times. According to Eccles. 3:4, there is "a time to mourn, and a time to dance." Dances were performed on both sacred and secular occasions, though the Hebrew mind would not likely have thought in these terms. The OT employs 11 terms to describe the act of dance.

DANIEL Personal name meaning "God is judge" or "God's judge." **1.** Son of David and Abigail the Carmelitess (1 Chron. 3:1); he is called Chileab in 2 Sam. 3:3. **2.** Priest of the Ithamar lineage (Ezra 8:2; Neh 10:6) who returned with Ezra from the Babylonian captivity. **3.** Daniel of Ezek. 14:14,20; 28:3 is spelled differently in Hebrew from all the other forms in the OT. This Daniel was a storied figure of antiquity mentioned with Noah and Job. **4.** The most common usage of "Daniel" refers to the hero of the book of Daniel. This young man of nobility was taken captive by Nebuchadnezzar, king of Babylon, and elevated to high rank in the Babylonian and Persian kingdoms. The Babylonians sought to remove all vestiges of Daniel's nationality and religion. For this reason, they sought to change the name of Daniel to Belteshazzar (Dan. 1:7; 2:26; 4:8-9,18-19; 5:12; 10:1).

Daniel would probably have celebrated his one hundredth birthday during the reign of Darius. He had outstanding physical attraction. He demonstrated at an early age propensities of knowledge, wisdom, and leadership. In addition to his wisdom, he was skilled in dream interpretation. Throughout his entire life he demonstrated an unshakable faith in his God.

DANIEL, BOOK OF In the English versions, Daniel appears as the last of four major prophetic books; in the Hebrew Bible, it is grouped with the section of Scripture known

Jewish men dancing during a private ceremony in the Court of the Men at the Wailing Wall in Jerusalem

as the *Hagiographa* or the Writings. The traditional position is that Daniel wrote the book in the sixth century BC, the prophecy is historically reliable, and its predictions are supernatural and accurate.

Theological Emphases Without doubt the principal theological theme of the book is the sovereignty of God. Every page reflects the author's conviction that his God is the Lord of individuals, nations, and all of history. Daniel also emphasizes the person and work of the Messiah (e.g., 7:13-14, 9:24-27). Eschatology is another prominent theme in Daniel's prophecies. Believers will experience tribulation in the last days (7:21,25; 9:27; 12:1), but the Messiah will appear and establish a glorious, eternal kingdom (2:44-45; 7:13-14,26-27; 9:24). In this wonderful new world, the saints will be rewarded and honored (12:2-3).

Structure That the book of Daniel should be divided according to the type of literature—the stories of Daniel (1:1–6:28) and the prophecies of Daniel (7:1–12:13)—is indicated by the chronological scheme set forth by the author of the book and by the fact that the author himself grouped homogeneous literary accounts together.

DANITE Resident and/or citizen of the city of Dan or member of the tribe of Dan.

DAN-JAAN Place-name of uncertain meaning in 2 Sam. 24:6.

DANNAH Place-name meaning "fortress." Town assigned to the tribe of Judah in the hill country (Josh. 15:49). Its location is uncertain.

DAPPLED Variegated gray color of the horses in the vision in Zech. 6:3,6. KJV translates the rare Hebrew term as "bay."

DARDA or **DARA** Personal name possibly meaning "pearl of knowledge." Famous wise man whose father is listed as Mahol in 1 Kgs. 4:31 but as Zerah in what appears to be a parallel list in 1 Chron. 2:6.

DARIC Persian gold coin equivalent to four days' wages, probably introduced by Darius I (522–486 BC) and possibly the earliest coined money used by the Jews who became acquainted with it during the exile. Offerings for the reconstruction of the temple were made in darics (Ezra 2:69 ESV; Neh. 7:70,72).

DARIUS Name of several Medo-Persian kings, three of whom are mentioned in the OT. **1.** Darius the Mede (Dan. 5:31), ruler who took Babylon from Belshazzar. Against his own will, he had Daniel thrown to the lions and later decreed that "in all my royal dominion, people must tremble in fear before the God of Daniel" (Dan. 6:26 CSB). **2.** Darius I (521–486 BC), also known as Darius Hystaspes or the Great, was both extremely cruel and generous. Darius seized power following the death of Cambyses II, son of Cyrus. This is the Darius of Ezra (Ezra 4–6; Haggai; Zech. 1–8), under whom the temple in Jerusalem was reconstructed, completed in the sixth year of his reign. Darius continued Cyrus's policy of restoring disenfranchised peoples who were victims of Assyrian and Babylonian conquests. Darius reaffirmed Cyrus's authorization and also provided for maintenance of the temple. **3.** Darius the Persian (Neh. 12:22), although scholars differ as to his identity.

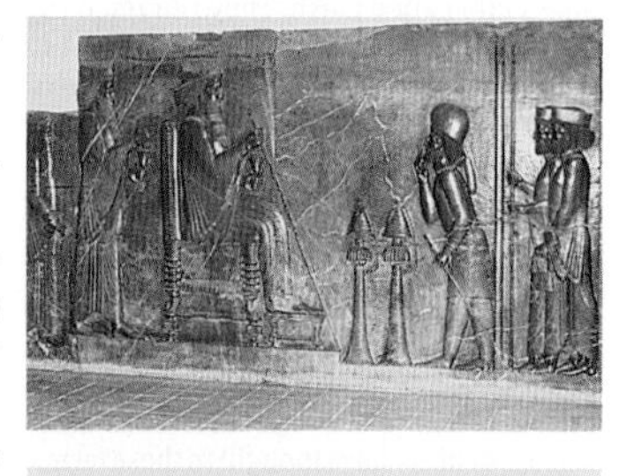

Relief of Darius I giving an audience

DARKNESS Absence of light is used in both physical and figurative senses in both the OT and NT. Darkness often has an ethical sense. Scripture speaks of ways of darkness (Prov. 2:13; 4:19), walking in darkness (John 8:12; 1 John 1:6; cp. 2 Cor. 6:14; Eph. 5:8), and works of darkness (Rom. 13:12; Eph. 5:11). In this ethical sense, God has no darkness in himself (1 John 1:5). Powers hostile to God can be termed darkness. People thus face a choice of whether to yield allegiance to God or to darkness (Luke 22:53; John 1:5; 3:19; Col. 1:13; 1 Thess. 5:5). Darkness also symbolizes ignorance, especially of God and of God's ways (Isa. 8:22; 9:2; John 12:46; Acts 26:18; 1 Thess. 5:4; 1 John 2:9). God's deliverance (either from ignorance or hostile powers) is described as lighting the darkness (Isa. 9:2; 29:18; 42:7-16; Mic. 7:8; 1 Pet. 2:9).

DARKON Personal name perhaps meaning "hard." A servant of Solomon whose descendants returned from exile with Zerubbabel about 537 BC (Ezra 2:56).

DATES Fruit of the date palm (*Phoenix dactylifera*), highly valued by desert travelers who consume dates fresh, dry them, or form them into cakes for a portable and easily storable food.

DATHAN Personal name meaning "fountain" or "warring." The son of Eliab from the tribe of Reuben, Dathan and his brother, Abiram, were leaders of a revolt challenging Moses's authority over the Israelites. The attempted coup failed, and Dathan and Abiram, along with their families, were swallowed up by the earth (Num. 16).

DAVID Personal name probably meaning "favorite" or "beloved." Shepherd, musician, poet, warrior, and loyal subject of King Saul, David became Israel's second king and the first king to unite Israel and Judah. He was the first king to receive the promise of a royal messiah in his line. David was pictured as the ideal king of God's people. David ruled from about 1005 to 965 BC.

The NT tells the story of Jesus as the story of the Son of God but also as the story of the Son of David from Jesus's birth (Matt. 1:1) until his final coming (Rev. 22:16). At least 12 times, the Gospels refer to Jesus as "Son of David." David was cited as an example of similar behavior by Jesus (Matt. 12:3), and David called him "Lord" (Luke 20:42-44). David thus took his place in the roll call of faith given in Heb. 11:32. This was "David the son of Jesse, . . . a man after my own heart, who will carry out all my will" (Acts 13:22 CSB).

DAY OF ATONEMENT Tenth day of the seventh month of the Jewish calendar (Sept.–Oct.) on which the high priest entered the inner sanctuary of the temple to make reconciling sacrifices for the sins of the entire nation (Lev. 16:16-28). The writer of Hebrews developed images from the Day of Atonement to stress the superiority of Christ's priesthood (8:6; 9:7,11-26). Hebrews 13:11-12 uses the picture of the bull and goat burned outside the camp as an illustration of Christ's suffering outside Jerusalem's city walls. According to one interpretation, Paul alluded to the day's ritual by speaking of Christ as a sin offering (2 Cor. 5:21).

DAY OF THE LORD Time when God reveals his sovereignty over human powers and human existence. The day of the Lord rests on the Hebrew term, *yom*, "day," the fifth most frequent noun used in the OT and one used with a variety of meanings.

The OT prophets used a term familiar to their audience, a term by which the audience expected light and salvation (Amos 5:18), but the prophets painted it as a day of darkness and judgment (Isa. 2:10-22; 13:6,9; Joel 1:15; 2:1-11,31; 3:14-15; Amos 5:20; Zeph. 1:7-8,14-18; Mal. 4:5). The OT language of the day of the Lord is thus aimed at warning sinners among God's people of the danger of trusting in traditional religion without commitment to God and his way of life.

New Testament writers took up the OT expression to point to Christ's final victory and the final judgment of sinners. In so doing, they used several different expressions (CSB): "day of Christ Jesus" (Phil. 1:6), "day of our Lord Jesus Christ" (1 Cor. 1:8); "day of the Lord" (1 Cor. 5:5; 1 Thess. 5:2); "day of Christ" (Phil. 1:10; 2:16); "day of judgment" (1 John 4:17); "this day" (1 Thess. 5:4); "that day" (2 Tim. 1:12); "day of wrath" (Rom. 2:5).

DAY'S JOURNEY Customary, though inexact, measure of distance traveled in a day. The distance varied with the terrain and with the circumstances of the traveler. The typical day's journey of the Jews was between 20 and 30 miles, though groups generally traveled only 10 miles per day (Gen. 30:36; 31:23; Exod. 3:18; 8:27; Deut. 1:2; Luke 2:44).

DAYSMAN KJV term for a mediator, arbitrator, or umpire (Job 9:33). In the Near East such mediators placed their hands on the heads of the parties in a dispute.

DEACON Term "deacon" comes from the Greek noun *diakonos*, which occurs 29 times in the NT, and is most commonly translated "servant" or "minister." This noun is derived from the verb "to serve" and is used to signify various types of service.

DEAD SEA Inland lake at the end of the Jordan Valley on the southeastern border of Canaan with no outlets for water it receives; known as Salt Sea, Sea of the Plain, and Eastern Sea. Its current English name was applied to it through writings after AD 100. Some modern translations use the designation "Dead Sea." It is about 50 miles long and 10 miles wide at its widest point. The surface of the sea is 1,292 feet below the level of the Mediterranean Sea.

Dead Sea Scroll fragment

The Dead Sea

DEAD SEA SCROLLS Discovered between 1947 and 1960 in a cave on the western Dead Sea shore near a ruin called Khirbet Qumran. Eleven caves from the Qumran area have since yielded manuscripts, mostly in small fragments. These were composed or copied between 200 BC and AD 70, mostly around the lifetime of Jesus, by a small community living at Qumran.

DEATH The biblical portrait of death is not that of a normal outworking of natural processes. Instead, the Bible presents human death as a reaffirmation that something has gone awry in God's created order. The Scriptures do not, however, picture death as a hopeless termination of human consciousness, but instead brim with the hope of resurrection. Biblical scholars group the Bible's teachings on death into three distinct but interrelated categories—physical, spiritual, and eternal.

DEBIR Personal and place-name meaning "back, behind." As a common noun, the Hebrew term refers to the back room of the temple, the holy of holies. **1.** King of Eglon who joined in Jerusalem-led coalition against Joshua and lost (Josh. 10:3). Nothing else about him is known. See *Eglon*. **2.** Important city in hill country of the tribe of Judah whose exact location is debated by archaeologists and geographers. Joshua annihilated its residents

(Josh. 10:38; cp. 11:21; 12:13). **3.** A town on the northern border of Judah (Josh. 15:7). This may be located at Thoghret ed-Debr, the "pass of Debir," 10 miles east of Jerusalem. **4.** A town in Gad east of the Jordan given various spellings in the Hebrew Bible: *Lidebor* (Josh. 13:26); *Lwo Debar* (2 Sam. 9:4-5); *Lo' Debar* (2 Sam. 17:27); *Lo' Dabar* (Amos 6:13).

DEBORAH Personal name meaning "bee." Deborah is the name of two women in the Bible. **1.** Rebekah's nurse (Gen. 35:8), who was buried by Rebekah's son, Jacob, at a place he named "Oak of Weeping." **2.** A judge of premonarchic Israel (Judg. 4–5). The wife of Lapidoth, she is identified as a prophetess, a judge, and as a "mother in Israel" (Judg. 5:7 CSB) because of her role in delivering God's people. After Moses, only Samuel filled the same combination of offices: prophet, judge, and military leader. Judges 5 contains a victory song Deborah composed to bless God for the victory over their enemies and to celebrate another woman's (see *Jael*) action to kill a commander (see *Sisera*) of an enemy army.

DECAPOLIS Place-name meaning "10 cities." A group of Greek cities mentioned in Matt. 4:25; Mark 5:20; 7:31, originally 10 in number but including more cities at a later time.

DECISION, VALLEY OF (Joel 3:14) See *Jehoshaphat, Valley of.*

DEDAN Personal and place-name of unknown meaning. **1.** The original ancestor of an Arabian tribe listed in the Table of Nations as a son of Cush (Gen. 10:7). See *Cush.* **2.** Grandson of Abraham (Gen. 25:3). Here, as in 10:7, Dedan's brother is Sheba. Three otherwise unknown Arabian tribes descended from Dedan, according to Gen. 25:3. **3.** Arabian tribe centered at al-Alula, 70 miles southwest of Tema and 400 miles from Jerusalem.

DEDANIM or **DEDANITE** Resident or citizen of the tribe of Dedan.

DEDICATION, FEAST OF Term for Hanukkah in John 10:22.

DEEP, THE English translation of the Hebrew term *tehom*. The deep constitutes the primeval waters of creation in Gen. 1:2. The waters of the deep can be destructive or constructive, curse or blessing. When the waters of the deep burst their bounds, the result is a flood (Gen. 7:11). On the other hand, the waters of the deep are a blessing, without which life could not continue. Deuteronomy 8:7 describes the promised land as a land of brooks, fountains, and deeps, which irrigate the land so that grain and fruit can be grown (Ezek. 31:4).

The Greek Bible or Septuagint translated *tehom* as "abyss," bringing it into relationship with the pit, the abode of the dead (Rom. 10:7) and place of evil spirits (Luke 8:31), including the beast of the apocalypse (Rev. 17:8).

DEER Antlered animal (all male and some female have antlers) with two large and two small hooves. It is believed that three species of deer lived in Israel in Bible times: red, fallow, and roe.

DEFILE To make ritually unclean.

DEGREES, SONG OF KJV phrase used in the titles of 15 psalms (Pss. 120–134). Modern speech translations render the phrase "Song of Ascents." Though the origin of the phrase is obscure, the generally accepted view is that the Hebrew term *ma'alot* (goings up) is a reference to pilgrims going up to Jerusalem for the three required festivals (Pss. 42:4; 122:4).

DEHAVITE KJV transliteration of Aramaic text in Ezra 4:9. Modern translators read the text as two Aramaic words—*di-hu'*—meaning "that is."

DEKAR KJV reads "son of Dekar" in 1 Kgs. 4:9, where modern translations transliterate the Hebrew text to read "Ben-deker."

DELAIAH Personal name meaning "the Lord rescued." **1.** Head of one of the 24 divisions of the priestly order organized by David (1 Chron. 24:18). **2.** Son of Shemaiah and a courtier who counseled Jehoiakim not to burn Jeremiah's scroll (Jer. 36:12,25).

3. One of the exiles who returned under Zerubbabel to Jerusalem (Ezra 2:60; Neh. 7:62). **4.** Descendant of David and son of Elioenai (1 Chron. 3:24). **5.** Contemporary of Nehemiah (Neh. 6:10).

DELILAH Personal name meaning "with long hair hanging down." A woman from the valley of Sorek who was loved by Samson. She betrayed him to the Philistines, who captured, blinded, and bound him (Judg. 16).

DEMAS Companion and coworker of Paul the apostle (Col. 4:14). Though in Philem. 24, Paul identified Demas as a "coworker," 2 Tim. 4:10 indicates that this man later deserted Paul, having "loved this present world" (CSB).

DEMETRIUS Personal name meaning "belonging to Demeter, the Greek goddess of crops." **1.** Silversmith in Ephesus who incited a riot directed against Paul because he feared that the apostle's preaching would threaten the sale of silver shrines of Diana, the patron goddess of Ephesus (Acts 19:24-41). **2.** Apparently a convert from the worship of Demeter, the god worshipped in the mystery religion at Eleusis near Athens. John commended him, saying, "Everyone speaks well of Demetrius—even the truth itself" (3 John 12 CSB).

DEMONIC POSSESSION Demons are identified in Scripture as fallen angels who joined Satan in his rebellion. They follow Satan, doing evil and wreaking havoc. They have limited power and like Satan are already defeated (Col. 2:15).

The NT distinguishes between demonic possession and physical disease. Matthew 4:24 states that Jesus healed "all those who were afflicted, those suffering from various diseases and intense pains, the demon-possessed, the epileptics, and the paralytics" (CSB).

The cure for demonic possession was faith in the power of Christ. Never were magic or rituals used to deliver one from demonic possession. The exorcisms of Jesus were accomplished by the power of his speech. He issued simple commands, such as "Be silent, and come out of him!" (Mark 1:25) or "You mute and deaf spirit, I command you: Come out of him and never enter him again!" (Mark 9:25 CSB).

DENARIUS Coin representing a typical day's wage for an ordinary laborer (Matt. 20:2). KJV translates it "penny." This unit of Roman currency is the most frequently mentioned coin in the NT.

DEN OF LIONS Place where lions live, at times a thicket (Jer. 50:44) or cave (Nah. 2:12). See *Lion*.

DEPUTY Official of secondary rank (1 Kgs. 22:47); KJV term for a Roman proconsul (Acts 13:7; 18:12; 19:38).

DERBE Important city in region of Lycaonia in province of Galatia in Asia Minor. It is apparently near modern Kerti Huyuk. The residents of Derbe and Lystra spoke a different language from the people to the north in Iconium. Paul visited Derbe on his first missionary journey (Acts 14:6), fleeing from Iconium. Persecution in Lystra led to a successful preaching mission in Derbe (14:20-21). On the second journey, Paul returned to Derbe (Acts 16:1). He apparently visited again on the third journey (18:23). Paul's fellow minister Gaius was from Derbe (20:4).

DESCENT Path down a mountain (Luke 19:37); a genealogy, line of ancestors (Heb. 7:3,6).

DESERT Areas with little rainfall in biblical times and lands inhabited by nomads with flocks and herds. Three major deserts figure in biblical events: the plateau east of the mountains to the east of the Jordan River; the area south of Edom; and the triangle bordered by Gaza, the Dead Sea, and the Red Sea.

DESIRE OF ALL NATIONS Phrase that Haggai used in his prophecy of a renewed temple (Hag. 2:7). Some translations (KJV, NIV) interpret the underlying Hebrew as a prophecy of the coming Messiah. Other translations render the phrase "treasure" (CSB, TEV, NRSV, REB) or "wealth" (NASB) of all nations in parallel to the gold and silver of 2:8.

Wasteland of the northern Negev in southern Israel

DESTINY Word used in modern translations for God's act in electing or predestinating people and nations.

DEUEL Personal name meaning "God knows." In Num. 1:14, the father of Eliasaph, the leader in the wilderness of the tribe of Gad.

DEUTERONOMY, BOOK OF English name of fifth book of OT taken from Greek translation meaning "second law." The title used in the Hebrew Bible, "these (are) the words" (two words in Hebrew), follows an ancient custom of using words from the first line of the text to designate a book. Deuteronomy is the last of five books of Law and should not be read in isolation from the other four books (Genesis, Exodus, Leviticus, Numbers). Pentateuch (five books) is the familiar title associated with these five books of Law, the first and most important division of the Hebrew Bible. By long-standing tradition, these books have been associated with Moses, the human instrument of God's deliverance of Israel from bondage in Egypt and the negotiator of the covenant between God and Israel.

The approaching death of Moses put urgency into his appeal for covenant renewal. He called for obedience through love to Yahweh, the loving God, who had established the covenant with Israel. Moses was convinced that only through a renewed relationship with God could the new generation of Israelites hope to succeed under Joshua's leadership in possessing the land. Deuteronomy is either quoted or alluded to nearly 200 times in the NT. Jesus resists Satan's three temptations in the wilderness by quoting from Deuteronomy.

Deuteronomy calls for a complete and undivided devotion to God. It sets forth the consequences of obedience and recognizes the inclination of God's people to forget who he is and what he has done for them. For that reason, Moses urges the people to continually be on guard against forgetting God and not to allow their children to be ignorant of him and his expectations.

DEVIL, SATAN, EVIL, DEMONIC Evil appears early in Genesis with the serpent figure (Gen. 3:1-5). While Genesis does not identify this figure as "Satan," Revelation alludes to him as such (Rev. 12:9). The Scriptures portray Satan as a personal being in direct opposition to God and his purposes. Satan is not equal to God nor does he threaten God's power (Isa. 45:5-7).

DEW Moisture that forms into drops of water on the earth during a cool night. Dew is used in the Bible as a symbol of refreshment (Deut. 32:2; Ps. 133:3); a symbol of the loving power of God that revives and invigorates (Prov. 19:12); a symbol of the sudden onset of an enemy (2 Sam. 17:12); a symbol of brotherly love and harmony (Ps. 133:3); a symbol of God's revelation (Judg. 6:36-40); and a symbol of God's blessing (Gen. 27:28).

DIADEM English translation of three Hebrew terms designating a head covering symbolizing authority and honor.

DIAMOND Precious stone used in jewelry and engraving. It is the hardest mineral known, formed of pure carbon crystals. Two Hebrew words stand behind English "diamond." *Yahelom* is a stone on the high priest's breastplate (Exod. 28:18; NIV, "emerald"; NRSV, "moonstone") and among the jewels of the king of Tyre (Ezek. 28:13). *Shamir* is the stone used on the point of an engraving tool to cut into stone surfaces (Jer. 17:1; NIV, "flint"; others suggest "emery"). The term also appears in Ezek. 3:9 and Zech. 7:12 as the hardest stone known.

DIANA Roman goddess with similar characteristics to the Greek Artemis. KJV reads "Diana" in Acts, where Greek and most modern translations read "Artemis."

DIASPORA Scattering of the Jews from the land of Palestine into other parts of the world. The term "dispersion" is also often used to describe this process.

DIBLAH or **DIBLATH** Place-name with variant manuscript spellings and English transliterations in Ezek. 6:14. The Hebrew term may mean "cake of figs."

DIBLAIM Personal or place-name meaning "two fig cakes." Hosea 1:3 lists Diblaim as a parent of Gomer, Hosea's harlot wife.

DIBON or **DIBON-GAD** Place-name possibly meaning "pining away" or "fence of tubes." **1.** Capital city of Moab captured by Moses (Num. 21:21-31). **2.** In Nehemiah's day (ca. 445 BC), Jews lived in a Dibon in Judah. This may be the same as Dimonah.

DIBRI Personal name meaning "talkative" or "gossip." Father of an Israelite woman who had a son with an Egyptian father. The son cursed God's name and was stoned to death (Lev. 24:10-23).

DIDRACHMA Greek coin worth two drachmas or a Jewish half shekel, the amount of the temple tax paid by every male Jew above age 19 (Matt. 17:24).

DIDYMUS Personal name meaning "twin." An alternative name for the apostle Thomas (John 11:16). It appears only in John's Gospel.

DIETING The book of Proverbs cautions that excessive eating and drinking is the mark of a fool (Prov. 23:20-21; cp. Eccles. 5:18; 9:7; 1 Cor. 15:32) and urges bodily restraint (Prov. 23:2; 25:16). The writer of Ecclesiastes noted that one who is blessed eats "at the proper time—for strength and not for drunkenness" (Eccles. 10:17 CSB). Daniel and his friends refused the rich foods of Babylon in favor of vegetables and water (Dan. 1:5-16) and were healthier as a result.

New Testament teaching holds that a person's body is the temple of the Holy Spirit (1 Cor. 6:19) and that it must therefore be subdued (1 Cor. 9:27) and cared for in a way that honors God (1 Cor. 6:20). For this reason, excessive eating is contrary to Christian discipline (Phil. 3:19).

DIGNITIES KJV translation of Greek *doxas* (literally, "glorious ones") in 2 Pet. 2:10. The people whom Peter condemned in his second letter willingly blasphemed the "dignities," who are either good angels or evil angels (cp. Jude 8).

DIKLAH Personal name apparently meaning "date palm." Grandson of Eber (Gen. 10:27).

DILEAN Place-name meaning "protrusion" or "ledge." Village in tribal territory of Judah (Josh. 15:38).

DILL Spice cultivated in Israel (Isa. 28:25-27). KJV translates "fitches"; NIV, "caraway." It was probably black cumin, *Nigella satina* (CSB). Jesus accused the scribes and Pharisees of tithing their dill but neglecting justice, mercy, and faith (Matt. 23:23).

DIMNAH Place-name meaning "manure." Town in tribal territory of Zebulun given to Levites (Josh. 21:35). First Chronicles 6:77 appears to refer to the same city as Rimmon (cp. Josh. 19:13). A scribe copying the text could easily confuse the two names.

DIMON Place-name perhaps meaning "blood." City in Moab on which Isaiah announced judgment (Isa. 15:9).

DIMONAH Place-name related to Hebrew word for blood. A town on southeast border of tribal allotment of Judah (Josh. 15:22). Some have suggested its location at Tell ed-Dheib near Aroer. It may be the same as Dibon mentioned in Neh. 11:25.

DINAH Personal name meaning "justice" or "artistically formed." The daughter of Jacob and Leah (Gen. 30:21). According to Gen. 34, she was sexually assaulted by a man named Shechem, who wished to marry her. Simeon and Levi, her brothers, took revenge by killing the male residents of the city of Shechem.

DINAITE KJV transliterations of Aramaic word in Ezra 4:9. Modern translations translate the word as "judges."

DINHABAH City name of unknown meaning. Residence of one of the earliest kings of Edom in period prior to Saul in Israel (Gen. 36:32). Nothing else is known of the city.

DIONYSIUS Athenian aristocrat who was converted to Christianity through the preaching of Paul the apostle (Acts 17:34). He was a member of the Areopagus, an elite and influential group of officials.

DIOTREPHES Personal name meaning "nurtured by Jove." An individual whose self-serving ambition is cited unfavorably (3 John 9). The writer of the letter declared that Diotrephes rejected the writer's authority.

DIPHATH NRSV, NASB reading of great grandson of Noah in 1 Chron. 1:6. KJV, CSB, NIV follow other Hebrew manuscripts and versions and Gen. 10:3 in reading Riphath.

DIRECTIONS The OT uses all the cardinal directions in several passages. God tells Abraham to look north and south, east and west (i.e., in all directions), and all that land will be his and his descendants' (Gen. 13:14). In the NT, ones from all directions, east and west, north and south, will sit at the table in God's kingdom (Luke 13:29).

DIRGE Modern translation term for lamentation.

DISCERNING OF SPIRITS One of the gifts of the Spirit (1 Cor. 12:10). It apparently refers to the God-given ability to tell whether a prophetic speech came from God's Spirit or from another source opposed to God.

DISCHARGE Modern translation term for bodily excretion that rendered one ceremonially unclean (Lev. 15:2-33: Num. 5:2; KJV, "issue"). A discharge rendered unclean the person and anything or anyone coming into contact with the source of uncleanness.

DISCIPLE Follower of Jesus Christ, especially the commissioned Twelve who followed Jesus during his earthly ministry. The term "disciple" comes to us in English from a Latin root. Its basic meaning is "learner" or "pupil." The term is virtually absent from the OT, though there are two related references (1 Chron. 25:8; Isa. 8:16).

DISCIPLINE In the Bible, discipline has a positive and essential place in the lives of God's people. God had prescribed a way of life for his people. They had to learn how to be obedient. The process by which God's people learned obedience was the "discipline of the Lord" (Deut. 11:2 CSB). Discipline, biblically understood, results in blessing. God's people learn how to serve him. Through praise and correction, their lives are shaped into a pattern of consistent obedience and love. Within "the discipline of the Lord," expressed in and through the Lord Jesus Christ, one can live the kind of life that is pleasing to God and of benefit to others.

DISEASES Physical and/or mental malfunctions that limit human functions and lessen the quality of life. Successful treatment of disease depends primarily on prompt, correct diagnosis, and the use of effective therapeutic agents. Unfortunately, people living in biblical times had limited means to diagnose and treat illness. The best-educated people in biblical times had a meager understanding of human anatomy and physiology and even less knowledge about the nature of disease and its effect on the body. No one knew about bacteria and viruses. This fact hampered diagnosis. Illness was often attributed to sin or to a curse by an enemy. The main diagnostic tools were observation and superficial physical examination. The physician had few aids to use in his work.

Jesus and the Treatment of Disease One of the major ministries of Jesus was the healing of ill persons. They flocked to him in large numbers, often after having tried all the remedies available in their day. They were desperate for help.

Jesus did not believe that all illness is the direct result of sin (John 9:1-3). He had the power, however, both to forgive sin and to heal (Matt. 9:1-8; cp. Mark 2:1-12; Luke 5:17-26). Ordinarily, he did not use any kind of secondary means to treat the afflicted, although on several occasions he used spittle (Mark 7:32-35; 8:22-25; John 9:6-7). Some of the illnesses treated by Jesus probably had a psychosomatic basis; but many others undoubtedly had organic causes, including birth defects, accidental injuries, and infections.

Regardless of the cause of their distress, people found that Jesus could truly help. There can be no doubt that the ability of Jesus to perform miracles is seen most vividly in his healing ministry. The blind, the deaf, the lame, and sufferers of all varieties found in him the help that was often not available through regular medical channels.

DISHAN Personal name meaning "bison" or "antelope." This may be a variant spelling/pronunciation of Dishon. A Horite chief and son of Seir (Gen. 36:21,28,30).

DISHON Name of Horite chief of Edom (Gen. 36:21,25-26,30). The name may be the same as Dishan with the variant spelling used to identify the separate individuals.

DISPENSATION An arrangement or management in which God places responsibility on humankind. As it is related to Jesus Christ, who had not been revealed for a long time (Eph. 3:5), the dispensation is new with regards to time. Paul indicated earlier in the epistle that there is coming a "dispensation of the fullness of the times" (1:10 KJV; cp. CSB, NASB), which appears as a future phenomenon. Colossians 1:25-29 indicates that there existed a previous dispensational arrangement different from the present one. This suggests that in Paul's thought at least three dispensations of God's dealings with humankind are evident: past, present, and future.

DISSIPATION Deceptive desires leading to a lifestyle without discipline resulting in the dizzy hangovers of drunkenness. The Greek word *apate* means "deception" caused by riches (Matt. 13:22) and sin (Heb. 3:13).

DISTAFF Part of the spindle used in spinning wool (Prov. 31:19). CSB: spinning staff.

DIVES Name sometimes given to the rich man of whom Jesus spoke in Luke 16:19-31. *Dives* actually is the Latin word for "rich" used in Luke 16:19 in the Vulgate translation. The idea that this was the name of the man emerged in medieval times.

DIVIDED KINGDOM Two political states of Judah and Israel that came into existence shortly after the death of Solomon (1 Kgs. 11:43) and survived together until the fall of Israel in 722 BC. The northern kingdom, known as Israel, and the southern kingdom, known as Judah, were operated as separate countries from approximately 924 BC until 722 BC (1 Kgs. 12).

DIVINATION AND MAGIC Practice of making decisions or foretelling the future by means of reading signs and omens. Several types of divination are mentioned in the Bible. God condemned divination and magic in every form. The law of Moses repeatedly condemns the practice. In Exod. 22:18 and Lev. 20:27, it brings the death penalty. People are exhorted to listen to God's prophets instead.

DIVINE FREEDOM One of God's unique attributes is freedom. Scripture declares, "Our God is in heaven and does whatever he pleases" (Ps. 115:3 CSB). God's actions are always voluntary. God cannot be compelled to act by any other person or exterior force. Only his nature and will are determinative for his actions (Isa. 42:21; Eph. 1:11).

DIVINE RETRIBUTION Repayment without stipulation of good or evil. The application of the word in theology is, however, almost always viewed as the response of a just and holy God to evil. Like other prominent theological terms (e.g., Trinity), the word is not found in the Bible, but the idea of God's repayment for evil is prominent in at least three ways.

First, the law of sowing and reaping is part of God's economy (Gal. 6:7-8). Second, coming judgment at the end of history includes repayment from God for rebellion. Finally, the justice of God's condemnation of sinners gives rise to the necessity of the grace of God in salvation and the substitutionary death of Jesus on the cross. God in his grace extends to sinners an offer of pardon rather than the retribution they deserve, because Jesus paid the price for human sin in his vicarious death, making it possible for the Father to be both "just" and still the "justifier" of the sinner who places personal faith in Jesus (Rom. 3:26).

DIVINERS' OAK Place visible from the gate of Shechem (Judg. 9:35,37).

DIVORCE Breaking of the marriage covenant. An action contrary to the pattern of "one man, one woman, one lifetime" revealed by God in Gen. 1:27; 2:21-25. The root idea implied a cutting of the marriage bond. While ancient cultures differed in details, most had a concept of marriage and a corresponding concept of divorce.

The NT also sheds light on the subject of divorce. The Lord Jesus stated that divorce, except in the case of sexual immorality, would cause complications for remarriage. An improper divorce would make the divorced wife and her future husband adulterers in their relationship (Matt. 5:31-32). In Matt. 19:3-12, Jesus stated that God did not intend for divorce to occur. Further, he stated that the Mosaic law allowed for divorce only because of the hardness of Israelite hearts. Jesus's disciples considered this a hard saying and said so; nevertheless, he affirmed his position on divorce (Matt. 19:7-12; Mark 10:4-12).

DIZAHAB Place-name meaning "place of gold." Place east of Jordan River used in Deut. 1:1 to locate where Moses spoke to Israel. Nothing else is known of it. It may have been located in Moab, in modern ed-Dhebe.

DOCTRINE Christian truth and teaching passed on from generation to generation as "the faith that was delivered to the saints" (Jude 3 CSB).

DODAI Personal name related to Hebrew word meaning "favorite" or "beloved." A military officer of David (1 Chron. 27:4). See *Dodo*.

DODANIM Great grandson of Noah and son of Javan in the Table of Nations (Gen. 10:4).

DODAVAH or **DODAVAHU** Personal name meaning "beloved of Yahweh." Father of Eliezer the prophet (2 Chron. 20:37).

DODO Personal name meaning "his beloved." **1.** Grandfather of Tola, the judge (Judg. 10:1). **2.** Father of Eleazar, one of David's three mighty men (2 Sam. 23:9). In 1 Chron. 27:4 he is called Dodai. **3.** Citizen of Bethlehem and father of Elhanan, one of David's warriors (2 Sam. 23:24).

DOE Modern translation where KJV has "hind" or "roe."

DOEG Personal name meaning "full of fear." An Edomite in the service of King Saul (1 Sam. 21:7).

DOG Considered an unclean animal; often wild, scavenger animal that ran in packs (Pss. 22:16-21; 59:6), but sometimes kept as domestic pet. Metaphorically, "dog" was a term of contempt (1 Sam. 17:43) and self-abasement (1 Sam. 24:14). Jesus used dogs to teach people to be discriminating in whom they chose to teach (Matt. 7:6). In Mark 7:27, Jesus probably was referring to the small dogs that people kept as pets. Jews contemptuously called Gentiles "dogs." Paul insulted his Judaizing opponents, calling them dogs (Phil. 3:2; cp. 2 Pet. 2:22; Rev. 22:15).

DOPHKAH Place-name perhaps meaning "(animal) drive." Station in the wilderness between Wilderness of Sin and Rephidim where Israel camped (Num. 33:12).

DOR Place-name meaning "dwelling." Canaanite city located at modern Khirbet el-Burj, 12 miles south of Mount Carmel. Dor lay in the territory assigned Asher, but the tribe of Manasseh claimed it (Josh. 17:11).

View of the ancient harbor at Dor in Israel

DORCAS Personal name meaning "gazelle." A Christian woman of Joppa who was known for her charitable works (Acts 9:36). She was also called Tabitha, an Aramaic name. When she died, distressed mourners sent for Peter, who restored her to life.

DOTHAN Place-name of uncertain meaning, also known as Dothaim. A city of the tribe of Manasseh, west of the Jordan, northeast of Samaria, southeast of Megiddo, and now identified as Tell Dotha. It was located in an area less productive for agriculture and was traversed by roads used for commerce. Dothan is the area to which Joseph traveled to find his brothers (Gen. 37:17).

DOVE A term applied rather loosely to many of the smaller species of pigeon. Because of the gentleness of the dove and because of its faithfulness to its mate, this bird is used as a descriptive title of one's beloved in the Song of Songs (2:14; 5:2; 6:9). In Matt. 10:16, the dove symbolizes innocence. All four Gospels describe the Spirit of God descending like a dove upon Jesus after his baptism (Matt. 3:16; Mark 1:10; Luke 3:22; John 1:32).

DOVE'S DUNG An item sold as food for an incredible price (2 Kgs. 6:25) during the siege of Samaria.

DOWRY Marriage present that ensured the new wife's financial security against the possibility her husband might forsake her or might die. The husband-to-be or his father paid the dowry or bride price to the bride's father to be kept for the bride.

DOXOLOGY Brief formula for expressing praise or glory to God. Biblical doxologies are found in many contexts, but one of their chief functions seems to have been as a conclusion to songs (Exod. 15:18), psalms (Ps. 146:10), and prayers (Matt. 6:13), where they possibly served as group responses to solo singing or recitation.

DRACHMA Greek term used to refer to silver coins (Luke 15:8-9). It was a Greek unit of silver coinage that, during the time of the NT, was considered equivalent to the Roman denarius. In 300 BC, a sheep cost one drachma, but apparently by NT times the drachma was worth much less.

DRAGNET Large fishing net equipped with a weighted bottom edge for touching ("dragging") the river or lake bottom and a top with wooden floats allowing the net to be spread across the water (Isa. 19:8). Jesus compared the kingdom of God to a dragnet, containing both good and bad fish until the time of separation and judgment (Matt. 13:47).

DRAGON Symbol of Satan in the NT. Revelation described it as a great, red monster with seven heads and ten horns. As in the OT texts, the dragon is put under guard (Rev. 20:1-3; Job 7:12) and later released for final destruction (Rev. 20:7-10; Isa. 27:1).

DRAWERS OF WATER Water carriers (Josh. 9:21,23,27).

DRESSER OF SYCAMORE TREES One of the occupations of the prophet Amos (Amos 7:14). The tending involved slitting the top of each piece of fruit to hasten its ripening and to produce a sweeter, more edible fruit.

DRIED GRAPES Raisins. Grapes were dried in clusters for a food that was easily stored and transported (1 Sam. 25:18; 30:12; 2 Sam. 16:1; 1 Chron. 12:40). Nazirites were prohibited from eating dried grapes (Num. 6:3).

DROMEDARY One-humped species of camel.

DROPSY Edema, a disease with fluid retention and swelling (Luke 14:2).

DRUNKENNESS Result of consuming a quantity of alcohol, the outcome being the impairment of faculties. This impairment may be mild (deep sleep) to severe (dizziness, vomiting, hallucination, and death). There are many cases of drunkenness in the OT. In the NT, the Lord explicitly warned against the use of alcohol (Luke 21:34). In Paul's letters, there are numerous warnings against the indulgence of alcohol (1 Cor. 5:11; 6:10; Gal. 5:21; Eph. 5:18).

DRUSILLA Wife of Felix, the Roman governor of Judea who heard Paul's case. Drusilla was a Jew and listened to Paul's arguments with her husband (Acts 24:24).

DULCIMER Apparently a Greek word used to name a musical instrument in Dan. 3:10. Many think the bagpipes are meant here (NASB). CSB and NRSV translate "drum."

DUMAH Place-name meaning "silence" or "permanent settlement." **1.** Son of Ishmael and the original ancestor of the Arabian tribe (Gen. 25:14) centered in the oases of Dumah, probably modern el-Gof, also called Dumat el-Gandel, meaning Dumah of the Rocks. **2.** City of the tribe of Judah (Josh. 15:52). It is probably modern Khirbet ed-Dome about nine miles southwest of Hebron. It may be mentioned in the Amarna letters.

DUNG Excrement of man or beast. "Dung" translates several different Hebrew and Greek words. An ash heap or rubbish heap was used to convey the haunt of the destitute (1 Sam. 2:8; Luke 14:35).

DUNG GATE Jerusalem landmark in the time of Nehemiah (Neh. 2:13; 3:13-14; 12:31). Located at the southwest corner of the wall, the gate was used for the disposal of garbage that was dumped into the Hinnom Valley below. Referred to as the Refuse Gate by KJV, NASB, and Rubbish Gate by TEV.

DURA Akkadian place-name meaning "circuit wall." Plain in Babylonia where King Nebuchadnezzar set up a mammoth golden image of a god or of himself (Dan. 3:1). The common place-name does not lend itself to an exact location.

DYEING Process of coloring materials. The dyeing process is not mentioned in Scripture, though dyed material is.

DYSENTERY Disease characterized by diarrhea, painful bowel spasms, and ulceration and infection of the bowels resulting in blood and pus in the excreta. Modern translations of Acts 28:8 render the "bloody flux" of the KJV as dysentery.

The Dung Gate in old Jerusalem

The mountainous landscape of the land of Edom

EAGLE The term "eagle" refers to several large birds of prey active in the daytime rather than at night. The Hebrew term translated "eagle" (*nesher*) also sometimes is translated "vulture." In Exod. 19:4 and Deut. 32:11, the eagle is used figuratively of God's protection and care.

EAR Physical organ of hearing. The ears appear in a variety of expressions in both Testaments. To incline the ear was to listen (2 Kgs. 19:16) or even to obey (Jer. 11:8). To give ear was to pay careful attention (Job 32:11). Sometimes the functions of the mind were attributed to the ear. Thus the ear exercised judgment (Job 12:11) and understanding (13:1).

EARNEST Sincerity and intensity of purpose (Luke 22:44; Jude 3) or a deposit paid to secure a purchase (2 Cor. 1:22; 5:5; Eph. 1:14).

EARTHQUAKE Shaking or trembling of the earth due to volcanic activity or, more often, the shifting of the earth's crust. Severe earthquakes produce such side effects as loud rumblings (Ezek. 3:12-13 RSV), openings in the earth's crust (Num. 16:32), and fires (Rev. 8:5).The Bible mentions an earthquake during the reign of Uzziah (Amos 1:1; Zech. 14:5). The oracles of Amos are dated two years before this earthquake.

EAST GATE This designation refers to three different gates. **1.** KJV refers to the East Gate of Jerusalem as leading to the Hinnom Valley (Jer. 19:2). **2.** The East Gate of the outer court of the temple. Since the temple faced east, this gate was the main entrance to the temple complex (Ezek. 47:1). **3.** The East Gate of the inner court of the temple. This gate was closed on the six working days but open on the Sabbath (Ezek. 46:1).

EAST SEA Ezekiel's expression for the Dead Sea (Ezek. 47:18).

EASTER The special celebration of the resurrection at Easter is the oldest Christian festival, except for the weekly Sunday celebration. In the early centuries, the annual observance was called the *pascha*, the Greek word for Passover, and focused on Christ as the paschal Lamb.

EBAL Personal name and place-name possibly meaning "bare." **1.** Grandson of Seir and son of clan leader Shobal among the Horite descendants living in Edom (Gen. 36:23). **2.** Son of Joktan in line of Shem (1 Chron. 1:22). He is called Obal in Gen. 10:28 through a scribal copying change. **3.** Mountain near Shechem on which Moses set up the curse for the covenant ceremony (Deut. 11:29; 27:13).

EBED Personal name meaning "servant." **1.** Father of Gaal, who led revolt in Shechem against Abimelech (Judg. 9:26-40). **2.** Clan leader who returned from exile under Ezra (Ezra 8:6).

EBED-MELECH Personal name meaning "servant of the king." An Ethiopian eunuch in the service of King Zedekiah of Judah (Jer. 38:7).

EBENEZER Personal name meaning "stone of help." The name of a site near Aphek where the Israelites camped before they fought in battle against the Philistines (1 Sam. 4:1).

EBER Personal name meaning "the opposite side." **1.** The ancestor of Abraham and the Hebrew people, and a descendant of Shem (Gen. 10:21-25; 11:14-17). **2.** A member of the tribe of Gad, called Heber by KJV (1 Chron. 5:13). The name entered Israel's record about 750 BC (v. 17). **3.** Clan leader in the tribe of Benjamin (1 Chron. 8:12). **4.** Another clan leader of Benjamin (1 Chron. 8:22). **5.** Head of priestly family of Amok (Neh. 12:20) in days of Jehoiakim (609–597 BC).

EBIASAPH Personal name meaning "my father has collected or taken in." A Levite descended from Kohath (1 Chron. 6:23).

EBLA Major ancient site located in Syria about 40 miles south of Aleppo. The discovery of more than 17,000 clay tablets in the mid-1970s revealed a major Syrian civilization in the mid-third millennium and brought the site worldwide prominence by the late 1970s. Valuable general information can be gleaned from Ebla for the study of the Bible. Ebla was a major religious center, and more than 500 gods are mentioned in the texts. The chief god was Dagon, a vegetation deity associated in the Bible with the Philistines (1 Sam. 5:2).

EBRON City in territory of Asher (Josh. 19:28), spelled Hebron in KJV. Several manuscripts in Josh. 19:28 plus the lists in Josh. 21:30; 1 Chron. 6:74 have Abdon.

ECBATANA Modern translation spelling of Achmetha. Capital of the ancient Median Empire, located in the Zagros Mountains in western Iran (Ezra 6:2).

ECCLESIASTES, BOOK OF Classified along with Job and Proverbs as one of the OT wisdom books. Traditionally Solomon has been identified as the author of Ecclesiastes.

Theme Probably no biblical book is so dominated by one leading theme as is Ecclesiastes. In 1:2, the author declares that "everything is meaningless" (NIV) or, better, "vanity" (KJV, NRSV, NASB, NKJV, ASV). CSB uses "futile." The Hebrew word translated thus is *hevel* (literally, "breath"), the key word in the book.

Interpretation Of all the books in the Bible, Ecclesiastes is usually considered to be the most problematic. The work has been called pessimistic, shocking, unorthodox, and even heretical. For example, certain statements in the book have been interpreted to deny life after death (3:18-21; 9:5-6,10). Yet, when these passages are considered in light of the overall theme of the book, it becomes clear that the author is not denying the existence of the human spirit after death but is stating an obvious fact: at death earthly life (life "under the sun") with its joys, sorrows, and opportunities is over. Earthly possessions and mere worldly endeavors are temporary and have no eternal value for believers or nonbelievers. Only what is done for God will endure (12:13-14).

ED Place-name meaning "witness." Altar that the tribes assigned territory east of the Jordan built as a witness that Yahweh is God of both the eastern and western tribes. The building resulted in a dispute between the two groups of tribes, but Phinehas, the priest, helped settle the dispute, ensuring the altar was a symbol and would not be used for burnt offering (Josh. 22:34). CSB, NASB, NIV, NRSV read "witness."

EDEN Garden of God. "Eden" appears 20 times in the OT but never in the NT. Fourteen appearances refer to the idyllic place of creation. In Genesis (2:8,10,15; 3:23-24; 4:16), the reference is to the region in which a garden was placed. Though details seem precise, identification of the rivers that flow from the river issuing forth from Eden cannot be accomplished with certainty. The Euphrates and the Tigris can be identified, but there is no agreement on the location of the Pishon and the Gihon.

EDER Place and personal name meaning "water puddle" or "herd." **1.** Tower near Bethlehem (Gen. 35:21; cp. v. 19). The exact location is not known. Micah referred to Jerusalem as the "tower of the flock," the same Hebrew expression as in Genesis (Mic. 4:8). **2.** A town in the southern limits of the tribal territory of Judah near Edom (Josh. 15:21). Its location is not known. **3.** A Levite of the clan of Merari (1 Chron. 23:23; 24:30). **4.** A leader of the tribe of Benjamin (1 Chron. 8:15); KJV spelling is Ader.

EDOM Area southeast and southwest of the Dead Sea, on opposite sides of the Arabah, was known as Edom in biblical times and was the home of the Edomites. The name "Edom" derives from a Semitic root that means "red" or "ruddy" and characterizes the red sandstone terrain of much of the area in question. The Israelites regarded the Edomites as close relatives, even more closely related to them than the Ammonites or Moabites. According to the biblical writers, enmity between Israel and Edom began with Jacob and Esau (when the former stole the latter's birthright) and was exacerbated at the time of the Israelite exodus from Egypt (when the Edomites refused the Israelites passage through their land). Be that as it may, much of the conflict also had to do with the fact that Edom was a constant threat to Judah's frontier and moreover blocked Judean access to the Gulf of Aqaba.

EDREI Place-name of unknown meaning. **1.** Royal city of Og, king of Bashan (Josh. 12:4). Invading Israel defeated Og there (Num. 21:33-35). It is also known from Egyptian records. Its location is modern Dera, halfway between Damascus and Amman. The clan of Machir in the tribe of Manasseh laid claim to the city (Josh. 13:31). **2.** Fortified city in the tribal territory of Naphtali (Josh. 19:37).

EGLAH Personal name meaning "heifer, young cow." David's wife and mother of his son Ithream (2 Sam. 3:5).

EGLAIM Place-name meaning "two cisterns." Place in Moab used by Isaiah to describe far limits of Moab's distress. It is modern Rugm el-Gilimeh, southeast of el-Kerak. It is distinct in location and Hebrew spelling from En-eglaim (Ezek. 47:10).

EGLATH-SHELISHIYAH Place-name meaning "the third heifer." Place apparently in Moab where Moab fugitives fled in Isaiah's description of disaster (Isa. 15:5).

EGLON 1. Moabite king who oppressed the Israelites (Judg. 3:12). Aided by the Amalekites and Ammonites, Eglon dominated Israel for 18 years. He was finally slain by the Benjaminite judge Ehud, who ran the obese monarch through with a short sword. **2.** Canaanite city whose king entered an alliance with four other Canaanite rulers against Gibeon (Josh. 10:3).

EGYPT Land in northeastern Africa, home to one of the earliest civilizations, and an important cultural and political influence on ancient Israel.

Egypt lies at the northeastern corner of Africa, separated from Palestine by the Sinai wilderness. In contrast to the modern nation, ancient Egypt was confined to the Nile River valley, a long, narrow ribbon of fertile land (the "black land") surrounded by uninhabitable desert (the "red land"). Egypt proper, from the first cataract of the Nile to the Mediterranean, is some 750 miles long.

From the Middle Kingdom (2040–1786 BC) onward, Egyptian history is contemporary with biblical events. Abraham's brief sojourn in Egypt (Gen. 12:10-20) during this period may be understood in light of a tomb painting at Beni Hasan showing visiting Asiatics in Egypt about 1900 BC.

Air view of the Nile River valley taken near Thebes. Notice the dramatic difference between the lands nourished by the Nile River and the deserts that surround the valley.

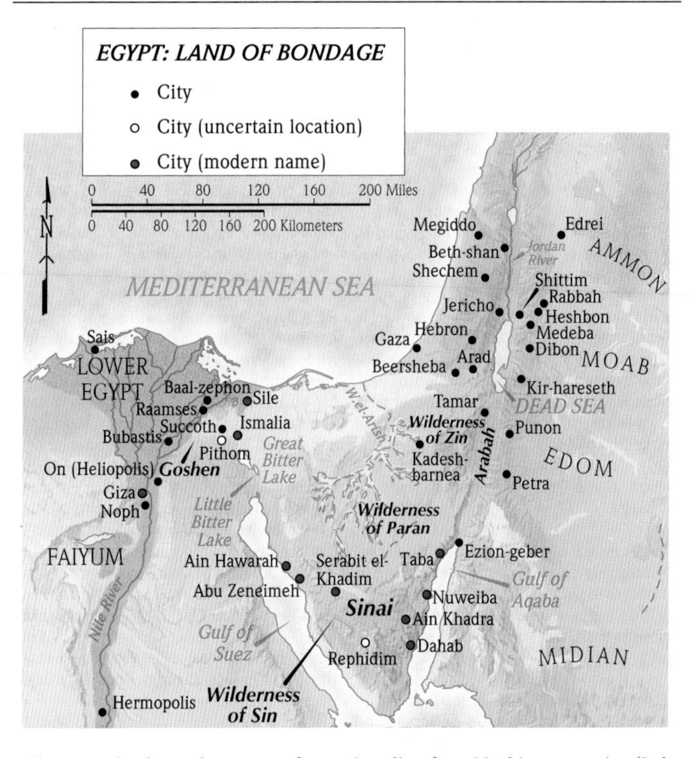

Six centuries later, documents from Akhetaton, the Amarna letters, represent diplomatic correspondence between local rulers in Egypt's sphere of influence and pharaoh's court. They especially illuminate the turbulent situation in Canaan which, depending upon one's preference for a fifteenth- or thirteenth-century date for the exodus, could be a century after or prior to the Israelite invasion.

EHI Personal name meaning "my brother." A son of Benjamin (Gen. 46:21), but he does not appear in the lists of Benjamin's sons in Num. 26:38-40; 1 Chron. 8:1-2.

EHUD Personal name meaning "unity, powerful." **1.** A left-handed Benjaminite whom the Lord raised up to deliver the Israelites from Moabite oppression (Judg. 3:15). By a ruse, he gained access to the Moabite King Eglon and assassinated him. **2.** Great grandson of Benjamin and clan leader in that tribe (1 Chron. 7:10). **3.** Clan leader in the tribe of Benjamin; the clan originally lived in Geba but were deported to Manahath (1 Chron. 8:6).

EKER Personal name meaning "root" or "offspring." Son of Jerahmeel and grandson of Hezron in the tribe of Judah (1 Chron. 2:27).

EKRON Northernmost of the five major Philistine cities known as the Pentapolis. Judges 1:18 reports that Judah captured Ekron along with other parts of the Philistine coast, but Ekron was certainly in Philistine hands at the time the ark was captured (1 Sam. 5:10). It was also the place to which the Philistines retreated after David slew Goliath (1 Sam. 17:52). Ahaziah, the son of King Ahab of Israel, called on the god of Ekron, Baal-zebub, when he was sick (2 Kgs. 1:2-16).

EL One of several words for God found in biblical Hebrew and the name of the high god among the Canaanites. The word is common to Hebrew, Aramaic, and Arabic, yet the origin and root from which the word was derived are obscure. "*El*" is a general term that expresses majesty or power. It occurs 238 times in the OT, most frequently in Psalms and Job. "El" is a synonym for the more frequent noun for God: Elohim. "El" refers to the God of Israel and in other passages to one of the pagan gods. "El" was frequently combined with nouns or adjectives to express the name for God with reference to particular attributes or characteristics of his being.

ELA Personal name of unknown meaning, perhaps related either to *'el*, Hebrew word for God, or to Elah, a slightly different Hebrew spelling not noted in KJV. Father of one of Solomon's district superintendents (1 Kgs. 4:18).

ELAH Personal name and place-name meaning "oak," "mighty tree," or "terebinth." **1.** Clan chief descended from Esau (Gen. 36:41) and thus an Edomite. **2.** A valley where Saul and his army set up battle lines against the Philistines (1 Sam. 17:2). The valley runs east and west just north of Socoh. There David defeated Goliath (1 Sam. 21:9). **3.** King of Israel (732–723 BC) killed while he was drunk during rebellion that Zimri, his general, led successfully (1 Kgs. 16:6-14). **4.** Father of Hoshea, who led a revolt and became king of Israel (732–723 BC) (2 Kgs. 15:30). **5.** Son of Caleb and father of Kenaz among clans of Judah (1 Chron. 4:15). **6.** Head of a clan from Benjamin who settled in Jerusalem after the exile (1 Chron. 9:8).

ELAM Personal name and place-name. **1.** Elam was a son of Shem, one of the sons of Noah (Gen. 10:22; 1 Chron. 1:17). He may have given his name to the region known as Elam. **2.** The region of Elam is on the western edge of ancient Persia, modern Iran. **3.** Clan head of the tribe of Benjamin living in Jerusalem (1 Chron. 8:24). **4.** Priestly gatekeeper under David (1 Chron. 26:3). **5.** Two clan leaders among the exiles who returned to Jerusalem with Zerubbabel in 537 BC (Ezra 2:7,31; cp. 8:7; 10:2,26). **6.** Postexilic leader who signed Nehemiah's covenant to obey God (Neh. 10:14). **7.** Priest who helped Nehemiah lead the people in celebrating the completion of the Jerusalem wall (Neh. 12:42).

ELASAH Personal name meaning "God has made." **1.** Son of Shaphan, the royal scribe. He took Jeremiah's message to the exiled community in Babylon while on a mission for King Zedekiah (Jer. 29:3). **2.** Descendant of Jerahmeel in tribe of Judah (1 Chron. 2:39-40); spelled "Eleasah" in English translations. **3.** Descendant of Saul and Jonathan in the tribe of Benjamin (1 Chron. 8:37; cp. 9:43); spelled "Eleasah" in English translations. **4.** Priest with a foreign wife who agreed to divorce her to avoid temptation of foreign gods in the time of Ezra (Ezra 10:22).

ELATH or **ELOTH** Place-name meaning "ram," "mighty trees," or "terebinth." Port city on northern end of Red Sea. Israel passed through it on way through Edom in wilderness (Deut. 2:8).

EL-BERITH Name of a god meaning "god of the covenant." A god worshipped in a temple at Shechem. It had a stronghold or citadel guarding it. There the citizens of Shechem sought protection when Abimelech attacked them, but Abimelech set the citadel on fire (Judg. 9:46-49). KJV translates "god Berith."

EL-BETHEL Place-name meaning "god of the house of El (god)." Either Bethel or place in or near Bethel, where Jacob built an altar to God as memorial to his previous visit to Bethel when he had seen a vision of God (Gen. 35:7; cp. 28:10-19). Apparently the name used for God was used as a place-name.

ELDAAH Personal name meaning "God has called," "God has sought," or "God of wisdom." Son of Midian and grandson of

Abraham, thus original ancestor of a clan of Midianites (Gen. 25:4).

ELDAD Personal name meaning "God loved." Along with Medad, he was one of 70 elders of Israel that God selected to help Moses, but the two did not meet at the tabernacle with the others. Still the Spirit came upon Eldad and Medad in the camp, and they prophesied. Joshua attempted to stop them, but Moses prayed that all God's people might have the Spirit (Num. 11:16-29).

ELDER Prominent member of both Jewish and early Christian communities. In the OT, "elder" usually translates the Hebrew word *zaqen* from a root that means "beard" or "chin." In the NT, the Greek word is *presbuteros*, which is transliterated in English as "presbyter" and from which the word "priest" was derived.

ELEAD Personal name meaning "God is a witness." Member of the tribe of Ephraim killed by men of Gath for stealing their cattle (1 Chron. 7:21).

ELEADAH Personal name meaning "God adorned himself." Modern translation spelling for KJV Eladah, a descendant of Ephraim (1 Chron. 7:20).

ELEALEH Moabite place-name meaning "God went up" or "high ground." Town the tribe of Reuben requested from Moses and strengthened (Num. 32:3,37). Isaiah announced judgment on the town (Isa. 15:4; 16:9; cp. Jer. 48:34).

ELEASAH Personal name meaning "God acted," or "God made," using same Hebrew spelling as Elasah. **1.** Member of the clan of Jerahmeel in the tribe of Judah (1 Chron. 2:39-40). **2.** Descendant of Saul and Jonathan in the tribe of Benjamin (1 Chron. 8:37; 9:43).

ELEAZAR Personal name meaning "God helps." **1.** The third son of Aaron (Exod. 6:23) and high priest of Israel (Num. 20:28). **2.** Son of Abinadab who was sanctified by the men of Kirjath-jearim to have responsibility for the ark of the Lord (1 Sam. 7:1). **3.** One of David's renowned warriors, the son of Dodo (2 Sam. 23:9). **4.** Son of Mahli who died having had no sons, only daughters (1 Chron. 23:21-22). **5.** Son of Phinehas who assisted in weighing out the silver and gold utensils in the house of God (Ezra 8:33). **6.** One of the sons of Parosh in a list of persons who had married foreign wives. He later put away his wife because of Ezra's reform banning foreign marriage (Ezra 10:25). **7.** Musician involved in the dedication of the wall of Jerusalem (Neh. 12:42). **8.** Son of Eliud and father of Matthan. He was an ancestor of Joseph the husband of Mary (Matt. 1:15).

ELECT LADY Recipient of John's second letter (2 John 1) sometimes understood to be an individual, but the phrase probably is a way of referring to a local church congregation.

ELECTION God's plan to bring salvation to his people and his world. The doctrine of election is at once one of the most central and one of the most misunderstood teachings of the Bible. At its most basic level, election refers to the purpose or plan of God whereby he has determined to effect his will. Thus election encompasses the entire range of divine activity from creation, God's decision to bring the world into being out of nothing, to the end time, the making anew of heaven and earth. The word "election" itself is derived from the Greek word *eklegomai*, which means, literally, "to choose something for oneself." This in turn corresponds to the Hebrew word *bachar*. The objects of divine selection are the elect ones, a concept found with increasing frequency in the later writings of the OT and at many places in the NT (Matt. 22:14; Luke 18:7; Col. 3:12; Rev. 17:14). The Bible also uses other words such as "choose," "predestinate," "foreordain," "determine," and "call" to indicate that God has entered into a special relationship with certain individuals and groups through whom he has decided to fulfill his purpose within the history of salvation.

EL-ELOHE-ISRAEL Divine name meaning "God, the God of Israel." Name that Jacob gave the altar he set up in the land he bought near Shechem (Gen. 33:20).

ELEMENTS, ELEMENTARY SPIRITS Greek term (*ta stoicheia*) used in a number of ways in ancient sources and in the NT.

First, "elements" could refer to the primary or elementary points of learning, especially for a religion or philosophy. Second, the term could refer to the four basic elements out of which all other materials were thought to have emerged: fire, air, water, and earth. Finally, the term came to be used in association with "elementary spirit-beings" who were thought by some to exercise a certain amount of control over the heavenly bodies—either for good or for evil.

ELEPHANTS While elephants are not specifically referred to in the Bible, ivory is mentioned in connection with King Solomon, that ivory was among the riches he imported (1 Kgs. 10:22). Ivory tusks were used in trading among nations in Ezek. 27:15, and in Rev. 18:12 ivory is again mentioned among products traded or bought. See *Ivory*.

ELHANAN Personal name meaning "God is gracious." The Bethlehemite who slew the brother of Goliath (2 Sam. 21:19).

ELI Personal name meaning "high." The priest at Shiloh who became the custodian of the child Samuel (1 Sam. 1:3). He was the father of Hophni and Phinehas. Eli's death was precipitated by the news of the death of his sons and the capture of the ark of God by the Philistines (1 Sam. 4:18).

ELI, ELI, LAMA SABACHTHANI This cry of Jesus on the cross, traditionally known as the "fourth word from the cross," means "My God, my God, why have you abandoned me?" (Matt. 27:46; Mark 15:34 CSB). It is a quotation from Ps. 22:1. The Markan form, *Eloi*, is closer to Aramaic than Matthew's more Hebraic *Eli*.

ELIAB Personal name meaning "God is father." **1.** Leader of the tribe of Zebulun under Moses (Num. 1:9). He brought the tribe's offering at the dedication of the altar (Num. 7:24). **2.** Member of the tribe of Reuben and father of Dathan and Abiram. **3.** First son of Jesse to pass by and be rejected when Samuel searched for king to replace Saul (1 Sam. 16:6). **4.** Levite in the line of Kohath and ancestor of Samuel (1 Chron. 6:27). The same person is apparently called Elihu in 1 Sam. 1:1 and Eliel in 1 Chron. 6:34. **5.** Levite appointed as a temple musician under David (1 Chron. 15:18,20; 16:5). **6.** Military leader from the tribe of Gad under David (1 Chron. 12:9).

ELIADA Personal name meaning "God has known." **1.** Son born to David after he established his rule in Jerusalem (2 Sam. 5:16). In 1 Chron. 14:7, he is listed as Beeliada ("Baal has known" or "the lord has known"). **2.** Father of Rezon, who established himself as king of Damascus after David conquered Zobah (1 Kgs. 11:23). **3.** Military commander of the tribe of Benjamin (2 Chron. 17:17) under King Jehoshaphat (873–848 BC).

ELIAHBA Personal name meaning "God hides in safety" or "my god is Chiba." A leading soldier in David's army (2 Sam. 23:32).

ELIAKIM Personal name meaning "God will raise up." **1.** Son of Hilkiah who was in charge of the household of King Hezekiah of Judah (2 Kgs. 18:18). **2.** Son of Josiah who was placed on the throne of Judah by Pharaoh Neco of Egypt (2 Kgs. 23:34). **3.** Priest who was involved in the dedication of the wall of Jerusalem (Neh. 12:41). **4.** Ancestor of Joseph, the husband of Mary (Matt. 1:13). **5.** Son of Melea, mentioned in Luke's genealogy of Jesus (Luke 3:30).

ELIAM Personal name meaning "God is an uncle or relative" or "God of the people." **1.** Father of Bathsheba (2 Sam. 11:3). The two parts of his name are reversed in 1 Chron. 3:5, becoming Ammiel. **2.** Leading warrior under David (2 Sam. 23:34).

ELIASAPH Personal name meaning "God has added." **1.** Leader of the tribe of Gad under Moses (Num. 1:14). **2.** Levite of the family of Gershon (Num. 3:24).

ELIASHIB Personal name meaning "God repays or leads back." **1.** Descendant of David in Judah after the return from exile in Babylon (1 Chron. 3:24). **2.** Leading priest under David (1 Chron. 24:12). **3.** High priest in time of

Nehemiah who led in rebuilding the Sheep Gate in the Jerusalem wall (Neh. 3:1). **4.** Priest in the time of Nehemiah who administered the temple storerooms and provided a place for Tobiah, Nehemiah's strong opponent (Neh. 13:4-9). This may be the Eliashib of Ezra 10:6. **5.** Levite and temple singer in Ezra's day who agreed to divorce his foreign wife to avoid tempting Israel to worship other gods (Ezra 10:24). **6.** Two Israelites who agreed to divorce their foreign wives under Ezra's leadership (Ezra 10:27,36).

ELIATHAH Personal name meaning "my God has come." A temple musician appointed under David to play and prophesy (1 Chron. 25:4).

ELIDAD Personal name meaning "God loved" or "My God is uncle or friend." The name in Hebrew is a variant spelling of Eldad. Representative of the tribe of Benjamin serving on committee that God chose to help Joshua and Eleazar divide the land of Canaan among the tribes (Num. 34:21).

ELIEHOENAI Personal name meaning "to Yaho [Yahweh] are my eyes" (cp. Ps. 123:2). **1.** One of the temple porters or gatekeepers under David (1 Chron. 26:3). **2.** One of the 12 clan heads who returned to Jerusalem from Babylon with Ezra (Ezra 8:4).

ELIEL Personal name meaning "my God is God" or "my God is El." **1.** Clan leader in the tribe of Manasseh east of the Jordan River (1 Chron. 5:23-24). **2.** Levite and ancestor of the singer Heman (1 Chron. 6:34). **3.** Member of the tribe of Benjamin (1 Chron. 8:20). **4.** Another Benjaminite (1 Chron. 8:22). **5.** Military leader under David (1 Chron. 11:46), not listed in 1 Sam. 23. **6.** Another military leader under David not listed in 1 Sam. 23 (1 Chron. 11:47). **7.** Warrior from the tribe of Gad who served under David in the wilderness (1 Chron. 12:11). **8.** Chief Levite in the time of David (1 Chron. 15:9,11). **9.** Overseer of temple offerings among the Levites (2 Chron. 31:13) under King Hezekiah (715–686 BC).

ELIENAI Abbreviated form of the Hebrew personal name Eliehoenai. The abbreviated form's literal meaning is "my God my eyes." A member of the tribe of Benjamin (1 Chron. 8:20).

ELIEZER Personal name meaning "God helps." **1.** Servant of Abram who would have been the patriarch's heir if Abram had remained childless (Gen. 15:2). **2.** Second son of Moses and Zipporah (Exod. 18:4). **3.** One of the sons of Becher the Benjaminite (1 Chron. 7:8). **4.** One of the priests who blew the trumpets when the ark of the covenant was brought to Jerusalem (1 Chron. 15:24). **5.** A ruler of the Reubenites (1 Chron. 27:16). **6.** Son of Dodavah, who prophesied against Jehoshaphat (2 Chron. 20:37). **7.** One of the leaders whom Ezra sent for (Ezra 8:16). **8.** Priest who put away his foreign wife (Ezra 10:18). **9.** Levite who put away his foreign wife (Ezra 10:23). **10.** Member of the clan of Harim who put away his foreign wife (Ezra 10:31). **11.** Son of Jorim mentioned in the genealogy of Jesus (Luke 3:29).

ELIHOREPH Personal name meaning "my God repays," or "my God is the giver of the autumn harvest," or borrowed from Egyptian, "Apis is my God." One of Solomon's two royal scribes with his brother Ahijah (1 Kgs. 4:3).

ELIHU Personal name meaning "he is God." **1.** Son of Barachel the Buzite who addressed Job after the latter's first three friends had ended their speeches (Job 32:2). **2.** Samuel's great grandfather (1 Sam. 1:1). **3.** Member of the tribe of Manasseh who defected to David (1 Chron. 12:20). **4.** Mighty military hero under David (1 Chron. 26:7). **5.** David's brother in charge of the tribe of Judah (1 Chron. 27:18).

ELIJAH Personal name meaning "my God is Yah." The prophet from the ninth century BC from Tishbe of Gilead in the northern kingdom has been called the grandest and the most romantic character that Israel ever produced (1 Kgs. 17:1–2 Kgs. 2:18). He was a complex man of the desert who counseled kings. His life is best understood when considered from four historical perspectives that at times are interrelated: his miracles, his struggle against baalism, his prophetic role, and his relationship to Messiah. Elijah appeared along with Moses on the Mount of Transfiguration with Jesus to discuss his "departure."

ELIKA Personal name meaning "my God has arisen" or "my God has vomited." One of David's military heroes from the village of Harod (2 Sam. 23:25).

ELIM Place-name meaning "trees." One of the encampments of the Israelites after the exodus from Egypt (Exod. 15:27). It was the first place where they found water.

ELIMELECH Personal name meaning "my God is king." Husband of Naomi, who led his family from Bethlehem to Moab to escape famine and then died in Moab. This

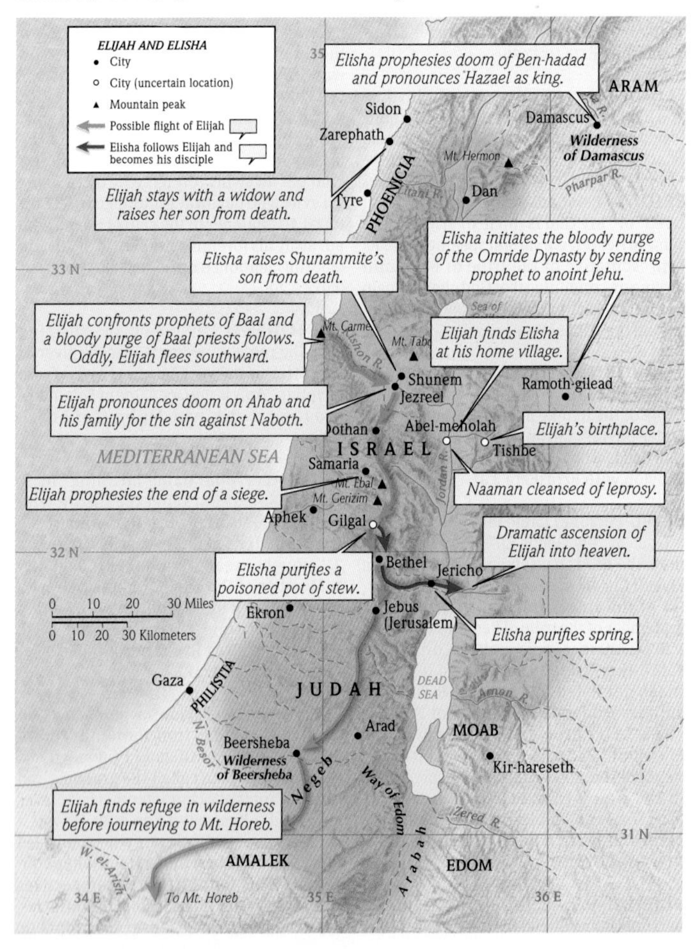

prepared the scene for the book of Ruth (Ruth 1:2-3; cp. 4:3).

ELIOENAI Personal name meaning "to Yo [Yahweh] are my eyes," a Hebrew spelling variant of Eliehoenai. **1.** Postexilic descendant of David, maintaining Israel's royal line (1 Chron. 3:23-24). **2.** Clan leader of the tribe of Simeon (1 Chron. 4:36). **3.** Grandson of Benjamin and thus great grandson of Jacob (1 Chron. 7:8). **4.** Priest who agreed under Ezra's leadership to divorce his foreign wife to protect the community from false worship (Ezra 10:22). **5.** Israelite who agreed to divorce his foreign wife (Ezra 10:27). **6.** Priest who led in the service of dedication and thanksgiving for the completion of repairs of the wall around Jerusalem (Neh. 12:41).

ELIPHAL Personal name meaning "God has judged." Military hero under David (1 Chron. 11:35). In 2 Sam. 23:34, the name appears as Eliphelet.

ELIPHAZ Personal name meaning "my god is gold." **1.** Son of Esau by his wife Adah, the daughter of Elon the Hittite (Gen. 36:4). **2.** One of three men who visited Job and engaged the sufferer in dialogue (Job 2:11). He is identified as a Temanite, meaning he was from Teman in Edom.

ELIPHELEH (KJV) or **ELIPHELEHU** Personal name meaning "God treated him with distinction." Levite and musician in temple under David (1 Chron. 15:18,21).

ELIPHELET Personal name meaning "God is deliverance." **1.** David's son born in Jerusalem (2 Sam. 5:16). He is apparently listed twice in both 1 Chron. 3:6,8 and 14:5,7, with an abbreviated Hebrew spelling in 14:5. **2.** Descendant of Saul and Jonathan in the tribe of Benjamin (1 Chron. 8:39). **3.** Clan leader who accompanied Ezra on his return from exile in Babylon (Ezra 8:13). **4.** Man who divorced his foreign wife under Ezra's leadership to avoid false worship among God's people (Ezra 10:33). **5.** Famous warrior under David (2 Sam. 23:34).

ELISABETH or **ELIZABETH** (modern American spelling) Personal name meaning "my God is good fortune" or "my God has sworn an oath." A woman descended from Aaron who was the wife of Zacharias the priest (Luke 1:5) and mother of John the Baptist.

ELISHA Personal name meaning "my God is salvation." A ninth-century BC Israelite prophet, son of Shaphat of Abel-meholah (1 Kgs. 19:16). Elisha was plowing one day when "Elijah walked by him and threw his mantle over him" (1 Kgs. 19:19 CSB). This action symbolically manifested God's plan to bestow the prophetic powers of Elijah upon Elisha. The chosen one understood the call of God for, "he left the oxen, ran to follow Elijah" (1 Kgs. 19:20). That Elisha felt the call of prophetic succession is again clear following Elijah's dramatic ascent into heaven. There Elisha "picked up the mantle of Elijah that had fallen off Elijah" (2 Kgs. 2:13).The beginning of Elisha's ministry should be dated to the last years of King Ahab's rule (1 Kgs. 19) or approximately 850 BC.

ELISHAH Place-name of unknown meaning. Elishah, or Alashiya as it appears in Hittite, Akkadian, and Ugaritic texts, is a name for all or part of the island of Cyprus, which exported copper and purple cloth.

ELISHAMA Personal name meaning "God heard." **1.** Leader of the tribe of Ephraim under Moses in the wilderness (Num. 1:10). **2.** David's son born after he captured and moved to Jerusalem (2 Sam. 5:16). He is apparently listed twice in 1 Chron. 3:6,8, though 1 Chron. 14:5 reads the first Elishama as Elishua, as in 2 Sam. 5:15. **3.** Royal scribe under King Jehoiakim (609–597 BC). Baruch's scroll of Jeremiah's preaching was stored in Elishama's room before it was taken to be read to the king (Jer. 36:12-21). **4.** Ancestor with royal bloodlines of Ishmael; the person who murdered Gedaliah and took over political control of Judah immediately after Babylon had destroyed Jerusalem (2 Kgs. 25:25). **5.** Descendant of the clan of Jerahmeel in the tribe of Judah (1 Chron. 2:41). **6.** Priest under King Jehoshaphat (873–848 BC). He taught the book of the law to the people of Judah at the king's request (2 Chron. 17:7-9).

ELISHAPHAT Personal name meaning "God had judged." Military captain who helped Jehoiada, the priest, overthrow Queen Athaliah and establish Joash (835–796 BC) as king of Judah (2 Chron. 23:1).

ELISHEBA Personal name meaning "God is good fortune." Wife of Aaron, the high priest (Exod. 6:23).

ELISHUA Personal name meaning "God is salvation." David's son born after he captured and moved to Jerusalem (2 Sam. 5:15).

ELIUD Personal name meaning "God is high and mighty." Great-great grandfather of Joseph, the earthly father of Jesus (Matt. 1:14-15).

ELIZAPHAN Personal name meaning "God has hidden or treasured up." **1.** Clan leader among the sons of Kohath among the Levites in the wilderness with Moses (Num. 3:30; cp. 1 Chron. 15:8; 2 Chron. 29:13). **2.** Representative of tribe of Zebulun on the council to help Joshua and Eleazar divide the land among the tribes (Num. 34:25).

ELIZUR Personal name meaning "God is a rock." Leader of the tribe of Reuben under Moses in the wilderness (Num. 1:5). He presented the tribe's offerings at the dedication of the altar (Num. 7:30-35).

ELKANAH Personal name meaning "God created." **1.** One of the sons of Korah, the priest (Exod. 6:24). **2.** Son of Jeroham. He became the father of Samuel (1 Sam. 1:1). **3.** Person named in a list of Levites (1 Chron. 6:23-26). **4.** Father of Asa who is mentioned in a list of Levites (1 Chron. 9:16). **5.** Benjaminite warrior who deserted Saul and joined David (1 Chron. 12:6). **6.** One of two gatekeepers for the ark of the covenant (1 Chron. 15:23). **7.** An official in the service of King Ahaz of Judah who was assassinated by Zichri the Ephraimite (2 Chron. 28:7).

ELKOSH Place-name of unknown meaning. Home of Nahum the prophet (Nah. 1:1). Although several traditions exist that identify various places as the site of Elkosh, its location remains unknown. That it was in Judea is fairly likely.

ELLASAR Babylonian place-name of unknown meaning. The capital city of King Arioch, who joined the eastern coalition against Sodom and Gomorrah, resulting in Abraham's involvement in war (Gen. 14:1).

ELMADAM or **ELMODAM** (KJV) Personal name of unknown meaning. An ancestor of Jesus Christ (Luke 3:28).

ELNAAM Personal name meaning "God is a delight." Father of military leaders under David (1 Chron. 11:46). He is not listed in 2 Sam. 23.

ELNATHAN Personal name meaning "God has given." **1.** Father of King Jehoiachin's mother (2 Kgs. 24:8). **2.** Possibly to be identified with 1, above. He was the member of King Jehoiakim's advisory staff who brought the prophet Uriah back to the king from Egypt for punishment (Jer. 26:22-23). He tried to prevent the king from burning Baruch's scroll of Jeremiah's preaching (Jer. 36:12-26). **3.** Three men of the same name plus a "Nathan" are listed in Ezra 8:16 as part of the delegation Ezra sent to search for Levites to return from Babylon to Jerusalem with him. Many Bible students feel that copying of the manuscripts has introduced extra names into the list.

ELOI Greek transliteration of Aramaic *'elohi*, "my God."

ELON Personal name and place-name meaning "great tree" or "tree of god" (cp. Gen. 12:6; Judg. 9:6,37). **1.** Son of Zebulun and grandson of Jacob (Gen. 46:14). A clan in Zebulun was thus named for him (Num. 26:26). **2.** Judge from the tribe of Zebulun (Judg. 12:11-12). **3.** City in tribal territory of Naphtali (Josh. 19:33), often transliterated into English as Allon. **4.** Site where Deborah, Rebekah's nurse, was buried, called "Allon-bachuth" or "the oak of weeping" (Gen. 35:8). **5.** A leader in the tribe of Simeon (1 Chron. 4:37).

A different Hebrew spelling underlies other examples of Elon in English translations. **1.** The Hittite father of Esau's wife Bashemath (Gen. 26:34). **2.** The Hittite father of Adah, Esau's wife (Gen. 36:2), Bashemath being listed as Ishmael's daughter (36:3). **3.** City in tribal territory of Dan (Josh. 19:43). It may be located at Khirbet Wadi Alin. It is probably the same place as Elon-beth-hanan (1 Kgs. 4:9), though some read Ajalon and Bethhanan or "Elon, and Beth-hanan" (REB).

ELPAAL Personal name meaning "God has made." A clan name in the tribe of Benjamin, mentioned twice in 1 Chron. 8 (vv. 11-12,18).

ELPARAN Place-name meaning "tree of Paran." The place where the eastern coalition of kings extended its victory over the Horites (Gen. 14:6). It is apparently a place in or near Elath.

ELPELET David's son born after he captured and moved to Jerusalem (1 Chron. 14:5). This is apparently an abbreviated spelling of Eliphelet.

ELTEKE or **ELTEKEH** Place-name meaning "place of meeting," "place of hearing," or "plea for rain." A city in Dan (Josh. 19:44) assigned to the Levites (21:23).

ELTEKON Place-name meaning "securing advice." Village in tribal territory of Judah in southern hill country (Josh. 15:59).

ELTOLAD Place-name meaning "plea for a child." Village in tribal territory of Judah (Josh. 15:30), given to tribe of Simeon (Josh. 19:4).

ELUL Sixth month of Hebrew year, name taken over from Akkadian. It included parts of August and September. See Neh. 6:15.

ELUZAI Personal name meaning "God is my strength." A member of King Saul's tribe of Benjamin who became a military leader for David, while he lived as a fugitive in Ziklag (1 Chron. 12:5).

ELYMAS Personal name possibly meaning "wise." A magician and false prophet also known as Barjesus (Acts 13:6-11). At Paphos on the island of Cyprus, Elymas tried to dissuade the deputy Sergius Paulus from listening to the words of Barnabas and Paul. He was denounced by Paul and stricken temporarily blind.

ELZABAD Personal name meaning "God made a gift." **1.** Soldier who fought for David while he was a fugitive in Ziklag (1 Chron. 12:12). **2.** Levite and grandson of Obed-edom, identified as a valiant man (1 Chron. 26:7). He was a porter or gatekeeper in the temple.

ELZAPHAN Personal name meaning "God has hidden or treasured up." An abbreviated form of Elizaphan. A son of Uzziel, Aaron's uncle (Exod. 6:22). He helped carry the dead bodies of Nadab and Abihu out of the wilderness camp after God punished them (Lev. 10:4-5).

EMBALMING Process of preserving bodies from decay. Embalming originated in Egypt and was seldom used by the Hebrews. The practice is rarely mentioned in the Bible, and the human remains unearthed in tombs in Israel generally show no signs of having been embalmed. In Gen. 50:2-3, it is recorded that Joseph ordered the embalming of Jacob's body and that "physicians" required 40 days to perform the process.

EMEK-KEZIZ Place-name meaning "the cut-off valley" or "the valley of gravel." It is listed as one of the cities assigned to the tribe of Benjamin (Josh. 18:21). Its location is not known.

EMERODS Archaic form of the word "hemorrhoids" used by the KJV for the disease(s) in Deut. 28:27 and 1 Sam. 5–6.

EMIM or **EMITES** (NIV) National name meaning "frightening ones." They lost a war to the eastern coalition of kings (Gen. 14:5) and are identified with a place in northern Moab, Shaveh Kiriathaim.

EMMAUS Place-name meaning "hot baths." A village that was the destination of two of Jesus's disciples on the day of his resurrection (Luke 24:13). As they traveled, they were joined by a person whom they later realized was the risen Christ. Emmaus was about 60 furlongs (approximately seven miles) from Jerusalem.

EMPEROR WORSHIP Practice of assigning the status of deity to current or deceased rulers. A specific NT example of emperor worship is the worship of the beast in the book of Revelation. Revelation 13 speaks of a beast that is given ruling authority. An image is made of the beast, and all are commanded to worship it (13:4,12,14-15; see also Dan. 8:4,8-12).

ENAIM or **ENAM** Place-name meaning "two eyes or springs." A village near Timnah, where Tamar seduced Judah (Gen. 38:14). It is probably the same as Enam in the tribal territory of Judah (Josh. 15:34).

ENAN Personal name meaning "eyes or springs." Father of Ahira, the leader of the tribe of Naphtali under Moses (Num. 1:15).

EN-DOR Place-name meaning "spring of Dor," that is, "spring of settlement." **1.** Home of witch who brought up Samuel from the grave (1 Sam. 28:7). Psalm 83:10 says Jabin died there (cp. Judg. 4–5). It is modern Khirbet Safsafe, three miles south of Mount Tabor. **2.** City the tribe of Manasseh claimed but could not conquer (Josh. 17:11; cp. Judg. 1:27).

EN-EGLAIM Place-name meaning "spring of the two calves." A spring near the Dead Sea where Ezekiel predicted a miracle, the salt waters being made fresh and becoming a paradise for fishing (Ezek. 47:10).

EN-GANNIM Place-name meaning "the spring of gardens." **1.** Town in the tribal territory of Judah located in the Shephelah (Josh. 15:34). It has been located at modern Beit Jemal, about two miles south of Beth-shemesh or at 'umm Giina, a mile southwest of Beth-shemesh. **2.** Town in tribal territory of Issachar designated as city for Levites (Josh. 19:21; 21:29).

EN-GEDI Place-name meaning "place of the young goat." A major oasis along the western side of the Dead Sea about 35 miles southeast of Jerusalem. The springs of En-gedi are full, and the vegetation is semitropical. Both biblical and extrabiblical sources describe En-gedi as a source of fine dates, aromatic plants used in perfumes, and medicinal plants (Song 1:14). When David was fleeing from Saul, he hid in the area of En-gedi (1 Sam. 23:29). Saul was in a cave near En-gedi when David cut off a piece of Saul's robe but spared his life (1 Sam. 24).

This natural waterfall, rare in Israel, is located at En-gedi on the west side of the Dead Sea.

ENGINE Catapult or battering ram.

ENGRAVE To impress deeply, to carve. Many materials were engraved including clay writing tablets (Isa. 8:1), metal, precious gems, stone (Zech. 3:9), and wood. Engraving was frequently done with an iron pen, a stylus, sometimes with a diamond point (Job 19:24; Jer. 17:1).

EN-HADDAH City in tribal lot of Issachar (Josh. 19:21). It is apparently el-Hadetheh about six miles east of Mount Tabor.

EN-HAKKORE Place-name meaning "spring of the partridge" or "spring of the caller." Place where God gave Samson water from the jawbone he had used to kill a thousand Philistines (Judg. 15:18-19). It is near Beth-shemesh.

EN-HAZOR Place-name meaning "spring of the enclosed village." A fortified city in the tribal territory of Naphtali (Josh. 19:37).

EN-MISHPAT Place-name meaning "spring of judgment." Another name for Kadesh, where the eastern coalition of kings defeated the Amalekites and Amorites.

ENOCH Personal name meaning "dedicated." **1.** The son of Jared who was taken up to God without dying (Gen. 5:18). He became the father of Methuselah. **2.** Son of Cain for whom Cain built a city and named it (Gen. 4:17-18).

ENON CITY TEV translation of Hazar-enon/enan (Ezek. 47:17).

ENOS or **ENOSH** Personal name meaning "humanity" or "a man." Son of Seth and therefore the grandson of Adam (Gen. 4:26). The period following his birth is identified as the time when people began to worship Yahweh. See Gen. 5:6-11.

EN-RIMMON Place-name meaning "spring of the pomegranate." A town in Judah (Neh. 11:29) where people lived in Nehemiah's day (ca. 445 BC).

EN-ROGEL Place-name meaning "spring of the fuller" or "spring of the foot." A border town between the tribal territory of Judah (Josh. 15:7) and that of Benjamin (Josh. 18:16).

EN-SHEMESH Place-name meaning "spring of the sun." Town on border between tribal territories of Judah (Josh. 15:7) and Benjamin (Josh. 18:17).

EN-TAPPUAH Place-name meaning "spring of apple." A spring near the town of Tappuah that marked the border of the tribe of Manasseh and Ephraim (Josh. 17:7).

ENVY Painful or resentful awareness of another's advantage joined with the desire to possess the same advantage. The advantage may concern material goods (Gen. 26:14) or social status (30:1).

EPAENETUS Personal name meaning "praise." The first Christian convert in Achaia and thus a friend with special meaning for Paul (Rom. 16:5).

EPAPHRAS Personal name meaning "lovely." A Christian preacher from whom Paul learned of the situation of the church in Colossae (Col. 1:7). He was a native of Colossae whose ministry especially involved Colossae, Laodicea, and Hierapolis. Later he was a companion of Paul during the latter's imprisonment.

EPAPHRODITUS Personal name meaning "favored by Aphrodite or Venus." A friend and fellow worker of Paul the apostle (Phil. 2:25). He had delivered to Paul a gift from the church at Philippi while the apostle was in prison. While he was with Paul, Epaphroditus became seriously ill; after his recovery, Paul sent him back to Philippi, urging the church there to receive him "with great joy" (Phil. 2:29 CSB).

EPHAH Personal name meaning "darkness." **1.** Son of Midian and grandson of Abraham (Gen. 25:4). **2.** Concubine of Caleb and mother of his children (1 Chron. 2:46). **3.** Son of Jahdai and apparently a descendant of Caleb (1 Chron. 2:47).

EPHAI Personal name meaning "bird." Father of men who joined Ishmael in revolt against and murder of Gedaliah, the governor of Judah after Babylon captured and destroyed Jerusalem in 586 BC (Jer. 40:8). Ephai was from Netophah near Bethlehem.

EPHER Personal name meaning "young deer." **1.** Son of Midian, grandson of Abraham through his wife Keturah, and clan father among the Midianites (Gen. 25:4). **2.** Descendant of Caleb in the tribe of Judah (1 Chron. 4:17). **3.** Original ancestor of clan in tribe of Manasseh (1 Chron. 5:24).

EPHES-DAMMIM Place-name meaning "end of bloodshed." Town between Shocoh and Azekah where Philistines gathered to fight Saul (1 Sam. 17:1) preceding David's killing of Goliath.

EPHESIANS, LETTER TO THE While it is not the longest of the Pauline Epistles, Ephesians is the one that best sets out the basic concepts of the Christian faith.

A traditional view is that Ephesians is one of four letters Paul wrote during his imprisonment in Rome, AD 61–62. The other three letters are Colossians, Philemon, and Philippians.

Paul's motive for writing this letter was the challenge that Christianity faced in confrontation with other religions and philosophies of the day. Paul was convinced that the religion he proclaimed was the only way of redemption from sin and of sonship to God.

Ephesians, like other letters of Paul, begins with theological affirmation and transitions to ethical implications of that theology. Paul opens the letter by praising God for his grace and his plan of redemption that is seen in Jesus's death, resurrection, and ascension to the Father's right hand. God's Spirit takes this word of truth about what God has done in Christ and applies it to individuals. The Spirit takes up residence in each believer and becomes the down payment of final and complete redemption. This redemption is not just an individual matter. God incorporates believers into the church, the body of Christ, a holy sanctuary in the Lord. It also brings reconciliation between Jews and Gentiles.

What God has done has consequences for personal life, calling for a complete transformation from the lifestyles of unbelievers. Without faith, the individual is devoted to selfish lust and earthly dissipation. The believer becomes like God in holiness, purity, and righteousness. A central element of this is human speech, speaking the truth and saying that which helps build up others. Anger and malice must turn to love, compassion, and forgiveness. Walking in the light means pleasing God and showing the sinfulness of evil deeds. This is the wise path avoiding spirits that make one drunk but turning to the one Spirit who leads to praise and worship. This changes one's role at home. Submission to one another becomes the key, a submission motivated by loyalty to Christ and love to the marital partner. That love follows the example of Christ's love for his church. Parents expect honor from children while training children in the Lord's way of love. Similarly, masters and servants respect and help one another.

To complete his letter, Paul called his readers to put on God's armor to avoid Satan's temptations. This will lead to a life of prayer for self and for other servants of God. This will lead to concern for and encouragement from other Christians. As usual, Paul concluded his letter with a benediction, praying for peace, love, faith, and grace for his beloved readers.

EPHESUS One of the largest and most impressive cities in the ancient world, a political, religious, and commercial center in Asia Minor. Associated with the ministries of Paul, Timothy, and the apostle John, the city played a significant role in the spread of early Christianity. Ephesus and its inhabitants are mentioned more than 20 times in the NT.

Location The ancient city of Ephesus, located in western Asia Minor at the mouth of the Cayster River, was an important seaport. Situated between the Maeander River to the south and the Hermus River to the north, Ephesus had excellent access to both river valleys that allowed it to flourish as a commercial center. Due to the accumulation of silt deposited by the river, the present site of the city is approximately five to six miles inland.

EPHLAL Personal name meaning "notched" or "cracked." Descendant of Jerahmeel in the tribe of Judah (1 Chron. 2:37).

EPHOD Priestly garment connected with seeking a word from God and used in a wrong way as an idol. The exact meaning and derivation of the term "ephod" are not clear. In early OT history, there are references to the ephod as a rather simple, linen garment, possibly a short skirt, apron, or loincloth. It is identified as a priestly garment (1 Sam.

The Great Theater at Ephesus as viewed from the Harbor Road

14:3; 22:18). It was worn by Samuel (1 Sam. 2:18) and by David when he danced before God on the occasion of the transfer of the ark of the covenant to David's capital city of Jerusalem (2 Sam. 6:14).

EPHPHATHA Aramaic expression that Jesus spoke when he healed a person who was deaf and had a speech impediment. It is translated "be opened." When Jesus had said it, the individual was healed (Mark 7:34).

EPHRAIM Personal and tribal name meaning "two fruit land" or "two pasture lands." The younger son of Joseph by the Egyptian Asenath, daughter of the priest of On (Gen. 41:52). Ephraim played an important role in Israelite history. He was the progenitor of the tribe of Ephraim, which occupied a region to the northwest of the Dead Sea.

Joshua was an Ephraimite (Josh. 19:50). Samuel was an Ephraimite (1 Sam. 1:1). Jeroboam I was an Ephraimite (1 Kgs. 12:25).

EPHRAIM, FOREST OF Densely wooded site of the battle between the forces of King David and the rebel army of Absalom (2 Sam. 18:6,8).

EPHRAIM GATE Entrance to Jerusalem located 400 cubits (ca. 200 yards) from the Corner Gate (2 Kgs. 14:13). The section of wall between these two gates was destroyed by King Jehoash of Israel in the eighth century BC. In Nehemiah's time the city square at the Ephraim Gate was one of the sites where booths for the celebration of the Feast of Tabernacles were set up (Neh. 8:16).

EPHRAIM, MOUNT KJV designation for the hill country belonging to the tribe of Ephraim.

EPHRAIN KJV reading of a city in 2 Chron. 13:19 following the earliest Hebrew scribal note. Hebrew text reads "Ephron," as do most modern translations.

EPHRATAH or **EPHRATH** or **EPHRATHAH** Place and personal name meaning "fruitful." **1.** Town near which Jacob buried his wife Rachel (Gen. 35:16-19; usually translated in English as Ephrath). Genesis 35:16 seems to indicate that Ephrath(ah) must have been near Bethel. This is supported by 1 Sam. 10:2; Jer. 31:15, which place Rachel's tomb near Ramah on the border between the tribal territories of Ephraim and Benjamin. Genesis 35:19, however, identifies Ephrath(ah) with Bethlehem (cp. Gen. 48:7). **2.** Caleb's wife (1 Chron. 2:50; spelled Ephrath in 2:19; cp. 4:4).

EPHRON Personal name and place-name meaning "dusty." **1.** Hittite who sold the cave of Machpelah to Abraham (Gen. 23:8-20). **2.** Mountain marking the tribal border of Judah with Benjamin (Josh. 15:9). It is located northwest of Jerusalem near Mozah at el-Qastel. **3.** City that King Abijah of Judah (913–910 BC) took from King Jeroboam of Israel (926–909 BC), according to spelling of Hebrew text (2 Chron. 13:19).

EPICUREANISM School of philosophy that emerged in Athens about 300 BC. The school of thought was founded by Epicurus who was born in 341 BC on the Greek island of Samos. Epicurus founded his school (The Garden) in Athens. Paul met Epicureans as he preached about Jesus and the resurrection in Athens (Acts 17:18). Epicurean philosophy centered on the search for happiness. Pleasure is the beginning and fulfillment of a happy life. To Epicurus, happiness could be achieved only through tranquility and a life of contemplation. The goal of Epicureanism was to acquire a trouble-free state of mind, to avoid the pains of the body, and especially mental anguish.

EPILEPSY Disorder marked by erratic electrical discharges of the central nervous system resulting in convulsions. In ancient times, epilepsy was thought to be triggered by the moon. The term in Matt. 4:24, translated as "epileptics" by most modern translations, is literally "moonstruck." The KJV term "lunatick" from the Latin *luna* (moon) assumes the same cause for the disorder. Many interpreters understand the symptoms of the boy in Mark 9:17-29 (inability to speak, salivation, grinding teeth, rigid body, convulsions) as expressions of epilepsy.

EPIPHANY Term comes from a Greek word which means "appearance" or "manifestation." In Western Christianity, the festival of Epiphany, observed on January 6, celebrates the manifestation of Christ to the Gentiles, the coming of the magi to see the child Jesus (Matt. 2:1-12). The Epiphany season also celebrates the baptism of Jesus, a recognition of his manifestation to humanity as the Son of God (Mark 1:9-11).

ER Personal name meaning "protector" or "watchful." **1.** Oldest son of Judah and grandson of Jacob (Gen. 38:3). He married Tamar but was so wicked that God killed him (Gen. 38:6-7). **2.** Grandson of Judah (1 Chron. 4:21).

ERAN Personal name meaning "of the city" or "watchful." Some of the earliest translations and the Samaritan Pentateuch read "Eden" rather than Eran. Eran was grandson of Ephraim and a clan leader in the tribe of Ephraim (Num. 26:36).

ERASTUS Personal name meaning "beloved." **1.** Disciple Paul sent with Timothy from Ephesus to Macedonia to strengthen the churches during his third missionary journey (Acts 19:22). **2.** City financial officer of Corinth who joined Paul in greeting the church at Rome (Rom. 16:23). **3.** Disciple who remained at Corinth and was not with Paul when he wrote Timothy (2 Tim. 4:20). He may have been identical with either of the other men named Erastus.

ERECH Hebrew transliteration of Akkadian place-name: Uruk, one of the oldest Sumerian cities founded before 3100 BC. The Genesis Table of Nations reports that Nimrod, the mighty hunter, included Erech in his kingdom (Gen. 10:10).

ERI Personal name meaning "of the city of" or "watchful." A son of Gad and grandson of Jacob (Gen. 46:16). Original ancestor of the clan of Erites (Num. 26:16).

ESAIAS KJV transliteration of Greek spelling of Isaiah in the NT.

ESARHADDON Assyrian royal name meaning "Ashur (the god) has given a brother." King of Assyria (681–669 BC).

ESAU Personal name whose meaning is not known. Son of Isaac and Rebekah; elder twin brother of Jacob (Gen. 25:24-26; 27:1,32,42; 1 Chron. 1:34); father of the Edomite nation (Gen. 26:34; 28:9; 32:3; Deut. 2:4-29; Mal. 1:2-3).

ESCHATOLOGY Derived from the combination of the Greek *eschatos*, meaning "last," and *logos*, meaning "word" or "significance." Refers to the biblical doctrine of last things. The doctrine of last things normally focuses on a discussion of the return of Christ at the end of the age, the coming judgments, various expressions of the kingdom of heaven and the kingdom of God, the nature of the glorified body, and the prospects for eternal destiny.

ESDRAELON Greek translation of the word "Jezreel," indicating the low-lying area that separates the mountains of Galilee from the mountains of Samaria.

Esdraelon, also called the Great Plain of Esdraelon or the Plain of Jezreel, is the area assigned to Zebulun and Issachar (Josh. 19:10-23). It extends from the Mediterranean Sea to the Jordan River at Beth-shean. Included are the Valley or Plain of Megiddo in the east and the valley of Jezreel in the west. Esdraelon is mentioned in the NT as Armageddon or har-Megiddon, meaning hill or city of Megiddo. Revelation 16:16 echoes the OT portrayal of Esdraelon as a place of war and tragedy. The final battle of the Lord will be waged there (Rev. 16:14-16; 19:19).

ESEK Place-name meaning "strife." A well that Isaac's servants dug in the valley near Gerar to find water for their herds (Gen. 26:18-24).

ESHAN or **ESHEAN** (KJV) Place-name meaning "I lean on." Town in the hill country assigned to the tribe of Judah (Josh. 15:52).

ESH-BAAL Personal name meaning "man of Baal." Son of Saul, the first king of Israel (1 Chron. 8:33; 9:39). In 2 Sam. 2:8, the name is Ish-bosheth, "man of shame," apparently an intentional corruption in the Hebrew tradition to avoid the name of the Canaanite god and to characterize the person with such a name.

ESHBAN Personal name of unknown meaning. An Edomite listed as a descendant of Seir the Horite (Gen. 36:26).

ESHCOL Place-name meaning "valley of grapes" or "cluster." **1.** A valley in Canaan that was explored by the 12 Israelites sent to spy out the land (Num. 13:23). From the valley of Eshcol, they brought back an exceptionally large cluster of grapes. **2.** Brother of Mamre and Aner (Gen. 14:13). He and his brothers were Amorites who were allies of Abram in the defeat of Chedorlaomer.

ESHEK Personal name meaning "oppression" or "strong." A member of the tribe of Benjamin descended from King Saul (1 Chron. 8:39).

The Great Plain of Esdraelon viewed from near Megiddo

ESHTAOL Place-name meaning "asking (for an oracle)." Town in lowlands of Shephelah of Judah allotted to the tribe of Judah (Josh. 15:33) but also to the tribe of Dan (Josh. 19:41). Near there, God's Spirit stirred Samson of the tribe of Dan (Judg. 13:25).

ESHTEMOA Place-name and personal name meaning "being heard." The name may indicate an ancient tradition of going to Eshtemoa to obtain an oracle or word of God from a prophet or priest. **1.** City in tribal allotment of Judah (Josh. 15:50, with variant Hebrew spelling). God set it aside for the Levites (Josh. 21:14). While living in exile in Ziklag, David sent some of the plunder from his victories to Eshtemoa (1 Sam. 30:28). **2.** Member of the clan of Caleb in the tribe of Judah (1 Chron. 4:17), probably listed as the clan father of those who settled in Eshtemoa.

ESHTEMOH Variant Hebrew spelling of Eshtemoa (Josh. 15:50).

ESHTON Personal name of uncertain meaning. Member of the tribe of Judah (1 Chron. 4:11-12).

ESLI Personal name of unknown meaning. Ancestor of Jesus (Luke 3:25), spelled Hesli in NASB. Some scholars equate him with Elioenai (1 Chron. 3:23).

ESSENES Members of a Jewish sect that existed in Palestine during the time of Christ. They are not mentioned in the NT. They were ascetics who practiced community of goods, generally shunned marriage, refrained from attending worship in the temple, and attached great importance to the study of the Scriptures. Many scholars associate the Dead Sea Scrolls discovered in 1947 with an Essene community.

The ruins of ancient Qumran probably inhabited by Essenes from 130 BC until AD 70

ESTHER Persian personal name meaning "a star." Since this is not the biblical Esther's given name at birth—Hadassah, meaning "myrtle" (Esth. 2:7)—some have suggested that the name Esther is linked to the planet Venus and the goddess Ishtar. Orphaned in childhood, she was raised by her cousin Mordecai among the Jews living in Persia. She became queen of King Ahasuerus, usually identified with Xerxes I (486–465/64 BC). Through divine providence, she interceded for and prevented the extermination of the Jewish population.

ESTHER, BOOK OF Placed by the Jews in the third section of the Hebrew Bible known as the Writings. While some debate over the book's canonical inclusion occurred because it never uses the name of God, the activity of the Lord was so obvious in the book that this objection was overruled.

The book of Esther provides the historical background for the feast of Purim. In plotting against the Jews, Haman, the prime minister of Persia under King Ahasuerus, cast lots (*purim* from Assyrian *puru*) to determine their fate (9:24-28). The story of God's preservation of his people through the courageous action of Ahasuerus's queen, Esther, is a reminder of his covenant with Abraham, that God will not only bless those who bless his people, but he will also curse those who curse them. The preservation of the Jews kept alive messianic expectations in the intertestamental period.

ETAM Place-name meaning "place of birds of prey." **1.** Rocky crag where Samson camped during his battles with the Philistines (Judg. 15:8-13), conferring there with men of Judah who wanted to bind him and hand him over to the Philistines. **2.** Town in territorial allotment of the tribe of Judah according to earliest Greek translation of the OT but omitted from present Hebrew manuscripts

(Josh. 15:59 REB). **3.** Member of the tribe of Judah and apparently clan father of town of same name associated with Jezreel (1 Chron. 4:3). **4.** Village assigned to Simeon (1 Chron. 4:32), though it is not listed in Simeon's tribal territory in Josh. 19:7. It may be modern Aitun, about 11 miles southwest of Hebron.

ETERNAL LIFE Life at its best, having infinite duration characterized by abiding fellowship with God. This important term in the NT is emphasized in the Gospel of John but also appears in the other Gospels and in Paul's writings. Eternal life in the NT eliminates the boundary line of death. Death is still a foe, but the one who has eternal life already experiences the kind of existence that will never end.

Yet in this expression, the emphasis is on the quality of life rather than on the unending duration of life. Probably some aspects of both quality and duration appear in every context, but some refer primarily to quality of life and others point to unending life or a life to be entered into in the future. In terms of quality, life is (1) life imparted by God; (2) transformation and renewal of life; (3) life fully opened to God and centered in him; (4) a constant overcoming of sin and moral evil; and (5) the complete removal of moral evil from the person and from the environment of that person.

ETHAM Place-name meaning "fort." The second station in Israel's wilderness wandering out of Egypt (Exod. 13:20; Num. 33:6-8). The nearby wilderness was called the wilderness of Etham (Num. 33:8).

ETHAN Personal name meaning "long-lived." **1.** Man so famous for his wisdom that Solomon's outstanding wisdom could be described as exceeding Ethan's (1 Kgs. 4:31). **2.** Levite and temple singer (1 Chron. 6:42,44; 15:17) and instrumentalist (1 Chron. 15:19). He is associated with Pss. 88 and 89 in their titles.

ETHANIM Canaanite name of the seventh month taken over by Israel (1 Kgs. 8:2), who also called the month Tishri. This was the first month of the civil year. Ethanim means "always flowing with water" and refers to the flooding streams fed by heavy fall rains.

ETH-BAAL Personal name meaning "with him is Baal." King of Sidon; father of Jezebel (1 Kgs. 16:31), who married Jeroboam II, king of Israel (793–753 BC). Through Jezebel's influence Baal worship pervaded the northern kingdom.

ETHER Place-name meaning "smoke of incense." **1.** Town in tribal territory of Judah (Josh. 15:42). **2.** Town occupied by the tribe of Simeon (Josh. 19:7).

ETHICS, CHRISTIAN Study of good behavior, motivation, and attitude in light of Jesus Christ and biblical revelation.

ETHIOPIA Region of Nubia just south of Egypt, from the first cataract of the Nile into the Sudan. Confusion has arisen between the names Ethiopia and Cush. The OT Hebrew (and Egyptian) name for the region was Cush. In some passages such as Gen. 2:13 and Isa. 11:11, various English versions alternate between Cush and Ethiopia. See *Cush*.

The biblical Ethiopia should not be confused with the modern nation of the same name somewhat farther to the southeast. In biblical times, Ethiopia was equivalent to Nubia, the region beyond the first cataract of the Nile south, or upstream, of Egypt.

The Ethiopian eunuch to whom Philip explained the gospel was a minister of "Candace, queen of the Ethiopians" (Acts 8:27 CSB). Candace should be understood as a title rather than a personal name.

ETHKAZIN Place-name perhaps meaning "time of the chieftain." Town in the tribal territory of Zebulun (Josh. 19:13).

ETHNAN Personal name meaning "gift." Member of the tribe of Judah (1 Chron. 4:7).

ETHNI Personal name meaning "I will give." Levite, ancestor of Asaph (1 Chron. 6:41).

EUBULUS Personal name meaning "good counsel." Companion of Paul who sent greetings to Timothy (2 Tim. 4:21).

EUNICE Personal name meaning "victorious." The mother of Timothy (2 Tim. 1:5). Paul commended both her and her mother, Lois, for their faith. She was a Jewish woman whose husband was a Gentile. No details are known about her conversion to Christianity.

EUNUCH A male deprived of the testes or external genitals. Such men were excluded from serving as priests (Lev. 21:20) and from membership in the congregation of Israel (Deut. 23:1). Part of Isaiah's vision of the messianic era was a picture of the eunuch no longer complaining of being "a dry tree," one without hope of descendants, because God would reward the faithful eunuch with a lasting monument and name in the temple that would be far better than sons or daughters (Isa. 56:45).

A eunuch for the sake "of the kingdom of heaven" (Matt. 19:12 CSB) is likely a metaphor for one choosing single life in order to be more useful in kingdom work (cp. 1 Cor. 7:32-34).

EUODIA or **EUODIAS** Female leader in the church at Philippi whose disagreement with Syntyche concerned Paul (Phil. 4:2-3). The name Euodia means either prosperous journey or pleasant fragrance.

EUPHRATES AND TIGRIS RIVERS Two of the greatest rivers of western Asia. They originate in the mountains of Armenia and unite about 90 miles from the Persian Gulf to form what is now called the Shatt-al-Arab that flows into the gulf. In ancient times, the Tigris flowed through its own mouth into the gulf. The Euphrates and Tigris were included among the four rivers of Paradise (Gen. 2:14).

EURAQUILO NASB transliteration of Greek name for northeast wind in Acts 27:14.

EUROCLYDON Noun meaning "southeast wind raising mighty waves." KJV reading of traditional Greek text in Acts 27:14, but most modern translations follow other Greek texts that read *Eurakulon*, the northeast wind.

EUTYCHUS Personal name meaning "good fortune." A young man who listened to Paul the apostle preach in Troas (Acts 20:9-10). Overcome with sleep, Eutychus fell from a third floor windowsill and was picked up dead. Paul, however, embraced the youth, and Eutychus was restored to life.

EVANGELISM Active calling of people to respond to the message of grace and commit oneself to God in Jesus Christ.

EVE Personal name meaning "life." The first woman created and thus original ancestor of all people (Gen. 3:20; cp. 4:1-2,25). She also faced the serpent's temptation first (Gen. 3:1;

Euphrates River

2 Cor. 11:3; 1 Tim. 2:13-14). Her fall illustrates the ease with which all persons fall into sin (2 Cor. 11:3).

EVERLASTING PUNISHMENT God's unending punishment of sinners beyond this life is known as eternal punishment. The Bible teaches that unrepentant, unforgiven sinners will be punished (Dan. 12:2; Matt. 10:15; John 5:28-29; Rom. 5:12-21).

Two common reasons are typically offered as grounds for denying everlasting punishment. One of these is that everlasting punishment denies God's eternal love. For God to allow his creatures to exist in eternal torment is a contradiction of his loving nature. Another argument against everlasting punishment is that endless torment contradicts God's sovereignty because he allows unbelievers to exist for eternity. As significant as these points are, they both seem to lack any support from the Bible.

God's intention for humanity is to live eternally in bliss and fellowship with God. Those who pervert this intention will and must experience the eternal consequences of that act.

EVI Personal name of uncertain meaning, perhaps "desire." King of Midian killed in battle by Israelites during wilderness wanderings (Num. 31:8). He apparently ruled as a vassal of Sihon (Josh. 13:21).

EVIL-MERODACH Babylonian royal name meaning "worshiper of Marduk." Babylonian king (562–560 BC) who treated Jehoiachin, king of Judah, with kindness (2 Kgs. 25:27). The Babylonian form of the name is Amel-marduk. He was the son of Nebuchadnezzar.

EXACTOR KJV term for a taskmaster or a tax collector used only at Isa. 60:17 CSB: overseer.

EXCOMMUNICATION Practice of temporarily or permanently excluding someone from the church as punishment for sin or apostasy.

EXECRATION Act of cursing; an object of cursing. The term appears in the KJV twice (Jer. 42:18; 44:12), both times in reference to the fate of the remnant who disobeyed God's word and sought safety in Egypt.

EXHORTATION Argument (Acts 2:40) or advice intended to incite hearers to action.

EXILE Events in which the northern tribes of Israel were taken into captivity by the Assyrians (beginning about 734 BC) and the southern tribes of Judah were taken into captivity by the Babylonians (beginning in 598 BC).

The prophets Hosea and Amos had prophesied the fall of Israel. These two prophets proclaimed that Israel's fall was due to moral and spiritual degeneration rather than to the superior military might of the Assyrian nation. Assyria was only the "rod of mine anger"' (Isa. 10:5 CSB).

More than a hundred years before the Babylon exile, Isaiah, the prophet, had predicted Judah's fall (Isa. 6:11-12; 8:14; 10:11). In addition, the prophets Micah, Zephaniah, Jeremiah, Habakkuk, and Ezekiel agreed that Judah would fall.

EXODUS Israel's escape from slavery in Egypt and journey toward the promised land under Moses. Historically and theologically this is the most important event in the OT. More than a hundred times in all parts of the OT except the Wisdom literature, Yahweh is proclaimed as "the one who brought you up from the land of Egypt, out of the house of bondage."

The Bible stresses that the exodus was the work of God. God brought the plagues on Egypt (Exod. 7:1-5). The miracle at the sea was never treated merely as a natural event or as Israel's victory alone. In the earliest recorded response to the event, Miriam sang, "Sing to the LORD, for he is highly exalted; he has thrown the horse and its rider into the sea" (Exod. 15:21 CSB).

The Date of the Exodus The Bible does not give an incontrovertible date for the exodus. The most commonly accepted early date (among conservatives) is 1446 BC. This is based on the following passage of 1 Kgs. 6:1, "Solomon began to build the temple for the Lord in the four hundred eightieth year after the Israelites came out of the land of Egypt, in the fourth year of his reign over Israel" (CSB).

Some scholars cite a combination of biblical and archaeological evidence to place the Exodus about two hundred years later.

The Pharaoh of the Exodus The pharaoh of the exodus is tied directly to the interpretation of the data for the dating of the exodus/conquest. If one takes the late exodus date (ca. 1270 BC), the pharaoh of the oppression would have been Seti I, and the pharaoh of the exodus would have been Ramesses II (1304–1237 BC). However, taking the early exodus date (ca. 1446 BC), the pharaoh of the oppression was Thutmose III, and the pharaoh of the exodus was Amenhotep II (1450–1425 BC).

If the statistics are correct that males over the age of twenty make up approximately 25 percent of the total population, then the Israelites numbered well over 2 million people at both the beginning and the end of the wilderness wanderings.

The exodus was the work of God. It was a historical event involving a superpower nation and an oppressed people. God acted redemptively in power, freedom, and love. When the kingdom of God did not come, the later prophets began to look for a second exodus. That expectation was fulfilled spiritually in Christ's redemptive act.

EXODUS, BOOK OF Central book of the OT, reporting God's basic saving act for Israel in the exodus from Egypt and his making of his covenant with the nation destined to be his kingdom of priests.

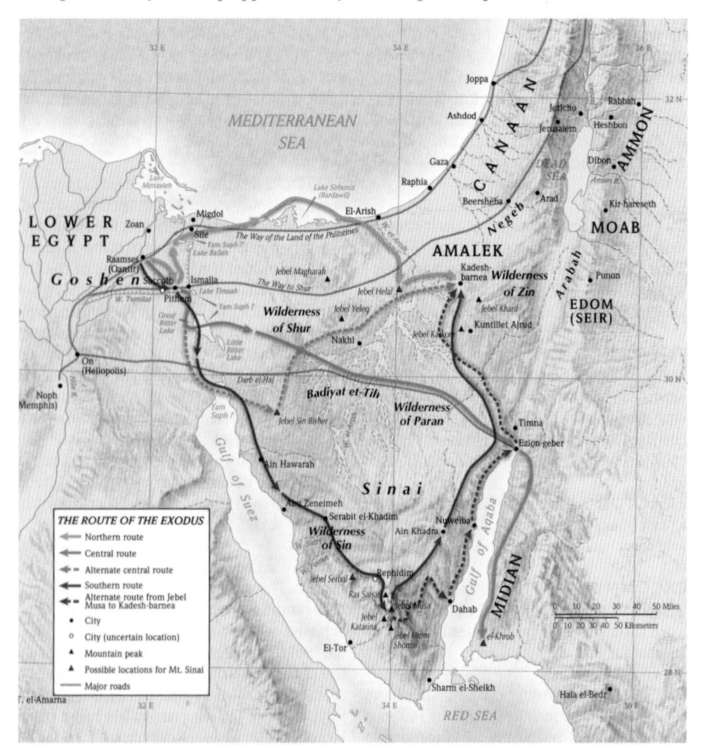

Jebel Musa, the traditional site of Mount Sinai

The book of Exodus is the second book of the OT and of the Pentateuch. Exodus takes up the story of the descendants of Jacob in Egypt, now under a hostile pharaoh and seen as feared foreigners instead of welcomed deliverers from famine. Israel thus became slave laborers in Egypt (chap. 1). Exodus is the account of how God raised up Moses as his instrument for delivering his people from slavery. Then the miracle of the Red Sea (or perhaps Sea of Reeds) became the greatest moment in Israel's history, the moment God created a nation for himself by delivering them from the strongest military power on earth (chap. 14).

Three months after Israel was delivered from Egypt, they came to Sinai, where God called them to become his covenant people, a holy nation to carry out Abraham's mission of blessing the nations. God gave the Ten Commandments and other laws central to the covenant (chaps. 19–23), and then confirmed the covenant in a mysterious ceremony (chap. 24). Moses went to the top of the mountain to receive the remainder of God's instructions, especially instructions for building the sacred place of worship, the tabernacle (chaps. 24–31). Impatient Israel got Aaron to build an object of worship they could see, so he made the golden calf. The people began worshiping. This angered God, who sent Moses back down to the people. Moses prayed for the people despite their sin but then saw the people's sinful actions and threw the tablets with the law to the ground, breaking them. Moses again went up and prayed for the people. God punished them but did not destroy them as he had threatened. God showed his continued presence in the Tent of Meeting and in letting his glory pass by Moses (chaps. 32–33). God then gave Moses the law on two new tablets of stone and renewed the covenant with the people, providing further basic laws for them. Such intense communication with God brought radiance to Moses's face (chap. 34). Moses then led Israel to celebrate the Sabbath and to build the tabernacle (chaps. 35–39). Moses set up the tabernacle and established worship in it. God blessed the action with his holy glorious presence (chap. 40). This provided the sign for Israel's future journeys, following God's cloud and fire.

EXORCISM Practice of expelling demons by means of some ritual act. Although the Hebrew Bible does make reference to demonic beings (Lev. 17:7; Deut. 32:17; Isa. 13:21; 34:14; 2 Chron. 11:15; Ps. 106:37 CSB, NRSV), there is no account of demons being cast out of a person or a place. In the NT, the demons were earthly powers or spirits allied with Satan. Jesus's power to exorcise demonstrated his power over Satan and is recorded in the Synoptic Gospels (Matt. 15:21-28; Mark 1:23-38; 5:1-20; 7:2430; 9:14-29). See *Demonic Possession*.

EXPIATION, PROPITIATION Terms that elaborate the meaning of atonement for sins. Expiation is the process by which sins are nullified or covered. Propitiation involves the satisfaction of an offended party—in this case—God. Sin evokes God's wrath, his eternal opposition to evil. Sin can't be expiated or covered until a prior issue has been addressed. Because God is just, he punishes sin. God is also compassionate, loving those who sin. Jesus's atonement for sin, his bearing the just punishment for sin, makes it possible for God to be "righteous and declare righteous" those who sin but who have faith in Jesus Christ (Rom. 3:26 CSB). Because Jesus is first the propitiation for sin, he can also be its expiation. Expiation without propitiation leaves God's righteousness in question.

EYELIDS OF THE MORNING Phrase meaning "the glow of dawn" used to describe the eyes of Leviathan (Job 41:18).

Sunrise ("eyelids of the morning") over the Mediterranean coast of Israel

EZBAI Personal name of unknown meaning. Father of one of David's military leaders (1 Chron. 11:37).

EZBON Personal name perhaps meaning "bare." Son of Gad and grandson of Jacob (Gen. 46:16).

EZEKIAS KJV spelling of Ezekiel in the NT following the Greek spelling there.

EZEKIEL Personal name meaning "God will strengthen." Ezekiel was a sixth-century BC prophet who ministered to the Judean exiles in Babylon. All that is known of Ezekiel derives from his book. He was a son of Buzi (1:3), taken captive to Babylon in 597 BC, along with King Jehoiachin and 10,000 others, including political and military leaders and skilled craftsmen (2 Kgs. 24:14-16). Ezekiel lived in his own house near the river Chebar, an irrigation canal that channeled the Euphrates River into surrounding arid areas. He was married and ministered from his own home (3:24; 8:1; 33:30-33). His wife died suddenly (24:18), but he was not allowed to mourn the loss.

EZEKIEL, BOOK OF Classified with the Major Prophets and placed in the OT canon following Lamentations. Ezekiel is a series of oracles delivered in a number of identifiable literary forms such as woe oracle, judgment oracle, riddle. Unlike Jeremiah, the order of Ezekiel is approximately chronological.

Ezekiel has sometimes been described as emotionally unstable, a victim of neurotic and psychotic abnormalities. Today scholars recognize that he was not a man on the verge of a breakdown but used deliberate rhetorical tactics to get his message across to a hardened and resistant audience. No prophet was as creative as Ezekiel in the strategies employed to communicate his message. Inspired by God, he crafted powerful word pictures (17:1-24; 19:1-14; 27:1-9), demolished populist slogans with impeccable logic (11:1-21; 18:1-32), played the role of prosecuting attorney (16:1-63; 23:1-49), and, like a watchman on the wall, warned them of certain doom (3:16-21; 7:1-27; 33:1-9). Once the judgment had fallen, he assumed a sympathetic stance, like a pastor (34:1-31), a bearer of good news (6:8-10; 36:16-38; 37:1-14), and like a second Moses, heralding a new constitution (40–48). But he also performed symbolic acts to expose the condition of the nation and her kings (chaps. 4–5; 12:1-20). Later he used the same strategy to declare his message of hope (37:15-28), but this was more than "street theater." In his own body, Ezekiel bore his message of doom (2:8–3:3; 3:22-27; 24:15-27; 33:21-22).

To evaluate Ezekiel's effectiveness, we must look to the events that followed his book. According to the internal evidence, Ezekiel delivered his last oracle in 571 BC (29:1), more than two decades after his call. Even then, there was no hint of positive response among the exiles. However, the following three decades witnessed a remarkable development: when Cyrus issued a decree in 538 BC, permitting the Judeans to return home and rebuild the temple, more than 40,000 people returned, totally weaned off idolatry and eager to rebuild (Ezra 2:64). Most likely they came through the ministry of Ezekiel, having experienced a widespread spiritual revival. Whether he lived long enough to witness these developments, we do not know. The preservation of his prophecies testifies to his impact on the exiles.

EZEL Place-name of uncertain meaning, perhaps, "disappearance." Rock where David hid from Saul and watched for Jonathan's signal (1 Sam. 20:19).

EZEM Place-name meaning "mighty" or "bone." Town in Judah's tribal territory but settled by tribe of Simeon (Josh. 15:29; 19:3; 1 Chron. 4:29). KJV spells Azem in Joshua.

EZER English spelling of two Hebrew names with different spellings and meanings. The first Hebrew meaning is "gathering" or "pile." Ezer was a leader in Edom and a descendant of Esau (Gen. 36:21,27,30). He was a Horite and lived in Seir or Edom.

The second Hebrew meaning is "help" or "hero." **1.** Descendant of Judah (1 Chron. 4:4) in the clan of Caleb. **2.** Son of Ephraim and grandson of Joseph. With his brother Elead, he was killed as he tried to take cattle from the inhabitants of Gath (1 Chron. 7:21). **3.** Member of tribe of Gad who joined David's wilderness army before he became king (1 Chron. 12:9). **4.** Person who helped Nehemiah repair the Jerusalem wall. His father had political authority over Mizpah (Neh. 3:19). **5.** Temple musician who helped Nehemiah dedicate the completion of the Jerusalem wall (Neh. 12:42, with a slightly different Hebrew spelling).

EZION-GABER (KJV, Num. 33:35-36; Deut. 2:8; 2 Chron. 20:36) or **EZION-GEBER** Port city of Edom located on the northern shore of the Gulf of Aqaba. It is first mentioned in the Bible among the cities on the route of the exodus (Num. 33:35-36; Deut. 2:8). Solomon used this city for ship-building purposes. During this time, it was a port from which ships manned by Phoenician sailors sailed to Ophir for gold and other riches (1 Kgs. 9:26-28; 10:11,22; 2 Chron. 8:17).

EZNITE Word of uncertain meaning describing the family or tribal relationship of Adino (2 Sam. 23:8).

EZRA Name "Ezra" means "Yahweh helps." Several had the name: a family head in Judah (1 Chron. 4:17), a priest in the return with

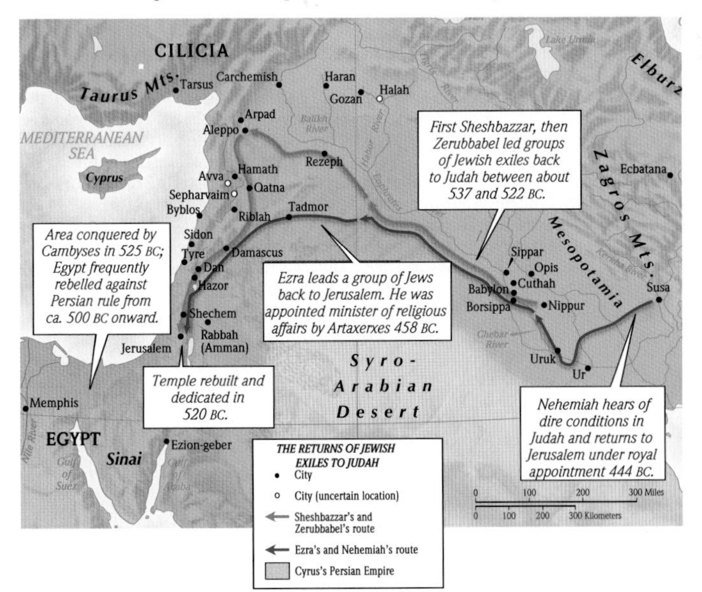

Zerubbabel (Neh. 12:1,13), and a prince at the dedication of Jerusalem's walls built by Nehemiah (Neh. 12:32-33). The most famous is the chief character in the book of Ezra: priest and scribe of the fifth century BC. He descended from Aaron through Phinehas and later Zadok (Ezra 7:1-5; 1 Chron. 6:4-14). Ezra was sent with a large company of Israelites to Jerusalem by King Artaxerxes of Persia in 458 BC (Ezra 7:7). His mission was "to study the law of the LORD, obey it, and teach its statutes and ordinances in Israel" (7:10 CSB).

Ezra was the main instigator of reform just after Israel's return from exile and one of the most important preservers and teachers of law in Jewish history. (He was probably the author of the books of Chronicles and Ezra and the final editor of the OT.) Additionally, he is the main source of information about the first return from exile.

EZRA, BOOK OF The book of Ezra is intimately connected with Chronicles and Nehemiah. The connection is so obvious that possibly one person wrote and compiled all three. This unknown person is referred to as the Chronicler. Ezra and Nehemiah were actually one book in the ancient Hebrew and Greek OT. Each book contains materials found in the other (e.g., the list in Ezra 2 is also in Neh. 7). Each book completes the other; Ezra's story is continued in Nehemiah (chaps. 8–10).

The book chronicles two major events, that of Zerubbabel and the group of returnees to Jerusalem who rebuilt the temple (chaps. 1–6), and the leadership of Ezra (chaps. 7–10, completed in Neh. 8–10), 60 years later. A great revival resulted.

Ezra's greatest contribution was his teaching, establishing, and implementing "the book of the law of the LORD" (Neh. 9:3) among the Jews. Ezra evidenced strong theology; he believed in the sovereignty of God, who could use a Cyrus, an Artaxerxes, and a Darius to accomplish his purposes. He believed in the faithfulness of God, who brought home the exiles who wanted to return. He believed in the sacredness and practicality of the Scriptures; he read them to his people and insisted that their teachings be carried out. He was a person of prayer; note his long confessional prayers (Ezra 9:5-15; Neh. 9:6-37). He was a preacher: he used a pulpit (Neh. 8:4); he publicly read the Scriptures; and he helped to interpret them to his congregation (8:8).

EZRAH Modern translation spelling of Ezra in 1 Chron. 4:17 to reflect different final letter in Hebrew spelling. This Ezra is a descendant of Judah about whom nothing else is known. The spelling of his name may be a Hebrew form, whereas the more common spelling is Aramaic.

EZRAHITE Term used to describe the family relationships of Ethan, a famous wise man (1 Kgs. 4:31). The precise meaning of the Hebrew word is debated. It may mean one born in the land with full citizenship rights and point to a Canaanite origin for Ethan. A related word appears in Exod. 12:19,49; Lev. 17:15; Josh. 8:33, and other places.

EZRI Personal name meaning "my help." Supervisor of royal farm labor under David (1 Chron. 27:26).

Floor mosaic of fish from church in Galilee, Israel

FABLE Short, fictitious story that uses animals or inanimate objects as characters to teach an ethical or practical lesson. Fables are rarely found in the Bible, but there are two clear examples in the OT. The fable of the trees of the forest selecting a king (Judg. 9:8-15) is designed to warn Israel of the dangers in selecting a weak and ruthless king. In 2 Kgs. 14:8-10 (2 Chron. 25:17-19), there is a fable addressed to Amaziah, king of Judah, about the folly of arrogance. In this story a thistle thinks that it is equal to the giant cedars of Lebanon and gets trampled by a wild beast of the forest.

FACE The word "face" has a variety of meanings. It is used literally to refer to the face of man or animals (Gen. 30:40), seraphim (Isa. 6:2), and the face of Christ (Matt. 17:2). Figuratively, it is used in reference to the face of the earth (Gen. 1:29), waters (Gen. 1:2), sky (Matt. 16:3), and moon (Job 26:9). Also, the word "face" is used theologically with regard to the "presence of God" (Gen. 32:30).

FAIR HAVENS An open bay on the southern coast of Crete near the city of Lasea. Protected only by small islands, it did not appear to be a safe harbor for winter, so the sailors of the ship carrying Paul to Rome decided to try to reach Phoenix. They refused to listen to Paul's warnings and were caught in a ferocious storm (Acts 27:8-20).

FAIRNESS Prerequisite for wisdom (Prov. 2:9-10) and therefore an important value for life (Ps. 99:4; Prov. 1:2-3). The prophets linked fairness with righteousness (Isa. 11:4; cp. Ps. 98:9) and saw that when fairness was lacking, life became tenuous and uncertain (Isa. 59:9-11; Mic. 3:9-12). Biblical persons who exhibited fairness in their words or actions include Jacob (Gen. 31:38-41), Solomon (1 Kgs. 3:16-27), Jesus (John 7:53–8:11), and the thief on the cross (Luke 23:40-41).

FAITH, FAITHFULNESS Faith is essentially trust, and faithfulness is dependability or trustworthiness. Throughout the Scriptures, faith is the trustful human response to God's self-revelation via his words and his actions. God initiates the relationship between himself and human beings. He expects people to trust him; failure to trust him was in essence the first sin (Gen. 3:1-7).

God's *modus operandi* during the OT and NT periods was to make himself knowable through words about how people can relate properly to him. Those words are not the object of the believer's faith; God is the object. But his words mediate faith in him. His words guide people to him. Without the words, no one would know how to respond properly to him. Old Testament believers praised God for revealing his word of salvation (Ps. 56:4).

FALL Traditional name for the first sin of Adam and Eve that brought judgment upon both nature and humanity.

Sin had immediate results in the couple's relationship; the "self-first" and "self-only" attitude displayed toward God affected the way they looked at each other. The couple also felt compelled to hide from God when they heard him walking in the garden. When loving trust characterized the couple's attitude, they were apparently comfortable in God's presence. After their sin, shame appropriately marked their relationships—both human and divine (Gen. 3:8).

The NT writers assumed the fallen state of both humans and nature. Both groan for redemption (Rom. 8:19-23). When comparing Adam and Christ, Paul declared that sin and death gained entrance into the world through Adam and that sin and death are now common to all people (Rom. 5:12; 6:23). Adam is pictured as a representative of humankind, all of whom share in his penalty (Rom. 5:19).

FALLOW GROUND Virgin soil or else soil that has not recently been planted (Jer. 4:3; Hos. 10:12).

FALSE APOSTLES Designation for Paul's opponents in 2 Cor. 11:13; also designated deceitful workers (11:13) and servants of Satan (11:15).

FALSE CHRISTS Imposters claiming to be the Messiah (Christ in Greek). Jesus associated the appearance of messianic pretenders with the fall of Jerusalem (Matt. 24:23-26; Mark 13:21-22). Jesus warned his followers to be skeptical of those who point to signs and omens to authenticate their false messianic claims. Jesus also urged disbelief of those claiming the Messiah was waiting in the wilderness or was in "the inner rooms" (perhaps a reference to the inner chambers of the temple complex).

FALSE PROPHET Person who spreads false messages and teachings, claiming to speak God's words. While the exact term "false prophet" only appears once in the OT (Isa. 44:25), references to false prophets are clear. The pages of the OT are filled with men and women who fit the description of a false prophet given in Jer. 14:14. Jesus and the apostles spoke many times about false prophets. In the Sermon on the Mount, Jesus taught about the marks of a false prophet and the consequences of being one (Matt. 7:15-23). The apostles instructed believers to be diligent in faith and understanding of Christian teachings, in order to discern false prophets when they arise (2 Pet. 1:10; 1:19-2:1; 1 John 4:1). The tests of a prophet are (1) Do their predictions come true (Jer. 28:9)? (2) Does the prophet have a divine commission (Jer. 29:9)? (3) Are the prophecies consistent with Scripture (2 Pet. 1:20-21; Rev. 22:18-19)? (4) Do the people benefit spiritually from the prophet's ministry (Jer. 23:13-14,32; 1 Pet. 4:11)?

Punishments for false prophets were just as severe in the NT as they were in the OT. Paul caused a false prophet to be stricken with blindness (Acts 13:6-12), but most other punishments were more permanent in nature. Jesus said the false prophets would be cut down and burned like a bad tree (Matt. 7:19). Second Peter 2:4 describes being cast into pits of darkness. The ultimate punishment appears in Rev. 19:20; 20:10—the false prophet, the beast, and the devil will be thrown into a lake of fire and brimstone and be tormented forever.

FALSE WORSHIP Broad category of acts and attitudes that includes worship, reverence, or religious honoring of any object, person, or entity other than the one true God. It also includes impure, improper, or other inappropriate acts directed toward the worship of the true God.

FAMILY A group of persons united by the ties of marriage, blood, or adoption, enabling interaction between members of the household in their respective social roles. God has ordained the family as the foundational institution of human society.

Old Testament The importance of the family unit in Israel is suggested by the fact that about half of the capital crimes were family related, including adultery, homosexuality, incest, persistent disobedience to or violence against one's parents, and rape (Lev. 20; Deut. 21–22). The basis for the family unit was the married couple (Gen. 2:4–5:1). From the union of the husband and wife, the family expanded to include the children, and also various relatives such as grandparents, and others.

Along with paternal authority over the family came responsibility to provide for and protect the family. The father was responsible for the religious and moral training of his children (Deut. 6:7,20-25; Exod. 12:26-27; Josh. 4:6-7), and before the law he acted as the family priest (Gen. 12:7-8; Job 1:2-5). After establishment of the Levitical priesthood, the father led the family in worship at the sites designated by God with the priests performing the sacrifices (1 Sam. 1). Moral purity was stressed for men and women in Israel with severe penalties for either party when sin occurred (Lev. 18; Prov. 5). The father was to give his daughter in marriage (Deut. 22:16; 1 Sam. 17:25; Jer. 29:6) to only an Israelite man, usually one from his own tribe. A daughter found to have been promiscuous before she married was to be stoned on her father's doorstep (Deut. 22:21).

Contrary to the practices of the surrounding nations, wives were not considered property. Though most marriages in the OT were arranged, this does not mean that they were loveless. The Song of Songs extols the joys of physical love between a husband and wife. God is used as an example of the perfect husband who loves his "wife" Israel (Hos. 1–2) and delights to care for her and make her happy.

A mother gave birth and reared the children, ran the home under her husband's authority, and generally served as her husband's helper (Gen. 2:18; Prov. 31:10-31). The importance of children in ancient Israel may be inferred from the law of Levirate marriage, which provided for the continuance of the family line (Deut. 25:5-10; Ps. 127:3-5). They were also the instruments by which the ancient traditions were passed on (Exod. 13:8-9,14; Deut. 4:9; 6:7). God delights to be praised by children (Ps. 8:2). Children were taught to respect their mothers as well as their fathers (Exod. 20:12; Deut. 5:16; 21:13; 27:16; Prov. 15:20; 23:22,25; 30:17) and to heed their instruction (Prov. 1:8; 6:20). Discipline was one way of showing love to one's children (Prov. 3:11-12; 13:24).

Polygamy (more specifically "polygyny") was one of the abnormal developments of the family in the OT and was first practiced by Lamech, a descendant of Cain. It is never cast in a positive light in Scripture but is a source of rivalry and bickering, as is seen in the lives of Abraham and Jacob (Gen. 16; 29–30). The exception was in the case of "Levirate marriage," that is, an unmarried male's marriage to the childless widow of his deceased brother.

New Testament Much of the NT teaching on the family is found in Paul's writings. Household ethics are described in Eph. 5–6 and Col. 3–4. In these texts, husbands are responsible for the physical, emotional, religious, and psychological health of wives. A wife's submission is in the marriage context.

Wives are called to be household administrators. As household managers, wives are responsible to give the family guidance and direction. Thus any decision made within the family without the counsel and guidance of the wife is unwise.

Family roles in the NT also include children, who are commanded to obey their parents (Eph. 6:14). Each member of the family has responsibilities. Jesus affirms the importance of children and their importance to him in Matt. 18:2-14; 19:13-14; Mark 10:14-16.

FAMINE AND DROUGHT Famine is an extreme shortage of food, and drought is an excessive dryness of land. The Bible reports or predicts the occurrence of several famines and droughts. While the Bible states that some famines and droughts are the judgment of God (2 Sam. 21:1; 1 Kgs. 17:1; 2 Kgs. 8:1; Jer. 14:12; Ezek. 5:12; Amos 4:6), not all such disasters are connected to divine punishment (Gen. 12:10; 26:1; Ruth 1:1; Acts 11:28). When God did send drought and famine on his people, it was for the purpose of bringing them to repentance (1 Kgs. 8:35-36; Hos. 2:8-23; Amos 4:6-8). Moreover, the OT contains promises that God will protect his faithful ones in times of famine (Job 5:20,22; Pss. 33:18-19; 37:18-19; Prov. 10:3).

FAN KJV term for a long wooden fork used to toss grain into the air so that the chaff is blown away. Shovels were also used for this purpose (Isa. 30:24). Modern translations render the underlying Hebrew and Greek terms "shovel," "winnowing fork," or "winnowing shovel."

FASTING Refraining from eating food. The Bible describes three main forms of fasting. The *normal fast* involves the total abstinence of food. Luke 4:2 reveals that Jesus "ate nothing"; afterward "he was hungry" (CSB). Jesus abstained from food but not from water. In Acts 9:9, we read of an *absolute fast* where for three days Paul "did not eat or drink" (CSB). The abstinence from both food and water seems to have lasted no more than three days (Ezra 10:6; Esth. 4:16). The *partial fast* in Dan. 10:3 emphasizes the restriction of diet rather than complete abstinence. The context implies that there were physical benefits resulting from this partial fast. However, this verse indicates that there was a revelation given to Daniel as a result of this time of fasting.

Fasting is to be done with the object of seeking to know God in a deeper experience (Isa. 58; Zech. 7:5). Fasting relates to a time of confession (Ps. 69:10). Fasting can be a time of seeking a deeper prayer experience and drawing near to God in prevailing prayer (Ezra 8:23; Joel 2:12). The early church often fasted in seeking God's will for leadership in the local church (Acts 13:2). When the early church wanted to know the mind of God, there was a time of prayer and fasting.

FATE That which must necessarily happen. The OT speaks of death as the common fate of humankind (Pss. 49:12; 81:15; Eccles. 2:14; 3:19; 9:2-3). The OT similarly speaks of violent death as the destiny of the wicked (Job 15:22; Isa. 65:12; Hos. 9:13).

FATHERLESS Person without a male parent, often rendered orphan by modern translations. Orphans are often mentioned with widows as representatives of the most helpless members of society (Exod. 22:22; Deut. 10:18; Ps. 146:9). God, however, has a special concern for orphans and widows (Deut. 10:18; Pss. 10:14-18; 146:9; Hos. 14:3) evidenced in the title "a father of the fatherless" (Ps. 68:5). Old Testament law provided for the material needs of orphans and widows who were to be fed from the third year's tithe (Deut. 14:28-29; 26:12-13), from sheaves left forgotten in the fields (24:19), and from fruit God commanded to be left on the trees and vines (24:20-21). Orphans and widows were to be included in the celebrations of the worshiping community (Deut. 16:11,14). God's people were repeatedly warned not to take advantage of orphans and widows (Exod. 22:22; Deut. 24:17; 27:19; Ps. 82:3; Isa. 1:17). In the NT, James defined worship acceptable to God as meeting the needs of orphans and widows (1:27).

FATHOM Measure of depth equaling six feet (Acts 27:28).

FATLINGS, FATTED Generally a young animal penned up to be fed for slaughter. Sometimes a general reference to the strongest or to the choice among a flock or herd is intended. In the parable of the loving father, a son is welcomed home with a banquet of a fatted calf (Luke 15:23,27,30). Fattened animals were used as a symbol for slaughter. In the NT, James pictured the oppressive rich as fattening their hearts for a day of slaughter, perhaps a reference to God's judgment on them (5:5).

FAWN Young deer; term used in modern translations for KJV's "hind" and "roe."

FEAR Natural emotional response to a perceived threat to one's security or general welfare. It ranges in degree of intensity from a sense of anxiety or worry to one of utter terror. It can be a useful emotion when it leads to appropriate caution or measures that would guard one's welfare. On the other hand, fear can be a hindrance to the enjoyment of life if it is induced by delusion or if it lingers and overpowers other more positive emotions such as love and joy, perhaps leading to an inability to engage in the normal activities of life. In the Bible, however, fear is perhaps more often than in popular culture regarded not as pure emotion but as wise behavior.

Attitude of Respect and Submission In some cases, "fear" carries with it the expectation of obedience. Respect or honor may be the sense in which Israel "feared" Solomon when they saw evidence that he possessed God's wisdom (1 Kgs. 3:28). Respect or reverence is also the proper attitude toward God's sanctuary (Lev. 19:30). Fear can be the opposite of treating someone or something as common, insignificant, irrelevant, or otherwise unworthy of attention (Esth. 5:9).

Fear of God Any of these senses—terror, honor, submission—may be involved when God is the object of fear, with the additional sense of worship. For those who are enemies rather than followers of the Lord, terror is most appropriate (Jer. 5:22). Such terror is limited by the fact that God is not capricious but acts consistently according to his righteous character and revealed will. Nevertheless, those guilty of idolatry and injustice have every reason to fear his coming wrath in judgment (Ps. 90:11; Isa. 13:6-11; 30:30-33; Zeph. 1:18; Heb. 10:26-31). Terror is the only reasonable response when confronted by a Being whose knowledge and power have no limits, unless one's safety has been assured. The Bible contains many cases of a divine or angelic appearance to which fear is the natural response (Exod. 3:6; 20:18-20; Dan. 10:10-12; Luke 1:12-13,30). Following the resurrection of Christ, for example, an angelic appearance caused the guards at the tomb to faint with fear, but the believing women were told they had nothing to fear (Matt. 28:4-5).

The proper attitude of believers toward God is often said to be respect, reverence, or awe rather than fear. The biblical terminology, however, is the same, and God's character remains unchanged. The description of God often translated "awesome" is literally "feared" or "fearful" (Exod. 15:11; Neh. 1:5; Job 37:22; Ps. 89:7; Dan. 9:4). Confining the believer's attitude toward God to "reverence" or "awe" rather than "fear" may lose sight of those aspects of the divine character that compel obedience—his perfect holiness and righteousness and his unlimited knowledge and power. Knowing that God's wrath has been satisfied in Christ relieves the believer from the fear of condemnation, but not from accountability to a holy God (2 Cor. 5:10-11; 7:1; 1 Tim. 5:20; 1 Pet. 1:17).

FEAR OF ISAAC Name or title that Jacob used, referring to God (Gen. 31:42; cp. 31:53; 46:1). Evidently the patriarchs used various names to refer to God until he revealed his personal name to Moses (Exod. 6:3). Some scholars translate the Hebrew expression "Kinsman of Isaac" or "Refuge of Isaac."

FELIX Procurator of Judea at the time Paul the apostle visited Jerusalem for the last time and was arrested there (Acts 23:24).

FELLOES (KJV, REB) Rim of a wheel (1 Kgs. 7:33).

FENCED CITY KJV term for a fortified or walled city.

FERRET White European polecat mentioned by KJV in Lev. 11:30. Other translations read "gecko."

FESTIVALS Regular religious celebrations remembering God's great acts of salvation in the history of his people. Traditionally called "feasts" in the English Bibles, these can conveniently be categorized according to frequency of celebration. Many of them were timed according to cycles of seven. The cycle of the week with its climax on the

Fenced city: city walls and buildings outside Hazor

seventh day provided the cyclical basis for much of Israel's worship; as the seventh day was observed, so was the seventh month (which contained four of the national festivals), and the seventh year, and the fiftieth year (the year of Jubilee), which followed seven cycles each of seven years.

Sabbath The seventh day of each week was listed among the festivals (Lev. 23:1-3). It functioned as a reminder of the Lord's rest at the end of the creation week (Gen. 2:3) and also of the deliverance from slavery in Egypt (Deut. 5:12-25). The Sabbath day was observed by strict rest from work from sunset until sunset (Exod. 20:8-11; Neh. 13:15-22). Each person was to remain in place and not engage in travel (Exod. 16:29; Lev. 23:3). Despite such restrictions even as kindling a fire (Exod. 35:3) or any work (Exod. 31:14; 35:2), the Sabbath was a joyful time (Isa. 58:13-14).

New Moon This festival was a monthly celebration characterized by special offerings, great in quantity and quality (Num. 28:11-15), and blowing of trumpets (Num. 10:10; Ps. 81:3). According to Amos 8:5, business ceased. The festivals of the new moon and Sabbath are often mentioned together in the OT (Isa. 1:13; 66:23; Ezek. 45:17; 46:1,3).

Passover The first of the three annual festivals was the Passover. It commemorated the final plague on Egypt when the firstborn of the Egyptians died and the Israelites were spared because of the blood smeared on their doorposts (Exod. 12). Passover took place on the fourteenth day (at evening) of the first month (Lev. 23:5).

During NT times, large crowds gathered in Jerusalem to observe this annual celebration. Jesus was crucified during the Passover event. He and his disciples ate a Passover meal together on the eve of his death. During this meal Jesus said, "This is my body" and "this cup is the new covenant in my blood" (Luke 22:19-20 CSB). The NT identifies Christ with the Passover sacrifice: "For Christ our Passover lamb has been sacrificed" (1 Cor. 5:7 CSB).

Feast of Weeks The second of the three annual festivals was Pentecost, also called the Feast of Weeks (Exod. 34:22; Deut. 16:10,16; 2 Chron. 8:13), the Feast of Harvest (Exod. 23:16), and the day of firstfruits (Num. 28:26; cp. Exod. 23:16; 34:22; Lev. 23:17). It was celebrated seven complete weeks, or 50 days, after Passover (Lev. 23:15-16; Deut. 16:9); therefore, it was given the name Pentecost (referring to 50).

Essentially a harvest celebration, the term "weeks" was used of the period of grain harvest from the barley harvest to the wheat harvest, a period of about seven weeks. In the NT, the Holy Spirit came upon the disciples at Pentecost (Acts 2:1-4), at the festive time when Jews from different countries were in Jerusalem to celebrate this annual feast.

The Day of Atonement The third annual festival came on the tenth day of the seventh month (Tishri–Sept./Oct.) and the fifth day before the Feast of Tabernacles (Lev. 16:1-34; Num. 29:7-11). According to Lev. 23:27-28, four main elements comprise this most significant feast. First, it was to be a "holy convocation," drawing the focus of the people to the altar of divine mercy. The holy One of Israel called the people of Israel to gather in his presence and give their undivided attention to him. Second, they were to "humble their souls" ("afflict your souls," Lev. 23:27 KJV). This was explained by later tradition to indicate fasting and repentance. Israel understood that this was a day for mourning over their sins. The seriousness of this requirement is reiterated in Lev. 23:29 (CSB): "If any person does not practice self-denial on this particular day, he is to be cut off from his people." Third, offerings are central to the Day of Atonement. The Bible devotes an entire chapter (Lev. 16) to them; they are also listed in Num. 29:7-11. In addition to these, when the day fell on a sabbath, the regular Sabbath offerings were offered. The fourth and final element of the day involved the prohibition of labor. The Day of Atonement was a "sabbath of rest" (Lev. 23:32), and the Israelites were forbidden to do any work at all. If they disobeyed, they were liable to capital punishment (Lev. 23:30).

The center point of this feast involved the high priest entering the holy of holies. Before entering, the high priest first bathed his entire body, going beyond the mere washing of hands and feet as required for other occasions. This washing symbolized his desire for purification. Rather than donning his usual robe and colorful garments (described in Exod. 28 and Lev. 8), he was commanded to wear special garments of linen. Also, the high priest sacrificed a bullock as a sin offering for himself and for his house (Lev. 16:6). After filling his censer with live coals from the altar, he entered the holy of holies where he placed incense on the coals. Then he took some of the blood from the slain bullock and sprinkled it on the mercy seat ("atonement cover," Lev. 16:13 NIV) and also on the ground in front of the ark, providing atonement for the priesthood (Lev. 16:14-15). Next he sacrificed a male goat as a sin offering for the people. Some of this blood was then also taken into the holy of holies and sprinkled there on behalf of the people (Lev. 16:15). Then he took another goat, called the "scapegoat" (for "escape goat"), laid his hands on its head, confessed over it the sins of Israel, and then released it into the desert where it symbolically carried away the sins of the people (Lev. 16:8,10). The remains of the sacrificial bullock and male goat were taken outside the city and burned, and the day was concluded with additional sacrifices.

According to Heb. 9–10, this ritual is a symbol of the atoning work of Christ, our great high Priest, who did not need to make any sacrifice for himself but shed his own blood for our sins. As the high priest of the OT entered the holy of holies with the blood of sacrificial animals, Jesus entered heaven itself to appear on our behalf in front of the Father (Heb. 9:11-12). Each year the high priest repeated his sin offerings for his own sin and the sins of the people, giving an annual reminder that perfect and permanent atonement had not yet been made; but Jesus, through his own blood, accomplished eternal redemption for his people (Heb. 9:12). Just as the sacrifice of the Day of Atonement was burned outside the camp of Israel, Jesus suffered outside the gate of Jerusalem so that he might redeem his people from sin (Heb. 13:11-12).

Feast of Tabernacles The fourth annual festival was the Feast of Tabernacles (2 Chron. 8:13; Ezra 3:4; Zech. 14:16), also called the Feast of Ingathering (Exod. 23:16; 34:22), the feast to the Lord (Lev. 23:39; Judg. 21:19). Sometimes it was simply called "the feast" (1 Kgs. 8:2; 2 Chron. 5:3; 7:8; Neh. 8:14; Isa. 30:29; Ezek. 45:23,25) because it was so well known. Its observance combined the ingathering of the labor of the field (Exod. 23:16), the fruit of the earth (Lev. 23:39), the ingathering of the threshing floor and winepress (Deut. 16:13), and the dwelling in booths (or "tabernacles"), which were to be joyful reminders to Israel (Lev. 23:41; Deut. 16:14). The "booth" in Scripture is not an image of privation and misery, but of protection, preservation, and shelter from heat and storm (Pss. 27:5; 31:20; Isa. 4:6). The rejoicing community included family, servants, widows, orphans, Levites, and sojourners (Deut. 16:13-15).

The feast began on the fifteenth day of Tishri (the seventh month), which was five days after the Day of Atonement. It lasted for seven days (Lev. 23:36; Deut. 16:13; Ezek. 45:25).

Feast of Trumpets Modern *Rosh Hashanah* is traced back to the so-called "Feast of Trumpets," the sounding of the trumpets on the first day of the seventh month (Tishri) of the religious calendar year (Lev. 23:24; Num. 29:1). The trumpet referred to here was the *shofar*, a ram's horn. It was distinctive from the silver trumpets blown on the other new moons.

This day evolved into the second most holy day on the modern Jewish religious calendar. It begins the "ten days of awe" before the Day of Atonement. According to Lev. 23:24-27, the celebration consisted of the blowing of trumpets, a time of rest, and "an offering by fire." The text itself says nothing specifically about a New Year's Day, and the term itself (*rosh hashanah*) is found only one time in Scripture (Ezek. 40:1) where it refers to the tenth day.

Purim Purim, commemorating the deliverance of the Jews from genocide through the efforts of Esther (Esth. 9:16-32), derives its name from the "lot" (*pur*) which Haman planned to cast in order to decide when he should carry into effect the decree issued by the king for the extermination of the Jews (9:24). In the apocryphal book of 2 Maccabees (15:36), it is called the Day of Mordecai. It was celebrated on the fourteenth day of Adar (March) by those in villages and unwalled towns and on the fifteenth day by those in fortified cities (Esth. 9:18-19). No mention of any religious observance is connected with the day; in later periods, the book of Esther was read in the synagogue on this day. It became a time for rejoicing and distribution of food and presents.

Hanukkah The other postexilic holiday was Hanukkah, a festival that began on the twenty-fifth day of Kislev (Dec.) and lasted eight days. Josephus referred to it as the Feast of Lights because a candle was lighted each successive day until a total of eight was reached. The festival commemorates the victories of Judas Maccabeus in 167 BC. At that time, when temple worship was reinstated after an interruption of three years, a celebration of eight days took place. The modern celebration does not greatly affect the routine duties of everyday life. This feast is referred to in John 10:22, where it is called the Feast of Dedication.

A Jewish mother and child celebrate the Jewish tradition of lighting of the candles at Hanukkah

Two festivals occurred less often than once a year: the Sabbatical Year and the Year of Jubilee.

Sabbatical Year Each seventh year, Israel celebrated a sabbath year for its fields. This involved a rest for the land from all cultivation (Exod. 23:10,11; Lev. 25:2-7; Deut. 15:1-11; 31:10-13). Other names for this festival were sabbath of rest (Lev. 25:4), year of rest (Lev. 25:5), year of release

(Deut. 15:9), and the seventh year (Deut. 15:9). The Sabbatical Year, like the Year of Jubilee, began on the first day of the month Tishri. This observance is attested by 1 Maccabees 6:49,53 and Josephus. Laws governing this year of rest included the following: (1) the soil, vineyards, and olive orchards were to enjoy complete rest (Exod. 23:10,11: Lev. 25:4-5); (2) the spontaneous growth of the fields or trees (Isa. 37:30) was for the free use of the hireling, stranger, servants, and cattle (Exod. 23:10-11; Lev. 25:6-7), fruitful harvest was promised for the sixth year (Lev. 25:20-22); (3) debts were released for all persons, with the exception of foreigners (Deut. 15:1-4) (probably this law did not forbid voluntary payment of debts, no one was to oppress a poor man); (4) finally, at the Feast of Tabernacles during this year, the law was to be read to the people in solemn assembly (Deut. 31:10-13). Jewish tradition interpreted 2 Chron. 36:21 to mean that the 70 years' captivity was intended to make up for not observing sabbatical years. After the captivity, this Sabbatical Year was carefully observed.

Year of Jubilee This was also called the Year of Liberty (Ezek. 46:17). Its relation to the Sabbatical Year and the general directions for its observance are found in Lev. 25:8-16,23-55. Its bearing on lands dedicated to the Lord is given in Lev. 27:16-25.

After the span of seven sabbaths of years, or seven times seven years (49 years), the trumpet was to sound throughout the land; and the Year of Jubilee was to be announced (Lev. 25:8-9). The law states three respects in which the Jubilee Year was to be observed: rest for the soil—no sowing, reaping, or gathering from the vine (Lev. 25:11); reversion of landed property (Lev. 25:10-34; 27:16-24)—all property in fields and houses located in villages or unwalled towns, which the owner had been forced to sell through poverty and which had not been redeemed, was to revert without payment to its original owner or his lawful heirs (exceptions noted in Lev. 25:29-30; 27:17-21); and redemption of slaves—every Israelite, who through poverty had sold himself to another Israelite or to a foreigner settled in the land, if he had not been able to redeem himself or had not been redeemed by a kinsman, was to go free with his children (Lev. 25:39-41).

FESTUS Successor of Felix as procurator of Judea (Acts 24:27); assumed this office at Nero's appointment in AD 60. He held it until his death in AD 62. Paul the apostle appealed to Porcius Festus for the opportunity of being tried before Caesar, and Festus granted that request.

FETTER Translation of several Hebrew and Greek terms referring to something that constrains, especially a shackle for the foot. Fetters were made of wood, bronze (Judg. 16:21; 2 Chron. 33:11), or iron (Ps. 149:8).

FEVER Elevated body temperature or disease accompanied by such symptoms. The "burning ague" (Lev. 26:16) is an acute fever marked by regular periods of fever, sweating, and then chills.

FIELD Unenclosed land. In the Hebrew definition of "field," both the use of land (pasture, Gen. 29:2; 31:4; cropland, Gen. 37:7; 47:24; hunting ground, Gen. 27:3,5) and the terrain (land, Num. 21:20, literal translation, "field of Moabi"; Judg. 9:32,36) were insignificant. The crucial distinction is between what is enclosed and what is open.

FIG, FIG TREE Important fruit and tree of the Holy Land. Adam and Eve used leaves from the plant to make clothing (Gen. 3:7). Jesus cursed a fig tree because it was without fruit (Mark 11:13-14,20-21).

FINGER OF GOD Picturesque expression of God at work. The finger of God writing the Ten Commandments illustrated God's giving the law without any mediation (Exod. 31:18; Deut. 9:10). Elsewhere the finger of God suggests God's power to bring plagues on Egypt (Exod. 8:19) and in making the heavens (Ps. 8:3). Jesus's statement, "If I drive out demons by the finger of God, then the kingdom of God has come upon you" (Luke 11:20 CSB), means that since Jesus cast out demons by the power of God, God's rule had become a reality among his hearers.

FINING POT KJV term for a crucible (CSB, NIV, NRSV) or smelting pot (REB), a vessel used to heat metal to a high temperature as part of the refining process (Prov. 17:3; 27:21).

FIRE The word "fire" in our English Bibles normally translates the Hebrew word *'esh* in the OT and the Greek word *pur* (the root from which such English terms as "pyromaniac" and "pure" are derived) in the NT. Both terms signify the physical manifestations of burning: heat, light, and flame. Throughout both the OT and NT, "fire" functions as a significant theological symbol. It is frequently associated with such important concepts as God's presence, divine judgment, and purification. In fact, in the OT, fire served as the primary means by which God manifested his presence and exercised judgment. Because of the sacrificial system, fire was an important aspect of early Israelite worship; it was the means by which animal sacrifices were offered up to God as a "pleasing aroma" (Gen. 1:8; Exod. 29:18,25,41).

The NT continues to portray God's presence in the form of fire especially in the person of the Holy Spirit. The outpouring of the Spirit at Pentecost was signaled by the appearance of fire on each believer's head (Acts 2:3). In his first letter to the Thessalonians, Paul warns believers not to "quench" the Holy Spirit (1 Thess. 5:19 KJV, NASB). The word "quench" often refers to extinguishing a fire. Since God so frequently indicated his presence by means of fire, fire became a metaphor for God emphasizing both his holiness and his retributive justice (Deut. 4:24; Heb. 12:29).

FIREPAN Utensil made of bronze (Exod. 27:3) or gold (1 Kgs. 7:50, KJV, "censers") used to carry live coals from the altar of burnt offering (Exod. 27:3; 38:3), as censers for burning incense (Num. 16:6,17), and as trays for collecting the burnt wicks from the tabernacle lamps (Exod. 25:38; 37:23; the "snuffdishes" of the KJV).

FIRKIN Unit of liquid measure (John 2:6). Firkin is an archaic English word that was used to translate a Greek term referring to a measure of approximately 10 gallons.

FIRMAMENT Great vault or expanse of sky that separates the upper and lower waters. God created the firmament on the second day to separate the "waters from the waters" (Gen. 1:6-7).

FIRSTBORN First son born to a couple and required to be specially dedicated to God. The firstborn son of newly married people was believed to represent the prime of human vigor (Gen. 49:3; Ps. 78:51). In memory of the death of Egypt's firstborn and the preservation of the firstborn of Israel, all the firstborn of Israel, both of man and beast, belonged to Yahweh (Exod. 13:2,15; cp. 12:12-16). This meant that the people of Israel attached unusual value to the eldest son and assigned special privileges and responsibilities to him. The birthright of a firstborn included a double portion of the estate and leadership of the family. As head of the house after his father's death, the eldest son customarily cared for his mother until her death, and he also provided for his sisters until their marriage.

FIRST RAIN KJV term at Deut. 11:14 for the early rain.

FISH, FISHING Animals living in water and breathing through gills; the profession and/or practice of catching fish to supply a family or society's need for food. Methods of catching fish included angling with a hook (Job 41:1), harpoons and spears (Job 41:7), use of dragnets (John 21:8), and thrown hand nets (Matt. 4:18).

Old Testament Fish are mentioned often but not by the different kinds. Fish were a favorite food and a chief source of protein (Num. 11:5; Neh. 13:16). The law regarded all fish with fins and scales as clean. Water animals that did not have fins and scales were unclean (Lev. 11:9-12).

Fish abounded in the inland waters of Palestine as well as in the Mediterranean.

References to fishing as an occupation are rare in the OT because, for the most part, in OT times the Mediterranean coast was controlled by the Philistines and Phoenicians. The Israelites depended largely on foreign trade for their fish (Neh. 13:16). Two OT texts (Song 7:4 KJV; Isa. 19:10 KJV) speak of fishpools and fishponds, possibly an indication of commercially raised fish or of fish farming.

The most famous OT fish was the great fish of the book of Jonah (1:17), one that God

Fishing boats on the Nile in Egypt

prepared especially for the occasion and one whose species the OT does not indicate.

New Testament During NT times, commercial fishing businesses were conducted on the Sea of Galilee by fishermen organized in guilds (Luke 5:7,11). Fishermen were hard workers, crude in manner, rough in speech and in their treatment of others (John 18:10). Fishermen owned their ships, took hirelings into their service, and sometimes joined to form companies (Mark 1:20; Luke 5:7).

Fish provided food for the common people (Matt. 14:17; 15:34). The risen Lord ate fish with the disciples in Jerusalem (Luke 24:42) and by the Sea of Galilee (John 21:13). The primary method of preparing fish was broiling (John 21:9). The most famous NT fish was the one used to pay the temple tax for Jesus and Peter (Matt. 17:27).

Theological In early Christian churches, the Greek word for fish (*ichthusro*) came to be interpreted as a cipher for Jesus. Combining the first letter of each successive Greek word for "Jesus Christ, Son of God, Savior" spells *ichthus*. We do not know when this cipher was first used; but once the identification was made, the fish became a standard Christian symbol.

FISH GATE A north gate of the second quarter of Jerusalem (Zeph. 1:10) mentioned in connection with fortifications built by Manasseh (2 Chron. 33:14). The gate was rebuilt during the time of Nehemiah (Neh. 3:3; 12:39). The name is perhaps derived from the proximity of the gate to the fish market (cp. Neh. 13:16-22).

FISHHOOK Curved or bent device of bone or iron used in biblical times for catching or holding fish (Job 41:1-2; Isa. 19:8 KJV, "angle"; Matt. 17:27). Habakkuk described God's people as helpless fish who would be captured by hooks (1:15) and nets. Amos 4:2 refers to the practice of ancient conquerors of leading captives with hooks through their lips. Such was the fate of Manasseh according to one interpretation (2 Chron. 33:11 CSB, NASB, NIV, TEV).

FITCHES KJV term for two different plants. The first is black cumin (Isa. 28:25,27). Ezekiel 4:9 refers to either spelt, an inferior type of wheat (CSB, NASB, NIV, TEV), or vetches (REB), a plant of the bean family.

FLAG KJV term for a water plant generally translated as "reed" (Exod. 2:3,5; Job 8:11) or rush (Isa. 19:6) by modern translations.

FLAGON Large, two-handled jar for storing wine (Isa. 22:24 KJV; Exod. 25:29; 37:16 REB, NRSV).

FLAX Plant (*Linum usitatissimumro*) used to make linen. The fibers of the flax stem are the most ancient of textile fibers. Flax was cultivated by the Egyptians before the exodus (Exod. 9:31) and by the Canaanites before the conquest (Josh. 2:6).

FLEET Group of ships. Solomon built a fleet of ships at Ezion-geber with the help of Hiram of Tyre (1 Kgs. 9:26-27; 10:11,22). KJV translated "fleet" as "navy" or "navy of ships." Solomon's fleet was used for commercial rather than military purposes.

FLESH The term "flesh," while prevalent in older English translations of the Bible such as the KJV and ASV (1901), has been replaced by numerous other terms in most modern English translations. Undoubtedly this shift is due to the wide variety of nuances the word "flesh" can have in the biblical context that are better rendered by other words in a modern setting. Nonetheless, such seemingly unrelated terms as "skin," "food," "meat," "relatives," "humankind," and "sinful nature" in modern English translations often render the same single word in the original languages: *basar* in Hebrew and *sarx* in Greek. Due to the obvious flexibility of the word, each of its primary meanings is listed below followed by an explanation and biblical examples.

"Flesh" as a Designation for the Body or Parts of the Body "Flesh" frequently refers to the skin or the body—all the material that covers the skeleton of humans and animals. For example, "flesh" clearly refers to the body as a whole in Lev. 14:9 where cleansed lepers are commanded to bathe "their flesh" in water. The psalmist also uses "flesh" in reference to his whole body when he says "my flesh trembles in fear of you" (Ps. 119:120 NIV).

Flesh as a Designation for Humankind or Blood Relatives Scripture occasionally uses the term "flesh" as a general designation for all living things. In Gen. 6:17, God warned that the flood he was about to bring upon the earth would destroy "all flesh." This included animals and human beings alike. More narrowly, "flesh" can be used as a designation for all humanity. The famous prophecy in Joel 2:28-32, which is quoted and fulfilled in Acts 2:17-21, promised that God's Spirit would be poured out on "all flesh." Clearly, in this case, only humanity is in view.

In an even narrower sense, "flesh" can refer to one's relatives. Leviticus 18:6, for example, employs the term in prohibitions against sexual intimacy with close family members.

Flesh as a Designation for the Sinful Nature In the NT, especially in the Pauline Epistles, the term "flesh" takes on a specialized theological meaning. Paul consistently uses the term "flesh" in reference to the fallen human nature that is incapable of conforming to God's holy expectations (Rom. 7:5,18; 8:3-9; Gal. 3:3). In this sense, "flesh" is unaided human effort—mere human strength without the power of the Holy Spirit. It is this "flesh" that offers sin a foothold in a believer's life (Rom. 8:3-4,9; Gal. 3:3; 5:16-17). Paul explains that the flesh and the Spirit are in conflict with each other within believers, necessitating the believer's denial of sinful desires and cooperation with the Holy Spirit (Rom. 8:13; Gal. 2:19-21; Col. 3:5).

Unfortunately, many have misunderstood Paul's specialized use of the term "flesh" and have taken the passages mentioned above to mean that our bodies are inherently evil. Nothing, however, could have been further from Paul's mind. Paul taught that Christ himself came in the flesh and yet lived a sinless life (Rom. 1:3; 1 Tim. 3:16). Furthermore, the body is God's creation and therefore is good when it is devoted to God in holy service (1 Tim 4:4). In fact, Paul referred to the believer's body as the temple of the Holy Spirit, indicating its sacred nature and purpose (1 Cor. 6:19-20). The notion that the physical body is inherently evil and therefore an obstacle to spirituality came not from Paul but from Plato.

FLOOD Genesis 6–9 tells the story of the flood that covered the whole earth and of Noah, the man used by God to save the world of humans and beasts. Both OT and NT texts seem clearly to teach that the flood was universal (Gen. 7:19-24; 2 Pet. 3:6,20). But that does not mean that any one way of arguing for a universal flood, such as the catastrophist approach, for instance, is the last word on the matter. Much work remains to be done. What can be said is that the scientific evidence for a flood, even for a universal flood, is strong and growing daily.

FLOWERS Colorful blooms containing a plant's reproductive organs. Flowers grew abundantly during springtime in the land of Israel. Flowers grew mostly in open fields, since flower gardens as we now know them were not cultivated. Flowers grew in crop fields and in groves of trees around houses. Numerous kinds of wild flowers could be found in the plains and mountains. The words "flower" and "flowers" refer to colorful blossoms, towering plants, open flowers, and flourishing flowers. The warm spring temperatures joined with the winter rains to produce beautiful, blooming plants and flowers. Biblical flowers of note:

Almond blossoms (Gen. 43:11; Exod. 25:33-34; 37:19-20; Num. 17:8; Eccles. 12:5). The almond tree, a member of the rose family, had beautiful pink blossoms that the Israelites used as models for engravers to adorn the cups of the golden lampstand.

Bulrush (Exod. 2:3; Job 8:11; Isa. 18:2; 35:7). Sometimes referred to as "flag," "papyrus" (CSB, NIV), "reed" (NASB), or "rush" (NEB). This tall, slender reedlike plant grew along the banks of the Nile and provided the earliest known material for making paper and covering the frames of boats (Isa. 18:2).

Calamus leaves (Exod. 30:23; Song 4:14; Isa. 43:24; Jer. 6:20; Ezek. 27:19). The leaves from this plant were a sweet-smelling cane or ginger grass. The leaves, when crushed, gave a much relished ginger smell. It was apparently imported from India for use in worship (Jer. 6:20). Several Hebrew expressions lie behind "calamus." The basic Hebrew term *qaneh* means "cane." It is modified in Exod. 30:23 by the word for balsam, apparently referring to sweet cane or *Cymbopogon.*

A similar plant may be meant by *qaneh tob* in Jer. 6:20, *tob* meaning either "good" or "perfumed." Elsewhere, *qaneh* occurs without modification and may refer to different types of cane. For example, in 1 Kgs. 14:15, the giant reed *Arundo donax* may be meant (cp. Job 40:21; Isa. 19:6; 35:7).

Cyclamen is one of the flowers found in Israel. The flowers appear between December and early May, but there is a single region near Jericho where the plants flower in the autumn.

Camphire flowers (sometimes referred to as henna)(Song 1:14; 4:13; 7:11). The camphire was a small plant or shrub that bore beautiful cream-colored flowers that hung in clusters like grapes and were highly scented. It was used for orange dye.

Caperberry flowers (Eccles. 12:5 CSB, NASB). The caperberry was a prickly shrub that produced lovely flowers and small, edible berries as it grew in rocks and walls. It was supposed to stimulate sexual desires and powers. KJV, NRSV, NIV, TEV translate the Hebrew term as "desire" in Eccles. 12:5, but REB and NASB follow recent Hebrew dictionaries in translating it "caperberry" or "caper-buds."

Cockle flowers (Job 31:40). Purplish red flowers of a noxious weed called the "cockle" or "darnel" (*Lolium tenulentumro*). This plant grew abundantly in Palestinian grain fields. Its Hebrew name is spelled like the Hebrew word for "stink" and thus is translated "stinkweed" by CSB and NASB.

Crocus (Song 2:1; Isa. 35:1). Spring flowering herb with a long yellow floral tube tinged with purple specks or

stripes. It is sometimes translated as "rose." Technically it was probably the asphodel (Isa. 35:2 REB).

Fitch (Isa. 28:25-27). KJV calls this flower the "fitch," but the better designation is probably the nutmeg flower. This flower was a member of the buttercup family and grew wildly in most Mediterranean lands. The plant was about two feet high and had bright blue flowers. The pods of the plant were used like pepper. Technically the plant is probably dill (NRSV, NASB, REB) or more precisely black cumin (*Nigella sativaro*). NIV translates "caraway." See *Fitches*.

Leek (Num. 11:5). Member of the lily family, a bulbous biennial plant with broad leaves. The bases of the leaves were eaten as food. The bulbs of this plant were used as seasoning. Israel relished the memory of leeks (*Allium porrumro*) from Egypt.

Lily (1 Kgs. 7:19,22,26; 2 Chron. 4:5; Songs 2:1-2,16; 5:13; 6:2-3; 7:2; Hos. 14:5). The term "lily" covered a wide range of flowers. The most common was *Lilius candidum*. The lily mentioned in Song 5:13 refers to a rare variety of lily that had a bloom similar to a glow-

Israel's Star of Bethlehem flower

ing flame. The "lily of the valley" (Song 2:1-2,16) is known as the Easter lily. The lily mentioned in Hos. 14:5 is more akin to an iris. The beautiful water lily or lotus was a favorite flower in Egypt and was used to decorate Solomon's temple (1 Kgs. 7:19,22,26; 2 Chron. 4:5). The "lilies of the field" (Matt. 6:28; Luke 12:27; CSB, wildflowers) were probably numerous kinds of colorful spring flowers such as the crown anemone.

Mandrake (Gen. 30:14-16; Song 7:13). The mandrake, an herb of the nightshade family, had a rosette of large leaves and mauve flowers during winter and fragrant and round yellow fruit during spring. The mandrake grew in fields and rough ground. It was considered to give sexual powers and probably can be identified as *Atropa Mandragora*, often used for medicine in ancient times.

Mint (Matt. 23:23; Luke 11:42). Aromatic plant with hairy leaves and dense white or pink flowers. Mint was used to flavor food. The Jews scattered it on the floors of houses and synagogues for its sweet smell.

Myrtle branches (Neh. 8:15; Isa. 41:19; 55:13; Zech. 1:8-11). Myrtle bushes (*Myrtus communisro*), which grew on Palestinian hillsides, had fragrant evergreen leaves and scented white flowers. The flowers on the myrtle branches were used as perfumes.

Pomegranate blossoms (Exod. 28:33; Num. 13:23; 1 Sam. 14:2; 1 Kgs. 7:18). Blossoms from the pomegranate tree (*Punica granatumro*) had dark green leaves with large orange-red blossoms. Decorators carved pomegranates on public buildings. The fruit symbolized fertility and was used to tan leather and for medicine.

The blossoms and fruit of a pomegranate tree growing in Israel. The pomegranate is one of the seven species with which the land of Israel is blessed (Deut. 8:8). It is a frequent theme in Jewish art and is found atop the columns on the façade to the temple.

Rose (Song 2:1; Isa. 35:1). Several varieties of roses could be found in Palestine. The rose was a member of the crocus family. Traditionally what is considered a rose is not the flower mentioned in Scripture. The "rose" is more generally considered an asphodel. See *Crocus*, above.

Saffron (Song 4:14) (*Curcumalonga* or *Crocus sativasro*). A species of crocus. In ancient times, the petals of the saffron flower were used to perfume banquet halls. The type meant in Song 4:14 may be an exotic plant imported from India.

Other Though not specifically mentioned by kind in the Bible, other varieties of flowers grew in the land of Israel. Appearing as early as January were the pink, white, and lilac blossoms of the cyclamen. Dominating many landscapes were the various shades of reds and pinks of the crown anemones, poppies, and mountain tulips. Some short-lived summer flowers were the yellow and white daisy-like chrysanthemums.

FODDER Feed for domestic animals. The Hebrew suggests a mixed feed, either of several grains (though barley was the common grain for livestock, Judg. 19:19; 1 Kgs. 4:28) or a mix of finely cut straw, barley, and beans formed into balls. Silage refers to fodder that has been moistened and allowed to ferment slightly (Isa. 30:24 NRSV). Fodder was salted to satisfy the animals' need for salt and to give a tastier feed.

FOOD There were only two main meals for the Jewish family. Breakfast was taken informally soon after getting up and normally consisted of a flat bread cake and a piece of cheese, dried fruit, or olives. Sometimes the bread was wrapped around the appetizer, and sometimes the bread was split open to make a bag where the morsels might be placed.

After the midday rest, the evening meal was prepared on the fire; a vegetable or lentil stew was made in the large cooking pot, herbs and salt being used to add to the flavor. Only on special occasions such as a sacrifice or festival day was any meat added to the stew, and only on very rare occasions was the meat roasted or game or fish eaten. At the close of the meal, fruit would be eaten and the wine would be drunk.

FOOL, FOOLISHNESS, AND FOLLY Translations of several uncomplimentary words that appear approximately 360 times throughout the OT and NT to describe unwise and ungodly people. The words are especially predominant in the Wisdom literature of the OT.

FOOT Part of the human and animal body used for walking. In Scripture, "foot" refers mainly to the human foot (Exod. 12:11; Acts 14:8). It may also be used of the feet of animals (Ezek. 1:7) or, anthropomorphically, of God's feet (Isa. 60:13).

FOOTMAN KJV translation of two unrelated Hebrew terms. The first refers to foot soldiers as distinguished from cavalry (2 Sam. 8:4), to soldiers in general (1 Sam. 4:10; 15:4), or to men of military age (Exod. 12:37). The second term refers to a runner who served in the honor guard that ran ahead of the king's chariot (1 Sam. 8:11; 2 Sam. 15:1), to the king's guards in general (1 Kgs. 14:27-28; 2 Kgs. 10:25), or to royal couriers (Esth. 3:13,15).

FOOTSTOOL Piece of furniture for resting the feet, especially for one seated on a throne (2 Chron. 9:18; James 2:3). The footstool of Tutankhamun of Egypt was carved with pictures of his enemies. Other pharaohs were portrayed with their feet on their enemies' heads. In Ps. 110:1, God makes the messianic King triumph over his enemies, who are then made his footstool.

FOOTWASHING An act necessary for comfort and cleanliness for any who had traveled ancient dusty roads wearing sandals. Customarily, a host provided guests with water for washing their own feet (Judg. 19:21; Luke 7:44, where the complaint was that Simon had not provided water). Footwashing was regarded as so lowly a task that it could not be required of a Hebrew slave.

FOREKNOW, FOREKNOWLEDGE Scripture reveals God as being omniscient, that is, having exhaustive knowledge of all things—past, present, and future. Both the OT and the NT testify to God's comprehensive knowledge. Nothing is hidden from God's sight (Heb. 4:13). God's foreknowledge is that aspect of God's omniscience that relates to the future. Scripture clearly indicates that God's knowledge is not limited to the past and present. He is the One who announces events before they occur, and he makes known the end from the beginning (Isa. 42:9; 46:10a). It is this knowledge of the future, among other things, that distinguishes God from the false gods (Isa. 44:68; 48:14). It was not the prophets' clairvoyance but God's foreknowledge that made possible their predictions.

FORERUNNER Greek term *prodromos* (one who runs ahead) occurs only once in the NT (Heb. 6:20) where it serves as a designation for Christ. In secular Greek, it was frequently used as a military term for advanced scouts or cavalry that prepared for a full assault. In English, forerunner indicates one who precedes and indicates the approach of another. In this sense, John the Baptist is termed the forerunner of Jesus, though the NT does not use this term of John.

FOREST Large, naturally wooded areas, characteristic of the central hill country, the Galilee, and the Bashan. Large expanses of forest covered the majority of the hills in the land of Israel during the OT period. Large portions of the forests around Jerusalem were destroyed during the Roman siege of the city in AD 70.

FORGIVENESS Term used to indicate pardon for a fault or offense; to excuse from payment for a debt owed. God is characterized early in the life of Israel as a God who both forgives and holds the guilty accountable (Exod. 34:7; cp. Neh. 9:17). He is the source of forgiveness for Israel at Sinai (Exod. 32:2; 34:9). He provides forgiveness for sin through the sacrificial system (Lev. 4:20,26,28,31; 5:10,13,16,18; 6:7; 19:22). The prophets held this same covenant grace out to Israel if she would only repent from her presumption on God's grace and her election (Dan. 9:9;

Isa. 33:74; Jer. 33:8; Mic. 7:8). The psalms reveal the God of Israel as the same God found in the Torah. He does not allow the guilty to go unpunished, yet he is a God of forgiveness.

Forgiveness is a vital idea for NT theology. John's baptism was for repentance and the forgiveness of sins (Mark 1:4; Luke 1:76-77). The idea is found in the confession of the Christchild's destiny (Matt. 1:21; Luke 1:77). It is the blood of Jesus's atonement that yields eternal forgiveness of sins (Matt. 26:28; Heb. 10:11-12; Lev. 16; 17:11). Jesus places enormous emphasis on horizontal (human to human) forgiveness. Because Christians have been redeemed, they are obligated to forgive as they have been forgiven (Col. 3:13).

The NT also speaks of a sin that will not be forgiven (Mark 3:29; Luke 12:10). Presumably the sin of indignantly categorizing the spirit of Jesus, whom Jesus identifies as the Holy Spirit, as demonic reveals the desire to vilify God and to deny him any place as sovereign.

FORK Two types of forks (pronged implements) are mentioned in Scripture: an implement used in the sacrificial cult and a farm tool used to winnow grain.

FORNICATION Various acts of sexual immorality.

FORT, FORTIFICATION Walled structures built for defense against enemy armies. Cities of the ancient world were fortified for defensive purposes as far back as archaeological records exist. The oldest fortifications in Israel are at Jericho, where a Neolithic stone tower and part of a wall have been dated to 7000 BC.

Masada, the site of a palace built by Herod the Great, provides its own natural fortification.

FORTUNATUS Corinthian Christian who together with Stephanus and Achaicus ministered to Paul at Ephesus (1 Cor. 16:17).

FORUM The open place of a market town or the town itself. The Forum of Appius (Acts 28:15) or market town of Appius was located 43 miles to the southeast of Rome on the Appian Way.

FOUNTAIN Spring of water flowing from a hole in the earth. The limestone rock of Palestine is especially suited for the formation of springs. In semiarid country springs are highly prized as water sources and often determine the location of settlements. The goodness of Canaan was seen in its abundant water supply, "a land of brooks of water, of

Fountain in the center of Cisterna, a possible site for Three Taverns, near the Forum of Appius

fountains and springs, flowing forth in valleys and hills" (Deut. 8:7 NASB).

FOWLER One who traps birds. All biblical references are figurative. A variety of means are mentioned in Scripture: snares (Pss. 91:3; 124:7); traps (Ps. 141:9; Jer. 5:26-27); ropes (Job 18:10 KJV, "snare"); and nets (Hos. 7:12). God is praised as One who delivers from the fowler's snare (Pss. 91:3; 124:7), an image of the power of the wicked.

FOX Doglike carnivorous mammal, smaller than the wolf with shorter legs (Neh. 4:3). It has large erect ears and a long bushy tail (Judg. 15:4). It is referenced as cunning and crafty (cp. Luke 13:32).

FRANKINCENSE Ingredient used in making the perfume for the most holy place in the tabernacle (Exod. 30:34). It is a resinous substance derived from certain trees in the balsam family. Frankincense was one of the gifts presented to the child Jesus by the magi (Matt. 2:11).

FREEWILL OFFERING Gift given at the impulse of the giver (Exod. 35:21-29; 36:3-7; Lev. 7:16). The distinctive marks of the freewill offering were the "stirred hearts" and "willing spirits" of the givers. The tabernacle was constructed using materials given as freewill offerings (Exod. 35:29).

FRIEND, FRIENDSHIP Close trusting relationship between two people. Nowhere does the Bible present a concise definition of "friend" or "friendship." Friendship may be simple association (Gen. 38:12; 2 Sam. 15:37) or loving companionship, the most recognizable example being that between David and Saul's son Jonathan (1 Sam. 18:1,3; 20:17; 2 Sam. 1:26).

Friendship, however, was not limited to earthly associates. The OT also affirms friendship between God and human persons. The relationship between God and Moses (Exod. 33:11) is likened to friendship because they conversed face to face.

In the NT, the predominant word for friend is *philos*. A derivative, *philia*, is often used for friendship. Jesus is described as the "friend of . . . sinners" (Matt. 11:19 CSB). He called his disciples "friends" (Luke 12:4; John 15:13-15).

FRINGE Tassels of twisted cords fastened to the four corners of the outer garment, worn by observant Jews as a reminder of covenant obligations (Num. 15:38,39; Deut. 22:12; cp. Zech. 8:23). The woman suffering from chronic hemorrhage touched the tassel of Jesus's cloak (Matt. 9:20; Luke 8:44).

FROG Amphibious animal specifically used by God as a plague against Pharaoh and his people (Exod. 8:2-15).

FRONTLETS Objects containing Scripture passages worn on the forehand and between the eyes, primarily at prayer times. Jews followed scriptural commands, literally, writing Exod. 13:1-16; Deut. 6:4-9; 11:13-21 on small scrolls, placing these in leather containers and placing these on their forehead and left arm (Exod. 13:9,16; Deut. 6:8; 11:18).

By NT times, the frontlets were known as phylacteries (Matt. 23:5).

A modern orthodox Jewish man praying at the Western Wall in Jerusalem wearing his frontlet

FULFILL Verb used in three senses that merit special attention: an ethical sense of observing or meeting requirements; a prophetic sense of corresponding to what was promised, predicted, or foreshadowed; and a temporal sense related to the arrival of times ordained by God.

FULLER One who thickens and shrinks newly shorn wool or newly woven cloth; also one who washes or bleaches clothing.

FURNITURE Equipment in a home used for rest, beautification, storage, and workspace.

Sacred Furniture Biblical interest in furniture focuses on the sacred furnishings of the tabernacle and the temple. We have in Exod. 25–27; 30; 37–38 a full description of the tabernacle with all its objects of furniture.

Common Furniture But this is not the case regarding the furniture of the common people living out their daily lives in their tents and houses. The Bible occasionally refers to basic furniture items such as beds, chairs, etc., but we have virtually nothing about manufacturers, building materials, designs, or appearances.

The Sea of Galilee as viewed from the northwest

GAAL Personal name meaning "abhorrence," "neglect," or perhaps "dung-beetle." Man who usurped Abimelech's leadership in Shechem but met sudden defeat from Abimelech and left the city (Judg. 9:26-41).

GAASH Place-name meaning "rising and falling noisily." A height in the hill country of Ephraim that cannot be located any more precisely. Joshua was buried there (Josh. 24:30). Hiddai, one of David's 30 military heroes, came from the brooks of Gaash (2 Sam. 23:30).

GABBAI Personal name traditionally interpreted as meaning "tax collector." Member of the tribe of Benjamin who settled in Jerusalem in the time of Nehemiah (Neh. 11:8).

GABBATHA English transliteration of Greek transliteration of Aramaic place-name meaning "elevation." A platform in front of the praetorian's or governor's palace in Jerusalem, where Pilate sat in judgment over Jesus (John 19:13), pronouncing the sentence to crucify Jesus.

GABRIEL Personal name meaning "strong man of God." The heavenly messenger who interpreted to Daniel the meaning of the vision of the ram and the goat. He appears four times in the Bible, each time bringing to human beings a message from the Lord. Twice he appeared to Daniel (8:15-27; 9:20-27). In the NT, he appeared to announce the births of John the Baptist (Luke 1:8-20) and Jesus (Luke 1:26-38).

GAD Personal name meaning "good fortune." **1.** Seventh son of Jacob and the progenitor of the tribe of Gad (Gen. 30:9-11). His mother was Leah's maid Zilpah. **2.** Syrian god known from inscriptions from Phoenicia and Palmyra and used in biblical names such as Baal-gad (Josh. 11:17) and Migdal-gad (Josh. 15:37). **3.** Prophet who advised David as he fled from Saul (1 Sam. 22:5) and who brought God's options for punishment after David took a census of Israel (2 Sam. 24:11-14).

GADARENE Resident of Gadara, one of the cities of Decapolis (Matt. 2:28; Mark 5:1 CSB: Gerasenes).

GADDI Personal name meaning "my good fortune." Spy from the tribe of Manasseh sent by Moses to examine the land of Canaan prior to Israel's conquest (Num. 13:11).

GADDIEL Personal name meaning "God is my good fortune." Spy from the tribe of Zebulun that Moses sent to examine Canaan, the land to be conquered (Num. 13:10).

GADFLY (Jer. 46:20 NIV, NRSV) Stinging insect (stinging fly, TEV), either a horsefly (*Tabanidae*, CSB, NASB) or a botfly (*Oestridae*).

GADI Personal name meaning "my good fortune." A variant Hebrew spelling of Gaddi using same word as Gadite. Father of Menahem, king of Israel (752–742 BC) (2 Kgs. 15:14,17).

GADITE Member of tribe of Gad.

GAHAM Personal name meaning "flame." Son of Nahor, Abraham's brother, by his concubine Reumah (Gen. 22:24).

GAHAR Personal name meaning "drought" or "small in spirit" or "red-faced." Clan head of family of temple servants who returned from Babylonian captivity with Zerubbabel about 537 BC (Ezra 2:47).

GAIUS Greek form of Latin name *Caius* meaning "I am glad, rejoice." **1.** Macedonian Christian who was one of Paul's traveling companions (Acts 19:29). **2.** Christian from Derbe who accompanied Paul the apostle into Asia (Acts 20:4). **3.** Paul the apostle's host in Corinth (Rom. 16:23). According to 1 Cor. 1:14, he was one of the individuals in Corinth whom Paul personally had baptized. **4.** The Christian John loved and to whom he addressed 3 John (3 John 1).

GALAL Personal name meaning "roll" or "turtle." **1.** Levite among those who settled in Jerusalem after the exile (1 Chron. 9:15). **2.** Grandfather of Adda, a Levite who led in Nehemiah's thanksgiving (Neh. 11:17).

GALATIA Geographical name derived from Gaul because its inhabitants were Celts or Galli (Gauls). The original settlement was in central Asia Minor. Paul visited Galatia (Acts 16:6; 18:23), though his precise route is not clear. It is not known whether he visited Phrygian-dominated cities or the true Galatians in the countryside or whether his letter was addressed to the original territory in the north or to the Roman province with its southern additions (cp. 1 Cor. 16:1; 2 Tim. 4:10, where some manuscripts have Gaul, and 1 Pet. 1:1).

GALATIANS, LETTER TO THE Galatians is Paul's most intense letter. His anger at their situation is evidenced by the omission of his usual expression of praise after the salutation. The Galatian churches were founded by Paul (4:13-15), but others, probably from Jerusalem, visited the Galatians espousing views contrary to what Paul had taught. Their teachings centered on the need to supplement faith in Christ with obedience to the law of Moses. Circumcision was required, since it marked the "conversion" of a Gentile male to Judaism. The false teachers were referred to as "Judaizers."

The letter can be divided into three main sections. In the first (Gal. 1:10–2:21), Paul defends his apostleship as given directly by God through Christ, not dependent on Jerusalem or those who were apostles before him. Paul concludes this section by stating the main argument of the epistle: Justification is by faith in Christ and the works of the law must not be added. Faith is living one's life in constant submission to Christ and in relationship to Christ. In fact, Paul says, "Christ lives in me." In the second section (3:1–5:12), he supports his thesis by appeals to the Galatians' own experience, inheritance practices, and the experiences of Abraham. Paul reminds them that Abraham was declared righteous when he was uncircumcised. He, too, had simply believed God and this faith was credited to him as righteousness (3:6-9). Reliance on the law placed one under the curse of the law (3:10-14). The purpose of Christ's work was to free (redeem) from the curse.

The third major section (5:13–6:10) contains Paul's appeal to live by the Spirit. They must not lose their spiritual freedom by giving in to sin. Life in the Spirit does not rule out moral absolutes. Paul's emphasis on justification by faith was an argument for the Galatians to live out their freedom. That freedom, however, must not be taken as meaning there is no moral accountability. The command that they not live by the law of Moses is not inconsistent with directions on how to live. The "works of the flesh" (5:19) are obvious and must be avoided. They must nurture the fruit of the Spirit (5:22-23a) and act in love toward each other. In this way they will fulfill the law of Christ.

The closing section is written in Paul's own hand and again challenges them not to return to dependence on the law (6:11-18).

GALEED Place-name meaning "pile for witness." Place where Jacob and his father-in-law Laban made a formal agreement or covenant determining the boundary line between their peoples and agreeing not to harm one another (Gen. 31:43-52). The place was also called Sahadutah and Mizpah.

GALILEAN Person who lived in Galilee. Dialect distinguished them from Jews in Jerusalem and Judah, particularly the difficulty in distinguishing the sounds of the gutturals that are important in Hebrew and Aramaic. Peter's Galilean style of speech set him apart from the courtyard crowd during Jesus's trial (Mark 14:70; cp. Acts 2:7).

GALILEE Place-name meaning "circle" or "region." The northern part of Palestine above the hill country of Ephraim and the hill country of Judah (Josh. 20:7). The term "Galilee" apparently was used prior to Israel's conquest, being mentioned in Egyptian records. It was used in Israel but not as a political designation. The tribes of Naphtali, Asher, Issachar, Zebulun, and Dan occupied the territory that covered approximately the 45-mile stretch between the Litani River in Lebanon and the valley of Jezreel in Israel, north to south, and from the Mediterranean Sea to the Jordan River, west to east.

In the time of Jesus's Galilee, Herod Antipas governed Galilee and Perea. Jesus devoted most of his earthly ministry to Galilee, being known as the Galilean (Matt. 26:69). After the fall of Jerusalem in AD 70, Galilee became the major center of Judaism, the Mishnah and Talmud being collected and written there.

GALILEE, SEA OF Place-name meaning "circle." A freshwater lake nestled in the hills of northern Israel. Its surface is nearly 700 feet below the level of the Mediterranean, some 30 miles to the west. The nearby hills of Galilee reach an altitude of 1,500 feet above sea level. To the east are the mountains of Gilead with peaks of more than 3,300 feet. To the north are the snow-covered Lebanon Mountains. Fed chiefly by the Jordan River, which originates in the foothills of the Lebanon Mountains, the Sea of Galilee is 13 miles long north and south and eight miles wide at its greatest east-west distance. Because of its location, it is subject to sudden and violent storms that are usually of short duration. In the OT, this sea is called Chinnereth. In NT times, it was also called the "lake of Gennesaret." Once John called it the "Sea of Tiberias" (6:1).

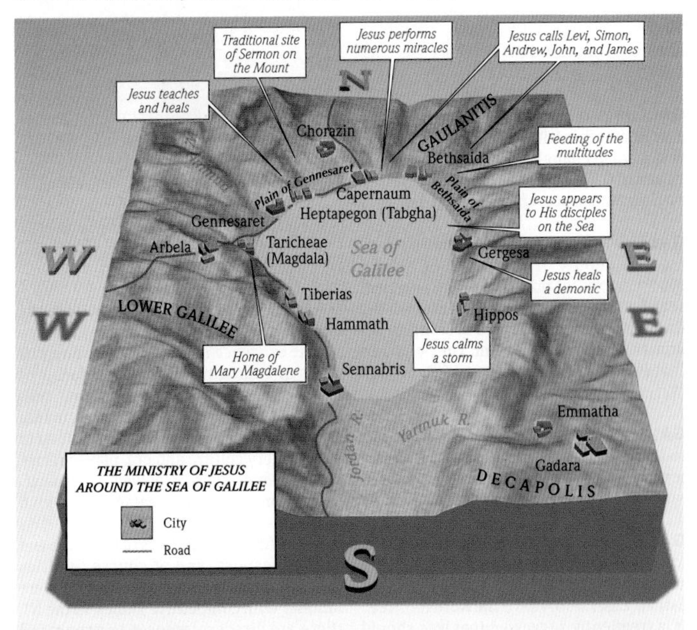

Capernaum, which played a major role in the ministry of Jesus, was a center of that industry. The other lake towns of importance were Bethsaida, which means "the fishing place," and Tiberias, a Gentile city constructed by Herod Antipas when Jesus was a young man.

GALL **1.** Bitter, poisonous herb (perhaps *Citrullus colocynthis*), the juice of which is thought to be the "hemlock" poison that Socrates drank. Gall was frequently linked with wormwood (Deut. 29:18; Jer. 9:15; 23:15; Lam. 3:19; Amos 6:12) to denote bitterness and tragedy. **2.** Expressed by two different Hebrew words, used in three senses in connection with the liver: (1) as an organ, either the liver or the gallbladder, through which a sword might pass when one was run through (Job 20:25); (2) as bile, a sticky, yellow-greenish, alkaline fluid secreted by the liver, which might be poured out on the ground when one was disemboweled (Job 16:13); (3) in a figurative sense (Job 13:26), for bitterness (bitter things, NASB, NIV, NRSV; bitter charges, REB, TEV; bitter accusations, CSB).

GALLIM Place-name meaning "piles." Village near Anathoth in tribal territory of Benjamin. Saul gave his daughter Michal as wife to a citizen of Gallim after taking her away from David (1 Sam. 25:44; cp. 2 Sam. 3:14-15).

GALLIO Personal name of unknown meaning. The deputy or proconsul of Achaia headquartered in Corinth, where his judgment seat has been discovered. Certain Jews brought Paul before Gallio seeking to get Roman punishment of him. They charged that Paul advocated an unlawful religion (Acts 18:12-17).

GALLON Word used by modern translations to transfer Greek *metretes* into modern terminology. A *metretes* contained about nine gallons (cp. John 2:6; KJV reads "firkin").

GALLOWS English translation referring to the platform on which a person was hanged. The Hebrew term translated "gallows" in Esther (2:23; 7:9-10; 9:25) is the word for "tree." It is frequently suggested that tree should be understood as "stake" and that those executed by the Persians were impaled rather than hung.

GAMALIEL Personal name meaning "God rewards with good." **1.** Son of Pedahzur; a leader of the tribe of Manasseh who helped Moses take the census in the wilderness (Num. 1:10; cp. 7:54-59). **2.** Highly regarded Pharisee who was a member of the Sanhedrin (Acts 5:34). He squelched a plan by the Sanhedrin to kill the apostles by reminding the members that interference with what the apostles were doing might prove to be opposition to God. **3.** A leading Jewish rabbi in the late first and early second centuries AD. He was the grandson of the Gamaliel mentioned in the book of Acts. He is credited with many of the adaptations in Judaism necessitated by the destruction of the temple in AD 70.

The interior of the traditional site of the tomb of Gamaliel

GAMES Archaeological finds from the ancient Near East provide ample evidence for the existence in antiquity of numerous types of games, including early forms of checkers and chess. Likewise, various children's toys found in Palestine confirm that Hebrew children, like their counterparts in nearly every culture and era, played recreational games. There is, however, no specific mention of organized games of any kind in the OT.

By the first century, Jews in Palestine and in the Diaspora, and of course Gentiles throughout the Mediterranean world, were familiar with competitive games. In the NT, there are direct references to games and competitions, particularly in the Pauline Epistles. For those living in first-century Corinth, illustrations from competitive games would be easily understood not only from everyday life, but also because it was the site of the Isthmian Games (AD 51), an event second only to the Olympics in prestige. Both Paul and the writer of Hebrews found illustrations of the Christian life in the competitive games of the first century.

Children in present-day Jerusalem playing a game in the street on the Via Dolorosa

GAMUL Personal name meaning "receiver of good deeds." Head of one of the priestly divisions in the temple under David and Solomon (1 Chron. 24:17).

GANGRENE Greek *gangraina* (2 Tim. 2:17) can refer either to gangrene, a death of soft tissue resulting from problems with blood flow (CSB, NASB, NRSV, REB) or to an ulcer (canker, KJV; open sore, TEV). In 2 Timothy, *gangraina* is used figuratively for false teachings that destroy people who accept them.

GARDEN In biblical times, an enclosed plot of ground on which flowers, vegetables, herbs, and fruit and nut trees were cultivated (Gen. 2:8; 1 Kgs. 21:2; Esth. 1:5; Isa. 51:3; John 18:1-2).

The garden of Eden (Gen. 2:8; 3:23-24) was planted by God (2:8) and entrusted to Adam for cultivating and keeping (2:15). Following their sin, Adam and Eve were banished from the garden; but "Eden, the garden of God" (Ezek. 28:13) continued as a symbol of bless-

The Garden of Gethsemane looking west toward the city wall of old Jerusalem

ing and bounty (Ezek.36:35; Joel 2:3). The "king's garden" in Jerusalem was located near a gate to the city that provided unobserved exit or escape (2 Kgs. 25:4; Neh. 3:15; Jer. 39:4; 52:7). The "garden" (John 18:1) called Gethsemane (Matt. 26:36; Mark 14:32) was a place where Jesus often met with his disciples (John 18:2) and where he was betrayed and arrested.

GAREB Personal name and place-name meaning "scabby." **1.** Member of David's personal army (2 Sam. 23:38). **2.** Hill in Jerusalem marking point of city wall which Jeremiah promised would be rebuilt (Jer. 31:39).

GARLAND In modern translations, two Hebrew terms and one Greek term, all referring to wreaths worn on the head. Garlands symbolized instruction or the benefit of wisdom (Prov. 1:8-9; 4:7-9).

GARMITE Title or designation meaning "my bone" used for Keilah in the tribe of Judah (1 Chron. 4:19). The Hebrew text and the exact meaning of Garmite are obscure.

GARNER KJV term for a barn, storehouse, or granary (Ps. 144:13; Joel 1:17; Matt. 3:12; Luke 3:17). To garner (Isa. 62:9 NASB, NRSV) means to gather (a crop) for storage.

GASH In modern translations, to cut the skin as a sign of mourning (CSB, NASB, Jer. 41:5; 47:5; 48:37) or in the worship of pagan deities (1 Kgs. 18:28).

GASHMU Aramaic form of *Geshem* used in Neh. 6:6.

GATAM Personal name of uncertain meaning. Son of Eliphaz and grandson of Esau (Gen. 36:11). He headed a clan of Edomites (Gen. 36:16).

GATE A gate, like a door, a wall, or a threshold, sets a boundary between that which is inside and that which is outside. "Gate" is the more prominent term since it provided the most common access into towns and villages, temples, and even houses. In reality, a gate serves both to allow access and to limit access. Open gates allowed entrance, though gatekeepers were often employed to ascertain that only authorized persons gained entry (1 Chron. 9:22). Shut gates offered protection and safety for those inside (Josh. 2:5). Because the gate was the primary means of entry, it was often the site where enemies assembled for attack or forced entry (Jer. 1:15).

The Damascus Gate at Jerusalem as seen from outside the old city walls

The Bible has several figurative or symbolic allusions to gates. Jacob, after his dream at Bethel, describes the place as "the house of God . . . the gate of heaven" (Gen. 28:17 CSB). In effect, for Jacob this spot marked a symbolic boundary between heaven and earth. Both Job and the psalmist speak of the gates of death (Job 38:17; Ps. 107:18). The gates of death mark the boundary between life and death. King Hezekiah in the book of Isaiah speaks of being consigned to the gates of Sheol the rest of his days, a clear reference to his death (Isa. 38:10). Jesus says of the church, "the gates of Hades will not overpower it" (Matt. 16:18 CSB). Hades, the realm of the underworld and the dead, has no power over Christ's church.

GATH One of the five cities that comprised the Philistine city-state system (1 Sam. 6:17). The inhabitants of Gath were referred to as the Gittites (1 Sam. 17:4; 2 Sam. 6:10-11). In addition to Gath, the other towns of the Philistine city-state system were Ekron, Ashdod, Ashkelon, and Gaza (1 Sam. 6:17). We may reasonably assume that Gath was the principal city among the five and served as the hub of the Pentapolis.

GATH-HEPHER Place-name meaning "winepress on the watering hole." A city on the eastern border of Zebulun's tribal allotment (Josh. 19:13). The prophet Jonah came from Gath-hepher (2 Kgs. 14:25). It is located at modern el-Meshed or nearby Khirbet ez-Zurra, three miles northeast of Nazareth.

GATH-RIMMON Place-name meaning "winepress on the pomegranate tree." Town in tribal territory of Dan (Josh. 19:45) and set aside for Levites (21:24).

GAZA Place-name meaning "strong." Philistine city on the coastal plain about three miles inland from the Mediterranean Sea. It was the southernmost town of the Philistine city-state system, which also included Ashkelon, Ashdod, Ekron, and Gath (1 Sam. 6:17).

GAZELLE Fleet-footed animal noted for its attractive eyes. Native to the Middle East, this animal resembles an antelope but is

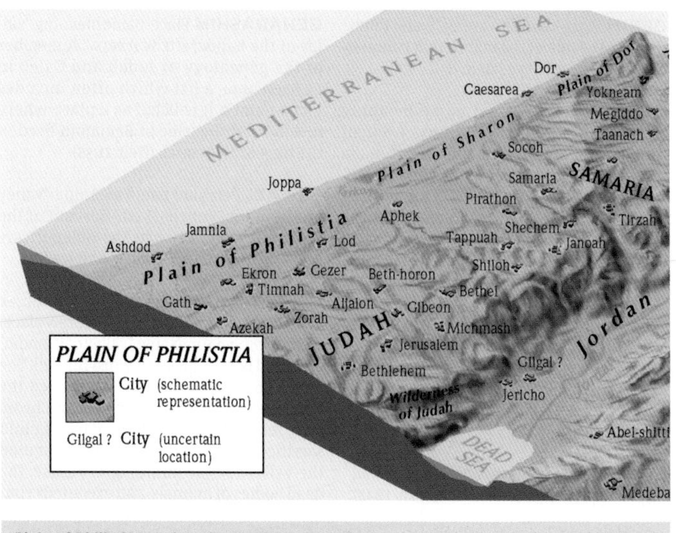

Plain of Philistia touches the Mediterranean Sea.

smaller. They were considered clean by the Israelites and thus were permitted as food (Deut. 12:15,22).

GAZER KJV spelling of Gezer based on Hebrew accented form (2 Sam. 5:25; 1 Chron. 14:16).

GAZEZ Personal name meaning "sheepshearing." Name of both Caleb's son and grandson (1 Chron. 2:46). As other names in the list represent cities in southern Judah occupied by the clan of Caleb, Gazez may also be a city, though nothing else is known about it.

GAZZAM Personal name meaning "caterpillar" or "bird of prey." Leader of a clan of temple servants who returned from Babylonian captivity with Zerubbabel (Ezra 2:48).

GEAR Context of Acts 27:17 indicates that the Greek term underlying "gear" (RSV) refers to some type of nautical equipment or apparatus.

GEBA Place-name meaning "hill" and variant Hebrew spelling of Gibeah, with which it is sometimes confused, though the two represent different towns in the territory of Benjamin. Geba was given to Benjamin (Josh. 18:24) but set aside for the Levites (21:17).

GEBAL Place-name meaning "mountain." **1.** Seaport known to Greeks as Byblos whose help for Tyre Ezekiel described (Ezek. 27:9). **2.** Member of a coalition against Israel that the psalmist lamented (Ps. 83:7). It is the northern part of Arabia near Petra in the mountainous country south of the Dead Sea. *The Genesis Apocryphon* from the Dead Sea Scrolls also mentions it.

GEBALITE Citizens of Gebal.

GEBER Personal name meaning "young man" or "hero." Solomon's district governor for Gilead beyond the Jordan (1 Kgs. 4:19) was the son of Uri. He collected provisions to supply the royal court. The district governor over Ramoth-gilead was Ben-geber or the son of Geber.

GEBIM Place-name meaning "water ditch." It lay on the line of the march that conquerors took against Jerusalem (Isa. 10:31).

GEDALIAH Personal name meaning "Yahweh has done great things." **1.** Son of Ahikam who was appointed ruler of Judah by Nebuchadnezzar of Babylon in 587 BC (2 Kgs. 25:22). **2.** Royal official under King Zedekiah (597–586 BC) who was with the group that got the king's permission to imprison Jeremiah in a cistern (Jer. 38). **3.** Temple singer and prophet who played the harp with his father Jeduthan and five brothers (1 Chron. 25:3). He headed one of the 24 divisions of temple servants (1 Chron. 25:9).

GEDEON KJV transliteration of Greek for Gideon in Heb. 11:32.

GEDER Place-name meaning "stone wall." City whose king Joshua killed (Josh. 12:13).

GEDERAH Place-name meaning "sheepfold" or "stone wall." A village in the Shephelah or valley of Judah (Josh. 15:36). Villagers were noted for skill in making pottery, much of which was made for the king (1 Chron. 4:23).

GEDERITE Citizen of Geder.

GEDEROTH Place-name meaning "walls." City in tribal allotment of Judah in the Shephelah or valley (Josh. 15:41).

GEDEROTHAIM Place-name meaning "two walls" or common noun referring to sheepfolds (cp. REB translation, namely both parts of Gederah). A town in the valley or Shephelah of Judah allotted to Judah (Josh. 15:36).

GEDOR Place-name meaning "wall." **1.** Town in hill country of Judah allotted to tribe of Judah (Josh. 15:58). It is located at Khirbet Judur three miles north of Hebron and Beth-zur and west of Tekoa. **2.** In 1 Chron. 4:18, Jered is the father of Gedor. **3.** The Gedor in 1 Chron. 4:39 probably represents an early copyist's change from Gerar, which is quite similar in appearance in Hebrew and appears in the earliest Greek translation.

GEHARASHIM Place-name meaning "valley of the handcrafts workers." A member of the genealogy of Judah and Caleb in 1 Chron. 4:14, a list which often includes place-names. It is listed as a place where members of the tribe of Benjamin lived in the time of Nehemiah (Neh. 11:35).

GEHAZI Personal name meaning "valley of vision" or "goggle-eyed." Servant of the prophet Elisha (2 Kgs. 4:12). The Bible portrays him as a man of questionable character.

GEHENNA English equivalent of the Greek word (*geena*) derived from the Hebrew place-name (*gehinnon*) meaning "valley of Hinnom" and used in NT times as a word for hell. The valley south of Jerusalem now called the Wadi er-Rababi (Josh. 15:8; 18:16; 2 Chron. 33:6; Jer. 32:35) became the place of child sacrifice to foreign gods. The Jews later used the valley for the dumping of refuse, the dead bodies of animals, and executed criminals. The NT uses "Gehenna" to speak of the place of final punishment.

View of the valley of Gehenna (Hinnom Valley) looking northeast toward the new city of Jerusalem

GELILOTH Place-name meaning "circles" or "regions." Border point north of Jerusalem in tribal allotment of Benjamin (Josh. 18:17). It appears to correspond to Gilgal in the description of Judah (Josh. 15:7).

GEMALLI Personal name meaning "my camel" or "camel driver." Spy who represented the tribe of Dan in searching out the land of Canaan (Num. 13:12).

GEMARIAH Personal name meaning "Yahweh has completed or carried out." **1.** Messenger King Zedekiah (597–586 BC) sent to Babylon. He carried a letter from Jeremiah to the exiles (Jer. 29:3). **2.** Son of Shaphan, the court scribe, who had a room in the temple, where Baruch read from Jeremiah's sermons to the congregation (Jer. 36:10). Later, Gemariah sought to keep the king from burning Jeremiah's scroll (v. 25).

GENEALOGIES Written or oral expressions of the descent of a person or persons from an ancestor or ancestors. Genealogies are presented in two forms: in concise lists or within narratives that will contain additional information. Biblical genealogies do not always name all the members of the family line. They serve a selective function, depending on the purpose(s) of the author.

GENERAL With reference to Sisera (Judg. 4:7) and Joab (1 Chron. 27:34), a general (NRSV) is the highest-ranking officer in command of an army. General, commander, and (chief) captain are used interchangeably for such an officer in English translations. KJV consistently translates "captain" or "chief captain."

GENERATION Period of time and its significant events comprising the life span of a person but also used to talk of a more indefinite time span. Two Hebrew words are at times translated "generation." The more significant of these is *toledot*, derived from the Hebrew verb meaning "to bear children." In the NT, "generation" refers to a specific contemporary audience. Jesus often used the term to describe the evil nature of the people he addressed (Matt. 11:16; 12:39; Luke 17:25). The message of the NT can be summarized: "to him be glory in the church and in Christ Jesus to all generations, forever and ever" (Eph. 3:21 CSB).

GENESIS, BOOK OF The first book of the Bible and the first of five written by Moses. Genesis describes the creation of all things by the mighty acts of the one true God, human rebellion, punishment, and restoration (Gen. 1–11:9). The remainder explains the origins of the people of God, Israel, and their place in God's plan of redemption (Gen. 11:10–50:26).

God is the central character of Genesis. He is sovereign Lord and Creator of all things. Genesis assumes the fact of divine creation but does not try to prove it. Genesis does not specify when creation occurred or exactly how long it took. Genesis eloquently teaches that God created all things, including Adam and Eve, by special creation for fellowship with himself. They were created innocent and with free wills. Freely they chose to disobey God, fell from innocence, and lost their freedom. Their fallen nature was passed to every other human being. The freedom of human wills is limited by fallen human nature. Humans are moral agents who make choices, but their wills are not free to obey God. Death came because of sin, and humanity was so corrupt that God wiped them out and started over with Noah. The second humanity also proved corrupt, and God confused their languages and scattered them. God's plan of redemption began to unfold by his calling of one man to found a family, one family chosen from among all the families of the earth. That family would be the source of blessing and salvation for all peoples. Through each generation in Genesis, God demonstrated that the promise depended only on his sovereign power and that no circumstance, person, family, or nation could thwart his purposes. Human sin could not destroy God's plan, but rather provided him opportunity to demonstrate his glory. Joseph may lie dead in a casket in Egypt, but his dying command was that his bones be carried home to Canaan when, not if, God brought his people again into the land he promised Abraham, Isaac, and Jacob.

GENNESARET Another name for the Sea of Galilee.

GENTILES People who are not part of God's chosen family at birth and thus can be considered "pagans." Though not synonymous in English, "Gentiles," "nations," "pagans," and "heathens" are variants chosen by translators to render *goyim* in Hebrew and *ethnoi* in Greek.

GENUBATH Personal name meaning "theft" or "foreign guest." Son of Hadad, king of Edom, and the sister of Tahpenes, the wife of Egypt's pharaoh (1 Kgs. 11:19-20). The name of the Egyptian pharaoh is not known.

GERA Personal name meaning "stranger," "alien," or "sojourner." **1.** Son of Benjamin and grandson of Jacob (Gen. 46:21). **2.** Grandson of Benjamin (1 Chron. 8:3,5). Son of Ehud and clan head in Geba who was exiled to Manahath (1 Chron. 8:6-7). **3.** Father of Ehud (Judg. 3:15). **4.** Father of Shimei, who cursed David (2 Sam. 16:5).

GERAH Smallest biblical measure of weight equaling one-twentieth of a shekel. Archaeological discoveries show a gerah weighed about half a gram.

GERAR Place-name possibly meaning "drag away." City located between Gaza and Beer-sheba. Abraham and Isaac made treaties with the king of Gerar (Gen. 20; 26).

GERASA Two places bear this name. One of them is referred to in the Bible; the other is not. According to some excellent ancient manuscript evidence, Mark 5:1 and Luke 8:26 located the healing of the demon-possessed man who lived among the tombs in "the country of the Gerasenes (Gadarenes)" ("Gerasenes" in CSB, NIV, NASB). This would point to a place-named Gerasa.

The other Gerasa was located some 26 miles north of present-day Amman in Jordan. Its ruins are among the most excellently preserved in the Middle East.

GERASENES Citizens of Gerasa.

GERGESENES KJV reading in Matt. 8:28. Modern translations read "Gadarenes."

GERIZIM AND EBAL Closely related place-names meaning "cut off ones" and "stripped one" or "baldy." Two mountains that form the sides of an important east-west pass in central Israel known as the valley of Shechem.

When the Israelites conquered central Israel, Joshua carried out the directive given by Moses and placed half of the tribes on Mount Gerizim to pronounce the blessing (Deut. 27:12) and the other half on Mount Ebal to pronounce the curses (Deut. 11:29; Josh. 8:30-35). Joshua built an altar on Ebal (Josh. 8:30).

GERSHOM Personal name meaning "sojourner there," "expelled one," or "protected of the god Shom." **1.** Firstborn son of Moses and Zipporah (Exod. 2:22). **2.** Son of Levi and head of a clan of Levitic priests (1 Chron. 6:16-20,43,62,71; 15:7). First Chronicles 23:14 shows that Moses's sons had been incorporated into the line of Levites (cp.

The ruins of ancient Gerasa located in the modern country of Jordan

1 Chron. 26:24). **3.** Man who accompanied Ezra on the return from Babylon to Jerusalem (Ezra 8:2).

GERSHOMITES NRSV term for "sons of Gershom" (1 Chron. 6:62,71).

GERSHON Personal name meaning "expelled" or "bell." Eldest son of Levi (Gen. 46:11). He was the progenitor of the Gershonites, who had specifically assigned responsibilities regarding the transporting of the tabernacle during the years of Israel's nomadic existence in the wilderness (cp. Exod. 6:16-17; Num. 3:17-25; 4:22-41; 7:7; 10:17; 26:57; Josh. 21:6,27).

GERSHONITE Descendant of Gershon.

GERUTH Part of a place-name meaning "hospitality" (Jer. 41:17) translated differently—KJV: "habitation of Chimham"; CSB, NASB, NRSV: "Geruth Chimham"; REB: "Kimham's holding."

GESHAM Personal name with variant spellings, perhaps meaning "rain." Son of Jahdai (1 Chron. 2:47).

GESHEM Personal name meaning "rain." Arabian ruler of Kedar who joined Sanballat and Tobiah in opposing Nehemiah's efforts to rebuild the wall of Jerusalem (Neh. 2:19; 6:1-19).

GESHUR Place-name perhaps meaning "bridge." Small Aramean city-state between Bashan and Hermon. It served as a buffer between Israel and Aram. David married Maacah, daughter of the king of Geshur, who became mother of Absalom (2 Sam. 3:3), which caused the two lands to be on friendly terms.

GETHER Aramean tribal name of uncertain meaning. They are Semites, their original ancestor being the grandson of Shem and great grandson of Noah (Gen. 10:23).

GETHSEMANE Place-name meaning "olive press." Place where Jesus went after the Last Supper, a garden outside the city, across the Kidron Valley, on the Mount of Olives (Matt. 26:36-56; Mark 14:32-52; Luke 22:39-53; John 18:1-14).Gethsemane was probably a remote walled garden (Jesus "entered" and "went out") where Jesus went often for prayer, rest, and fellowship with his disciples.

Looking toward the Garden of Gethsemane with the Church of All Nations in the center of the photo

GEUEL Personal name meaning "pride of God." Spy from the tribe of Gad whom Moses sent to inspect the land before conquering it (Num. 13:15).

GEZER An important city in the biblical period, located on a main juncture of the Via Maris, the Way of the Sea. It guarded the Aijalon Valley and the route from the coast up to Jerusalem and the Judean Hills. Joshua defeated the king of Gezer who was part of a Canaanite coalition (Josh. 10:33). Gezer remained in Canaanite hands throughout the period of the judges (Josh. 16:10; Judg. 1:29). David fought against the Philistines near Gezer (2 Sam. 5:25; 1 Chron. 20:4).

GHOST KJV uses "ghost" in two senses, for the human life force and for God's Holy Spirit. KJV never uses "ghost" for the disembodied spirits of the dead. All 11 OT KJV references involve the phrase "give up the ghost" (e.g., Gen. 25:8; 35:29), which means to cease breathing or simply to die. This phrase occurs eight times in the NT (Matt. 27:50; Acts 5:5; 12:23). The predominant NT use is for the Holy Spirit.

GIAH Place-name meaning "bubbling." Place where David's general, Joab, confronted Abner, Saul's general, after Abner killed Joab's brother Asahel (2 Sam. 2:24).

GIANTS Persons of unusual stature who often are reputed to possess great strength and power. The earliest biblical reference to giants is to the *nephilim* born to the "daughters of men" and the "sons of God" (Gen. 6:1-4).

A second class of giants who inhabited pre-Israelite Palestine was the *repha'im*. Their last survivor was Og, king of Bashan (Deut. 3:11,13).

GIBBAR Personal name meaning "young, powerful man." A man whose 95 descendants returned from Babylonian captivity with Zerubbabel in 537 BC (Ezra 2:20). The corresponding list in Neh. 7:25 has Gibeon.

GIBBETHON Place-name meaning "arched," "hill," or "mound." City in the tribal territory of Dan (Josh. 19:44) but assigned to the Levites (Josh. 21:23).

GIBEA Personal name meaning "hill." Son of Caleb by his concubine Maacah (1 Chron. 2:49).

GIBEAH Place-name meaning "a hill," closely related to names of Geba and Gibeon. Gibeah or Gibeath was the name of four different places in the OT. **1.** City in hill country of Judah allotted to tribe of Judah (Josh. 15:57). **2.** City closely connected with Phinehas, the high priest and grandson of Aaron. Phinehas buried his father Eleazar there (Josh. 24:33). **3.** The ark was lodged on a hill (Hb. *Gibeah*) during the period between its return by the Philistines and David's initial effort to move it to Jerusalem (2 Sam. 6:3-4). **4.** The most significant Gibeah was the city in the tribal territory of Benjamin (Josh. 18:28). A bloody civil war between Benjamin and the other Israelite tribes broke out when the men of Gibeah raped a traveling Levite's concubine (Judg. 19:1–21:25).

GIBEATH Alternative Hebrew spelling for Gibeah (Josh. 18:28) preserved in KJV spelling.

GIBEATH-ELOHIM Place-name meaning "hill of God."

GIBEATH-HAARALOTH Place-name meaning "hill of foreskins." KJV translates the place-name in Josh. 5:3, while modern translations transliterate it. Joshua used traditional flint stone knives rather than more modern metal ones to circumcise the Israelite generation about to conquer Canaan.

GIBEON Place-name meaning "hill place." This "great city" (Josh. 10:2) played a significant role in OT history, especially during the conquest of Canaan. Archaeology has demonstrated that the city was a thriving industrial area that made it a primary community in Canaan.

GIDDALTI Personal name meaning "I brought from there" or "I made great, praised." Son of Heman to whom David gave the task of prophesying through playing musical instruments (1 Chron. 25:4). He became a leader of a clan of temple musicians (1 Chron. 25:29).

GIDDEL Personal name meaning "he made great, praised." **1.** Clan leader of a group of temple servants who returned from the Babylonian captivity with Zerubbabel about 537 BC (Ezra 2:47). **2.** Original clan father of a group of royal servants who returned from the Babylonian exile with Zerubbabel about 537 BC (Ezra 2:56).

GIDEON Personal name meaning "one who cuts to pieces." The fifth major judge of 12th-century Israel. He was also called Jerubbaal and was the son of Joash of the tribe of Manasseh. He judged for 40 years (Judg. 6:11–8:35). Gideon was given the task of delivering the Israelites from the Midianites and Amalekites, desert nomads who repeatedly raided the country. Gideon was not a willing volunteer, but God gave him more than enough evidence that he was being called to this task. God then gave Gideon a strategy for getting the job done. Although Gideon is counted among the men and women of faith (Heb. 11:32), some of his actions in later life had the result that Gideon's family did not follow his God (Judg. 8:33).

GIDEONI Personal name meaning "one who cuts down or cuts to pieces." Father of Abidan, a leader of the tribe of Benjamin during the encampment in the wilderness (Num. 1:11; 2:22; 7:60; 10:24).

GIDOM Place-name meaning "cleared land." Place where tribes of Israel punished the tribe of Benjamin by killing 2,000 of Benjamin's soldiers (Judg. 20:45) for grossly mistreating a traveling Levite and his concubine.

GIFT, GIVING Favor or item bestowed on someone. Gifts were given on numerous occasions for a variety of purposes: as dowry for a wife (Gen. 34:12); as tribute to a military conqueror (2 Sam. 8:2); as bribes (Exod. 23:8; Prov. 17:8; Isa. 1:23); as rewards for faithful service and to ensure future loyalty (Dan. 2:48); and as relief for the poor (Esth. 9:22).

Both OT and NT witness to God as the giver of every good gift (1 Chron. 29:14; James 1:17). Human life is God's gift (Job 1:21), as are all things necessary for physical life.

Scripture also witnesses to God's gifts as evidence of a special providence. In the OT, such gifts include the promised land (Gen. 12:7), including its successful conquest (Deut. 2:36), possessing its cities (Deut. 6:10) and its spoils (Deut. 20:14); the Sabbath (Exod. 16:29); the promises (1 Kgs. 8:56); the covenants (2 Kgs. 17:15); the law (Exod. 24:12); and peace (Lev. 26:6). In the NT, God's special providence is especially evident in the gift of God's Son (John 3:16) and of God's Holy Spirit (Luke 11:13). God makes relationship with himself possible by giving his people

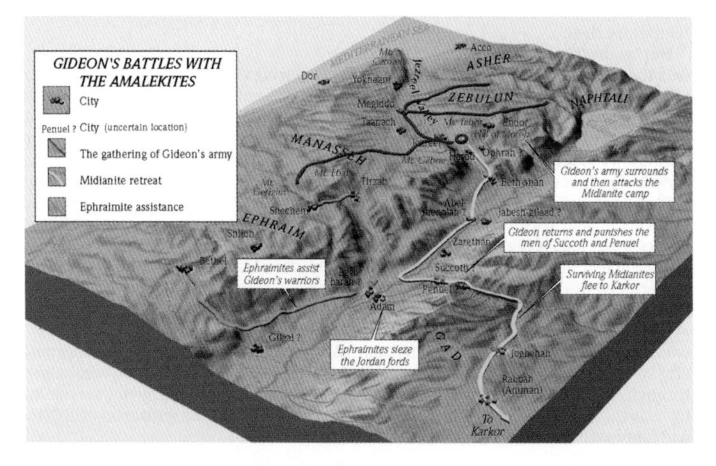

wisdom (1 Kgs. 4:29), understanding (1 Kgs. 3:9), a new heart (1 Sam. 10:9), and a good Spirit to teach them (Neh. 9:20). The NT expresses these gifts as the power to become children of God (John 1:12), justification from sin (Rom. 3:24; 5:15-17), and eternal life (John 10:28; Rom. 6:23).

Both Testaments witness to God's gift of leadership to God's people as priests (Num. 8:19; Zech. 3:7); Davidic kings (2 Chron. 13:5); deliverers (2 Kgs. 13:5); shepherds with Godlike hearts (Jer. 3:15); apostles, prophets, evangelists, and pastor-teachers (Eph. 4:11-12). Paul spoke of God's giving the ministry of reconciliation (2 Cor. 5:18), authority for building up the church (2 Cor. 10:8), and grace for sharing the gospel with the Gentiles (Eph. 3:8). The NT also stresses God's gift of spiritual abilities to every believer (Rom. 12:6; 1 Cor. 12:4; 1 Pet. 4:10).

God's gifts should prompt the proper response from the recipients. This response includes not boasting (1 Cor. 4:7; Eph. 2:8); amazement at God's inexpressible goodness (2 Cor. 9:15); the using of gifts for the furtherance of Christ's kingdom (1 Tim. 4:14; 2 Tim. 1:6-11); and a life of good works (Eph. 2:10).

The pool of Siloam in Jerusalem. The pool was built in the eighth century BC by King Hezekiah to bring water from the Gihon Spring into Jerusalem.

GIHON Place-name meaning "gushing fountain." The primary water supply for Jerusalem and one of the four rivers into which the river of Eden divided (Gen. 2:13). The river cannot be identified with any contemporary river.

During the OT period, the spring of Gihon was the primary water supply for the city of Jerusalem. The name comes from a Hebrew word meaning "a bursting forth" and is descriptive of the spring that is located in the Kidron Valley. It does not produce a steady flow, but gushes out at irregular intervals, twice a day in the dry season to four or five times in the rainy season. Water issues from a crack 16 feet long in the rock. At some point in the ancient past, a wall was built at the eastern end of the crack, diverting water into a cave at the other end.

In the Jebusite period before David, a shaft went from the spring to a pool under the city. Water jugs were let down into the pool through another vertical shaft. This probably was the way Joab entered into the city and captured it for David (2 Sam. 5:8; 1 Chron. 11:6). During the early Israelite occupation, water was collected outside the city walls in an open basin called the "upper pool" (Isa. 7:3). An open aqueduct carried water from there to the "old pool" at the southern end of the city (Isa. 22:11; cp. Isa. 8:6). Along this conduit Isaiah confronted Ahaz (Isa. 7:3), and later Sennacherib's army demanded the city's surrender (2 Kgs. 18:17). Before Sennacherib's arrival, Hezekiah plugged the aqueduct and dug his famous water tunnel (2 Kgs. 20:20; 2 Chron. 32:30).

GILALAI Personal name perhaps meaning "rolled away." Temple musician who helped Nehemiah lead the thanksgiving service for the completion of the Jerusalem wall (Neh. 12:36).

GILBOA Place-name of uncertain meaning, perhaps "hill country" or "bubbling fountain." Location of an Israelite encampment (1 Sam. 28:4). The Israelites under Saul were preparing to do battle against the Philistines. At Mount Gilboa, Saul and his three sons were slain (1 Sam. 31:8). David sang a lament over the Gilboa tragedy (2 Sam. 1:17-27). Mount Gilboa has been identified with modern Jebel Fuqus, on the eastern side of the Plain of Esdraelon.

GILEAD Place and personal name meaning "raw" or "rugged." **1.** The north-central section of the Transjordanian highlands. The name may originally have applied to a very small area. Usage of the name then grew and could be applied in different contexts depending on present political situations (cp. Judg. 10:17; Hos. 6:8). Physically, Gilead is a rugged country; the Hebrew name *Gil'ad* may be translated "rugged." Some of its peaks reach higher than 3,500 feet. It also has plains with grassland suitable for cattle, and in antiquity the northern half of the region particularly was heavily forested. The King's Highway, an important international trade route, passed through Gilead. Gilead was an agriculturally significant region as well. It was famous especially for its flocks and herds and also for the balm of Gilead, an aromatic and medicinal preparation, probably derived from the resin of a small balsam tree. **2.** Great grandson of Joseph and original clan leader in the tribe of Manasseh (Num. 26:28-32; 36:1).

GILGAL Place-name meaning "circle" and probably referring to a circle of stones or a circular altar. Such a circle of stones could be found almost anywhere in ancient Israel and led easily to naming towns Gilgal. The many references to Gilgal in the OT cannot thus be definitely connected to the same town, since several different Gilgals may well have existed. **1.** Gilgal is most closely associated with Joshua, but the number of Gilgals involved continues an unsolved question. After crossing the Jordan, Joshua established the first camp at Gilgal (Josh. 4:19). There Joshua took 12 stones from the bed of the river to set up a memorial for the miraculous crossing. Gilgal, the first foothold on Canaan soil, became Israel's first worship place, where they were circumcised and

The rugged hill country of Gilead

observed the Passover. There God appeared to Joshua and affirmed his mission (Josh. 5). **2.** Elijah and Elisha were associated closely with Gilgal. At one time Elisha made his headquarters there (2 Kgs. 4:38), where Elijah was taken up into heaven (2 Kgs. 2:1). This was apparently Tell Jiljulieh about three miles southeast of Shiloh, though it could still be Joshua's original Gilgal. **3.** Gilgal of the nations is mentioned as a royal city near Dor (Josh. 12:23).

GILO RSV, TEV spelling of Giloh to refer to Gilonite (2 Sam. 23:34).

GILOH Place-name meaning "uncovered" or "revealed." Town in tribal allotment of Judah in Judean hills (Josh. 15:51). David's counselor Ahithophel came from Giloh (2 Sam. 15:12). Some scholars locate it at Khirbet Jala in the suburbs of Jerusalem, but most think Giloh was farther south.

GIMZO Place-name of uncertain meaning. Town in the Shephelah or valley of Judah that the Philistines captured from King Ahaz of Judah (735–715 BC), leading him to ask Assyria for help and to pay tribute to them (2 Chron. 28:18).

GIN KJV term for a trap or snare. With the exception of Amos 3:5, all scriptural uses are figurative, either of the fate of the wicked (Job 18:9; Isa. 8:14) or of the schemes of the wicked (Pss. 140:5; 141:9).

GINATH Place-name or personal name meaning "wall" or "enclosure." Father of Tibni, the favorite of half of Israel for kingship when Omri became king about 885 BC (1 Kgs. 16:21).

GINNETHO KJV spelling in Neh. 12:4 of Levite who returned from Babylonian captivity with Zerubbabel about 537 BC. Hebrew texts have various spellings followed by modern translations: Ginnethon (NIV; REB); Ginnethoi (CSB, NASB, TEV, NRSV).

GIRDLE Several items of clothing in KJV. **1.** An ornate sash worn by the officiating priests (Exod. 28:4,40) and by the wealthy of Jerusalem (Isa. 3:24). **2.** A decorated band (NRSV), woven belt (TEV, NASB), or waistband (CSB, NIV, REB) for the high priest's ephod (Exod. 28:8,27-28). **3.** A belt on which a sword or bow might be carried (1 Sam. 18:4; 2 Sam. 20:8; perhaps Isa. 5:27); a leather belt forming part of the proverbial garb of the prophets (2 Kgs. 1:8; Matt. 3:4). **4.** An undergarment (Job 12:18; Jer. 13:1-11), often rendered "waistcloth" or "loincloth."

To gird up one's loins means literally to tuck the loose ends of one's outer garment into one's belt. Loins were girded in preparation for running (1 Kgs. 18:46), for battle (Isa. 5:27), or for service for a master (Luke 12:35). The call to "gird up your minds" (1 Pet. 1:13 NASB) means to be spiritually alert and prepared.

GIRGASHITE or **GIRGASITE** Tribal name possibly meaning "sojourner with a deity." One on the list of original tribal groups inhabiting Canaan, traced back to Canaan, son of Ham and grandson of Noah (Gen. 10:16). The Ugaritic texts from Ras Shamra also apparently mention them.

GISHPA or **GISPA** (KJV) Personal name of uncertain meaning. Supervisor of temple servants in the days of Nehemiah (Neh. 11:21). It does not appear in the lists in Chronicles and Ezra, so some Bible students think the name is a copyist's change from Hasupha, which the Jews would have pronounced similarly (Ezra 2:43; Neh. 7:46).

GITTAH-HEPHER KJV spelling for Gath-hepher (Josh. 19:13) based on a variant Hebrew spelling in the text.

GITTAIM Place-name meaning "two winepresses." City to which people of Beeroth fled after Israel entered Canaan. The Bible does not tell the precise time (2 Sam. 4:3). After the exile, part of the tribe of Benjamin settled there (Neh. 11:33). This could be the same as the Gath of 1 Chron. 7:21; 8:13, but that is not certain.

GITTITH Word of uncertain meaning used in the titles of Pss. 8; 81; 84. It may represent a musical instrument resembling a Spanish guitar, a musical tune, or a rite or ceremony as part of a festival.

GIZONITE Citizen of Gizah or Gizon, a place not otherwise mentioned. It may be modern Bethgiz southwest of Latrun. David had military leaders from there (1 Chron. 11:34), though Gizonite does not appear in the parallel in 2 Sam. 23:34.

GIZRITE Citizen of Gezer. Also Gezerite.

GLAD TIDINGS KJV phrase for good news (Luke 1:19). A synonym for "gospel" as the news Jesus brought of God's kingdom (Luke 8:1; Acts 13:32; Rom. 10:15).

GLASS Amorphous substance, usually transparent or translucent. Glass has a long history in the Middle East. Transparent glass was not made until NT times as a luxury item. Corinth became known for the production of glass after the time of Paul. John probably had the transparent variety of glass in mind when he wrote Revelation. He described the walls and streets of the new Jerusalem being made of pure gold. The gold of the walls and streets was so pure that it was as clear as glass (Rev. 21:18,21). John also described the sea as being like glass (Rev. 4:6; 15:2). Here the reference is probably not so much to transparency as to calmness.

GLEANING Process of gathering grain or produce left in a field, vineyard, or orchard by reapers or pickers. Mosaic law required leaving this portion so that the poor and aliens might have a means of earning a living (Lev. 19:9-10; 23:22; Deut. 24:19-21; cp. Ruth 2).

GLEDE KJV term for an unclean bird of prey (Deut. 14:13).

GLORY Weighty importance and shining majesty that accompany God's presence. The basic meaning of the Hebrew word *kavod* is heavy in weight (cp. 1 Sam. 4:18; Prov. 27:3). The NT uses *doxa* to express glory and limits the meaning to God's glory. In classical Greek, *doxa* means opinion, conjecture, expectation, and then praise. The NT carries forward the OT meaning of divine power and majesty (Acts 7:2; Eph. 1:17; 2 Pet. 1:17). The NT extends this to Christ as having divine glory (Luke 9:32; John 1:14; 1 Cor. 2:8; 2 Thess. 2:14). Divine glory means that humans do not seek glory for themselves (Matt. 6:2; John 5:44; 1 Thess. 2:6). They only look to receive praise and honor from Christ (Rom. 2:7; 5:2; 1 Thess. 2:19; Phil. 2:16).

GLOSSOLALIA Technical term for speaking in tongues (Gk. *glossa*).

GLUTTON One habitually given to greedy and voracious eating. Gluttony was associated with stubbornness, rebellion, disobedience, drunkenness, and wastefulness (Deut. 21:20).

GNASHING OF TEETH Grating one's teeth together. In the OT, gnashing of teeth was an expression of anger reserved for the wicked and for one's enemies (Job 16:9; Pss. 35:16; 37:12; Lam. 2:16). In the NT, gnashing of teeth is associated with the place of future punishment (Matt. 8:12; 13:42,50).

GNOSTICISM Modern designation for certain dualistic religious and philosophical perspectives that existed prior to the establishment of Christianity and for the specific systems of belief characterized by these ideas, which emerged in the second century and later. The term "Gnosticism" is derived from the Greek word *gnosis* (knowledge) because secret knowledge was such a crucial doctrine in Gnosticism.

GOAD Rod, generally about eight feet long, with a pointed end used to control oxen.

GOAH Place-name meaning "low" (as in a sound made by a cow) or "bellow." A place, apparently on the west side of Jerusalem, where Jeremiah promised the walls would be restored after the Babylonian destruction (Jer. 31:39).

GOAT Hollow-horned, cud-chewing mammal with long, floppy ears, usually covered with long, black hair. Sometimes, they were speckled. One type of goat mentioned in the Bible has been identified as the Syrian or Mamber goat.

GOATH KJV and REB transliteration of Hebrew in Jer. 31:39 for Goah.

GOATSKIN Hide of goats that desert dwellers used for clothing (Heb. 11:37) and for containers for water (Gen. 21:14) and wine (Josh. 9:4).

GOB Place-name meaning "back" or "mountain crest." Site where David and his men fought two battles with the Philistines, killing Philistine giants (2 Sam. 21:18-19).

GOBLET KJV term for a bowl-shaped drinking vessel without handles (Song 7:2).

GOD Personal Creator and Lord of the universe, the Redeemer of his people, the ultimate author and principal subject of Scripture, and the object of the church's confession, worship, and service.

Knowledge of God At the heart of the biblical presentation of God is that God alone is the personal Creator and Lord, and that if he is to be known truly by his creatures, he must take the initiative in making himself known to us (1 Cor. 2:10-11; Heb. 1:1-2). No doubt his existence and power are disclosed in the created order, even though that order has been deeply scarred by human rebellion and its consequences (Ps. 19:1-2; Rom. 1:19-20; Gen. 3:18; Rom. 8:19-22). But Scripture is also very clear that apart from God's own gracious self-disclosure, both in Word and action, we could not know him in any true sense. In truth, God is incomprehensible, one that we cannot totally fathom (Pss. 139:6; 145:3; Rom. 11:33-36). But this in no way implies that we cannot know God truly. For in creating us in his image and giving us a Word, revelation of himself, even though we cannot know God fully, we may know him truly (Deut. 29:29).

Nature of God God is both transcendent over and immanent in his world. God is presented as the Lord who is exalted above and over his world, that is, transcendent (Pss. 7:17; 9:2; 21:7; 97:9; 1 Kgs. 8:27; Isa. 6:1; Rev. 4:3). Second, God is infinite, sovereign, and personal. By infinite, Scripture presents God as having every attribute or quality to the most perfect degree as well as not being bound by any of the limitations of space or time that apply to us, his creatures. Third, God is Triune. Distinctive to biblical theism is the conviction that the covenant Lord is as truly three as he is one. Although the word "trinity" is not found in Scripture, theologians have employed it to do justice to the biblical teaching that God is not only one in nature, but also three in person. As one follows the self-revelation of God in redemptive history, we discover not only the oneness of God (Deut. 6:4-5; Isa. 44:6), but also the affirmation that the Father is God (John 20:17), the Son is God (John 1:1,14; Rom. 9:5; Col. 2:9), and the Holy Spirit is God (Gen. 1:2; Acts 5:3-4; 1 Cor. 3:16).

Character of God Throughout Scripture, in God's dealings with human beings, we see God's character fully revealed and displayed. There are at least two statements that must be affirmed concerning the character of God.

First, God's character is holy love. It is important never to separate the holiness of God from the love of God. God is holy (Lev. 11:44; Isa. 6:3; Rev. 4:8). In the first instance, the word "holy" conveys the meaning of separateness and transcendence. However, it is the secondary meaning of "holiness" that speaks of God's moral purity in the sense of God's separateness from sin. In this latter sense, as the holy one, God is pure, righteous, and just. That is why Scripture repeatedly emphasizes that our sin and God's holiness are incompatible. His eyes are too pure to look on evil and he cannot tolerate wrong (Exod. 34:7; Rom. 1:32; 2:8-16). Thus, our sins effectively separate us from him, so that his face is hidden from us (Isa. 59:1-2). Closely related to God's holiness is his wrath, that is, his holy reaction to evil (Rom. 1:18-32; John 3:36). The wrath of God, unlike the holiness of God, is not one of the intrinsic perfections of God; rather, it is a function of his holiness against sin. Where there is no sin, there is no wrath, but there will always be holiness.

Nevertheless, God is also love. Often divine holiness and love are set over against each other, but in Scripture this is never the case. This is best seen in the context of the affirmation "God is love" (1 John 4:8). John, in this context, does not view the love of God as mere sentimentality or a blind overlooking of our sin; rather, he views divine love as that which loves the unlovely and undeserving. In fact, the supreme display of God's love is found in the Father giving his own dear Son as our propitiatory sacrifice that turns back God's holy anger against us and satisfies the demands of justice on our behalf (1 John 4:8-10). Thus, in the cross of Christ we see the greatest demonstration of both the holiness and love of God fully expressed, where justice and grace come together, and God remains both just and the justifier of those who have faith in Christ Jesus (Rom. 3:21-26).

Second, God's character is that of moral perfection. In all of God's dealings with his creation and with his people, God displays the wonder, beauty, and perfection of his own character. Ultimately the purpose of human existence, and especially of God's redeemed people, the church, is to live before this great and glorious God in adoration, love, and praise and to find in him alone our all in all (Ps. 73:23-28; Rom. 11:33-36).

GOD FEARER The term used to describe the Gentiles mentioned in Acts who were drawn to the Jewish religion, perhaps for ethical and moral reasons or because they were attracted to Jewish monotheism and worship practices. "God fearers" took part in Jewish practices such as tithing and regular prayers (Acts 10:2-4) and were apparently welcome to take part in some synagogue services.

GODHEAD Word used with reference to God when one speaks of God's divine nature or essence or of the three persons of the Trinity.

GODLESSNESS Attitude and style of life that excludes God from thought and ignores or deliberately violates God's laws. Romans 1:20-32 is a classic characterization of godlessness.

GODLINESS The term appears most frequently in the writings of Paul, specifically the Pastoral Epistles. Paul encouraged Timothy to pursue "godliness" in an active manner (1 Tim. 6:11). He emphasized the value of godliness by contrasting it to physical training (1 Tim. 4:8). Whereas physical training has benefit for this life, Paul noted that godliness would benefit the believer in this life and in the life to come.

GOD OF THE FATHERS Technical phrase used as a general designation of the God of the patriarchs—Abraham, Isaac, and Jacob.

GOG AND MAGOG In Ezek. 38–39, Gog of the land of Magog is the leader of the forces of evil in an apocalyptic conflict against Yahweh. In Rev. 20:8 Gog and Magog appear together in parallel construction as forces fighting for Satan after his 1,000-year bondage. The identity of Gog and Magog has been the subject of an extraordinary amount of speculation. In general, however, attempts to relate these figures to modern individuals or states have been unconvincing.

GOIIM Proper name meaning "nation," particularly a "Gentile, foreign nation." **1.** Land where King Tidal joined the eastern coalition against a coalition from Sodom and Gomorrah. This action led to a war in which Abraham became involved (Gen. 14:1). **2.** Joshua 12:23 lists a king of Goiim in Gilgal as one Joshua conquered. **3.** Isaiah 9:1 refers to Galilee of the nations/Gentiles. This may represent the Hebrew way of referring to Assyria's governmental district that the Assyrians called Megiddo.

GOLAN Place-name meaning "circle" or "enclosure." A city of refuge for people who unintentionally killed someone, located in Bashan for the part of the tribe of Manasseh living east of the Jordan River (Deut. 4:43). It was also a city for the Levites (Josh. 21:27), located at modern Sahem el-Jolan on the eastern bank of the River el-Allan.

GOLDEN CALF See *Calves, Golden.*

GOLDEN RULE Name usually given to the command of Jesus recorded in Matt. 7:12 (cp. Luke 6:31)—"whatever you want others to do for you, do also the same for them" (CSB). The designation "Golden Rule" does not appear in the Bible, and its origin in English is difficult to trace. The principle of the Golden Rule can be found in many religions, but Jesus's wording of it was original and unique.

GOLGOTHA See *Calvary.*

GOLIATH In 1 Sam. 17:4, the huge Philistine champion who baited the Israelite army under Saul in the valley of Elah for 40 days. He was slain by the youthful David.

Azekah in the valley of Elah where young David killed Goliath

GOMER Personal name meaning "complete, enough," or "burning coal." **1.** Daughter of Diblaim and wife of Hosea the prophet (Hos. 1:3). She is described in Hos. 1:2 as "a wife of promiscuity" (CSB). **2.** Son of Japheth and grandson of Noah in the Table of Nations (Gen. 10:2).

GONG Loud percussion instrument, perhaps like a type of cymbal used in the temple worship (1 Cor. 13:1; KJV, brass). The Greek is literally "noisy brass," referring to the metal from which the instrument was made.

GOOD In contrast to the Greek view of "the good" as an ideal, the biblical concept focuses on concrete experiences of what God has done and is doing in the lives of God's people.

GOODMAN KJV term for a husband or for the head of a household.

GOPHER WOOD In Gen. 6:14, the material out of which Noah was instructed to construct the ark.

GOSHEN **1.** The phrase, "land of Goshen," appears in the general description of territory occupied by Joshua's forces (Josh. 10:41; 11:16). **2.** The "land of Goshen" may have been

The fertile land of Goshen in the delta country of northern Egypt

named after the city of Goshen located in the district of Debir (Josh. 15:51). **3.** Goshen is primarily recognized as an area in the northeast sector of the Nile Delta. It was occupied by the Hebrews from the time of Joseph until the exodus.

GOSPEL The term "gospel" occurs frequently in the NT in both noun and verb forms, literally meaning "good news" or "proclaiming good news." The gospel in the NT is the message about the kingdom of God established in the life, death, and resurrection of Jesus the Messiah, who is enthroned as Lord of all. This good news describes events to which all Scripture points and declares that all principalities and powers are defeated once and for all by Jesus the Messiah. Finally, all of humanity will be judged according to their reception or rejection of this good news.

GOSPELS, SYNOPTIC The collective name for the Gospels of Matthew, Mark, and Luke. The term "synoptic" means "with the same eye," thus "with the same viewpoint."

GOURD Inedible fruit with a hard rind of the genera *Lagenaria* or *Cucurbita*. Gourd motifs were used in the ornamentation of the interior of the temple (1 Kgs. 6:18; KJV, knops) and of the rim of the bronze sea (1 Kgs. 7:24).

GOVERNOR Generally an appointed civil official charged with the oversight of a designated territory.

GOZAN Place-name of uncertain meaning, possibly, "quarry." A Syrian city-state to which the Assyrians exiled many of the people from Israel after they defeated Israel in 732 BC (1 Chron. 5:26) and 722 BC (2 Kgs. 17:6; 18:11).

GRACE Undeserved acceptance and love received from another. Although the biblical words for "grace" are used in a variety of ways, the most characteristic use is to refer to an undeserved favor granted by a superior to an inferior. When used of divine grace toward humankind, it refers to the undeserved favor of God in providing salvation for those deserving condemnation. In the more specific Christian sense, it speaks of the saving activity of God that is manifested in the gift of his Son to die in the place of sinners.

GRANARY Storage facility for threshed and winnowed grain.

Storage facilities at Knossos, Crete. Oil, wine, and grain were stored here.

GRASS Herbage suitable for consumption by grazing animals (Job 6:5). English translations use "grass" to translate at least five Hebrew words.

GRATE, GRATING Framework of crisscrossed bars. The grating of the tabernacle altar was made of bronze and held rings through which carrying poles could be inserted (Exod. 27:4-7; 35:16; 38:4-5,30; 39:39).

GRAVE Pit or cave in which a dead body is buried. In Hebrew thought, graves were not simply places to deposit human remains. They were in a sense extensions of Sheol, the place of the dead. Since the realm of Sheol was threatening and since each grave was an individual expression of Sheol, the Israelites avoided burial sites when possible and treated them with circumspection. They performed purification rites when contact was unavoidable.

GRAVING TOOL Sharp implement used to finish shaping the rough form of a statue cast from a mold (Exod. 32:4) or used for engraving tablets with writing (Jer. 17:1).

GRAY Usually a reference to hair color (Prov. 16:31; 20:29).

GRECIAN Proper adjective referring to things or to people with origins in Greece. In the NT, this refers to Jews who had adopted the Greek culture and language. They formed a significant part of the early church and created problems because of prejudice within the church (Acts 6:1; 9:29).

GREECE Located between the Italian Peninsula and Asia Minor, Greece itself is a peninsula, with the Adriatic and Ionian Seas on the west and the Aegean Sea on the east. Very few references to Greece appear in the OT with most of them being found in the book of Daniel (Dan. 8:21; 10:20; 11:2; Zech. 9:13). This is not true of the NT, however, especially in regard to Paul's ministry. Some of his most fruitful work was done in Greek cities: Philippi, Thessalonica, Berea, Athens, and Corinth.

The Greek influence on the NT and Christianity is immeasurable. Koine, the Greek of the streets, is the language of the NT. At least five NT books are written to churches in Greek cities (Philippians, 1 and 2 Thessalonians, 1 and 2 Corinthians). All the other books in the NT are written in the Greek language. As the Christian gospel moved out into the Mediterranean world, it had to communicate its values to people who were steeped in Greek culture and religion. Both gained from the relationship, with people being transformed by the gospel and Christianity gaining a vehicle for its spread.

Looking through a gate into the ancient city of Corinth

GREED Excessive or reprehensible desire to acquire; covetousness.

GREETING A salutation on meeting; an expression of good wishes at the opening (or, in Hellenistic times, also the close) of a letter. Among Semitic peoples, the usual greeting was and is "peace": "Peace to you, and peace to your family, and peace to all that is yours" (1 Sam. 25:5-6 CSB; cp. Luke 10:5).

GREYHOUND (KJV, Prov. 30:31). Modern translations read "strutting cock" or rooster.

GRIDDLE Flat surface on which food is cooked by dry heat (Lev. 2:5; 6:21; 7:9 modern translations; KJV, pan).

GRIEF AND MOURNING Practices and emotions associated with the experience of the death of a loved one or of another catastrophe or tragedy. After Jesus watched Mary and her friends weeping, we are told, "Jesus wept" (John 11:35). Weeping was then, as now, the primary indication of grief. Tears are repeatedly mentioned (Pss. 42:3; 56:8). The loud lamentation (wail) was also a feature of mourning, as the prophet who cried, "Alas! My brother!" (1 Kgs. 13:30; cp. Exod. 12:30; Jer. 22:18; Mark 5:38).

Sometimes they tore either their inner or outer garment (Gen. 37:29,34; Job 1:20; 2:12). They might refrain from washing and other normal activities (2 Sam. 14:2), and they often put on sackcloth. Mourners would typically sit barefoot on the ground with their hands on their heads (Mic. 1:8; 2 Sam. 12:20; 13:19; Ezek. 24:17) and smear their heads or bodies with dust or ashes (Josh. 7:6; Jer. 6:26; Lam. 2:10; Ezek. 27:30; Esth. 4:1). They might even cut their hair, beard, or skin (Jer. 16:6; 41:5; Mic. 1:16), though disfiguring the body in this way was forbidden since it was a pagan practice (Lev. 19:27-28; 21:5; Deut. 14:1). Fasting was sometimes involved, usually only during the day (2 Sam. 1:12; 3:35), typically for seven days (Gen. 50:10; 1 Sam. 31:13). Food, however, was brought by friends since it could not be prepared in a house rendered unclean by the presence of the dead (Jer. 16:7).

Not only did the actual relatives mourn, but they might hire professional mourners (Eccles. 12:5; Amos 5:16). Reference to "the mourning women" in Jer. 9:17 suggests that there were certain techniques that these women practiced. Jesus went to Jairus's house to heal his daughter and "saw the flute players and a crowd lamenting loudly" (Matt. 9:23 CSB).

GRISLED KJV term for dappled (spotted) gray (Gen. 31:10,12).

GROVE In Gen. 21:33, a tree planted in Beer-sheba by Abraham. More than likely it was a tamarisk. The KJV also uses the word "grove" to translate the term *Asherah*.

GUARDIAN Adult responsible for the person and property of a minor (2 Kgs. 10:1,5). The Greek term *epitropos*, translated "guardian" at Gal. 4:2 (KJV, tutor), is a general word for a manager.

GUDGODAH Place-name of uncertain meaning. A stop on the Israelites' wilderness journey (Deut. 10:7).

GUILE Crafty or deceitful cunning; treachery; duplicity; deceit. Jesus pronounced Nathanael "a true Israelite in whom there is no deceit (guile)" (John 1:47 CSB; cp. John 1:51 with Gen. 28:12). Paul encouraged Christians to be "guileless as to what is evil" (Rom. 16:19 NRSV; cp. 1 Pet. 2:1), that is, innocent or naive when it comes to evil.

GUILT Responsibility of an individual or a group for an offense or wrongdoing. The Bible teaches that the violation of God's moral law (i.e., sin; 1 John 3:4), whether in act or attitude, results in an immediate state of culpability before God requiring either punishment or expiation. Sin results in guilt whether or not the sinner is a member of God's redemptive community. Whereas this covenant community is further accountable to obey God's written law, all men are accountable to God's moral law (Rom. 2:14-15).

God's righteousness demands that the guilt resulting from sin cannot just be overlooked (Prov. 11:21; Hab. 1:13). The "wages" for sin is death (Rom. 6:23), and God cannot leave the guilty unpunished and still be righteous (Exod. 34:7). The only way God can forgive sin in us is to impute that sin to Christ and punish it in him: "God presented [Jesus] to demonstrate his righteousness at the present time, so that he would be righteous and declare righteous the one who has faith in Jesus" (Rom. 3:26 CSB; see also Isa. 53:6,12; John 1:29). The result is that one who is "in Christ" by faith has been freed of his guilt so that there is "no condemnation" (Rom. 8:1).

The presence or absence of the feeling or realization of one's guilt is not a reliable indication of true guilt, because the heart is more deceitful than anything else (Jer. 17:9). Some who are "self-righteous," that is, with no sense of guilt, may nevertheless be guilty (Matt. 5:20; 9:10-13), and those plagued by self-doubt may nevertheless be right with God (cp. 1 Cor. 8:7). On the other hand, the

Bible gives several examples of the emotional anguish caused by sin (Pss. 32:1-5; 38; 51; Matt. 27:35; Luke 22:62). See *Atonement; Christ; Expiation, Propitiation; Forgiveness; Reconciliation; Sin.*

GULF Term used by the KJV and REB for the gorge or pit (CSB, chasm) separating the rich man's place of torment from Lazarus's place of comfort in the presence of Abraham (Luke 16:26).

GUM Yellow to yellowish-brown product formed from the excretions of certain plants. Gum was an item of the Ishmaelites' caravan trade with Egypt (Gen. 37:25; KJV, spicery) and was regarded as one of the choice products of the land (Gen. 43:11).

GUNI Personal name meaning "black-winged partridge." **1.** Son of Naphtali and grandson of Jacob (Gen. 46:24), thus head of the Gunite clan (Num. 26:48). **2.** Member of the tribe of Gad (1 Chron. 5:15). (Also: Gunite.)

GUR Place-name meaning "foreign sojourner" or "young animal." An unidentified mountain road near Ibleam where Jehu's men caught up with and mortally wounded Ahaziah, king of Judah (841 BC) (2 Kgs. 9:27).

GUR-BAAL Place-name meaning "foreign sojourner of Baal" or "young animal of Baal." An Arabian or Bedouin city where God helped King Uzziah of Judah (792–740 BC) attack (2 Chron. 26:7).

GUTTER KJV translation of two Hebrew terms. That in Gen. 30:38,41 is rendered (drinking) "troughs" (CSB, NIV, REB, NRSV TEV) or "runnels," "a small stream" (RSV). The term used at 2 Sam. 5:8 is rendered "water shaft" (CSB, NIV, NRSV) or "water tunnel" (NASB, TEV).

Jewish men of the Orthodox tradition are prohibited from cutting off the hair above their ears.

HAAHASHTARI Personal and national name in Persian language meaning "kingdom." Son of Ashhur, member of the tribe of Judah (1 Chron. 4:6).

HABAIAH Personal name meaning "Yahweh hides, keeps safe." Clan leader of exiled priests who returned from Babylon to Jerusalem with Zerubbabel about 537 BC (Ezra 2:61).

HABAKKUK Prophet of the late seventh century BC, contemporary to Jeremiah. One explanation has his name based on a root meaning "to embrace." The Greek OT spelling "Hambakoum" suggests a root meaning "plant" or "vegetable."

Other than his work as a prophet, nothing for certain of a personal nature is known about Habakkuk. Tradition makes him a priest of the tribe of Levi.

HABAKKUK, BOOK OF One of the 12 Minor Prophets. After a brief statement identifying the prophet (1:1), the book falls into three distinct divisions: (1) Prophet's Questions and the Lord's Answers (1:2–2:5); (2) Five Woes against Tyrants (2:6-20); (3) Prayer of Habakkuk (3:1-19).

The first question, Why does violence rule where there should be justice? (1:2-5), expressed the prophet's sense of dismay, either about conditions within his own land caused by Jehoiakim or by the oppression of weak countries by stronger powers. In light of what follows, internal injustice seems to have been the object of his concern. In response, the Lord told the prophet that he was at work sending the Chaldeans as the instrument of his judgment (1:5-11).

The prophet shrank from such an idea and posed another question: Lord, to punish us how can you use someone more sinful than we are? (1:12-17). When the answer was not forthcoming immediately, he took his stand in the watchtower to wait for it. It was worth the wait: "Behold, as for the proud one, his soul is not right within him; but the righteous will live by his faith" (2:4 NASB). The term "faith" has more of the sense of faithfulness or conviction that results in action.

Habakkuk had a significant influence on the apostle Paul. Habakkuk's declaration that "the righteous (just) will live by his faith" (2:4) was taken by Paul as a central element in his theology. As he did with many OT passages, he used it with a slightly different emphasis. Through Paul, this passage came alive for an Augustinian monk named Martin Luther, setting off the Protestant Reformation, one of history's greatest religious upheavals. Thus a so-called "Minor" prophet had a major influence on those who followed him.

HABERGEON Short coat of mail covering the neck and shoulder worn as defensive armor.

HABITATION Dwelling place; home; KJV translation of 10 different Hebrew words.

HABOR Akkadian river name. A major tributary of the Euphrates River (2 Kgs. 17:6).

HACALIAH or **HACHALIAH** (KJV) Personal name meaning "wait confidently on Yahweh." Father of Nehemiah.

HACHMON Clan name meaning "wisdom." Original ancestor of an Israelite clan called the Hachmonites (1 Chron. 27:32).

HADAD Personal name meaning "mighty." **1.** An Edomite king (Gen. 36:35). The name Hadad was borne by several members of the royal household of Edom. **2.** Hadad was also the name of the chief deity of the Ugaritic pantheon. This deity was identified as a storm-god.

HADAD-EZER Syrian royal name meaning "Hadad (god) helps" (2 Sam. 8:3-13).

HADAD-RIMMON Names of two Syrian gods combined into one word (Zech. 12:11).

HADAR Apparently a copyist's change of the name Hadad, a Syrian god, in Gen. 36:39 and in some manuscripts of Gen. 25:15.

HADAR-EZER Copying change in some manuscripts for Hadad-ezer.

HADASHAH Town name meaning "new" (Josh. 15:37).

HADASSAH Personal name meaning "myrtle." In Esth. 2:7, another name for Esther.

HADATTAH Place-name meaning "new." Part of name Hazor-hadattah (Josh. 15:25).

HADES The Greek noun *hades* is used 61 times in the Greek OT (Septuagint) to translate the Hebrew term *sheol*, which refers to the grave or the realm of the dead (Gen. 37:35; 1 Sam. 2:6; Prov. 15:24; cp. Ps. 16:10 and Acts 2:27,31). The picture generally presented by *Sheol* is the tomb, where the bodies of the dead lie in silence.

Hades in the NT, on the other hand, can represent a place of torment for the wicked. Jesus uses the term in this way in his condemnation of Capernaum in Matt. 11:23 (parallel Luke 10:15) and in the parable of the rich man and Lazarus in Luke 16:23 where the rich man is said to be "in Hades."

HADID Place-name meaning "fast" or "sharpened." Home of people returning from exile with Zerubbabel (Ezra 2:33).

HADLAI Personal name meaning "quit" or "fat sack." Leader in the tribe of Ephraim and father of Amasa (2 Chron. 28:12).

HADORAM Personal and tribal name perhaps meaning "Hadad (god) is exalted." **1.** Arabic tribe descended from Shem through Eber and thus distantly related to Hebrews according to the Table of Nations (Gen. 10:27). **2.** Son of Tou, city-state ruler in Hamath of Syria. Hadoram brought tribute to David after David had defeated Hadad-ezer of Zobah (1 Chron. 18:10). **3.** Taskmaster "in charge of the forced labor" (2 Chron. 10:18) under Rehoboam, Solomon's son and successor as king of Judah.

HADRACH City-state name of uncertain meaning. Zechariah 9:1 claims this Syrian city-state will become a part of God's territory, though the precise meaning of the verse is difficult to interpret.

HAELEPH Place-name meaning "the ox." KJV reads the initial "h" as the Hebrew definite article and thus has "Eleph." Some interpreters combine the preceding town name in Josh. 18:28 to read "Zelah Haeleph" as one town, following early Greek manuscript evidence.

HAFT KJV term for the hilt or handle of a dagger (Judg. 3:22).

HAGAB Personal name meaning "grasshopper" or "chamberlain." Clan of temple servants who returned to Jerusalem from Babylonian exile with Zerubbabel (Ezra 2:46).

HAGABA Clan of temple servants who returned home from Babylonian exile with Zerubbabel about 537 BC (Ezra 2:45).

HAGAR Personal name meaning "stranger." The personal servant of Sarah who was given as a concubine to Abraham and became the mother of Ishmael (Gen. 16:1-16; 21:8-21; 25:12; Gal. 4:24-25). Despairing in the desert, Hagar encounters a heavenly being whom she calls "El-roi," meaning "God sees me" (16:13).

HAGARITE Name of nomadic tribe whom the tribe of Reuben defeated east of the Jordan River (1 Chron. 5:10,19-20).

HAGGADAH and **HALAKAH** In Judaism, rabbinic teaching is divided into two categories: halakah and haggadah (also spelled aggadah). Both of these terms refer to the oral teaching of the rabbis. Halakah refers to the legal teachings that are considered authoritative for religious life. Haggadah refers to the remaining nonlegal teachings.

HAGGAI Personal name of one of the "postexilic" (sixth-century) prophets and of the book preserving his preaching. The name probably means that he was born on one of the Jewish feast days. He and the prophet Zechariah roused the people of Judah to finish the temple under Zerubbabel's leadership.

HAGGAI, BOOK OF One of the so-called Minor Prophets (also collectively known as "the Twelve"). It consists of four addresses the prophet delivered to the postexilic community of Judah and its leaders, Zerubbabel the governor and Joshua the high priest. The addresses are precisely dated according to the year of the Persian ruler and the month and day of the Jewish calendar.

Historical Background The Persian ruler Cyrus had freed the Jews to return from Babylonian exile shortly after he conquered Babylon in October 539 BC. He had also promised to help them rebuild their temple in Jerusalem that the Babylonians had destroyed in 586 BC. The temple foundation was laid fairly quickly under Zerubbabel's leadership, who eventually replaced Sheshbazzar as governor. This initial success was met not only with celebration but also with sadness when this temple was compared with Solomon's (Ezra 1–3; Hag. 2:3; Zech. 4:10). This is the first hint that perhaps this restoration would not satisfy entirely the prophetic announcements of Israel's glorious restoration.

Message and Purpose The leaders and people of Judah allowed external opposition, discouragement, and self-interest to keep them from completing the task of rebuilding the Lord's temple (1:2-4; 2:3). So they and their offerings to the Lord were defiled and displeasing to him (2:14). The Lord's command through Haggai was to "build the house" for the pleasure and glory of God (1:8). Toward that end, the Lord exhorted them not to fear but to be strong and to work (2:4-5). Finally, by a parable, Haggai instructed them of the need to dedicate themselves and their work to the Lord (2:11-16). The Lord called upon them to recognize his chastisement in the deprivation they had been experiencing (1:5-6,9-11; 2:16-17). He also informed the people that the completion of the temple would bring him pleasure and glory (1:8). He further assured them of their success because of his presence (1:13-14; 2:4-5). He promised them that he would reward their renewed work and dedication to him by glorifying the temple and granting them peace (2:6-9) and blessing (2:18-19). Finally, he promised to restore the Davidic throne on the earth through a descendant of Zerubbabel (2:20-23).

HAGGEDOLIM Personal name meaning "the great ones." Zabdiel, a leading priest, was the son of Haggedolim (Neh. 11:14; KJV, "the great men"; TEV, "a leading family").

HAGGERI KJV transliteration of Hebrew for Hagarite in 1 Chron. 11:38.

HAGGI, HAGGITE Personal name meaning "my festival," indicating birth on a holy day. Son of Gad and grandson of Jacob and thus original ancestor of clan of Haggites (Gen. 46:16; Num. 26:15).

HAGGIAH Personal name meaning "Yahweh is my festival." A Levite in the line of Merari (1 Chron. 6:30).

HAGGITE Member of clan of Haggi.

HAGGITH Personal name meaning "festival." Wife of David and mother of Adonijah, who was born at Hebron (1 Sam. 3:4).

HAGIOGRAPHA Greek term meaning "holy writings," used as a designation for the third and final major division of the Hebrew Bible. The Hagiographa in their Hebrew order include Psalms, Proverbs, and

Job; the "five scrolls" (*Megilloth*) read at major festivals, namely, Song of Songs, Ruth, Lamentations, Ecclesiastes, and Esther; Daniel; and Ezra-Nehemiah and Chronicles. These books were the last portion of the Hebrew Bible to be recognized as canonical. Luke 24:44 uses "psalms" as a designation for these writings.

HAGRI Tribal or personal name probably referring to the Hagarites (1 Chron. 11:38) or a miscopying of "the Gaddite" from 2 Sam. 23:36.

HAHIROTH Reading of some manuscripts and translations for Pi-hahiroth in Num. 33:8.

HAIR Covering of the human head and of animals. Ordinarily human hair is meant in biblical references (Num. 6:5), though animal hair (wool) may be in mind (Matt. 3:4). Beautiful hair has always been desirable for both women and men (Song 5:11). In OT times, both men and women wore their hair long. Both Samson and Absalom were greatly admired for their long locks (Judg. 16:13; 2 Sam. 14:25-26). In the NT era, men wore their hair much shorter than did women (1 Cor. 11:14-15). Gray hair and white hair were respected signs of age (Prov. 20:29). But baldness could be considered embarrassing or even humiliating (2 Kgs. 2:23; Ezek. 7:18).

HAKELDAMA NASB, NRSV spelling for Aceldama or Akeldama (Acts 1:19).

HAKKATAN Personal name meaning "the small one, the lesser." Father of the clan leader who accompanied Ezra from Babylon to Jerusalem about 458 BC (Ezra 8:12).

HAKKORE TEV reading of En-hakkore (Judg. 15:19), translating *En* as "spring."

HAKKOZ Personal and clan name meaning "the thorn." **1.** Clan leader in the tribe of Judah (1 Chron. 4:8). **2.** Clan of priests (1 Chron. 24:10; cp. Neh. 3:4,21).

HAKUPHA Personal name meaning "bent." Original ancestor of clan of temple servants (Ezra 2:51).

HALAH City-state or region in northern Mesopotamia to which Assyrians exiled some leaders of the northern kingdom after capturing Samaria in 722 BC (2 Kgs. 17:6).

HALAK Place-name meaning "barren" or "naked." Mountain marking southern extent of Joshua's conquests (Josh. 11:17; 12:7). It is identified with Jebel Halak, about 40 miles southwest of the Dead Sea in Edom.

HALF TRIBE Used to designate a segment of the tribe of Manasseh that received territory on both sides of the Jordan River. The term usually refers to that part of Manasseh dwelling to the east of the Jordan along with Reuben and Gad (Num. 32:33; Deut. 3:13; Josh. 1:12; 4:12; 22:1).

HALF-SHEKEL TAX Temple tax required annually of every Israelite 20 years of age and older (Exod. 30:13,15; 38:26). Such payment brought atonement, but atonement price was equal for all (30:15). At Matt. 17:24 this tax is called the *didrachma* ("the two drachma") tax. The coin in the fish's mouth was a stater, a coin worth four drachmas or the temple tax for two (17:27).

HALHUL Place-name perhaps meaning "circles." Town in hill country of Judah assigned to the tribe of Judah (Josh. 15:58).

HALI Place-name meaning "jewel." Border town assigned to tribe of Asher (Josh. 19:25).

HALL Large, usually imposing building, often used for governmental functions; the chief room in such a structure. NIV uses hall for the main room of the temple (1 Kgs. 6:3,5,17,33). Other translations have house (KJV), nave (NASB, NRSV), or sanctuary (CSB, REB).

HALLEL Song of praise. The name derives from the Hebrew "Praise thou." The singing of psalms of praise was a special duty of the Levites (2 Chron. 7:6; Ezra 3:11). The "Egyptian" Hallel (Pss. 113–118) was recited in homes as part of the Passover celebration (cp. Ps. 114:1; Matt. 26:30). The "Great Hallel" was recited in the temple as the Passover lambs were being slain and at feasts of Pentecost,

Tabernacles, and Dedication. Scholars disagree as to the original extent of the "Great Hallel" with some limiting the Hallel to Ps. 136, some including Ps. 135, and still others including the "Songs of Ascents" (Pss. 120–134).

HALLELUJAH Exclamation of praise that recurs frequently in the book of Psalms; meaning "Praise Yahweh!"

HALLOHESH Personal name meaning "the exorcist." Father of Shallum, who helped Nehemiah repair the Jerusalem wall (Neh. 3:12; 10:24).

HALLOW To make holy; to set apart for holy use; to revere.

HALT Term that KJV sometimes uses as alternate translation for "lame" (Matt. 18:8; Mark 9:45; Luke 14:21; John 5:3).

HAM Personal name meaning "hot." Second of Noah's three sons (Gen. 5:32). Following the flood, he discovered Noah, his father, naked and drunken and reported it to Shem and Japheth (Gen. 9:20-29). When Noah learned of the incident, he pronounced a curse on Canaan the son of Ham. Ham became the original ancestor of the Cushites, the Egyptians, and the Canaanites (Gen. 10:6).

HAMAN Personal name meaning "magnificent." The Agagite who became prime minister under the Persian king Ahasuerus (Esth. 3:1). He was a fierce enemy of the Jews, and he devised a plot to exterminate them. In particular, he had a gallows erected on which he hoped to hang Mordecai because Mordecai would not bow to him. Through the intervention of Queen Esther, however, his scheme was unmasked, and he was hanged on the gallows he had designed for Mordecai the Jew.

HAMATH Place-name meaning "fortress" or "citadel." City-state located in the valley of the Orontes River, roughly 120 miles north of Damascus. The southern boundary of Hamath served as the northern boundary of Israel during the reigns of Solomon (1 Kgs. 8:65; 2 Chron. 8:4) and Jeroboam II (2 Kgs. 14:25,28). The "entrance of Hamath" was treated as the northern border of Israel (Num. 34:8; Josh. 13:5; Ezek. 47:15-17,20; 48:1) and served as an accepted geographical expression (Num. 13:21; Judg. 3:3).

HAMATH-ZOBAH Place-name meaning "hot place of Zobah." City that Solomon captured in Syria (2 Chron. 8:3). Both Hamath and Zobah are cities in Syria that David controlled (2 Sam. 8).

HAMMATH Place-name meaning "hot spot," probably due to hot spring, and personal name meaning "hot one." **1.** Fortified city in the tribal territory of Naphtali (Josh. 19:35); probably the same as the Levitical town of Hammoth-dor (21:32). **2.** Original ancestor of Kenites and Rechabites (1 Chron. 2:55; KJV reads "Hamath"; TEV, REB see a verbal construction meaning "intermarried" or "connected by marriage").

HAMMEDATHA Personal name meaning "given by the god." Father of Haman, the villain of the book of Esther (Esth. 3:1).

HAMMELECH According to KJV, personal name translated "the king" (Jer. 36:26; 38:6). Modern translations read "son of the king."

HAMMER A striking tool. Mallets of bone and wood were used (Judg. 5:26), though these have not normally been preserved. Hammers were used in cutting stone (1 Kgs. 6:7), working common and precious metals (Isa. 41:7; 44:12), and for woodworking (Jer. 10:4). The hammer was a symbol of power. God's word is pictured as a hammer (Jer. 23:29). Babylon is mocked as a hammer whose strength has failed (Jer. 50:23).

HAMMOLEKETH (KJV, NIV, REB) Personal name meaning "queen." Sister of Gilead in genealogy of Manasseh in the unparalleled list of 1 Chron. 7:18.

HAMMON Place-name meaning "hot spot," probably from a hot spring. Town in tribal allotment of Asher (Josh. 19:28).

HAMMUEL Personal name meaning "El is my father-in-law" or "God is hot with anger." Member of the tribe of Simeon (1 Chron. 4:26).

HAMMURABI King of Babylon about 1700 BC who issued a famous code of law. The Hammurabi code resembles Hebrew law in form, style, and general content. Thus some scholars believe the Hebrews were influenced by Hammurabi's code through the Canaanites among whom they settled. Whatever the similarities, important differences are obvious. First, the Hammurabi code presupposes an aristocratic class system that did not prevail in Israel. Second, Israel could never have viewed the state as the custodian of the law. Third, Hebrew law is characterized by a more humane spirit. Fourth, Hebrew law maintains a high ethical emphasis. Fifth, the pervading religious fervor makes the Hebrew code unique. Sixth, Hebrew law is set within a covenant relationship.

HAMON-GOG Place-name meaning "horde of Gog." Place where Ezekiel predicted burial of defeated army of Gog (Ezek. 39:11,15).

HAMONAH Place-name meaning "horde." Town in valley of Hamon-gog where Israel would bury the defeated army of Gog (Ezek. 39:16).

HAMOR Personal name meaning "donkey" or "ass." In Gen. 33:19, the father of Shechem.

HAMRAN Personal name of uncertain meaning, perhaps "vineyard." Member of the family of Esau (1 Chron. 1:41). KJV spells the name "Amram."

HAMSTRING To cripple by cutting the leg tendons. Horses captured in war were frequently hamstrung (KJV, hough) (Josh. 11:6,9; 2 Sam. 8:4; 1 Chron. 18:4). The hamstringing of oxen (Gen. 49:6 modern translations) is an example of rash anger.

HAMUL Personal name meaning "pitied, spared" or "El is father-in-law" or "El is hot, angry." Son of Pharez and grandson of Judah (Gen. 46:12) and thus a clan leader in Judah (Num. 26:21).

HAMUTAL Personal name meaning "father-in-law or kindred of the dew." Mother of King Jehoahaz (2 Kgs. 23:31) and King Zedekiah (2 Kgs. 24:18) of Judah.

HANAMEEL Personal name meaning "God is gracious." Uncle of Jeremiah from whom the prophet bought the field in Anathoth (Jer. 32:7-12). Jeremiah's act symbolized God's long-range plans to restore the people to the land after exile.

HANAN Personal name meaning "gracious." Personal name probably originally connected to divine name such as El, Yahweh, or Baal. **1.** Clan or guild of prophets or priests living in the temple. Jeremiah used their temple chamber for his meeting with the Rechabites (Jer. 35:4). **2.** Clan of temple servants who returned to Jerusalem from Babylonian exile with Zerubbabel about 537 BC (Ezra 2:46). **3.** Man whom Nehemiah appointed as assistant temple treasurer to receive and disperse tithes brought to care for the Levites (Neh. 13:13). **4.** One of David's military heroes (1 Chron. 11:43). **5.** Levite who instructed the people in the Lord's law while Ezra read it (Neh. 8:7). **6.** Levite who sealed Nehemiah's covenant to obey God's law (Neh. 10:10). **7.** Another signer of Nehemiah's covenant (Neh. 10:22). **8.** Another who signed Nehemiah's covenant (Neh. 10:26). **9.** Member of the tribe of Benjamin (1 Chron. 8:23). **10.** Descendant of Saul in the tribe of Benjamin (1 Chron. 8:38).

HANANEEL (KJV) or **HANANEL** Place-name meaning "God is gracious." Tower marking northern wall of Jerusalem. Jeremiah predicted its rebuilding in the day of the Lord to come (Jer. 31:38; cp. Zech. 14:10).

HANANI Personal name meaning "my grace" or a shortened form of "Yahweh is gracious." **1.** Father of Prophet Jehu (1 Kgs. 16:1,7; 2 Chron. 19:2). **2.** Man who agreed under Ezra's leadership to divorce his foreign wife to protect the Jews from temptation to worship idols (Ezra 10:20). **3.** Nehemiah's brother who reported the poor conditions in Jerusalem to him while Nehemiah was still in Persia (Neh. 1:2). **4.** Priest musician at dedication of Jerusalem walls (Neh. 12:36). **5.** Temple musician and descendant of Heman (1 Chron. 25:4). Some would equate him with 4, above. **6.** Original leader of one course of temple musicians (1 Chron. 25:25). **7.** Prophetic seer who condemned King Asa of Judah

sole authority, using his Cushite wife as an excuse (Num. 12).

HAZIEL Personal name meaning "God saw." A leading Levite in the time of David (1 Chron. 23:9).

HAZO Abbreviated form of personal name Haziel meaning "God saw." Son of Abraham's brother Nahor (Gen. 22:22).

HAZOR Place-name meaning "enclosed settlement." **1.** Hazor was located in upper Galilee on the site now known as Tell el-Qedah, 10 miles north of the Sea of Galilee and 5 miles southwest of Lake Huleh. Hazor was the dominant and largest city-state in ancient Canaan. Joshua defeated the Canaanite forces, slew the leaders, including Jabin, and burned the city of Hazor. Modern archaeology lends support to this biblical account. First Kings 9:15 mentions that Solomon rebuilt the walls of Hazor, Megiddo, and Gezer. Excavations have discovered conclusive evidence to support this short portion of Scripture. **2.** Town in tribal inheritance of Judah (Josh. 15:23), probably to be read with earliest Greek translation as Hazor-Ithnan. This may be modern el-Jebariyeh. **3.** Town in southern part of tribal inheritance of Judah, probably to be read as Hazor-Hadattah (Josh. 15:25) with most modern translations. This may be modern el-Hudeira near the Dead Sea's southern end. **4.** Town identified with Hezron (Josh. 15:25). **5.** Town where part of the tribe of Benjamin lived in time of Nehemiah (Neh. 11:33). **6.** Name of "kingdoms" that Nebuchadnezzar of Babylon threatened (Jer. 49:28-33).

HAZOR-HADDATTAH Place-name meaning "new Hazor." Town in tribal territory of Judah (Josh. 15:25). Its location is not known.

HAZZOBEBAH NIV rendering of the name of the son of Coz (or Kos) and grandson of Helah (1 Chron. 4:8).

HE Fifth letter of the Hebrew alphabet; it carries the numerical value five. In Judaism, *he* is used as an abbreviation for the divine name Yahweh (Tetragrammaton).

HEAD Literally, the uppermost part of the body, considered to be the seat of life but not of the intellect; figuratively refers to first,

Overview of the excavations at Tel el-Qedah (ancient Hazor) north of the Sea of Gaililee.

top, or chief. The Jewish notion was that the heart was the center or seat of the intellect. "Head" meant the physical head of a person (Gen. 48:18; Mark 6:24) or of animals, such as a bull's head (Lev. 1:4). It was often used to represent the whole person (Acts 18:6). Achish made David "keeper of mine head" (KJV), that is, his bodyguard (1 Sam. 28:2).

HEAD OF THE CHURCH Title for Christ (Eph. 4:15; Col. 1:18). Christ's headship includes the idea of his authority (1:22; 5:23) and of the submission required of the church (5:24). Also in view is the character of Christ's relationship with the church. Unlike self-seeking human lords (Luke 22:25), Christ exercises his authority for the church (Eph. 1:22), nourishing and caring for the church as one cares for one's own body (5:29).

HEADSTONE KJV term for a top stone (NASB) or capstone (CSB, NIV) at Zech. 4:7. New Testament writers spoke of Christ as a stone rejected by the builders that has become the head of the corner (Acts 4:11; 1 Pet. 2:7). Here, head of the corner refers either to a capstone (coping), a keystone of an arch, or to a cornerstone.

HEALING, DIVINE God's work through instruments and ways he chooses to bring health to persons sick physically, emotionally, and spiritually. Nearly one-fifth of the Gospels report Jesus's miracles and the discussions they occasioned. The Gospels record 14 distinct instances of physical and mental healing. Jesus commissioned his disciples to continue his basic ministry, including healing (Matt. 10:5-10; Mark 6:7-13; Luke 9:1-6). In the book of Acts, the healing ministry continued.

HEART Center of the physical, mental, and spiritual life of humans. The word "heart" refers to the physical organ and is considered to be the center of the physical life. Eating and drinking are spoken of as strengthening the heart (Gen. 18:5; Judg. 19:5; Acts 14:17).The believer is commanded to love God "with all your heart" (Mark 12:30; cp. Deut. 6:5). Paul taught that the purpose of God's command is love that comes from a "pure heart" (1 Tim. 1:5 CSB). The heart is spoken of in Scripture as the center of the moral and spiritual life. The conscience, for instance, is associated with the heart.

On the negative side, depravity is said to issue from the heart: "The heart is more deceitful than all anything else and incurable—who can understand it?" (Jer. 17:9 CSB). Jesus said that out of the heart come evil thoughts, murder, adultery, fornication, theft, false witness, slander (Matt. 15:19). In other words, defilement comes from within rather than from without.

Because the heart is at the root of the problem, this is the place where God does his work in the individual. For instance, the work of the law is "written on their hearts," and conscience is the proof of this (Rom. 2:15 CSB). The heart is the field where seed (the Word of God) is sown (Matt. 13:19; Luke 8:15).

The heart is the dwelling place of God. Two persons of the Trinity are said to reside in the heart of the believer. God has given us the "down payment" of the Spirit "in our hearts" (2 Cor. 1:22 CSB). Ephesians 3:17 expresses the desire that "Christ may dwell in your hearts through faith" (CSB). The love of God "has been poured out in our hearts through the Holy Spirit who was given to us" (Rom. 5:5 CSB).

HEATH Shrubby, evergreen plant of the heather family, used by the KJV (Jer. 17:6; 48:6). Various translations have been offered: juniper (CSB, NASB); bush (NIV); shrub (NRSV, 17:6).

HEAVE OFFERING See *Sacrifice and Offerings*.

HEAVEN Part of God's creation above the earth and the waters including "air" and "space" and serving as home for God and his heavenly creatures. The word "heaven" occurs more frequently in Revelation than in any other NT book. The Revelation addresses heaven from the standpoints of the struggle between good and evil and of God's rule from heaven. The most popular passage dealing with heaven is Rev. 21:1–22:5. In this passage, heaven is portrayed in three different images: (1) the tabernacle (21:1-8), (2) the city (21:9-27), and (3) the garden (22:1-5). The image of the tabernacle portrays heavenly life as perfect fellowship with God. The symbolism of the city portrays heavenly life as perfect protection. The image of the garden shows heavenly life as perfect provision.

HEBER Personal name meaning "companion." **1.** Grandson of Asher and great grandson of Jacob (Gen. 46:17). He was the original clan ancestor of the Heberites (Num. 26:45). **2.** A Kenite related to family of Moses's wife (Judg. 4:11). **3.** A member of the tribe of Judah in a Hebrew text (1 Chron. 4:18), which apparently lists two mothers of Heber, one an Egyptian. **4.** A member of the tribe of Benjamin (1 Chron. 8:17). **5.** A different Hebrew word lies behind Eber (1 Chron. 5:13; 8:22), which KJV spells Heber. The Heber in Luke 3:35 (KJV) is the Eber of Gen. 11:15.

HEBREW A descendant of Eber. It differentiates early Israelites from foreigners. After David founded the monarchy, the term "Hebrew" seems to disappear from the Hebrew language. The designation apparently begins with Abraham (Gen. 14:13).

HEBREW LANGUAGE The language in which the canonical books of the OT were written, except for the Aramaic sections in Ezra 4:8–6:18; 7:12-26; Dan. 2:4b–7:28; Jer. 10:11, and a few other words and phrases from Aramaic and other languages. The language is not called "Hebrew" in the OT. Rather, it is known as "the language (literally, 'lip') of Canaan" (Isa. 19:18) or as "Judean" (NASB), that is, the language of Judah (Neh. 13:24; Isa. 36:11).

HEBREWS, LETTER TO THE Both the author of Hebrews and the historical situation that prompted its writing are matters of speculation. Although Paul's name is included in the title in some manuscripts, the author never mentions his name. Nor does the author identify his recipients or their location. The date of the letter is also uncertain. The author labeled himself and his audience as second-generation Christians, who heard the word from those who had known Jesus (Heb. 2:3b).

The main theme of Hebrews is found early in chapter 1. The God who spoke to the Israelites is the same God who spoke through Jesus (1:1-2). And when God speaks, his people ought to listen, a message reiterated in the climactic warning passage of the letter: "See to it that you do not reject the one who speaks" (12:25 CSB). Related to this is the warning against apostasy. This issue is present in all the warning passages, but the focal point of discussion usually is 6:4-8. The passage leaves no doubt that those who fall away will be punished for their disobedience. What is often overlooked, however, is that the text is far from explicit about what they are falling away from and what the punishment will be.

The most common assumption is that they have fallen away from salvation and that the burning (6:8) refers to eternal destruction. However, Herschel Hobbs's contention that these believers were in danger of falling away from God's world mission and that the punishment will be loss of opportunity is credible. The theme of God's mission can be seen in other passages, such as the failed attempt at Kadesh-barnea to enter the prom-

The Gezer Calendar is believed to be the oldest Hebrew inscription found to date. The inscription is on a limestone tablet and dates from 925 BC.

ised land to fulfill their calling (chaps. 3–4). Another often suggested solution looks at those who fall away as phenomenological believers; in other words, they appeared to be believers but were not. A difficulty with this position is the strong language the author used in 6:4-5 to describe these people.

In what may be the climax of the whole letter (13:10-16), the author reintroduced the themes of high priest, altar, and Day of Atonement sacrifice, all of which were central images in chapters 8–10. In this passage, these images were used to call the hearers outside their security zone. The synagogue might represent physical security for the audience, but Jesus was outside, suffering for the people. His people needed to be outside with him.

Other theological themes give support to the call to obedience. One such theme is the nature of Christ: Jesus is God's ultimate, superior revelation of himself. He is superior to angels, Moses, and the earthly priests, and his sacrifice is superior to anything offered in the temple. Through careful exposition of OT passages, the author points out the temporal nature of the priesthood, the temple sacrificial system, and the initial covenant between God and his people. Jesus as the perfect high priest offered a once-for-all sacrifice that initiated the new covenant foretold by Jeremiah.

HEBRON Place-name and personal name meaning "association" or "league." A major city in the hill country of Judah about 19 miles south of Jerusalem and 15 miles west of the Dead Sea.

After his separation from Lot, Abraham moved to Hebron. At that time, the area was known as Mamre and was associated with the Amorites (Gen. 13:18; 14:13; 23:19). Abraham apparently remained at Mamre until after the destruction of Sodom and Gomorrah. When Sarah died, the place was called Kirjath-arba. The population was predominantly Hittite (Gen. 23:2; Josh. 14:15; 15:54; Judg. 1:10). From them Abraham purchased a field with a burial plot inside the Cave of Machpelah. Abraham and Sarah, Isaac and Rebekah, and Jacob and Leah were buried there (Gen. 23:19; 25:9; 35:29; 49:31; 50:13).

The mosque of the patriarchs at Hebron built over the traditional site of the Cave of Machpelah

Four centuries later, when Moses sent the 12 spies into Canaan, the tribe of Anak lived in Hebron. After the death of Saul, David settled in the city (2 Sam. 2:3) and made it his capital during the seven years he ruled only Judah (1 Kgs. 2:11). His son Absalom launched an abortive revolt against David from Hebron (2 Sam. 15:10).

HEDGEHOG NASB, NRSV translation of the Hebrew *qippod*, a term of uncertain meaning (Isa. 14:23; 34:11; Zeph. 2:14). The term refers to the hedgehog (or porcupine) or to a type of bird.

HEEL, LIFTED HIS To lift one's heel against someone is to turn one's back and join rank with the enemies. Jesus applied the expression to Judas, who accepted Jesus's hospitality but then plotted his arrest (John 13:18).

HEGAI Persian name of unknown meaning. Eunuch in charge of King Ahasuerus's harem who befriended Esther (Esth. 2:8-9,15).

HEGE KJV spelling of Hegai in Esth. 2:3, based on variant spelling in Hebrew text.

HEGLAM NRSV interpretation of Hebrew text in 1 Chron. 8:7; a proper name, giving a second name to Gera what other versions translate as "who deported them."

HEIFER Young cow, especially one that has not yet calved.

HELAH Personal name meaning "jewelry for the neck." Wife of Ashur in the tribe of Judah (1 Chron. 4:5,7).

HELAM Place-name meaning "their army." Helam is the region, rather than a city, where David defeated the army of Hadadezer and thus gained control of Syria (2 Sam. 10:15-19).

HELBAH Place-name meaning "forest." City in tribal territory of Asher that Asher could not drive out (Judg. 1:31).

HELBON Place-name meaning "forest." City known for its trade in wine, mentioned in Ezekiel's lament over Tyre (Ezek. 27:18).

HELDAI Personal name meaning "mole." **1.** Officer in charge of David's army for the twelfth month of the year (1 Chron. 27:15). **2.** Man who returned from exile in Babylon, apparently with a gift of silver and gold, which God told Zechariah to take and have made into a crown for Joshua, the high priest (Zech. 6:10).

HELEB Personal name meaning "fat" or "the best." One of David's military heroes (2 Sam. 23:29).

HELEK Personal name meaning "portion." Son of Gilead from the tribe of Manasseh and original clan ancestor of the Helekites (Num. 26:30). The clan received an allotment in the tribe's share of the promised land (Josh. 17:2).

HELEM Personal name meaning "beat, strike." Member of the tribe of Asher (1 Chron. 7:35).

HELEPH Place-name meaning "replacement settlement" or "settlement of reeds." Border city of the tribal allotment of Naphtali (Josh. 19:33).

HELEZ Personal name perhaps meaning "ready for battle." **1.** David's military hero (2 Sam. 23:26) in charge of the army for the seventh month (1 Chron. 27:10). **2.** Member of the family of Caleb and Jerahmeel in the tribe of Judah (1 Chron. 2:39).

HELI Hebrew personal name meaning "high." The son of Matthat and father of Joseph, Jesus's earthly father (Luke 3:23-24).

HELIOPOLIS 1. Greek name for Egyptian city that meant "city of the sun." Its name in Egyptian means "pillar town" and was rendered in Akkadian as *Ana* and in Hebrew as *On* or *Awen* (Gen. 41:45; 46:20; Ezek. 30:17). **2.** Ancient city of Baalbek ("Lord of the Valley") located in the Beqaa Valley of Lebanon about 50 miles east of Beirut. Although it was a very ancient city, it was renamed Heliopolis in the third or second century BC.

HELKAI Personal name meaning "my portion." Priest when Joiakim was high priest one generation after the return from the exile under Zerubbabel (Neh. 12:15).

HELKATH Place-name meaning "flat place." Border town in the tribal allotment of Asher (Josh. 19:25) given to the Levites (21:31).

HELKATH-HAZZURIM Place-name meaning "field of flint stones" or "field of battle." Site of "play" (2 Sam. 2:14) battle between young warriors of Saul and those of David leading to defeat of Ish-bosheth's army (2:12-17).

HELL Usually understood as the final abode of the unrighteous dead wherein the ungodly suffer eternal punishment; the term translates one OT word and several NT words.

HELLENISM Used to describe any influence of classical Greek thought on Western heritage. The Hellenistic culture of Alexandria strongly impacted Jewish and Christian communities. The Koine Greek language became the *lingua franca*, an influence seen in the Greek terms used to name the Jewish "synagogue" (*sunagoge*) and the NT "church" (*ekklesia*). In about 275 BC, Jewish scholars produced the first translation of the Hebrew Scriptures, the Greek Septuagint (LXX). The Greek language was crucial in the spread of the gospel. NT authors used and quoted from the Septuagint, and the NT was written in Koine Greek. Some passages in the NT seem to reflect Greek thought as well as Greek terminology. Greek influence shows in the use of *logos* in John 1:1-14, a term Stoic philosophers used to describe the creative order of the universe.

Harbor at Alexandria. In Alexandria the Septuagint was translated about 275 BC.

HELLENISTS Group of early Christians whose language and culture were Greek rather than Hebrew. One of the first conflicts among believers in the early church was between those with a Greek background and those who had grown up in the Hebrew tradition (Acts 6:1; 9:29).

HELON Personal name meaning "powerful." Father of the leader of the tribe of Zebulun under Moses (Num. 1:9).

HELPER NASB translation of *parakletos*, a distinctive title for the Holy Spirit in the Gospel of John (14:16,26; 15:26; 16:7). Other versions translate the term "Comforter" (KJV), "Advocate" (NEB), or "Counselor" (CSB, RSV, NIV).

HELPMEET KJV term for woman as a helper precisely adapted to man (Gen. 2:18). Modern translations supply various equivalents: help suitable for him (NASB, NIV); help as his partner (NRSV); "helper corresponding to him" (CSB). The noun translated "help" or "partner" does not suggest subordination. Elsewhere the term is used of God as Help (1 Chron. 12:18; Pss. 30:10; 54:4; 121:1) or of military allies (Jer. 47:4; Nah. 3:9). The adjective "meet" (translated "suitable," "comparable," or "corresponding") stresses that woman, unlike the animals (Gen. 2:20), can be truly one with man (2:24), that is, enjoy full fellowship and partnership in humanity's God-given task (Gen. 1:27-28) of rule and dominion.

HELVE KJV term used for the handle of an ax (Deut. 19:5).

HEMAM Personal name of uncertain meaning. Descendant of Seir (Gen. 36:22).

HEMAN Personal name meaning "faithful." **1.** In Gen. 36:22, one of the sons of Lotan mentioned among the descendants of Esau. **2.** In 1 Kgs. 4:31, a notable sage to whose wisdom that of Solomon is compared. **3.** In 1 Chron. 6:33, the son of Joel, a Kohathite.

HEMDAN Personal name meaning "beauty, charm." Descendant of Seir and thus an Edomite (Gen. 36:26).

HEMLOCK KJV translation of two Hebrew terms. Modern translations agree in translating that in Hos. 10:4 as poisonous weed(s). The term at Amos 6:12 is translated as "bitterness" (NASB margins, NIV), "poison" (REB), and "wormwood" (CSB, NRSV, NASB).

HEMORRHAGE Heavy or uncontrollable bleeding. The KJV translates the underlying Hebrew and Greek terms as "issue of blood" (Lev. 12:7; Matt. 9:20) or "fountain of blood" (Mark 5:29).

HEMORRHOIDS Mass of dilated veins and swollen tissue in the vicinity of the anus. The KJV translators understood the affliction of Deut. 28:27; 1 Sam. 5:6,9,12 as hemorrhoids (or emerods).

HENA Place-name of uncertain meaning. City Sennacherib, king of Assyria, captured prior to threatening Hezekiah and Jerusalem in 701 BC (2 Kgs. 18:34).

HENADAD Personal name meaning "grace of Hadad (the god)." Clan of Levites who supervised the rebuilding of the temple under Zerubbabel after 537 BC (Ezra 3:9). Clan members also helped Nehemiah rebuild Jerusalem's walls (Neh. 3:18,24) and signed Nehemiah's covenant of obedience (Neh. 10:10).

HEPHER Personal name meaning "well" or "shame." **1.** Original family ancestor in clan of Gilead and father of Zelophehad (Num. 26:28-37). He belonged to the tribe of Manasseh (Josh. 17:1-2). **2.** A hero in David's wilderness army (1 Chron. 11:36). **3.** Member of the tribe of Judah (1 Chron. 4:6).

HEPHZIBAH Personal name meaning "my delight is in her." **1.** In 2 Kgs. 21:1, the mother of Manasseh, king of Judah. **2.** In Isa. 62:4, it is used as a symbolic name for Jerusalem.

HERBS, BITTER Salad of bitter herbs was eaten as part of the Passover observance (Exod. 12:8; Num. 9:11).

HERES Place-name meaning "sun." A mountain pass over which Gideon traveled in returning from his battle with the Midianites (Judg. 8:13).

HERESH Personal name meaning "unable to speak." Levite who lived near Jerusalem after the return from exile about 537 BC (1 Chron. 9:15).

HERESY Opinion or doctrine not in line with the accepted teaching of a church; the opposite of orthodoxy. Our English word is derived from a Greek word that has the basic idea of "choice."

HERETH Modern translation spelling of Hareth; place-name meaning "cut in to." Forest in which David hid from Saul after settling his parents with the king of Moab (1 Sam. 22:4-5).

HERMAS Christian to whom Paul sent greetings (Rom. 16:14). His name, the variant spelling of the Greek god Hermes, may indicate he was a slave, since many slaves were named for gods.

HERMES In Acts 14:12, the Greek deity for whom the superstitious people at Lystra took Paul. KJV uses the god's Latin name, Mercurius. Hermes was known as a messenger of the gods and was associated with eloquence. Paul's role as chief speaker made the Lystrans think of Hermes.

HERMOGENES Personal name meaning "born of Hermes." Follower who deserted Paul, apparently while he was in prison in Ephesus (2 Tim. 1:15). Paul's statement indicates acute disappointment in Hermogenes but does not say he became an apostate.

HERMON, MOUNT Place-name meaning "devoted mountain." At 9,100 feet above sea level, Hermon is the highest mountain in Syria. It can be seen from as far away as the Dead Sea—120 miles. The range is approximately 28 miles in length and reaches a width of 15 miles. Its peak is covered with snow two-thirds of the year. The mount is significant for four reasons. (1) It was the northern border of the Amorite kingdom (Deut. 3:8; 4:48).

View of Mount Hermon from the ancient city-mound of Hazor in northern Galilee

(2) It marked the northern limits of Joshua's victorious campaigns (Josh. 11:17; 12:1; 13:5). (3) It has always been regarded as a sacred mountain. (4) Some scholars believe the transfiguration of Jesus occurred on Hermon.

HEROD Name given to the family ruling Palestine immediately before and to some degree during the first half of the first Christian century. The most prominent family member and ruler was called Herod the Great, an Idumaean who was appointed king of the Jews in 40 BC and ruled until his death in 4 BC. Herod was ruler of Judea when Jesus was born (Matt. 2:1).

This aqueduct built by Herod the Great brought fresh water to Caesarea Maritima.

HERODIAN Member of an aristocratic Jewish group who favored the policies of Herod Antipas and thus supported the Roman government. Apparently they lived in Galilee, where Antipas ruled, and joined the Jerusalem religious authorities in opposing Jesus (Matt. 22:15-22; Mark 12:13-17).

HERODIAS Wife of Herod Antipas (Mark 6:17).

HERODION Christian man to whom Paul the apostle sent a greeting (Rom. 16:11). Paul referred to him as a kinsman.

HERODIUM A fortress-palace built by Herod the Great about four miles southeast of Bethlehem. Herod was buried there.

HERON Any of a family of wading birds with long necks and legs (*Areidae*), regarded as unclean (Lev. 11:19; Deut. 14:18).

HESED Personal name meaning "grace" or "covenant love." Father of one of Solomon's district governors (1 Kgs. 4:10 KJV).

HESHBON Place-name meaning "reckoning." City in Moab ruled by Sihon and captured by Moses (Num. 21:21-30).

HESHMON Place-name meaning "flat field." Town in tribal territory of Judah (Josh. 15:27).

HETH Personal name of unknown meaning. Son of Canaan, great grandson of Noah, and original ancestor of the Hittites, some of the original inhabitants of Canaan (Gen. 10:15).

HETHLON Place-name of unknown meaning on the northern border of Israel's promised land, according to Ezekiel's vision (Ezek. 47:15).

HEW To cut with blows from a heavy cutting instrument. The references to "hewers of wood" together with "drawers of water" (Josh. 9:21,23,27; Deut. 29:11) probably refer to those who gathered firewood. Such work was a despised task relegated to foreigners and slaves.

HEXATEUCH Modern designation for the first six books of the OT viewed as a literary unity.

HEZEKIAH Son and successor of Ahaz as king of Judah (716/15–687/86 BC). Hezekiah began his reign when he was 25 years old. Hezekiah died in 687/86 BC. Manasseh, his son, succeeded him, although Manasseh had become co-regent with Hezekiah about 696 BC.

In 711 BC, just a few years after Hezekiah had become king, Sargon II of Assyria captured Ashdod. Hezekiah anticipated the time when he would have to confront Assyrian armies. Hezekiah fortified the city of Jerusalem and organized an army. Knowing that a source of water was crucial, Hezekiah constructed a tunnel through solid rock from the spring of Gihon to the Siloam pool. The city wall was extended to enclose this important source of water.

Hezekiah consistently demonstrated both faith in and obedience to God. "Not one of the kings of Judah was like him, either before him or after him" (2 Kgs. 18:5 CSB).

The Gihon Spring in the Kidron Valley. King Hezekiah built a tunnel from the spring to the pool of Siloam that he also built to provide water for Jerusalem.

HEZION Personal name meaning "vision." Grandfather of King Ben-hadad of Damascus (1 Kgs. 15:18).

HEZIR Personal name meaning "wild pig." Ugaritic texts apparently show that the name came from the profession of herding swine. **1.** Leader of one of the 24 courses of priests (1 Chron. 24:15). **2.** Levite who signed Nehemiah's covenant to obey God's law (Neh. 10:20).

HEZRAI or **HEZRO** Personal name meaning "his stalk" or "stem." KJV reading of name of one of David's warriors (2 Sam. 23:35).

HEZRON Personal and place-name meaning "camping place" or "reeds." **1.** Son of Reuben, grandson of Jacob (Gen. 46:9), and original clan ancestor of Hezronites (Num.

26:6). **2.** Grandson of Judah, great grandson of Jacob (Gen. 46:12), original clan ancestor of Hezronites (Num. 26:21) through whom David was born (Ruth 4:19).

HIDDAI Personal name, perhaps a short form for Hodai, meaning "my majesty." One of David's warriors (2 Sam. 23:30).

HIDDEKEL Hebrew name for the third river flowing from the garden of Eden (Gen. 2:14). Most modern translations translate it as Tigris.

HIEL Personal name meaning "God lives" or, following the Greek translation, a short form of Ahiel, "brother of God." Man from Bethel who rebuilt Jericho at the price of the life of two of his sons (1 Kgs. 16:34), fulfilling the divine curse Joshua issued when he destroyed Jericho (Josh. 6:26).

HIERAPOLIS Place-name meaning "sacred city." Site of early church where Epaphras worked (Col. 4:13). The city was 12 miles northwest of Colossae.

HIGGAION Transliteration of Hebrew word meaning "whispering" (Lam. 3:62 NASB) or "meditation" (Ps. 19:14) or musical sound a stringed instrument produces (Ps. 92:3). It appears as a worship notation with uncertain meaning in Ps. 9:16. It may mean to play quietly or to pause for meditation.

HIGHEST KJV designation for God (Luke 1:32,35,76; 6:35). Modern translations prefer "Most High" (CSB, NASB, NIV, NRSV) or "Most High God" (TEV).

HIGH GATE, HIGHER GATE KJV designations for a gate of the Jerusalem temple (2 Kgs. 15:35; 2 Chron. 23:20; 27:3).

HIGH HEAPS KJV translation of a Hebrew term that occurs only at Jer. 31:21. Modern translations render the term as guideposts (NASB, NIV, NRSV) or signpost (REB).

HIGH PLACE Elevated site, usually found on the top of a mountain or hill; most high places were Canaanite places of pagan worship.

Mineral deposits from the hot springs of Hierapolis used as a health spa during the Roman period

Stone fragments of what is probably an altar base at the high place in Lachish

HIGH PRIEST One in charge of the temple (or tabernacle) worship. A number of terms are used to refer to the high priest: the priest (Exod. 31:10); the anointed priest (Lev. 4:3); the priest who is chief among his brethren

(Lev. 21:10); chief priest (2 Chron. 26:20); and high priest (2 Kgs. 12:10). The high priesthood was a hereditary office based on Lev. 16:32). Normally, the high priest served for life (Num. 18:7; 25:11-13; 35:25,28; Neh. 12:10-11), though as early as Solomon's reign a high priest was dismissed for political reasons (1 Kgs. 2:27).

During the Roman period, Annas (high priest AD 6–15) was clearly the most powerful priestly figure. Even when deposed by the Romans, Annas succeeded in having five of his sons and a son-in-law, Joseph Caiaphas (high priest AD 18–36/37) appointed high priests.

HIGHWAY A road, especially an elevated road (Isa. 62:10). In addition to literal uses, there are figurative uses, especially in Isaiah.

HILEN Place-name, perhaps meaning "power." City in tribal territory of Judah given to Levites (1 Chron. 6:58).

HILKIAH Personal name meaning "Yah's portion." **1.** Father of Amaziah (1 Chron. 6:45). He was a Levite who lived before the time of David the king. **2.** Levite and temple servant who lived during the time of David (1 Chron. 26:11). **3.** Father of Eliakim, who was in charge of the household of King Hezekiah (2 Kgs. 18:18). **4.** Father of Jeremiah the prophet (Jer. 1:1). **5.** Father of Gemariah, who was an emissary from Zedekiah to Nebuchadnezzar, king of Babylon (Jer. 29:3). **6.** High priest who aided in Josiah's reform movement (2 Kgs. 22:4). **7.** Person who stood with Ezra the scribe at the reading of the law (Neh. 8:4). **8.** Priest among the exiles who returned (Neh. 12:7).

HILL OF GOD (Hb. *Gibeat-elohim*) Site of a Philistine garrison and of a place of worship. Here Saul met a band of ecstatic prophets and joined them in their frenzy (1 Sam. 10:5).

HILL OF THE FORESKINS (Hb. *Gibeat-haaraloth*) Place near Gilgal where Joshua circumcised the Israelites born during the wilderness wandering (Josh. 5:3).

HILLEL Personal name meaning "praise." **1.** Father of the judge Abdon (Judg. 12:13). **2.** Influential rabbi and Talmudic scholar who flourished just prior to the time of the ministry of Jesus. He and his colleague Shammai presided over the two most important rabbinic schools of their time.

HIN Unit of liquid measure reckoned as one-sixth of a bath (Exod. 29:40). It would have been approximately equivalent to a gallon.

HIND Female deer; doe (Prov. 5:19). "To make my feet like hinds' feet" (KJV, NASB) is a common expression (2 Sam. 22:34; Ps. 18:33; Hab. 3:19) of God's care in dangerous situations.

HINNOM, VALLEY OF Place-name of uncertain meaning; also called the valley of the son(s) of Hinnom. The valley lies in close proximity to Jerusalem (2 Kgs. 23:10), just south of the ancient city (Josh. 15:8). The valley had a somewhat unglamorous history during the OT period. The worshipers of the pagan deities, Baal and Molech, practiced child sacrifice there (2 Kgs. 23:10).

The Hinnom (or Gehenna) Valley in Jerusalem, just south of the ancient city

HIP Part of the body where the thigh and torso connect. Jacob's hip came out of socket when he wrestled with God at the Jabbok (Gen. 32:25). The Israelites commemorated this encounter by not eating the thigh muscle on the hip socket (Gen. 32:32).

HIPPOPOTAMUS Large, thick-skinned, amphibious, cud-chewing mammal of the family *Hippopotamidae*. The Hebrew *behemoth* (Job 40:15-24) is sometimes understood as the hippopotamus (NASB, TEV margins).

HIRAH Personal name of unknown meaning. A friend of Judah, the son of Jacob, whom Judah was visiting when he met Shuah, who bore three of his sons (Gen. 38:1-12).

HIRAM Personal name apparently meaning "brother of the lofty one." **1.** King of Tyre, associated with David and Solomon in building the temple. **2.** Craftsman who did artistic metal work for Solomon's temple (1 Kgs. 7:13-45). He lived in Tyre, his father's hometown, but had a widowed Jewish mother from the tribe of Naphtali.

HISS Sound made by forcing breath between the tongue and teeth in mockery or to ward off demons. In the OT, an army or nation hissed at their enemy's city or land that suffered defeat or disaster (Jer. 19:8).

HITTITES Non-Semitic minority within the population of Canaan who frequently became involved in the affairs of the Israelites. Hittites, along with the Hivites, were people of Indo-European origin, identified within the population of Canaan (as "sons" of Canaan) in the Table of Nations (Gen. 10:15,17).

HIVITES A name that occurs 25 times in the Bible though not in texts outside the Bible. Most frequently the name appears in the list of nations God would drive out of the land during the Israelite conquest (e.g., Deut. 7:1).

HIZKI Personal name meaning "my strength" or a shortened form of "Yah is my strength." Modern translation spelling of Hezeki, a Benjaminite (1 Chron. 8:17).

HIZKIAH Personal name meaning "Yah is my strength." **1.** Abbreviated form in Hebrew for Hezekiah and used as alternate spelling of the king's name (2 Kgs. 18; Prov. 25:1). **2.** Apparently the Hebrew name of a clan that returned from Babylonian exile with Zerubbabel about 537 BC. **3.** A descendant of David living after the return from exile (1 Chron. 3:23).

HIZKIJAH KJV spelling of Hizkiah in Neh. 10:17. Modern translations usually use "Hezekiah."

HOARFROST or **HOAR FROST** KJV terms for frost, from "hoar" (white) and "frost" (Exod. 16:14; Job 38:29; Ps. 147:16).

HOBAB Personal name meaning "beloved" or "cunning." Father-in-law of Moses (Num. 10:29; Judg. 4:11). Some uncertainty exists concerning the identity of Moses's father-in-law. Jethro (Exod. 3:1; 18:2) and Reuel (Exod. 2:18) are also given as names for the father-in-law of the great lawgiver.

HOBAH Place-name probably meaning "guilt" in Hebrew but "land of reeds" in Akkadian. Town in Syria to which Abraham pursued the coalition of eastern kings who kidnapped Lot (Gen. 14:15).

HOBAIAH Personal name meaning "Yah hides." Clan of priests in time of Zerubbabel who did not have family records to prove their descent from pure priestly lines and were excluded from the priesthood (Ezra 2:61; Neh. 7:63).

HOD Personal name meaning "majesty." Member of the tribe of Asher (1 Chron. 7:37).

HODAIAH KJV, REB spelling of Hodaviah (1 Chron. 3:24).

HODAVIAH Personal name meaning "praise Yah." **1.** The final generation of the sons of David that the Chronicler listed (1 Chron. 3:24). **2.** Original ancestor of clan in the half tribe of Manasseh living east of the Jordan (1 Chron. 5:24). **3.** A member of the tribe of Benjamin (1 Chron. 9:7). **4.** A clan of Levites

ed by sin (Gen. 4). Humanity remained body and soul, but the inmost being was particularly impacted by sin. The human heart, the core of one's being, is sinful (Gen. 6:5; Jer. 17:9; Mark 7:20-23) and the mind is darkened (Eph. 4:17-19). The human will is in bondage to sin (Rom. 3:10-11; 2 Tim. 2:25-26); the human conscience is defiled (Titus 1:15); desires are twisted (Eph. 2:3; Titus 3:3). Simply put, humanity is universally dead in sin (Eph. 2:1), in a state of hostility toward God (Rom. 5:10), and subject to physical death followed by eternal judgment (Rom. 5:12-21; 8:10; 14:12; Heb. 9:27).

God in his grace did not leave humanity to perish eternally but provided for redemption. Humanity's participation in salvation begins at the individual level, when one places conscious faith in Jesus Christ. Saving faith includes a recognition of who Jesus is (fully divine and human Son of God), trust in the merits of his atoning death, and submission of the will to him. This is all made possible by God who, according to his eternal and gracious purpose, enables sinful humanity to believe (Eph. 2:4-9; 1 Tim. 1:14; Titus 3:5).

Humanity's participation in salvation will be consummated at the end of the age with resurrection and entry into the eternal state (1 Cor. 15:50-57). Scripture emphasizes the perfect conformity of the believer to Christ (1 John 3:2), eternal fellowship with God (John 14:2-3), and the joyful, worshipful assembly of all the redeemed (Rev. 7:9). This, of course, does not include all of humanity. Those who do not believe in Jesus Christ will spend an eternity suffering the just wrath of God (John 3:36; 2 Thess. 1:9).

HUMILITY The personal quality of being free from arrogance and pride and having an accurate estimate of one's worth.

HUMP Fleshy mound on the back of a camel where food is stored in the form of fat. Isaiah 30:6 refers to burdens carried on camels' humps (KJV, bunches).

HUMTAH Place-name meaning "lizards." Town in hill country of Judah in tribal territory of Judah (Josh. 15:54). Its exact location is not known.

HUNCHBACK One with a humped (curved or crooked) back. According to the Holiness Code, a hunchback was excluded from priestly service though allowed to eat the priests' holy food (Lev. 21:20). REB translates using the unique Hebrew term, "misshapen brows."

HUNDRED, TOWER OF (KJV "Tower of Meah") Tower located on the north wall of Jerusalem that was restored by Nehemiah (Neh. 3:1; 12:39). The name perhaps refers to the height of the tower (100 cubits), the number of its steps, or the number of troops in its garrison. It may have been part of the temple fortress (Neh. 2:8).

HUNDREDWEIGHT Unit of weight equal to 100 pounds (Rev. 16:21 REB, RSV).

HUNT, HUNTER To pursue game for food or pleasure. Hunting was an important supplementary food source, especially in the seminomadic stage of civilization. Genesis mentions several hunters by name, none of whom are Israelite ancestors (Nimrod, 10:9; Ishmael, 21:20; Esau, 25:27), perhaps suggesting that hunting was more characteristic of Israel's neighbors than of Israel. Hunting was, however, regulated by Mosaic law. The blood of captured game was to be poured out on the ground (Lev. 17:13). Deuteronomy 14:3-5 outlines what game was permitted as ritually clean food.

HUPHAM Original ancestor of the clan of Benjamin in the wilderness (Num. 26:39).

HUPPAH Personal name meaning "shelter" or "roof" or "bridal chamber." Leader of thirteenth course of priests under David (1 Chron. 24:13).

HUPPIM Personal name of unknown meaning. Son of Benjamin and grandson of Jacob (Gen. 46:21).

HUR Personal name of uncertain meaning, perhaps "white one" or "Horite" or perhaps derived from the name of the Egyptian god Horus. **1.** Israelite leader who accompanied Moses and Aaron to the top of the mountain in the fight against the Amalekites (Exod. 17:10-12). **2.** King of Midian whom Israel slew as they moved toward the promised land (Num. 31:8). **3.** District governor under Solomon over Mount Ephraim in charge of providing the royal table with provisions one month a year (1 Kgs. 4:8). His name may also be translated Ben-hur. **4.** Administrator over half the district of Jerusalem under Nehemiah or father of the administrator (Neh. 3:9).

HURAI Variant reading in 1 Chron. 11:32 for David's warrior Hiddai in the parallel passage (2 Sam. 23:30).

HURAM Personal name probably shortened from Ahuram meaning "exalted brother." **1.** Chronicler's spelling of Hiram, king of Tyre (2 Chron. 2). **2.** Descendant of Benjamin, often identified with Hupham of Num. 26:39.

HURAMABI Personal name perhaps meaning "my father is an exalted brother." NASB, NIV, NRSV, CSB name for Huram/Hiram, the skilled artisan that Hiram, king of Tyre, sent to Solomon to help build the temple (2 Chron. 2:13).

HURI Personal name of uncertain meaning, perhaps "white one," "linen maker," "Horite," or "my Horus" (Egyptian god). A member of the tribe of Gad (1 Chron. 5:14).

HUSBANDMAN KJV term for one who tills the soil; a farmer.

HUSHAH Personal name and place-name meaning "hurry." Member of the tribe of Judah (1 Chron. 4:4).

HUSHAI Personal name meaning "quick," "from Hushah," or "gift of brotherhood." The clan became a part of Israel as a clan of the tribe of Benjamin living in Archi southwest of Bethel (Josh. 16:2).

HUSHAM Personal name, perhaps meaning "large-nosed" or "with haste." One of the early kings of Edom (Gen. 36:34) from Teman.

HUSHIM Personal name meaning "hurried ones." **1.** Son of Dan and grandson of Jacob (Gen. 46:23). **2.** Member of the tribe of Benjamin (1 Chron. 7:12). **3.** Wife of Shaharaim of the tribe of Benjamin (1 Chron. 8:8) and mother of Abitub and Elpaal (1 Chron. 8:11).

HUT Modern translations' rendering for a lean-to or temporary shelter; shack (Isa. 1:8; 24:20). The image of Isa. 1:8 stresses the isolation of Jerusalem, the sole survivor of the cities of Judah (1:7-9). Isaiah 24:20 illustrates God's power in judgment in the picture of the earth's swaying like an unstable hut before the Lord.

HYACINTH Stone regarded as precious in ancient times. The hyacinth is sometimes identified with the sapphire (Rev. 9:17 NRSV, TEV) or turquoise (Exod. 28:19; Rev. 9:17; 21:20 REB; Exod. 28:19; Rev. 21:20 TEV). Others identify the hyacinth with zircon, a brown to grayish gem, or essonite, a yellow to brown garnet.

HYENA Any of a group of stocky built, carnivorous mammals of the genus *Hyaena*, located zoologically between the felines and canines. It is a striped scavenger looking much like a fox.

HYKSOS Racial name from the Greek form of an Egyptian word meaning "rulers of foreign lands" given to kings of the Fifteenth and Sixteenth Dynasties of Egypt.

HYMENAEUS or **HYMENEUS** (KJV) Personal name of the Greek god of marriage. Name of a fellow worker of Paul whose faith weakened and whose lifestyle changed, leading Paul to deliver him to Satan (1 Tim. 1:20). That probably means Paul led the church to dismiss Hymenaeus from the membership to purify the church, remove further temptation from the church, and to lead Hymenaeus to restored faith, repentance, and renewed church membership. Along with Philetus, Hymenaeus taught that the resurrection had already occurred (2 Tim. 2:17-18; cp. 1 Cor. 5).

HYMN A song of praise to God.

HYPOCRISY Pretense to being what one really is not, especially the pretense of being a better person than one really is.

HYRAX Small mammal making its home in the rock cliffs (Ps. 104:18; Prov. 30:26 NIV, CSB).

HYSSOP Small (about 27 inches), bushy plant, probably *Origanum Maru L.*, the Syrian marjoram. Stalks of hyssop bear numerous small white flowers in bunches. Hyssop was thus well suited for use as a "brush" to dab the lintels of Israelite homes with the blood of the Passover lambs (Exod. 12:22). A branch of hyssop bore the sponge used to offer vinegar to Christ at his crucifixion (John 19:29; Matt. 27:48 and Mark 15:36 mention a reed).

I

A vase handle in the shape of a beautiful winged ibex

IBEX Species of wild goat with large curved horns, native to high mountain areas. The ibex has been identified as the wild goat of the Bible (1 Sam. 24:2; Ps. 104:18).

IBHAR Personal name meaning "he elected." Son born to David after he moved to Jerusalem (2 Sam. 5:15).

IBLEAM Place-name meaning "he swallowed the people." City in tribal territory of Issachar but given to the tribe of Manasseh (Josh. 17:11).

IBNEIAH Personal name meaning "Yah builds." Benjaminite who returned from exile and settled in Jerusalem (1 Chron. 9:8).

IBNIJAH Personal name meaning "Yah builds," a variant spelling of Ibneiah. Ancestor of a Benjaminite returning from exile and living in Jerusalem (1 Chron. 9:8).

IBRI Personal name meaning "Hebrew." A Levite under King David (1 Chron. 24:27).

IBSAM Personal name akin to balsam, meaning "sweet smelling" in modern translations. KJV spelling is Jibsam. Member of the tribe of Issachar (1 Chron. 7:2).

IBZAN Personal name, perhaps meaning "quick, agile." Judge of Israel from Bethlehem who participated in royal practice of marrying children to foreigners (Judg. 12:8-10).

ICHABOD Personal name meaning "where is the glory?" The son of Phinehas, Eli's son (1 Sam. 4:21). His birth seems to have been precipitated by the news of the death of his father and the capture of the ark of the covenant in battle against the Philistines. The mother of Ichabod died immediately after the child's birth.

ICONIUM City of Asia Minor visited by Barnabas and Paul during the first missionary journey (Acts 13:51). Paul endured sufferings and persecution at Iconium (2 Tim. 3:11).

IDALAH Place-name of uncertain meaning, perhaps "jackal" or "memorial." Town in tribal territory of Zebulun (Josh. 19:15).

IDBASH Personal name meaning "sweet as honey." Son of Etam in the tribe of Judah (1 Chron. 4:3).

IDDO English spelling of four different Hebrew personal names. **1.** Name of uncertain meaning. Person with authority in the exilic community during the Persian period to whom Ezra sent messengers to secure Levites to join him in the return to Jerusalem (Ezra 8:17-20). **2.** Personal name, perhaps meaning "his praise." Leader of the eastern half of the tribe of Manasseh under David (1 Chron. 27:21). **3.** Name, perhaps meaning "Yahweh adorns himself." A prophet whose records the chronicler consults for more information about Solomon and Jeroboam (2 Chron. 9:29), Rehoboam (2 Chron. 12:15),

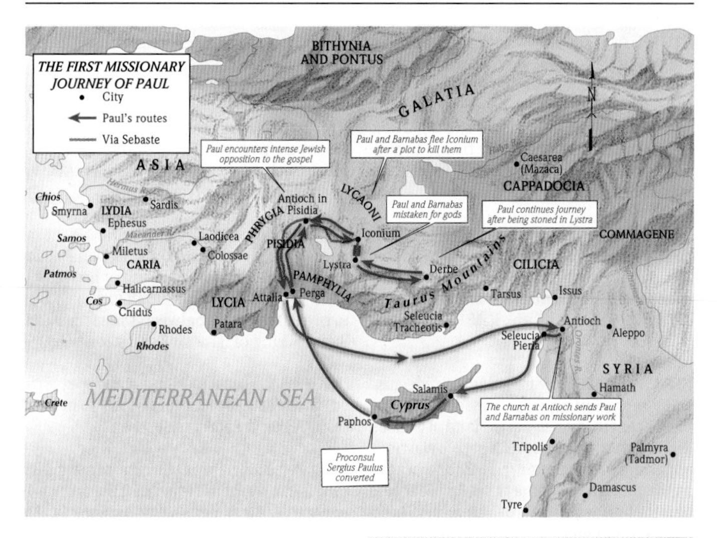

and Abijah (2 Chron. 13:22). **4.** Grandfather of Zechariah, the prophet (Zech. 1:1,7 with different Hebrew spellings). Ezra (5:1; 6:14) put Zechariah as Iddo's son, using "son" to mean descendant, as often in Hebrew. **5.** Father of Solomon's district supervisor who supplied the royal court provisions for one month a year in the area of Mahanaim (1 Kgs. 4:14). **6.** A Levite (1 Chron. 6:21).

IDLE Not engaged in earning a living; depending on the labor and generosity of others for support. Scripture distinguishes between those unwilling to work who should not eat (2 Thess. 3:10) and those unable to earn a living (e.g., "true" widows, 1 Tim. 5:9) for whom the community of faith is responsible.

IDOL Physical or material image or form representing a reality or being considered divine and thus an object of worship. In the Bible, various terms are used to refer to idols or idolatry: "image," either graven (carved) or cast, "statue," "abomination." Both Testaments condemn idols, but with idols the OT expresses more concern than the NT, probably reflecting the fact that the threat of idolatry was more pronounced for the people of the OT (Exod. 20:4-5 NASB).

Allat, the moon goddess of Syria and later northern Arabia

IDUMEA In Isa. 34:5, a nation destined for judgment. "Idumea" is the term used for Edom in the Greek version of the OT and in the writings of the Jewish historian Josephus. The region was southeast of the Dead Sea. The Herods came originally from Idumea. Crowds from Idumea followed Jesus early in his ministry (Mark 3:8).

IEZER Personal name meaning "where is help" or a short form of "my father is help." (Hb. *Aviezer*, Josh. 17:2). Son of Gilead in the tribe of Manasseh and original clan ancestor of Iezerites (Num. 26:30). KJV, REB spelling is Jeezer.

IGAL Personal name meaning "he redeems." **1.** Spy representing tribe of Issachar whom Moses sent to investigate the land of Canaan (Num. 13:7). **2.** One of David's heroic warriors, apparently a foreigner from Zobah (2 Sam. 23:36), though his name is spelled Joel, and he is the brother, not son, of Nathan in 1 Chron. 11:38. **3.** Descendant of David in the postexilic community (about 470 BC) and thus bearer of the messianic line and hope (1 Chron. 3:22).

IGDALIAH Personal name meaning "Yahweh is great." Ancestor of the prophets whose chamber in the temple Jeremiah used to test the Rechabites' loyalty to their oath not to drink wine (Jer. 35:4).

IIM Place-name meaning "ruins." **1.** Town on southern border of tribal territory of Judah (Josh. 15:29). **2.** Used in Num. 33:45 (KJV) as abbreviation for Iye-abarim.

IJON Place-name meaning "ruin." Place in northern Israel captured by King Ben-hadad of Damascus. This was a result of his agreement with King Asa of Judah (910–869 BC) to break the treaty between Damascus and Baasha, king of Israel (1 Kgs. 15:20).

IKKESH Personal name meaning "perverted, false." Father of one of David's 30 heroes from Tekoa (2 Sam. 23:26).

ILAI Personal name of uncertain meaning. One of David's military heroes (1 Chron. 11:29), apparently the same as Zalmon (2 Sam. 23:28).

ILLYRICUM Place-name of uncertain meaning. A district in the Roman Empire between the Danube River and the Adriatic Sea. The Romans divided it into Dalmatia and Pannonia. Illyricum represented the

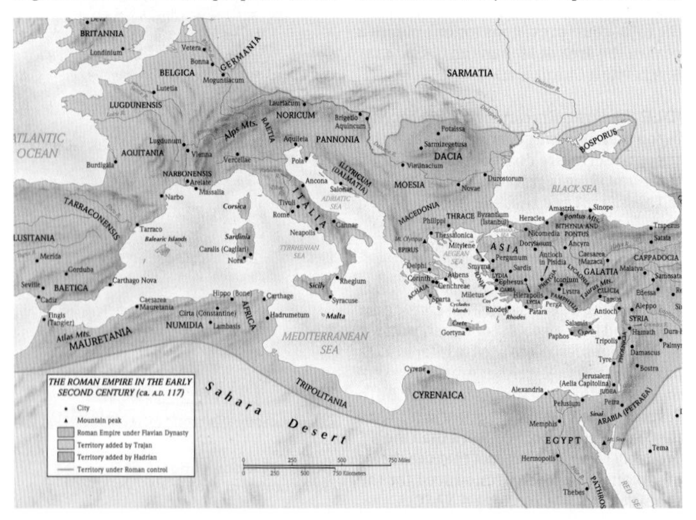

northeastern limits of Paul's missionary work (Rom. 15:19), though the Bible nowhere mentions his specific work there.

IMAGE OF GOD Biblical designation for the unique nature, status, and worth of all human beings as created by God. See *Humanity*.

IMAGERY, CHAMBER OF KJV phrase (Ezek. 8:12) understood as "room of his carved images" (NASB) or "shrine of his idol" (CSB). The picture of the representatives of Israel worshiping idols within the Jerusalem temple in Ezekiel's vision (8:3,12) symbolizes the people's unfaithfulness to God.

IMAGINATION KJV term for thought as the prelude to action, frequently in the sense of plotting or devising evil; can also refer to stubbornness, from the Hebrew words meaning "formed" or "twisted."

IMLA or **IMLAH** Personal name meaning "he fills," appearing in different spelling in Kings and Chronicles. Father of the prophet Micaiah (1 Kgs. 22:8).

IMMANUEL Personal name meaning "God with us." Name of son to be born in Isaiah's prophecy to King Ahaz (Isa. 7:14) and fulfilled in the birth of Jesus (Matt. 1:22-23).

IMMER Personal name probably meaning "lamb." **1.** Father of Pashhur, the priest and temple administrator (Jer. 20:1). **2.** Priest whose son Zadok helped Nehemiah repair Jerusalem's walls (Neh. 3:29). **3.** Leader of priestly division under David (1 Chron. 24:14).

IMMORALITY Any illicit sexual activity outside of marriage. Both in the OT and in the NT, the word has a figurative meaning as well, referring to idolatry or unfaithfulness to God.

IMMORTALITY Quality or state of being exempt from death. In the true sense of the word, only God is immortal (1 Tim. 1:17; 6:16; 2 Tim. 1:10), for only God is living in the true sense of the word. Humans may be considered immortal only insofar as immortality is the gift of God.

IMMUTABILITY OF GOD The unchangeability of God. In biblical theology, God is described as unchanging in his nature and in his character. This includes God's being (essence), purposes, and promises.

IMNA Personal name meaning "he defends." A member of the tribe of Asher (1 Chron. 7:35).

IMNAH Personal name meaning "he allots for" or "on the right hand, good fortune." **1.** Son of Asher and original ancestor of the Imnites (Num. 26:44; KJV, Jimna). **2.** Levite in the time of King Hezekiah (2 Chron. 31:14).

IMPEDIMENT IN SPEECH Disturbance of the vocal organs resulting in the inability to produce intelligible sounds (Mark 7:32). In Jesus's healing of a man who "had difficulty speaking" (CSB; NIV, "hardly talk"), the crowds recognized a fulfillment of Isa. 35:5-6.

IMPERISHABLE Not subject to decay; ever-enduring. Imperishable (KJV, incorruption) describes the spiritual resurrection body that, unlike the physical body, is not subject to the decay associated with death (1 Cor. 15:42-54).

IMPORTUNITY Troublesome urgency; excessive persistence. In Luke 11:8, importunity results in a favorable response to a midnight request for bread (KJV, RSV).

IMPOTENT Lacking power, strength, or vigor; helpless. Impotence in the KJV never refers to sexual inability. Modern translations replace "impotent" with other terms: "cripple" (Acts 4:9 NIV); "disabled" (John 5:3 CSB, NIV; Acts 4:9 CSB); "invalid" (John 5:3 NRSV); "sick" (John 5:3,7; Acts 4:9 NASB).

IMPRECATION, IMPRECATORY PSALMS Act of invoking a curse. In the Imprecatory Psalms, the author calls for God to bring misfortune and disaster upon the enemies (Pss. 5; 11; 17; 35; 55; 59; 69; 109; 137; 140). Some of the theological principles underlying these psalms are (1) the principle that vengeance belongs to God (Deut. 32:35; Ps. 94:1), which excludes personal retaliation and necessitates appeal to God to punish the wicked (cp. Rom. 12:19); (2) the principle that God's righteousness demands judgment on the wicked (Pss. 5:6; 11:5-6); (3) the principle that God's covenant love for the people of God necessitates intervention on their part (Pss. 5:7; 59:10,16-17); and (4) the principle of prayer that believers trust God with all their thoughts and desires.

IMPUTE, IMPUTATION Setting to someone's account or reckoning something to another person. God reckoned righteousness to believing Abraham (Gen. 15:6). This means that God credited to Abraham that which he did not have in himself (Rom. 4:3-5). The imputation of righteousness lies at the heart of the biblical doctrine of salvation. This righteousness is seen in Christ who purchased redemption. God grants righteousness to those who have faith in Christ (Rom. 1:17; 3:21-26; 10:3; 2 Cor. 5:21; Phil. 3:9). This righteousness imputed or reckoned to believers is, strictly speaking, an alien righteousness. It is not the believer's own righteousness but God's righteousness imputed to the believer. So, as Luther said, believers are simultaneously righteous and sinful.

IMRAH Personal name meaning "he is obstinate." Member of the tribe of Asher (1 Chron. 7:36).

IMRI Short form of personal name "Amariah" meaning "Yah has spoken." **1.** Ancestor of a clan from the tribe of Judah living in Jerusalem after the return from exile (1 Chron. 9:4). **2.** Father of Zaccur, who helped Nehemiah rebuild Jerusalem's wall (Neh. 3:2).

INCANTATIONS Chants used by magicians to control evil spirits and thus heal the sick or afflict enemies. Mosaic law prohibited the casting of spells (Deut. 18:10-11). The complaint that the wicked are like a snake, immune to the cunning enchanter, perhaps refers to the futility of incantations (Ps. 58:3-5). The Babylonians hoped to gain success and terrorize their enemies by means of incantations (Isa. 47:12). Isaiah warned their incantations would be of no avail (47:9). The tongue muttering wickedness perhaps refers to incantations (Isa. 59:3). The books of magic of Acts 19:19 were likely collections of incantations.

INCARNATION God's becoming human; the union of divinity and humanity in Jesus of Nazareth. Incarnation (Lat. *incarnatio*, being or taking flesh), while a biblical idea, is not a biblical term. Its Christian use derives from the Latin version of John 1:14 and appears repeatedly in Latin Christian authors from about AD 300 onward.

As a biblical teaching, incarnation refers to the affirmation that God, in one of the modes of his existence as Trinity and without in any way ceasing to be the one God, has revealed himself to humanity for its salvation by becoming human. Jesus, the Man from Nazareth, is the incarnate Word or Son of God, the focus of the God-human encounter. As the God-Man, he mediates God to humans; as the Man-God, he represents humans to God. By faith-union with him, men and women, as adopted children of God, participate in his filial relation to God as Father.

Formulation of the Doctrine The problem of the incarnation begins with John's assertion, "the Word became flesh" (John 1:14). Clear expression of the relation of the Word to the flesh, of divinity to humanity within the person of Jesus, became a matter of major concern during the first five centuries of the Christian era. The unsystematized affirmations of the NT were refined through controversy, a process that culminated in the ecumenical councils of Nicaea (AD 325), Constantinople (AD 381), Ephesus (AD 431), and Chalcedon (AD 451).

The mystery of the incarnation continues, and the statements of the first four councils of the Christian church preserve that mystery. Jesus, God incarnate, was one Person in two natures—fully divine and fully human. See *Christ*.

INCENSE Mixture of aromatic spices prepared to be burned in connection with the offering of sacrifices (Exod. 25:6). The incense used in worship was to be prepared according to exacting specifications and was to be offered only by the high priest. According to Luke 1:8-20, Zacharias was burning incense in the temple when he was visited by the angel Gabriel.

INCEST Sexual intercourse between persons too closely related for normal marriage. The twofold theological rationale for the prohibition of incestuous unions is the divine claim "I am the LORD your God" (Lev. 18:2,4,6) and the note that such behavior characterized the Egyptians and Canaanites whom God judged (Lev. 18:3,24-25).

Penalties for various forms of incest included childlessness (Lev. 20:20-21), exclusion from the covenant people (Lev. 18:29; 20:17-18; cp. 1 Cor. 5:2,5), and death (Lev. 20:11-12,14). In patriarchal times, marriage to a half sister (Gen. 20:12) and marriage to rival sisters (Gen. 29:21-30) were permissible, though such marriages proved troublesome to both Abraham and Jacob. Scriptural accounts of incest include Gen. 19:31-35; 35:22; and 2 Sam. 13.

INCH A unit of measure equal to a twelfth of a foot. Eighteen inches (Gen. 6:16 NIV, TEV) is the equivalent of a cubit.

INCONTINENCY, INCONTINENT KJV term for the lack of self-control (1 Cor. 7:5). Incontinent (2 Tim. 3:3) means lacking self-control (CSB, NASB), profligate (NRSV), or even violent (TEV).

INDIA Eastern boundary of the Persian Empire of Ahasuerus (Xerxes) (Esth. 1:1; 8:9). Biblical references to India refer to the Punjab, the area of Pakistan and northwest India drained by the Indus River and its tributaries. India was possibly a port of call for Solomon's fleet (1 Kgs. 10:22). Trade between India and the biblical lands began before 2000 BC.

INFANT BAPTISM Rite of initiation performed on infants born into Christian families, also called "paedobaptism." While there is no explicit record of infant baptism in the NT, it was an established practice in the church by the third century.

Adherents of believer's baptism argue against paedobaptism on the basis that: (1) the clear pattern in the NT is that baptism is preceded by repentance and faith (e.g., Acts 2:38; 8:12; 18:8); (2) it is not clear that household baptisms included infants; and (3) the NT parallel to circumcision is not baptism but circumcision of the heart (Rom. 2:29; Col. 2:11), which points to an inward spiritual reality based upon a confession of faith that is impossible for infants.

INFLAMMATION Response to cellular injury characterized by redness, infiltration of white blood cells, heat, and frequently pain. Inflammation was one of the curses upon those disobedient to the covenant (Deut. 28:22; cp. Lev. 13:28).

INGATHERING, FEAST OF Alternate name for the Feast of Tabernacles (Booths) (Exod. 23:16; 34:22). See *Festivals*.

INHERITANCE Legal transmission of property after death. The Hebrew Bible has no exclusive term for "inheritance." The words often translated "inherit" mean more generally "take possession." Only in context can they be taken to mean "inheritance." The Greek word in the NT does refer to the disposition of property after death, but its use in the NT often reflects the OT background more than normal Greek usage.

INK Writing fluid. Ink for writing on papyrus (a plant product) was made of soot or lampblack mixed with gum arabic (Jer. 36:18; 2 Cor. 3:3; 2 John 12; 3 John 13). Red ink was made by replacing lampblack with red iron oxide. Because such ink did not stick well to parchment (a leather product), another ink was made from nutgalls mixed with iron sulfate.

INKHORN KJV term for a case in which ingredients for making ink were kept (Ezek. 9:2-3,11). A scribe customarily carried his inkhorn in his belt.

INLET Bay or recess in the shore of a sea or lake. When Deborah and Barak went to battle against Sisera, the tribe of Asher stayed at home "by his inlets" ("landings," NRSV; "harbors," CSB; Judg. 5:17).

INN Different kinds of shelters or dwellings. In the OT, the Hebrew word translated "inn" or "lodging place" might refer to a camping place for an individual (Jer. 9:2), a family on a journey (Exod. 4:24), an entire caravan (Gen. 42:27; 43:21), or an army (Josh. 4:3,8). In these passages (with the possible exception of the reference in Jeremiah), the presence of a building is not implied. Often the reference is only to a convenient piece of ground near a spring. It is doubtful that inns in the sense of public inns with a building existed in OT times.

By the time of Christ, the situation is quite different. Public inns existed in Greek times and throughout the Roman period. The Greek word for "inn" in the NT implies some type of stopping place for travelers. At times it refers to a public inn. Such an inn of the first century consisted primarily of a walled-in area with a well. A larger inn might have small rooms surrounding the court. People and animals stayed together.

INNKEEPER One who serves as the host or hostess at an inn. The innkeeper of Luke 10:35 was responsible for providing food and medical care. A Targum (early Aramaic free translation) on Josh. 2:1 identifies Rahab as an innkeeper.

INSCRIPTION Words or letters carved, engraved, or printed on a surface (Mark 15:26; Luke 23:38; superscription, KJV). Pilate likely intended the inscription above the cross ("the King of the Jews") in a derogatory sense: "see the defeated King of the Jews." According to John 19:21, the Jewish leadership found the inscription offensive. The Gospel writers saw in Pilate's mockery the truth about Jesus who in his suffering and death fulfilled his messianic role.

INSECTS Air-breathing arthropods that make up the class *Hexapoda*. Representatives are found on land and in water. They have three distinct body parts (head, thorax, and abdomen) as well as three pairs of legs, one pair of antennae, and usually one or two pairs of wings. Insects are found often in the story of God's dealings with his people. These occurrences help the reader to understand the life of an ancient people. Insects are a part of the Bible because they were a part of life. Yet the references to these small creatures do more than give information. From them the reader can learn much about God.

God's sovereignty is reflected in his use of hornets to accomplish his divine purpose of driving Israel's enemies out of Canaan. He also could chasten the chosen people

Hieroglyphic inscriptions on a temple wall at Karnak in Egypt

with a locust if they should disobey. The absence of advanced methods of insect control reminds us of Israel's utter dependence upon God. The Lord would inspire his servants to use the lowly ant and locust as examples for humankind to follow. The wisdom writers would use even the disgusting fly larva to remind humanity of its mortality.

INSPECTION GATE Jerusalem city gate (Neh. 3:31 CSB, NASB, NIV). The KJV refers to the gate as the Miphkad Gate.

INSPIRATION OF SCRIPTURE "All Scripture is inspired by God" (2 Tim. 3:16 CSB). Paul's Greek suggests that Scripture is a divine "spiration" (that which God has breathed out, the product of his creative breath). Paul's point, then, is not that Scripture is inspiring to read (it is that), nor that the authors were inspired (they were), but that Scripture's origin means it is the very Word of God.

Theories of Inspiration Historically biblical inspiration has been reckoned in four ways. (1) The Bible is only inspired like other good books with human authors. This is neither what Scripture says nor what the church has believed. (2) The Bible is only partially inspired by God. Proponents hold that only the theological (not the scientific or historical) portions of Scripture are inspired, or that Scripture is just a record of God's saving historical acts, or that the Bible contains the word of God rather than being that word. But inspiration ensures that Scripture itself is the revealed word of God, not only testifying of God's redemptive work but also interpreting it. (3) The Bible is divinely inspired without use of human authors. Mechanical dictation theory renders Scripture analogous to myths regarding the origins of the Quran or Book of Mormon, and runs contrary to what the Bible says of its origins. (4) The Bible is divinely inspired because God concurrently worked with human authors to produce the very written message he desired. This classical view teaches the Holy Spirit superintended more than 40 authors from widely divergent backgrounds (shepherds, kings, prophets, fishermen, etc.), spanning a period of approximately a millennium and a half, to produce with supernatural congruity not just the thoughts but the very words of God to humanity.

INSTRUCTION Teaching or exhortation on aspects of Christian life and thought directed to persons who have already made a faith commitment. Instruction (*didache*) is frequently distinguished from missionary preaching (*kerugma*). Matthew's Gospel says of Jesus, "He was teaching them like one who had authority" (7:29 CSB). The Sermon on the Mount (Matt. 5–7) in particular is the rock-solid foundational teaching for Christian life (7:24-27). Jesus himself admonished his disciples to make disciples, baptizing them in the name of the Father, the Son, and the Holy Spirit, "teaching them to observe everything I have commanded you" (Matt. 28:20 CSB).

INSTRUMENT KJV term for a tool, utensil (1 Chron. 28:14), weapon (Gen. 49:5; 1 Chron. 12:33,37), or musical instrument (1 Chron. 15:16; 16:42; 23:5).

INSULT To treat with insolence, indignity, or contempt. The term does not appear in the KJV but becomes increasingly frequent in more recent translations, where it replaces terms such as "abuse, mock, revile, reproach," or "ridicule."

INTEGRITY Faithful support of a standard of values. Terms that occur in parallel with integrity (Hb. *tom*, *tomim*) suggest its shades of meaning: righteousness (Ps. 7:8); uprightness (Ps. 25:21); without wavering (Ps. 26:1 CSB, NRSV, NASB, NIV); blameless (Ps. 101:2 CSB, NRSV, Hebrew uses *tom* twice in verse, otherwise translated "integrity"). In the NT, integrity occurs only at Titus 2:7 (CSB, NRSV, NIV, REB) in reference to teaching. The idea of singleness of heart or mind is frequent (Matt. 5:8; 6:22; James 1:7-8; 4:8).

INTERCESSION Act of intervening or mediating between differing parties, particularly the act of praying to God on behalf of another person. In the OT, the Hebrew verb *paga'* is used of such pleading or interceding (Gen. 23:8; Isa. 53:12; 59:16; Jer. 7:16; 15:11; 27:18; 36:25). More general terms such as *palal*, "pray," or *chalah*, "appease," are also sometimes translated "intercede" (1 Sam. 7:5; 1 Kgs. 13:6). In the NT, the Greek term is *entungkano* and its derivatives (Rom. 8:26-27,34; 1 Tim. 2:1; Heb. 7:25).

INTEREST Sum of money a borrower pays for use of loaned capital. Mosaic law prohibited the charging of interest to fellow Israelites (Exod. 22:25; Lev. 25:36-37; Deut. 23:19). Interest could be charged to foreigners (Deut. 23:20). The motive in lending without interest to fellow Israelites was to prevent the formation of a permanent underclass in Israel.

INTERTESTAMENTAL HISTORY AND LITERATURE Events and writings originating after the final prophet mentioned in the OT (Malachi, about 450 BC) and before the birth of Christ (about 4 BC). The Intertestamental Period can be divided into three sections: The Greek Period, 323 BC to 167 BC; the Period of Independence, 167–63 BC; and the Roman Period, 63 BC through the time of the NT.

Literature The Jews produced many writings during the Intertestamental Period. These writings can be divided into three groups. The Apocrypha are writings that were included, for the most part, in the Greek translation of the OT, the Septuagint. They were translated into Latin and became a part of the Latin Vulgate, the authoritative Latin Bible. A second group of writings is the Pseudepigrapha. It is a larger collection than the Apocrypha, but there is no final agreement as to which writings should be included in it. Fifty-two writings are included in the two volumes, *The Old Testament Pseudepigrapha*, edited by James H. Charlesworth. The final group of writings from this period is the Qumran scrolls, popularly known as the Dead Sea Scrolls. The first knowledge of these came with the discovery of manuscripts in a cave above the Dead Sea in 1947. During subsequent years, fragments of manuscripts have been found in at least 11 caves in the area. These writings include OT manuscripts, writings of the Qumran sect, and writings copied and used by the sect that came from other sources. These writings show us something of the life and beliefs of one group of Jews in the last two centuries before Jesus.

IPHDEIAH or **IPHEDEIAH** Personal name meaning "Yah redeems." Member of the tribe of Benjamin who lived in Jerusalem (1 Chron. 8:25).

IPHTAH Place-name meaning "he opened." Town in the tribal territory of Judah in the Shephelah (Josh. 15:43).

IPHTAHEL Place-name meaning "God opens." Valley separating tribal territories of Zebulun and Asher (Josh. 19:14,27).

IR Personal name meaning "city" or "donkey's calf." Member of the tribe of Benjamin (1 Chron. 7:12).

IRA Personal name meaning "city" or "donkey's colt." **1.** Priest under David (2 Sam. 20:26). **2.** Two of David's military heroes were named Ira (2 Sam. 23:26,38). Ira from Tekoa was also an officer in charge of the sixth month's "national guard" army (1 Chron. 27:9).

IRAD Personal name of uncertain meaning. Son of Enoch (Gen. 4:18).

IRAM Personal name of uncertain meaning. Tribal leader in Edom (Gen. 36:43).

IRI Personal name meaning "my city" or "my donkey's colt." Leader in the tribe of Benjamin (1 Chron. 7:7).

IRIJAH Personal name meaning "Yah sees." Army captain who accused Jeremiah of treason and turned him over to the authorities for punishment (Jer. 37:13) about 586 BC.

IRNAHASH Place-name meaning "city of the snake" or "city of bronze." First Chronicles 4:12 lists it as a personal name in the descendants of Judah, basing a genealogy on the Table of Nations (Gen. 10) and other lists of cities.

IRON Metal that was a basic material for weapons and tools in the biblical period. The Iron Age began in Israel about 1200 BC, though introduction of this metal into daily life occurred slowly. The Bible mentions iron in conjunction with Moses and with the Canaanite conquest, but at this time iron was rare and used mainly for jewelry. The availability of iron was a sign of the richness of the promised land (Deut. 8:9), and articles of iron were indications of wealth (Deut. 3:11; Josh. 6:19).

IRON Place-name meaning "fearful." Town in tribal territory of Naphtali (Josh. 19:38), sometimes spelled Yiron (RSV, TEV, NASB).

IRONSMITH One who works with iron, one who smelts ore or works cast pieces. Barzillai (2 Sam. 17:27-29; 19:31-39), whose name means "man of iron," perhaps served as David's ironsmith.

IRPEEL Place-name meaning "God heals." Town in tribal territory of Benjamin (Josh. 18:27). Location is not known.

IRRIGATION Transportation of water by man-made means such as canals, dams, aqueducts, and cisterns. The dry climate of the ancient Near East made the transportation of water, often across long distances, a necessity. Large canal systems crossed the lands of Egypt and Mesopotamia, providing the vast amounts of water necessary to support crops during the dry months of March to October. In Egypt, the second highest official, the vizier, oversaw the maintenance of canals and the allocation of water to the provinces.

At the second cataract of the Nile River a scene of primitive irrigation with the use of manpower

IRSHEMESH Place-name meaning "city of the sun." Town in tribal territory of Dan (Josh. 19:41) on the border of the tribe of Judah (Josh. 15:10, called Beth-shemesh or house of the sun).

IRU Personal name meaning "donkey's colt" or "they protect." Son of Caleb (1 Chron. 4:15).

ISAAC Personal name meaning "laughter." Only son of Abraham by Sarah and a patriarch of the nation of Israel.

Old Testament Isaac was the child of a promise from God, born when Abraham was 100 years old and Sarah was 90 (Gen. 17:17; 21:5). After waiting years for the fulfillment of God's promise of a son, God tested Abraham's faith once again by commanding him to sacrifice Isaac (Gen. 22:1-19).

Isaac married Rebekah (Gen. 24), who bore him twin sons, Esau and Jacob (Gen. 25:21-28). Though less significant than Abraham and Jacob, Isaac was revered as one of the Israelite patriarchs (Exod. 3:6; 1 Kgs. 18:36; Jer. 33:26).

New Testament In the NT, Isaac appears in the genealogies of Jesus (Matt. 1:2; Luke 3:34), as one of the three great patriarchs (Matt. 8:11; Luke 13:28; Acts 3:13) and as an example of faith (Heb. 11:20). Isaac's sacrifice by Abraham (Heb. 11:17-18; James 2:21), in which Isaac was obedient to the point of death, serves as a type looking forward to Christ and as an example for Christians. Paul reminded believers that "you too, brothers and sisters, like Isaac, are children of promise" (Gal. 4:28 CSB).

ISAIAH Personal name meaning "Yahweh saves." Isaiah ministered primarily to the southern kingdom of Judah, although he was interested in the affairs of the northern kingdom of Israel during its time of demise and ultimate fall in 722/21 BC. According to Isa. 1:1, the prophet ministered under the Judahite kings of Uzziah, Jotham, Ahaz, and Hezekiah. Neither the beginning nor closing dates of Isaiah's prophesying can be discerned with certainty. Isaiah 6 dates the temple vision of Isaiah to the year of Uzziah's death in 740 BC. The close of Isaiah's ministry cannot be dated with certainty. The last datable prophecy records the Sennacherib crisis of 701 BC (chaps. 36–37), although the prophet may have continued to minister beyond this point. The Assumption of Isaiah, an apocryphal book, preserves the tradition that the prophet was sawn in half at the command of Manasseh, who began to reign around 689 BC.

Isaiah was the son of Amoz (1:1). Jewish tradition mentions Amoz as the brother of King Amaziah of Judah. If this assumption is correct, Isaiah and Uzziah were cousins, thus making Isaiah a member of the nobility. This family connection would explain the impact of Uzziah's death (chap. 6) on the prophet as well as the apparent ready access Isaiah had to the kings to whom he ministered.

Isaiah was married to "the prophetess" (8:3) and had at least two sons, Shear-jashub, "A remnant will return" (7:3) and Maher-shalal-hash-baz, "Speed the spoil; hasten the prey" (8:3). The sons' names were symbolic and served as warnings to Isaiah's generation of God's coming judgment against Judah's rebellion.

ISAIAH, BOOK OF The book of Isaiah stands at the head of the classical prophetic books both in the order of the English canon and the Hebrew canon. The English division of Scripture into the Major Prophets and the Minor Prophets places Isaiah first among the Major Prophets. In the Hebrew canon, Isaiah appears first among the Latter Prophets, the section including also the books of Jeremiah, Ezekiel, and "the Twelve" (i.e., the Minor Prophets).

Division of the Book Of particular scholarly interest is the question of the division of the book and the related issues of authorship. In the late eighteenth century, different theories regarding the authorship of Isaiah emerged. The issue of authorship is directly related to the division of the book into sections. Different sections of Isaiah do contain different emphases, issues, vocabulary, style, and even historical perspectives. However, whether these differences demand different authors for the book is debated.

Isaiah 1–39 The issues and events found in Isa. 1–39 clearly relate to the times of Isaiah as an eighth-century prophet. In fact, in some of the oracles, Isaiah relates the story in first person (chaps. 6 and 8). Other oracles, although told in third person, refer to incidents in Isaiah's lifetime (chaps. 20; 36–39). The historical background of Isa. 1–39 involves Assyrian aggression and attempts on the part of Assyria to expand control into the areas of Israel and Judah. Isaiah 7 and 8 clearly have Assyrian interference in the region as their historical basis. Assyria is mentioned specifically in chapter 10, as well as chapters 20 and 36–37. Assyria is the major international power in the region in chapters 1–39.

Another indication that Isa. 1–39 comes from the time of the prophet Isaiah is the frequent occurrence of the prophet's name (occurs 16 times in 1–39). Isaiah interacts with various people on several occasions in these chapters. The clear intent of the text is to show Isaiah acting and prophesying during the first 39 chapters.

A major emphasis in this section of the book is the prediction of exile because of the nation's rebellion against God. The clearest statement of this is Isa. 39:5-7. In the early chapters of Isaiah, judgment has not yet come upon the people, but it is predicted.

Isaiah 40–66 The situation changes in Isa. 40–66. The prophet's name does not appear at all nor is any indication given that the prophet is acting or speaking. Of greater importance is the change in the major world power. Assyria is no longer the emphasis; Babylon is now the power. Babylon and Babylon's gods receive attention (chaps. 46–48). The mention of Cyrus (45:1), the Persian king who conquered Babylon, presumes a Babylonian background.

The judgment upon God's people for their sin that was prophesied in chapters 1–39 is depicted as having already happened in Isa. 40–66. Jerusalem had received God's judgment (40:2) and was in ruins (44:26,28). God had given Judah into Babylon's hand (47:5-6). Jerusalem had drunk the cup of God's wrath (51:17). The temple had been destroyed (63:18; 64:10-11). The historical perspective of chapters 40–66 seems clearly different from the perspective found in chapters 1–39. The explanation for this, some argue, is that Isaiah prophesied extensively about these future events; others, that someone(s) later appended what befell Judah as the consummation of what the prophet had earlier predicted. Clearly, the latter chapters need to be interpreted in the light of the events of the sixth-century exile to Babylon and return while the earlier chapters need to be interpreted based on events in the eighth century.

Although many scholars would divide the book of Isaiah among two or more authors, other scholars hold to single authorship of the book. The designation as "single author" may be misleading. Few would argue that Isaiah personally penned every word. Rather, this view holds that the messages themselves derive from the prophet Isaiah, leaving open the possibility that Isaiah's disciples later organized or put the prophet's oracles in writing.

The NT includes quotations and allusions from Isaiah on several occasions. In each instance, no indication is given that the book should be divided. For example, John 12:38-40 alludes to both Isa. 53:1 and Isa. 6:10, indicating both were spoken by Isaiah. Likewise, the Dead Sea Scrolls shed light on the unity of the book. Among the discoveries at Qumran was a complete copy of Isaiah. The particular placement of Isa. 40 is interesting. Chapter 39 ends on the next to the last line on the page. Chapter 40 begins on the last line. If a break ever existed between chapters 39 and 40, the copyists at Qumran did not indicate it.

Messiah is a key theme in Isaiah. The messiah of Isaiah is an enigmatic figure. Sometimes this image is a branch (11:1), other times a kingly figure (9:6-7), and other times a suffering servant (50:6; 53:3-6). Isaiah, however, never made a distinct connection between the messianic passages dealing with kingship and those having the suffering servant motif. The messiah and the suffering servant themes seem contradictory, at least initially. The messiah would rule while the servant suffered and died for the nation. From the NT perspective, one can easily see how Jesus fulfilled both images in his ministry. The church, knowing how Jesus suffered, yet believing he would also return to rule, combined the concepts into the ministry of the ultimate Messiah, the Christ.

ISCAH Personal name, perhaps meaning "they look." Daughter of Haran and sister of Milcah (Nahor's wife) and Lot (Gen. 11:29).

ISCARIOT Personal name transliterated from Hebrew into Greek and meaning "man of Kerioth," or perhaps a name derived from Latin and meaning "assassin" or "bandit." Surname of both the disciple Judas who betrayed Jesus (Mark 3:19) and of his father Simon (John 6:71).

ISH-BOSHETH Personal name meaning "man of shame." Son of Saul; his successor as king of Israel (2 Sam. 2:8). After Saul's death, Abner, the commander of Saul's army, proclaimed Ish-bosheth king. He reigned for two years. His own captains finally murdered him (2 Sam. 4:1-7).

ISHBAH Personal name meaning "he soothes." Member of tribe of Judah known as father of the town of Eshtemoa (1 Chron. 4:17).

ISHBAK Personal name meaning "come before, excel." Son of Abraham and Keturah (Gen. 25:2).

ISHBI-BENOB Personal name meaning "inhabitant of Nob." Philistine who tried to kill David in battle (2 Sam. 21:16-17).

ISHHOD Personal name meaning "man of vigor and vitality." Member of the tribe of Manasseh, east of the Jordan (1 Chron. 7:18).

ISHI Personal name meaning "my deliverer or salvation." **1.** Descendant of Jerahmeel in the tribe of Judah (1 Chron. 2:31). **2.** Member of the tribe of Judah (1 Chron. 4:20). **3.** Father of military leaders of the tribe of Simeon who successfully fought the Amalekites (1 Chron. 4:42). **4.** Clan leader in the tribe of Manasseh, east of the Jordan (1 Chron. 5:24). **5.** Transliteration of Hosea's wordplay between "my man" or "my husband" (Hb. *ishi*) and "my master" or "my lord" (Hb. *baali*) (Hos. 2:16 KJV, NASB). Hosea looked to the day when Israel would quit worshiping or even pronouncing the name of Baal and would be totally faithful to Yahweh as "her man" and "her master."

ISHMA Short form of Ishmael meaning "God hears." Member of the tribe of Judah (1 Chron. 4:3).

ISHMAEL Personal name meaning "God hears." Son of Abraham by the Egyptian concubine Hagar (Gen. 16:11). He became the progenitor of the Ishmaelite peoples. The description in Gen. 16:12 points to an unruly and contentious disposition. Genesis 21:20 explains that God was with Ishmael and that he became an archer.

ISHMAELITE Tribal name for descendants of Ishmael. According to Gen. 25:12-16, Ishmael was the father of 12 sons. The Ishmaelites were regarded as an ethnic group, generally referring to the nomadic tribes of northern Arabia.

ISHMAIAH Long and short form of personal name meaning "Yah(weh) hears." **1.** Military hero from Gibeon in charge of David's 30 select warriors (1 Chron. 12:4). **2.** Head of the tribe of Zebulun under David (1 Chron. 27:19).

ISHMERAI Short form of personal name meaning "Yah protects." Member of the tribe of Benjamin (1 Chron. 8:18).

ISHPAH Personal name, perhaps meaning "baldhead." Member of the tribe of Benjamin (1 Chron. 8:16).

ISHPAN Personal name of uncertain meaning. Member of the tribe of Benjamin (1 Chron. 8:22).

ISHTAR Mesopotamian goddess of fertility and war. The goddess is perhaps the "Queen of heaven" of Jer. 7:18; 44:17-19,25; Ezek. 8:14.

ISHTOB Personal name meaning "man of good" or "man of Tob." KJV follows early translations in interpreting this as a proper name (2 Sam. 10:6,8).

ISHVAH Personal name meaning "he is equal" or "he satisfies." Son of Asher (Gen. 46:17).

ISHVI Personal name meaning "he is equal," "he satisfies," or "he rules." Son of Asher (Gen. 46:17) and original clan ancestor of Ishvites (Num. 26:44).

ISLAND Tract of land surrounded by water. The Hebrews were not a seafaring people and so easily equated the Mediterranean islands with the ends of the earth. Scripture mentions many islands by name.

ISMACHIAH Personal name meaning "Yahweh supports." Priest and administrator in the temple under Cononiah and Shimei when Hezekiah was king of Judah (2 Chron. 31:13).

ISRAEL **1.** Name of the northern kingdom after Jeroboam led the northern tribes to separate from the southern tribes and form a separate kingdom (1 Kgs. 12). **2.** Personal name meaning "God strives," "God rules," "God heals," or "he strives against God." Name that God gave Jacob after he wrestled with the divine messenger (Gen. 32:28).

ISRAEL, LAND OF The most common name in the OT for the land where the history of Israel takes place is Canaan. It occupies about 9,500 square miles, an area about the size of Vermont or the country of Belgium. Canaan, or Palestine, reaches from the Mediterranean Sea on the west, to the Great Arabian Desert on the east, to the Lebanon and Anti-Lebanon Mountains on the north, and the Sinai Desert on the south. It is about 150 miles from north to south and 75 miles from east to west. The very location of Israel profoundly affected what was to happen to her over the centuries, for she sat uncomfortably in the middle of the Fertile Crescent (including Egypt, Palestine, Mesopotamia, Anatolia, and Armenia or, to use modern names: Egypt, Lebanon, Syria, Turkey, Jordan, Iraq, and Iran). This area was the very matrix of humankind, a veritable cradle for civilization.

Due to its strategic location, it served as a land bridge between Asia and Africa, a meeting place, and a contested battlefield for many ancient powers, including Egypt, Assyria, Babylonia, Medo-Persia, Greece, and Rome. To this day, it remains one of the most geopolitically sensitive and important areas of the world.

From west to east, the topographical features are the coastal plain, Galilee and the central hill country, flowing in a south-

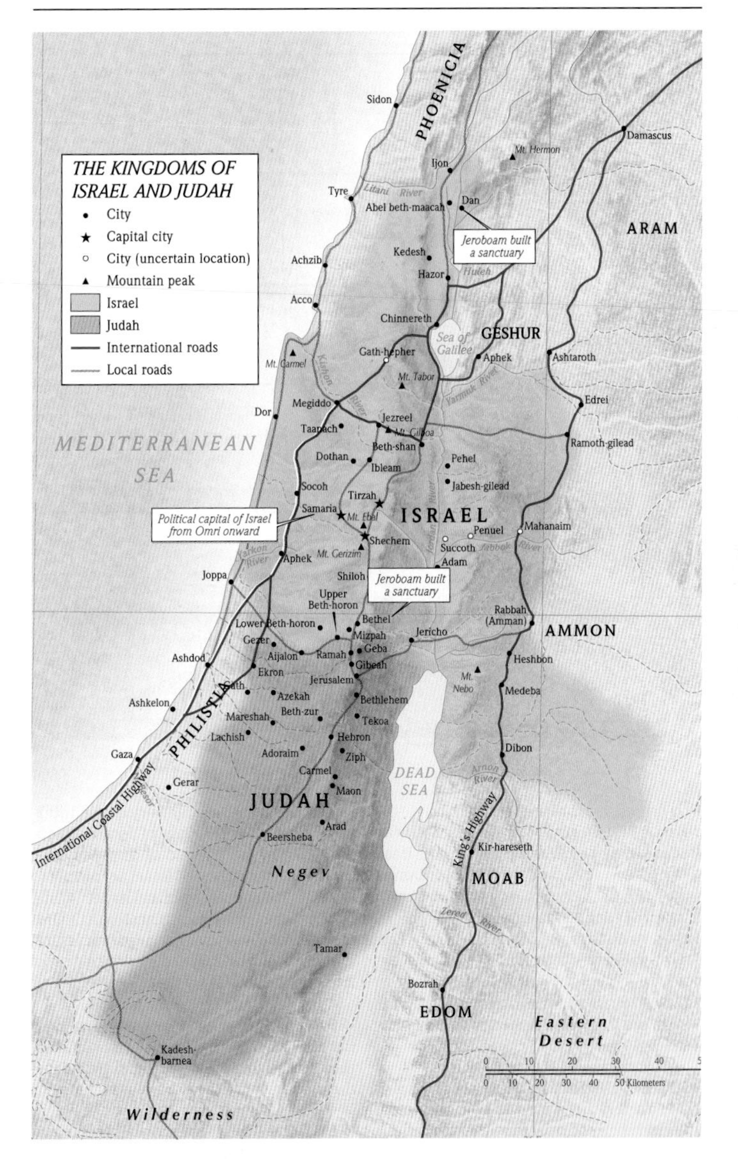
THE KINGDOMS OF ISRAEL AND JUDAH
City
Capital city
City (uncertain location)
Mountain peak
Israel
Judah
International roads
Local roads
PHOENICIA
Sidon
Tyre
Damascus
Mt. Hermon
Ijon
Dan
Abel beth-maacah
Jeroboam built a sanctuary
ARAM
Kedesh
Achzib
Hazor
Acco
Chinnereth
Sea of Galilee
GESHUR
Gath-hepher
Aphek
Ashtaroth
Mt. Carmel
Mt. Tabor
Edrei
Megiddo
Dor
Jezreel
Taanach
Mt. Gilboa
Ramoth-gilead
MEDITERRANEAN SEA
Beth-shan
Dothan
Pehel
Ibleam
Jabesh-gilead
Socoh
Tirzah
Samaria
ISRAEL
Political capital of Israel from Omri onward
Mt. Ebal
Penuel
Mahanaim
Shechem
Succoth
Aphek
Mt. Gerizim
Adam
Joppa
Shiloh
Jeroboam built a sanctuary
Upper Beth-horon
Bethel
Rabbah (Amman)
Lower Beth-horon
Jericho
AMMON
Gezer
Mizpah
Geba
Ashdod
Aijalon
Ramah
Heshbon
Gibeah
Ekron
Jerusalem
Gath
Mt. Nebo
Azekah
Medeba
Bethlehem
Ashkelon
Beth-zur
Mareshah
Tekoa
PHILISTIA
Lachish
Hebron
Gaza
Adoraim
Dibon
Ziph
Carmel
DEAD SEA
Gerar
Maon
JUDAH
Arad
International Coastal Highway
Beersheba
King's Highway
Kir-hareseth
Negev
MOAB
Zered River
Tamar
Bozrah
EDOM
Eastern Desert
Kadesh-barnea
Wilderness
50 Kilometers

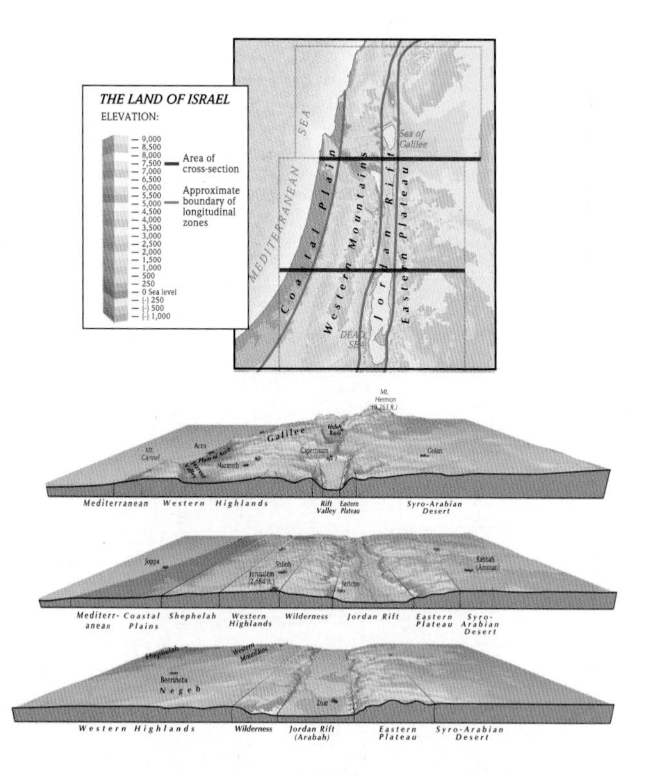

erly direction from the Lebanon range; the Jordan Rift Valley, continuous with the Bekaa Valley, continuing south to the Dead Sea in the Arabah; and the Transjordanian highlands as the southern continuation of the Anti-Lebanon Mountains in Phoenicia/Lebanon on into the Moab-Edom plateau. It is an arid and exotic land of great variety. Mountains in the north are in stark contrast to the Arabah and the lowest point on the earth, the Dead Sea, some 1,300 feet below sea level.

ISRAEL, SPIRITUAL The phrase "spiritual Israel" is often used as a description of the church in contrast to national or ethnic Israel. It refers to all believers in all times regardless of ethnic identity. Some interpreters see Paul's language of "Israel according to the flesh" (1 Cor. 10:18) as necessarily implying its antithesis, "Israel according to the Spirit," and thus, "spiritual Israel." While Paul's phrase may be suggestive, it is not conclusive. The idea of a "spiritual Israel" must rest on the basis of evidence drawn from texts viewed together.

ISSACHAR Personal name meaning "man for hire" or "hireling." Ninth son of Jacob, the fifth borne by Leah (Gen. 30:18). He became the progenitor of the tribe of Issachar.

ISSARON Transliteration of Hebrew word meaning "a tenth." A dry measure equal to one-tenth of an ephah (Exod. 29:40; Lev. 14:10,21; 23:13,17; 24:5; Num. 15:4) or about two quarts. KJV translates "a tenth deal."

ISSHIAH Personal name meaning "let Yahweh forget." In Hebrew, the name appears in a longer form in 1 Chron. 12:6. **1.** Leader in the tribe of Issachar (1 Chron. 7:3). **2.** Soldier from Saul's tribe of Benjamin who joined David at Ziklag while he hid from Saul (1 Chron. 12:6). **3.** Member of the Kohath branch of Levites (1 Chron. 23:20; 24:24-25). **4.** Descendant of Moses among the Levites (1 Chron. 24:21; cp. 23:13-17).

ISSHIJAH Personal name meaning "let Yahweh forget." Same Hebrew name as Isshiah. Israelite who had married a foreign wife, threatening Israel's total allegiance to Yahweh in the time of Ezra (Ezra 10:31).

ISSUE KJV term referring to offspring (Gen. 48:6; Isa. 22:24; Matt. 22:25; cp. 2 Kgs. 20:18; Isa. 39:7) or to a bodily discharge (Lev. 15:2-30; Matt. 9:20).

ITALIAN COHORT Name of the archery unit of the Roman army to which the Gentile centurion Cornelius belonged (Acts. 10:1). CSB: Italian Regiment.

ITALY Boot-shaped peninsula between Greece and Spain that extends from the Alps on the north to the Mediterranean Sea on the south. Italy is named in the NT in Acts 18:2; 27:1,6 and Heb. 13:24.

ITHAI Personal name, perhaps meaning "with me." A member of David's 30 elite military heroes (2 Sam. 23:29 NIV; CSB, NASB, Ittai).

ITHAMAR Personal name of uncertain meaning, perhaps "island of palms," or "where is Tamar," or shortened form of "father of Tamar (palms)." Fourth son of Aaron the priest (Exod. 6:23; 38:21).

ITHIEL Personal name meaning "with me is God." **1.** Member of the tribe of Benjamin in the time of Nehemiah after the return from exile (Neh. 11:7). **2.** Person to whom Prov. 30 is addressed, following standard Hebrew text (KJV, NASB, NIV, CSB).

ITHLAH Place-name, perhaps meaning "he hangs." Town in tribal territory of Dan (Josh. 19:42).

ITHMAH Personal name meaning "orphan." Moabite soldier in David's army (1 Chron. 11:46).

ITHNAN Place-name meaning "flowing constantly." Town on southern border of tribal territory of Judah (Josh. 15:23).

ITHRA Personal name meaning "remnant" or "abundance." He was the father of Amasa and the general that Absalom appointed to replace David's general Joab when he revolted against his father (2 Sam. 17:25).

ITHRAN Personal name meaning "remnant" or "abundance." **1.** A Horite leader who lived in Edom (Gen. 36:26). **2.** Leader in the tribe of Asher (1 Chron. 7:37). He may be the same as the similarly spelled Jether (1 Chron. 7:38).

ITHREAM Personal name meaning "remnant of the people." David's son born in Hebron to Eglah, David's wife (2 Sam. 3:5).

ITHRITE Clan name meaning "of Jether." Descendants of Jether or Jethro (Exod. 4:18) or a clan whose home was Kiriath-jearim (1 Chron. 2:53). The latter may have been Hivites (cp. Josh. 9:7,17). Two of David's 30 valiant warriors were Ithrites (2 Sam. 23:38).

ITTAI Personal name meaning "with God." **1.** Gittite (from Gath) soldier who demonstrated loyalty to David by accompanying the latter in flight from Jerusalem after the outbreak of a rebellion led by David's son Absalom (2 Sam. 15:19-22). **2.** One of the select 30 of David's army (2 Sam. 23:29) and son of Ribai of Gibeah from the tribe of Benjamin.

ITURAEA or **ITUREA** Place-name meaning "related to Jetur." Region over which Herod Philip was governor when John the Baptist began his public ministry (Luke 3:1). It was located northeast of Galilee between the Lebanon and Anti-Lebanon Mountains, though its precise boundaries are almost impossible to determine.

IVORY English translation of the Hebrew word that means "tooth." Ivory was used for decoration on thrones, beds, houses, and the decks of ships (1 Kgs. 10:18; 22:39; 2 Chron. 9:17; Ps. 45:8; Ezek. 27:6,15; Amos 3:15; 6:4). Archaeologists in Israel have unearthed numerous articles made of ivory: boxes, gaming boards, figurines, spoons, and combs.

IYE-ABARIM Place-name meaning "ruins of the crossings." Station in the wilderness wanderings (Num. 21:11) near Moab.

IYIM Modern translations spelling of Iim (Num. 33:45), a shortened form of Iye-abarim.

IZHAR Personal name meaning "olive oil" or "he sparkles." **1.** Son of Kohath and grandson of Levi, thus original ancestor of a priestly clan (Exod. 6:18). He was father of Korah (Num. 16:1; cp. 1 Chron. 23:18). **2.** Written Hebrew text of 1 Chron. 4:7 names Izhar as a member of the tribe of Judah.

IZHARITE Clan of Levites descended from Izhar.

IZLIAH Personal name meaning "long-lived" or "Yahweh delivers." Leader in the tribe of Benjamin living in Jerusalem after the return from exile (1 Chron. 8:18).

IZRAHIAH Personal name meaning "Yahweh shines forth." Member of the tribe of Issachar (1 Chron. 7:3).

IZRAHITE Clan designation in 1 Chron. 27:8 for which the text tradition gives several variants: Harorite (1 Chron. 11:27 KJV); Harodite (2 Sam. 23:25 KJV).

IZRI Clan leader of fourth course of temple musicians (1 Chron. 25:11). He is probably the same as Zeri (25:3), the name change occurring in copying the text.

IZZIAH Personal name meaning "Yah sprinkled." Priest who repented of marrying a foreign woman and thus tempting Israel with foreign gods in the time of Ezra (Ezra 10:25).

The Jabbok River between Jerash and Amman. Near this river Jacob wrestled with the angel.

JAAKAN Personal name meaning "to be fast." Descendant of Esau and thus tribal ancestor of Edomites (1 Chron. 1:42).

JABAL Personal name meaning "stream." Son of Lamech by Adah (Gen. 4:20). A descendant of Cain, he was the first nomad, the progenitor of tent dwellers and herdsmen.

JABBOK Place-name meaning "flowing." River near which Jacob wrestled through the night with God (Gen. 32:22). A tributary of the Jordan River, some sections of the Jabbok served as the western boundary of Ammon.

JABESH or **JABESH-GILEAD** Place-name meaning "dry, rugged" or "dry place of Gilead." City whose residents, with the exception of 400 virgins, were put to death by an army of Israelites (Judg. 21:8-12). The 400 women who were spared became wives for the Benjaminites. King Saul's rescue of the people of Jabesh-gilead from Nahash the Ammonite marked the effective beginning of the Israelite monarchy (1 Sam. 11:1-11).

JABEZ Personal and place-name with a connotation of pain, hurt, and sorrow. **1.** Home of scribes whose location is not known (1 Chron. 2:55). **2.** Israelite who asked God for blessing and received it (1 Chron. 4:9-10). He illustrates the power of prayer.

JABIN Personal name meaning "he understands." **1.** Leader of northern coalition of kings who attacked Joshua at the water of Merom and met their death (Josh. 11:1-11). **2.** Many scholars believe that a dynasty of kings in Hazor carried the name Jabin.

JACHIN AND BOAZ Proper names meaning "he establishes" and "agile." In 1 Kgs. 7:21, the names of two bronze pillars that stood on either side of the entrance to Solomon's temple. They may have been 27 feet high and 6 feet in diameter with a 10-foot capital on top. See *Temple*.

JACINTH Semiprecious stone. Some English translations give "jacinth" as a gem in the high priest's breastplate (Exod. 28:19 CSB, NASB, NIV, NRSV), the color of one of the riders' breastplates (Rev. 9:17 KJV), and the eleventh foundation stone of the new Jerusalem (Rev. 21:20 CSB, KJV, NASB, NIV, NRSV).

JACKAL A carnivorous mammal resembling the wolf but smaller. The same Hebrew word is translated both "jackal" and "fox" (Judg. 15:4, REB has "jackals"; CSB, NIV has "foxes"). Most biblical references associate jackals with desert ruins. For a city or nation to be made the haunt or lair of jackals is for it to be utterly destroyed (Isa. 13:22; Jer. 9:11).

JACOB Personal name built on the Hebrew noun for "heel" meaning "he grasps the heel" or "he cheats, supplants" (Gen. 25:26; 27:36). Original ancestor of the nation of Israel and father of the 12 ancestors of the 12 tribes of Israel (Gen. 25:1–Exod. 1:5). He was the son of Isaac and Rebekah, younger twin brother of Esau, and husband of Leah and Rachel (Gen. 25:21-26; 29:21-30). God changed his name to "Israel" (Gen. 32:28; 49:2).

Living up to his name, Jacob cheated his older brother, Esau, out of his birthright, or the inheritance rights of the older son. Rebekah had to arrange for Jacob to flee to her ancestral home in Paddan-aram to escape Esau's wrath (27:41–28:5). A lonely night in Bethel, interrupted by a vision from God, brought reality home to Jacob. Life had to include wrestling with God and assuming responsibility as the heir of God's promises to Abraham (28:10-22). Jacob made an oath, binding himself to God.

In Aram with his mother's family, the deceiver Jacob met deception. Laban tricked him into marrying Leah, the elder daughter, before he got his beloved Rachel, the younger. He labored 14 years for his wives (29:1-30). Six more years of labor let Jacob return the deception and gain wealth at the expense of his father-in-law, who continued his deception, changing Jacob's wages 10 times (31:7,41). Amid the family infighting, both men prospered financially, and Jacob's family grew. Eventually he had 12 sons from four different wives (29:31–30:24). Prosperous and confident, he made plans to return to his home in Canaan with his wives, children, and livestock.

As Jacob approached his homeland, a band of angels met him at Mahanaim (32:1-2). They probably symbolized God's protection and encouragement as he headed southward to meet his brother, Esau, for the first time in 20 years. Esau's seemingly hostile advance prompted a call for clear evidence of God's protection. Shrewdly, Jacob sent an enormous gift to his brother. After crossing the Jabbok River, Jacob met One who wrestled with him until daybreak (chap. 32). The two struggled without one gaining advantage, until the Opponent dislocated Jacob's hip. Jacob refused to release his Antagonist. Clinging to him, Jacob demanded a blessing. The Opponent emphasized his superiority by renaming Jacob, who became Israel, the one on whose behalf God strives. Jacob named the place Peniel (face of God), because he had seen God face to face and his life had been spared (32:30).

Jacob's fear of meeting Esau proved groundless. Esau was willing to forget the wrongs of the past. So Jacob set out for Shechem. From Shechem, he returned to Bethel. Once again he received the promises that God had originally given to Abraham. Losses and grief characterized this period of his life. The death of his mother's nurse (35:8; 24:59) was followed by the death of his beloved wife Rachel while giving birth to Benjamin at Ephrath (35:19; 48:7). About the same time, Reuben forfeited the honor of being the eldest son by sexual misconduct (35:22). Finally, the death of Jacob's father, who had been robbed of companionship with both sons, brought Jacob and Esau together again at the family burial site in Hebron.

When severe famine gripped Canaan, Jacob and his sons set out for Egypt. At Beersheba, Jacob received further assurance of God's favor (46:1-4). Jacob lived in Egypt, in the "land of Goshen" until his death. Jacob bestowed the blessing not only upon his favorite son Joseph, but also upon Joseph's two sons, Ephraim and Manasseh. He was finally laid to rest at Hebron in the cave Abraham had purchased as a burial site (50:12-14).

God did not choose Jacob because of what he was but because of what he could become. His life is a long history of discipline, chastisement, and purification by affliction. Not one of his misdeeds went unpunished. He sowed deception and reaped the same, first from Laban and then from his own sons. But God was at work in his life, building a nation through him and his descendants.

JACOB'S WELL Place in Samaria where Jesus stopped to rest as he traveled from Judea to Galilee (John 4:6). There he met and conversed with a Samaritan woman on the subject of living water.

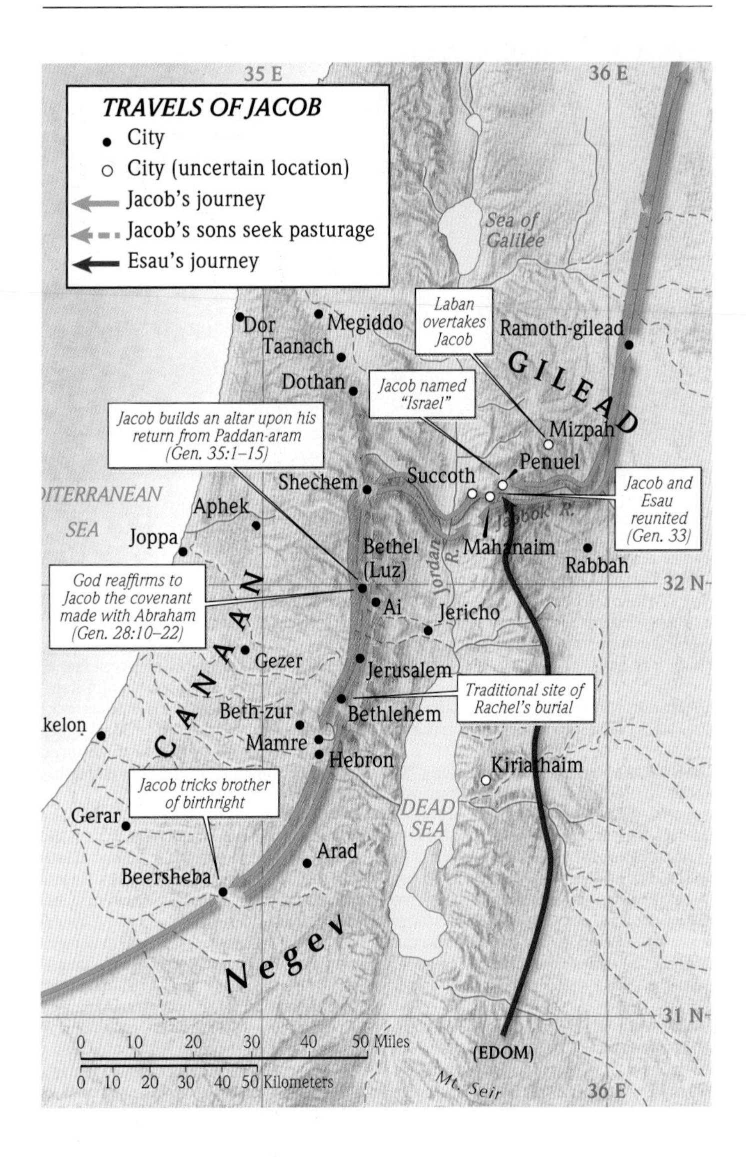
TRAVELS OF JACOB
City
City (uncertain location)
Jacob's journey
Jacob's sons seek pasturage
Esau's journey
35 E
36 E
Sea of Galilee
Laban overtakes Jacob
Dor
Megiddo
Taanach
Dothan
Ramoth-gilead
GILEAD
Jacob named "Israel"
Mizpah
Jacob builds an altar upon his return from Paddan-aram (Gen. 35:1–15)
Penuel
Shechem
Succoth
Jacob and Esau reunited (Gen. 33)
ITERRANEAN SEA
Aphek
Joppa
Jabbok R.
Bethel (Luz)
Jordan R.
Mahanaim
Rabbah
32 N
God reaffirms to Jacob the covenant made with Abraham (Gen. 28:10–22)
Ai
Jericho
CANAAN
Gezer
Jerusalem
Traditional site of Rachel's burial
Beth-zur
Bethlehem
kelon
Mamre
Hebron
Kiriathaim
Jacob tricks brother of birthright
DEAD SEA
Gerar
Arad
Beersheba
Negev
31 N
0 10 20 30 40 50 Miles
0 10 20 30 40 50 Kilometers
(EDOM)
Mt. Seir

The traditional site of Jacob's Well in the city of Sychar

JAEL Personal name meaning "mountain goat." Wife of Heber the Kenite (Judg. 4:17), she assassinated the Canaanite leader Sisera. Her action is celebrated in the Song of Deborah (Judg. 5:24-27).

JAH Short form of divine name Yahweh in Ps. 68:4 (KJV) and in many proper names.

JAHAZIEL Personal name meaning "Yah looks." **1.** Benjaminite military hero who supported David against Saul (1 Chron. 12:4). **2.** Priest whom David appointed to blow the trumpet before the ark (1 Chron. 16:6). **3.** Levite of the clan of Hebron (1 Chron. 23:19; 24:23). **4.** Levite and a son of Asaph who received the Spirit of the Lord and prophesied (2 Chron. 20:14-19). **5.** Clan leader who led 300 men among the exiles returning to Jerusalem with Ezra (Ezra 8:5).

JAIR Abbreviated place-name meaning "Jah shines forth." **1.** Son of Manasseh who took possession of a number of villages in Gilead (Num. 32:41). **2.** A Gileadite who judged Israel for 22 years (Judg. 10:3-5). **3.** Father of El-hanan (1 Chron. 20:5) whose name comes from a different Hebrew word possibly meaning "Jah protects." **4.** Benjaminite who was the ancestor of Mordecai, Esther's guardian (Esth. 2:5).

JAIRUS Greek form of Hebrew personal name "Jair" meaning "Jah will enlighten." Synagogue official who came to Jesus seeking healing for his daughter (Mark 5:22). Taking the girl by the hand, Jesus restored her to life, showing his power over death.

JAMES English form of Jacob, and the name of three men of the NT. **1.** James, the son of Zebedee and brother of John (Matt. 4:21; 10:2; Mark 1:19; 3:17; Luke 5:10). As one of the 12 disciples of Jesus (Acts 1:13), he, with Peter and John, formed Jesus's innermost circle of associates. These three were present when Jesus raised Jairus's daughter (Mark 5:37; Luke 8:51), witnessed the transfiguration (Matt. 17:1; Mark 9:2), and were summoned by Christ for support during his agony in Gethsemane (Matt. 26:36-37; Mark 14:32-34). Perhaps because of James's and John's fiery fanaticism, evidenced as they sought to call down fire from heaven on the Samaritan village refusing to receive Jesus and the disciples (Luke 9:52-54), Jesus called the brothers "Boanerges" or "sons of thunder" (Mark 3:17). James's zeal was revealed in a more selfish manner as he and John (their mother, on their behalf, in Matt. 20:20-21) sought special positions of honor for the time of Christ's glory (Mark 10:35-40). James was the first of the 12 to be martyred (Acts 12:2). His execution (ca. AD 44), by order of King Herod Agrippa I of Judea, was part of a larger persecution in which Peter was arrested (Acts 12:1-3). **2.** James, the son of Alphaeus, one of the 12 disciples of Jesus (Matt. 10:3; Acts 1:13). He is not distinguished by name in any occasion reported in the Gospels or Acts. He may be "James the younger," whose mother, Mary, was among the women at Jesus's crucifixion and tomb (Matt. 27:56; Mark 15:40; 16:1; Luke 24:10). **3.** James, the half brother of Jesus. During the Lord's ministry, the brothers of Jesus (Matt. 13:55) were not believers (John 7:3-5; cp. Luke 8:19-21). Paul specifically mentioned a resurrection appearance by Jesus to James (1 Cor. 15:7). After the resurrection and ascension, the brothers are said to have been with the Twelve and the other believers in Jerusalem (Acts 1:14). In time, James assumed the leadership of the Jerusalem church. In a Jerusalem conference called regarding Paul's Gentile mission, James presided as spokesman for the Jerusalem church (Acts 15). See *James, Letter from.*

JAMES, LETTER FROM Letter from James belongs to the section of the NT usually described as the General Epistles. Tradition of the early church universally ascribes the text to James, the pastor of the church in Jerusalem; James, the half brother of Jesus. The letter is one of exhortation for practical Christianity. The author stated principles of conduct and then frequently provided poignant illustrations. The author's concerns were clearly more practical and less abstract than those of any other NT writer.

JANNES AND JAMBRES Two men who opposed Moses and Aaron (2 Tim. 3:8). Though the names do not appear in the OT, rabbinic tradition identified Jannes and Jambres as being among those Egyptian magicians who sought to duplicate for Pharaoh the miracles performed by Moses (Exod. 7:11).

JAPHETH Personal name meaning "may he have space." One of Noah's three sons (Gen. 5:32). Genesis 10:2 identifies Japheth's sons as Gomer, Magog, Madai, Javan, Tubal, Meshech, and Tiras. These names point to Japheth as having been the progenitor of the Indo-European peoples who lived north and west of Israel. See *Noah; Table of Nations.*

JAPHIA Place-name and personal name meaning "place situated high above" or "may [God] bring shining light." **1.** Border town of tribal territory of Zebulun (Josh. 19:12). **2.** King of Lachish who joined southern coalition against Joshua and were killed by the cave of Makkedah (Josh. 10:1-27,31-32). **3.** Son born to David in Jerusalem by unnamed wife (2 Sam. 5:15).

JASHAR, BOOK OF An ancient written collection of poetry quoted by Bible authors (Josh. 10:12–13).

JASHOBEAM Personal name meaning "the uncle (or people) will return." Warrior of Saul's tribe of Benjamin who supported David at Ziklag as he fled from King Saul (1 Chron. 12:6).

JASON Personal name often used by Jews as a substitute for Hebrew Joshua or Joseph and also used by Gentiles. **1.** Paul's host in Thessalonica (Acts 17:5). He was brought up on charges before the city officials when the angry Jewish mob was unable to find Paul (Acts 17:6-7). The Jason mentioned in Rom. 16:21 may have been the same person. **2.** Jewish high priest during the final years of Seleucid control of Palestine.

JASPER Green chalcedony. Jasper commonly translates two Hebrew terms and one Greek term. The first term is used for the sixth stone in the headdress of the king of Tyre (Ezek. 28:13). The second term is used for a stone in the high priest's breastplate (Exod. 28:20; 39:13). The third term describes the face of the One seated on the throne (Rev. 4:3) and the glory of the new Jerusalem (Rev. 21:11,18-19).

JAVAN Personal name meaning "Greece." Son of Japheth (Gen. 10:2) and father of Elishah, Tarshish, Kittim, and Dodanim (Gen. 10:4), thus the original ancestor of Greek peoples. Elsewhere in the OT, the name Javan is used to denote Greece.

JAVELIN Light spear thrown as a weapon (1 Sam. 18:10–11).

JAZER Place-name meaning "may he help." Amorite city-state that Israel conquered while marching across the land east of the Jordan River toward the promised land (Num. 21:32). The tribe of Gad rebuilt and settled Jazer (Num. 32:35; cp. Josh. 13:25). Joshua assigned it to the Levites (Josh. 21:39).

JEALOUSY Used in three senses in Scripture: (1) as intolerance of rivalry or unfaithfulness; (2) as a disposition suspicious of rivalry or unfaithfulness; and (3) as hostility toward a rival or one believed to enjoy an advantage, a sense of envy. God is jealous for his people Israel in the first sense. That is, he is intolerant of rival gods (Exod. 20:5; Deut. 4:24; 5:9). One expression of God's jealousy for Israel is God's protection of his people from enemies.

JEALOUSY, ORDEAL OF Test to determine guilt or innocence of a wife suspected of adultery but who had not been caught in the act (Num. 5:11-31). The ordeal consisted of two parts: "a grain offering of memorial, a reminder of iniquity" (5:15 NASB) and "the water of bitterness that brings a curse" (5:18). See *Bitter Water*.

JEBUS Place-name meaning "trodden under foot." Name of tribe originally occupying Jerusalem and then of the city of Jebus (Judg. 19:10; cp. Josh. 18:28; 1 Chron. 11:4). See *Jebusi* or *Jebusites; Jerusalem*.

JEBUSI (Josh. 18:16,28 KJV) or **JEBUSITES** Clan who originally controlled Jerusalem before David conquered the city. In the time of the judges, Jerusalem was attacked and burned by the men of Judah (Judg. 1:8), but the Jebusites were not expelled. In later years, David captured the city and made it his capital. David purchased a stone threshing floor from a Jebusite named Araunah (2 Sam. 24:16-24), and this later became the site of Solomon's temple. The remnants of the Jebusites became bondservants during Solomon's reign (1 Kgs. 9:20-21).

JEDUTHUN Personal name meaning "praise." Prophetic musician and Levite in the service of King David (1 Chron. 25:1). Three psalms (39; 62; 77) include his name in their titles. The exact nature of Jeduthun's relationship to these psalms is uncertain.

JEHOAHAZ Personal name meaning "Yahweh grasps hold." Two kings of Judah and one king of Israel bore this name. **1.** In 2 Chron. 21:17, the son and successor of Jehoram as king of Judah (841 BC). He is more frequently referred to as Ahaziah. **2.** In 2 Kgs. 10:35, the son and successor of Jehu as king of Israel (814–798 BC). His reign is summarized in 2 Kgs. 13. **3.** In 2 Kgs. 23:30, the son and successor of Josiah as king of Judah (609 BC). He is also known as Shallum.

JEHOASH Personal name meaning "Yahweh gave." Variant spelling of Joash. See *Joash*.

JEHOIACHIN Personal name meaning "Yahweh establishes." Son and successor of Jehoiakim as king of Judah (2 Kgs. 24:6). He was 18 years old when he came to the throne late in 598 BC, and he reigned for three months in Jerusalem before being taken into captivity by Nebuchadnezzar of Babylon. Jehoiachin's original name seems to have been Jeconiah or Coniah. He retained the title "king of Judah" even in exile, but he never returned to Judah to exercise rule. Nevertheless, he was ultimately released from prison by Evil-merodach of Babylon and accorded some honor in the land of his captivity (2 Kgs. 25:27-30).

JEHOIADA Personal name meaning "Yahweh knows" or "Yahweh concerns himself for." **1.** Priest who led the coup in which Queen Athaliah, who had usurped the throne of Judah, was slain and Joash (Jehoash), the legitimate heir to the monarchy, was enthroned (2 Kgs. 11:4). Since Joash was only seven years old, Jehoiada evidently acted as regent for a number of years. He influenced the young king to restore the temple. **2.** Father of Benaiah, David's military leader (2 Sam. 8:18). **3.** Leading priest in the time of Jeremiah (Jer. 29:25-26).

JEHOIAKIM Personal name meaning "Yahweh has caused to stand." Son of Josiah who succeeded Jehoahaz as king of Judah (609–597 BC). Jehoiakim was a throne name given to him by Pharaoh Neco of Egypt, who deposed his brother Jehoahaz. His original name had been Eliakim (2 Kgs. 23:34). After reigning for 11 years, Jehoiakim was succeeded by his son Jehoiachin.

JEHONADAB Personal name meaning "Yahweh incites" or "Yahweh offers himself freely." Son of Rechab who supported Jehu in the latter's bloody purge of the house of Ahab (2 Kgs. 10:15). He was representative of a group of austere ultraconservatives known as the Rechabites. See *Rechabites*.

JEHORAM Personal name meaning "Yahweh is exalted." Alternate form of Joram. See *Joram*.

JEHOSHABEATH Variant form of Jehosheba. See *Jehosheba*.

JEHOSHAPHAT Personal name meaning "Yahweh judged." **1.** Son and successor of Asa as king of Judah (1 Kgs. 15:24). He occupied the throne for 25 years (873–848 BC). He was an able ruler and a faithful worshiper of Yahweh (1 Kings 22:42-43). Nevertheless, he made an alliance with Ahab, king of Israel, which proved to be disastrous. This alliance involved a marriage between Jehoshaphat's son Jehoram and Ahab's daughter Athaliah. Athaliah's influence in Judah finally proved to be horrific. **2.** Father of Jehu (2 Kgs. 9:2,14). **3.** Official at David's court (2 Sam. 8:16), called the "recorder" or "secretary of state" (REB). **4.** Solomon's official in tribal territory of Issachar in charge of providing provisions for the royal court one month a year (1 Kgs. 4:17).

JEHOSHAPHAT, VALLEY OF Place-name meaning "valley where Yahweh judged." Place to which the Lord summons the nations for judgment (Joel 3:2).

JEHOSHEBA Personal name meaning "Yahweh is fullness or fortune." Sister of King Ahaziah who, after his death, took young Joash and protected him from Queen Athaliah (2 Kgs. 11:2).

Valley of Jehoshaphat (Kidron Valley) in Jerusalem showing the Church of All Nations

JEHOSHUA (Num. 13:16 KJV) See *Joshua.*

JEHOVAH English transliteration of Hebrew text's current reading of the divine name Yahweh.

JEHOVAH-JIREH Place-name meaning "Yahweh will provide." The name Abraham gave to the place where the Lord provided a sacrifice in place of Isaac (Gen. 22:14).

JEHOVAH-NISSI Transliteration of place-name meaning "Yahweh is my banner." Name Moses gave to the altar he built after defeating the Amalekites (Exod. 17:15).

JEHOVAH-SHALOM Place-name meaning "Yahweh is peace." Name Gideon gave to the altar he built at Ophrah (Judg. 6:24).

JEHOVAH-SHAMMA Transliteration of a Hebrew name (Ezek. 48:35, margin) meaning "The LORD is there." The Jerusalem of Ezekiel's vision was known by this name (cp. Isa. 60:19-20; Rev. 21:3).

JEHOVAH-TSIDKENU Hebrew name meaning "The LORD [is] our righteousness" (Jer. 23:6; 33:16, margin). The name is applied to a future Davidic king who would lead his people in righteousness and thus bring peace (23:6).

JEHU Personal name meaning "Yah is he." **1.** Son of Jehoshaphat and king of Israel (841–814 BC). He was a commander of the army when Elisha the prophet sent one of the sons of the prophets to Ramoth-gilead to anoint him as king (2 Kgs. 9:1-10). Jehu embarked on a violent and bloody course that finally led him to the throne. He was responsible for the deaths of Joram, king of Israel; Ahaziah, king of Judah; Jezebel, still powerful former queen of Israel, and some 70 surviving members of the household of Israel's late King Ahab. Jehu established a

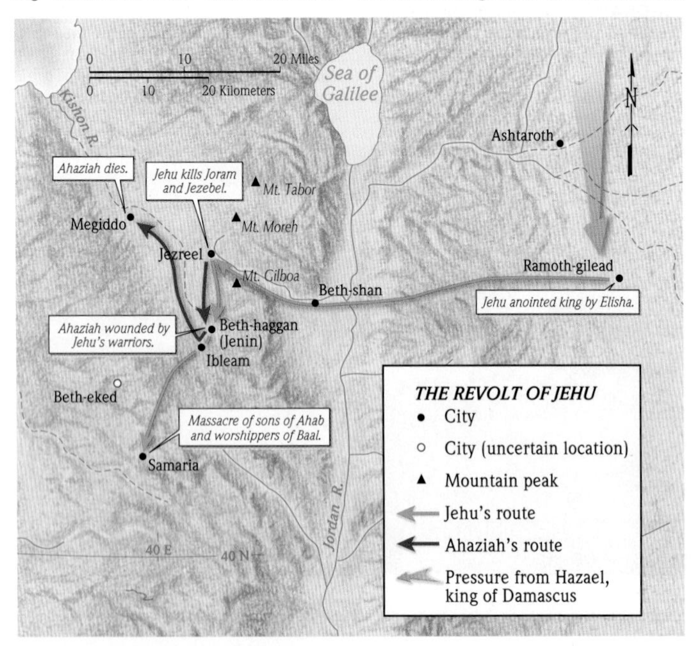

strong dynasty in Israel. He and his descendants held the throne for approximately a century. **2.** Prophet who proclaimed God's judgment on King Baasha of Israel (1 Kgs. 16:1-12). **3.** Member of David's army at Ziklag (1 Chron. 12:3). **4.** Leader of the tribe of Simeon (1 Chron. 4:35).

JEPHTHAH Personal name meaning "he will open." One of Israel's judges about 1100 BC (Judg. 11:1–12:7). A Gileadite, he was driven from his home because he was "the son of a harlot" (Judg. 11:1). He lived and raided in the land of Tob with a band of outlaws, becoming known as a "mighty warrior." When the Ammonites moved against Israel, Jephthah's people asked him to return and lead them. His victory over the Ammonites came about after a vow he made to offer as a burnt offering the first living thing he saw upon his return from the battle. Even though it was his daughter who greeted him, Jephthah did fulfill his vow. Jephthah is hailed by the author of Hebrews as a hero of faith (Heb. 11:32).

JERASH Modern Arabic name of Gerasa. See *Gerasa*.

Sunset at Jerash (ancient Gerasa)

JERBOA Any of several species of leaping rodents having long hind legs and long tails. The REB includes the jerboa among the unclean animals of Lev. 11:29.

JEREMIAH, THE PROPHET Jeremiah was called to be a prophet in the thirteenth year of King Josiah (627/6 BC) (Jer. 1:2). He was active under the Kings Jehoahaz/Shallum (609 BC) (22:11), Jehoiakim (609–597 BC) (Jer. 1:3; 22:18; 26:1; 35:1; 36:1,9), Jehoiachin/Jeconiah/Coniah (597 BC) (22:24; 24:1; 27:20; 28:4; 29:2; 37:1), and Zedekiah (597–586 BC) (1:3; 21:1; 27:1-12; 28:1; 32:1; 34:2; 37–38; 39:4; 52:8). When Jerusalem was destroyed by the Babylonians in 587 BC, Jeremiah moved to Mizpah, the capital of Gedaliah, the newly appointed Jewish governor of the Babylonian province of Judah (40:5). When Gedaliah was assassinated (41:1-2), Jeremiah was deported to Egypt against his will by Jewish officers who had survived the catastrophes (42:1–43:7). In Egypt, he continued to preach against the Egyptians (43:8-13) and his compatriots (44:1-30).

Jeremiah recommended national surrender to the rule of the Babylonian Empire and called Nebuchadnezzar, Babylon's emperor and Judah's most hated enemy, the Lord's "servant" (25:9; 27:6). He even incited his compatriots to desert to the enemy (21:8-9). He was accused of treason and convicted (37:12-13; 38:1-6), and yet the most aggressive oracles against Babylon are attributed to him (chaps. 50–51). Enemies challenged his prophetic honesty and the inspiration of his message (43:1-3; 29:24), and yet kings and nobles sought his advice (21:1-2; 37:3; 38:14; 42:1-2).

He constantly proclaimed God's judgment upon Judah and Jerusalem, and yet he was also a prophet of hope, proclaiming oracles of salvation, conditioned (3:22–4:2) or unconditioned (30–31; 32:36-38; 33:6; 34:4). God forbade him to intercede for his people (7:16; 11:14; 14:11; cp. 15:1); yet he interceded (14:7-9,19-22). God ordered him to live without marriage and family (16:2). He had to stay away from the company of merrymakers (15:17) and from houses of feasting (16:8). He complained to and argued with God (12:1-17), complaining about the misery of his prophetic office (20:7-18). At the same time, he

Round Neolithic (New Stone Age) defense tower at Old Testament Jericho

sang hymns of praise to God (20:13). See *Jeremiah, Book of*; *Lamentations*.

JEREMIAH, BOOK OF A prophetic book of the OT, written by the prophet Jeremiah, which stimulates the search for the will of God in moments when all the institutions and religious representatives normally in charge of administrating God's will are discredited. The nation of Judah would fall to the Babylonians, the prophet emphasized, unless they turned back from their idolatry to worship the one true God.

Jeremiah declared that God's justice and righteousness cannot be usurped by his people. He can be a stumbling block even for his prophet (Jer. 12:1-6; 20:7-12). Execution of judgment and destruction is not God's delight. God himself suffers pain because of the alienation between himself and his people (2:1-37). Better than the prophet was able to admit, the apostate members of God's people remembered a correct notion of the nature of God. He continued to be their Father, and his anger would not last forever (3:4,12-13). Judah and Jerusalem would be carried away as captives to a foreign land. But this was not God's last word. His faithfulness prevails and creates new hope where all hope is lost (chaps. 30–33).

JERICHO Place-name meaning "moon." Apparently the oldest city in the world and the first city Israel conquered under Joshua. Jericho is situated in the lower Jordan Valley, which, according to Gen. 13:10, "was well-watered everywhere like the LORD's garden" (CSB). The OT town lies beneath Tell es-Sultan near one of Palestine's strongest springs. The combination of rich alluvial soil, the perennial spring, and constant sunshine made Jericho an attractive place for settlement. Jericho could be called "city of palms" (Deut. 34:3; Judg. 1:16; 3:13; 2 Chron. 28:15) and has plenty of palm trees today. Only about 6.4 inches of rain fall there per year. Jericho was an oasis situated in a hot plain.

New Testament Jericho, founded by Herod the Great, was about 1.5 miles south of the location of OT Jericho. In NT times, Jericho was famous for its balm (an aromatic gum

Reconstruction of Herod the Great's winter palace at Jericho. The palace had a commanding view of New Testament Jericho and the arid, fertile Jordan River.

known for its medicinal qualities). This, along with its being the winter capital, made it a wealthy city.

JEROBOAM Personal name possibly meaning "he who contends for justice for the people" or "may the people multiply." **1.** First king of the northern kingdom Israel about 926–909 BC. Jeroboam managed the laborers Solomon had conscripted for his huge building projects (1 Kgs. 11:28). During Solomon's reign Ahijah, a prophet from Shiloh, predicted that Jeroboam would become king over 10 of the 12 tribes. Seizing upon the people's resentment toward Solomon's high-handed policies at his death, Jeroboam led the 10 northern tribes to revolt against the house of David. They then crowned Jeroboam king. Jeroboam became the example of evil kings in Israel because he built temples in Dan and Bethel with golden calves representing God's presence. **2.** Powerful king of Israel in the dynasty of Jehu about 793–753 BC (2 Kgs. 14:23-29). He managed to restore prosperity and territory to a weak nation but continued the religious practices of Jeroboam I and thus met condemnation from the biblical writers.

JERUBBAAL Personal name meaning "Baal judges." Another name for Gideon (Judg. 6:32). See *Gideon.*

JERUSALEM Jerusalem is a city set high on a plateau in the hills of Judah, considered sacred by Judaism, Christianity, and Islam. Its biblical-theological significance lies in its status as Yahweh's chosen center of his divine kingship and of the human kingship of David and his sons, Yahweh's vice-regents. Besides the name "Jerusalem," the city is also called "the City of David" and "Zion" (originally referring to a part of the city, the "stronghold of Zion" that David captured from the Jebusites; see 2 Sam. 5:6-10).

The city (known earlier as Jebus for its inhabitants, the Jebusites; see Judg. 19:10-11) was captured in Joshua's time (Judg. 1:8), but the Jebusites were not driven out (Josh. 15:63; Judg. 1:21). After David captured it and made it Israel's capital (1 Chron. 11:4-9), David brought the ark of the covenant into Jerusalem (2 Sam. 6:17) and made it the seat of his kingdom. Jerusalem came to be "the city of our God," "the city of the great King," "the city of Yahweh of hosts" (Ps. 48). Under Solomon, the temple was constructed in Jerusalem (2 Chron. 3-7) and the nation reached its political and economic zenith with Jerusalem at the center (2 Chron. 9).

Since the people abandoned God, he eventually abandoned his chosen city to the Babylonians in 586 BC (2 Kgs. 23:26-27). Yet judgment was not his final word. The Persian king Cyrus (decree in 538 BC) was the Lord's servant in facilitating the return of many exiles and the rebuilding of the city and the temple (Isa. 44:26-28; 45:13; Ezra 6; Neh. 1–6). Moreover, the future salvation of Jerusalem would exceed the temporal restoration of the postexilic community. All peoples would come to it (Isa. 2:2-4; Jer. 3:17). God's new work for Jerusalem would usher in nothing less than a new age (Isa. 65:18-25; Zech. 14:8-21).

The NT portrays the various Jerusalem-related prophecies as fulfilled in and through Jesus, Israel's Messiah. In the Gospels, Jerusalem takes on ironic, contrasting roles. On one hand, it is "the city of the great King" (Matt. 5:35) and "the holy city" (Matt. 4:5; 27:53). On the other hand, it is the city "who kills the prophets and stones those who are sent to her" (Luke 13:34 CSB). While there were those who longed for "the redemption of Jerusalem" (Luke 2:38), the city and its inhabitants will face judgment because they did not recognize the time of divine visitation by Jesus (Luke 19:41-44). Indeed Jesus's mis-

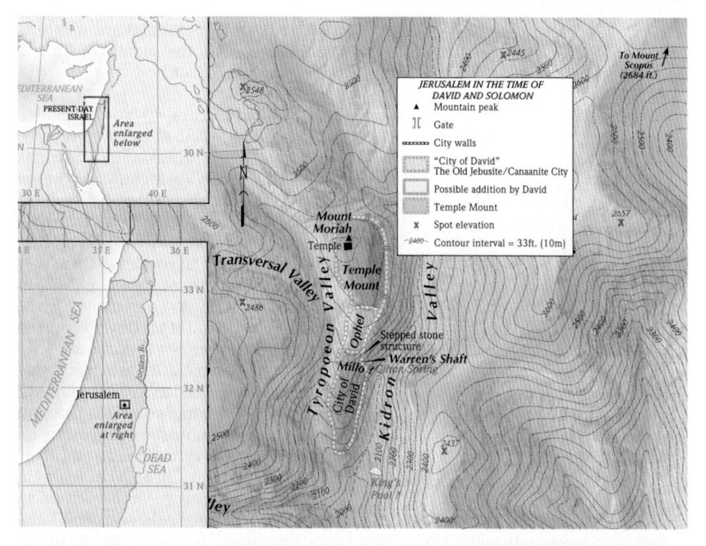

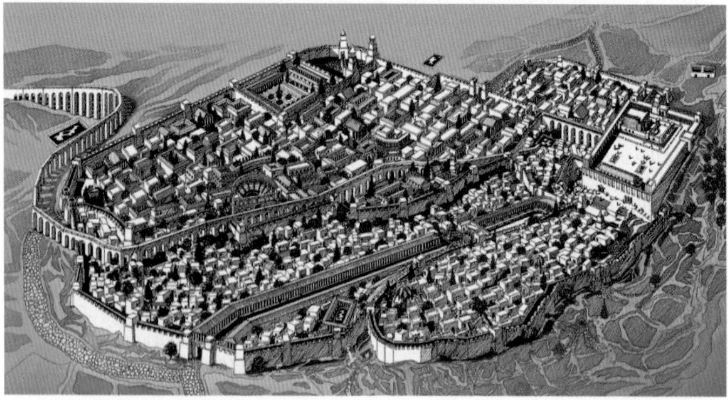

Jerusalem in the time of Jesus

sion ended in his rejection by Jerusalem's rulers and his death outside the city walls (Mark 8:31; 10:32-34).

The promises of the Lord's reign ("the kingdom of God") and of the salvation of his people, both Jews and Gentiles, find their fulfillment in Jesus's death and resurrection and in the dawning of the new heaven and new earth. Biblical hope is now focused on "the city of the living God (the heavenly Jerusalem)" (Heb. 12:22 CSB).

JESHURUN Proper name meaning "upright" or "straight." Poetic name for Israel (Deut. 32:15; 33:5,26; Isa. 44:2).

JESSE Personal name meaning "man" or "manly." Father of David the king (1 Sam. 16:1). He was a Judahite who lived in Bethlehem, the son of Obed and the grandson of Boaz and Ruth (1 Sam. 16:1; Ruth 4:17). He is mentioned in the genealogies of Jesus in the Gospels of Matthew and Luke.

JESUS CHRIST Jesus's proper name derives from the Hebrew "Joshua," meaning "Yahweh saves" or "salvation is from Yahweh" (Matt. 1:21). *Christ* is the Greek term for "anointed," equivalent to the Hebrew *Messiah*. This anointed Savior is also Immanuel, "God is with us" (Matt. 1:23; Isa. 7:14). Paul's favorite term for Jesus was *kurios*, "Lord," and the earliest Christian confession was that "Jesus is Lord." The sublime introduction of Jesus in the prologue to John's Gospel presents him as the *logos*, the "Word" who created all things (1:3) and who became flesh and dwelt among us (1:14). He is the life (1:4) and the light of humankind (1:4); the glory of God (1:14); the only begotten Son of God who makes the Father known (1:18).

The Gospels record Jesus's own self-designation as Son of Man, the title he frequently used to speak of his humiliation, his identification with sinful humankind, his death on behalf of sinners, and his glorious return. While Jesus was the Son of Man in respect to his ministry and passion, he is also Son of God, the uniquely begotten one sent from God himself (Mark 1:1; John 3:16). The book of Hebrews shows Jesus as God's great high priest (3:1; 4:14) who both makes sacrifice for his people and who is himself the sacrifice (10:10-14). Hebrews also presents Jesus as the creator of all things (1:2), the perfect representation of God (1:3), and the apostle of our confession (3:1). The metaphors used of Jesus, particularly in John's Gospel, speak poignantly to the indispensable need for a person to know Jesus. He is the water of life (John 4:14), the bread of life (6:41), the light (8:12), the door (10:7), the way, the truth, and the life (14:6).

Jesus was fully human. He was not partially human nor did he function at times as a human and at times as God nor did he merely appear to be human. He was at once both man and God. The evidence for Jesus's humanity in Scripture is abundant. He displayed physical symptoms that all humans experience: fatigue (John 4:6), sleep (Matt. 8:24), hunger (Matt. 21:18), and suffering (Luke 22:43-44). Jesus also experienced the emotional reactions of humankind: compassion (Luke 7:13), weeping (Luke 19:41), anger and indignation (Mark 3:5), grief (Matt. 26:37), and joy (John 15:11).

Yet Jesus was not just a real man; he was also a unique person. He differed from all other people in two ways. First, he was born to a virgin; he had no human father. He was conceived by the Holy Spirit in Mary's womb (Matt. 1:18-25). Second, unlike any other person, Jesus was without sin. He claimed to be sinless (John 8:46), and there is never a record of his confessing sin, though he told us to confess ours (Matt. 6:12). Other biblical writers ascribe sinlessness to Jesus. Paul said that Jesus became sin for us but that he personally knew no sin (2 Cor. 5:21). The writer of Hebrews says that Jesus never sinned (Heb. 4:15), and Peter affirmed that Jesus the righteous died for the unrighteous (1 Pet. 3:18).

Throughout the centuries, few people have denied the existence of the man Jesus. A fierce battle has always raged, however, over the supernatural nature of Jesus. If Jesus was virgin born and sinless, then a supernatural element is already introduced into his nature that sets him apart from all other people. Further, his resurrection denotes that this is a person who transcends time and space. The gospel accounts record many eyewitnesses to the resurrected Christ (Matt. 28:1-10; John 20:19-31), and all attempts to refute such accounts fall short. However, the NT goes beyond these implicit references to deity and clearly states that Christ is divine.

The demands of loyalty from his followers (Luke 9:57-62) and the claims that he will judge the world (John 5:27) sound strange if they come from a mere man. He also claimed that he could forgive sins (Mark 2:5), and he declared that in the judgment people will be condemned or approved according to their attitude toward the people who represent him (Matt. 25:31-46). Scripture says that Jesus created (John 1:3) and now sustains all things (Col. 1:17). He even has the power to raise the dead (John 5:25). Angels and people worship him (Heb. 1:6; Matt. 2:2). He possesses equality with the persons of the Trinity (John 14:23; 2 Cor. 13:14).

Beyond these assertions, the NT provides even clearer evidence regarding the deity of Christ. He is called God in Heb. 1:8. John's prologue (1:1-18) affirms that Jesus is from the beginning, that he is "with" (literally "face to face") God, and that he is God. The Gospel of John declares Jesus to be equal in nature with God the Father but distinct in person. Another important passage is John 5:16-29. During a controversy with the Jews about healing a man on the Sabbath, the Jews sought to kill him because he blasphemed in making himself equal with God. Rather than correcting them for mistaking his identity, Jesus went on to make even further claims regarding his deity: he has power to give life to people (v. 21), all judgment is handed over to him (v. 22), and all should honor the Son with the same honor they bestow upon the Father (v. 23).

Jesus was a master teacher. Crowds that claimed no loyalty to him were forced to admit, "No man ever spoke like this!" (John 7:46 CSB). At the close of his compelling Sermon on the Mount, the multitudes were amazed at how he taught (Matt. 7:29). He taught mainly about his Father and the kingdom that he had ushered in. He explained what that kingdom is like and the absolute obedience and love his followers are to have as citizens of the kingdom. His teaching often enraged the religious leaders of his day because they did not understand that he was

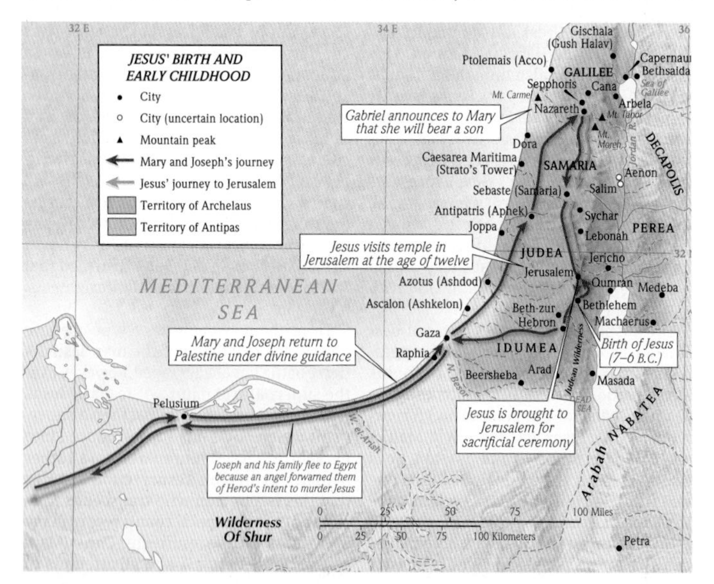

the promised Messiah who appeared to usher in the kingdom through his death, resurrection, and second coming. He stressed that the kingdom, though inaugurated at his first appearing, will find its consummation in his second coming (Matt. 24–25). Until then, his disciples are to conduct themselves as salt and light in a dark, sinful world (Matt. 5–7). Often he spoke in parables, helping people to understand by using common things to illustrate spiritual truths.

Jesus's mighty works validated his unique and divine nature. He backed up his claims to deity by demonstrating his power over sickness and disease, over nature, and over life and death itself. One great miracle that demonstrates conclusively his claim to deity is his resurrection from the dead. Death could not hold him. He rose from the dead and showed himself alive by many "convincing proofs" (Acts 1:3 CSB). Despite rigorous attempts by liberalism to expunge the miracles from the Gospels, it is impossible to eliminate these supernatural elements from Jesus's life without damaging the credibility of the gospel records about him.

Christianity affirms that Jesus is the only way to God (John 14:6; Acts 4:12). This view seems intolerant in light of our pluralistic, relativistic age. Yet one must deal with Jesus Christ either as the Lord God whom he claimed to be or as an imposter who somehow was deceived as to his own identity.

JESUS, LIFE AND MINISTRY The story of Jesus begins abruptly in the Gospel of Mark when he presented himself at the Jordan River to the desert prophet John the Baptist as a candidate for baptism. All that is said about his origin is that he came to the river "from Nazareth" (Mark 1:9). "Jesus of Nazareth" was a designation that followed him to the day of his death (John 19:19). Matthew's Gospel demonstrates that although Nazareth was Jesus's home when he came to John for baptism, he was not born there. Rather, he was born (as the Jewish messiah must be) in Bethlehem, the "city of David," as a descendant of David's royal line (Matt. 1:1-17; 2:1-6). However, he grew up in Nazareth.

Even after the momentous events associated with Jesus's baptism in the Jordan River—the descent of God's Spirit on him like a dove and the voice from heaven announcing, "You are my beloved Son; with you I am well pleased" (Mark 1:10-11 CSB)—his identity as Son of God remained hidden from those around him. We have no evidence

The traditional site on the Jordan River where Jesus was baptized

that anyone except Jesus, and possibly John the Baptist, either heard the voice or saw the dove. Ironically, the first intimation after the baptism that he was more than simply "Jesus of Nazareth" came not from his family or friends or from the religious leaders of Israel, but from the devil!

Twice the devil challenged him: "If you are the Son of God, tell this stone to become bread" (Luke 4:3 CSB), and (on the pinnacle of the temple in Jerusalem), "If you are the Son of God, throw yourself down from here" (Luke 4:9 CSB). Jesus made no attempt to defend or make use of his divine sonship but appealed instead to an authority to which any devout Jew of his day might have appealed—the holy Scriptures—and through them to the God of Israel.

Two things about this temptation story have a special bearing on the ministry of Jesus as a whole.

First, the God-centered character of his message continued in the proclamation he began in Galilee when he returned home from the desert: "The time is fulfilled, and the kingdom of God has come near. Repent and believe the good news!" (Mark 1:15 CSB). Mark called this proclamation "the good news of God" (Mark 1:14). John's Gospel presented Jesus as reminding his hearers again and again that he had come not to glorify or proclaim himself, but solely to make known "the Father," or "him who sent me" (John 4:34; 5:19, 30; 6:38; 7:16-18,28; 8:28,42,50; 14:10,28).

Second, the issue of Jesus's identity continued to be raised first by the powers of evil. Just as the devil challenged Jesus in the desert as "Son of God," so in the course of his ministry the demons (or the demon-possessed) confronted him with words such as "What do you have to do with us, Jesus of Nazareth? ... I know who you are—the Holy One of God" (Mark 1:24), or "What do you have to do with me, Jesus, Son of the Most High God?" (Mark 5:7 CSB).

The mystery of Jesus's person emerged in pronouncements of this kind, but Jesus seemed not to want the question of his identity raised prematurely. He silenced the demons (Mark 1:25,34; 3:12); and when he healed the sick, he frequently told the people who were cured not to speak of it to anyone (Mark 1:43-44; 7:36a). The more he urged silence, however, the faster the word of his healing power spread (Mark 1:45; 7:36b). The crowds appear to have concluded that he must be the Messiah, the anointed King of David's line expected to come and deliver the Jews from Roman rule. If Jesus was playing out the role of Messiah, the Gospels present him as a strangely reluctant Messiah.

At one point, when the crowds tried to "take him by force to make him king, he withdrew again to the mountain by himself" (John 6:15 CSB). Seldom, if ever, did he apply to himself the customary terms "Messiah" or "Son of God." He had instead a way of using the emphatic "I" when it was not grammatically necessary and a habit sometimes of referring to himself indirectly and mysteriously as "Son of Man." In the Aramaic language spoken by Jesus, "son of man" meant simply "a certain man," or "someone."

Though he made no explicit messianic claims and avoided the ready-made titles of honor that the Jews customarily applied to the Messiah, Jesus spoke and acted with the authority of God himself. He gave sight to the blind and hearing to the deaf; he enabled the lame to walk. When he touched the unclean, he made them clean. He even raised the dead to life. In teaching the crowds that gathered around him, he did not hesitate to say boldly, "You have heard that it was said ... but I tell you" (Matt. 5:21-22,27-28,31-34,38-39,43-44). So radical was he toward the accepted traditions, that he found it necessary to state at the outset: "Don't think that I came to abolish the Law or the Prophets. I did not come to abolish but to fulfill" (Matt. 5:17 CSB).

Jesus's primary mission was to reach the lost sheep of Israel. Through their carelessness about the law, the religious leaders had become the enemies of God; but God loved his enemies. Jesus's conviction was that both he and his disciples must love them, too (Matt. 5:38-48). Jesus was challenged on one occasion for enjoying table fellowship with social outcasts (known to the religious Jews as "sinners") in the house of Levi, the tax collector in Capernaum. He replied to this criticism: "It is not those who are well who need a doctor, but those who are sick. I didn't come to call the righteous, but sinners" (Mark 2:17 CSB). Such an exuberant celebration of divine mercy must have seemed to religious leaders a serious lowering of ancient ethical standards and a damaging compromise of the holiness of God.

We have little evidence that Jesus included non-Jews among the "sinners" to whom he was sent. Despite the reference in Luke 4:25-27 to Elijah and Elisha and their ministry to foreigners, Jesus explicitly denied that he was sent to Gentiles or Samaritans (Matt. 15:24). Yet the principle "not to the righteous, but to sinners" (Matt. 9:13) made the extension of the good news of the kingdom of God to the Gentiles after Jesus's resurrection a natural one. Even during Jesus's lifetime, he responded to the initiatives of Gentiles seeking his help (Matt. 8:5-13; Luke 7:1-10), sometimes in such a way as to put Israel to shame (Matt. 8:10).

The gospel accounts of Jesus's last days in Jerusalem correspond in broad outline to his predictions of his death. He seems to have come to Jerusalem for the last time in the knowledge that he would die there. Though he received a royal welcome from crowds who looked to him as the long-expected Messiah (Mark 11:9-10; John 12:13), no evidence points to this as the reason for his arrest. Rather, his action in driving the money changers out of the Jerusalem temple (Matt 21:12-16; Mark 11:15-17), as well as certain of his pronouncements about the temple, aroused the authorities to act decisively against him.

During his last week in Jerusalem, Jesus had predicted the temple's destruction (Matt. 24:1-2; Luke 21:5-6) and claimed that "I will destroy this temple made with human hands, and in three days I will build another not made by hands" (Mark 14:58 CSB). Jesus's intention to establish a new community as a "temple," or dwelling place of God (Matt. 16:18; John 2:19), was perceived as a threat to Judaism and to the temple that stood as its embodiment. On this basis, he was arrested and charged as a deceiver of the people.

During a hearing before the Sanhedrin, or Jewish ruling council, Jesus spoke of himself as "Son of Man seated at the right hand of Power and coming with the clouds of heaven" (Mark 14:62 CSB). Though the high priest called this blasphemy and the Sanhedrin agreed that such behavior deserved death, the results of the hearing seem to have been inconclusive. The high priest and his cohorts apparently found no formal charges they

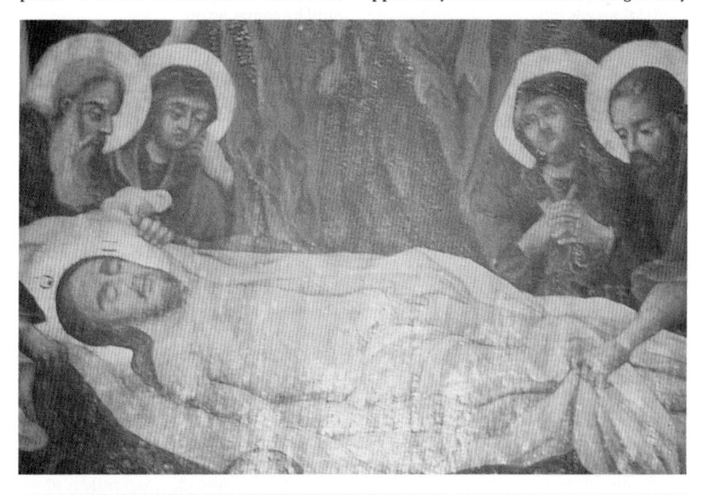

Painting from the fifteenth or sixteenth century showing the burial of Jesus, seen at the Church of the Holy Sepulchre in Jerusalem

could make stick. The Sanhedrin decided, therefore, to send Jesus to Pontius Pilate, the Roman governor, with charges against him that the Romans would take seriously: "We found this man misleading our nation, opposing payment of taxes to Caesar, and saying that he himself is the Messiah, a king" (Luke 23:2 CSB). Jesus's execution is therefore attributable neither to the Jewish people as a whole, nor to the Sanhedrin, but rather to a small group of priests who manipulated the Romans into doing what they were not able to accomplish within the framework of their law.

Though Pilate pronounced Jesus innocent three times (Luke 23:4,14,22), he was maneuvered into sentencing Jesus with the thinly veiled threat: "If you release this man, you are not Caesar's friend. Anyone who makes himself a king opposes Caesar!" (John 19:12 CSB). Consequently Jesus was crucified between two thieves, fulfilling his own prediction that "as Moses lifted up the snake in the wilderness, so the Son of Man must be lifted up" (John 3:14 CSB). Most of his disciples fled at his arrest; only a group of women and one disciple, called the disciple whom he loved, were present at the cross when he died (John 19:25-27).

The story did not end with the death of Jesus. His body was placed in a new tomb that belonged to a secret disciple named Joseph of Arimathea (John 19:38-42). Two days later, the morning after the Sabbath, some of the women who had remained faithful to Jesus came to the tomb. They discovered the stone over the entrance to the tomb rolled away and the body of Jesus gone. According to Mark, a young man was there (16:5; tradition calls him an angel) and told the women to send word to the rest of the disciples to go and meet Jesus in Galilee, just as he had promised them (Mark 16:7; 14:28). According to Matthew, the young man's word was confirmed to the women by the risen Jesus himself. When they brought word to the 11 disciples (the Twelve minus Judas, the betrayer), the disciples went to a mountain in Galilee, where the risen Jesus appeared to them as a group. He commanded them to make more disciples, teaching and baptizing among the Gentiles (Matt. 28:16-20).

According to Luke, the risen Jesus appeared to the gathered disciples already in Jerusalem on the same day he was raised and before that to two disciples walking to the neighboring town of Emmaus. According to John, there was an appearance in Jerusalem on Sunday to one of the women, Mary Magdalene, another on the same day to the gathered disciples, another a week later (still in Jerusalem) to the same group plus Thomas, and a fourth appearance, at an unstated time, by the lake of Galilee, in which Jesus reenacted the initial call of the disciples by providing them miraculously with an enormous catch of fish.

Luke adds in the book of Acts that the appearances of the risen Jesus continued over a period of 40 days in which he instructed them about the kingdom of God. The disciples' experience of the living Jesus transformed them from a scattered and cowardly band of disillusioned visionaries into the nucleus of a coherent movement able to challenge and change forever the Roman Empire within a few short decades.

Even today, the story of Jesus is not over; he continues to fulfill his mission wherever his name is confessed and his teaching is obeyed. Christians believe that he will do so until he comes again.

JETHRO Personal name meaning "excess" or "superiority." Priest of Midian and the father-in-law of Moses (Exod. 3:1). In Exod. 2:18, his name is Reuel; in Num. 10:29, it is Hobab. The deity whom he served is not explicitly identified; in Exod. 18:11, however, he declared Yahweh to be greater than all gods.

JEWISH PARTIES IN THE NEW TESTAMENT Judaism in NT times included several different groups, or parties, such as the Pharisees, Sadducees, Herodians, and Zealots.

Pharisees The term "Pharisee" means "separated ones." Perhaps it means that they separated themselves from the masses or that they separated themselves to the study and interpretation of the law. They saw the way to God as being through obedience to the law. They were the progressives of the day, willing to adopt new ideas and adapt the law to new situations. The Pharisees accepted all the OT as authoritative. They affirmed the reality of angels and demons. They had a firm belief in life beyond the grave and a resurrection of the body. They were missionary, seeking the conversion of Gentiles (Matt. 23:15). They had little interest in politics. The Pharisees opposed Jesus because he refused to accept their interpretations of the oral law.

Sadducees The Sadducees were the party of the wealthy and of the high priestly families. They were in charge of the temple, its services, and concessions. They claimed to be descendants of Zadok, high priest of Solomon. They stood in opposition to the Pharisees. They were social conservatives, seeking to preserve the practices of the past. They opposed the oral law, accepting the Pentateuch as the ultimate authority. The Sadducees were materialistic in their outlook. They did not believe in life after death or rewards or punishment beyond this life. They denied the existence of angels and demons. They did not believe that God is concerned with what people do. Rather, people are totally free. The Sadducees were politically oriented, supporters of ruling powers, whether Seleucids or Romans. They tolerated no threats to their position and wealth, so they strongly opposed Jesus.

Herodians The Herodians are mentioned only three times in the NT (Matt. 22:16; Mark 3:6; 12:13). In Mark, they joined the Pharisees in a plot to kill Jesus. The other references are to Pharisees and Herodians together asking Jesus about paying taxes to Caesar. They were Jews who supported Herod Antipas or sought to have a descendant of Herod the Great given authority over Palestine. At this time, Judea and Samaria were under Roman governors.

Zealots The Zealots were the extreme wing of the Pharisees. In contrast with other Pharisees, they believed only God had the right to rule over the Jews. They were willing to fight and die for that belief. For them nationalistic patriotism and religion were inseparable. Simon, one of the disciples, is called Zealot (Luke 6:15).

JEZEBEL Personal name meaning "where is the prince?" perhaps derived from Phoenician name meaning "Baal is the prince." Wife of King Ahab of Israel (874–853 BC), who brought the worship of Baal from Sidon where her father Ethbaal was king (1 Kgs. 16:31). Jezebel tried to destroy all God's prophets in Israel (1 Kgs. 18:4) while installing prophets of Baal and Asherah (1 Kgs. 18:19) as part of the royal household. Jezebel was killed by her own servants when Jehu overthrew the dynasty of Ahab (2 Kgs. 9:30-37). Jezebel's name became so associated with wickedness that the false prophetess in the church at Thyatira was labeled "Jezebel" (Rev. 2:20).

JEZREEL Personal and place-name meaning "God sows." **1.** The valley of Jezreel that separates Galilee from Samaria, including the valley of Esdraelon. **2.** Northern city of Jezreel and the site of the royal residence of Omri and Ahab (1 Kgs. 21). **3.** The southern city of Jezreel located in the vicinity of Ziph (1 Sam. 25:43). **4.** Name given by Hosea to his son as a symbol to indicate the evil nature of the dynasty of Jehu (Hos. 1:4-5; 1:10–2:1).

The valley of Jezreel (Esdraelon or Megiddo) as viewed from the top of the Megiddo tel

JOAB Personal name meaning "Yahweh is father." Military commander during most of David's reign. David's nephew, he was loyal to David and ruthless in achieving his objectives. Joab successfully led David's armies against the Ammonites (2 Sam. 10). During this campaign, David sent his infamous order to Joab to have Uriah, the husband of Bathsheba, killed (2 Sam. 11). When Absalom led a rebellion, Joab remained loyal to David. Joab killed Absalom against the clear orders of David (2 Sam. 18:14). Joab murdered his cousin Amasa, whom David had named commander (2 Sam. 20:10). He opposed David's plan for a census but carried it out when ordered to do so (2 Sam. 24:1-9). When David was dying, Joab supported Adonijah's claim to the throne (1 Kgs. 1). David named Solomon king and told him to avenge Abner (King Saul's commander) and Amasa by killing Joab. Although Joab fled to the tabernacle for sanctuary, Solomon ordered Benaiah to kill Joab (1 Kgs. 2).

JOANNA Personal name meaning "Yahweh's gift." **1.** One of the women who came to Jesus's tomb on the Sunday following the crucifixion and reported to the 11 that he had risen (Luke 8:3). **2.** The son of Rhesa mentioned in the genealogy of Jesus (Luke 3:27 KJV).

JOASH Personal name meaning "Yahweh gives." **1.** Father of Gideon (Judg. 6:11). **2.** A son of Shelah (1 Chron. 4:21-22). **3.** A son of Becher (1 Chron. 7:8). **4.** One of David's warriors (1 Chron. 12:3). **5.** One of David's officers who was in charge of the stores of oil (1 Chron. 27:28). **6.** A son of Ahab king of Israel and one of those to whom Micaiah the prophet was handed over (1 Kgs. 22:26). **7.** Infant son of King Ahaziah of Judah who survived the bloodbath carried out by Athaliah, the queen mother, following the murder of Ahaziah (2 Kgs. 11:2). Joash was hidden by Jehosheba his aunt for six years, then proclaimed as the legitimate ruler of Judah in a move instigated by Jehoiada. Athaliah was executed, and Joash took the throne at the age of seven. **8.** Son and successor of Jehoahaz as king of Israel (2 Kgs. 13:10). He ruled for 16 years during the early part of the eighth century BC. His son Jeroboam II succeeded him on the throne.

JOB, BOOK OF This OT book is most frequently pictured as a drama that deals with the age-old question of human suffering. It consists of a series of debates between Job and his three friends, with Job searching for answers on why he, who claimed to be a righteous man, lost all his possessions, his children, and his health. Through his ordeal, Job learns that God still controls the world, even a world with unexplainable suffering. The human mind cannot have perfect understanding, but God can be trusted to treat us with justice and fairness. In the final analysis, God is sovereign, and God does not owe us an explanation for his actions.

JOCHEBED Personal name meaning "Yahweh's glory." Wife of Amram and the mother of Miriam, Aaron, and Moses (Exod. 6:20).

JOEL Personal name meaning "Yah is God." **1.** Son of Samuel who became an evil judge (1 Sam. 8). **2.** Levite (1 Chron. 6:36). **3.** Member(s) of the tribe of Reuben (1 Chron. 5:4,8). **4.** Leader among the Levites under David (1 Chron. 15:7,11,17). **5.** Member of the tribe of Simeon (1 Chron. 4:35). **6.** Leader of the tribe of Gad (1 Chron. 5:12). **7.** Leader of the tribe of Issachar (1 Chron. 7:3). **8.** Military hero under David (1 Chron. 11:38). **9.** Leader of the western half of the tribe of Manasseh under David (1 Chron. 27:20). **10.** Levite who helped King Hezekiah cleanse the temple (2 Chron. 29:12). **11.** Israelite whom Ezra condemned for having a foreign wife (Ezra 10:43). **12.** Leader of the people from the tribe of Benjamin living in Jerusalem in time of Nehemiah (Neh. 11:9). **13.** Prophet whose preaching ministry produced the book of Joel.

JOEL, BOOK OF This OT book describes a terrible locust plague that devastated the land of Israel. The prophet interpreted this disaster as a symbol of the coming day of God's judgment. Then when the people repented of their sin and turned to the Lord, he answered that he would show pity and remove their plague (2:18-27). The clear message of the book is that the Creator of the universe is in complete control of nature and can use calamities to bring his people to repentance. Joel also predicted a time when God's Spirit would fall upon his people. On the day of Pentecost, the apostle Peter proclaimed that this new day of Spirit-filled people predicted by the prophet Joel had arrived (Acts 2:17-21).

JOHN THE APOSTLE A disciple of Jesus, brother of James, and leader in the early church. John is always mentioned among the first four apostles in the lists of the Twelve (Mark 3:17). John is also among the "inner three" (with Peter and James) who were with Jesus on special occasions in the Synoptic Gospels: the raising of Jairus's daughter (Mark 5:37), the transfiguration (Mark 9:2), and the garden of Gethsemane (Mark 14:32-33). The apostle John appears four times in the book of Acts, and each time he is with Peter (1:13; 3:1-11; 4:13-20; 8:14). After Peter healed the man, they were arrested, imprisoned, and then released. They were "uneducated and untrained men" (Acts 4:13 CSB), but they answered their accusers boldly (Acts 4:20).

Five books of the NT have been attributed to John the apostle: the gospel, three letters, and Revelation. In each case, the traditional view that the apostle was the author of these books can be traced to writers in the second century. Neither the Gospel nor the letters identify their author by name.

JOHN THE BAPTIST Prophet from a priestly family who preached a message of repentance, announced the coming of the Messiah, baptized Jesus, and was beheaded

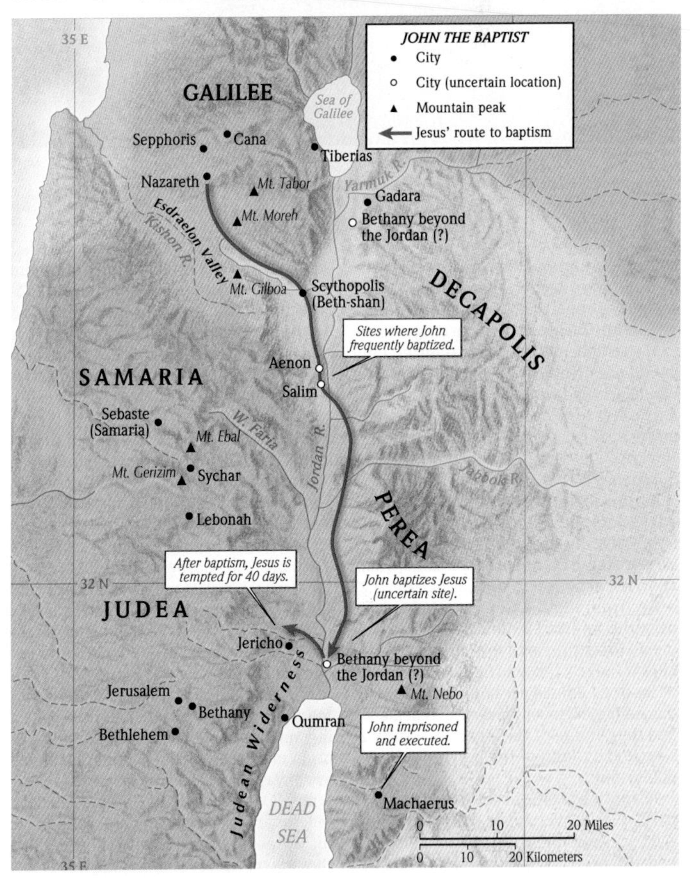

Machaerus, Herod's fortress-palace where John the Baptist was imprisoned and beheaded

by Herod Antipas. Luke 1:5-80 records the birth of John. Zechariah, his father, was a priest. The angel Gabriel announced John's birth while Zechariah was burning incense in the temple. According to Gabriel, John would not drink wine or strong drink. He would be filled with the Holy Spirit, and as a prophet he would have the spirit and power of Elijah. His role would be to prepare the Lord's people for the coming of the Messiah.

Mark 1:3-4 records that John was in the wilderness until the time of his public ministry. There he ate locusts and wild honey. He wore the dress of a prophet, camel's hair, and a leather girdle (Matt. 3:4; cp. 2 Kgs. 1:8).

According to the Gospel of Luke, John began his ministry around the Jordan River in the fifteenth year of the reign of Tiberius Caesar (Luke 3:1-3), which must have been ad 26 or 27. John's preaching emphasized the coming judgment, the need for repentance, and the coming of the Messiah. Jesus was baptized by John at the beginning of his public ministry.

According to the Gospel of John, the ministry of Jesus overlapped with that of John (3:22-24), and some of Jesus's first disciples had also been disciples of John the Baptist (John 1:35-37). Jesus even identified John with the eschatological role of Elijah (Mark 9:12-13). John was vigorous in his attacks on Herod Antipas, Roman ruler over Palestine, because of his sensual lifestyle. Herod had him arrested and eventually executed. John's death is recorded in detail in Mark 6:14-29.

JOHN, GOSPEL OF The fourth Gospel in the NT, noted for its distinctiveness when compared with the Synoptic Gospels—Matthew, Mark, and Luke. Unlike the other three Gospels, John emphasizes the deity of Jesus from the beginning of his Gospel. The prologue to his Gospel affirms that Jesus is the eternal Word (*logos*) who was both with God and was God. Jesus is the Word incarnate (John 1:14). Jesus uses the significant phrase "I am" seven times in John, claiming the personal name of God as his own.

Knowing and *believing* are key terms for John. Knowledge of God comes from believing and knowing Jesus. Both these words occur more than 90 times in this Gospel and are always used as verbs. Jesus's teaching reminds us that knowing God and believing in Jesus are expressed in action. John wrote his Gospel to assure fearful believers that they must believe Jesus and the words that he spoke. Further, he calls on others who sense a spiritual thirst to come to the One who gives the life-giving water. In him one finds light, life, and love.

JOHN, LETTERS FROM Three short letters in the NT that are attributed to John, the apostle of Jesus.

First John This letter was written to a church or group of churches in crisis—being attacked by false teaching (cp. 2:18-28; 4:1-6; 5:6-7). False teachers had compromised the person and work of Jesus Christ. They did not confess Jesus of Nazareth as the Christ (2:22) and denied that Jesus had come in the flesh (4:2-3). John affirmed that Jesus had indeed come to earth in human form because John had seen him with his own eyes (1:1-2). To know Christ, according to John, is to keep his commandments or to walk in the light of his truth (2:6). Furthermore, a person cannot be in the light and hate his brother or love the world (2:7-17).

Second John Only 245 words in the Greek text, 2 John is an excellent example of hortatory (or exhortation) discourse. The "elect lady" to whom the letter is addressed (v. 1)—most likely a reference to a local church—must continue to walk in the truth, love one another, and be on guard against false teachers (the deceiver and the antichrist of v. 7). The church must not extend hospitality to those who deny "the coming of Jesus Christ in the flesh" (v. 7 CSB).

Third John This is a personal letter that revolves around three individuals: Gaius (the recipient), Diotrephes (the troubler), and Demetrius (probably the bearer of the letter). It contains a word of exhortation to Gaius encouraging him not to imitate the bad example of Diotrephes but to continue the good work he is doing of receiving and supporting the traveling teachers/missionaries.

JOKTAN Personal name meaning "watchful" or "he is small." Son of Eber in line from Shem in the Table of Nations (Gen. 10:25-26).

JONAH Personal name meaning "dove." God used Jonah to deliver a warning of God's judgment to the pagan citizens of Nineveh, capital of the Assyrian Empire. Jonah also prophesied in the northern kingdom during the time of Jeroboam II (793–753 BC; see 2 Kgs. 14:25).

JONAH, BOOK OF This OT book tells about how God used a prejudiced and narrow-minded prophet to show that his grace extends to all people, Gentiles as well as Jews. At first Jonah refused to answer God's call to preach God's message of judgment and repentance to the citizens of Nineveh, capital city of the cruel Assyrian Empire. God mercifully delivered him from drowning by having Jonah swallowed by a great fish and delivered on dry land. Finally, Jonah did preach to the Ninevites, only to sulk and pout when the people repented and turned to the Lord. The message of the book is that God is concerned for all human beings (1 Tim. 2:1-6) and has the right to show mercy to whomever he wills (Rom. 9:15).

JONATHAN Personal name meaning "Yahweh gave." **1.** Levite who served as priest of Micah in Ephraim and later with the tribe of Dan (Judg. 17–18). **2.** Eldest son of King Saul and friend of David. Jonathan made a covenant with David and warned him about his father's plot against David's life (1 Sam. 9:1-2). Jonathan was killed by the Philistines in a battle at Mount Gilboa (1 Sam. 31:1-2). In later years, after David became king of Judah, he showed kindness to Jonathan's son, Mephibosheth (2 Sam. 9:1-13). **3.** Son of Abiathar the priest in service to David (1 Kgs. 1:42-43). **4.** An uncle of David who functioned as counselor and scribe in the royal court (1 Chron. 27:32). **5.** Son of Shimea who killed a Philistine giant (1 Chron. 20:7). **6.** One of David's 30 mighty men (2 Sam. 23:32-33). **7.** A royal treasurer in reign of David; called Jehonathan (KJV) in 1 Chron. 27:25. **8.** "House of Jonathan," referring to a scribe or secretary where Jeremiah was imprisoned (Jer. 38:26). **9.** Son of Kareah, "Johanan"; possibly same as 8, above. (Jer. 40:8). **10.** Father of Ebed, a returned exile (Ezra 8:6). **11.** Priest during high priesthood of Joiakim (Neh. 12:14). **12.** Priest, son of Joiada (Neh. 12:11). **13.** Priest who played musical instruments (Neh. 12:35). **14.** Son of Asahel who supported foreign marriages in time of Ezra (Ezra 10:15). **15.** Descendant of Jerahmeel (1 Chron. 2:32-33).

JOPPA Place-name meaning "beautiful." Situated on the Mediterranean coast, Joppa is located about 35 miles northwest of Jerusalem. In Joppa, Simon Peter was praying on the flat roof of a house when he saw in a trance what seemed to be "a large sheet coming down, being lowered by its four corners" (Acts 10:11 CSB). Through this encounter with God, he learned that the Gentile world was a fit audience for the gospel.

The ancient seaport of Joppa (Jaffa)

Traditional house of Simon the Tanner in Joppa where Peter received a vision from God

JORAM Personal name meaning "Yahweh is exalted." Name of a king of Israel (849–843 BC) and a king of Judah (850–843 BC). Joram of Judah was succeeded on the throne by his son, whose name was Ahaziah; Joram of Israel came to the throne at the death of his brother, who was also named Ahaziah. The account of the reign of Joram (Jehoram) of Israel is found in 2 Kgs. 3. He led a coalition with Judah and Edom, advised by Elisha, to defeat Moab. The reign of Joram of Judah is treated in 2 Kgs. 8. He married the daughter of Ahab of Israel and brought Baal worship to Judah.

JORDAN RIVER Place-name meaning "the descender." River forming geographical division separating eastern and western tribes of Israel. It is the longest and most important river of Palestine. The first mention of the Jordan in the Bible occurs in the story of Abram and Lot. Upon his separation from Abram, Lot chose for himself "the entire plain of the Jordan" (Gen. 13:11 CSB). Under the leadership of Joshua, Israel crossed the Jordan "on dry ground" (Josh. 3:15-17). During the period of the judges and the early monarchy, the possession of the fords of the Jordan more than once meant the difference between defeat and victory. The Jordan was a strong line of defense, not to be easily forded. The Jordan River is also featured in the miracles of Elijah and Elisha.

The Jordan River flows south from Mount Hermon through Israel, finally emptying into the Dead Sea.

The essential story of the Gospels begins at the Jordan River, where John the Baptist came preaching the coming kingdom of heaven. The most important NT event relating to the Jordan is the baptism of Jesus, performed by John the Baptist (Mark 1:9).

JOSEPH Personal name meaning "adding." **1.** Son of Jacob by Jacob's favorite wife, Rachel. As the child of Jacob's old age, Joseph became his favorite son. This and dreams which showed his rule over his family inspired the envy of his brothers, who sold Joseph to a caravan of Ishmaelites (Gen. 37). Joseph was taken to Egypt, where he eventually became second in command to the pharaoh because of his prediction of a coming famine and his recommendation on how to solve this problem (Gen. 41:39-45). Later, under Joseph's patronage, his father Jacob moved the rest of his family to Egypt (Gen. 46:1–47:12). Joseph died in Egypt but was embalmed and later buried in Shechem (Gen. 50:26; Josh. 24:32). While in Egypt, Joseph became the father of two sons, Manasseh and Ephraim (Gen. 41:50-52), who were counted as sons of Jacob (48:5-6) and whose tribes dominated the northern nation of Israel. The name Joseph is used later in the OT as a reference to the tribes of Ephraim and Manasseh (1 Kgs. 11:28) or as a designation for the whole northern kingdom (Zech. 10:6). **2.** A spy from the tribe of Issachar (Num. 13:7). **3.** A Levite of the sons of Asaph (1 Chron. 25:2). **4.** A contemporary of Ezra with a foreign wife (Ezra 10:42). **5.** A priest in the days of high priest Joiakim (Neh. 12:14). **6.** Husband of Mary, mother of Jesus. Upon learning of Mary's pregnancy, he sought to put her away without public disgrace. But after assurances from the Lord in a dream, he took Mary to his ancestral home, Bethlehem, was with her at Jesus's birth, and shared in the naming, circumcision, and dedication of the child (Luke 2:8-33). Joseph does not appear later in the Gospels, and it is likely that he died before Jesus launched his public ministry. **7.** Joseph of Arimathea, a rich member of the Sanhedrin and a secret disciple of Jesus. After the crucifixion, he requested Jesus's body from Pilate and laid it in his own unused tomb (John 19:38-42). **8.** Two different Josephs mentioned in the genealogy of Jesus (Luke 3:24,30). **9.** Another name for both Barsabbas (Acts 1:23) and Barnabas (Acts 4:36).

JOSES Personal name. **1.** One of the "brothers" of Jesus (Mark 6:3). **2.** The brother of James the Less (Mark 15:40).

JOSHUA Personal name meaning "Yahweh delivered." **1.** Moses's successor who led the Israelites to take control of the promised land. Joshua was on Mount Sinai when

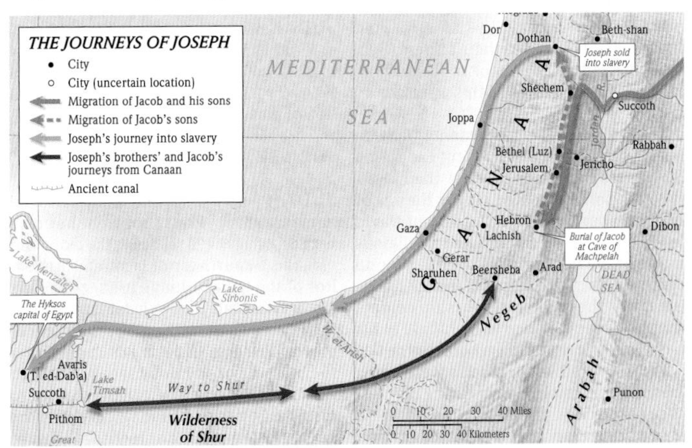

Moses received the Law (Exod. 32:17). He was also one of the 12 spies Moses sent to investigate Canaan (Num. 13:8). He and Caleb returned with a positive, minority report. Of all the adults alive at that time, only the two of them were allowed by God to live to enter the land of Canaan (Num. 14:28-30,38). **2.** High priest of community who returned from Babylonian exile in 538 BC. Called Jeshua. He began building the temple but quit when strong opposition arose and appealed to King Artaxerxes (Ezra 3:8–4:24). Later correspondence led King Darius to recover Cyrus's proclamation authorizing the rebuilding of the temple. This came after Jeshua followed the prophetic preaching of Zechariah and Haggai and renewed efforts to rebuild the temple, finally finishing in 515 bc. Jeshua was apparently one of two anointed ones of Zechariah's vision (Zech. 4:14; cp. 6:12-13).

JOSHUA, BOOK OF This OT book points backward to the exodus as well as forward to the time of the judges and the monarchy. The book is named after the successor to Moses and one of the greatest military leaders of the OT, Joshua the son of Nun. However, the central character of the book is not Joshua but God. He fights for Israel and drives out the enemy before them. He is a faithful God who desires a true covenant relationship with his chosen people. God promised that he would give Israel the land that he had pledged to their fathers (Gen. 15:18-21; Exod. 3:8). The book of Joshua documents how God fulfilled this promise.

JOSIAH Personal name meaning "Yahweh heals." Judah's king from about 640 to 609 BC who led the people to renew their loyalty to the Lord. Anointed king at the age of eight, he began to seek the God of David (2 Chron. 34:3). Josiah initiated a religious purge of Judah during his twelfth year on the throne (34:3-7). This purge included tearing down the Canaanite worship centers that had been taken over by Judah. In his eighteenth year as king, a book of the law was discovered while repairs were being made on the temple. Upon hearing the message of the book, Josiah tore his clothes, a sign of repentance, and humbled himself before God. The reading of this book prompted Josiah to instigate the most far-reaching religious reforms in Israel's history.

JOTHAM Personal name meaning "Yahweh has shown himself to be perfect." **1.** Son of Gideon who survived the mass killing of Gideon's sons by Abimelech, their half brother (Judg. 9:5). Afterward, when Abimelech had been hailed as king at Shechem, Jotham addressed a fable to the people of Shechem designed to mock the idea of Abimelech acting as a king. **2.** Son and successor of Uzziah (750–732 BC) as king of Judah (2 Kgs. 15:32). His reign was marked by building projects, material prosperity, and military successes.

JOY State of delight and well-being that results from knowing and serving God. Joy is the fruit of a right relation with God. It is not something people can create by their own efforts. God himself knows joy, and he wants his people to know joy. Psalm 104:31 speaks of God rejoicing in his creative works. Isaiah 65:18 speaks of God rejoicing over his redeemed people who will be to him "a joy." Joy is a fruit of a Spirit-led life (Gal. 5:22). When a person walks with the Lord, he can continue to rejoice even when troubles come. Jesus spoke of those who could rejoice even when persecuted and killed (Matt. 5:12).

JUBAL Personal name meaning "a ram," as a "ram's horn" used as a musical instrument. Son of Lamech and full brother of Jabal (Gen. 4:19-21). He is associated with the invention of musical instruments.

JUBILEE See *Festivals*.

JUDAH Personal, tribal, and territorial name meaning "Praise Yahweh" but may have originally been related to the mountain of Jehud. **1.** Fourth son of Jacob and progenitor of the tribe of Judah (Gen. 29:35). His mother was Leah. Though Judah is prominent in the Genesis narratives, he seldom occupies center stage. Genesis 49:8-12 preserves the blessing of Judah by Jacob. Through Judah ran the genealogical line that led to Jesus. **2.** The tribe of Judah occupied the strategically important territory west of

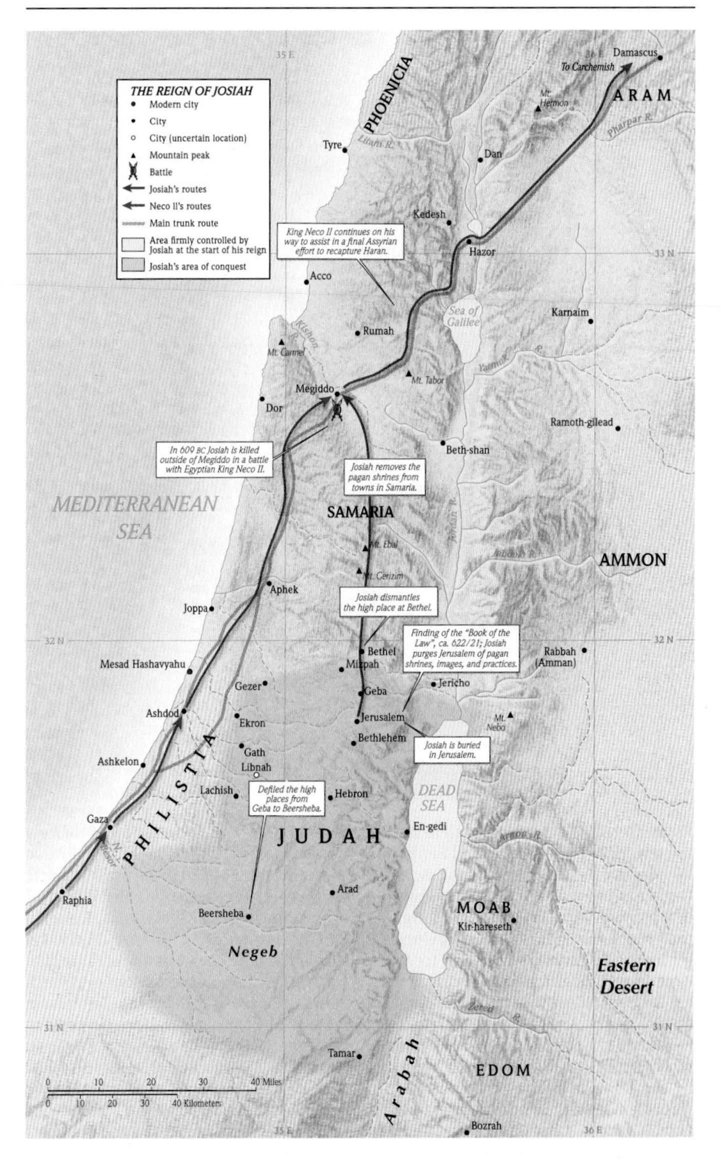

THE REIGN OF JOSIAH
Modern city
City
City (uncertain location)
Mountain peak
Battle
Josiah's routes
Neco II's routes
Main trunk route
Area firmly controlled by Josiah at the start of his reign
Josiah's area of conquest
King Neco II continues on his way to assist in a final Assyrian effort to recapture Haran.
In 609 BC Josiah is killed outside of Megiddo in a battle with Egyptian King Neco II.
Josiah removes the pagan shrines from towns in Samaria.
Josiah dismantles the high place at Bethel.
Finding of the "Book of the Law", ca. 622/21; Josiah purges Jerusalem of pagan shrines, images, and practices.
Josiah is buried in Jerusalem.
Defiled the high places from Geba to Beersheba.
Damascus
To Carchemish
ARAM
Mt. Hermon
Pharpar R.
PHOENICIA
Tyre
Litani R.
Dan
Kedesh
Hazor
Acco
Sea of Galilee
Karnaim
Rumah
Kishon R.
Mt. Carmel
Yarmuk R.
Mt. Tabor
Megiddo
Dor
Ramoth-gilead
Beth-shan
MEDITERRANEAN SEA
SAMARIA
Jordan R.
Mt. Ebal
Jabbok R.
AMMON
Mt. Gerizim
Aphek
Joppa
Bethel
Rabbah (Amman)
Mesad Hashavyahu
Mizpah
Jericho
Gezer
Geba
Ashdod
Jerusalem
Mt. Nebo
Ekron
Bethlehem
Gath
Ashkelon
Libnah
PHILISTIA
Lachish
Hebron
DEAD SEA
Gaza
En-gedi
JUDAH
Arnon R.
Arad
Raphia
Beersheba
MOAB
Kir-hareseth
Negeb
Eastern Desert
Zered R.
Tamar
Arabah
EDOM
Bozrah
35 E
36 E
33 N
32 N
31 N
0 10 20 30 40 Miles
0 10 20 30 40 Kilometers

the Dead Sea. The city of Jerusalem was on the border between Judah and Benjamin. David was from the tribe of Judah. **3.** When the kingdom was divided following the death of Solomon, the southern kingdom took the name Judah. **4.** The province set up by the Persian government to rule a conquered Judean kingdom (Neh. 5:14; Hag. 1:1). **5.** Priest whose sons helped Zerubbabel and Joshua restore the temple (Ezra 3:9; cp. Neh. 12:8). **6.** Levite whom Ezra condemned for having foreign wife (Ezra 10:23). **7.** Member of the tribe of Benjamin who lived in Jerusalem after the return from exile (Neh. 11:9). **8.** Priestly musician who helped in Nehemiah's celebration (Neh. 12:36).

JUDAS Greek transliteration of Hebrew personal name Judah meaning "Praise Yahweh." **1.** "Brother" of Jesus (Mark 6:3). **2.** Judas of Galilee, who was killed in a revolt against the Romans (Acts 5:37). **3.** A man in Damascus visited by Paul (Acts 9:7-12). **4.** Judas, surnamed Barsabbas, was one of those chosen by the church of Jerusalem to go with Paul and Barnabas to deliver the letter from James to the church at Antioch concerning the important matter of Gentile salvation (Acts 15:22). **5.** An apostle of Jesus, also called Lebbaeus Thaddaeus (Matt. 10:3; Mark 3:18). **6.** Judas Iscariot, who betrayed Jesus. All of the Gospels place him at the end of the list of disciples because of his role as betrayer.

Iscariot is an Aramaic word that means "man of Kerioth," a town near Hebron. He was the only disciple from Judea. He acted as treasurer for the disciples but was known as a miser and a thief (John 12:4-6).

JUDE, EPISTLE OF A NT letter of only 25 verses that addresses the problem of false teachings in the early church. Jude emphasized that the Lord will judge evil intruders who are attempting to corrupt the true faith. The message of judgment strikes many in our world as intolerant, unloving, and contrary to the message of love proclaimed elsewhere in the NT. But some of the most beautiful statements about God's sustaining grace are found in Jude (vv. 1,24-25), and they shine with a greater brilliance when contrasted with the false teachers who have departed from the true Christian faith. Jude called on believers to contend for the faith that was transmitted to them (v. 3) and not to abandon God's love.

JUDEA Place-name meaning "Jewish." In Ezra 5:8, the Aramaic designation of a province that varied in size with changing political circumstances, but always included the city of Jerusalem and the territory surrounding it. The area, formerly called Judah, was first given the name Judea following the Babylonian exile. In Roman times, Judea, Samaria, and Galilee were generally considered to be the three main geographical divisions of Palestine.

JUDGE (OFFICE) 1. An official with authority to administer justice by trying cases. **2.** One who usurps the prerogative of a judge. **3.** A military deliverer in the period between Joshua and David. Moses served as the judge of Israel, both deciding between persons and teaching Israel God's statutes (Exod. 18:15-16). Elders of a community frequently served as judges at the city gate (Deut. 22:15; 25:7). During the monarchy, the king served as the supreme judge (2 Sam. 15:2-3) and appointed local judges (2 Chron. 19:5), along with an appeals process (2 Chron. 19:8-11). Following the exile, King Artaxerxes of Persia gave the priest Ezra the authority to appoint judges in Judea (Ezra 7:25). God is the ultimate Judge of all the earth (James 4:12). As God's representative, Christ functions as Judge as well (1 Pet. 4:5).

JUDGES, BOOK OF A historical book of the OT that describes a dark period in the life of Israel. The nation fell into worship of pagan gods and refused to follow the com-

Sunset over the Judean hills

mands of the Lord. God would punish the people by sending a foreign nation to oppress them. Then they would repent and cry out for deliverance. God would respond by sending a judge, or military deliverer, to overthrow the enemy. This cycle of sin-oppression-repentance-deliverance occurs throughout the book (4:1–3). The best-known judges of the book of Judges are Gideon (6:1–8:35) and Samson (13:1–16:31).

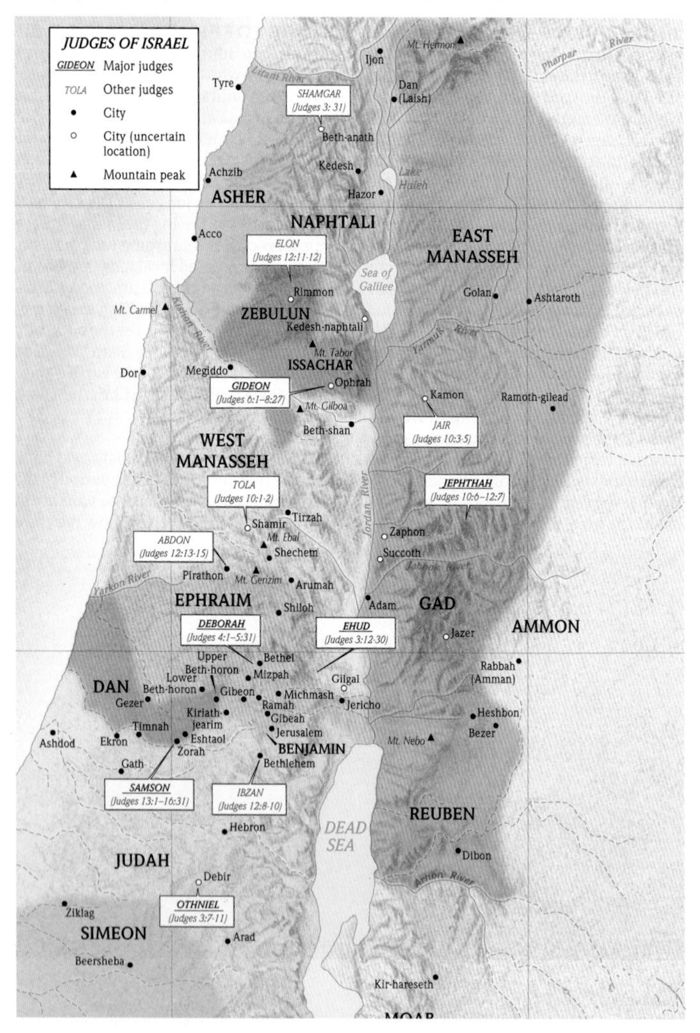

JUDGING The interpretation of Matt. 7:1 that Christians should not make value judgments of the behavior of others is shown to be erroneous by multiple commands in Scripture to do exactly that (e.g., Matt. 7:15-20; 1 Tim. 3:10). But Christians are to judge others constructively with humility and gentleness (Gal. 6:1). We are forbidden to judge hypocritically, that is, when such judgment entails intolerance of another's sin coupled with blindness of one's own (Matt. 7:1-5; Rom. 2:1-4) or when human judgment impinges on God's prerogative as judge (1 Cor. 4:5). Instructions on proper exercise of judgment include (1) the call to judge reputed prophets by their fruits (Matt. 7:15-17), (2) encouragement for Christians to arbitrate between fellow believers who have a dispute rather than going to pagan law courts (1 Cor. 6:1-6), and (3) instructions regarding church cases (Matt. 18:15-20). First Corinthians 5:3-5 illustrates the function of a church court.

JUDGMENT DAY Appointed time in the future when God will intervene in history for the purpose of judging the wicked and upholding the righteous. In OT texts, nations are pictured as being judged during this time. Yet in the NT, the judgment seems to be more for individuals. In the OT, Yahweh is pictured as the Judge, while the Judge is Christ in the NT. Generally the NT understands the day of judgment as being closely associated with the second coming of Christ, resurrection of the dead, and the coming kingdom of God. The day of judgment is often referred to as the "day of Christ" (Phil. 1:10; 2:16) or "day of the Lord" (1 Cor. 5:5). The Gospels point to Christ as the agent who will judge humankind (Matt. 16:27; 19:28; 25:31; Luke 9:26; 17:24; 22:69). The day of judgment will be a time when all humankind throughout eternity will be judged. On this day, the living and dead of all humanity shall stand and make an account to God (1 Pet. 4:5).

JULIUS A Roman centurion assigned the responsibility of escorting Paul to Rome (Acts 27:1).

JUPITER Latin name of Zeus, king of Greek gods. The people of Lystra responded to Paul's healing of a crippled man by claiming the gods had come to earth. They referred to Barnabas as Zeus, or Jupiter (Acts 14:12-13 KJV).

The temple of Jupiter at Baalbek (Heliopolis)

JUSTICE Order that God seeks to reestablish in his creation where all people are treated fairly and impartially. As the sovereign Creator of the universe, God is just (Gen. 18:25; Deut. 32:4), particularly as the defender of all the oppressed of the earth (Jer. 49:11). Justice thus is universal (Ps. 9:7-9) and applies to each covenant or dispensation. Jesus affirmed for his day the centrality of the OT demand for justice (Matt. 23:23). Justice is the work of the NT people of God (James 1:27). God's justice is not a distant external standard. It is the source of all human justice (2 Chron. 19:6,9). Justice is grace received and grace shared (2 Cor. 9:8-10). Various needy groups are the recipients of justice. These groups include widows, orphans, resident aliens (also called "sojourners" or "strangers"), wage earners, the poor, prisoners, slaves, and the sick (Job 29:12-17; Mal. 3:5).

JUSTIFICATION Divine, forensic act of God, based on the work of Christ upon the cross, whereby a sinner is pronounced righteous by the imputation of the righteousness of Christ. The doctrine of justification is developed most fully by the apostle Paul as the central truth explaining how both Jew and Gentile can be made right before God on the exact same basis—faith in Jesus Christ.

The term "justification" does not mean "to subjectively change into a righteous person" but instead "to declare righteous" upon the act of faith based upon the work of another—the divine substitute, Jesus Christ. Justification then involves both the forensic, legal declaration of the righteousness of the believer and the imputation of the righteousness of Christ as the grounds and basis of their acceptance. The fact that it is the righteousness of Christ which is imputed to the believer accounts for the resulting perfection of the relationship between the believer and God: "Therefore, since we have been declared righteous by faith, we have peace with God through our Lord Jesus Christ" (Rom. 5:1 CSB). Justification is wholly the work of God, obtained solely by faith alone (Rom. 3:28).

JUSTUS Common Jewish personal name. **1.** Surname of Joseph Barsabbas, one of two men put forward to replace Judas Iscariot among the Twelve (Acts 1:23). **2.** A pious man, probably a Roman citizen, whose home adjoined the synagogue in Corinth (Acts 18:7). Paul left the synagogue and moved into the home of Titius Justus. **3.** Surname of a fellow minister with Paul (Col. 4:11).

JUVENILE DELINQUENCY God expects parents to control their children and children to obey their parents (Eph. 6:1-4). But even in the Bible, this did not always happen. The sons of Eli (1 Sam. 2:22-25), the boys who jeered at Elisha (2 Kgs. 2:23-24), and the prodigal son (Luke 15:12-13) are all examples of juvenile delinquency. The Mosaic law categorized striking (Exod. 21:15), cursing (Exod. 21:17) and dishonoring (Deut. 27:16) one's parents as acts of familial rebellion and mandated that a son who refused correction should be stoned in public (Deut. 21:18-21).

In spite of the responsibility placed on parents for child rearing (Deut. 6:7), the Bible recognizes that, ultimately, children are responsible for their own actions (Ezek. 18:10-13). Jesus used the example of the prodigal son to teach that everyone stands delinquent before God and must come to him for forgiveness (Luke 15:11-32).

Iron Age fortress in the area of ancient Kadesh-barnea

KADESH or **KADESH-BARNEA** Place-name meaning "consecrated." The site where the Hebrews stayed for most of the 38 years after leaving Mount Sinai and before entering the promised land. Moses sent out the 12 spies into Canaan from Kadesh-barnea (Num. 13:3-21,26). The Hebrews also attempted their abortive southern penetration into Canaan from there (Num. 13:26; 14:40-45).

KARKOR Place-name meaning "soft, level ground." A mountainous village in the eastern region of Gilead during the period of the judges. Gideon and 300 Israelite men conducted their second surprise attack on the Midianites at Karkor.

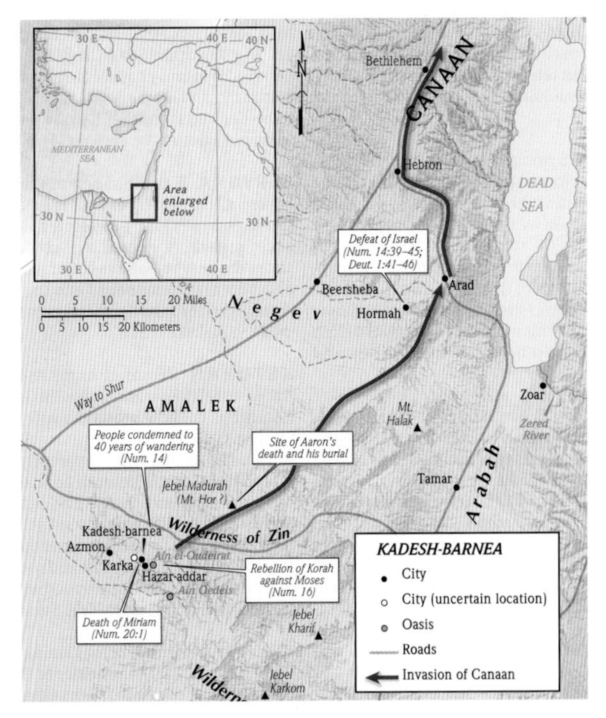

KEDAR Personal name meaning "mighty" or "swarthy" or "black." The second son of Ishmael and a grandson of Abraham (Gen. 25:13; 1 Chron. 1:29). The name occurs later in the Bible presumably as a reference to a tribe that took its name from Kedar. Apparently the descendants of Kedar occupied the area south of Palestine and east of Egypt (Gen. 25:18).

KEDESH Place-name meaning "sacred place" or "sanctuary." **1.** A city in the southern part of Judah (Josh. 15:23), probably the same as Kadesh-barnea. **2.** Canaanite town in eastern Galilee defeated by Joshua (Josh. 12:22). **3.** City in Issachar allotted to the Gershonite Levites (1 Chron. 6:72).

KEILAH Personal and place-name, perhaps meaning "fortress." **1.** Descendant of Caleb (1 Chron. 4:19). **2.** Fortified city in the lowland plain (Shephelah) of the territory of Judah. David rescued the city from a Philistine attack but later withdrew, fearing the populace would hand him over to Saul (1 Sam. 23:1-13).

KENITES Nomadic tribe, probably of blacksmiths, whose land, along with that of the Kadmonites and Kenizzites, was promised to Abraham by the Lord (Gen. 15:19). Their home was the southeastern hill country of Judah. Balaam pronounced doom and captivity for them (Num. 24:21-22). Moses's father-in-law, Jethro, is described as a Kenite (Judg. 1:16). This association suggests a close relationship between the Kenites and Midianites.

KENIZZITE Clan name of uncertain meaning. God promised Abraham that the Israelites would dispossess this group (Gen. 15:19). The Kenizzites lived in the Negev, the southern desert region of Judah, before the conquest of the land by Joshua. The tribe of Judah absorbed some of the Kenizzites and Edom absorbed others. The Kenizzites probably derived their name from Kenaz—a descendant of Esau (Gen. 36:11,15).

KENOSIS View asserting that the eternal Son of God by virtue of the incarnation gave up some or all of the divine attributes that were incommensurate with a fully human existence. This view is primarily based on Phil. 2:5-11, especially verse 7, which states that Christ "emptied himself." The idea of self-emptying is taken from the Greek verb *kenooi,* which means "make empty." Although the kenosis view of Christ sought to do full justice to the real humanity of Jesus, in reality it is a serious assault on the true deity of Jesus Christ. Most evangelicals have resisted the kenotic view and have replaced it with what may be termed a subkenotic view, stating that what Christ laid aside in the incarnation was not some or all of the divine attributes, such as omniscience, omnipotence, and omnipresence. Instead, what Christ "emptied himself" of was the independent use of these attributes in order to live a normal human life. See *Incarnation.*

KERIOTH Place-name meaning "cities." A fortified city of Moab (Jer. 48:24,41; Amos 2:2, KJV, Kirioth). Judas, the disciple who betrayed Jesus, may have been from Kerioth. Many scholars take the designation "Iscariot" to be derived from the Hebrew meaning "man of Kerioth."

KERYGMA Transliteration of the Greek *kerugma*, "the content of what is preached"; "the message"; closely connected with the act of preaching. Repentance comes, God saves those who believe (1 Cor. 1:21), and believers are strengthened and confirmed (Rom. 16:25) through the message preached (Matt. 12:41; Luke 11:32).

KETURAH Personal name meaning "incense" or "the perfumed one." In Gen. 25:1, Keturah is called Abraham's wife, while 1 Chron. 1:32 calls her a concubine. She was Abraham's second wife, apparently taken after Sarah's death. Keturah bore six sons to Abraham, the most notable being Midian. The list of Keturah's children substantiates the link between the Hebrews and the tribes that inhabited the areas east and southeast of Canaan. As children of a second wife, they were viewed as inferior to Isaac, Sarah's son.

KEY(S) An instrument for gaining access (Judg. 3:25). In the OT, the holder of the keys had the power to admit or deny entrance to the house of God (1 Chron. 9:22-27; Isa. 22:22). In late Judaism, this key imagery was extended to angelic beings and to God as keepers of the keys of heaven and hell. In the NT, keys are used only figuratively as a symbol of access (Luke 11:52) or of authority, particularly the authority of Christ over the final destiny of persons. The risen Christ holds the key of David and controls access to the New Jerusalem (Rev. 3:7). By overcoming death, he has the keys to the world of the dead (Rev. 1:18).

KIBROTH-HATTAAVAH Place-name meaning "graves of craving, lust, gluttony." The first stopping place of the Israelites after they left Sinai (Num. 33:16). The Israelites craved meat, which the Lord gave them (Num. 11:31), but because they overindulged, an epidemic broke out and many Israelites died. The dead were buried there, giving the place its name (Num. 11:34; Deut. 9:22; Ps. 78:30-31).

KIBZAIM Place-name meaning "double gathering" or "double heap." One of the Levitical cities in the tribal territory of Ephraim also designated as a city of refuge (Josh. 21:22).

KIDNEYS The kidneys are often associated with the heart as constituting the center of human personality (Pss. 7:9; 26:2; Rev. 2:23). The Hebrews believed the kidneys were the seat of the emotions (Job 19:27; Ps. 73:21; Prov. 23:16). The kidneys were also used figuratively as the source of the knowledge and understanding of the moral life (Ps. 16:7; Jer. 12:2).

KIDRON VALLEY Place-name meaning "turbid, dusky, gloomy." Deep ravine beside Jerusalem separating the temple mount and the city of David on the west from the Mount of Olives on the east. David crossed the brook of Kidron when he fled Jerusalem to escape from Absalom (2 Sam. 15:23). After the Last Supper, Jesus went through the Kidron Valley on his way to the Mount of Olives (John 18:1).

KINDNESS In the OT, this word is a translation of the Hebrew term *chesed*. Throughout the OT, the idea of *chesed* is that of compassion and faithfulness to one's obligations as well as to relatives, friends, and even to slaves (Gen. 21:23; 39:21; 1 Sam. 15:6). Kindness can be in the form of kind deeds done for another person. In the NT, kindness is translated from the Greek word *chrestotes*. This word can describe gentleness, goodness, uprightness, generosity, and graciousness. The NT describes kindness as an attribute of God (Titus 3:4; CSB, love). The Lord's people should possess kindness and not refuse to dispense it to others (Matt. 5:7; 1 Tim. 5:9).

KING, CHRIST AS Biblical teaching that Jesus of Nazareth fulfilled the OT promises of a perfect King and reigns over his people and the universe. The OT hope for the future included a vision of a new king like David, called "the anointed one," or "the Messiah" (2 Sam. 7:16; 22:51). When Jesus Christ was born, his birth was announced in these categories. His earthly ministry then amplified these themes (Matt. 4:17; Luke 1:32-33). Similarly, John the Baptist proclaimed the presence of God's kingdom in the coming of Jesus (Matt. 3).

KING, KINGSHIP Male monarch of a major territorial unit; especially one whose position is hereditary and who rules for life. From the time of Joshua to the time of Saul, the judges led Israel. Their leadership was temporary and local in nature, their main function being to lead those parts of Israel threatened by some outside force until the threat was gone. As Israel became more settled in Canaan, the people began to feel a need for a hereditary and totalitarian leadership. The first national leader was King Saul.

Israel, unlike most other nations, placed limitations on the power of its kings (1 Sam. 8:10-18). It was normal for the elders of the nation to make a covenant with the king (2 Sam. 5:3; 2 Kgs. 11:17) in which the rights and duties of the king were recorded and deposited in the sanctuary—possibly at the time of Meroda anointment ceremony (1 Sam. 10:25). It was clearly understood that the king was not exempt from observing civil laws (1 Kgs. 21:4), nor was the king the absolute lord of life and death. The prophetic denunciation of certain kings demonstrates that they were subject to the law (2 Sam.

12:1-15; 1 Kgs. 21:17-24; cp. Deut. 17:14-20). Israel's faith included the confession that God was its ultimate King. The earthly king derived his authority from God as the Lord's anointed (1 Sam. 16:6; 2 Sam. 1:14).

KINGDOM OF GOD Concept of God's kingly or sovereign rule, encompassing both the realm over which rule is exerted (Matt. 24:7) and the exercise of authority to reign (Rev. 17:12,17-18). God rules sovereignly over all his works as King. He desires his rule to be acknowledged in a bond or relationship of love, loyalty, spirit, and trust. The fullest revelation of God's divine rule is in the person of Jesus Christ. His birth was heralded as the birth of a king (Luke 1:32-33). The crucifixion was perceived as the death of a king (Mark 15:26-32). Jesus preached that God's kingdom was at hand (Matt. 11:12). His miracles, preaching, forgiving sins, and resurrection are an inbreaking of God's sovereign rule in this dark, evil age.

KINGS, BOOKS OF Covering the time frame between the final days of King David and the end of the nation of Judah, the books of 1 and 2 Kings are a vital part of the history of Israel. The title of these books is indicative of their contents: the kings and the kingdoms of Israel and Judah. The historical beginning point for the narrative of 1 Kings is approximately 970 BC. The final event in 2 Kings—Evil-merodach's release of King Jehoiachin from prison—occurs in approximately 560 BC. Thus the narrative of 1 and 2 Kings spans 410 years of history. These 410 years witness monumental changes within the nation of Israel, including the division of the kingdom in 930 BC, the height of the monarchy under Solomon (970–930 BC), and the exiles of both Israel and Judah (722 BC and 587/586 BC).

The author of 1 and 2 Kings gave a qualitative judgment regarding how well each king followed God's covenant. All of the kings of the northern kingdom of Israel were wicked kings, while the kings of Judah continued the dynasty of King David and were generally more obedient to the commands of the Lord. While the history of God's people was fraught with failure, God remained faithful to his promise. Even though both nations went into exile, God remembered his covenant with Abraham, and he preserved his people. God would bring his ultimate redemption to pass in the future in the person of his Son, Jesus Christ.

KING'S GARDEN Place in Jerusalem adjacent to and probably irrigated by the overflow of the Pool of Shelah (Siloam) (Neh. 3:15).

KING'S HIGHWAY Major transportation route east of the Jordan River. Literally "the way of the king," this highway has been in continuous use for more than 3,000 years. It runs from Damascus to the Gulf of Aqaba and is the main caravan route for the Transjordan. It is mentioned in Num. 20:17 and 21:22 as the route Moses and the Israelites would take through Edom and the land of Sihon.

KING'S POOL Probably the same as the Pool of Shelah, a reservoir in the king's garden in Jerusalem (Neh. 2:14). It was rebuilt by Shallum, ruler of the district of Mizpah (Neh. 3:15).

KINSMAN This term usually refers to a blood relative. Certain obligations were laid on the kinsman. In the case of an untimely death of a husband without a son, the law of levirate marriage specified that the husband's brother was obligated to marry his widow to raise up a male descendant for his deceased brother and thus perpetuate the family name and inheritance. The living brother was the dead brother's *go'el*—his redeemer (Gen. 38:8; Deut. 25:5-10; Ruth 3:9-12).

The kinsman was also the blood avenger. A wrong done to a single member of the family was considered a crime against the entire tribe or clan. The clan had an obligation, therefore, to punish the wrongdoer. In the case of a murder committed, the kinsman should seek vengeance. The kinsman was also responsible to redeem the estate that his nearest relative might have sold because of poverty (Lev. 25:25; Ruth 4:4). It was the kinsman's responsibility also to ransom a kinsman who had sold himself into slavery (Lev. 25:47-48).

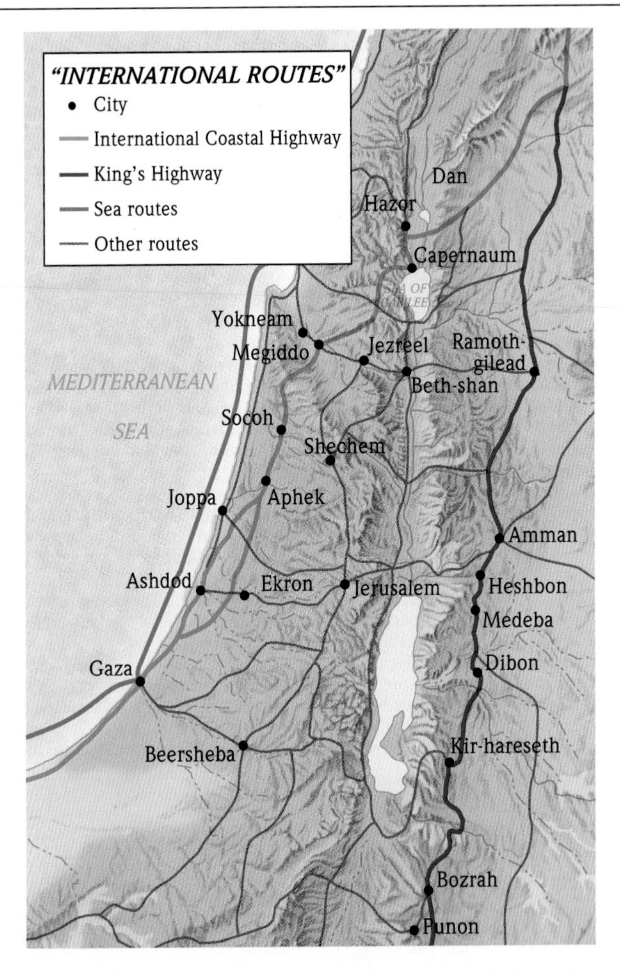

KIRIATH Place-name meaning "city" in tribal territory of Benjamin (Josh. 18:28; KJV, Kirjath). The same as Kiriath-jearim (Josh. 18:28).

KIRIATHAIM Place-name meaning "double city" or "two cities." **1.** Levitical city and city of refuge in the tribal territory of Naphtali (1 Chron. 6:76; KJV, Kirjathaim). **2.** City taken from the Emim by Chedorlaomer (Gen. 14:5, Shaveh-kiriathaim means "the plain of Kiriathaim"). Later the Israelites took it from the Amorites and assigned it to the tribe of Reuben (Num. 32:37; Josh. 13:19).

KIRIATH-ARBA Place-name meaning "city of Arba" or "city of four." The ancient name for the city of Hebron, the chief city in the hill country of Judah (Josh. 15:54). It was both a Levitical city (Josh. 21:11) and a city of refuge (Josh. 20:7). Caleb captured the city for Israel (Josh. 15:13-14).

KIRIATH-JEARIM Place-name meaning "city of forests." After the Philistines returned the ark of the covenant to the Israelites, it was kept at Kiriath-jearim for a time (1 Sam. 6:21–7:2). David attempted to move the ark to Jerusalem from there, but because he did so improperly, God struck Uzzah dead (2 Sam. 6:1-8).

KISHON Place-name meaning "curving, winding." A small river that flows through the valley of Jezreel. At the Kishon, Deborah and Barak defeated the Canaanite Sisera when his chariots became mired in the river marshes (Judg. 4:7,13; 5:21). Later the river was the place where Elijah brought the prophets of Baal to be executed following God's display and victory on Mount Carmel (1 Kgs. 18:40).

KISS The touching of the lips to another person's lips, cheeks, shoulders, hands, or feet as a gesture of friendship, acceptance, respect, and reverence. The location of the kiss carried different meanings as Jesus made clear in the episode of the woman kissing his feet (Luke 7:36-50). With the exception of three occurrences (Prov. 7:13; Song 1:2; 8:1), the term is used without any erotic overtones. The holy kiss was widely practiced among the early Christians as a manner of greeting, a sign of acceptance, and an impartation of blessing. This custom could well have been used to express the unity of the Christian fellowship. The kiss still survives in the Near Eastern culture as a sign of love, respect, and reverence.

KITE Bird of prey, best described as a scavenger of the hawk family. It was medium-sized with red coloring (Deut. 14:13; Isa. 34:15). This bird was considered unclean and not for human consumption.

KITTIM Tribal name for the island of Cyprus, sometimes spelled Chittim. Genesis 10:4 traces the roots of the people of Kittim to Noah's son Japheth. Jeremiah and Ezekiel both mention it in their prophecies (Jer. 2:10; Ezek. 27:6; cp. Isa. 23:1,12).

KNEAD, KNEADING BOWL Process of making bread dough by mixing flour, water, and oil along with a piece of the previous day's dough with the hands in a kneading bowl or trough. The mixture was allowed to stand in the bowl to rise and ferment (Exod. 12:34).

KNEEL Common posture when requesting a blessing from a person believed able to bestow the blessing. The Hebrew word for *kneel* comes from the same root as the word

Limassol, a modern city on the southern coast of Cyprus. Kittim or Chittim was the tribal name of Cyprus.

for *bless*. Kneeling is also considered a sign of reverence, obedience, or respect. Kneeling was the posture of prayer (Dan. 6:10; Eph. 3:14), acknowledging a superior (Mark 1:40), or worship of God (1 Kgs. 8:54), Jesus (Phil. 2:10), or idols (1 Kgs. 19:18).

KNIFE Small instrument made of flint, copper, bronze, or iron used mainly for domestic purposes. Knives were used most commonly for killing and skinning animals and for killing sacrificial animals (1 Sam. 9:24).

KNOB/KNOP Ornamental detail on the seven-branched lampstand in the tabernacle (Exod. 25:31-36). Some suggest that the knob was an imitation of the almond. The word may also refer to the capital of a column (Zeph. 2:14).

Large, wide-bladed knife from the Roman era

KNOWLEDGE God knows all things (Job 21:22; Ps. 139:1-18); his understanding is beyond measure (Ps. 147:5). He knows the thoughts of our minds and the secrets of our hearts (Pss. 44:21; 94:11). He knows past events (Gen. 30:22), present happenings (Job 31:4), and future events (Zech. 13:1; Luke 1:33). The Bible also speaks often about human knowledge. Knowledge of God is the greatest knowledge (Prov. 9:10) and is the chief duty of humankind (Hos. 6:6). In the OT, the Israelites know God through what he does for his people (Deut. 4:32-39; Hos. 2:19-20). In the NT, one knows God through knowledge of Jesus Christ (John 8:19; Col. 2:2-3). The apostle Paul closely connected knowledge to faith. Knowledge gives direction, conviction, and assurance to faith (2 Cor. 4:14).

KOHATH Personal name of unknown meaning. The second son of Levi (Gen. 46:11) and father of Amram, Izhar, Hebron, and Uzziel (Exod. 6:18), who became the heads of the Kohathite branch of the Levitical priesthood.

KOHATHITES Descendants of Kohath, the son of Levi (Exod. 6:16). Since Kohath was the grandfather of Aaron, Moses, and Miriam (Exod. 6:20; Num. 26:59), the Kohathites were considered the most important of the three major Levitical families: Kohathites, Gershonites, and Merarites. The Kohathites, along with the Gershonites and Merarites, were placed around the tabernacle and were charged with caring for and moving it. David appointed 120 Kohathites to bring the ark to Jerusalem (1 Chron. 15:5).

KOHELETH English transliteration of the Hebrew title of Ecclesiastes (also spelled Qoheleth). Koheleth is a Hebrew word that is translated as preacher (KJV, RSV, NASB), teacher (CSB, NIV, NRSV), speaker (REB), or philosopher (TEV) in Eccles. 1:1.

KOPH Nineteenth letter of Hebrew alphabet. Used as a heading for Ps. 119:145-152. Each verse in this section begins with the letter Koph (KJV), Qoph (NASB, NIV), or Qof (CSB).

KOR A dry measure equal to a homer or to about 6.3 imperial bushels, though estimates vary greatly. It apparently represented the load a donkey could carry.

KORAH Personal name meaning "bald." **1.** Son of Esau (Gen. 36:5,14) who became chief of a clan of Edom (Gen. 36:18). **2.** Grandson of Esau, son of Eliphaz, and chief of a clan of Edom (1 Chron. 1:36). **3.** Leader of rebellion against Moses and Aaron while Israel was camped in the wilderness of Paran (Num. 16). Korah, Dathan, and Abiram led a confederacy of 250 princes of the people against Aaron's claim to the priesthood and Moses's claim to authority in general. The rebels contended that the entire congregation was sanctified and therefore qualified to perform priestly functions. As punishment for their insubordination, God caused the earth to open and swallow the leaders and their property. A fire from the Lord consumed the 250 followers. **4.** Levite descended from Izhar, of the family of Kohath (Exod. 6:21), probably to be identified with 3, above. The sons of Korah and Asaph were the two most prominent groups of temple singers (cp. 2 Chron. 20:19). Many of the psalms with the heading "A Psalm of the Sons of Korah" may have been taken from their hymnbook (Pss. 42; 44–49; 84–85; 87–88). **5.** Son of Hebron in the lineage of Caleb (1 Chron. 2:43). **6.** Possibly a town in Judah near Hebron. The five Korahites who joined David at Ziklag may have been persons from this town (1 Chron. 12:6).

The definitive line of a wall at Lachish running from the south going northeast up to the high place

LABAN Personal name meaning "white." Rebekah's brother (Gen. 24:29) and father of Leah and Rachel (Gen. 29:16). Laban agreed to give his daughter, Rachel, as payment for Jacob's seven years of labor. But Laban deceived Jacob, making him marry the older daughter, Leah. After Jacob worked an additional seven years, Laban allowed him to marry Rachel (Gen. 29:15-30).

LACE Ornamental braid used as a trim. Blue or purple cords were used to fasten the high priest's breastpiece to the ephod (Exod. 39:21) and the golden plate to his turban (Exod. 28:37).

LACHISH An important OT city located in the Shephelah ("lowlands") southwest of Jerusalem. The Israelites under Joshua's command killed the king of Lachish and conquered his city (Josh. 10:5,23,32-33). Later Lachish was apportioned to the tribe of Judah (Josh. 15:39). The "Lachish letters"—a group of messages in ancient Hebrew inscribed with ink on pottery shards dating to around 590 BC—are among the most significant finds from Lachish. They provide important linguistic and historical information about this period.

LAISH Personal and place-name meaning "strong" or "lion." **1.** Father of Paltiel/Palti (Phalti in KJV) and father-in-law of Michal, King Saul's daughter, after Saul took her from David and gave her to Palti (1 Sam. 19:11-12; 25:44). **2.** Originally a Canaanite city in northern Palestine known for its quiet, isolated lifestyle (Judg. 18:7). It was spied out by the Danites as a place to live after the Philistines forced them from the coastal region. The Danites renamed the city and area Dan. **3.** Town apparently in tribal territory of Benjamin mentioned by Isaiah (Isa. 10:30).

LAMB OF GOD Title bestowed on Jesus by John the Baptist (John 1:29). The expression comes from the important place that the "lamb" occupied in the sacrifices of the Jewish people. A lamb was used for sacrifice during the annual Passover (Exod. 12:1-36) as well as in the daily sacrifices of Israel (Lev. 14:12-21). Christ fulfilled the promise made by the prophet Isaiah (see Isa. 53) that God would provide a sacrifice who would bear the curse of sin and provide salvation for the world.

LAME, LAMENESS Physical condition in which walking is difficult or impossible. A proverb excluding the blind and lame from "the house" (i.e., the temple) is traced to the assault on Jerusalem (2 Sam. 5:8). In the NT, the healing of lame people was an important part of Jesus's messianic work (Matt. 15:29-31). By healing lame people in the temple, Jesus restored these excluded ones to full participation in the worshiping community (Matt. 21:14).

LAMECH Personal name meaning "powerful." The son of Methuselah and father of Noah (Gen. 4:18; 5:25,29). His two sons are credited with the rise of the nomadic way of life, music, and metalworking.

LAMED Twelfth letter of the Hebrew alphabet used as a heading for Ps. 119:89-96. Each verse in this section of the psalm begins with the letter *lamed.*

LAMENTATIONS, BOOK OF An OT book consisting of poetic laments over the destruction of Jerusalem and the temple in 587 BC (Lam. 2:7) and over the pitiable condition of the people of Judah that resulted (Lam. 2:11). The misery after the destruction is all the more deplorable compared to the glory beforehand (Lam. 1:1). The author calls on the people to recognize that because of their sin God is just in what he has done (Lam. 1:5), so the people should turn to him, repent, and appeal for mercy (Lam. 2:18). It was probably written by the prophet Jeremiah. The fall of Jerusalem is recorded in 2 Kgs. 25 and Jer. 52. Lamentations expresses the deep emotions that issued from this tragedy.

LAMPS, LIGHTING, LAMPSTAND Archaeologists have discovered numerous examples of these lighting implements used in ancient times. These lamps were of the open-bowl design with a pinched spout to support the wick. Lamps burned olive oil almost exclusively (Exod. 25:6). A golden lampstand with three branches extending from either side of the central tier was placed in the tabernacle (Exod. 25:31-40). Each branch may have had a seven-spouted lamp (Zech. 4:2). This seven-branched candelabrum (menorah), supporting seven lamps, became symbolic of the nation of Israel.

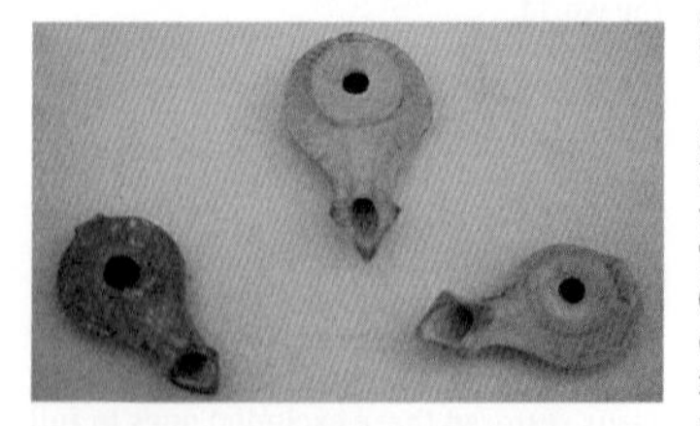

First-century BC pottery oil lamps

LANCE, LANCET Weapon consisting of a long shaft with a metal head; javelin; spear (Judg. 5:8 NASB; 1 Kgs. 18:28 RSV; Jer. 50:42 KJV; Jer. 46:4 CSB).

LANDMARK Pillar or heap of stones serving as a boundary marker (Gen. 31:51-52). Moving the landmark meant changing the traditional land allotments (Josh. 13–19) and cheating a poor landowner of what little land he owned.

LANGUAGES OF THE BIBLE The OT was first written in Hebrew with the exceptions of much of Ezra 4–7 and Daniel 2:4b–7:28, which appear in Aramaic. The NT was written in Greek, though Jesus and the early believers may have spoken Aramaic.

Hebrew is a Semitic language related to Phoenician and the dialects of ancient Canaan. Semitic languages have the ability to convey abundant meaning through few words. Importance rests on the verb, which generally comes first in the sentence because action is the most significant element. Similarly, modifiers (such as adjectives) follow nouns, lending greater weight to the nouns.

Aramaic is similar to Hebrew and shares a considerable vocabulary with it. It began as the language of Syria and was gradually adopted as the language of international communication. After about 600 BC, it replaced Hebrew as the spoken language of Palestine. Hebrew then continued as the religious language of the Jews, but the Aramaic alphabet was borrowed for writing it.

Greek belongs to the Indo-European language group. It spread throughout the Mediterranean world after about 335 BC with the conquests of Alexander the Great. The NT is written in a dialect called *koine* (meaning "common"), which was the dialect of the common person. New Testament Greek is heavily infused with Semitic thought modes, and many Aramaic words are rendered with Greek letters (e.g., *talitha koum,* Mark 5:41; *ephphatha,* Mark 7:34; *Eloi, Eloi, lemá sabach-*

tháni, Mark 15:34; *maranatha*, 1 Cor. 16:22). So also are such Latin words as *kenturion* (centurion) and *denarion* (denarius). Greek's accurateness of expression and widespread usage made it the ideal tongue for the early communication of the gospel.

LAODICEA City in southwest Asia Minor on an ancient highway running from Ephesus to Syria ten miles west of Colossae and six miles south of Hierapolis. Christian communities existed in all three cities (Col. 2:1; 4:13-16). Laodicea was well known in the ancient world for its textile industry, the production of black wool, and its banking industry. As one of the seven churches of Asia Minor, the church at Laodicea was criticized for its spiritual lethargy or lukewarmness (Rev. 3:14-22).

An unexcavated Roman theater, smaller of the two theaters at ancient Laodicea

LAPWING Bird with a short bill and a crest of feathers on its head. The lapwing is known for its irregular flapping flight and shrill cry. KJV included the lapwing among the unclean birds (Deut. 14:18). Modern translations generally identify this bird as the hoopoe.

LASCIVIOUSNESS KJV term for an unbridled expression of sexual urges (2 Cor. 12:21; Gal. 5:19). RSV translates the underlying Greek as "licentiousness"; NASB, "sensuality." Other translations use a variety of terms: "debauchery," "indecency," "lewdness."

LASHARON Place-name meaning "belonging to Sharon." One of the towns whose king was killed by Joshua during his conquest of Canaan (Josh. 12:18).

LAST SUPPER The last meal Christ shared with his disciples before the crucifixion (Mark 14:12-31). The event marked the institution of the Lord's Supper, which is to be celebrated until Christ returns. The meal focuses on Jesus's impending death and anticipates his resurrection. The bread served to his disciples by Jesus is a symbol of his body to be broken for his people. The wine is a symbol of his blood of the covenant to be poured out on the cross for the forgiveness of sins.

LATCHET KJV term for a leather thong or strap that fastened sandals. Untying sandals was a slave's task that could not be required of a disciple. John the Baptist thus claimed for himself a position lower than that of a slave before Jesus (John 1:27).

LATRINE Receptacle, generally a pit, used as a toilet (2 Kgs. 10:27; KJV, draught house). Jehu demonstrated his utter contempt for Baal by ordering that his temple be destroyed and converted into a latrine.

The public latrine of ancient Ephesus

LAUGH To express joy or scorn with a chuckle or explosive sound. Laughter is central to the account of the birth of Isaac. Both Abraham (Gen. 17:17) and Sarah (Gen. 18:12) laughed in contempt and disbelief at God's promise that Sarah would bear a son. The name Isaac (from the Hebrew word for laughter) served as a joyful reminder that the last laugh was on those slow to believe (Gen. 21:3,6).

LAVER Large basin or bowl used in purification rites. The priests used the laver for washing their hands and feet before priestly service (Exod. 40:30-31). Levites also used water from this laver to purify themselves (Num. 8:7). Solomon's temple featured a large laver, the molten sea (1 Chron. 4:2-5), and 10 smaller lavers (1 Kgs. 7:38-39).

LAW, TEN COMMANDMENTS, TORAH Few expressions in the Bible are more significant yet more misunderstood than "law." Biblical interpreters apply the word to specific commandments, customs, legal judgments, collections of regulations/ordinances, the book of Deuteronomy (which means "second law"), the entire complex of regulations revealed at Sinai, the Pentateuch (in contrast to the Prophets), and the OT as a whole as opposed to the NT.

The contrast between the OT, in which God's people were under the law, and the NT, where God's people are under grace, seems to determine many people's understanding of Scripture. Appeal is sometimes made to John 1:17, "For the law was given through Moses; grace and truth came through Jesus Christ" (CSB). However, a closer look at the biblical evidence raises questions about the common perception of the old covenant as a works-oriented system.

It is important to remember that God and Moses perceived obedience to the laws, not as a way of or precondition to salvation, but as the grateful response of those who had already been saved. God did not reveal the law to the Israelites in Egypt and then tell them that as soon as they had measured up to this standard he would rescue them. On the contrary, by grace alone, through faith they crossed the Red Sea to freedom. All that was required was belief in God's promise that he would hold up the walls of water on either side and see them safely through to the other shore.

In the OT, obedience to the law was an expression of covenant relationship. Israel's primary commitment was not to a code of laws but to the God who graciously called Israel to himself. They were to obey "his voice." In fact, he did not reveal his will to the people until he heard their declaration of complete and unconditional servitude to him as covenant lord (Exod. 19:8).

God's revelation of the law to Israel was a supreme act of grace and a unique sign of privilege (Deut. 4:6-8). In contrast to the nations who worshipped gods of wood and stone who never spoke (Deut. 4:28; Ps. 115:4-8), Israel's God had spoken, clearly revealing to his people what he deemed an acceptable response to him. Accordingly, for the genuinely faithful in Israel, obedience to the law was not a burden but a delight because of their deep gratitude for God's saving grace and covenant relationship (Ps. 24:3-6).

The laws were perceived as comprehensible and achievable (Deut. 30:11-20) by those whose hearts were right with God. God did not impose upon his people an impossibly high standard but revealed to them in great detail a system of behavior that was righteous and gracious (Deut. 4:6-8). At the same time, there is a recognition of human depravity and the need for divine enablement for covenant faithfulness. Jeremiah anticipated a future new covenant when all Israel will love God and demonstrate with their lives that his law or *tora* has been written on their hearts (Jer. 31:31-34). God had a realistic view of his people. Recognizing their propensity to sin, within the law he graciously provided a way of forgiveness and communion through the sacrificial and ceremonial ritual.

Of course, these facts about the law did not prevent the Israelites from perverting obedience to the law into a condition for blessing and a condition for salvation. The prophets constantly railed against their people for substituting external rituals prescribed by the law for true piety, which is demonstrated first in moral obedience (Isa. 1:10-17; Hos. 6:6; Mic. 6:6-8). In every age, Israelites misused the law, thinking that performance of rituals obligated God to receive them favorably. They imagined that God looked upon their hearts through the lenses of their sacrifices. They persisted in violating the moral laws even while they continued to observe the ceremonial regulations (Isa. 1; Jer. 7). In the end, Moses's predictions of disaster in Deut. 4 and 29–30 proved true in the exile of Judah in 586 BC.

Like Moses and the psalmists, the NT views God's original revelation of the law to Israel as a climactic moment of grace. Accordingly, when Jesus and Paul appear to be critical of the law, we should ask whether their struggle was with the law itself or with misuse of the law. From the beginning, Israelites had perverted the law by treating the law as a precondition of entrance into the kingdom of God rather than as a response to his grace. They also misrepresented the law by adhering to the law's legal requirements as a matter of duty rather than a grateful expression of heartfelt covenant love for God and one's neighbor. In addition, they treated physical descent from Abraham and membership in the Jewish nation as a guarantee of divine favor, rather than spiritual descent by faith as the precondition to blessing. It is to these abuses that many of the critical words concerning the law are addressed in the NT.

With Christ's first coming, many aspects of the law are brought to complete fruition. As the eschatological fulfillment of the old covenant, in his person Jesus brings to an end the ceremonial sacrifices and festivals and transforms old covenant customs into new covenant realities. Baptism, the sign of the covenant made with the church, appears to replace circumcision, the sign of the covenant made with physical Israel. The Lord's Supper replaces the Passover meal (Luke 22:13-20) and anticipates the eschatological covenant meal (Rev. 19:6-10). But other aspects of the law were to remain in force until Christ's return. When we read the OT law, we should always be open to both continuities and discontinuities with NT demands.

As God's Son who fulfills the law and as the Lord of the covenant originally made with Israel at Sinai, Jesus has the perfect perspective on the law and the authority to declare its intention. He declared that God's demands cannot be reduced to a list of rules, but they involve the commitment of one's whole being to him and a genuine concern for the well-being of others.

The writings of Paul are the source of most of the confusion on the NT's view of the law. He spoke of the law as a way of death, in contrast to the Spirit that gives life (Rom. 7:10), and the law as a curse from which Christ has redeemed us (Gal. 3:13). He contrasted the letter (of the old covenant), which kills, with the Spirit (of the new covenant), that delivers life (2 Cor. 3:6). Such statements are difficult to reconcile with Moses's and the psalmists' celebration of the law as the supreme gift of grace and the way of life for God's people. But when we understand Paul correctly, we will discover his perspective to be in line with that of Moses.

Paul agrees with Moses in affirming the law, declaring that without it we would not know what sin is (Rom. 7:7), evaluating it as holy, just, and good (1 Tim. 1:8), and rooting his understanding of the ethical implications of the gospel firmly in the Torah (2 Cor. 6:14-18). Furthermore, Paul, like Jesus, captures the spirit of the OT law by reducing its demands to love for God and one's neighbor (Gal. 5:13).

Paul declared that the problem was not with the law, but with himself, because the law of sin inside him constantly waged war against the law of God. The glorious news of the gospel is that God through Christ lifts the curse of sin, which the law says we deserve. But this does not mean that the law has been suspended as a fundamental statement of God's moral will. The law served as a reflection of God's very nature. Since his nature does not change, neither does his moral will. Accordingly, those who fulfill the "Law of Christ," and those who love God with all their hearts and their neighbors as themselves will fulfill the essence of the law.

LAWLESS, LAWLESSNESS Terms that describe people not restrained or controlled by law, especially God's law. As rebellion against God, sin is lawlessness (1 John 3:4). Those responsible for Christ's death are characterized as lawless (Acts 2:23), as are Gentiles in their idolatry (1 Pet. 4:3). The leader of the eschatological (end-time) rebellion is called the man of lawlessness (2 Thess. 2:3). The lawless one is already at work but is presently restrained (2 Thess. 2:6-7). The lawless one will be revealed before the return of Christ—who will destroy him with his breath (2 Thess. 2:8).

LAWYER An interpreter of the Mosaic law. Characterization of the lawyers is especially harsh in Luke's Gospel: they rejected God's purpose by refusing John's baptism (Luke

7:30); they burdened others without offering any relief (Luke 11:45-46); and they refused God's offer of salvation and hindered others from accepting it (Luke 11:52-53).

LAYING ON OF HANDS Symbolic ceremonial act used to invoke a divine blessing or establish a connection for the purpose of sacrifice, ordination, or to impart spiritual gifts. In the OT, this ceremony was associated with priestly sacrifices (Lev. 16:21). Moses laid his hands on Joshua to identify him as Moses's successor and to symbolize that he was imparting his authority to Joshua (Num. 27:18-23). In the NT, laying on of hands also signified the appointment of persons to specific tasks, such as the ordination of the "seven" in Acts 6:6. It was used in the commissioning of Barnabas and Saul for their mission (Acts 13:3). First Timothy 4:14 speaks of Timothy receiving a spiritual gift from elders who laid their hands on him. Paul mentions the spiritual gift that Timothy received "through the laying on of my hands" (2 Tim. 1:6 CSB). These references show that Timothy received authority, the spirit of power, love, and self-discipline, through the laying on of hands (1:7).

LAZARUS Personal name meaning "one whom God helps." **1.** One of the principal characters in a parable Jesus told to warn the selfish rich that justice will eventually prevail (Luke 16:19-31). **2.** Lazarus of Bethany, a personal friend of Jesus and the brother of Mary and Martha (John 11:1-3). To show the glory of God, Jesus raised Lazarus from the dead after he had been in the tomb for four days. Lazarus was at the Passover celebration in Bethany six days later. He was targeted for murder by the chief priests because of his notoriety (John 12:9-11).

LEAH Personal name meaning "wild cow" or "gazelle." Older daughter of Laban (Gen. 29:16) and Jacob's first wife. Jacob had asked for the younger Rachel's hand but was tricked by her father, Laban, into marrying Leah. Leah bore six sons to Jacob (Reuben, Simeon, Levi, Judah, Issachar, Zebulun) and a daughter (Dinah) (Gen. 29:31-35; 30:17-21). Her handmaid, Zilpah, bore two sons to Jacob (Gad, Asher) (Gen. 30:9-13).

LEANNOTH Transliteration of Hebrew word in title of Ps. 88 possibly meaning "to sing" or "for the poor," "for the sick." It may be part of the title of a tune to which the psalm was sung. Its meaning is uncertain.

LEATHER Animal skins tanned and used for clothing. Elijah the prophet was recognized by his hairy garment and leather belt or girdle (2 Kgs. 1:8). The similar dress of John

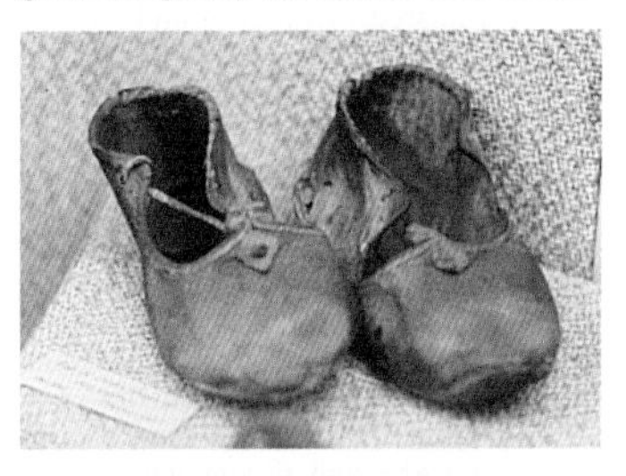

A child's leather shoes fromEgypt (Roman era)

The traditional site of the tomb of Lazarus in Bethany

the Baptist marked him as a prophet (Matt. 3:4; Mark 1:6).

LEAVEN Small portion of fermented dough used to ferment other dough and often symbolizing a corruptive influence. The common bread of OT times was made with leaven. Unleavened bread was also prepared in times of haste (1 Sam. 28:24) and was required for the Feast of Unleavened Bread that was celebrated in conjunction with the Passover festival (Lev. 23:4-8). This unleavened bread reminded the Israelites of their hasty departure from Egypt and warned them against corruptive influences (Exod. 12:14-20). In the NT, leaven is a symbol of any evil influence. Jesus warned his disciples against the leaven of the Pharisees, their teaching and hypocrisy (Luke 12:1).

LEBANON Place-name meaning "white" or perhaps "white mountain." A small country at the eastern end of the Mediterranean Sea and the western end of Asia. Lebanon is often mentioned in the OT as the northern boundary of Israel (Josh. 1:4), dividing it from Phoenicia and Syria. It was a proverbially lush land, noted for its magnificent forests (Isa. 60:13), especially the "cedars of Lebanon" (Isa. 2:13). These cedars, as well as other woods of Lebanon, were used in great abundance in the construction of David's palace and Solomon's temple and palace buildings (1 Kgs. 7:2).

LEEKS An Egyptian food eaten by the Hebrews during their captivity. After a steady diet of manna in the wilderness, they were ready to return to slavery and the foods of servitude (Num. 11:5).

LEES Solid matter that settles out of wine during the fermentation process. In Palestine, wine was allowed to remain on the lees to increase its strength and flavor. Such wine "on the lees" was preferred to the newly fermented product. To drink dregs or lees is to endure the bitterness of judgment or punishment (Ps. 75:8).

LEGION In the NT, a term referring to a collection of demons (Luke 8:30) and the host of angels (Matt. 26:53). Behind this usage was a Roman military term. Legions were made up of the best soldiers in the army. At different times in Rome's history, the legion numbered between 4,500 and 6,000 soldiers.

LEHI Place-name meaning "chin" or "jawbone." City where Samson killed 1,000 Philistines with the jawbone of a donkey and where God provided water from the jawbone (Judg. 15).

LEISURE TIME The Bible recognizes the need for regularly scheduled breaks from work. The weekly Sabbath (Exod. 20:8-11) and several yearly festivals (Deut. 16:1-17) were intended to focus on Israel's spiritual needs but also provided breaks from physical labor. The Bible cautions against the misuse of leisure time, which leads to idleness (Prov. 19:15), excessive partying (Isa. 5:11-12), or troublemaking (Prov. 6:10-15).

LEMUEL Personal name meaning "devoted to God." A king who received words of wisdom from his mother concerning wine, women, and the legal rights of the weak and poor (Prov. 31:1-9).

LEOPARD Large cat with yellow fur containing black spots. Known for its gracefulness and speed, it was common in Palestine in OT times, especially in the forests of Lebanon. Two sites in the OT suggest habitats of leopards—Beth-nimrah ("leopards' house," Num. 32:36) and "waters of Nimrim" ("waters of leopards," Jer. 48:34). The lurking, noiseless movement of the leopard symbolizes God's wrath (Hos. 13:7).

LEPROSY Generic term applied to a variety of skin disorders, ranging from psoriasis to true leprosy. Its symptoms ranged from white patches on the skin to running sores and even the loss of fingers and toes. For the Hebrews, leprosy was a dreaded malady that rendered its victims ceremonially unclean or unfit to worship God (Lev. 13:3). Anyone who came in contact with a leper was also considered unclean. Therefore, lepers were isolated from the rest of the community. Even houses and clothing could have "leprosy" and, thus, be unclean (Lev. 14:33-57). Jesus did not consider this distinction between clean and unclean valid. He touched and healed lepers (Mark 1:40-45) and even commanded his disciples to do so (Matt. 10:8). See *Diseases*.

LEVI Personal name meaning "a joining." **1.** Third son of Jacob and Leah (Gen. 29:34) and original ancestor of Israel's priests. He is characterized in Scripture as savage and merciless, avenging the rape of his sister, Dinah, by annihilating the male population of an entire city (Gen. 34:25-31). Later, Jacob spoke harshly of Levi rather than blessing him (Gen. 49:5-7). After the people of Israel sinned in the wilderness by making the molten calf, Moses commanded the people of Levi to slaughter those who had participated in the debacle (Exod. 32:28). Levi's descendants became a tribe of priests. **2.** Name of two of Jesus's ancestors (Luke 3:24,29). **3.** A tax collector in Capernaum who became a follower of Jesus (Mark 2:14); another name for Matthew.

LEVIATHAN Name of an ancient sea creature that means "coiled one." Isaiah 27:1 refers to Leviathan as "the monster that is in the sea" (CSB). Psalm 74:14 mentions a many-headed Leviathan among the supernatural enemies of God dwelling in the sea. Job 3:8; 41:1-9 present the sea creature as a formidable foe that should not be aroused. Yet Leviathan was created by God and subject to him (Ps. 104:24-30).

LEVIRATE LAW, LEVIRATE MARRIAGE Legal provision requiring a dead man's brother (levirate) to marry the deceased's childless widow and father a son who would carry on the family name (Deut. 25:5-10). The practice is an important element in the story of Ruth (Ruth 4:1-11).

LEVITES Assistants to the priests in Israel's sacrificial system. Originally Israel's priests and temple personnel were to be drawn from the firstborn of every family in Israel (Exod. 13:11-15). Later God chose the tribe of Levi to carry out this responsibility for Israel (Num. 3:11-13). The Levites were not given a tribal inheritance in the promised land, since God was considered their inheritance. They were placed in 48 Levitical cities throughout the land (Num. 18:20; 35:1-8). The tithe of the rest of the nation was used to provide for their material needs (Num. 18:24-32).

During the wilderness journey, the Levites were in charge of taking down the tabernacle, transporting it, setting it up, and conducting worship at the tent where God dwelt (Num. 1:47-54; 3:14-39). In some passages (Deut. 17:9,18; 24:8) the terms "priest" and "Levite" (or Levitical priests) seem identical, but in Exod. 28 and Lev. 8–10, it is clear that only the family of Aaron fulfilled the priestly duties of offering sacrifices in the tabernacle. Because there appears to be a different way of handling the relationship between the priests and the Levites in these texts, interpreters differ in the way they understand the Levites. Although it is possible that the role of the Levites changed or that the distinction between the priests and Levites was not maintained in each period with equal strictness, the interpretation that maintains a general distinction between the priests and Levites seems to fit most texts.

The Levites assisted the priests in their responsibilities (Num. 16:9) by preparing grain offerings and the showbread, by purifying all the holy instruments used in the temple, by singing praises to the Lord at morning and evening offerings, by assisting the priests with burnt offerings on Sabbaths and feast days, and by taking care of the temple precinct and the chambers of the priests (1 Chron. 6:31-48; 2 Chron. 29:12-19). See *Levitical Cities*.

LEVITICAL CITIES Residence and pasturelands provided the priestly tribe of Levi in lieu of a tribal inheritance. Because of their priestly duties, the tribe of Levi did not receive any part of the land of Canaan as an inheritance (Josh. 18:7). To compensate them for this, they received the tithes of Israelites for their support (Num. 18:21), and 48 cities were allotted to them from the inheritance of the other tribes. On the average, four cities from each tribe were Levitical cities.

These cities did not cease to belong to the tribes within which they were located. The Levites were simply allowed to live in them and have fields to pasture their herds. Although 6 of the 48 cities were asylums for

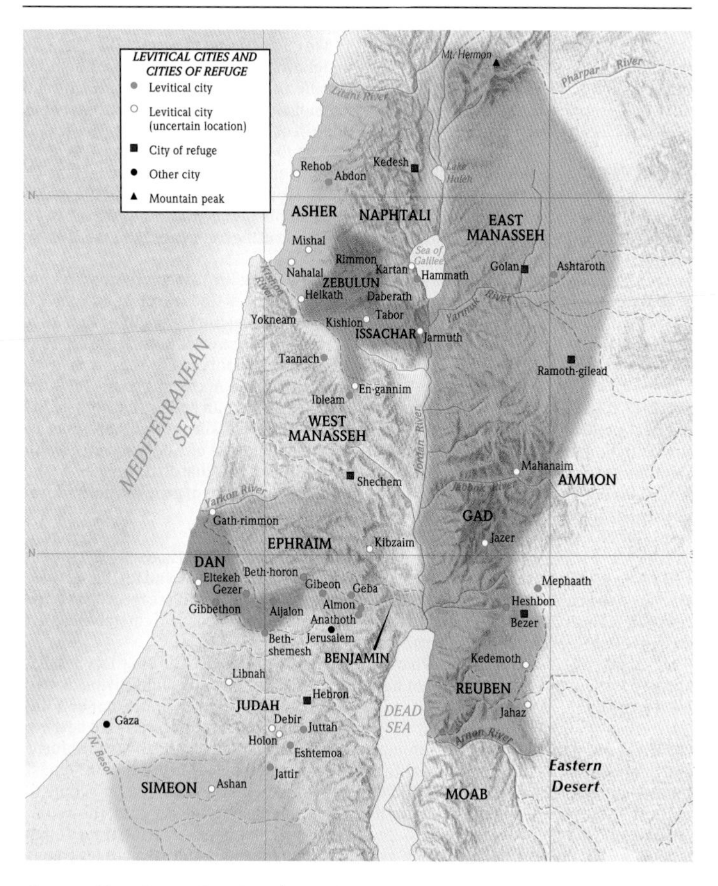

those guilty of manslaughter (Kedesh, Shechem, Hebron in Canaan, Bezer, Ramoth-gilead, and Golan), Levitical cities and cities of refuge were not synonymous. The privilege of asylum for persons who had committed manslaughter was not extended to all 48 Levitical cities. Living among the tribes in these cities meant the Levites could better infiltrate each of the tribes to instruct them in God's covenant. Since the Levites had no steady income, the cities were also provided for their economic relief and support. See *Cities of Refuge.*

LEVITICUS, BOOK OF Third book of the OT containing instructions for priests and worship. These regulations are referred to as the ceremonial law—how to observe the rituals and regulations that were considered important acts of worship for God's people, the nation of Israel. Leviticus describes the establishment of the priesthood through Aaron, his sons, and their successors. The priests were to preside at the tabernacle and temple when various sacrifices were presented by the people to offer thanksgiving to their Creator and to atone for their sins.

One of the most important themes of Leviticus is holiness. God's people were to be different than pagan worshipers and wholly dedicated to God's service. They worshipped a holy God, and he expected his people to be holy.

LEWDNESS Lust; sexual unchastity; licentiousness. Lewdness sometimes refers to an especially heinous crime such as brutal gang rape resulting in murder (Judg. 19:25-27), murder by priests (Hos. 6:9), or any vicious crime (Acts 18:14). Most often lewdness is used figuratively for idolatry (Hos. 2:10).

LIBERTINE KJV transliteration of Greek for "freedmen" (Acts 6:9).

LIBERTY, LIBERATION Freedom from physical, political, and spiritual oppression. One of the dominant themes of the OT is that Yahweh is the God who liberated the Israelites from their bondage in Egypt. In the NT, God liberates people from bondage to sin through Jesus Christ.

LIBYA Large land area between Egypt and Tunisia. The people who inhabited the territory in biblical days are referred to variously as Chub (Ezek. 30:5), Put (Nah. 3:9), Phut (Ezek. 27:10), and Libyans (Acts 2:10). Pharaoh Shishak I (about 950 BC) is thought to have been a Libyan.

LIFE The animating force in both animals and humans (Gen. 1:20). Only God has life in the absolute sense. He is the living God (Matt. 16:16). All other life depends on him for its creation and maintenance (Acts 17:25). God is spoken of as the God of life or as life-giving (Deut. 32:40). In contrast to God, the idols are dead (Jer. 10:8-10,14), and so are those who depend on these pagan symbols for life (Ps. 135:18).

No possibility of life exists when God withholds his breath or spirit (Job 34:14-15). Thus, God is Lord of both life and death (James 4:15). Life is something that only God can give (Ps. 139:13-14) and sustain (Ps. 119:116). Thus every life is solely the possession of God. Jesus warned that "one's life is not in the abundance of his possessions" (Luke 12:15 CSB). He brought wholeness into physical life.

We come to God to receive life. We walk in fellowship with God, and in his light we see life. Otherwise, we are devoid of life and cannot see. The proper response to life as the gift of God is to live life in service to God (Isa. 38:10-20) by obeying the Law (Lev. 18:5), doing God's will (Matt. 7:21), and feeding on God's Word (Matt. 4:4). Only that life which lives in obedience to God deserves to be called life in the true sense of the word (Ezek. 18:1-32).

The genuine life that comes from Jesus to those who obey God is true or eternal life. Just as physical life is the gift of God, so is eternal life (Rom. 6:23). Eternal life refers as much to the quality of life one has as to the quantity of life. According to the Bible, all people will have an endless duration of life either in the blessing of God's presence or in the damnation of God's absence (John 5:28-29). The thing that distinguishes the life of these two groups of people is not its duration but its quality.

LIFE, BOOK OF Heavenly document mentioned in Ps. 139:16 and further defined in the NT (Rev. 13:8). In it are recorded by God the names and deeds of righteous people.

LIFE, ORIGIN OF The Bible teaches that all matter (John 1:3), including living matter, was created by God *ex nihilo* (out of nothing—Heb. 11:3) through a series of decisive acts (Ps. 148:5; Rev. 4:11). Plants and animals were created in self-reproducing "kinds" (Gen. 1:11-12,21,24). God created people to bring glory to himself (Isa. 43:7). The psalmist stood in wonder at the intricate design of the human body and saw it as testimony of God's creative power (Ps. 139:13-15).

LIFE SPAN The life expectancy in industrialized Western countries closely approximates the natural life span of humankind according to Ps. 90:10: "Our lives last seventy years or, if we are strong, eighty years" (CSB). While modern medicine, improved health care, and a healthy diet can increase this natural limit somewhat, it is unreasonable to assume that people can ever live as long as several centuries, which was the case with the patriarchs before the flood (Gen. 5:3-31). After the flood, the recorded life span of the descendants of Noah gradually decreased so that the patriarchs lived only twice today's normal span (Gen. 25:7-8; 47:28; 50:26).

LIFE SUPPORT (ARTIFICIAL) The Bible does not speak directly to the issue of life support by artificial means, but it does provide principles relevant to the time of one's death. Only God gives life, and only God should take life away (Exod. 20:13; Job 1:21). Human life is a sacred and precious gift because each person is created in the image of God (Ps. 8:5).These principles suggest that extreme measures to artificially prolong life encroach upon the prerogative of God to control life and death. For the same reason, any and all forms of euthanasia are contrary to the teaching of Scripture. Yet there comes a God-appointed time for everyone to die (Eccles. 3:2). Although Christians value life highly, they need not fear death (Heb. 2:14-15).

LIGHT, LIGHT OF THE WORLD Light is one of the Bible's most complex symbols. Light is linked with instruction (Ps. 119:105,130), truth (Ps. 43:3), good (Isa. 5:20), salvation (Isa. 49:6), life (Job 33:28,30), peace (Isa. 45:7), rejoicing (Ps. 97:11), covenant (Isa. 42:6), justice and righteousness (Isa. 59:9), God's presence and favor (Ps. 89:15), and the glory of Yahweh (Isa. 60:1-3). Apocalyptic visions of the end are associated with the extinguishing of light (Matt. 24:29). In the new age, the new Jerusalem "does not need the sun or the moon to shine on it, because the glory of God illuminates it, and its lamp is the Lamb" (Rev. 21:23 CSB).

On the first day, God created light (Gen. 1:3), which implies that light existed before the sun and other luminaries (Gen. 1:14-18). God himself is the source of light (Ps. 104:2). This light probably signified the divine presence in the same way as the luminous cloud of the Shekinah glory (Exod. 24:15-18).

The identification of light with the divine presence of the Shekinah glory sheds light on the meaning of light in the Gospel of John and 1 John. In the person of Jesus, "the true light that gives light to everyone, was coming into the world" (John 1:9 CSB). The only begotten God, who is in the bosom of the Father, has made the Father known (John 1:18) because he "became flesh and dwelt among us" (John 1:14).

In Jesus God was made manifest because in him the Shekinah glory had returned to reside among us, and this glory consisted of fullness of grace and truth (John 1:16-17). Light thus signifies Jesus's glory, which is fullness of grace and truth. Jesus is "the light of the world," and his followers will have "the light of life" (the truth that brings life; John 8:12). Jesus, who is the light, the embodiment of grace and truth, also brings salvation (John 12:35-36,46-47) and the doing of God's works (John 9:4-5). This salvation and doing of God's works comes from guidance and instruction from the light (John 12:35,47).

The attribution of God (rather than the Word) as light in 1 John 1:5 falls into place in this line of interpretation. Not only is the only begotten God characterized by fullness of grace and truth, but his Father, whom he makes known as characterized by fullness of grace and truth, is as well (John 1:17-18). John can thus affirm that those who do not do the truth do not have fellowship with God, who is light (1 John 1:6).

LIGHTNING Flash of light resulting from a discharge of static electricity in the atmosphere. God is the Maker of lightning and thunder (Job 28:26), which reveal God's power and majesty (Ps. 77:18). Lightning and thunder frequently accompany a revelation of God (Ezek. 1:13-14). In poetic language, God's voice is identified with the thunder (Job 37:3-5). Lightning serves as an illustration of Christ's clearly visible coming (Matt. 24:26-27) and of Satan's fall (Luke 10:18).

LIKENESS Quality or state of being like; resemblance. Old Testament passages center on two truths: (1) God is wholly other and cannot be properly compared to any likeness (Isa. 40:18).

(2) Humanity is created in the image and likeness of God (Gen. 1:26). The first truth forms the basis for the prohibition of making any graven images (Deut. 4:16-18). Interpreters have identified the image of God in man with the ability to think rationally, to form relationships with other humans

and with God or with the exercise of dominion over creation (Ps. 8:5-8). See *Image of God.*

LILY Any of a number of distinctive flowers ranging from the lotus of the Nile (1 Kgs. 7:19) to wild field flowers in Palestine (Matt. 6:28). See *Flowers.*

LIME White, caustic solid consisting primarily of calcium oxide obtained by heating limestone or shells to a high temperature. Lime was used as a plaster (Deut. 27:2,4). Burning someone's bones to lime amounts to complete annihilation (Isa. 33:12) and was regarded as an especially heinous crime (Amos 2:1).

LINE Tool used for measuring length or distance; a plumb line; a cord; a row. References to a plumb line refer to judgment (Isa. 34:11) upon those who failed to meet God's high standards (Isa. 28:17).

Line is used in the sense of a cord in the story of Rahab and the spies (Josh. 2:18,21).

LINEN Most common fabric used in the ancient Near East. It was spun from the flax plant and bleached before being woven into clothing, bedding, curtains, and burial shrouds. The tabernacle curtains (Exod. 26:1) and the high priest's garments (Exod. 28:6) were of finely woven linen. See *Flax.*

LINTEL Wooden crossbeam over a doorway. The people of Israel were to avoid the death angel sent by the Lord by sprinkling the blood of the sacrificial lamb on the lintel and the doorposts (Exod. 12:22-23).

LION Large flesh-eating cat that was once common in Israel (Judg. 14:18; 1 Sam. 17:34-35) but is no longer found in the Middle East. A sign of the tribe of Judah. One of the most well-known biblical stories is about Daniel being cast into a den of lions (Dan. 6:16-23).

LIPS In the OT, lips frequently show the character of a person. There are flattering and lying lips (Ps. 12:2); joyful lips (Ps. 63:5); righteous lips (Prov. 16:13); and fearful lips (Hab. 3:16). Uncircumcised lips (Exod. 6:12 KJV) probably refer to stammering lips or lack of fluency in speech (Exod. 4:10).

LITTLE OWL Any species of owl other than the great owl; included in the unclean birds of Lev. 11:17. See *Owl.*

LIVER According to the CSB and NASB, the lobe of the liver was offered to God with the other choice parts of the burnt offering (Lev. 3:4,10,15). The ancients examined livers to discern the future. The only scriptural mention of the practice concerns the king of Babylon (Ezek. 21:21).

LIVING BEINGS, LIVING CREATURES Creatures in Ezekiel's first vision (Ezek. 1:5,13-15,19-20,22; 3:13; 10:15,17,20) later identified as cherubim (10:20). There were four creatures, each having a human form but with four faces. Perhaps the best interpretation views the creatures as a pictorial representation of the total sovereignty of God. The book of Revelation develops a similar image to portray God's total sovereignty (Rev. 4:1-8).

The Lion of Amphipolis, a statue erected to look over the burial site of battle casualties

LO-AMMI Symbolic personal name meaning "not my people." Son of Hosea the prophet whose name God gave to symbolize Israel's lost relationship with him because of their sin and broken covenant (Hos. 1:9).

LOAN Because of Israel's experience as slaves in Egypt, its moral code made special provision for the poor (Exod. 22:21-24). Thus loans were to be gestures of generosity, not acts for profit at the expense of the poor (Lev. 25:35-37). The OT forbade charging interest to fellow Israelites (Lev. 25:35-38), but sojourners or foreigners could be charged interest (Deut. 23:20). Laws for collateral focused on protecting the debtor. The pledge must not threaten the debtor's dignity (Deut. 24:10-11), livelihood (Deut. 24:6), or family (Job 24:1-3,9). Years of release and the Jubilee Year (Exod. 23:10-11) provided a systematic means for addressing long-term economic hardship by returning family property, freeing slaves, and canceling debts.

LOCUST An insect similar to the grasshopper that periodically multiplies to astronomical numbers in the Middle East. As the swarm moves across the land, it devours all vegetation. The locust plague is a symbol of God's judgment (Joel 2:1,11,25). The image of the locust plague also symbolized being overwhelmed by a large and powerful army (Judg. 6:5).

LOD Place-name of unknown meaning, later called Lydda, 11 miles southeast of Joppa. Returning Jewish exiles settled there about 537 BC (Neh. 11:35). See *Lydda*.

LOGOS John in his Gospel deliberately used *logos* (translated "Word") to describe Jesus (John 1:1). The Greek word *logos* ("word") ordinarily refers to an explanation or reason for something otherwise meaningless. But the OT concept of the "word" (*davar*) of God is foundational for understanding John's usage of this word in reference to Jesus. The Hebrews saw the word of God not as merely words but as a powerful and effectual means of accomplishing God's purposes (Isa. 40:8). By his word God spoke the world into existence (Gen. 1:3-31). God communicated his word directly to persons, especially in the Law (Deut. 5:4-5) and the Prophets (Jer. 1:4,11). The wise person lives in accordance with the word of God (Ps. 106:24).

Writing under the inspiration of the Holy Spirit, John poured new meaning into the concept of *Logos*. In relation to God, Jesus as the *Logos* was not merely an angel or created being who was the agent of creation, nor another word from God or wisdom from God; rather he was God himself (John 1:1-4). In relation to humanity, Jesus the *Logos* was not an impersonal principle, but he was a personal Savior who took on human flesh in the incarnation (John 1:4-14). By depicting Jesus as the *Logos*, John portrays him as the pre-existent Creator of the universe, with God, and identical to God. From this perspective of Jesus's divinity and eternity, any view of Jesus as a mere prophet or teacher is impossible (Col. 1:13-20; Rev. 19:13).

In other NT texts, *logos* refers to Scripture, particularly as proclaimed in gospel preaching (Heb. 4:12). The preaching of the gospel brings order and meaning to lives shattered by sin. Those who put faith in Jesus, the *Logos*, will be welcomed into the family of God (John 1:11-12).

LOINS Midsection of the human body. The OT sometimes speaks of the loins as the seat of physical strength (Nah. 2:1). Tying up the long, lower garments about the waist or loins indicated readiness for travel (1 Kgs. 18:46). In the NT, to gird up one's loins is used in the figurative sense of preparedness (Eph. 6:14).

LOIS Personal name, perhaps meaning "more desirable" or "better." The mother of Eunice and grandmother of Timothy (2 Tim. 1:5).

LOOKING GLASS KJV term for a hand mirror (Exod. 38:8). Mirrors were made of polished metal (Job 37:18), which yielded a distorted image (1 Cor. 13:12).

LOOM Implement used for weaving thread into cloth. The weaving of cloth was an important industry in the ancient world. Job compared the brevity of life to the speed of the weaver's shuttle (Job 7:6). See *Cloth, Clothing*.

LOOPS The inner and outer coverings of the tabernacle were made of two large curtains held together by 50 clasps that passed through curved sections of blue cord for the inner tent or of leather for the outer tent (Exod. 36:11-12,17).

LORD English rendering of several Hebrew and Greek words. Generally the term refers to one who has power or authority. *Jehovah* (or Yahweh; Hebrew *YHWH*, "self-existent") is the name of God most frequently used in the Hebrew Scriptures. This word or title is commonly represented by LORD (in small capital letters) in English translations of the Bible. The Jews meticulously avoided every mention of this name and substituted another word, *'Adonai*.

The importance of this name of God cannot be overstated. Exodus 3:14 furnishes a clue to the meaning of the word. When Moses through the burning bush received his commission to be the deliverer of Israel, God communicated to him the name to give as the credentials of his mission: "God replied to Moses, 'I AM WHO I AM. This is what you are to say to the Israelites: I AM has sent me to you" (CSB). The root idea behind this name is uncreated existence. When it is said that God's name is "I am," more than simple existence is affirmed. He *is* in a sense in which no other being is. He is, and the cause of his being is in himself. *He is because he is.* This name affirms God's lordship over his people (Exod. 34:23), as well as his power over the whole creation (Josh. 3:13). By this name, God avows his superiority over all other gods (Deut. 10:17).

'Adonai is another important designation for God as Lord in the OT. It derives from the Hebrew word *'Adon*, an early word denoting ownership, hence, absolute control. *'Adon* is not properly a divine title as it is used of humans in some places. It is applied to God as the owner and governor of the whole earth (Ps. 114:7). It is sometimes used as a term of respect (like our "sir") but with a pronoun attached ("my lord"). It often occurs in the plural. *'Adonai* is, in the emphatic form, "the Lord."

Kurios is the word normally used in the NT to speak of Jesus as Lord. The word, however, has a wide range of reference, being used of God (Acts 2:34), of Jesus (Luke 10:1), of humans (Acts 16:19), and of angels (Acts 10:4). When characters in the Gospels speak of Jesus as Lord, they often mean no more than "sir." At other times, the designation *kurios* expresses a full confession of faith, as in Thomas's declaration, "My Lord and my God!" (John 20:28 CSB). "The Lord" came to be used as a simple yet profound designation of Christ in Luke and Acts. "The Lord Jesus" was used frequently in Acts as well (4:33) to speak of faith in Christ as Lord (16:31) and to identify baptism as being performed in the name of the Lord Jesus (8:16; 19:5). The phrase "Jesus is Lord" was the earliest Christian confession of faith. Peter declared that God had made Jesus both Lord and Christ (Acts 2:36).

Paul often used a fuller phrase to speak of Jesus's lordship: "the Lord Jesus Christ." It is significant that he used this in conjunction with the mention of God the Father and the Holy Spirit (2 Cor. 13:14). At other times, Paul used the simpler formulas "the Lord Jesus" (2 Thess. 1:7) and "our Lord Jesus" (1 Thess. 3:13). In contrast to the many false gods and lords of pagans, there is for Christians one God, the Father, and one Lord, Jesus Christ (1 Cor. 8:5-6).

LORD'S DAY Designation for Sunday, the first day of the week (Rev. 1:10). Because the first day of the week was the day on which the early Christians celebrated the Lord's Supper, it became known as the Lord's Day, the distinctively Christian day of worship. The earliest account of a first-day worship experience is found in Acts 20:7-12. Here Paul joined the Christians of Troas on the evening of the first day of the week for the breaking of bread (probably a reference to the Lord's Supper). Sunday became the standard day for Christian worship, probably because the resurrection of Jesus took place on that day.

LORD'S PRAYER Words Jesus used to teach his followers to pray. Jesus's prayer life caused one of his disciples to ask for instruction in prayer. What followed (Luke 11:2-13) was a teaching on prayer in which the disciples were told why to pray and what to pray for. The Lord's Prayer is a model of how believers should pray. To pray in this way is a distinguishing mark of Jesus's disciples. The Lord's Prayer is a community's prayer: "*Our* Father"; "Give *us*"; Forgive *us*"; "Deliver *us*." It is the prayer of the community of Jesus's disciples. This model prayer for Christians is not praise, thanksgiving, meditation, or contemplation, but petition. It is asking God for something. A prayer of petition assumes a certain view of God. A God to whom one prays in this way is assumed to be in control; God is able to answer. He is also assumed to be good; he *wants* to answer.

LORD'S SUPPER Church ordinance where unleavened bread and the fruit of the vine memorialize the death of the Lord Jesus and anticipate his second coming. Jesus established the Lord's Supper before his crucifixion while observing the Passover with his disciples (Matt. 26:26-29). Paul used the phrase "Lord's Supper" in 1 Cor. 11:20. In observing the Lord's Supper, church members eat unleavened bread and drink the "fruit of the vine" to symbolize the body and blood of Christ. This memorial meal is to be observed until Christ comes again.

LO-RUHAMAH Symbolic personal name meaning "without love." Name that God gave Hosea for his daughter to symbolize that Israel, by rebelling against God and serving foreign gods, had rejected God's love (Hos. 1:6).

LOT Personal name meaning "concealed." Nephew of Abraham (Gen. 11:27). When Abraham left Haran for Canaan, he was accompanied by Lot and Lot's household (Gen. 12:5). After traveling throughout Canaan and into Egypt, Abraham and Lot finally settled in Canaan between Bethel and Ai, about 10 miles north of Jerusalem (Gen. 13:3). Abraham and Lot acquired herds and flocks so large that the land was unable to support both (Gen. 13:2,5-6). Abraham suggested that they separate, and he allowed Lot to take his choice of the land. Lot chose the well-watered Jordan Valley where the city of Sodom was located (13:8-12).

Sometime after this, two angels visited Lot in the city of Sodom. They warned Lot to leave the city because God intended to destroy Sodom and its sister city Gomorrah because of the wickedness of the people

Stone relief of the Lord's Supper

(Gen. 18:20). When the townsmen heard that two strangers were staying with Lot, they wanted to have sexual relations with them. Lot protected his guests and offered them his daughters instead. The angels urged Lot to take his family into the nearby hills to escape the judgment that God promised to send upon the city. During their flight from Sodom, Lot's wife looked at the destruction and turned to a pillar of salt (Gen. 19:1-29).

After Sodom and Gomorrah were destroyed, Lot's daughters feared they would never have children, so they tricked their father into having intercourse with them. The son of the elder daughter was called Moab, and he became the father of the Moabites. The son of the younger daughter was named Ben-ammi, and he became the father of the Ammonites (Gen. 19:30-38). These two tribes became enemies of the Israelites in later years. In the NT, the story of Lot is used to show the faithfulness of God to rescue his people (2 Pet. 2:7-9).

LOTS Objects used to determine God's will. Matthias was chosen as Judas's successor by casting lots (Acts 1:26). The apostles' prayer immediately before they cast the lots shows the belief that God would express his will through this method. In the OT, Saul was chosen as Israel's first king through the use of lots (1 Sam. 10:20-24). When Joshua summoned the people to stand before the Lord to find the guilty party after the defeat at Ai, he may have used lots (Josh. 7:10-15). God commanded that the promised land be divided by lots (Num. 26:52-56).

LOVE Unselfish, loyal, and benevolent intention and commitment toward another person. The concept of the love of God is deeply rooted in the Bible. The Hebrew term *chesed* refers to covenant love. Jehovah is the God who remembers and keeps his covenants in spite of the treachery of people. His faithfulness in keeping his promises proves his love for Israel and all humanity.

In NT times, three words for love were used by the Greek-speaking world. The first is *eros*, referring to erotic or sexual love. This word is not used in the NT or in the Septuagint. It was commonly used in Greek literature of the time. The word *phileo* refers to tender affection, such as toward a friend or family member. It is very common in the NT. It is used to express God the Father's love for Jesus (John 5:20), God's love for an individual believer (John 16:27), and Jesus's love for a disciple (John 20:2).

The word *agapao* (and its cognate *agape*) was used by believers to denote the unconditional love of God and is used interchangeably with *phileo* to designate God's love for Jesus (John 3:35), God's love for an individual believer (John 14:21), and Christ's love for a disciple (John 13:23). Biblical love has God as its object, true motivator, and source. Love is a fruit of the Holy Spirit (Gal. 5:22) and is not directed toward the world or the things of the world. The ultimate example of God's love is the Lord Jesus Christ, who said, "I give you a new commandment: Love one another. Just as I have loved you, you are also to love one another" (John 13:34 CSB). The definitive statement on love in Paul's writings occurs in 1 Cor. 13. Paul declared that rhetorical ability, preaching, knowledge, mountain-moving faith, charity toward the poor, and even martyrdom are nothing without *agape*.

LOVE FEAST Fellowship meal that the Christian community celebrated with joy in conjunction with the Lord's Supper. It served as a practical expression of the *koinonia* or communion that characterized the church's life. The only explicit NT reference to the *agape* meal is found in Jude 12, but allusions to the practice may be seen in other NT texts. Acts 2:46 mentions that the early believers, while celebrating the Lord's Supper, took their food "with gladness and simplicity of heart," implying a social meal was connected with this celebration.

LOVING-KINDNESS Occasional translation of the Hebrew *chesed*. The OT's highest expression for love. It is variously called God's election, covenant-keeping, or steadfast love. It is a love that remains constant regardless of the circumstances. See *Kindness; Love*.

LUBIM Racial name of uncertain meaning apparently applied to all white North Africans, especially the inhabitants of Libya (Dan. 11:43). Many English translations read "Libyans." See *Libya*.

LUCIFER Latin translation (followed by the KJV) of the Hebrew word for "day star" in Isa. 14:12, where the word is used as a title for the king of Babylon, who had exalted himself as a god. The prophet taunted the king by calling him "son of the dawn" (NIV, NASB), a play on a Hebrew term which could refer to a pagan god but normally indicated the light that appeared briefly before dawn.

LUCIUS Personal name of uncertain meaning. **1.** Christian prophet from Cyrene who helped lead the church at Antioch to set apart Saul and Barnabas for missionary service (Acts 13:1). **2.** Relative of Paul who sent greetings to the church at Rome (Rom. 16:21).

LUD Racial name for person from Lydia (pl. Ludim). **1.** Son of Egypt in the Table of Nations (Gen. 10:13) and apparently a people living near Egypt or under the political influence of Egypt. **2.** Son of Shem and grandson of Noah in Table of Nations (Gen. 10:22). See *Lydia*.

LUKE Author of the Third Gospel and the book of Acts in the NT; traveling companion of the apostle Paul. Many scholars believe Luke wrote his Gospel and the book of Acts while in Rome with Paul during the apostle's first Roman imprisonment. Apparently Luke remained nearby or with Paul also during the apostle's second Roman imprisonment. Shortly before his martyrdom, Paul wrote that "only Luke is with me" (2 Tim. 4:11). Paul identified Luke as a physician (Col. 4:14) and distinguished Luke from those "of the circumcision" (Col. 4:11), perhaps meaning that he was a Gentile.

LUKE, GOSPEL OF Third Gospel and longest book in the NT. Luke is the first of a two-part work dedicated to the "most honorable Theophilus" (Luke 1:3 CSB; Acts 1:1). The book of Acts is a sequel to Luke, with the author explaining in Acts that Luke dealt in his Gospel with "all that Jesus began to do and teach until the day he was taken up" (Acts 1:1-2 CSB). It was written by Luke the physician (Col. 4:14), a missionary associate of the apostle Paul.

Luke wrote his Gospel to confirm for Theophilus the certainty of the things Theophilus had been taught (Luke 1:1-4). His target audience was Gentile inquirers and Christians who needed strengthening in the faith. His Gospel emphasized the universal redemption available to all people through Christ. Samaritans enter the kingdom (17:11-19) as well as Gentiles (23:47). Publicans, sinners, and outcasts (7:37-50) are welcome along with Jews (1:33) and respectable people (11:37). Both the poor (6:20) and rich (23:50) can have redemption. Luke especially notes Christ's high regard for women. Mary and Elizabeth are central figures in chapters 1 and 2. Luke included the story of Christ's kind dealings with the widow of Nain (7:11-18) and the sinful woman who anointed him (7:36-50). He also related Jesus's parable of the widow who persevered (18:1-8).

LUKEWARM Tepid; neither hot nor cold (Rev. 3:16). The city of Laodicea received its water from an aqueduct several miles long. The lukewarm water that arrived at the city served as an appropriate illustration of a tasteless, good-for-nothing Christianity.

LUNATIC Term for epilepsy or insanity (Matt. 17:15). The term "lunacy" derives from the Latin *luna* (moon) and reflects the popular notion that the mental state of the "lunatic" fluctuated with the changing phases of the moon.

LUST A strong craving or desire, especially sexual desire. The unregenerate (preconversion) life is governed by deceitful lusts or desires (Eph. 4:22). Following conversion, such fleshly desires compete with spiritual desires for control of the individual (2 Tim. 2:22). Part of God's judgment on sin is to give persons over to their own fleshly desires (Rom. 1:24). Only the presence of the Holy Spirit in the life of the believer makes victory over sinful desires possible (Rom. 8:1-2). See *Concupiscence*.

LUTE Stringed instrument with a large, pear-shaped body and a neck. NRSV used "lute" to translate two Hebrew terms (Pss.

92:3; 150:3). NASB translated the first term as "10-stringed lute" and the second as "harp." The KJV translated both terms as psaltery. See *Music, Instruments, Dancing*.

LUZ Place-name meaning "almond tree." **1.** Original name of Bethel (Gen. 28:19). **2.** City in the land of the Hittites founded by a man who showed the tribe of Joseph how to conquer Bethel (Judg. 1:25-26).

LYCAONIA Roman province in the interior of Asia Minor including cities of Lystra, Iconium, and Derbe (Acts 14:1-23).

LYCIA Place-name indicating the projection on the southern coast of Asia Minor between Caria and Pamphylia (Acts 27:5).

LYDDA Place-name of uncertain meaning. Known as Lod in the OT (1 Chron. 8:12), Lydda was located at the intersection of the caravan routes from Egypt to Babylon and the road from Joppa to Jerusalem. The church spread to Lydda early (Acts 9:32) as the result of Peter's ministry.

LYDIA A place-name and personal name of uncertain meaning. **1.** Country in Asia Minor whose citizens were named by Ezekiel as "men of war" or mercenaries who fought to defend Tyre (27:10) and who made an alliance with Egypt (30:5). **2.** The first convert to Christ under the preaching of Paul at Philippi (Acts 16:14). Her name originally might have been the designation of her home, "a woman of Lydia." She hosted Paul and his entourage in Philippi after her conversion.

LYE A cleaning substance similar to soap (Jer. 2:22).

LYSANIAS Personal name of unknown meaning. Roman tetrarch of Abilene at the beginning of John the Baptist's ministry about AD 25–30 (Luke 3:1). See *Abilene*.

LYSIAS Second name or birth name of Roman tribune or army captain who helped Paul escape the Jews and appear before Felix, the governor (Acts 23:26). See *Claudius*.

LYSTRA City in south central Asia Minor where Paul healed a crippled man (Acts 14:8-10). It was probably the home of Timothy, one of Paul's missionary associates (Acts 16:1).

The south city gate (possibly Hellenistic) at Perga of Pamphylia, the port from which Mark returned home

MACEDONIA A mountainous country north of Greece to which the apostle Paul was beckoned by the vision of a man pleading, "Come over to Macedonia and help us!" (Acts 16:9 CSB). Responding to the vision, Paul and his missionary associate, Silas, went to the city of Philippi. They were received by Lydia, a God fearer from Thyatira, and founded the first Christian community in Europe (Acts 16:14-15).

MACHIR Personal name meaning "sold." **1.** Head of the family called the Machirites (Num. 26:29). Machir was allotted the territory of Bashan and Gilead, east of the Jordan River (Josh. 17:1). **2.** Member of the tribe of Manasseh who provided assistance for Mephibosheth the son of Jonathan (2 Sam. 9:4-5) and also David during Absalom's rebellion (2 Sam. 17:27-29).

MACHPELAH Place-name meaning "the double cave." A field and cave located near Hebron purchased by Abraham that became the burial site for Sarah (Gen. 23:19), Abraham (25:9), Isaac, Rebekah, Jacob, Leah, and probably other members of the family. Jacob requested burial there before he died in Egypt and was returned there by his sons (Gen. 49:29-30; 50:13).

MAGADAN Site on the Sea of Galilee (Matt. 15:39). At Mark 8:10 most translations follow other Greek manuscripts reading Dalmanutha. KJV follows the received text of its day in reading Magdala. The location of Magadan, if it is a correct reading, is not known.

MAGDALA Place-name, perhaps meaning "tower." City on the western shore of the Sea of Galilee and home of Mary Magdalene, or "Mary of Magdala" (Matt. 27:56).

MAGGOT Soft-bodied, legless grub that is the intermediate stage of some insects (Isa. 14:11). The term emphasizes human mortality.

MAGI Eastern wise men, priests, and astrologers who were expert in interpreting dreams and other "magic arts." The phrase is used of those men who came to Palestine to find and honor Jesus, the newborn King (Matt. 2). They may have been from Babylon, Persia, or the Arabian Desert. Matthew gives no number, names, or royal positions to the magi.

MAGISTRATE Governmental official with administrative and judicial responsibilities. In the OT, the term perhaps signified a judge (Ezra 7:25). In the NT, magistrates were military commanders and civil officials of a Greek city (Acts 16:20,22,35-36,38).

MAGNIFICAT Latin word meaning "magnify." The first word in Latin of Mary's psalm of praise that she would be the earthly mother of Jesus (Luke 1:46-55) and thus the title of the psalm.

MAGOG See *Gog and Magog*.

MAHALATH-LEANNOTH A phrase in the title of a psalm perhaps giving a choreographic instruction or referring to an antiphonal performance by two groups answering and responding to each other (Ps. 88).

MAHANAIM Place-name meaning "two camps." Levitical city in the hill country of Gilead on the border of Gad and eastern Manasseh (Josh. 13:26,30; 21:38). It served as a refuge for Ish-bosheth after Saul's death (2 Sam. 2:8-9) and for David when Absalom usurped the throne (2 Sam. 17:24-27).

MAHER-SHALAL-HASH-BAZ Personal name meaning "quick to the plunder, swift to the spoil" (Isa. 8:1). Symbolic name Isaiah gave his son to warn Judah of the danger posed by the nations of Syria and Israel. The context of Isaiah's prophecy was that these two enemies of Judah would be destroyed before they could attack the southern kingdom. Assyria defeated Syria in 732 BC and Israel in 722 BC.

MAHLON Personal name meaning "sickly." One of the two sons of Elimelech and Naomi (Ruth 1:2,5); the husband of Ruth the Moabitess (4:9-10). Mahlon died while the family was sojourning in Moab to escape a famine in their homeland of Israel.

MAID, MAIDEN A young, unmarried woman, especially of the servant class (Ruth 2:8). The word for "maid" sometimes refers to a female slave or a virgin.

MAIMED Mutilated, disfigured, or seriously injured, especially by loss of a limb (Matt. 18:8). The maimed had difficulty finding work and relied on the generosity of others (Luke 14:13). Christ, the Good Shepherd, cared for the maimed in his healing ministry (Matt. 15:30-31).

MAKKEDAH Place-name meaning "place of shepherds." A Canaanite city where Joshua defeated the combined forces of five Canaanite kings (Josh. 10:10). Joshua captured the city, killing all its inhabitants (10:28).

MALACHI, BOOK OF The last prophetic book of the OT. Malachi prophesied during the dark days after the exile when the Jewish captives had returned from the exile and resettled their homeland. It was a time of indifference and spiritual apathy. Blaming their economic and social troubles on the Lord's supposed unfaithfulness to them, the people were treating one another faithlessly (especially husbands treating their wives) and were profaning the temple by marrying pagan women. They were also withholding their tithes from the temple. Malachi calls the people to turn from their spiritual apathy and correct their wrong attitudes of worship by trusting God with genuine faith as living Lord. This includes honoring the Lord's name with tithes and offerings and being faithful to covenants made with fellow believers, especially marriage covenants.

MALCAM or **MALCHAM** Name meaning "their king." **1.** A Benjaminite (1 Chron. 8:9). **2.** Chief god of the Ammonites (Zeph. 1:5, KJV; Malcam, RSV and NASB margins). The Hebrew *malcam* is sometimes seen as a deliberate scribal misspelling of Milcom (cp. Jer. 49:1,3; Zeph. 1:5), the common name for the god of the Ammonites (Zeph. 1:5).

MALCHUS Personal name meaning "king." High priest's servant whose ear was cut off by Peter (John 18:10).

MALEFACTORS KJV word that denotes the two criminals who were crucified beside Jesus (Luke 23:32-33,39).

MALICE Vicious intention or desire to hurt someone. Malice is characteristic of preconversion life in opposition to God (Rom. 1:29). Christians are called upon to rid their lives of malice (Eph. 4:31-32).

MALLOW Two plants mentioned in the Bible: **1.** A salt marsh plant and unpleasant food (Job 30:4). **2.** A flowering plant whose fading petals provide an image for the unrighteous, according to one interpretation of Job 24:24 (NRSV, REB).

MAMMON Aramaic word for "money," "worldly goods," or "profit." Jesus declared, "Ye cannot serve God and mammon" (KJV), meaning that no one can be a slave of God and worldly wealth at the same time. Concentration on making money is incompatible with total devotion to God and his service (Col. 3:5).

MAMRE Place-name meaning "grazing land." Abraham and his family sojourned in Canaan in this area. Mamre was famous for its oak trees. Abraham purchased a cave (Machpelah) for a family burial plot just east of Mamre (Gen. 23:9-18).

MAN OF LAWLESSNESS or **MAN OF SIN** (KJV) Ultimate opponent of Christ (2 Thess. 2:3). Modern translations follow other manuscripts in reading "man of lawlessness."

MANAEN Greek form of Menahem ("comforter"). A prophet and teacher in the early church at Antioch (Acts 13:1).

MANASSEH Personal name meaning "God has caused me to forget" (trouble). **1.** A son of Joseph (Gen. 41:50-51). Along with Joseph's other son Ephraim, Manasseh became one of the 12 tribes of Israel and received a portion of the land. Half of the tribe of Manasseh settled on the east bank of the Jordan River and half on the west. **2.** King of Judah (696–642 BC) who led the people into worship of false gods. Second Kings blames Manasseh for Judah's ultimate destruction and exile (2 Kgs. 21:10-16).

MANDRAKE Small plant viewed as an aphrodisiac and fertility drug. It is often called love apple or devil's apple. A barren Rachel bargained with Reuben (Leah's oldest son) for mandrakes that he had found (Gen. 30:14-16).

MANGER Feeding trough used for livestock. The place where Jesus was laid after his birth (Luke 2:16). Archaeologists have discovered stone mangers in the horse stables of King Ahab of Israel at Megiddo. Other ancient mangers were made of masonry.

MANNA Grainlike substance, considered to be food from heaven, which sustained the Israelites in the wilderness and foreshadowed Christ, the true Bread from heaven. The small round grains or flakes, which appeared around the Israelites' camp each morning with the dew, were ground and baked into cakes or boiled (Exod. 16:13-36). The name *manna* may have come from the question the Israelites asked when they first saw it: "What is it (*man hu*)?"

MANOAH Personal name meaning "rest." A member of the tribe of Dan and the father of Samson (Judg. 13). Manoah asked God for a son when his wife could not produce an heir.

MANSERVANT KJV, RSV word for a male servant or slave.

MANSLAYER One guilty of involuntary manslaughter; one who accidentally causes another's death (Deut. 19:1-10). English translations distinguish manslayer from murderer although the underlying Hebrew term (*ratsach*) is the same (cp. Exod. 20:13).

MANTLE Robe, cape, veil, or loose-fitting tunic worn as an outer garment. Many of the prophets wore mantles (1 Kgs. 19:13). The transference of the mantle from Elijah to Elisha signified the passing of prophetic responsibility and God's accompanying power.

MAONITES A tribal group that oppressed Israel during the period of the judges (Judg. 10:12). These Maonites were perhaps the Meunites, a band of marauding Arabs from south of the Dead Sea in the vicinity of Ma'an. After the period of the judges, the Meunites were attacked by King Hezekiah (1 Chron. 4:41) and King Uzziah (2 Chron. 26:7) of Judah.

MARA Personal name meaning "bitter," chosen by Naomi to reflect God's bitter dealings with her in the death of her husband and sons (Ruth 1:20-21).

MARAH Place-name meaning "bitter." Place in the Wilderness of Shur, so named because of the bitter water found there by the wandering Israelites (Exod. 15:23). At God's command, Moses cast a tree into the water to make it miraculously sweet and drinkable.

MARANATHA Aramaic expression meaning "Our Lord, come" or "Our Lord has come"

(1 Cor. 16:22), depending on the way the word is divided. The phrase probably reveals the expectant hope in which early Christians lived, watching for the imminent return of Christ.

MARCUS Latin form of Mark ("large hammer") used by the KJV at Col. 4:10; Philem. 24; and 1 Pet. 5:13. See *Mark, John*.

MARDUK Chief god of Babylon, sometimes called Merodach or Bel, the Babylonian equivalent of Baal, meaning "lord." He was credited with creation, a feat reenacted each new year and celebrated with a festival. The prophets mocked Marduk and his worshipers as products of human craftsmen who would lead Babylon to defeat and exile (Isa. 46:1; Jer. 51:47).

MARK, JOHN Author of the Second Gospel and an early missionary leader. John Mark, as Luke calls him in Acts, was the son of Mary, in whose house the church was meeting when Peter was miraculously freed from prison in Acts 12. Commonly called by his Greek name, Mark, in the NT, John was probably his Jewish name. Mark was a cousin of Barnabas (Col. 4:10) and a companion of Barnabas and Paul on their first missionary journey. On the first missionary journey, Mark ministered with the group on Cyprus, the home territory of Barnabas and also a place with family connections for Mark. However, when they left for Pamphylia, Mark returned to Jerusalem.

Mark was the cause of the split between Paul and Barnabas when Mark's participation in the second missionary journey was debated (Acts 15:39). Barnabas sided with his cousin, while Paul refused to take Mark since he had left them on the first journey. Later, however, Paul indicated that Mark was with him (in Rome likely) as Paul sent letters to the Colossians (Col. 4:10) and Philemon (Philem. 24). Mark was also summoned to be with Paul in 2 Tim. 4:11. Whatever rift existed earlier had been healed and their friendship renewed.

Mark is closely related to Peter. In 1 Pet. 5:13, Peter refers to Mark, his "son," as being with him in Rome (Babylon). Early church tradition supports the strong association between Peter and Mark. In the early second century, Papias mentioned that Mark was Peter's interpreter. Other early church figures associate Mark with Peter and note that the Gospel of Mark was based upon Peter's preaching.

MARK, GOSPEL OF Second book of the NT and shortest Gospel account of the ministry of Jesus. According to early church tradition, Mark—also known as John Mark—recorded and arranged the "memories" of Peter, producing a Gospel based on apostolic witness. Mark became an important assistant to both Paul and Peter, preaching the good news to Gentiles and preserving the gospel message for later Christians. Mark wrote his Gospel for Gentile Christians. He explains Jewish customs in detail for the benefit of readers unfamiliar with Judaism (Mark 7:3-4; 12:18).

Mark has been called the "Gospel of action." Jesus is constantly on the move. Mark apparently had more interest in the work of Jesus than in his words. Thus he omitted the Sermon on the Mount. Jesus taught as he moved from region to region, using the circumstances of his travel as valuable lessons for his disciples (8:14-21). Geographical references serve only to trace the expansive parameters of his ministry. According to Mark's "motion" picture, Jesus moved quickly—as if he were a man whose days were numbered.

MARKETPLACE Narrow streets and clustered buildings of most towns and villages in ancient Palestine left little room for a public marketplace. Shops were built into

Modern produce vendors at a busy market in Tel Aviv

private residences or clustered in the gate area to form bazaars (1 Kgs. 20:34). Merchants operated booths just inside the city gate or hawked their merchandise outside the gate area in an open space or square. This area also served as a marshaling place for troops (2 Chron. 32:6) and the site for public meetings (Neh. 8:1), victory celebrations (Deut. 13:16), and the display of captives (2 Sam. 21:12).

MARRIAGE The sacred, covenantal union of one man and one woman formed when the two swore before God an oath of lifelong loyalty and love to each other. God instituted the first marriage in the garden of Eden when he gave Eve to Adam as his wife (Gen. 2:18-25). That later marriages were to follow the pattern of the first is indicated by the concluding divine instruction (see Matt. 19:4-6): "This is why a man leaves his father and mother and bonds with his wife, and they become one flesh" (Gen. 2:24 CSB). A unique unity between Adam and Eve was seen in that the two became "one flesh." The oneness of marriage separated the couple from others as a distinct family unit.

If one's main purpose is to glorify God and enjoy our relationship with him forever (1 Cor. 10:31), clearly this is the chief purpose of marriage. Paul explains in Eph. 5:21-33 that the marriage relationship is to be patterned after that of Christ and the church. A husband and wife are to display in their relationship the nature of our relationship with Christ, our divine Husband, as his bride, the church. This same principle may also be inferred from the OT, where the marriage relationship was one of the key analogies used to describe Yahweh's relationship with Israel (Jer. 2:1; 3:6; 31:32; Hos. 1–3). Marriage is also God's unique gift to provide the framework for intimate companionship, as a means for procreation of the human race and as the channel of sexual expression according to biblical standards.

The Bible describes the marriage that pleases God in terms of mutual submission empowered by the Holy Spirit (Eph. 5:18-21; see also Phil. 2:1-4). Such a marriage also provides the marital fulfillment and companionship God intends. However, mutual submission is to be expressed differently by the husband and the wife. The husband is to practice self-denying, nurturing love patterned after that of Christ (Eph. 5:25-33). He is the initiator and is responsible for leading his wife with wisdom and understanding. He is also to protect, provide for, and honor her (Col. 3:19). A wife, on the other hand, is to express her submission by following her husband's leadership with respect (Eph. 5:22-24,33), maintaining a pure and reverent life with "a gentle and quiet spirit" (1 Pet. 3:1-6).

MARROW Soft tissue within bone cavities. The image of the dividing of joints and marrow pictures the power of Scripture to penetrate a person's thoughts and motives (Heb. 4:12).

Mars Hill, where Paul was invited to address the intellectuals of Athens at the Areopagus

MARS HILL Prominent hill overlooking the city of Athens where the philosophers of the city gathered to discuss their ideas. Paul discussed religion with the leading minds of Athens on Mars Hill. He used the altar to an "unknown god" to present Jesus to them (Acts 17:22).

MARTHA Personal name meaning "lady [of the house]" or "mistress." Sister of Mary and Lazarus of Bethany and follower of Jesus. True to her name, Martha is portrayed as a person in charge: she welcomed Jesus as a guest in her home (Luke 10:38); she was concerned with meeting the obligations of a hostess, whether preparing food (John 12:2) or greeting guests (John 11:20). Luke 10:38-42 contrasts Martha's activist discipleship with Mary's contemplative discipleship. Jesus's gentle rebuke of Martha serves as a perpetual reminder not to major on minor matters.

MARTYR Transliteration of the Greek word *martus*, meaning "witness." The messages and oracles of God were often rejected, resulting in the messenger's maltreatment or death (1 Kgs. 19:2). Witnesses also bear testimony about moral, religious, or spiritual truths so important that one would give his life for those truths. The NT refers three times to a martyr in this sense (Acts 22:20; Rev. 2:13; 17:6).

MARY Personal name of seven women in the NT. **1.** Mary, the earthly mother of Jesus. Mary was a young woman, a virgin, living in Nazareth, and a relative of Elizabeth, mother of John the Baptist (Luke 1:5; 2:26). She had been pledged to marry a carpenter named Joseph. The angel Gabriel appeared to her, announcing she would give birth to "the Son of the Most High" who would sit on "the throne of his father David" (Luke 1:32 CSB). When Mary raised the issue of her virginity, the angel indicated the conception would be supernatural (Luke 1:34-35). Subsequently, Mary visited Elizabeth (Luke 1:39-45). Later, after journeying to Bethlehem and giving birth to Jesus (Luke 2:1-20), Mary and Joseph presented the baby to the Lord at the temple (Luke 2:22-38). Matthew indicates that Mary, Joseph, and Jesus lived in Bethlehem until the visit of the magi, when the threat posed by Herod forced them to take refuge in Egypt (Matt. 2:1-18). The family then lived in Nazareth in Galilee (Matt. 2:19-23). Mary was present at the cross when Jesus committed her care to John, who took her into his home (John 19:26-27). After the ascension, Mary and her sons were with the disciples in Jerusalem as they waited for the promised coming of the Holy Spirit (Acts 1:14). **2.** Mary Magdalene, one of the women who followed and supported Jesus (Mark 15:41). She was from Magdala in Galilee. She experienced dramatic healing when seven demons came out of her (Luke 8:2). She was a key witness to Jesus's death (Matt. 27:56), burial (Mark 15:47), and the empty tomb (Luke 24:1-10), and was the first to encounter the risen Christ (John 20:1-18). She has been identified as a sinful woman, perhaps a prostitute and the "sinful woman" of Luke 7:36-50. However, there is no evidence for this assumption. **3.** Mary of Bethany, sister of Martha and Lazarus. Jesus commended Mary for her interest in his teaching (Luke 10:38-42). Mary later anointed the feet of Jesus with perfume (John 12:1-8). **4.** Mother of James the Younger, Joses, and Salome. This Mary is also identified as an eyewitness to the death, burial, and resurrection of Jesus (Mark 15:40–16:1). **5.** Wife of Clopas. This Mary also was a witness to the death of Jesus and may be the same Mary as 4, above (John 19:25). **6.** Mother of John Mark. When Peter was freed from prison in Acts 12, he went to the house of Mary, mother of John Mark, where the disciples were meeting. **7.** A believer in Rome greeted by Paul (Rom. 16:6).

"Mary's House" in Ephesus, where tradition says that Mary the mother of Jesus lived out her last days

MASKIL A word of uncertain meaning in the titles of Pss. 32; 42; 44; 45; 52–55; 74; 78; 88; 89; 142. The word may have given directions for the melody in which these psalms were to be sung.

MASONS Building craftsmen using brick or stone. The professional mason in Israel first appears in the Bible in David's time. The Bible suggests that no Israelites were skilled in the art of quarrying, squaring, and setting fine building stones in David's

Examples of Herodian masonry are visible around the Temple Mount in Jerusalem

time. David relied upon the king of Tyre for craftsmen (1 Chron. 22:2-4,14-18).

MASSAH Place-name meaning "to test, try." Stopping place near Mount Sinai where the people put God to the test by demanding water (Exod. 17:7). Massah became a reminder of Israel's disobedience or hardness of heart (Ps. 95:8).

MATTANIAH Personal name meaning "gift of Yah." **1.** Tabernacle musician in David's time (1 Chron. 25:4). **2.** Ancestor of Jahaziel (2 Chron. 20:14). **3.** Levite who participated in King Hezekiah's religious reforms (2 Chron. 29:13). **4.** Original name of King Zedekiah of Judah (2 Kgs. 24:17). **5.** Asaphite who returned from exile (1 Chron. 9:15). **6.** Levitic leader of the temple choir in Zerubbabel's time (Neh. 11:17,22). **7.** Levitic temple gatekeeper (Neh. 12:25). **8.** Father of the Levite Shemaiah (Neh. 12:35). **9.** Grandfather of Hanan (Neh. 13:13). **10–13.** Four men who returned from exile with foreign wives (Ezra 10:26-27,30,37). Some of 5–13 may be identical.

MATTHEW Personal name meaning "the gift of Yahweh." A tax collector who became an apostle of Jesus (Matt. 9:9; 10:3). Matthew is the same person as Levi (Luke 5:27). From earliest times, Christians affirmed that Matthew wrote the Gospel that bears his name.

MATTHEW, GOSPEL OF Opening book of the NT that was written to show the Jewish people that Jesus was the Messiah promised in the OT. In Matthew's genealogy of Jesus, he traces him to two of the greatest personalities in the history of the Jewish people—Abraham (Matt. 1:2) and David (Matt. 1:6). Another purpose of this Gospel was to show that Jesus had the power to command his disciples to spread his gospel throughout all the world (Matt. 28:16-20). Matthew also contains the teachings of Jesus known as the Sermon on the Mount (Matt. 5:1–7:29). It includes his teachings on subjects such as true happiness (5:2-12), prayer and fasting (6:1-18), and building life on a secure foundation (7:24-27).

MATTHIAS Shortened form of Mattathias ("gift of Yah"). Follower of Jesus who was chosen by lot to succeed Judas as an apostle (Acts 1:20-26). This selection was regarded as necessary to fulfill Scripture concerning the band of apostles (Ps. 69:25).

MAW KJV term for the fourth stomach of a cud-chewing animal. The maw was among the choice cuts of meat reserved for the priests (Deut. 18:3). Modern translations render as "stomach" (CSB, NASB, REB, NRSV) or "inner parts" (NIV).

MAZZAROTH Puzzling term in Job 38:32. Either a proper name for a constellation (KJV, NRSV), a collective term for the 12 signs of the Zodiac (KJV margin, REB), or a general term meaning constellation or stars (CSB, NASB, NIV, TEV).

MEADOW Tract of grassland, especially moist, low-lying pasture. In modern translations, "meadows" illustrate God's blessing (Ps. 65:13 NASB, NIV, NRSV [pastures, CSB]; Isa. 30:23; 44:4 NIV). Meadows are also used in pictures of God's judgment (Jer. 25:37 NIV; Hos. 9:13 NASB; Zeph. 2:6 NRSV).

MEASURING LINE Cord used to measure length (2 Chron. 4:3). References to a measuring line point to the restoration of Jerusalem (Zech. 2:1).

MEASURING REED Ezekiel's measuring reed was a cane about 10 feet long used as a measuring tool (Ezek. 40:3,5-8).

MEAT OFFERING KJV term for a food offering in contrast to a drink offering or libation (1 Chron. 21:23). Modern translations render the term as "grain offering."

MEAT TO IDOLS Offerings of animal flesh sacrificed to a pagan god. Most religions of the ancient Near East had laws regarding offering sacrifices to the gods. A problem arose in the church when Gentile converts ate meat that had been offered to idols. The Jerusalem council decided that Christians should abstain from eating meat offered to idols so as not to cause weak believers to stumble (Acts 15:29). Paul echoed this sentiment (1 Cor. 8:13).

MEDEBA A Moabite town captured by the Amorites, then by the Israelites (Num. 21:23-30), and allotted later to the tribe of Reuben (Josh. 13:9,16).

MEDES, MEDIA Inhabitants of an ancient kingdom west of Assyria who descended from Japheth, the grandson of Noah (Gen 10:2). The Medes were first reported in history by King Shalmaneser III of Assyria about 850 BC. At this time they were a group of nomadic tribes rather than a state or kingdom. After the Assyrian Empire fell to the Babylonians, Babylon and Media divided the Assyrian Empire with Media taking the land east and north of the Tigris River. The Medes turned their attention to the north and toward Asia Minor. The end of the Median kingdom came with the rise of Cyrus II, founder of the Persian Empire. Though conquered by the Persians, the Medes continued to hold a place of honor in the Persian Empire. Media was the second most important portion of the empire after Persia itself.

Biblical references frequently combine "the Medes and the Persians" (Dan. 5:28). The kings of the Persian Empire are called "the kings of Media and Persia" (Dan. 8:20). The most famous Mede in Scripture was Darius the Mede (Dan. 5:31; 9:1). Media is sometimes referred to as the instrument of God, especially against Babylon (Jer. 51:11,28), but the Medes also had to drink the cup of God's judgment (Jer. 25:25). Their final appearance in Scripture is the presence of Jews or Jewish converts from there at Pentecost (Acts. 2:9).

MEDIATOR One who stands between two or more parties to negotiate and establish agreement. The idea of a mediator or the need for mediation is prevalent throughout the OT. Abraham entered into negotiations with God for mercy toward Sodom (Gen. 18:22-32), and Joab mediated between David and Absalom (2 Sam. 14:1-23). Most commonly it was the prophet, priest, or king who stood in this role. The prophets were representatives of God to the people and often had the task of pronouncing God's judgment or good news to the Israelites. Priests mediated for man in the presence of God (Lev. 9:7).

God the Son became incarnate as a man and fulfilled the role as the perfect mediator between God and man. Paul declares that man is unable to commune with God unless he come to God through Jesus because there is only one mediator "between God and humanity, the man Christ Jesus" (1 Tim. 2:5 CSB). Christ, who is superior to Moses (Heb. 3:1-6), mediates a new covenant (Heb. 8:6) based upon his "once for all" substitutionary death on the cross that guarantees a better covenant (Heb. 7:22).

MEDITATION Deep thought or reflection upon some truth or supposition. A righteous person contemplates God or his great spiritual truths (Pss. 63:6; 143:5). He hopes to please God by meditation (Ps. 19:14). Thus meditation by God's people is a reverent act of worship. Through it they commune with God and are renewed spiritually. Meditation is an important part of the Christian's relationship with Christ.

MEDITERRANEAN SEA Some of the most important nations of ancient times were either on the shores of the Mediterranean Sea or operated in its 2,200 miles of water. These included Israel, Syria, Greece, Rome, Egypt, Philistia, and Phoenicia. The Mediterranean Sea served as the western border for the land of Canaan (Num. 34:6) and the territory of Judah (Josh. 15:12). Following the conquest of Palestine by Pompey in 63 BC, traffic on the Mediterranean increased. This development helped to make possible the missionary activity of Paul, Silas, Barnabas, and others. Paul made

Sunset over the Mediterranean Sea

three missionary journeys across the Mediterranean. Under Roman arrest, Paul made his final voyage across the Mediterranean Sea and shipwrecked (Acts 27). Paul's work involved such Mediterranean cities as Caesarea, Antioch, Troas, Corinth, Tyre, Sidon, Syracuse, Rome, and Ephesus. Designated in the OT and the NT simply as "the sea" (Acts 10:6), the Mediterranean was also called the "Western Sea" (Deut. 11:24 RSV, NIV) and the "Sea of the Philistines" (Exod. 23:31).

MEDIUM A person possessed by (Lev. 20:6) or consulting (Deut. 18:11) a ghost or spirit of the dead, especially for information about the future. Acting as a medium was punishable by stoning (Lev. 20:27); consulting a medium, by exclusion from the congregation of Israel (Lev. 20:6). The transformation of King Saul from a person who expelled mediums (1 Sam. 28:3) to one who consulted a medium at En-dor (1 Sam. 28:8-19) graphically illustrates his fall.

MEEKNESS Humility and gentleness, usually exhibited during suffering and accompanied by faith in God. While God can be described as "meek" or "gentle" in his dealings with humanity (Ps. 18:35), meekness is primarily a character trait associated with people (Prov. 22:4). In the OT, God often promises deliverance or salvation to the "meek," who are righteous persons suffering injustice, poverty, or oppression (Pss. 25:9; 147:6; Isa. 11:4). In the NT, Jesus is presented as the supreme example of meekness (Matt. 11:29). Humble and faithful ("meek") disciples, although suffering the same rejection as their Messiah, will one day be vindicated by God (Matt. 5:5,11-12). Meekness is part of the "fruit of the Spirit," which is produced in believers by the Holy Spirit (Gal. 5:23). See *Humility*.

MEGIDDO Place-name, perhaps meaning "place of troops." One of the most strategic cities of Canaan since it guarded the main pass through the Carmel mountain range. This range was an obstacle along the international coastal highway that connected Egypt with Mesopotamia. After the conquest of Canaan by the Israelites, the city was allotted to Manasseh (Josh. 17:11), but it was not secured by the tribe. By the time of Solomon, though, the city was firmly Israelite, since he fortified the city (1 Kgs. 9:15), including his mighty six-chambered gate that followed the pattern of his other two key fortress cities of Hazor and Gezer. The Mount of Megiddo (har-Megiddon thus "Armageddon") will be where the kings of the world are gathered for the final battle in the last day of the Lord (Rev. 16:16).

Megiddo overlooking the valley of Jezreel

MEHUNIM KJV form of Meunim or Meunites, an Arab tribe whose name probably comes from the city of Ma'an about 12 miles southeast of Petra. The Meunites raided Judah during the reign of Jehoshaphat (873–849 BC) according to 2 Chron. 20:1 (CSB, NASB, NIV, REB, NRSV). The Meunites are listed as temple servants in the postexilic period (Neh. 7:52). They were perhaps the descendants of prisoners of war.

MELCHIZEDEK Personal name meaning "Zedek is my king" or "my king is righteousness." Mysterious priest and king of Salem who blessed Abraham in the name of "God Most High." In return, Abraham gave Melchizedek a tenth of everything (Gen. 14:20). Melchizedek and Abraham both worshipped the one true God. Abraham also appeared to recognize the role of Melchizedek as a priest. The writer of Hebrews made several references in chapters 5–7 to Jesus's priesthood being of the "order of Melchizedek" as opposed to Levitical in nature. Only Jesus, whose life could not be destroyed by death, fit the description of a priest of "the order of Melchizedek."

MEM Thirteenth letter of the Hebrew alphabet that serves as the heading for Ps. 119:97-104. Each of these verses begins with this letter.

MEMORIAL Something that serves as a reminder. God's covenant name (Yahweh) was to be a "memorial name" (Exod. 3:15 NASB), a reminder of God's liberation of his people. The Passover served as a similar reminder (Exod. 13:9). In the NT, the Lord's Supper serves as a reminder of Christ's sacrificial death and an assurance of his future coming (Matt. 26:13; 1 Cor. 11:25-26).

MEMPHIS Place-name meaning "the abode of the good one." An ancient capital of Egypt (Jer. 46:19) located just south of modern Cairo on the west bank of the Nile River. For more than 300 years, Memphis was the principal city of Egypt. Gradually, other cities grew in importance, and Memphis was eclipsed as the seat of power. Many of the royal pyramids of the Egyptian kings and the famous Sphinx are located near Memphis.

One of several small sphinxes located at Memphis on the Nile River in Egypt

MENAHEM Personal name meaning "consoler." King of Israel (reigned 752–742 BC) who assassinated Shallum to take the throne (2 Kgs. 15:10-14). After becoming king,

Menahem attacked and destroyed one of Israel's cities because it resisted his rule (2 Kgs. 15:16). He paid tribute to Tiglath-pileser III, the king of Assyria. This is the first mention of the Assyrian monarch in the biblical record. It is possible that Menahem obtained the throne of Israel with Tiglath-pileser's help. See *Tiglath-pileser*.

MENE, MENE, TEKEL, UPHARSIN Strange inscription written on the palace wall of King Belshazzar of Babylon that was interpreted by the prophet Daniel. He told the king that it meant "numbered, weighed, and divided," or Belshazzar and his kingdom had been weighed in the balance and found wanting. The kingdom would be divided and given to his enemies, the Medes and Persians. The overthrow occurred that very night (Dan. 5:30).

MENORAH Candelabrum used in Jewish worship, specifically the seven-branched lampstand used in the tabernacle (Exod. 25:31-35).

MEPHIBOSHETH Personal name meaning "shame destroyer" or "image breaker." **1.** Son of Jonathan and grandson of King Saul. Crippled at age five after his father was killed by the Philistines, Mephibosheth was granted special position and privilege in David's court (2 Sam. 9). **2.** Son of King Saul who was delivered by David to the Gibeonites to be hanged, in retaliation for Saul's earlier slaughter of a band of Gibeonites (2 Sam. 21:1-9).

MERAB Personal name from the root "to become many." Elder daughter of King Saul (1 Sam. 14:49), who was twice promised to David in exchange for killing Goliath (1 Sam. 17:25) and for fighting the Lord's battles against the Philistines (1 Sam. 18:17-19). Saul reneged on his promise and gave Merab to another man.

MERARI Personal name meaning "bitterness" or "gall." Third son of Levi (1 Chron. 23:6) and ancestor of a division of priests, the Merarites.

MERARITES Major division of priests descended from Merari, the third son of Levi. The Merarites and Gershonites were responsible for the set-up, breakdown, and transport of the tabernacle (Num. 10:17). The Merarites received an allotment of 12 cities from the tribes of Reuben, Gad, and Zebulun, including Ramoth-gilead, a city of refuge (1 Chron. 6:63,77-81). Representatives of the Merarites participated in David's move of the ark to Jerusalem (1 Chron. 15:6), served as tabernacle musicians (1 Chron. 15:17,19) and gatekeepers (1 Chron. 26:10,19), shared in Hezekiah's (2 Chron. 29:12) and Josiah's (2 Chron. 34:12) reforms, and returned from exile to assist in building the new temple (Ezra 8:19).

MERCHANT Buyer and seller of goods for profit. With the exception of the period of Solomon (1 Kgs. 10:15,22), Israel was not known as a nation of merchants. The majority of OT references to merchants are to nations other than Israel. Businessmen of Tyre sold fish and all kinds of merchandise in postexilic Jerusalem (Neh. 13:16). Tyre's trading partners included 22 nations or peoples encompassing Asia Minor, Palestine, Syria, Arabia, and Mesopotamia. Some merchants generated great wealth. The prophets railed against the pride that accompanied their material successes (Ezek. 27).

Trajan's Market in Rome, a large second-century AD "shopping center" where merchants sold their wares

MERCURIUS Roman name for the pagan god Mercury. The people of Lystra referred to the apostle Paul by this name (Acts 14:12).

MERCY SEAT Slab of pure gold measuring about 45 inches by 27 inches that sat atop the ark of the covenant. It was the base for the golden cherubim (Exod. 25:17-19,21) and symbolized the throne from which God ruled Israel (Lev. 16:2; Num. 7:89). On the Day of Atonement, the high priest sprinkled the blood of a sacrificial lamb on the mercy seat as a plea for forgiveness for the sins of the nation (Lev. 16:15). The Hebrew word for "mercy seat" means literally "to wipe out" or "cover over."

MERCY An attribute of God. On the human level, it is best described as a person's consideration of the condition and needs of his fellow man. It is an essential disposition of a covenant people, especially Israel and the church. In the OT, God's mercy was not primarily given to people outside his covenant community but was expressed mainly toward his people Israel. It also became the expected attitude and action of the people of Israel toward one another. This expectation was passed on to the church and became a chief characteristic of the lifestyle of believers. Jesus made it an essential part of his Christian manifesto in the Sermon on the Mount (Matt. 5:7).

Mercy as given by God is the foundation of forgiveness. God is not seen as displaying an emotion called mercy but as taking merciful action. This action was taken as Israel was in need: provisions such as manna in the wilderness (Exod. 13:31-35), protection such as the Shepherd who keeps Israel and does not sleep (Ps. 121), and deliverance (Ps. 56:12-23) as Yahweh who delivered his people from Egypt (1 Sam. 10:18). Mercy has never been the benefit of God's people because of their merit but is always the gift of God.

MERIBBAAL Personal name meaning perhaps "opponent of Baal" or "Baal defends." The original name of Mephibosheth, Jonathan's son (1 Chron. 8:34).

MERODACH Hebrew form of Marduk, the chief god of Babylon, also called Bel, corresponding to the Semitic Baal or "Lord" (Jer. 50:2). Merodach is an element in the names of the Babylonian kings Merodach-baladan (2 Kgs. 20:12; Isa. 39:1) and Evil-merodach (2 Kgs. 25:27; Jer. 52:31).

MERODACH-BALADAN Personal name meaning "god Marduk gave an heir." King of Babylon who sent envoys to King Hezekiah of Judah (2 Kgs. 20:12-13). Hezekiah showed these agents the palace treasure house and treasuries, an action condemned by the prophet Isaiah (2 Kgs. 20:12-19).

MEROM Place-name meaning "high place." Place in Galilee where Joshua led Israel to defeat a coalition of Canaanite tribes under King Jabin of Hazor (Josh. 11:1-7).

MESHA Personal and place-name. **1.** Ruler of Moab who led a rebellion against the northern kingdom of Israel (2 Kgs. 3:4-27). Mesha succeeded in seizing Israelite border towns and in fortifying towns on his frontier. An alliance of Israel, Judah, and Edom, however, outflanked his defenses and attacked Mesha from the rear. Mesha retreated to Kir-hareseth, where he sacrificed his firstborn son to his god Chemosh on the city walls. In response the Israelites lifted their siege and returned home. **2.** Descendant of Benjamin living in Moab (1 Chron. 8:9). **3.** Descendant of Caleb in the tribe of Judah (1 Chron. 2:42). **4.** City in the territory of the Joktanites (Gen. 10:30).

MESHACH Personal name. One of Daniel's friends exiled to Babylon after the fall of Jehoiakim in 597 BC (Dan. 1:6-7). His Hebrew name was Mishael ("Who is what God is") but was changed to Meshach (perhaps "Who is what Aku is") to mock Israel's God. Declining the rich food of the king's table, he and his friends proved that the simple fare of vegetables and water was superior to the king's rich food. After refusing to bow to the king's golden image, he, Shadrach, and Abednego were thrown into a flaming furnace but were delivered by God (Dan. 3).

MESOPOTAMIA The area between the Tigris and Euphrates Rivers. This region was the homeland of the patriarchs (Gen. 11:31–12:4; 28:6). A Mesopotamian king subdued Israel for a time during the period of the judges (Judg. 3:8). Mesopotamia supplied mercenary chariots and cavalry for the Ammonites' war with David (1 Chron. 19:6; superscription of Ps. 60). Both the northern kingdom of Israel (1 Chron. 5:26) and the southern kingdom of Judah (2 Kgs. 24:14-16) went into exile in Mesopotamia.

MESSENGER One sent with a message. The Hebrew and Greek terms for "messenger" are frequently rendered "angel," the heavenly messengers of God. The prophets (Isa. 44:26; Hag. 1:13) and priests (Mal. 2:7) are termed messengers in their role as bearers of God's message for humanity. Sometimes messengers made advance travel arrangements for their master (Luke 9:52). The gospel writers applied this preparatory function to John the Baptist (Mark 1:2).

MESSIAH Transliteration of Hebrew word meaning "anointed one" that was translated into Greek as *Christos*. "Christ" or Messiah is a name that expresses the church's link with Israel through the OT and the faith that sees Jesus Christ as the bearer of salvation for the world. "Anointed" carries several senses in the OT. All have to do with installing a person in an office in a way that the person will be regarded as accredited by Yahweh, Israel's God. Prophets such as Elisha were set apart in this way (1 Kgs. 19:16). Israelite kings were particularly hailed as Yahweh's anointed (Judg. 9:8), beginning with Saul (1 Sam. 9–10 NIV) and especially referring to David (2 Sam. 2:4; 5:3) and Solomon (1 Kgs. 1:39). The king in Israel thus became a sacred person to whom loyalty and respect were to be accorded (1 Sam. 24:6,10).

The king, especially in the Psalms, became idealized as a divine son (Ps. 2:2,7) and enjoyed God's protecting favor (Ps. 18:50). His dynasty would not fail (Ps. 132:17), and the people were encouraged to pray to God on his behalf (Ps. 84:9). The fall of Jerusalem in 586 BC led to great confusion, especially when Yahweh's anointed was taken into exile as a prisoner (Lam. 4:20) and his authority as king rejected by the nations (Ps. 89:38,51).

After the exile, the Israelite priesthood came into prominence. In the absence of a king, the high priest took on a central role in the community. The rite of anointing was the outward sign of his authority to function as God's representative. This authority was traced back to Aaron and his sons (Exod. 29:7-9). The high priest was the anointed-priest (Lev. 4:3,5,16) and even, in one place, a "messiah" (Zech. 4:14). In the exilic and postexilic ages, the expectation of a coming Messiah came into sharper focus, beginning with Jeremiah's and Ezekiel's vision of a Messiah who would combine the traits of royalty and priestly dignity (Jer. 33:14-18; Ezek. 46:1-8).

In John 4:29, a question is posed about Jesus: "Could this be the Messiah?" (CSB). The issue of the Messiah's identity and role was much debated among the Jews in the first century. In the Synoptic Gospels, the way Jesus acted and spoke led naturally to the dialogue at Caesarea Philippi. Jesus asked his disciples, "Who do you say that I am?" a question to which Peter replied, "You are the Messiah" (Mark 8:29 CSB). Mark made clear that Jesus took an attitude of distinct reserve and caution to this title since it carried overtones of political power. Jesus, therefore, accepted Peter's confession with great reluctance since with it went the disciple's objection that the Messiah could not suffer (Mark 9:32). For Peter, Messiah was a title of a glorious personage both nationalistic and victorious in battle. Jesus, on the other hand, saw his destiny in terms of a suffering Son of man and Servant of God (Mark 10:33-34).

The course of Jesus's ministry is one in which he sought to wean the disciples away from the traditional notion of a warrior Messiah. Instead, Jesus tried to instill in their minds the prospect that the road to his future glory was bound to run by way of the cross, with its experience of rejection, suffering, and humiliation. After the trial, before his Jewish judges (Matt. 26:63-66), he went to the cross as a crucified Messiah because the Jewish leaders failed to perceive the nature of messiahship as Jesus understood it. Pilate sentenced him as a messianic pretender who claimed (according to the false charges brought against him) to be a rival to Caesar (John 19:14-15). It was only after the resurrection that the disciples were in a position to see how Jesus was truly a king Messiah and how Jesus then opened their minds to what true messiahship meant (Luke

24:45-46). The national title "Messiah" then took on a broader connotation, involving a kingly role that was to embrace all peoples (Luke 24:46-47). See *Christ, Christology; Jesus Christ.*

MESSIANIC SECRET Term that Bible students use to describe Jesus's commands not to reveal who he was after his performance of messianic wonders. Mark used the unveiling of the messiahship of Jesus as the unifying theme of his Gospel. Demons demonstrated that they recognized Jesus immediately: "I know who you are—the Holy One of God!" (Mark 1:24 CSB); nevertheless, Jesus suppressed their confession. He prohibited public profession by those who experienced miraculous healing (Mark 8:26). The parables of Jesus were offered in order to keep "outsiders" from learning the secret (Mark 4:11-12). Even the disciples, once they related that they understood the "secret of the kingdom of God" (Mark 4:11), were sworn to silence (Mark 9:9).

Perhaps Jesus avoided the title because of the popular messianic expectations of the people. They were looking for a political deliverer. Some believe that Jesus prohibited messianic proclamation so he could continue to move about freely in public. The only parable of Jesus that Mark recorded exclusively may provide a clue to the purpose of the messianic secret. Jesus introduced the parable of the secret growing seed (Mark 4:26-29) with the proverb: "For there is nothing hidden that will not be revealed, and nothing concealed that will not be brought to light" (4:22 CSB). Like the seed that is covered by ground, the secret of Jesus's identity would be concealed for a season. The disciples needed time to recognize Jesus as Messiah (Mark 4:41; 6:52; 8:17-21). They also needed time to come to terms with the fact that his messianic suffering would precede messianic glory (Mark 9:31-32). Complete human understanding of the messianic secret would be possible only after the resurrection (Mark 9:9-10). See *Christ, Christology; Jesus Christ; Messiah.*

METHUSELAH Personal name meaning either "man of the javelin" or "worshiper of Selah." A son of Enoch and grandfather of Noah (Gen. 5:21,26-29) who died at the age of 969 (Gen. 5:27), making him the oldest man in the Bible.

MEZUZAH Hebrew word for "doorpost." Ancient doors pivoted on posts set in sockets. The blood of the Passover lamb was to be applied to doorposts (Exod. 12:7,22-23). Today the word *mezuzah* refers to small scrolls inscribed with Deut. 6:4-9 and 11:13-21 and placed in a container attached to the doorjambs of Jewish homes.

MICAH Abbreviated form of the personal name Micaiah, meaning "Who is like Yahweh?" **1.** Ephraimite whose home shrine was the source of Dan's idolatrous worship (Judg. 17–18). **2.** Descendant of Reuben (1 Chron. 5:5). **3.** Descendant of King Saul (2 Sam. 9:12 KJV, Micha). **4.** Leader of a family of Levites in David's time (1 Chron. 23:20). **5.** Father of Abdon, a contemporary of King Josiah of Judah (2 Kgs. 22:12, Micaiah). **6.** Prophet of the eighth century BC who came from Moresheth (NRSV, CSB), which probably should be identified with Moresheth-gath. Micah prophesied during the reigns of Jotham (750–732 BC), Ahaz (735–715 BC), and Hezekiah (715–686 BC), kings of Judah. Even though Micah ministered in Judah, some of his messages were directed toward the northern kingdom of Israel.

MICAH, BOOK OF A short prophetic book of the OT in which the prophet Micah condemned the rich for oppressing the poor, criticized unjust business practices, denounced the idolatry of the people, and predicted the destruction of Judah as an act of God's judgment. At the same time, he proclaimed messages of hope. Judgment would come, but afterward God would restore a remnant of the people devoted to him (7:14-20). Perhaps Micah is best known for its prediction that the Messiah would be born in Bethlehem (Mic. 5:2). Matthew saw in Micah's hope for a new ruler a description of Christ (Matt. 2:6).

MICAIAH Personal name meaning "who is like Yahweh?" **1.** Prophet who predicted the death of King Ahab and the scattering of Israel's forces at Ramoth-gilead (1 Kgs.

View of the gorge at Michmash

22:7-28). **2.** Form of Michaiah preferred by modern translations.

MICHAEL Personal name meaning "who is like God?" **1.** Father of one of the 12 Israelite spies (Num. 13:13). **2-3.** Two Gadites (1 Chron. 5:13-14). **4.** Ancestor of Asaph (1 Chron. 6:40). **5.** Leader of the tribe of Issachar (1 Chron. 7:3). **6.** Leader of the tribe of Benjamin (1 Chron. 8:16). **7.** Manassite who defected to David's army (1 Chron. 12:20). **8.** Son of King Jehoshaphat (2 Chron. 21:2). **9.** Ancestor of one of those who returned from exile with Ezra (Ezra 8:8). **10.** Archangel who served as the guardian of the nation of Israel (Dan. 12:1). Together with Gabriel, Michael fought for Israel against the prince of Persia. In Rev. 12:7, Michael commands the forces of God against the forces of the dragon in a war in heaven. See *Angel*; *Archangel*.

MICHAL Personal name meaning "Who is like God?" King Saul's younger daughter (1 Sam. 14:49), given to David in marriage for killing 100 Philistines (1 Sam. 18:20-29). Michal criticized King David for dancing before the ark of the covenant as he brought the sacred chest to Jerusalem. As punishment Michal was never allowed to bear children (2 Sam. 6:16-23). Saul gave Michal as wife to a citizen of Gallim after taking her away from David.

MICHMASH Place-name meaning "hidden place." City in Benjamin about seven miles northeast of Jerusalem that served as a staging area, first for King Saul (1 Sam. 13:2) and then for the Philistine army. Before the battle began, Jonathan and his armor bearer sneaked into the Philistine camp, killed 20 sentries, and set off great confusion, resulting in the Philistines fighting one another (1 Sam. 14:20).

MICHTAM KJV form of Miktam. A heading for Pss. 16; 56–60. The term may be a musical notation or a title for psalms connected with expiation of sin.

MIDDLE WALL Term found in Eph. 2:14 and variously translated as "middle wall of partition" (KJV); "dividing wall of hostility" (CSB, NRSV, NIV); "barrier of the dividing wall" (NASB); "barrier of enmity which separated them" (REB). There are several possible interpretations of this word. **1.** The wall that separated the inner and outer courts of the temple and prevented Jews and Gentiles from worshiping together. **2.** The curtain that separated the holy of holies from the rest of the temple. This curtain was torn at the death of Jesus (Mark 15:38) and is representative of the separation of all humanity from God. **3.** The "fence" consisting of detailed commandments and oral interpretations erected around the law by its interpreters to ensure its faithful observation. **4.** The cosmic barrier that separates God and people, people themselves, and other powers in the universe (Eph. 1:20-21)—angels, dominions, principalities. **5.** Echoing Isa. 59:2, the term refers to the separation of humanity from God as a result of sin.

No one interpretation is sufficient by itself. The writer of Ephesians emphasized that every conceivable barrier that exists between people and between God and humanity has been destroyed by Jesus Christ.

MIDIAN, MIDIANITES Personal and clan name meaning "strife." Midian was the son of Abraham by his concubine Keturah (Gen. 25:2). Abraham sent him and his brothers away to the east, leading to the association of the Midianites with the "children of the east" (Judg. 6:3). The people of Israel had both good and bad relationships with the Midianites. When Moses fled from Pharaoh, he went east to Midian (Exod. 2:15). Here he met Jethro, the priest of Midian, and married his daughter. In the time of the judges, the Midianites along with the Amalekites began to raid Israel. Gideon drove them out and killed their leaders (Judg. 6–8). They never again threatened Israel, but Midian did harbor Solomon's enemy Hadad (1 Kgs. 11:18).

MIDRASH Jewish interpretations of the OT included a form called midrash. The word was used to denote the process of biblical interpretation or the written expression of that interpretation. According to early rabbinic tradition, Hillel the Elder formulated seven rules that guided Jewish biblical interpretation. These rules were sensible guidelines for understanding the Bible. Examples of the application of each rule appear in the NT. Later rabbis formulated many other rules that resulted in wild, fanciful interpretations that lost all connection with the literary and historical context of the passage under discussion.

The NT contains midrash and is midrashic in the sense that many portions of the NT offer interpretations of specific OT texts that follow the normal patterns of exegesis suggested by ancient rabbis. The study of midrash may offer the interpreter of Scripture insight into the methods of interpretation used throughout Jewish history. As the student examines the strengths and weaknesses of these approaches to interpretation, he may learn how a person's culture and worldview impact his understanding of the Bible and how he may more "accurately interpret the word of truth."

MIDWIFE Woman who assisted in the delivery of a baby (Exod. 1:15-21). The duties of the midwife likely included cutting the umbilical cord, washing and salting the infant, and wrapping the child in cloths (Ezek. 16:4).

MIGHTY MEN As applied to the descendants of the Nephilim, "mighty men" likely indicates men of great size (Gen. 6:4). Elsewhere the phrase refers to valiant warriors, especially to the elite groups of three and of 30 who served David (1 Kgs. 1:10,38).

MILCOM Name of a pagan god meaning "king" or "their king." Apparently this was a form created by Hebrew scribes to avoid pronouncing the name of the national god of Ammon (1 Kgs. 11:5,7), who may have been identified with Chemosh, the god of Moab. Solomon built sanctuaries to Milcom on the Mount of Olives at the request of his foreign wives, reviving the ancient cult (1 Kgs. 11:5,33). See *Chemosh; Moab; Molech.*

MILDEW Fungus causing a whitish growth on plants. The Hebrew term rendered "mildew" means "paleness." The term may refer to the yellowing of leaves as a result of drought rather than to a fungus (1 Kgs. 8:37). Mildew is one of the agricultural plagues God sent to encourage repentance.

MILETUM (KJV) or **MILETUS** Ancient city on the west coast of Asia Minor that served as the port for Ephesus. Paul met with the elders of the church at Ephesus in Miletus (Acts 20:15-17). See *Ephesus.*

Reconstruction of the Asian city of Miletus as it appeared in the first century AD

MILK Nourishing liquid and its by-products, a staple of the Hebrew diet. Most often milk came from sheep and goats (Deut. 32:14); cow's milk was also known (Isa. 7:21-22). Butter and cheese were known among the ancients (1 Sam. 17:18) as well as curdled, sour milk, which still forms one of the main foods of the poorer classes in Arabia and Syria. This soured milk was carried by travelers who mixed it with meat, dried it, and then dissolved it in water to make a refreshing drink such as that set before his visitors by Abraham (Gen. 18:8).

MILL Two circular stones used to grind grain. The grain is fed into a hole in the upper stone and gradually works down between the stones for grinding. It was forbidden to take millstones as a pledge because they were essential for sustaining life (Deut. 24:6).

MILLENNIUM This expression, taken from Latin words, means 1,000 years. The Bible passage that mentions the "thousand years" is Rev. 20:1-7, where the word appears six times. There are three schools of thought about the millennium: amillennialism, premillennialism, and postmillennialism. The prefixes "a," "pre," and "post" suggest different views of the timing of the Lord Jesus Christ's second coming in relation to the "thousand years."

Postmillennialists argue that Christ returns *after* the thousand years. Premillennialists

Rotary mills at Capernaum

argue that Christ comes *before* the thousand years. Amillennialists, much like postmillennialists, also contend that the Lord comes after the thousand years, but they understand the thousand years differently. For the amillennialist, as the prefix suggests, there really is no literal thousand years. Instead, the whole interadvent period between the first and second comings of Christ is taken to be the "millennium." Some postmillennialists argue with the amillennialists that the millennium may not be a literal thousand years, yet they generally agree with the premillennialists that the millennium is yet future. There are many variations even among adherents to the same broad view of the millennium.

Despite differences on the details, all evangelicals are firmly committed to the literal second coming of Jesus Christ.

MILLET A small cereal grain. Millet makes a poor quality bread and is normally mixed with other grains (Ezek. 4:9).

MILLO Hebrew word meaning "filling" that describes a stone terrace system used in ancient construction. **1.** A Canaanite sanctuary built upon an artificial platform or fill and thus named "House of the Filling" (Judg. 9:6,20). **2.** A tower built by David near Jerusalem for defensive purposes (2 Sam. 5:9). It was improved by King Solomon because of a threat from Assyria (1 Kgs. 9:15).

MIND The seat of human reflection, understanding, reasoning, feeling, and decision making. Philippians 1:27 says believers are to be of "one mind [soul]" (KJV). Hebrews 12:3 urges believers not to "faint in your minds [souls]" (KJV). These passages show that the mind is considered to be the center of the human personality. The mind can be evil. It is described as "reprobate" (Rom. 1:28 KJV), "fleshly" (Col. 2:18), "vain" (Eph. 4:17), "corrupt" (2 Tim. 3:8), and "defiled" (Titus 1:15). On the other hand, believers are commanded to love God with all their minds (Matt. 22:37). This is possible because the mind can be empowered by the Holy Spirit (Rom. 12:2) and because God's laws under the new covenant are put into our minds (Heb. 8:10).

MINERALS AND METALS Inorganic elements or compounds found naturally in nature. A number of precious stones, minerals, and metals are mentioned in the Bible.

Precious Stones The Bible contains three extensive lists of precious stones: the 12 stones in Aaron's breastpiece (Exod. 39:10-13), the treasures of the king of Tyre (Ezek. 28:13), and the stones in the foundation of the new Jerusalem (Rev. 21:18-21). Other lists are found in Job 28:15-19; Isa. 54:11-12; and Ezek. 27:16. The precise identification of some of the terms is unclear, and they are rendered differently in various English translations of the Bible.

Adamant This Hebrew word is sometimes translated "diamond" (Jer. 17:1 CSB, KJV, NRSV, REB, NASB). The stone was "harder than flint" (Ezek. 3:9) and may be emery (Ezek. 3:9 NASB) or an imaginary stone of impenetrable hardness. It is perhaps best translated "the hardest stone" (Ezek. 3:9 NRSV).

Agate Multicolored and banded form of chalcedony. It was on Aaron's breastpiece (Exod. 28:19) and by some translations is the third stone in the foundation of the new Jerusalem (Rev. 21:19 NRSV).

Amethyst (Exod. 28:19; 39:12; Rev. 21:20) Identical with modern amethyst, a blue-violet form of quartz.

Beryl Most translations indicate beryl is the first stone in the fourth row of Aaron's breastpiece (Exod. 28:20; 39:13; REB "topaz"; NIV "chrysolite"). The word also occurs in the list of the king of Tyre's jewels (Ezek. 28:13; RSV, NIV "chrysolite"; NRSV "beryl"; REB "topaz").

Mineral deposits from the hot mineral springs at Hierapolis

Carbuncle In KJV, RSV, the third stone in Aaron's breastpiece (Exod. 28:17; 39:10; REB "green feldspar"; CSB, NASB, NRSV "emerald"; TEV "garnet"; NIV "beryl") and material for the gates of the restored Jerusalem (Isa. 54:12; REB "garnet"; NIV "sparkling jewels").

Carnelian (KJV and sometimes RSV, NASB "sardius") A clear to brownish red variety of chalcedony. NRSV reading for one of the stones of the king of Tyre (Ezek. 28:13; NASB, TEV, NIV "ruby"; REB "sardin") and the sixth stone in the foundation of the new Jerusalem wall (Rev. 21:20; cp. 4:3).

Chalcedony Alternate translation for agate as the third stone in the foundation of the new Jerusalem (Rev. 21:19 CSB, KJV, NASB, REB, NIV). This non-crystalline form of quartz has many varieties, including agate, carnelian, chrysoprase, flint, jasper, and onyx.

Chrysolite (Rev. 21:20) Represents various yellowish minerals. It replaces the KJV rendering "beryl" frequently in the RSV (Ezek. 1:16; 10:9; 28:13) and throughout the NIV but not in NRSV. REB reads "topaz."

Chrysoprase or Chrysoprasus (KJV) Apple-green variety of chalcedony, the tenth stone in the foundation of the new Jerusalem (Rev. 21:20).

Coral (Job 28:18; Ezek. 27:16) Calcium carbonate formed by the action of marine animals. CSB. NRSV, REB, NASB translated a second word as coral (Lam. 4:7 KJV, NIV "rubies").

Crystal Refers to quartz, the two Hebrew words so translated being related to "ice." In Job 28:18, KJV has "pearls," the NIV "jasper," but NRSV, NASB read "crystal," while REB has "alabaster." The glassy sea (Rev. 4:6) and river of life (Rev. 22:1) are compared to crystal.

Diamond Stone in the high priest's breastpiece (Exod. 28:18; 39:11; REB "jade"; NIV "emerald") and one of the jewels of the king of Tyre (Ezek. 28:13; NRSV, REB "jasper"; NIV "emerald"). It is not clear, however, if diamonds were known in the ancient Near East, and the translation is uncertain.

Emerald Bright green variety of beryl. A stone in the high priest's breastpiece and one of the stones of the king of Tyre (Exod. 28:18; 39:11; Ezek. 28:13; REB "purple garnet"; NASB, NIV, NRSV "turquoise"), with NRSV translating another word as "emerald" in Ezek. 28:13. The rainbow around the throne is compared to an emerald (Rev. 4:3), which was also a stone in the foundation of the new Jerusalem (Rev. 21:19).

Jacinth Transparent red to brown form of zirconium silicate. It appears in Aaron's breastpiece (Exod. 28:19; 39:12; KJV "ligure"; REB, TEV "turquoise") and the foundation of the new Jerusalem (Rev. 21:20).

Jasper (Exod. 28:20; 39:13; Rev. 21:11,18-19) A red, yellow, brown, or green opaque variety of chalcedony. In the RSV at Ezek. 28:13, "jasper" translates the word elsewhere rendered "diamond" (REB "jade"), but NRSV reads "moonstone" with the sixth stone jasper as in other translations.

Lapis Lazuli Not one mineral but a combination of minerals that yields an azure to green-blue stone popular in Egypt for jewelry. It is an alternate translation for sapphire (NASB in Ezek. 28:13; NIV marginal notes).

Onyx A flat-banded variety of chalcedony; sardonyx includes layers of carnelian. Onyx was used on the ephod (Exod. 25:7; 28:9; 35:27; 39:6) and in the high priest's breastpiece (Exod. 28:20; 39:13). It was provided for the settings of the temple (1 Chron. 29:2) and was one of the precious stones of the king of Tyre (Ezek. 28:13).

Pearl (Job 28:18 CSB, NASB, NRSV; KJV, NIV "rubies"; REB "red coral") Formed around foreign matter in some shellfish. In the NT, "pearl" is a simile for the kingdom of God (Matt. 13:46), a metaphor for truth (Matt. 7:6), and a symbol of immodesty (1 Tim. 2:9). Pearl is also material for the gates of the new Jerusalem (Rev. 21:21).

Ruby Red variety of corundum, or aluminum oxide. The first stone of Aaron's breastpiece is sometimes translated "ruby" (Exod. 28:17; 39:10 NASB, NIV; KJV, RSV, REB "sardius"; CSB, NRSV "carnelian"). It also appears as a stone of the king of Tyre (Ezek. 28:13 NASB, NIV; REB, KJV "sardius"; CSB, NRSV "carnelian").

Sapphire (Exod. 24:10; Lam. 4:7; Rev. 21:19) The Hebrew *sappir* is a blue variety of corundum. It is possible that *sappir* refers to lapis lazuli (NIV marginal notes) rather than true sapphire.

Topaz Stone in Aaron's breastpiece (Exod. 28:17; 39:10); also mentioned in the wisdom list (Job 28:19) and the list of the king of Tyre's precious stones (Ezek. 28:13). True topaz is an aluminum floro silicate and quite hard, but the OT topaz may refer to peridot, a magnesium olivine. The ninth decorative stone of the new Jerusalem wall foundation is topaz (Rev. 21:20). See *Beryl, Chrysolite,* above.

Turquoise Sky-blue to bluish-green base phosphate of copper and aluminum was mined in the Sinai by the Egyptians and was a highly valued stone in antiquity. Turquoise is sometimes substituted for emerald (Exod. 28:18 CSB, NASB, NIV) or jacinth (Exod. 28:19; 39:11 REB, TEV).

The following minerals are mentioned in the Bible.

Alabaster A fine-grained gypsum, but Egyptian alabaster was crystalline calcium carbonate with a similar appearance. Alabaster may be mentioned once in the Song of Songs (5:15 CSB, NRSV, NASB; KJV, REB, NIV "marble"). In the NT (Mark 14:3), it refers to containers for precious ointment.

Brimstone Refers to sulfur (CSB, NRSV, NIV). Burning sulfur deposits created extreme heat, molten flows, and noxious fumes, providing a graphic picture of the destruction and suffering of divine judgment (Isa. 30:33; Luke 17:29).

Salt Sodium chloride is an abundant mineral, used as a seasoning for food (Job 6:6) and offerings (Ezek. 43:24). As a preservative, salt was symbolic of covenants (2 Chron. 13:5). Both meanings are present in Jesus's comparison of the disciples to salt (Matt. 5:13). Salt was also a symbol of desolation and barrenness, perhaps because of the barrenness of the Dead Sea, the biblical Salt Sea.

Soda (Prov. 25:20 NASB, NIV; Jer. 2:22 REB, NIV), or nitre (KJV), is probably sodium or potassium carbonate. Other translations prefer lye (Jer. 2:22 CSB, NRSV, NASB). In Prov. 25:20, the Hebrew text refers to vinegar or lye or soda, but some modern translations follow the earliest Greek translation in reading "vinegar on a wound" (NRSV, REB; TEV "salt in a wound"; CSB "vinegar on soda").

The following metals are mentioned in the Bible.

Brass Relatively modern alloy of copper and tin. Brass in the KJV should be rendered "copper" or "bronze." RSV substitutes bronze, retaining brass only in a few places (Lev. 26:19; Deut. 28:23; Isa. 48:4; NRSV using brass only in Isa. 48:4; CSB only in Rev. 18:12). NIV does not use brass.

Bronze Usual translation of the Hebrew word that can indicate either copper or bronze. An alloy of copper and tin, and stronger than both, bronze was the most common metal used to make utensils in the ancient Near East. The Bible mentions armor (1 Sam. 17:5-6), shackles (2 Kgs. 25:7), cymbals (1 Chron. 15:19), gates (Isa. 45:2), and idols (Rev. 9:20), as well as other bronze objects.

Copper Usually alloyed with tin to make bronze, which had greater strength. The KJV uses copper only in Ezra 8:27 (CSB, NRSV, NIV "bronze"). See *Ezion-gaber*.

Gold Valued and used because of its rarity, beauty, and workability. A number of Israel's worship objects were solid gold or gilded (Exod. 37). Gold occurs in the Bible more frequently than any other metal, being used for jewelry (1 Tim. 2:9), idols, scepters, worship utensils, and money (Matt. 10:9; Acts 3:6). The new Jerusalem is described as made of gold (Rev. 21:18,21).

Iron A more difficult metal to smelt than copper, it did not come into widespread use until about the time of Israel's conquest of Canaan. The Canaanites' "iron chariots" (Judg. 4:3 CSB) represented a technological advantage over Israel; the Philistines may have enjoyed an iron-working monopoly (1 Sam. 17:7). Iron was used where strength was essential and became a symbol of hardness and strength (Ps. 2:9).

Lead Gray metal of extremely high density (Exod. 15:10) used for weights, heavy covers (Zech. 5:7-8), and plumb lines (Amos 7:7-8). Lead is quite pliable and useful for inlays such as lettering in rock (Job 19:24). It was also used in the refining of silver (Jer. 6:27-30).

Silver Silver was a measure of wealth (Zeph. 1:18). By Solomon's day, it was common in Israel (1 Kgs. 10:27) and was the standard monetary unit, being weighed in shekels, talents, and minas (Exod. 21:32). Silver was used for objects in Israel's worship (Exod. 36:24), idols (Ps. 115:4), and jewelry (Song 1:11).

Tin (Num. 31:22; Ezek. 22:18,20) Sometimes confused with lead; articles of pure tin were rare. It was principally used in making bronze, an alloy of tin and copper.

MINGLED PEOPLE KJV term for foreigners who are perhaps of mixed race and are associated with a dominant population (Ezek. 30:5).

MINISTER, MINISTRY One who serves another. God's call to Abram (Gen. 12) contains the foundations of ministry. God's promise was to begin with Abram and Sarai and from them make a nation that would be a blessing to all nations. For Christians, Jesus is the supreme model of a minister. In his inaugural sermon in the synagogue at Nazareth, Jesus read from the prophet Isaiah, summarizing the purpose of his ministry (Luke 4:18-19). Although Jesus had all authority in heaven and on earth, his style of leadership and ministry was not one of dominating his followers (Mark 10:42) but one of service. On one occasion, when James and John sought prominent places in Jesus's kingdom, he reminded them, "For even the Son of Man did not come to be served, but to serve, and to give his life as a ransom for many" (Mark 10:45 CSB).

Jesus's intention was that his ministry would continue through his people, the church. God through the Holy Spirit gives a variety of roles and gifts to those in the church for the purpose of ministry. These include preaching, evangelism, teaching, pastoral care, and administration.

MINSTREL KJV term for musician (Matt. 9:23). Modern translations have "flute players" or "musicians." Professional musicians were hired to assist in mourning at funerals. See *Grief and Mourning*.

MINT AND CUMIN Mint is a sweet-smelling herb for seasoning food. Cumin is a caraway-like herb used in seasonings and in medicine (Matt. 23:23).

MIRACLES, SIGNS, WONDERS Events that involve an immediate and powerful action of God designed to reveal his character or purposes. Words used in the Scriptures to describe the miraculous include "sign," "wonder," "work," "mighty work," "portent," and "power." The basic nature of a sign is that it points people to God. "Wonders" describe God's supernatural activity, a special manifestation of his power (Exod. 7:3). New Testament writers also used *dunamis*, power or inherent ability, to refer to activity of supernatural origin or character (Mark 6:2; Heb. 2:4). "Work" (*ergon*) is also used in the NT in the sense of "miracle." John the Baptist heard of the "works" of Jesus while he was in prison (Matt. 11:2).

Contemporary philosophical and theological arguments over the possibility of the miraculous reflect the altered worldview of the past several centuries—from a theistic to a nontheistic concept of the universe. We live in a world that seems intent on squeezing the supernatural out of the realm of reality. The people of the Bible did not face this problem. The biblical perspective on the universe is that it is created, sustained, and providentially governed by God. The Bible makes no clear-cut distinction between the natural and supernatural. In the "natural" event, the Bible views God as working providentially; whereas, in the miraculous, God works in striking ways to call attention to himself or his purposes.

One's view of the miraculous is related to one's view of the universe. A mechanistic perspective believes the world is controlled by unalterable natural laws and cannot allow for the possibility of miracles. Christians in every century have refused to have their universe so limited. They have affirmed the continuing miraculous work of God in the universe he created, continues to care for, uses to reveal himself, and has promised to redeem.

MIRIAM Personal name meaning "bitter," "God's gift," "beloved," or "defiant." **1.** Sister of Moses and Aaron. She played a key role in the rescue of the baby Moses (Exod. 2:4-8) and in the experience of the exodus and the wilderness community. After crossing the Red Sea, she assumed the role of prophetess and led the women in singing a song of victory (Exod. 15:20-21). Miriam sided with Aaron in an act of rebellion against Moses. God chastened her by striking her with leprosy, but granted healing following Moses's intercessory prayer and a seven-day quarantine (Num. 12:15). **2.** Member of the clan of Caleb in the tribe of Judah (1 Chron. 4:17).

MIRROR Polished or smooth surface that produces images by reflection. In Bible times, mirrors were made of polished metal (Job 37:18). The apostle Paul spoke of the unclear reflections seen in such mirrors (1 Cor. 13:12).

Bronze mirror with a bone handle from the Etruscan culture (ca. 350 BC)

MISHNAH A term that refers to the teaching about the oral law (halakah) passed on by a particular teacher (rabbi). According to the Mishnah itself, oral tradition and its teachings go all the way back to Moses, who received the halakah from God on Mount Sinai and passed it on to subsequent generations. The Mishnah has helped scholars reconstruct specific elements in the Judaism of Palestine at the time of Jesus. It has also been helpful in understanding the development of Judaism during the period of establishment and growth of the early Christian church.

MISSION(S) Task on which God sends a person whom he has called, particularly a mission to introduce another group of people to salvation in Christ. In the Christian context, the person sent is called a missionary. The mission of the churches is to send missionaries to all parts of the world until everyone has had the opportunity to hear the message of Jesus and accept him as Lord.

Mission is an important OT concept. Its foundation lies in the

understanding that the transcendent God is also the God who is involved in history. He is the God who acts. The record of his involvement in history indicates that his work is both revelatory and redemptive. People know who God is by what he has done. Since the fall (Gen. 3), God's primary activity has been redemptive (Josh. 24:2-15). God sends his messengers to the house of Israel and his prophets as his spokesmen to all nations.

God's mission concern is inclusive, not exclusive. His interest has been in all people, not just in Israel. When God called Abraham and his descendants, they were chosen, not to be exclusive vessels, but to be a means of blessing "all the peoples on earth" (Gen. 12:3 CSB). Later God told Israel that they had been elected as God's chosen people (Exod. 19:3-6). They were to be the recipient and guardian of God's special revelation (Heb. 1:1-3) and the channel through which the Redeemer would enter the stream of human history (Isa. 49:1-10).

The NT brings to a crescendo the Bible's symphonic theme of mission. The mission begins with Jesus who was sent to earth to reveal the Father (John 1:18), to glorify him (John 13:31), to bring the kingdom of God on earth (Matt. 12:22-32), and to make God's love and mercy known to a lost world. He came to seek and save the lost (Luke 19:10). Through his teachings Jesus made clear that his mission was to continue after he ascended. Each of the Gospels and Acts contain an account of his mandate to his followers, telling them to go to all the world, make disciples, baptize them, and preach the gospel (Matt. 28:19-20; Mark 16:15-16; Luke 24:46-49; John 20:21-22; Acts 1:8). Jesus assumed that the church would reach out beyond itself. The church was to cross all barriers—to reach out to all ethnic groups,

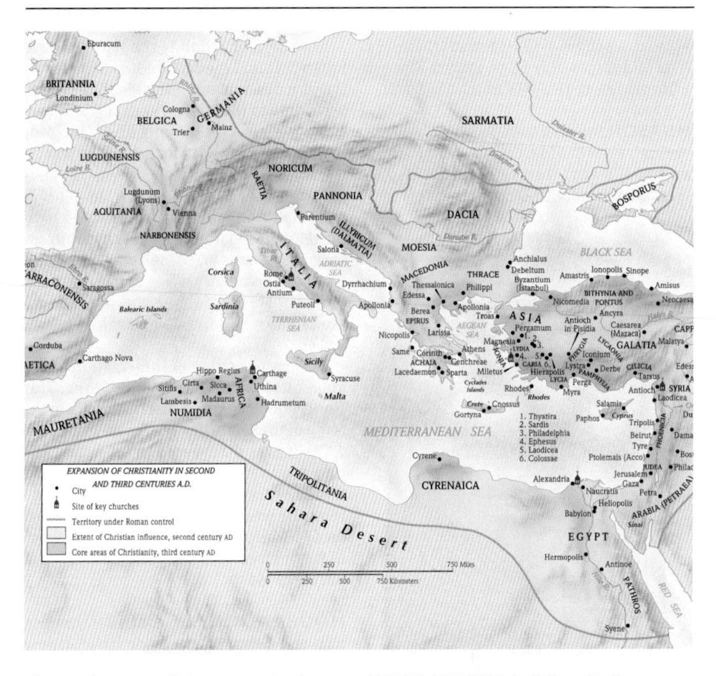

clans, tribes, social classes, and cultures. The message of salvation was to be shared with all people everywhere.

MIST The mist of Gen. 2:6 refers to subterranean waters welling up and watering the ground. In Job 36:27, rain distills from the mist or fog rising from the earth. Mist is often symbolic of something that disappears quickly (James 4:14; 2 Pet. 2:17).

MITRE KJV term for a type of headdress, probably a turban. The mitre was part of the high priest's distinctive clothing (Exod. 28:4,36-39) and was required dress on the Day of Atonement (Lev. 16:4).

MITYLENE Place-name meaning "purity." Chief city of the Aegean island of Lesbos southeast of Asia Minor. Paul stopped at Mitylene on his return trip to Syria from Achaia during his third missionary journey (Acts 20:14).

MIXED MULTITUDE Term for foreigners who associate themselves with a dominant ethnic group. The term is used for those foreigners who joined the Israelites in the exodus from Egypt (Exod. 12:38), who became associated with the people of Judah during the exile (Neh. 13:3), or who were associated with the Egyptians (Jer. 25:20) or Babylonians (Jer. 50:37). See *Mingled People*.

MIZPAH or **MIZPEH** Place-name meaning "watchtower" or "lookout." **1.** Place in Gilead where Laban and Jacob made a covenant and set up a pillar (Gen. 31:49). This Mizpah was also the hometown of Jephthah, a judge of Israel (Judg. 11). **2.** A district near Mount Hermon (Josh. 11:3-8). **3.** A city in the lowland plain of Judah (Josh. 15:38). **4.** A city of Benjamin where Saul was first presented to Israel as its new king (1 Sam. 10:17).

MIZRAIM Hebrew word for Egypt (Gen. 12:10; 25:18). **1.** Son of Ham (Gen. 10:6,13). **2.** The

Mushri, a people of Cilicia in southeastern Asia Minor (possibly 1 Kgs. 10:28; 2 Kgs. 7:6; 2 Chron. 1:16-17 TEV; NIV note). See *Egypt*.

MNASON Personal name meaning "remembering"; variant of Jason. Native of Cyprus, and Paul's host during his final trip to Jerusalem in about AD 60 (Acts 21:16).

The Moabite Stone found at Dibon. In the inscription, Mesha, king of Moab, gives thanks to Chemosh for delivering Moab out of the hands of Israel.

MOAB AND THE MOABITE STONE Personal and national name and monument that Moab left behind. The narrow strip of land east of the Dead Sea was known in biblical times as "Moab." The history of the Moabites was intertwined with that of Israel. Moreover, the Israelites regarded the Moabites as close relatives, as implied by Gen. 19:30-38. There were peaceful interchanges as well as conflicts between the Israelites and Moabites during the time of the judges. The story of Ruth illustrates peaceful relations, while the episode of Ehud and Eglon illustrates conflict (Judg. 3:12-30).

King Saul of Judah is reported to have fought against the Moabites (1 Sam. 14:47). David, a descendant of the Moabitess Ruth according to the biblical genealogies (Ruth 4:18-22), placed his parents under the protection of the king of Moab while he was on the run from Saul (1 Sam. 22:3-4). Yet he is reported to have defeated the Moabites in battle later on and to have executed two-thirds of the Moabite prisoners by arbitrary selection (2 Sam. 8:2). Moab was represented among Solomon's wives, and the worship of Chemosh, the Moabite god, was accommodated in Solomon's Jerusalem (1 Kgs. 11:1-8).

Our major source of information about ancient Moab is the Moabite Stone. This stone, which bears an inscription from the reign of the same King Mesha mentioned in 2 Kgs. 3, was discovered in 1868, near the ruins of ancient Dibon. The monument reports the major accomplishments of King Mesha's reign. He boasts especially of having recovered Moabite independence from Israel and of having restored Moabite control over northern Moab.

MODERATION Self-control; calmness; temperateness (Phil. 4:5). Modern translations read "forbearance" (RSV), "forbearing spirit" (NASB), "gentleness" (NIV, NRSV), "graciousness" (CSB), and "consideration of others" (REB).

MOLE Large rodent. In Lev. 11:30, some translate the Hebrew word as "chameleon" (CSB, NIV, NASB, RSV). Others translate "mole" in Lev. 11:29 (NASB, NEB) or in Isa. 2:20 (CSB, NASB, RSV, KJV).

MOLECH A pagan Ammonite god to whom human sacrifices were made. Leviticus 20:5 condemns those who are "prostituting themselves with Molech" (CSB). Israelites are commanded not to "sacrifice any of your children in the fire to Molech" (Lev. 18:21 CSB), apparently a reference to the sacrifices of children in the valley of Hinnom.

MOLTEN SEA (KJV) Large bronze basin with water for the ceremonial washing of priests that stood in the courtyard southeast of Solomon's temple (1 Kgs. 7:23-26). The basin was cast by Hiram of Tyre who was responsible for all the bronze work in the temple (1 Kgs. 7:13-14). This basin was more than 14 feet in diameter, more than 7 feet high, and more than 43 feet in circumference. It held about 12,000 gallons. After the fall of Jerusalem in 587 BC, the basin was broken up and taken to Babylon (Jer. 52:17).

MONEY CHANGERS Persons who sold or exchanged foreign money for Jewish money acceptable in temple worship. Some exchangers profited greatly from this business and lent their money along with what others invested with them. Money changers set up tables in the temple court of the Gentiles in the time of Jesus to provide this service for worshipers. In anger at this corruption of the purpose of the temple, Jesus drove them, along with the sellers of sacrificial animals, out of the temple court (Matt. 21:12).

MONKEY Small, long-tailed primate. TEV, REB include monkeys among the exotic animals brought as gifts to King Solomon (2 Chron. 9:21). CSB, NIV, NRSV notes read "baboons." CSB, KJV, NASB, NRSV render the Hebrew term "peacocks."

MONOTHEISM/POLYTHEISM Competing systems of religious belief that only one god exists or that many gods exist. The first commandment demanded of the Israelites, "Do not have other gods besides me" (Exod. 20:3 CSB). This requirement seems to assume that other gods besides Yahweh existed. However, it was only acknowledging that most people believed in the existence of many gods, and it also demanded that the people who followed the Mosaic commandments should reject such beliefs. The Lord who brought Israel out of the land of Egypt would allow no compromise in the loyalty of the people. That kind of belief system is commonly called henotheism.

In contrast to Israel's strict commitment to the Lord alone, the surrounding nations believed in numerous gods whose activities influenced their lives. A good example of this is the Canaanite religious system. Principal among the gods of the Canaanite pantheon were El, the great father figure, and Baal, the younger hero, along with several other gods. The Canaanites believed that the fertility of the land depended on the fertility of Baal and his consort.

A move away from henotheism and polytheism appears first in the OT among the prophets. Competition between the people of Israel and the people of Phoenicia was highlighted by a competition for loyalty of the people between the Lord and Baal. That competition came to its sharpest focus in the contest between Elijah, the Lord's prophet, and the prophets of Baal on Mount Carmel, with Yahweh emerging victorious (1 Kgs. 18).

The pressure of the exile challenged Yahweh's claim as the only God. If the Lord is really God, how could the people of the Lord lose their independence and their land to a foreign people? Would the success of the Babylonians not suggest that the Lord, the God of the Judeans, had been defeated by Marduk, the god of the Babylonians? The prophets' response was that the exile was the result of Israel's own God using the Babylonians as an instrument of punishment against the Lord's own people since they had violated the terms of the covenant. This opened the door for a theological position that asserted the existence of only one God who is Lord not only of Israel but also of all the rest of the world. This is known as monotheism.

The beautiful poetry of Isa. 40–66 represents the height of Israel's monotheism. For the first time in the OT literature, a prophet argued that no other gods exist (Isa. 45:5-6). With that poetry, Israel reached a fully developed monotheism.

MOON Light in the night sky created by God and controlling the calendar (Gen. 1:14-19). Two of Israel's greatest festivals were celebrated at the beginning of the full moon: the Passover in the spring and the Feast of Booths in the fall. Each month they celebrated the "new moon" with a little more festivity than a regular Sabbath (Num. 28:11-15). Yet the OT strongly teaches against worshiping the moon (Deut. 4:19) as did Israel's neighbors. The moon was nothing more than an object created by Yahweh and had no power over people.

MORAL DECLINE The Bible teaches that in the latter days the world will be gripped by an unprecedented decline in morals. False teaching will allow wickedness to grow, resulting in apathy (Matt. 24:12) and hostility (2 Tim. 3:1-5) toward the things of Christ. Religion will become a pretense for personal gain rather than an expression of true devotion to God (2 Tim. 3:5), and as a result the standards of moral behavior rooted in the Bible will be held to be irrelevant. These are the kind of activities that people have always done in opposition to God, but they will be more intense and worldwide in scope.

MORDECAI Personal name meaning "little man." **1.** Esther's cousin and the mastermind behind her rise to power and subsequent victory over the evil Haman. A descendant of the Amalekite king Agag, Haman sought to destroy the Jewish race. Mordecai, a descendant of King Saul's family, led Esther to thwart the attempt. Haman was hanged on the gallows he had built for Mordecai. **2.** A man who returned from Babylon to Jerusalem with Zerubbabel (Ezra 2:2; Neh. 7:7).

MOREH Place-name meaning "instruction" or "archers." **1.** Abraham's first encampment in the land of Canaan. Here he built an altar after God had appeared to him and entered into covenant (Gen. 12:6-7). In later years, God set forth at Moreh the blessings and curses on Israel regarding their keeping of the commandments (Deut. 11:26-30). Joshua set up a memorial stone under the oak at Moreh as a reminder of the covenant between God and his people (Josh. 24:26). **2.** Hill in tribal territory of Issachar where Gideon reduced his troops by testing the way they drank water (Judg. 7:1).

The hill of Moreh

MORESHETH or **MORESHETH-GATH** Place-name meaning "inheritance of Gath." Home of the prophet Micah (Mic. 1:1). The city was apparently located near Philistine Gath. This may be the Gath that King Rehoboam fortified (2 Chron. 11:8).

MORIAH Rocky outcropping in Jerusalem located north of the ancient city of David. It was on this rock that Abraham would have sacrificed Isaac as a burnt offering, but God intervened and provided a ram (Gen. 22:2,13). Centuries later, King Solomon built the temple on this site (1 Chron. 28:3-6).

MORTAR A vessel used to crush grain, herbs, and olives (Num. 11:8). Mortar was also a claylike building material (Exod. 1:14), used to secure brick or stone.

A stone mortar for grinding grain or other substances at Lachish

MOSES Personal name meaning "drawn out of the water." Leader of the Israelites in their exodus from Egyptian slavery and oppression and their later sojourn in the wilderness as they journeyed toward the promised land.

The story of Moses begins in Exod. 1 with an account of events in Egypt that affected Moses's people. Since the Israelites had grown to be so numerous, the Egyptian pharaoh feared their power. To control them he launched an official policy of oppression. When the oppression failed to curb their population growth, he decreed that all male Hebrew babies were to be cast into the Nile (Exod. 1:22). Moses was born after this decree was issued, so his life began under the pharaoh's judgment of death.

His mother acted to protect her baby from the pharaoh's death decree. She placed Moses in a basket in the river. The pharaoh's own daughter came to the river, found the ark, and recognized the child as a Hebrew. Eventually she adopted the baby as her own child and hired Moses's own mother to take care of him (Exod. 2:10).

Rock traditionally considered the Rock of Rephidim that Moses struck to get water for the Israelites

Moses grew to maturity in the palace of the Egyptian king. But he was forced to flee to the land of Midian when he killed an Egyptian supervisor who was brutalizing a Hebrew slave. Soon after arriving in Midian, Moses witnessed the aggression of male shepherds against female shepherds who had already drawn water for their sheep. Moses saved the oppressed shepherds, whose father, the priest of Midian, invited him to live and work under the protection of the Midianite's hospitality. Eventually one of the Midianite's daughters became Moses's wife. In the idyllic peace of the Midianite's hospitality, Moses took care of Jethro's sheep, fathered a child, and lived at a distance from his own people (Exod. 2).

The event at the burning bush while Moses worked as a shepherd introduced him to the critical character of his heroic work. The burning bush caught Moses's attention. There Moses met the God of the fathers who offered Moses a distinctive name as the essential key for Moses's authority—"I am who I am." This strange formulation played on God's promise to Moses to be present with him in his special commission. God sent Moses back to the Egyptian pharaoh to secure the release of his people from oppression.

The negotiation narratives depict Moses in one scene of failure after another. Moses posed his demands to the pharaoh, announced a sign that undergirded the demands, secured some concession from the pharaoh on the basis of the negotiations, but failed to win the release of the people. The final scene is hardly a new stage in the negotiations. To the contrary, God killed the firstborn of every Egyptian family, passing over the Israelite families. In the agony of this death scene, the Egyptians drove the Israelites out of Egypt (Exod. 12:30-36).

Moses led the people into the wilderness, only to have the pursuing Egyptians trap the Israelites at the Red Sea. But God, who had promised divine presence for the people, defeated the enemy at the sea. Then God proved his presence with his people. He met their needs for food and water in the hostile wilderness. Even the serpents and the Amalekites failed to frustrate the wilderness journey of the Israelites under Moses's leadership. Exodus 17:8-13 shows Moses to be faithful in the execution of his leadership responsibilities. Numbers 12:1-16 shows Moses to be meek, a leader of integrity who fulfilled the duties of his office despite opposition from members of his own family.

At Mount Sinai, also known as Mount Horeb, God delivered the law through Moses that would serve as the instruction book for his people (Exod. 20:1-24). The law showed each new generation how to follow Moses's teaching in a new setting in the life of the people. The law of Moses became a model for Israelite society. Indeed, Israel's historians told the entire story of Israel under the influence of the Moses model and suggested that the Davidic kings should have constructed their leadership for Israel under the influence of the Moses model.

The death of Moses is marked by tragic loneliness, yet graced with God's presence. Because of Moses's sin (Num. 20:1-13), God denied Moses the privilege of entering the promised land. Deuteronomy 34 reports the death scene. Moses left his people to climb another mountain. Atop that mountain, away from the people whom he served so long, Moses died (Deut. 34:1-8). God attended this servant at his death. Indeed, God buried him. Only God knows where the burial place is.

The Moses saga served as a model for future leaders in Israel. Jeroboam I created a new kingdom, distinct from the Davidic kingdom centered in Jerusalem. The sign of his kingship included the golden calves of Aaron. Josiah modeled a reformation in Jerusalem on the basis of the Mosaic model. As the new Moses, he almost succeeded in uniting the people of the south with the people of the north. Perhaps the most important OT figure that must be interpreted as a new Moses is the servant of Isa. 40–66, the model for understanding Jesus in the NT.

Stream in the Wilderness of Zin that local tradition says was formed when Moses and Aaron hit the rock

MOST HIGH Translation of the Hebrew word *'Elyon*. It is used in conjunction with other divine names such as El (Gen. 14:18) and Yahweh (Ps. 7:17) to speak of God as the Supreme Being. See *Names of God*.

MOTE Archaic English word (KJV) referring to a small particle or speck. Jesus used the word in his Sermon on the Mount to contrast a slight moral fault one may enjoy pointing out in others, while neglecting one's own more heinous fault, represented by the "log," "plank," or "beam" in one's own eye (Matt. 7:3-5).

MOTH Literally "consumer" or "waster," an insect whose destructive power illustrates the result of sin (Ps. 39:11) and the judgment of God (Hos. 5:12). The moth's weakness speaks of the frailty of man (Job 4:19). Jesus urged his followers to avoid the temptation to accumulate wealth on earth where the moth could destroy it but to lay up treasures in heaven (Matt. 6:19-20). See *Insects*.

MOTHER The Bible refers to every aspect of motherhood: conception (Gen. 4:1), pregnancy (Luke 1:24), the pain of childbirth (Gen. 3:16), and nursing (1 Sam. 1:23). A new mother was considered to be ritually unclean, and an offering was prescribed for her purification (Lev. 12; cp. Luke 2:22-24). The book of Proverbs (31:1) indicates that even in ancient times mothers shared with fathers the responsibility for instructing and disciplining children. Mothers have the same right to obedience and respect as fathers (Lev. 19:3), and in OT times death was the fate of those who cursed or assaulted parents (Deut. 21:18-21). Jesus enforced the fifth commandment and protected it against scribal evasion (Matt. 15:3-6).

Motherly virtues are often extolled: compassion for children (Isa. 49:15), comfort of children (Isa. 66:13), and sorrow for children (Jer. 31:15, quoted in Matt. 2:18). The fact that God would use a human mother to bring his Son into the world has bestowed upon motherhood its greatest honor. Jesus set an example for all to follow by the provision he made for his mother (John 19:25-27). Jesus made it plain, however, that devotion to God must take precedence over that of a mother (Matt. 12:46-50). Even the OT (Gen. 2:24) indicated that a man's devotion to his wife supersedes that to his mother.

In addition to the literal sense, the word "mother" is often used metaphorically. Israel is compared to an unfaithful mother (Isa.

Church of the Beatitudes on the traditional site of the Sermon on the Mount by the Sea of Galilee

50:1). Revelation 17:5 calls Babylon (Rome) the mother of harlots (those who are unfaithful to God). A city is the "mother" of her people (2 Sam. 20:19). Deborah was the "mother" (or deliverer) of Israel. In a more dramatic vein, the heavenly Jerusalem is the "mother" of Christians (Gal. 4:26). Jesus spoke of his compassion for Jerusalem as being like that of a mother hen for her chicks (Matt. 23:37). Paul compared his ministry to a mother in labor (Gal. 4:19) and a nursing mother (1 Thess. 2:7).

MOUNT OF THE BEATITUDES The "Horns of Hattin" near Capernaum that tradition identifies as the site of the Sermon on the Mount (Matt. 5:1–7:29).

MOUNTAIN The geography of Bible lands featured high mountains and deep rifts. Many important events in the Bible took place on or near mountains. God called Moses to his work at Mount Horeb, sometimes called "the mountain of God." A part of God's call was the promise that the Israelite people would worship there upon their escape from Egypt (Exod. 3:1-12). After the exodus, God commanded Moses to gather the people at Mount Sinai (probably identical to Horeb). There God gave the law including the Ten Commandments to Moses. Other OT mountain episodes include Aaron's death on Mount Hor (Num. 33:38), the death of Moses on Mount Nebo (Deut. 34:1-8), and Elijah's defeat of the prophets of Baal on Mount Carmel (1 Kgs. 18:15-40). The term "mountain" is also used symbolically. It is a natural image for stability (Ps. 30:7), obstacles (Zech. 4:7), and God's power (Ps. 121:1-2). God will remove all obstacles when his redemption is complete "and every mountain and hill will be leveled" (Isa. 40:4 CSB).

Lightning strikes over the traditional location for Mount Sinai, Jebel Musa. The monastery of St. Catherine, built on the traditional spot where Moses saw the burning bush, is in the center of the photograph.

MOUSE Rodent listed among the unclean animals (Lev. 11:29). Mice were apparently feared as carriers of the plague (1 Sam. 6:4).

MOUTH The word is used as a synonym for lips (2 Kgs. 4:34). The phrase "the mouth of the LORD has spoken" serves as a frequent reminder of the reliability of a prophetic message (Jer. 9:12). Fire (2 Sam. 22:9) or a sword (Rev. 1:16) proceeding from the mouth of God pictures the effectiveness of God's word of judgment.

MUFFLER KJV term for a scarf (Isa. 3:19, NRSV). The item was part of the finery of Jerusalem socialites.

MULE Hybrid animal produced by the union of a male ass and a female horse. Since the Mosaic law forbade crossbreeding (Lev. 19:19), the Israelites imported mules (Ezek. 27:14). They were used as war animals, for riding, and for carrying burdens (2 Kgs. 5:17). They were especially good for moving heavy burdens in mountainous areas. David chose a mule to symbolize royalty for Solomon's coronation (1 Kgs. 1:33), possibly because the Israelites did not have horses.

MURDER Intentional taking of human life. People are created in the image of God, and human life is viewed as a sacred trust. It is because of this that taking human life is viewed as a serious crime in the Bible. The prohibition against murder is found in the Ten Commandments, the heart of Hebrew law (Exod. 20:13). The OT (Gen. 9:6) prescribed that a murderer should be prepared to forfeit his own life. In Num. 35:16-31, careful attention is given to determining whether a killing is to be classified as murder. According to Jesus, murder in the heart is also a serious matter (Matt. 5:21-22). Murder really begins when one loses respect for another human being. Spitting in the face of another, looking with contempt upon another, and unleashing one's anger are signs that a murderous spirit is present.

MUSIC, INSTRUMENTS, DANCING Expression of the full range of human emotions vocally or instrumentally through music was an important part of the lives of biblical people. Celebration through dance found a natural place in both the religious and secular life of ancient Israel.

Music The first reference to music in the Bible occurs in Gen. 4:21. Lamech's son, Jubal, "was the father of all who play the lyre and the flute" (CSB). Jubal brought the advent of music to the portrayal of cultural advance. The name Jubal is related to the Hebrew word for "ram" (*yovel*), the horns of which served as a signaling instrument in ancient Israel. The joy of music is evidenced by its prominent role in the celebrations of life. A farewell might be said "with joy and singing, with tambourines and lyres" (Gen. 31:27 CSB); a homecoming welcomed "with tambourines and dancing" (Judg. 11:34 CSB). Victory in warfare provided impetus for numerous songs. The song of Miriam, one of the oldest poetic verses in the OT, celebrated the defeat of Pharaoh at the Sea (Exod. 15:21).

The establishment of the monarchy about 1025 BC brought a new dimension to the musical tradition of ancient Israel. Professional musicians took their place at court (1 Kgs. 1:34,39-40) and in religious ritual. Worship featured trumpet calls (cp. Num. 10:10) and songs of thanksgiving, expressions of praise and petition sung after the offering of sacrifices (2 Chron. 29:25-30).

The psalms show not only the emotional range of music from lament to praise but also provide words for some of the songs used in temple worship. Guilds of musicians, known through reference to their founders in some psalm headings (e.g., "the sons of Korah"), were devoted to the discipline of liturgical music.

Musical Instruments Pictorial representations as well as remains from instruments discovered through archaeology give us information about ancient musical instruments. The most common musical instrument in the Bible is the shofar (ram's horn). It was a signaling instrument in times of peace and war (Judg. 3:27).The shofar announced the new moons and Sabbaths, warned of approaching danger, signaled the death of nobility, and was sounded in national celebrations (1 Kgs. 1:34). Other musical instruments mentioned in the Bible are the trumpet, known as the instrument of the priests (Num. 10:2-10); the lyre, a rectangular stringed instrument (2 Sam. 6:5); the harp, another stringed instrument (2 Chron. 9:11); the flute, also called "pipes," a wind instrument best described as a primitive clarinet (1 Kgs. 1:39-40); and the timbrel or tambourine, a percussion instrument (Ps. 150). The cymbal, another percussion instrument, is mentioned in the NT (1 Cor. 13:1).

Dancing Dancing had a prominent place in the life and worship of Israel. Pictured in the homecoming welcome of victorious soldiers by women, dancing could be accompanied by song and instrumental music (1 Sam. 18:6).

MUSTARD Large plant whose seeds were once thought to be the smallest in the plant world. Jesus used the mustard plant in a parable to symbolize the rapid growth of the kingdom of God (Matt. 13:31-32), and its seed as a simile for faith (Matt. 17:20).

MUTENESS Inability to speak. God made Ezekiel mute (Ezek. 3:26) in response to Israel's failure to listen to his message. Daniel became speechless in response to the appearance of a heavenly messenger (Dan. 10:15). Zechariah's muteness (Luke 1:20,22) served as a sign of the truthfulness of Gabriel's message as well as a punishment for Zechariah's unbelief. Symbolically, to be mute means to hold one's peace (Isa. 53:7), especially in the face of injustice.

MUTH-LABBEN Hebrew phrase in the title of Ps. 9 that means "death of the son." The phrase likely refers to the tune to which the psalm was sung.

MYRA A city in the province of Lysia in southeastern Asia Minor. Myra was a stopping point on Paul's voyage to Rome (Acts 27:5-6).

MYRRH Aromatic resin used as an ingredient in anointing oil (Exod. 30:23), applied as perfume (Esth. 2:12), placed in clothes to deodorize them (Ps. 45:8), given as a gift (Matt. 2:11), and used to embalm bodies (John 19:39).

MYSIA Northwest region of Asia Minor (Acts 16:7). Hindered from mission work in Bythinia, Paul passed through Mysia before embarking on his mission to Macedonia (Acts 16:6-11).

The Treasury building of ancient Petra, the Nabatean capital

NAAM Personal name meaning "pleasantness." Descendant of Caleb in the tribe of Judah (1 Chron. 4:15).

NAAMAH Name *meaning* "pleasant" or "delightful." **1.** Sister of Tubal-cain (Gen. 4:22). **2.** Ammonite wife of Solomon and mother of Rehoboam (1 Kgs. 14:21,31; 2 Chron. 12:13). **3.** Village in the Shephelah district of Judah (Josh. 15:41).

NAAMAN Personal name meaning "pleasantness." **1.** Syrian general cured of leprosy under the direction of the prophet Elisha (2 Kgs. 5). Naaman's leprosy apparently was not contagious nor was it seen as the result of some moral sin. Following his cleansing, he professed faith in Israel's God. **2.** A son (Gen. 46:21) and/or grandson (Num. 26:40) of Benjamin, who became head of a clan called Naamites.

NAAMATHITE Title meaning "resident of Na'ameh," given to Zophar, one of Job's three friends (Job 2:11; 11:1; 20:1; 42:9).

NAARAH Name meaning "girl" or "mill." **1.** Wife of Ashur (1 Chron. 4:5-6). **2.** Form of place-name Naarath preferred by modern translations.

NAARAI Personal name meaning "attendant of Yah." One of David's 30 elite warriors (1 Chron. 11:37). The parallel account gives the name Paarai (2 Sam. 23:35).

NAARAN City allotted to Ephraim, likely identical with Naarah (1 Chron. 7:28; cp. Josh. 16:7).

NAARATH KJV form of Naarah, a city in the tribal territory of Ephraim just north of Jericho (Josh. 16:7).

NABAL Personal name meaning "fool" or "rude, ill-bred."

NABATEANS Arabic people whose origins are unknown. Although not mentioned in the Bible, they greatly influenced Palestine during intertestamental and NT times. They appear to have infiltrated ancient Edom and Moab from a homeland southeast of Petra. That city later became their capital.

NABONIDUS Personal name meaning "Nabu is awe-inspiring." Last king of the Neo-Babylonian Empire (555–539 BC).

NABOPOLASSAR Personal name meaning "Nabu, protect the son." King (626–605 BC) who revolted from the Assyrians and established the Neo-Babylonian Empire. He rebelled in 627 BC and established his capital in Babylon.

NABOTH Personal name, perhaps meaning "sprout." Owner of a vineyard in the Jezreel Valley adjacent to the country palace of King Ahab, who desired the property for a vegetable garden. Naboth refused to sell on the grounds that the property was a family inheritance (1 Kgs. 21:3-4). Hebrew law allowed only farmland to be leased for the number of crops until the Jubilee Year (Lev. 25:15-16). Farmland was not to be sold in perpetuity (Lev. 25:23). Jezebel, who had no regard for Israel's laws, plotted Naboth's judicial murder on the charge that he had blasphemed God and the king (1 Kgs. 21:8-14). Naboth's murder evoked God's judgment on Ahab and his family (1 Kgs. 21:17-24).

NACON or **NACHON** (KJV) Place-name meaning "firm" or "prepared." Threshing floor between Baal-judah (Kiriath-jearim) and Jerusalem (2 Sam. 6:6).

NADAB Personal name meaning "willing" or "liberal." **1.** Aaron's eldest son (Exod. 6:23; Num. 3:2; 1 Chron. 6:3), who participated in the ratification of the covenant (Exod. 24:1,9), served as a priest (Exod. 28:1), and was consumed by fire along with his brother Abihu for offering unholy fire before the Lord (Lev. 10:1-7; Num. 26:61). **2.** Descendant of Judah and Tamar (1 Chron. 2:28,30). **3.** Descendant of Benjamin and great-uncle of Saul (1 Chron. 8:30; 9:36). **4.** Son of Rehoboam (1 Kgs. 14:20) and idolatrous king of Israel (901–900 BC).

NAG HAMMADI Modern Egyptian village 300 miles south of Cairo and about 60 miles north of Luxor or ancient Thebes. Because of the close proximity of Nag Hammadi to the site of an important discovery of ancient documents relating to Gnosticism, the collection of documents is usually referred to as the Nag Hammadi Documents or Library.

NAGGAI or **NAGGE** (KJV) Personal name, perhaps meaning "splendor of the sun." Ancestor of Jesus (Luke 3:25).

NAHALAL Place-name meaning "pasture" with alternate forms: Nahallal (Josh. 19:15 KJV); Nahalol (Judg. 1:30). Town Zebulun's territory allotted to the Levites (Josh. 19:15; 21:35). The Israelites did not drive out the Canaanite inhabitants of the city (Judg. 1:30).

NAHALIEL Place-name meaning "palm grove of God," "torrent valley of God," or, less likely, "God is my inheritance." One of Israel's stopping places in Transjordan (Num. 21:19).

NAHAM Personal name meaning "consolation." Either the brother (KJV, REB) or brother-in-law (CSB, NASB, NIV, NRSV) of Hodiah (1 Chron. 4:19).

NAHAMANI Personal name meaning "comfort." Exile who returned with Zerubbabel (Neh. 7:7). The name does not appear in the parallel list (Ezra 2:2).

NAHARAI or **NAHARI** (KJV) Personal name meaning "intelligent" or "snorting." One of David's 30 elite warriors; he served as armor-bearer to Joab (2 Sam. 23:37; 1 Chron. 11:39).

NAHASH Personal name meaning "serpent" or perhaps "magnificence." **1.** Ammonite ruler whose assault of Jabesh-Gilead set the stage for Saul's consolidation of power as king (1 Sam. 11:1-11). **2.** Mother of Abigail the sister of David, also aunt of Joab (2 Sam. 17:25).

NAHATH Personal name meaning "descent," "rest," "quietness," or even "pure, clear." **1.** Edomite clan chief (Gen. 36:13,17; 1 Chron. 1:37). **2.** Levite (1 Chron. 6:26), possibly identical with Toah (1 Chron. 6:34) and Tohu (1 Sam. 1:1). **3.** Overseer in Hezekiah's time (2 Chron. 31:13).

NAHBI Personal name meaning "hidden" or "timid." Naphtali's representative among the 12 spies sent to survey Canaan (Num. 13:14).

NAHOR Personal name meaning "snore, snort." **1.** Son of Serug, father of Terah, and grandfather of Abraham (Gen. 11:22-26). **2.** Son of Terah and brother of Abraham (Gen. 11:26). **3.** City in Mesopotamia where Abraham's servant sought and found a wife for Isaac (Gen. 24:10).

NAHSHON Personal name meaning "serpent." Leader of the tribe of Judah during the wilderness years (Num. 1:7; 2:3; 7:12,17; 10:14), brother-in-law of Aaron (Exod. 6:23), and an ancestor of King David (Ruth 4:20-22) and of Jesus (Matt. 1:4; Luke 3:32).

NAHUM, BOOK OF Personal name "Nahum" means "comfort, encourage." He was a Hebrew prophet, and the OT book that bears his name contains some of his messages. Very little biographical information is known about the prophet Nahum. He is called an Elkoshite (1:1), but the location of Elkosh is unknown.

The date of the prophet's ministry can be placed between 600 and 700 BC by two events mentioned in his book. Nahum 3:8 refers to the destruction of the Egyptian capital, No-amon or Thebes, in 663 BC and indicates that the prophet was active after this time. In chapter 2 he looked forward to the destruction of Nineveh, which took place in 612 BC. Nahum, therefore, prophesied after 650 BC, probably close to the time of the fall of Nineveh.

Historical Background Since about 730 BC, Israel and Judah had been Assyrian vassals. Almost a century later, the Assyrian Empire began its decline. Many vassal nations revolted along with Josiah of Judah (2 Kgs. 22–23). A coalition of Medes, Babylonians, and Scythians attacked Assyrians and in 612 BC destroyed the capital, Nineveh. The Assyrians formed a coalition with the Egyptians, but in 605 BC they were defeated.

The Prophet's Message The Assyrian oppression caused the people to ask how God could allow such inhumanity to go unanswered. Nahum responded to Assyrian tyranny with a message marked by its vivid language. Assyria's might had been heavy upon Judah, but Nahum announced that God would destroy them.

While the book of Nahum is harsh and deals with the unpleasantness of war, it served to give hope to the people of Judah. They had been subjected to the cruel domination of Assyria for over a century, but now their faith in God to act on their behalf could be bolstered through God's response. God's justness was reaffirmed.

NAIL **1.** Keratinous covering of the top ends of fingers and toes. If an Israelite desired to marry a prisoner of war, she was to cut her nails either as a sign of mourning for her parents or as part of her purification on entering the community of Israel (Deut. 21:12). **2.** Metal fasteners used in construction and for decoration (1 Chron. 22:3; 2 Chron. 3:9; Isa. 41:7; Jer. 10:4). The earliest nails were made of bronze. With the introduction of iron, larger nails were made of iron. Smaller nails continued to be made of bronze. Nails were sometimes plaited with precious metal and nail heads decorated with gold foil when used for ornament (cp. 2 Chron. 3:9). The nails used in the crucifixion of Jesus were likely iron spikes five to seven inches long (John 20:25). **3.** KJV used nail (pin) as an alternate translation for a Hebrew term modern translations consistently render "peg" (Exod. 35:18; Judg. 4:21-22; Zech. 10:4).

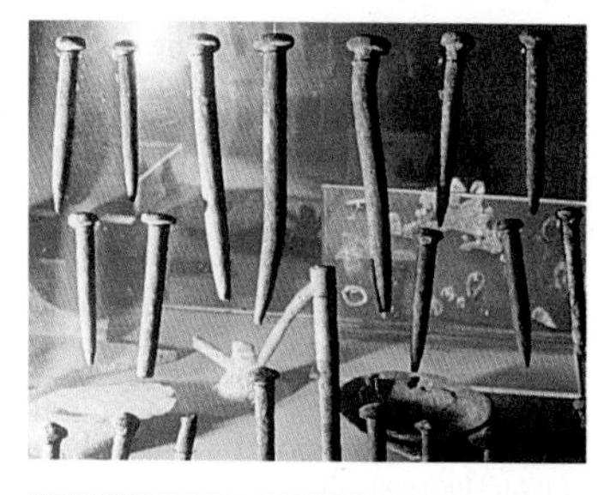

Nails from Roman times

NAIN Place-name meaning "pleasant." Village in southwest Galilee where Jesus raised a widow's son (Luke 7:11-15). The ancient town sat on a hillside overlooking the Plain of Esdraelon.

NAIOTH Place-name meaning "dwelling." The name refers either to a building or district in the city of Ramah that housed the prophetic school that Samuel led (1 Sam. 19:18-24). David sought refuge from Saul at Naioth. Three groups of royal messengers and finally Saul himself fell victim to prophetic frenzy when they attempted to capture David there.

NAKED Being without clothes (Gen. 2:25; Job 1:21; Eccles. 5:15; Amos 2:16; Mic. 1:8) or else poorly clothed (Deut. 28:48; Matt. 25:36-44; James 2:15). The phrase "to uncover the nakedness of" means to have sexual intercourse (Lev. 18:6-19; 20:11,17-21). Nakedness frequently occurs in conjunction with shame (Gen. 3:7; 9:21-27; Isa. 47:3; Ezek. 16:8,36-37).

NAMES OF GOD The name of God holds an important key to understanding the doctrine of God and the doctrine of revelation. The name of God is a personal disclosure and reveals his relationship with his people. His name is known only because he chooses to make it known. To the Hebrew mind, God was both hidden and revealed, transcendent and immanent. Even though he was mysterious, lofty, and unapproachable, he bridged the gap with humankind by revealing his name.

NAMING In biblical tradition the task of naming a child generally fell to the mother (Gen. 29:31–30:24; 1 Sam. 1:20) but could be performed by the father (Gen. 16:15; Exod. 2:22) and in exceptional cases by nonparental figures (Exod. 2:10; Ruth 4:17). Naming could be attributed to God originating through a divine birth announcement (Gen. 17:19; Luke 1:13). Naming took place near birth in the OT and on the eighth day accompanying circumcision in NT narratives (Luke 1:59; 2:21).

The biblical concept of naming was rooted in the ancient world's understanding that

NAMES OF GOD

Name	Reference	Meaning
Hebrew Names		
Adonai	Ps. 2:4	Lord, Master
El-Shaddai	Gen. 17:1-2	All Powerful God
El-Elyon	Gen. 14:18-20	Most High God/Exalted One
El-Olam	Gen. 21:33	The Eternal God
El-Berith	Judg. 9:46	God of the Covenant
El-Roi	Gen. 16:13	God Who Sees Me
Qedosh Yisra'el	Isa. 1:4	The Holy One of Israel
Shapat	Gen. 18:25	Judge/Ruler
Yahweh-Jireh	Gen. 22:14	Yahweh Provides
Yahweh-Nissi	Exod. 17:15	Yahweh My Banner
Yahweh-Mekaddesh	Exod. 31:13	Yahweh Sanctifies
Yahweh-Shalom	Judg. 6:24	Yahweh My Peace
Yahweh-Sabaoth	1 Sam. 1:3	Yahweh of Armies
Yahweh-Rohi	Ps. 23:1	Yahweh My Shepherd
Yahweh-Shammah	Ezek. 48:35	Yahweh Is There
Yahweh-Tsidkenu	Jer. 23:6	Yahweh Our Righteousness
Aramaic Names		
Attiq yomin	Dan. 7:9	Ancient of Days
Illaya	Dan. 7:25	Most High

a name expressed essence. To know the name of a person was to know that person's total character and nature. Revealing character and destiny, personal names might express hopes for the child's future. Changing of name could occur at divine or human initiative, revealing a transformation in character or destiny (Gen. 17:5,15; 32:28; Matt. 16:17-18).

NAOMI Personal name meaning "my pleasantness." Wife of Elimelech and mother-in-law to Orpah and Ruth (Ruth 1:2,4). Naomi suffered the deaths of her husband and two sons while in Moab. Her matchmaking between Ruth and Boaz was successful, and she became a forebear of David, Israel's greatest king (Ruth 4:21-22).

NAPHATH-DOR or **NAPHOTH-DOR** Designation of the region surrounding the coastal city of Dor about 15 miles west of Megiddo (Josh. 12:23; 1 Kgs. 4:11).

NAPHISH Personal name meaning "refreshed." A son of Ishmael and ancestor of a northwest Arabian tribe of the same name (Gen. 25:15; 1 Chron. 1:31). The tribe dwelt in Transjordan before being displaced by Reuben, Gad, and the half tribe of Manasseh (1 Chron. 5:19).

NAPHTALI Personal name meaning "wrestler." Sixth son of Jacob and second son by his concubine Bilhah (Gen. 30:6-8). In blessing him, Jacob likened Naphtali to a hind let loose (49:21), probably a reference to unbridled energy. The tribe that bears his name inhabited a territory north of the Sea of Galilee that extended along the northwest side of Jordan beyond Lake Huleh (Josh. 19:32-39).

NAPHTUHIM Residents of Naphtuh, an unidentified geographic area (Gen. 10:13; 1 Chron. 1:11; Naphtuhites, NIV and REB). The Naphtuhim were most likely residents of the Nile Delta or inhabitants of the oases to the west of the Nile Valley.

NARCISSUS Common name among both slaves and freedmen meaning "daffodil." The Narcissus of Rom. 16:11 headed a household, perhaps including slaves and/or associated freedmen, which included some Christians.

NARD Expensive fragrance derived from the roots of the herb *nardostachys jatamansi*. The term appears twice in the Song of Songs (1:12 ESV; 4:13-14) and in two of the Gospel accounts of the woman anointing Jesus at Simon's house in Bethany (Mark 14:3; John 12:3; "spikenard," KJV). The disciples rebuked her for this action, stating that the ointment could have been sold for a sizable sum and the proceeds donated to the poor.

NATHAN Personal name meaning "gift." **1.** Prophet in royal court during reign of David and early years of Solomon. **2.** Son of David, born in Jerusalem (2 Sam. 5:14; 1 Chron. 14:4). His mother was Bathsheba (Bath-shua) (1 Chron. 3:5). He is in the genealogy of Jesus Christ (Luke 3:31). **3.** Nathan of Zobah, father of Igal, one of David's mighty men (2 Sam. 23:36). He may be the same as Nathan the brother of Joel (1 Chron. 11:38), within another list of David's mighty men. **4.** The two Nathans mentioned as fathers of Azariah and Zabud may be the same man and identified as the prophet Nathan (1 Kgs. 4:5) during Solomon's reign. **5.** Returning exile whom Ezra sent on a mission to secure ministers for God's house (Ezra 8:15-17). He may be the same exile who had married a foreign wife and put her away (Ezra 10:39).

NATHAN-MELECH Personal name meaning "the king has given" or perhaps "Melech [the god Molech] has given." Nathan-Melech served as an official of King Josiah (2 Kgs. 23:11).

NATHANAEL Personal name meaning "giver of God." An Israelite whom Jesus complimented as being guileless (John 1:47) and who, in turn, confessed the Lord as being the Son of God and King of Israel (v. 49). Nathanael was from Cana of Galilee (John 21:2) and apparently became one of the inner core of disciples who followed Jesus.

NATIVES Term used by several modern translations (NASB, REB, NRSV) to designate the inhabitants of Malta (Acts 28:2). Barbarous people (KJV) reflects the Greek *barbaroi*, which designates the islanders as non-Greek speaking. NIV reads "islanders"; CSB "local people."

NATURAL According to nature. **1.** Natural use (Rom. 1:26-27 KJV; natural relations, RSV) refers to heterosexual relations, thus "natural intercourse" (NRSV, REB). **2.** Natural affection refers specifically to affection for family members. Those lacking natural affection (*astorgoi*) are unloving to their families or generally inhuman or unsociable (Rom. 1:31; 2 Tim. 3:3). **3.** Natural branches refer to original or native branches as opposed to engrafted ones (Rom. 11:21,24). **4.** Natural or unspiritual person (1 Cor. 2:14) is one not open to receiving gifts from God's Spirit or to discerning spiritual matters (contrast 2:15). This contrast between the spiritual and natural is also evidenced by James 3:15 (NASB) and Jude 19 (NIV). **5.** The natural face (James 1:23) is literally the face of one's birth. To see one's natural face is to see oneself as one actually is.

NAUM KJV form of Nahum, an ancestor of Christ (Luke 3:25).

NAVE 1. Term used by some modern translations (NASB, NRSV) for the main room of the temple between the vestibule and the holy of holies (1 Kgs. 6:3,5,17; 7:50; 2 Chron. 3:4-5,13; 4:22). KJV referred to this room as the temple or house. **2.** KJV used "nave" for the center of a wheel through which an axle passes (1 Kgs. 7:33). Modern translations render the underlying Hebrew as "rim."

NAVEL 1. Depression in the middle of the belly marking the place where the umbilical cord was formerly attached. Ezekiel 16:4 graphically portrays Jerusalem's hopeless state before God's adoption in the image of a child whose umbilical cord (navel string) is not cut. **2.** Hebrew expression for "midst of the land" or "center of the earth" (NRSV) in Judg. 9:37; Ezek. 38:12.

NAZARETH, NAZARENE Place-name meaning "branch." Nazareth did not enjoy a place of prominence until its association with Jesus. It does not appear in the OT. As he became known as "Jesus of Nazareth" (Matt. 26:71; Luke 18:37; 24:19; John 1:45; Acts 2:22; 3:6; 10:38), his hometown became fixed in Christian memory. Nazareth was located in lower Galilee about halfway between the Sea of Galilee and the Mediterranean Sea.

Nazareth did not possess a good reputation, as reflected in the question of Nathanael, himself a Galilean (John 1:46). The early church received similar scorn as the Nazarene sect (Acts 24:5).

An overview of modern Nazareth from the southwest

Such lack of respect was likely due to an unpolished dialect, a lack of culture, and quite possibly a measure of irreligion and moral laxity. Jesus was rejected by his townspeople near the beginning of his public ministry, being cast out of the synagogue at Nazareth (Luke 4:16-30; Matt. 13:54-58; Mark 6:1-6).

NAZIRITE Member of a class of individuals especially devoted to God. The Hebrew term means consecration, devotion, and separation. Two traditional forms of the Nazirite are found. One was based on a vow by the individual for a specific period; the other was a lifelong devotion following the revelatory experience of a parent that announced the impending birth of a child.

The lifelong Nazirites in biblical tradition included Samson (Judg. 13), Samuel (1 Sam. 1), and John the Baptist (Luke 1:15-17). In the NT, Paul took the Nazirite vow for a specific period of time (Acts 18:18; 21:22-26). Amos 2:12 shows an ethical concern for protecting the status of the Nazirite.

NEAH Place-name meaning "settlement." Border town in the tribal territory of Zebulun (Josh. 19:13).

NEAPOLIS Name meaning "new city," of the seaport of Philippi (Acts 16:11). Neapolis (modern Kavala) is located about 10 miles from Philippi in northeastern Macedonia. The city sits on a neck of land between two bays, both of which serve as harbors.

NEARIAH Personal name, perhaps meaning "Yah's young man." **1.** Descendant of David (1 Chron. 3:22-23). **2.** Commander of Hezekiah's forces who defeated the Amalekites (1 Chron. 4:42-43).

NEBAI Personal name meaning "projecting" or "fruitful." One of the witnesses to Ezra's renewal of the covenant (Neh. 10:19).

NEBAIOTH or **NEBAJOTH** (KJV) Personal name meaning "fruitfulness." Son of Ishmael and ancestor of an Arab tribe of the same name (Gen. 25:13; 28:9; 36:3). KJV used the alternate form Nebajoth in 1 Chron. 1:29; Isa. 60:7.

NEBALLAT Place-name, perhaps meaning "blessed with life." The name perhaps derives from Nabu-uballit, the personal name of an Assyrian governor of Samaria. Neballat was resettled by Benjaminites after the exile (Neh. 11:34).

NEBAT Personal name meaning "God has regarded." Father of Jeroboam I (1 Kgs. 11:26; 12:2,15). Nebat was from Zeredah about 10 miles west of Shiloh.

NEBO Place-name and divine name meaning "height." **1.** Babylonian god of speech, writing, and water. Worship of Nebo was popular during the Neo-Babylonian era (612–539 BC). Isaiah mocked parades featuring the idol of Nebo (Isa. 46:1). **2.** Moabite city located southwest of Heshbon. The tribes Reuben and Gad requested the area around Nebo for their flocks (Num. 32:2-3). It was held by Israel until recaptured by King Mesha about 850 BC. **3.** Town reinhabited by exiles returning from Babylon (Ezra 2:29). The site has been identified with Nob. **4.** Mountain about 12 miles east of the mouth of the Jordan River from which Moses viewed the promised land (Deut. 32:49). It rises more than 4,000 feet above the Dead Sea and gives an excellent view of the southwest, west, and as far north as Mount Hermon.

The Jordan Valley from the top of Mount Nebo looking toward Jericho

NEBUCHADNEZZAR Personal name meaning "Nabu protects." King of Babylon 605–562 BC. He was the son of Nabopolassar and inherited the throne upon the death of his father. Nebuchadnezzar served as a general under his father and was a brilliant strategist. His victory over the Egyptian forces at Carchemish (605) signaled the completion of Babylon's conquest of Palestine (Jer. 46:1-2).

NEBUSHASBAN, NEBUSHAZBAN Variant transliterations of personal name meaning "Nabu save me." High official of Nebuchadnezzar involved in the fall of Jerusalem (Jer. 39:13).

NEBUZARADAN Personal name meaning "Nabu has given offspring." An officer in the Babylonian army during King Nebuchadnezzar's reign. His title is given as "captain of the guard" (bodyguard, Jer. 39:13), an uncertain designation. He led his troops in a siege of Jerusalem in 587 BC (2 Kgs. 25:8-9), burned the city's buildings, tore down its walls, and carried away the people into exile. Four years later, he returned and deported still more citizens (Jer. 52:30).

NECHO KJV form of Neco (2 Chron. 35:20,22; 36:4). KJV used the hyphenated form Pharaoh-necho at Jer. 46:2.

NECHOH KJV alternate form of Neco. This form always occurs in the hyphenated form Pharaoh-nechoh (2 Kgs. 23:29,33-35).

NECK Portion of the body connecting the head to the torso. To put one's feet on the neck of an enemy is a sign of complete victory (Josh. 10:24). A yoke placed on the neck is a frequent emblem of servitude (Gen. 27:40; Deut. 28:48; Isa. 10:27). To fall upon someone's neck with weeping or kissing is a special sign of tenderness (Gen. 33:4; 45:14; cp. Luke 15:20). To be stiff-necked or to harden one's neck is a common picture of stubborn disobedience (Exod. 32:9; 33:3,5).

NECKLACE Ornament worn around the neck (Song 1:10; Ezek. 16:11). The gift of a gold necklace is sometimes the sign of installation to a high office (Gen. 41:42; Dan. 5:29).

NECO Second Pharaoh (609–594 BC) of the 26th Dynasty of Egypt whose forces killed Josiah in battle (2 Kgs. 23:29-35; 2 Chron. 35:20-24) and who installed Jehoiakim as king of Judah in his place (2 Kgs. 23:34-35).

NECROMANCY Conjuring the spirits of the dead to predict or influence future events.

NEDABIAH Personal name meaning "Yah is generous." Son of Jeconiah, the exiled king of Judah (1 Chron. 3:18).

NEEDLE Small slender instrument used in sewing with an eye at one end through which thread is passed. The needles of NT times were similar in size to modern needles with the exception of our smallest needles. Needles were most often made of bronze, though bone and ivory were also used. Jesus's teaching that "it is easier for a camel to go through the eye of a needle than for a rich person to enter the kingdom of God" (Matt. 19:24 CSB; cp. Mark 10:25; Luke 18:25) illustrates the impossibility of a rich person's being saved apart from the intervention of God who does the impossible (Matt. 19:26).

NEEDLEWORK Decorative work sewn upon cloth. Needlework was used in the decoration of the screens for the tabernacle door (Exod. 26:36; 36:37) and for the gate to its court (Exod. 27:16; 38:18) as well as for Aaron's girdle (Exod. 28:39; 39:29).

NEESINGS KJV term meaning "sneezings" or "sneezes" (Job 41:18).

NEGEB or **NEGEV** (preferred sp.) Place-name meaning "dry" and referring to an arid region in southern Palestine and coming to

View of the Negev from Beer-sheba, the most important city of the Negev.

Cross-sectional view of the Negev/Negeb in relation to the Dead Sea, Judah, and the Mediterranean Sea.

mean "south." During biblical times it was more populated than today, indicating either more rainfall then or better conservation of the resources. It was the land of the Amalekites during Abraham's day (Gen. 14:7). There he exiled Hagar (21:14). The Israelites wandered in the Negev after a futile attempt to enter Canaan (Num. 14:44-45). David incorporated it into his kingdom, and Solomon established fortresses in the region.

NEGINAH, NEGINOTH Neginoth, the plural form of Neginah, is used as a technical term in the superscriptions of several psalms (Pss. 4; 6; 54–55; 61; 67; 76) and as the subscription of Hab. 3:19. The term is generally understood to specify the instrumentation needed for performance "with stringed instruments" (cp. Isa. 38:20; Lam. 5:14). Other references suggest that *neginah* designates a taunt song (Job 30:9; Ps. 69:12; Lam. 3:14).

NEHELAM, NEHELAMITE Either a family name or a reference to the home of the false prophet Shemaiah (Jer. 29:24,31-32). The name is perhaps a play on the Hebrew word for dreamer (cp. Jer. 23:25,32).

NEHEMIAH Personal name meaning "Yah comforts or encourages" and name of OT book featuring work of Nehemiah. **1.** Leader who was among the first to return with Zerubbabel from exile to Judah in about 538 BC (Ezra 2:2; Neh. 7:7). **2.** Son of Azbuk, "ruler of half the district of Beth-zur" (Neh. 3:16 CSB), one who helped Nehemiah son of Hachaliah with rebuilding the walls of Jerusalem. **3.** Nehemiah, the son of Hachaliah, is the main character in the book that bears his name. He was a contemporary of Ezra and Malachi, Socrates in Greece (470–399 BC).

NEHEMIAH, BOOK OF Nehemiah and Ezra were one book in the ancient Hebrew and Greek OT and probably were not divided until after the interbiblical period. Jewish tradition says Ezra or Nehemiah was the author. Because of the close connection between Chronicles and Ezra-Nehemiah, one person might have written or compiled all three books. Those who follow this argument refer to the author as the Chronicler.

The literary style of Nehemiah is similar to that in Ezra. There are many lists (chaps. 3; 10:1-27; 11; 12:1-26). The author/compiler wove Ezra's and Nehemiah's stories together, Ezra being featured in Neh. 8.

The book has four major sections: the rebuilding of Jerusalem's walls (chaps. 1–7), the Great Revival (chaps. 8–10), population and census information (chaps. 11–12), and the reforms of Nehemiah (chap. 13). Nehemiah made two visits from King Artaxerxes to Jerusalem (2:1-6; 13:6-7). His first, 445 BC, was to repair the walls; they were in a state of disrepair almost a century after the first arrival from exile in 538 BC. The second was a problem-solving trip in the thirty-second year of Artaxerxes (13:6), 432 BC.

NEHILOTH Technical musical term in the superscription of Ps. 5. The term is generally understood to specify the instrumentation for the psalm, "with flutes."

NEHUSHTA Personal name meaning "serpent" or "bronze." Mother of King Jehoiachin of Judah (2 Kgs. 24:8). As queen mother, she was among those deported in the first exile (24:12,15).

NEHUSHTAN Name of a "brazen serpent" destroyed by King Hezekiah as part of an attempt to reform Judah's life and worship (2 Kgs. 18:4). The object was believed to be the one Moses fashioned to relieve a plague in the Israelite camp during the exodus (Num. 21:8-9).

NEIEL Name meaning "dwelling place of God." Town assigned to Asher (Josh. 19:27).

NEIGH Loud, prolonged cry of a horse used as a figure of approaching battle (Jer. 8:16) or of unbridled sexual desire (Jer. 5:8; 13:27; 50:11).

NEKEB KJV transliteration of a Hebrew term meaning tunnel, shaft, or mine (Josh. 19:33).

NEKODA Personal name meaning "speckled." **1.** Family of temple servants returning to Jerusalem after the exile (Ezra 2:48; Neh. 7:50). **2.** Family who returned from exile but were unable to establish their Israelite descent (Neh. 7:62).

NEMUEL **1.** Ancestor of a family of Simeonites, the Nemuelites (Num. 26:12; 1 Chron. 4:24); this Nemuel is also called Jemuel (Gen. 46:10; Exod. 6:15) **2.** A Reubenite (Num. 26:9).

NEPHEG Personal name meaning "boaster." **1.** A Levite (Exod. 6:21). **2.** Son born to David in Jerusalem (2 Sam. 5:15; 1 Chron. 3:7; 14:6).

NEPHEW **1.** The son of one's brother or sister. KJV never used "nephew" in this sense, but CSB, NASB, NIV used it in this sense for Lot (Gen. 12:5; 14:12). **2.** When KJV translation was being made, "nephew" was used in the broader sense of a lineal descendant, especially a grandson (Judg. 12:14; Job 18:19; Isa. 14:22; 1 Tim. 5:4).

NEPHILIM Transliteration of a Hebrew word that designates a class of beings mentioned in Gen. 6:4 and Num. 13:33. Some interpreters believe the word is related to *naphal* meaning "to fall." In Gen. 6:4, the term refers to "heroes of old" (NRSV) so some have concluded that these are beings that have fallen from heaven and married the daughters of men. However, the text does not state that explicitly. At most it says that the Nephilim were on the earth during the days when the sons of God married the daughters of mankind. When the 12 spies were sent to Canaan, they saw giants whom they called the Nephilim, beside whom they seemed small, as "grasshoppers." There is no attempt to relate these people to the Nephilim of Gen. 6.

NEPHISIM Family of temple servants who returned from exile (Ezra 2:50), probably identical with the Nephushesim (Nephishesim, KJV) of Neh. 7:52.

NEPHTHALIM Greek form of Naphtali, son of Jacob and tribe, used by the KJV (Matt. 4:13,15; Rev. 7:6).

NEPHTOAH Name meaning "opening," found only in the phrase "Waters of Nephtoah." Boundary marker for Judah and Benjamin (Josh. 15:9; 18:15).

NER Personal name meaning "light." Father of Saul's general Abner and grandfather of Saul (1 Sam. 14:51; 26:5,14; 2 Sam. 2:8; 1 Chron. 9:36).

NEREUS Personal name borrowed from Greek mythology where Nereus is the sea god who fathers the Nereids (sea nymphs). The NT Nereus was a Roman Christian, possibly the son of Philogus and Julia (Rom. 16:15).

NERGAL Name, perhaps a form of "Ne-urugal" (Lord of the great city). Following the fall of the northern kingdom of Israel, the Assyrians resettled Samaria with Mesopotamian peoples who brought their gods, including Nergal, with them (2 Kgs. 17:30).

NERGAL-SHAREZER A personal name meaning "Nergal, protect the king." He is mentioned as being among the officers of Nebuchadnezzar's court who helped destroy Jerusalem in 586 BC (Jer. 39:3,13). He was a son-in-law of Nebuchadnezzar who usurped the Babylonian throne following the death of Evil-merodach.

NERI Personal name meaning "lamp." An ancestor of Jesus (Luke 3:27).

NERIAH Personal name meaning "Yahweh is light." Father of two men who assisted Jeremiah: Baruch the scribe (Jer. 32:12; 36:4-19) and Seraiah the quartermaster (Jer. 51:59).

NERO Personal name meaning "brave." Roman emperor AD 54–68. Nero became emperor in AD 54 at the age of 17. During Nero's rule, the Great Fire broke out in Rome (AD 64). Much of the city was destroyed, including Nero's palace. The story, probably true in part, goes that Nero fiddled while Rome burned. Nero took measures to provide relief for those affected by the fire. Still he could not dispel the rumor that he had the fire set. People knew that he planned to build a much larger palace for himself, and they reasoned that he used the fire to clear off the land. Nero felt the need to divert suspicion to another group. He selected the Christians as his scapegoats. He claimed that they had set the fire. A systematic persecution of the Christians followed. Because of his lifestyle and the persecution, many Christians viewed him as the antichrist.

NEST Hollow container fashioned by a bird to contain its eggs and young. Nest is often used as a simile or metaphor for a human dwelling (Num. 24:21; Job 29:18; Hab. 2:9; Prov. 27:8). The term translated "nest" (Matt. 8:20; Luke 9:58) suggests a leafy "tent" rather than a nest.

NET **1.** Loosely woven mesh of twine or cord used for catching birds, fish, or other prey. **2.** Netting or network refers to grillwork used as part of the ornament of the altar of burnt offering (Exod. 27:4-5; 38:4) and of the capitals of the temple columns (1 Kgs. 7:17-20).

NETAIM Name meaning "plantings." Site of a royal pottery works (1 Chron. 4:23).

NETHANEEL or **NETHANEL** Personal name meaning "given by God." **1.** Leader of the tribe Issachar and a son of Zuar (Num. 1:8). He commanded an army of 54,400 men (2:5-6). **2.** Fourth son of Jesse and brother of King David (1 Chron. 2:14). **3.** One of several priests to blow the trumpet before the ark of God (1 Chron. 15:24). **4.** Prince of Judah whom King Jehoshaphat sent out with others to teach the law of God in the cities of Judah (2 Chron. 17:7-9). **5.** Levite and father of Shemaiah who recorded the names and order of the people who would minister in the temple (1 Chron. 24:6). **6.** Fifth son of Obed-edom who was a gatekeeper in the temple (1 Chron. 26:4). **7.** Levite who contributed to the Passover offering when Josiah was king (2 Chron. 35:9). **8.** Priest and son of Pashur who had married a foreign wife while exiled in Babylon (Ezra 10:22). He might have participated in the dedication of the wall around Jerusalem (Neh. 12:36). **9.** Head of the priestly family of Jedaiah when Joiakim was high priest (Neh. 12:21). **10.** Priest, one of Asaph's associates, who played a trumpet, in dedicating the rebuilding of Jerusalem's wall (Neh. 12:36). Some identify him with 8, above.

NETHANIAH Personal name meaning "given of Yah." **1.** Son of Asaph who served in a company of prophets established by David. They issued their message with harps, psalteries, and cymbals (1 Chron. 25:1-2). **2.** Levite sent along with Jehoshaphat's princes to teach from the book of the law of God in all the cities of Judah (2 Chron. 17:7-9). **3.** Father of Jehudi sent to Baruch by the princes of Jehoiakim (Jer. 36:14). **4.** Father of Ishmael who killed Gedaliah (2 Kgs. 25:23-25; Jer. 40:8,14-16; 41).

NETHINIM Name meaning "those given (to the priests and Levites)," which Ezra and Nehemiah apply to persons of foreign extraction who performed menial tasks in the temple. Representatives of the Nethinim returned from exile with Zerubbabel in 538 BC (Ezra 2:43-54; Neh. 7:46-56). The lists of returnees contain many foreign names suggesting their origin as prisoners of war. Despite their foreign origin, the Nethinim appear to be accepted as part of the people of Israel. They were prohibited from mixed marriages with the people of the land (Neh. 10:28-30) and shared in the responsibility for repair of the Jerusalem city walls (Neh. 3:26; contrast Ezra 4:1-3). The Nethinim resided in the Ophel district of Jerusalem, likely near the water gate (Neh. 3:26), a site conducive with their task as water bearers.

NETOPHAH Name meaning "dropping." A village and surrounding district in the hill country of Judah (2 Sam. 23:28-29; 1 Chron. 11:30; 27:13; Neh. 7:26).

NETTLE Two different Hebrew words are sometimes translated "nettle" (other times "weeds," "thistles" [CSB]). Nettles are coarse plants with stinging hairs belonging to the family *Urtica*; generally, any prickly or stinging plant (Job 30:7; Prov. 24:31; Isa. 34:13; Hos. 9:6; Zeph. 2:9). Nettles are used as a sign of desolation and judgment.

NEW BIRTH Term referring to God's impartation of spiritual life to sinners. It is synonymous with regeneration and finds its origin in John 3:1-10. There Jesus told Nicodemus, "Unless someone is born again, he cannot see the kingdom of God" (v. 3 CSB). When Jesus chastised Nicodemus for his dismay at this teaching: "Are you a teacher of Israel and don't know these things?" (v. 10; cp. Ezek. 36:26-27), Jesus indicated that the idea of the new birth is rooted in the OT. The new birth is caused by the gracious and sovereign act of God apart from human cooperation (John 1:13; Eph. 2:4-5). God brings the new birth about through the preaching of the word of God (1 Pet. 1:23; James 1:18). The result of the new birth is a changed life (2 Cor. 5:17), which includes saving faith and repentance (Eph. 2:8; Acts 11:18; 16:14) and obedience to God's law (1 John 3:9).

NEW GATE A gate of the Jerusalem temple (Jer. 26:10; 36:10), which should perhaps be identified with the Upper Gate that Jothan built (2 Kgs. 15:35) and/or with the Upper Benjamin Gate (Jer. 20:2).

NEW TESTAMENT Second major division of the Christian Bible with 27 separate works (called "books") attributed to at least eight different writers. Four accounts of Jesus's life are at the core. The first three Gospels (called "Synoptic") are very similar in content and order. The Fourth Gospel has a completely different perspective. A history of selected events in the early church (Acts) is followed by 20 letters to churches and individuals and one apocalypse. The letters deal mainly with the interpretation of God's act of salvation in Jesus Christ. Matters of discipline, proper Christian behavior, and church polity also are included. The apocalypse is a coded message of hope to the church of the first century that has been reinterpreted by each succeeding generation of Christians for their own situations.

NEZIAH Personal name meaning "faithful" or "illustrious." Head of a family of temple servants (Nethinim) who returned from exile (Ezra 2:54; Neh. 7:56).

NEZIB Name meaning "garrison," "idol," "pillar," or "standing place." Village in the Shephelah district of Judah (Josh. 15:43).

NIBHAZ Deity worshipped by the residents of Avva whom the Assyrians used to resettle the area about Samaria after the fall of that city in 722 BC (2 Kgs. 17:31).

NIBSHAN Name meaning "prophesy." Town assigned to the tribe of Judah (Josh. 15:62).

NICANOR Personal name meaning "conqueror." One of seven Hellenists "full of faith and the Holy Spirit" (CSB) chosen to administer food to the Greek-speaking widows of the Jerusalem church (Acts 6:3).

NICODEMUS Personal name meaning "innocent of blood." John identifies Nicodemus as a Pharisee, "a ruler of the Jews" (John 3:1), that is, a member of the Sanhedrin, the Jewish ruling council, and as "a teacher of Israel" (John 3:10), that is, an authority on the interpretation of the Hebrew Scriptures. Nicodemus's coming at night suggests his timidity and his trek from the darkness of his own sin and ignorance to the light of Jesus (John 3:2).

True to his name, Nicodemus defended Christ before his peers (John 7:51), who were unaware that one of their number might have believed in him (v. 48). Their response is a twofold rebuke that may be paraphrased "Are you a Galilean peasant?" and "Are you ignorant of the Scriptures?" (v. 52).

The reference to Nicodemus's initial coming at night highlights his later public participation in Jesus's burial (John 19:39-41). Nicodemus's contribution was enough aloes and spices to prepare a king for burial, and so he did. On one level, the burial was a simple act of Pharisaic piety (cp. Tobit 1:17). On a deeper level, it recognized that in his suffering and death Christ fulfilled his role as King of the Jews.

NICOLAITANS Heretical group in the early church who taught immorality and idolatry. They are condemned in Rev. 2:6,15 for their practices in Ephesus and Pergamum. Thyatira apparently had resisted the false prophecy they preached (Rev. 2:20-25). The Nicolaitans have been linked to the type of heresy taught by Balaam (Num. 25:1-2; 2 Pet. 2:15), especially the pagan feasts and orgies that they apparently propagated in the first-century church.

NICOLAS or **NICOLAUS** Personal name meaning "conqueror of people." A "convert from Antioch," one of seven Hellenists chosen to administer food to the Greek-speaking widows of the Jerusalem church (Acts 6:5 CSB).

NICOPOLIS Place-name meaning "city of victory," shared by many cities in the ancient world. The site in which Paul most likely wintered (Titus 3:12) was Nicopolis in Epirus in northwest Greece.

NIGER Latin nickname meaning "black." Surname of Simeon (KJV, Symeon), one of the teacher-prophets of the early church at Antioch (Acts 13:1).

NIGHT MONSTER Translation (NASB, ASV) of the Hebrew term *Lilith* (Isa. 34:14 NRSV). The term occurs only here in Scripture unless textual emendations are accepted (Job 18:15; Isa. 2:18).

NIGHT WATCH Ancient division of time (Pss. 90:4; 119:148; Lam. 2:19; Matt. 14:25). According to the later Jewish system, the night was divided into three watches (evening, midnight, and morning). The Greco-Roman system added a fourth (crowing of the rooster, CSB) between midnight and morning (Mark 13:35). The fourth watch (Matt. 14:25; Mark 6:48) designates the time just before dawn.

NILE RIVER Major river considered the "life" of ancient Egypt. The Egyptian Nile is formed by the union of the White Nile that flows out of Lake Victoria in Tanzania and the Blue Nile from Lake Tana in Ethiopia. These join at Khartum in the Sudan and are later fed by the Atbara. Thereafter the Nile flows 1,675 miles northward to the Mediterranean Sea without any further tributary.

The Nile is the basis of Egypt's wealth, indeed of its very life. It is the only river to flow northward across the Sahara. Egypt was unique as an agricultural community in not being dependent on rainfall. The secret was the black silt deposited on the fields by the annual flood caused when the Blue Nile was swollen by the run-off from the winter rains in Ethiopia. This silt was remarkably fertile. Irrigation waters, raised laboriously from the river, let the Egyptians produce many varieties of crops in large quantities (Num. 11:5; Gen. 42:1-2). If the winter rains failed, the consequent small or nonexistent inundation resulted in disastrous famine: some are recorded as lasting over a number of years (cp. Gen. 41).

NIMRAH Place-name meaning "clear (water)." Alternate form of Beth-nimrah (Num. 32:36) used at Num. 32:3.

NIMRIM Place-name meaning "leopards" or "basins of clear waters." The name occurs in the phrase "Waters of Nimrim" (Isa. 15:6; Jer. 48:34), the stream upon which Moab's agricultural productivity depended.

NIMROD Personal name meaning "we shall rebel." Son of Cush or Ethiopia (Gen. 10:8-10; 1 Chron. 1:10). A hunter and builder of the kingdom of Babel whom some Bible students have linked to Tukulti-ninurta, an Assyrian king (ca. 1246–1206 BC).

NIMSHI Personal name meaning "weasel." Grandfather of Jehu (2 Kgs. 9:2,14). Elsewhere Jehu is called the son of Nimshi (1 Kgs. 19:16; 2 Kgs. 9:20; 2 Chron. 22:7). Either "son" is used loosely in the sense of descendant, or a variant tradition is involved.

NINEVE (KJV, Luke 11:32) or **NINEVEH** Greatest of the capitals of the ancient Assyrian Empire, which flourished from about 800 to 612 BC. It was located on the left bank of

Restored gate at the site of the ancient city of Nineveh of Assyria

the Tigris River in northeastern Mesopotamia (Iraq today). Nineveh is first mentioned in the OT as one of the cities established by Nimrod (Gen. 10:9-12). It was the enemy city to which God called the reluctant Prophet Jonah in the eighth century BC. The book of Jonah calls it "the great city" (1:2; 4:11), and "an exceedingly great city" (3:3). The final biblical references are from Nahum, who prophesied the overthrow of the "bloody city" by the attack of the allied Medes and Chaldeans in 612 BC. By 500 BC, the prophet's words (Nah. 3:7) "Nineveh is devastated" (CSB) were echoed by the Greek historian Herodotus who spoke of the Tigris as "the river on which the town of Nineveh formerly stood."

NIPPUR City located in Mesopotamia, approximately 50 miles southeast of the ancient city of Babylon and approximately 100 miles south of modern Baghdad, Iraq.

NISAN Foreign term used after the exile for the first month of the Hebrew calendar (Neh. 2:1; Esth. 3:7). This month that falls within March and April was formerly called Abib.

NISROCH God worshipped by the Assyrian king Sennacherib (2 Kgs. 19:37; Isa. 37:38).

NOADIAH Personal name meaning "Yah has met." **1.** Levite who returned from exile and served as a temple treasurer (Ezra 8:33). **2.** Prophetess who discouraged Nehemiah's building of the walls of Jerusalem (Neh. 6:14).

NOAH Personal name of uncertain meaning, related to "rest." **1.** Son of Lamech, a descendant of Adam in the line of Seth, and a survivor of the flood. A good and righteous man, Noah was the father of Shem, Ham, and Japheth who were born when he was 500 years old. God warned Noah that God was going to wipe humankind from the face of the earth. Because Noah walked with God and stood blameless among the people of that time, God gave him specific instructions for building the ark by which Noah and his family would survive the coming flood. Hebrews 11:7 affirms Noah's actions of faith in building the ark. The references to Noah in 1 Pet. 3:20 and 2 Pet. 2:5 speak of Noah and those of his family who were saved in the flood. **2.** One of Zelophehad's five daughters (Num. 26:33). Of the tribe of Manasseh, these daughters received an inheritance in the land in their father's name even though he had died with no male offspring (27:1-11). This was most unusual in that time.

NOB City in Benjamin likely situated between Anathoth and Jerusalem (Neh. 11:31-32; Isa. 10:32).

NOBAH Personal name meaning "barking" or "howling." **1.** Leader of the tribe of Manasseh who conquered Kenath in Gilead (Num. 32:42). **2.** Town in Gilead, formerly Kenath (Num. 32:42). Site is perhaps identical with Kanawat about 60 miles east of the Sea of Galilee. **3.** Town in Gilead (Judg. 8:10-11) to the east of Succoth and Penuel and west of the king's highway (KJV, "the way of them that dwell in tents"; NRSV, "caravan route").

NOD Place-name meaning "wandering." After murdering his brother Abel, Cain was condemned to be "a fugitive and a wanderer on the earth" (Gen. 4:12,14 NRSV). Nod is located "away from the presence of the LORD" and "east of Eden" (Gen. 4:16). The text is not so much interested in fixing the physical location of Nod as in emphasizing the "lostness" of the wanderer Cain.

NODAB Name meaning "nobility." Tribe conquered by Reuben, Gad, and the half tribe of Manasseh (1 Chron. 5:19).

NOGAH Personal name meaning "brilliance" or "luster." Son born to David in Jerusalem (1 Chron. 3:7; 14:6).

NOHAH Personal name meaning "quiet." Son of Benjamin (1 Chron. 8:2). The name is omitted from the parallel list (Gen. 46:21).

NOON Middle of the day, specifically 12 o'clock noon. Noon is frequently associated with death and destruction (2 Sam. 4:5; 1 Kgs. 20:16; 2 Kgs. 4:20; Ps. 91:6; Jer. 6:4; 15:8; 20:16; Zeph. 2:4). Noon is also associated with blessings and vindication (Job 11:17; Ps. 37:6; Isa. 58:10).

NOPH Variant form of Moph, the Hebrew term for Memphis (Isa. 19:13; Jer. 2:16; 44:1; 46:14,19; Ezek. 30:13,16).

NOPHAH Place-name meaning "blast." Nophah passed from Moabite to Ammonite to Israelite control (Num. 21:30).

NORTH GATE Designation of two gates in Ezekiel's vision of the renewed temple, a gate entering the outer court (Ezek. 8:14; 44:4; 46:9; 47:2) and a gate entering the inner court (Ezek. 40:35,40,44).

NOSE Part of the face between the eyes and mouth that bears the nostrils and covers the nasal cavity. Jewelry was worn in the nose (Gen. 24:47; Isa. 3:21; Ezek. 16:12). Prisoners of war were sometimes led captive with hooks in their noses (2 Kgs. 19:28; Isa. 37:29).

NUBIANS Residents of an ancient kingdom along the Nile in southern Egypt and northern Sudan (Dan. 11:43 NIV; also NRSV margin).

NUMBER SYSTEMS AND NUMBER SYMBOLISM The Hebrews did not develop the symbols to represent numbers until the postexilic period (after 539 BC). In all preexilic inscriptions, small numbers are represented by individual strokes (e.g., //// for four). Larger numbers were either represented with Egyptian symbols, or the name of the number was written out ("four" for the number 4).

Biblical passages show that the Hebrews were well acquainted with the four basic mathematical operations of addition (Num. 1:20-46), subtraction (Gen. 18:28-33), multiplication (Num. 7:84-86), and division (Num. 31:27). The Hebrews also used fractions such as a half (Gen. 24:22), a third (Num. 15:6), and a fourth (Exod. 29:40).

In addition to their usage to designate specific numbers or quantities, many numbers in the Bible came to have a symbolic meaning. Thus seven came to symbolize completeness and perfection.

Multiples of seven frequently had symbolic meaning. The Year of Jubilee came after the completion of every 49 years. Jesus sent out the 70 (Luke 10:1-17). Seventy years is specified as the length of the exile (Jer. 25:12; 29:10; Dan. 9:2). The messianic kingdom was to be inaugurated after a period of 70 weeks of years had passed (Dan. 9:24).

After seven, the most significant number for the Bible is undoubtedly 12. The Sumerians used 12 as one base for their number system. Both the calendar and the signs of the zodiac reflect this 12-base number system. The tribes of Israel and Jesus's disciples numbered 12. Multiples of 12 are also important. There were 24 divisions of priests (1 Chron. 24:4) and 24 elders around the heavenly throne (Rev. 4:4). Seventy-two elders, when one includes Eldad and Medad, were given a portion of God's spirit that rested on Moses, and they prophesied (Num. 11:24-26). An apocryphal tradition holds that 72 Jewish scholars, six from each of the 12 tribes, translated the OT into Greek, to give us the version we call today the Septuagint (abbreviated LXX). The 144,000 servants of God (Rev. 7:4) were made up of 12,000 from each of the 12 tribes of Israel.

Three as a symbolic number often indicated completeness. The created cosmos had three elements: heaven, earth, and underworld. Three Persons make up the Godhead: Father, Son, and Holy Spirit.

Four was often used as a sacred number. Significant biblical references to four include the four corners of the earth (Isa. 11:12), the four winds (Jer. 49:36), four rivers that flowed out of Eden to water the world (Gen. 2:10-14), and four living creatures surrounding God (Ezek. 1; Rev. 4:6-7). God sent forth the four horsemen of the Apocalypse (Rev. 6:1-8) to bring devastation to the earth. The most significant multiple of four is 40, which often represented a large number or a long period of time. Rain flooded the earth for 40 days (Gen. 7:12). For 40 days, Jesus withstood Satan's temptations (Mark 1:13). Forty years represented approximately a generation. Thus all the adults who had rebelled against God at Sinai died during the 40 years of the Wilderness Wandering period. By age 40, a person had reached maturity (Exod. 2:11; Acts 7:23).

NUMBERS, BOOK OF Fourth in the chronological series of the Torah, Numbers carries the title *Bemidhbar* ("in the wilderness") in the original Hebrew text. The book carries the title Numbers in English translations as a result of the early Greek title *ARIQMOI* and the Latin title *Numeri*. In both instances, the title reflects a focus on the censuses taken to account for the number of fighting men in each tribe.

Numbers is a book of transition, in which the conditional nature of the Sinaitic covenant is most clearly demonstrated to the generation of adults who escaped Egyptian bondage. The older generation chose disobedience, which carried a death sentence in the wilderness. More time elapses historically in this book than the other books combined that relate to the exodus from Egypt (Exodus, Leviticus, Deuteronomy). The nearly 40 years of wandering take place in Numbers as a result of Israel's disobedience and lack of faith in the covenant God, *YHWH* (Yahweh).

This book is essential for understanding the reasons for the second giving of the commandments (see Exod. 20 and Deut. 5). Were it not for the death sentence on the adults, it would not have been necessary for Moses to reintroduce the Law and the commandments to another generation who would take the promised land.

Numbers also records historical details that are only alluded to by other biblical writers. In Ps. 95:8, for example, the writer gives the command "Do not harden your hearts as at Meribah, as on that day at Massah in the wilderness" (CSB). The context indicates a reference to Israel's choice to accept the spies' majority report (Num. 14). Another incident found in Numbers is the fashioning of the bronze snake (Num. 21). Jesus refers to this event during his instruction of Nicodemus.

NUN 1. Father of Joshua (Exod. 33:11; Num. 11:28; 13:8,16). **2.** Fourteenth letter of the Hebrew alphabet that serves as a heading for Ps. 119:105-112. Each verse of this section begins with "nun."

NYMPHA or **NYMPHAS** Christian host of a house church, likely in Laodicea (Col. 4:15). Because the name occurs only in the accusative case, it is not possible to determine whether it is masculine or feminine.

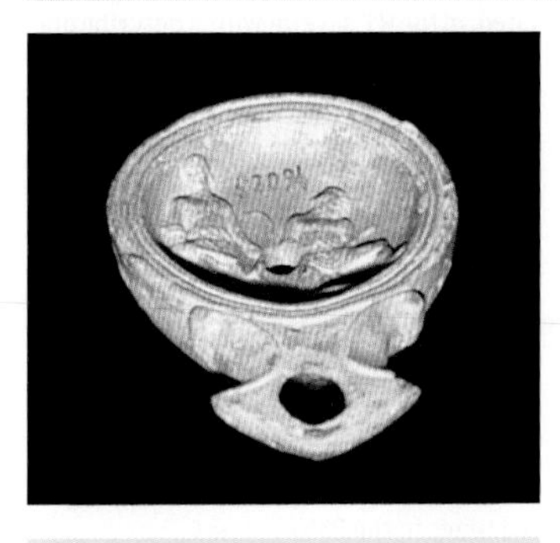

Ancient oil lamp decorated with two human figures

OARSMEN NIV term for those who row a galley (Ezek. 27:8,26).

OATHS Statements by which a person promises or guarantees that a vow will be kept or that a statement is, in fact, true. In the OT, the name of God was invoked as the One who would guarantee the results or veracity of a statement. Oaths were often accompanied and evidenced by the raising of a hand or hands toward heaven or by placing the hand under the thigh (Gen. 14:22; 24:2-3; Dan. 12:7).

Jesus did not use oaths to confirm the authority of his teaching. He pointed to a higher ethic that rests upon the integrity of the child of God as one not needing to prove his veracity by affirming an oath. So in the Sermon on the Mount, Jesus exhorts his followers to refrain from oaths, and, "But let your word 'yes' mean 'yes' and your 'no' mean 'no.' Anything more than this is from the evil one" (Matt. 5:36-37 CSB).

The admonition of Jesus to his followers to have honesty in their speech does not discount the use of oaths in the NT. Though Jesus did not use oaths when Caiaphas placed him under oath, he accepted the challenge and declared himself to be the promised Messiah of Israel (Matt. 26:63-64).

OBADIAH Personal name meaning "Yahweh's servant." **1.** Person in charge of Ahab's palace. He was devoted to Yahweh and saved Yahweh's prophets from Jezebel's wrath. He was the go-between for Elijah and Ahab (1 Kgs. 18:3-16). **2.** Descendant of David through Hananiah (1 Chron. 3:21). **3.** Son of Izrahiah of the tribe of Issachar (1 Chron. 7:3). **4.** Son of Azel of the tribe of Benjamin (1 Chron. 8:38; 9:44). **5.** Levite who returned to Jerusalem with the first of the Babylonian exiles (1 Chron. 9:16). **6.** Gadite who joined David, along with Ezer and Eliab. Obadiah was second in command behind Ezer (1 Chron. 12:8-9). **7.** Father of Ishmaiah, an officer from the tribe of Zebulun who served in David's army (1 Chron. 27:19). **8.** One of five officials Jehoshaphat sent throughout the cities of Judah to teach "the book of the LORD's instruction" (2 Chron. 17:7-9 CSB). See *Jehoshaphat*. **9.** Levite descended from Merari appointed by Josiah to oversee the repairing of the temple (2 Chron. 34:12). See *Josiah*. **10.** Priest who returned from Babylonian exile to Jerusalem with Ezra (Ezra 8:9). He joined other priests along with princes and Levites in putting his seal upon the covenant (Neh. 9:38) made between the people and God (Neh. 10:5). **11.** Gatekeeper and guardian of "the ward" (KJV), "the storerooms at the city gates" (CSB) during the leadership of Ezra and Nehemiah (Neh. 12:25). **12.** The prophet Obadiah, most likely none of the above. See *Book of Obadiah*.

OBADIAH, BOOK OF Shortest book of the Minor Prophets, preserving the message of the prophet Obadiah.

Historically, the book belongs to the early postexilic period at the end of the sixth century BC. Its central section, verses 10-14, deals with the fall of Jerusalem to the Babylonians in 586 BC., concentrating on the part the Edomites played in that tragic event. Edom was a state to the southeast of Judah. Despite treaty ties ("brother," v. 10), the Edomites, along with others, had failed to come to Judah's aid and had even helped Babylon by looting Jerusalem and handing over refugees.

Moreover, the Edomites filled the vacuum caused by Judah's exile by moving west and annexing the Negev to the south of Judah and even its southern territory (cp. v. 19).

Judah reacted with a strong sense of grievance. Obadiah's oracle responded to an underlying impassioned prayer of lament, like Pss. 74; 79; or 137, in which Judah appealed to God to act as providential trial Judge and Savior to set right the situation.

Like the book of Revelation, which proclaims the downfall of the persecuting Roman Empire, the aim of Obadiah is to sustain faith in God's moral government and hope in the eventual triumph of his just will. It brings a pastoral message to aching hearts that God is on the throne and cares for his own.

OBAL Personal name meaning "stout." Son of Joktan and ancestor of an Arab tribe (Gen. 10:28). At 1 Chron. 1:22, the name takes the alternate form Ebal.

OBED Personal name meaning "serving." **1.** Son of Boaz and Ruth (Ruth 4:13-17), father of Jesse, and grandfather of King David. He was an ancestor of Jesus Christ (Matt. 1:5; Luke 3:32). **2.** Son of Ephal and father of Jehu (1 Chron. 2:37-38). **3.** One of David's mighty men (1 Chron. 11:47). **4.** Gatekeeper in Solomon's temple (1 Chron. 26:7). **5.** Father of Azariah, a commander assisting in coronation of King Josiah (2 Chron. 23).

OBED-EDOM Personal name meaning "serving Edom." **1.** Philistine from Gath who apparently was loyal to David and Israel. At Obed-edom's house, David left the ark of the covenant following the death of Uzzah at the hand of God (2 Sam. 6:6-11). **2.** Levite who served as both gatekeeper and musician in the tabernacle in Jerusalem during David's reign (1 Chron. 15:18,24; 16:5). His duties related especially to the ark of the covenant. A guild of Levites may have adopted the name Obed-edom as their title as keepers of the ark. **3.** Member of the Korahites (1 Chron. 26:1,4-8) who kept the south gate of the temple (v. 15). **4.** Keeper of the sacred vessels of the temple. Joash of Israel took with him the sacred vessels to Samaria following his capture of Jerusalem and of Amaziah king of Judah (2 Chron. 25:23-24).

OBEDIENCE To hear God's Word and act accordingly. The word translated "obey" in the OT means "to hear" and is often so translated. In the NT, several words describe obedience. One word means "to hear or to listen in a state of submission." Another NT word often translated "obey" means "to trust." The person's obedient response to God's Word is a response of trust or faith. To really hear God's Word is to obey God's Word (Exod. 19:5; Jer. 7:23).

OBEISANCE To bow down with one's face to the ground as a sign of homage and submission. KJV and RSV translate the Hebrew *shachah* as "obeisance" when the object of homage is a person but as "worship" when the object of homage is God or other gods (84 times in the RSV).

OBIL Personal name of uncertain meaning, perhaps "camel driver," "tender," or "mourner." Overseer in charge of David's camels (1 Chron. 27:30).

OBLATION Gift offered at an altar or shrine, especially a voluntary gift not involving blood.

OBOTH Place-name meaning "fathers" or "water skins." A wilderness station (Num. 21:10-11; 33:43-44).

OBSCENE OBJECT REB translation for an object the queen mother Maacah erected for the worship of Asherah, a fertility goddess (1 Kgs. 15:13; 2 Chron. 15:16). CSB, "obscene image."

OBSCURITY KJV term for gloom or darkness (Isa. 29:18; 58:10; 59:9).

OBSERVER OF TIMES KJV term for a soothsayer (Deut. 18:10,14; cp. Lev. 19:26; 2 Kgs. 21:6; 2 Chron. 33:6).

OCHRAN or **OCRAN** Personal name meaning "troubler." Father of Pagiel, a leader of the tribe of Asher (Num. 1:13; 2:27; 7:72,77; 10:26).

ODED Personal name of uncertain meaning, perhaps "counter," "restorer," or "timekeeper." **1.** Father of the prophet Azariah (2 Chron. 15:1). **2.** Prophet in the time of Ahaz who urged the Israelites to release the people of Judah they had taken as prisoners of war (2 Chron. 28:8-15).

ODOR Scent of fragrance, usually in the phrase "pleasing odor" (KJV, "sweet savour"; CSB, "pleasing aroma"). A synonym for a burnt offering (Num. 28:1-2).

OFFAL NIV term for the waste remaining from the butchering of a sacrificial animal (Exod. 29:14; Lev. 4:11; 8:17; 16:27; Num. 19:5; Mal. 2:3). Other translations render the underlying Hebrew as "dung."

OFFENSE Translates several Hebrew and Greek terms. The following two senses predominate. **1.** That which causes indignation or disgust (Gen. 31:36). Here offense approximates crime (Deut. 19:15; 22:26), guilt (Hos. 5:15), trespass (Rom. 5:15,17-18,20), or sin (2 Cor. 11:7). Christ is said to be a rock of offense in this sense (Rom. 9:33; Gal. 5:11; 1 Pet. 2:8). What was especially offensive was the claim that an accursed one was the Messiah and that faith in this crucified one and not works was necessary for salvation. **2.** That which serves as a hindrance (Matt. 16:23) or obstacle (2 Cor. 6:3). This hindrance is often temptation to sin (Matt. 18:7; Luke 17:1).

OFFSCOURING That which is removed by scouring: the dregs, filth, garbage, refuse, or scum (Lam. 3:45; 1 Cor. 4:13).

OG Amorite king of Bashan defeated by the Israelites before they crossed the Jordan (Num. 21:33-35; Deut. 1:4; 3:1-13).

OHAD Personal name meaning "unity." Son of Simeon (Gen. 46:10; Exod. 6:15). The name is omitted in parallel lists (Num. 26:12-14; 1 Chron. 4:24).

OHEL Personal name meaning "tent," "family (of God)," or "(God is) shelter." Descendant of David (1 Chron. 3:20).

OHOLAH Personal name meaning "tent dweller." A woman's name Ezekiel used to portray Samaria (Ezek. 23:1-10).

OHOLIAB Personal name meaning "father's tent." Danite craftsman, designer, and embroiderer who assisted Bezalel in supervision of the construction of the tabernacle and its equipment (Exod. 31:6; 35:34; 36:1-2; esp. 38:23).

OHOLIBAH Personal name meaning "tent worshiper." Younger sister in the allegory of Ezek. 23 identified with Jerusalem (23:4,11-49). The sexual misconduct of these sisters represents Israel's and Judah's embrace of idolatry.

OHOLIBAMAH Personal name meaning "tent of the high place" or "tent dweller of the false cult." **1.** Hivite daughter of Anah and wife of Esau (Gen. 36:2). **2.** Edomite leader descended from Esau (Gen. 36:41).

OIL Indispensable commodity in the ancient Near East for food, medicine, fuel, and ritual. Oil was considered a blessing given by God (Deut. 11:14), and the olive tree was a characteristic of the land that God gave to Israel (Deut. 8:8).

OINTMENT Perfumed unguents or salves of various kinds used as cosmetics, medicine, and in religious ceremonies. The use of ointments and perfumes appears to have been a common practice in the ancient Near East including the Hebrews.

OLD GATE KJV, CSB, NASB, NRSV designation for a Jerusalem city gate repaired in Nehemiah's time (Neh. 3:6; 12:39). This rendering is doubtful on grammatical grounds (the adjective and noun do not agree).

OLD TESTAMENT First part of the Christian Bible. The Hebrew Scriptures. For Jews it is the complete Bible, sometimes called Tanak for its three parts (Torah or Law, Nebiim or Prophets, Ketubim or Writings). It tells the history of the nation of Israel and God's dealings with them to the return from exile in Babylon. Christians see its complement in the NT, which reveals Jesus Christ as the fulfillment of OT prophecy.

OLD TESTAMENT QUOTATIONS IN THE NEW TESTAMENT Influence of the OT is seen throughout the NT. The NT writers included approximately 250 express OT quotations. If one includes indirect or partial quotations, the number jumps to more than 1,000. It is clear that the writers of the NT were concerned with demonstrating the continuity between the OT Scriptures and the faith they proclaimed. They were convinced that in Jesus the OT promises had been fulfilled.

OLIVES, MOUNT OF Mountain ridge 2.5 miles long that towers over the eastern side of Jerusalem; more precisely, the middle of the three peaks forming the ridge. Heavily covered with olive trees, the ridge juts out in a north-south direction (like a spur) from the range of mountains running down the center of the region.

Both the central Mount of Olives and Mount Scopus, the peak on its northern side, rise more than 200 feet above the Temple Mount across the Kidron Valley. It provided a lookout base and signaling point for armies defending Jerusalem.

David crossed the Mount of Olives when fleeing Absalom (2 Sam. 15:30). Ezekiel saw the cherubim chariot land there (Ezek. 11:22-23). Zechariah described how the Mount of Olives would move to form a huge valley on the Day of the Lord (Zech. 14:3-5). Many crucial events in Jesus's life occurred on the Mount of Olives (Matt. 26:30; Mark 11:1-2; Luke 4:5; 22:39-46; Acts 1:9-12).

The western slope of the Mount of Olives on which Jesus gave his Olivet discourse

OLIVET DISCOURSE Jesus's major sermon preached on the Mount of Olives; Jesus gave instructions concerning the end of the age and the destruction of Jerusalem. The discourse (Matt. 24–25; Mark 13) is in part an apocalypse because it uses symbolic, visionary language that makes it a difficult passage to understand. Parts of it appear scattered throughout Luke 12–21.

OLYMPAS Perhaps a shortened form of Olympiodorus (gift of Olympus). Christian whom Paul greeted in Rom. 16:15. Olympas was apparently a member of a house church including the others mentioned in 16:15.

OMAR Personal name meaning "talkative." Son of Eliphaz and ancestor of an Edomite clan of the same name (Gen. 36:11,15; 1 Chron. 1:36).

OMEGA Last letter in the Greek alphabet. Together with the first letter, alpha, omega designates God and Christ as the all-encompassing "Reality" (Rev. 1:8; 21:6; 22:13).

OMEN **1.** Sign used by diviners to predict the future. The Israelites were prohibited from interpreting omens (Deut. 18:10 CSB, NASB, NIV). **2.** Sign indicating a future event. Ahab's reference to Ben-hadad as "my brother" was understood as an omen or sign of Ahab's favor (1 Kgs. 20:33).

The faithful witness of Christians in the face of opposition is likewise an omen or sign pointed to the salvation of believers and the destruction of God's enemies (Phil. 1:28).

OMER **1.** Unit of dry measure equal to one-tenth of an ephah or a little more than two quarts (Exod. 16:13-36). See *Weights and Measures.* **2.** First sheaf (omer) of the barley harvest that was elevated as an offering (Lev. 23:9-15).

OMNIPOTENCE State of being all-powerful, which is true only of God. Scripture often affirms that all power belongs to God (Ps. 147:5), that all things are possible for God (Luke 1:37; Matt. 19:26), and that God's power exceeds what humans can ask or think (Eph. 3:20).

OMNIPRESENCE Being present everywhere at once, a unique attribute of God.

OMNISCIENCE Having all knowledge, a unique attribute of God. God knows us intimately (Ps. 139:1-6; Matt. 6:4,6,8). Such knowledge is cause for alarm for the unrighteous but for confidence for God's saints (Job 23:10; Pss. 34:15-16; 90:8; Prov. 15:3; 1 Pet. 3:12).

OMRI Personal name meaning "pilgrim" or "life." **1.** King of Israel 885–874 BC and founder of the Omride dynasty, which ruled the northern kingdom until 842. **2.** Officer of the tribe of Issachar under David (1 Chron. 27:18). **3.** Grandson of Benjamin (1 Chron. 7:8).

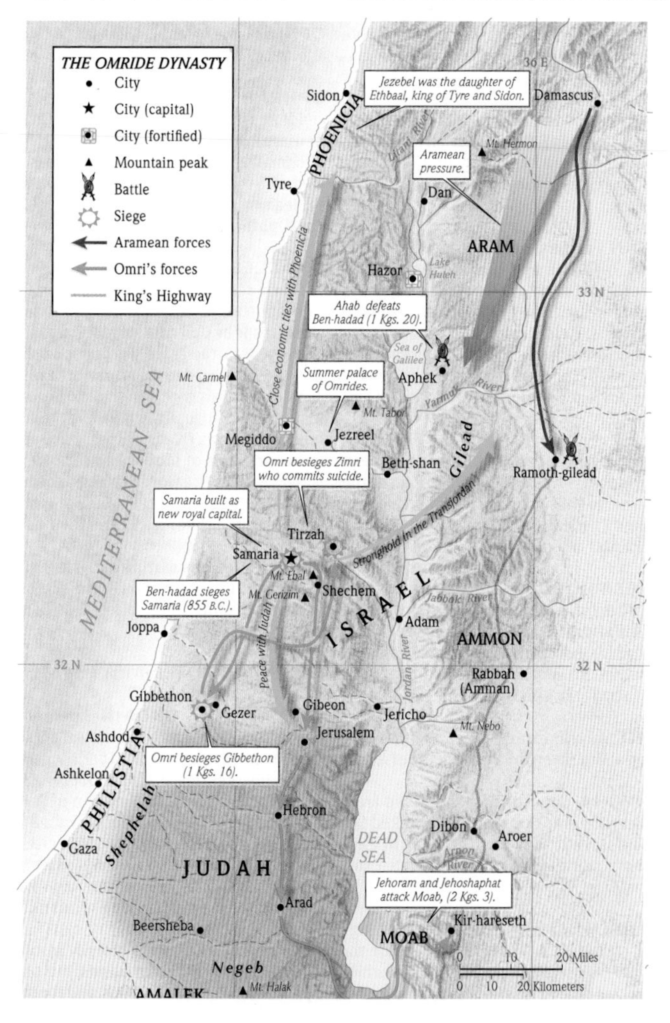

4. Grandfather of a member of the tribe of Judah who returned to Jerusalem from exile about 537 BC.

ON Egyptian place-name meaning "city of the pillar," called in Greek Heliopolis or "city of the sun" and in Hebrew Beth-shemesh, "city of the sun" (Jer. 43:13), and Aven. It was the cult center for the worship of the sun-god Re (Atum).

ONAM Personal name meaning "vigorous." **1.** Ancestor of an Edomite subclan (Gen. 36:23; 1 Chron. 1:40). **2.** Ancestor of a family of Jerahmeelites, a subclan of Judah (1 Chron. 2:26,28).

ONAN Personal name meaning "power." A son of Judah and his Canaanite wife, Shuah (Gen. 38:2-8). Following the death of his older brother, Er, Onan was to have married the widow and produce a son who would carry on Er's name. Onan repeatedly failed to complete the responsibilities of the marriage and therefore God killed him (38:8-10).

ONESIMUS Personal name that may mean "profitable." The slave for whom Paul wrote his letter to Philemon. Later, Onesimus accompanied Thychius in bearing Paul's letter to the church at Colossae (Col. 4:7-9).

ONESIPHORUS Personal name meaning "profit bearing." Ephesian Christian praised for his effort to seek out the place of Paul's arrest, his disregard of the shame connected with befriending one in chains, and his past service in Ephesus (2 Tim. 1:16-18).

ONO Name meaning "grief." Benjaminite town about seven miles southeast of Joppa.

ONYCHA Spice probably derived from the closing flaps or the shell of a Red Sea mollusk that was used in the incense reserved for the worship of Yahweh (Exod. 30:34).

OPHEL Place-name meaning "swelling," "fat," "bulge," or "mound." It became the proper name of a portion of the hill on which the city of David was built (2 Chron. 27:3).

OPHIR Place-name and personal name meaning "dusty." Place famous in the ancient Near East for its trade, especially in gold. Solomon's ships with help from Phoenician sailors brought precious goods from Ophir (1 Kgs. 9:28; 10:11; cp. 1 Kgs. 22:48).

OPHNI Name meaning "high place." Town allotted to Benjamin (Josh. 18:24).

OPHRAH Name meaning "fawn." **1.** Descendant of Judah (1 Chron. 4:14). **2.** City in Benjamin (Josh. 18:23), likely north of Michmash (1 Sam. 13:17-18). **3.** Town associated with the Abiezer clan of Manasseh who settled west of the Jordan (Judg. 6:11,24; 8:32). This Ophrah was the home of Gideon.

ORACLES Communications from God. The term refers both to divine responses to a question asked of God and to pronouncements made by God without his being asked. In one sense, oracles were prophecies since they often referred to the future; but oracles sometimes dealt with decisions to be made in the present. Usually in the Bible the communication was from Yahweh, the God of Israel. In times of idol worship, however, Israelites did seek a word or pronouncement from false gods (Hos. 4:12). Many of Israel's neighbors sought oracles from their gods.

ORCHARD Grove of fruit (Neh. 9:25; Eccles. 2:5) or nut trees (Song 6:11). An enclosed orchard is sometimes called a garden or park.

ORDINANCES See *Baptism; Lord's Supper.*

ORDINATION, ORDAIN Appointing, consecrating, or commissioning of persons for special service to the Lord and his people. Four primary examples provide OT precedents for ordination: the consecration of Aaron and his sons as priests to God (Exod. 28–29; Lev. 8–9), the dedication of the Levites as servants of God (Num. 8:5-14), the appointment of 70 elders to assist Moses (Num. 11:16-17,24-25), and the commissioning of Joshua as Moses's successor (Num. 27:18-23). The NT practice of ordination is generally associated with the laying on of hands, but other appointments, consecrations, and commissionings must be considered even if they lack formal investiture.

OREB AND ZEEB Personal names meaning "raven" and "wolf." Two Midianite princes captured and executed by the Ephraimites following Gideon's rout of their forces (Judg. 7:24–8:3).

OREN Personal name meaning "cedar." Member of the Jerahmeelite clan of Judah (1 Chron. 2:25).

ORGAN KJV term for a musical instrument that modern translations identify as a pipe or shrill flute (Gen. 4:21; Job 21:12; 30:31; Ps. 150:4).

ORION Constellation bearing the name of a giant Greek hunter who, according to myth, was bound and placed in the heavens. Job 38:31 perhaps alludes to this myth. God is consistently portrayed as the creator of the Orion constellation (Job 9:9; Amos 5:8). The plural of the Hebrew term for Orion is rendered "constellations" at Isa. 13:10.

ORNAN Personal name meaning "prince." Alternate name of Araunah (1 Chron. 21:15,18,20-25,28; 2 Chron. 3:1).

ORONTES RIVER Principal river of Syria which originates east of the Lebanon ridge, rises near Heliopolis (Baalbek) in the Beka Valley of Lebanon, and flows north some 250 miles through Syria and Turkey before turning southwest into the Mediterranean south of Antioch-on-the-Orontes (Antakya) to reach the coast just south of ancient Seleucia, the seaport of Antioch.

ORPAH Personal name meaning "neck," "girl with a full mane," or "rain cloud." Daughter-in-law of Naomi who returned to her people and gods after Naomi twice requested that she go (Ruth 1:4-15).

ORYX Large, straight-horned antelope.

OSEE Greek form of Hosea used by KJV (Rom. 9:25).

OSHEA KJV alternate form of Hoshea (Joshua) at Num. 13:8,16.

OSNAPPAR or **OSNAPPER** Assyrian king who repopulated Samaria with foreigners following its capture in 722 BC (Ezra 4:10). Osnappar is most often identified with Ashurbanipal. KJV used the form Asnapper.

OSPRAY, OSPREY Large, flesh-eating hawk included in lists of unclean birds (Lev. 11:13; Deut. 14:12 KJV, NRSV).

OSSIFRAGE English applies "ossifrage" to three birds: the bearded vulture; the osprey; and the giant petrel. The KJV included the ossifrage among the unclean birds (Lev. 11:13; Deut. 14:12).

OSTIA Roman city at the mouth of the Tiber about 15 miles from Rome that, following construction of an artificial harbor by Claudius (AD 41–54), served as the principal harbor for Rome.

OSTRACA Potsherds (pottery fragments), especially fragments used as an inexpensive writing material.

OSTRICH The ostrich, the largest of birds, is a swift, flightless fowl. One passage in Job (39:13-18) describes some of the characteristic habits of the ostrich.

OTHNI Personal name, perhaps meaning "force" or "power." Levitic gatekeeper (1 Chron. 26:7).

OTHNIEL Name meaning "God is powerful." **1.** First of Israel's judges or deliverers. Othniel received Caleb's daughter Achsah as his wife as a reward for his capture of Kiriath-sepher (Debir) (Josh. 15:15-19; Judg. 1:11-15). **2.** Clan name associated with a resident of Netophah (1 Chron. 27:15).

OUCHES KJV term for (filigree) settings for precious stones (Exod. 28:11,13-14,25; 39:6,13,16,18).

OUTCAST Scripture never employs "outcast" in the now common sense of one rejected by society. "Outcasts" often has the technical sense of Diaspora. NASB employs "outcast" for one excommunicated from the synagogue (John 16:2).

OUTLANDISH KJV term meaning "foreign" (Neh. 13:26).

OVEN Device used for baking food, especially bread (Lev. 2:4; Exod. 8:3). Ancient ovens were cylindrical structures of burnt clay two to three feet in diameter. A fire was built on pebbles in the oven bottom. Bread was baked by either placing the dough against the oven walls or upon the heated pebbles. Dried grass (Matt. 6:30; Luke 12:28), thorny shrubs, and animal dung were often used as fuels.

Large domed oven

OVERLIVE KJV term meaning "outlive" (Josh. 24:31).

OVERPASS KJV term (Jer. 5:28) meaning either "surpass" previous limits or bounds (NASB, NIV, RSV, TEV) or else "pass over" in the sense of overlook (NASB margin, REB).

OVERRUN Term meaning "outrun" (2 Sam. 18:23; Ps. 105:30 CSB).

OVERSEER Superintendent or supervisor. Various translations use "overseer" for a variety of secular positions. CSB, NASB, and NIV employ "overseer" for the bishop of the KJV, NRSV (Phil. 1:1; 1 Tim. 3:1-2; Titus 1:7).

OWL Bird of prey belonging to the order *Strigiformes*, which are generally nocturnal. Hebrew terms for various bird species cannot be identified precisely with English terms.

OWNERSHIP Possession of property. Two general principles guided Israelite laws of ownership: (1) all things ultimately belong to God, and (2) land possession is purely a business matter. After the division of the land among the 12 tribes, individual plots were given to family groups or clans. If the occasion demanded it, the land could be redivided at a later time. Land sales and transfers were recorded by scribes on leather or papyrus scrolls, on clay tablets, or in the presence of witnesses with the symbolic removal of a sandal (Ruth 4:7) or the stepping onto the land by the new owner. Land passed from father to son but could be given to a daughter. Private lands ultimately reverted to the king if not used for several years (2 Kgs. 8).

Private ownership continued in much the same fashion during the NT era. Bills of sale and land deeds written on papyrus scrolls from this period have been discovered, attesting to the exchange of private lands. Often the sale of private land was subject to royal approval. The Romans oversaw the control of lands in Palestine, requiring heavy taxes from owners. The early Christian community existed through the generosity of those members who sold many of their possessions to help poorer believers.

OX Large, often domesticated, bovine. In the OT, it was extremely valuable as a work animal. Permitted as food, they were also offered as sacrifices (Deut. 14:4-6; Lev. 17:3-4).

OZEM Personal name meaning "irritable" or "strength." **1.** Sixth son of Jesse (1 Chron. 2:15). **2.** Fourth son of Jerahmeel (1 Chron. 2:25).

OZIAS Greek form of Uzziah used by KJV (Matt. 1:8-9).

OZNI Personal name meaning "my hearing" or "attentive." Ancestor of a Gadite family, the Oznites (Num. 26:16).

PQ

The altar of Zeus, the highest god in the Greek pantheon

PAARAI Personal name meaning "revelation of Yahweh." One of David's 30 elite warriors (2 Sam. 23:35) designated an Arbite, a resident of Arbah (Josh. 15:52). The parallel list has the name "Naarai" (1 Chron. 11:37).

PADAN-ARAM (KJV) or **PADDAN-ARAM** Place-name, perhaps meaning "way of Syria," "field of Syria," or "plow of Syria." The land from where Abraham journeyed to Canaan. One of the principal cities was Haran. Later Abraham sent his steward to Paddan-aram (Gen. 25:20) to seek a wife for Isaac (Gen. 24:1-9), and Jacob fled there and married into Laban and Rebekah's branch of the patriarchal family (28:2-5).

PADDLE KJV term for a digging tool (Deut. 23:13). Modern translations render the term as something to dig with (NIV), spade (NASB), stick (RSV, TEV), or trowel (NRSV, REB). The Israelites were required to respect God's presence in their camp by burying their excrement.

PADON Personal name meaning "redemption." Ancestor of a family of postexilic temple servants (Ezra 2:44; Neh. 7:47).

PAGANS Those who worship a god or gods other than the living God to whom the Bible witnesses. NIV, REB, and RSV sometimes use "pagans" as the translation of the Greek *ethnoi* (1 Cor. 5:1; 10:20), which is generally translated "Gentiles" (so KJV, CSB, NASB). In English, "Gentile" relates to ethnic background while "pagan" refers to religious affiliation.

PAGIEL Personal name meaning "fortune of God," "God is entreated," or "God meets." Wilderness leader of the tribe of Asher (Num. 1:13; 2:27; 7:72,77; 10:26).

PAHATH-MOAB Title meaning "governor of Moab." A family of returned exiles likely descended from the Hebrew governor of Moab in the time of David (2 Sam. 8:2; Ezra 2:6; 8:4; 10:30; Neh. 7:11; 10:14).

PAI Place-name meaning "groaning." Alternate form of Pau used at 1 Chron. 1:50 (cp. Gen. 36:39).

PAINT Mixture of pigment and liquid used to apply a closely adhering, colorful coat to a surface. Most scriptural references are to painting the eyes.

PALACE Residence of a monarch or noble. KJV often used "palace" in passages where modern translations have substituted a term more appropriate to the context.

PALAL Personal name meaning "God comes to judge." One of those assisting in Nehemiah's repair of the wall (Neh. 3:25).

PALANQUIN REB, RSV term for an enclosed seat or couch carried on servants' shoulders (Song 3:9). Other translations include: carriage (CSB, NIV), chariot (KJV), and sedan chair (NASB).

PALESTINA KJV alternate name for Philistia (Exod. 15:14; Isa. 14:29,31).

PALESTINE Geographical designation for the land of the Bible, particularly land west of Jordan River that God allotted to Israel for an inheritance (Josh. 13–19). Various terms have been used to designate that small but significant land known in the early OT era as "Canaan" (Gen. 12:5) and often referred to as the promised land (Deut. 9:28). The area was designated "Israel" and "Judah" at the division of the kingdoms in 931 BC. By NT times, the land had been divided into provincial designations: Judea, Samaria, Galilee, and others. Generally the region was considered to be a part of Syria. See *Israel.*

Palestine is derived from the name *Pelishtim* or "Philistines." The Greeks, familiar primarily with the coastal area, applied the name "Palestine" to the entire southeastern Mediterranean region. Although the word "Palestine" (or "Palestina") is found four times in the KJV (Exod. 15:14; Isa. 14:29,31; Joel 3:4), these are references to the territory of the Philistines and so properly designate only the strip of coastland occupied by that people.

Climate Palestine lies in the semitropical belt between 30 degrees 15 feet and 33 degrees 15 feet north latitude. Temperatures are normally high in the summer and mild in the winter, but these generalizations are modified by both elevation and distance from the coast. Variety is the necessary word in describing Palestinian weather, for in spite of its relatively small size, the geographical configuration of the area produces a diversity of conditions. Because of the Mediterranean influence, the coastal plain has an average annual temperature of 57 degrees at Joppa. Jerusalem, only 35 miles away, has an annual average of 63 degrees. Its elevation of 2,500 feet above sea level causes the difference. Jericho is only 17 miles farther east, but it is 3,400 feet lower (900 feet below sea level), consequently having a tropical climate and very low humidity. Here bitterly cold desert nights offset rather warm desert days. Similarly, much of the area around the Sea of Galilee experiences temperate conditions, while the Dead Sea region is known for its strings of 100 degrees-plus summer days.

Palestine is a land of two seasons, a dry season and a rainy season, with intervening transitional periods. The dry season lasts from mid-May to mid-October. From June through August, no rain falls except in the extreme north. Moderate, regular winds blow usually from the west or southwest. The breezes reach Jerusalem by noon, Jericho in early afternoon, and the Transjordan plateau by midafternoon. The air carries much moisture, but atmospheric conditions are such that precipitation does not occur. However, the humidity is evident from the extremely heavy dew that forms five nights out of six in July.

With late October, the "early rain" so often mentioned in Scripture begins to fall. November is punctuated with heavy thunderstorms. The months of December through February are marked by heavy showers, but it is not a time of unrelenting rain. Rainy days alternate with fair days and beautiful sunshine. The cold is not severe, with occasional frost in the higher elevations from December to February. In Jerusalem, snow may fall twice during the course of the winter months.

All of Palestine experiences extremely disagreeable warm conditions occasionally. The sirocco wind (the "east wind" of Gen. 41:6 and Ezek. 19:12) blowing from the southeast during the transition months (May–June, September–October) brings dust-laden clouds across the land. It dries vegetation and has a withering effect on people and animals. On occasion, the temperature may rise 30 degrees Fahrenheit and the humidity fall to less than 10 percent.

Along the coastal plain, the daily temperature fluctuation is rather limited because of the Mediterranean breezes. In the mountains and in Rift Valley, the daily fluctuation is much greater.

PALLET Small, usually straw-filled mattress light enough to be carried. All biblical references are found in accounts or summaries of the healing of people with disabilities (Mark 2:4-12; John 5:8-12; Acts 5:15). The "bedridden" man of Acts 9:33 was one who had lain on a pallet for eight years.

PALLU Personal name meaning "conspicuous," "wonder," or "distinguished." Second son of Reuben (Gen. 46:9; Exod. 6:14; Num. 26:5,8; 1 Chron. 5:3). KJV used the alternate spelling Phallu in Genesis.

PALMERWORM Caterpillar stage of a species of locust (Joel 1:4; 2:25; Amos 4:9). See *Insects.*

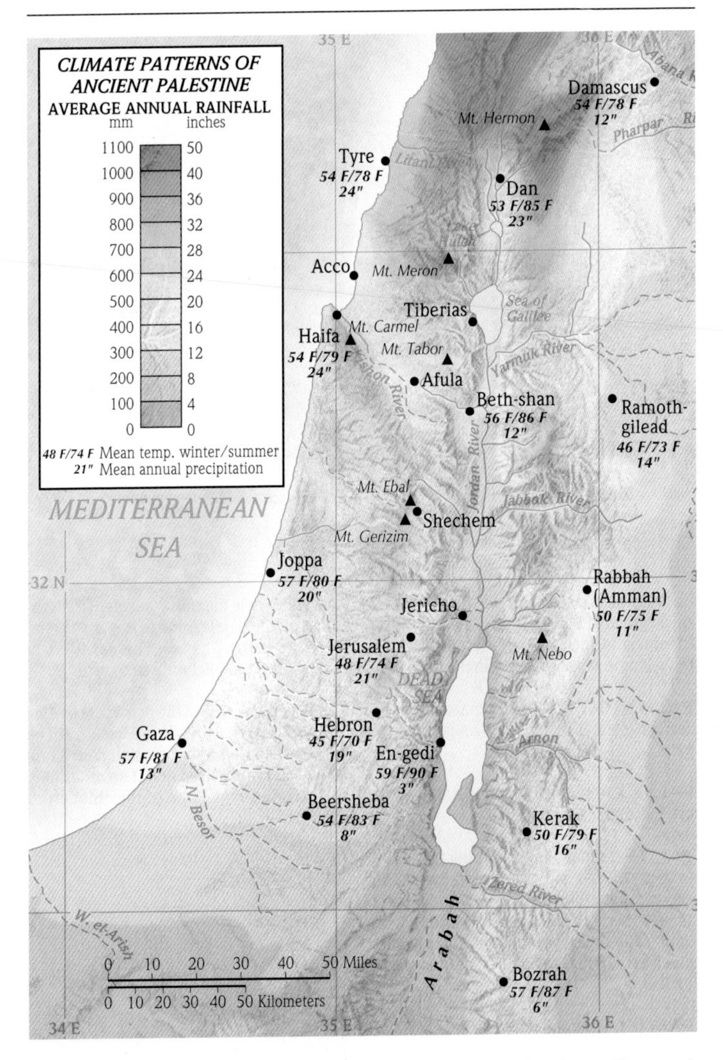

PALMS Date palm (*Phoenix dactylifera*) was among the earliest cultivated trees. Five-thousand-year-old inscriptions from Mesopotamia give instruction for their cultivation. Palms are characteristic of oases and watered places (Exod. 15:27; Num. 33:9). The fruit of the date palm is highly valued by desert travelers since it may be consumed fresh or dried or made into cakes for a portable and easily storable food. Palms were

Palm trees in the Wadi Feiran on the Sinai Peninsula

used in the construction of the booths for the Festival of Booths (Lev. 23:40; Neh. 8:15). In John 12:13, the crowd used palm branches to welcome Jesus to Jerusalem.

PALMS, CITY OF Alternate name for Jericho (Deut. 34:3; Judg. 1:16; 3:13; 2 Chron. 28:15).

PALSY KJV term for paralysis (Matt. 4:24; 9:2; Luke 5:18; Acts 8:7).

PALTI Personal name meaning "my deliverance." **1.** Benjamin's representative among the 12 spies sent to survey Canaan (Num. 13:9). **2.** Second husband of Michal, King Saul's daughter who had previously been given in marriage to David (1 Sam. 25:44; KJV, Phalti).

PALTIEL Personal name meaning "God is (my) deliverance." **1.** Leader of Issachar whom Moses appointed to assist Joshua and Eliezer in distribution of land to the tribes west of the Jordan (Num. 34:26). **2.** Fuller form of the name of Saul's son-in-law (2 Sam. 3:15-16).

PALTITE Title meaning "resident of Beth-pelet," given to Helez, one of David's 30 elite warriors (2 Sam. 23:26). The parallels in 1 Chronicles read Pelonite (11:27; 27:10).

PAMPHYLIA One of the provinces of Asia Minor. Located in what is now southern Turkey, Pamphylia was a small district on the coast. It measured about 80 miles long and 20 miles wide. One of the chief cities

The road north from Antalia to Isparta in the Roman province of Pamphylia (modern Turkey)

was Perga, where John Mark left Paul and Barnabas during the first missionary journey (Acts 13:13).

PAPER, PAPYRUS Popular writing material invented by the Egyptians and used by scribes from 2500 BC to AD 700.

The English word "paper" is derived from the word *papyrus*. The papyrus plant once grew in abundance along the Nile Delta ("Does papyrus grow where there is no marsh?" [Job 8:11 CSB]), providing the Egyptians with an inexpensive writing material that was exported throughout the Mediterranean world.

By AD 100, papyrus was used to make codices (books). The codex format—a stack of papyrus sheets, bound at one end—proved to be more economical than the roll since a scribe could only write on one side of the roll. A codex was also less cumbersome, considering the transportation of rolls and the difficulty of cross-referencing. Eventually, papyrus was replaced by the more expensive and yet more durable parchment (animal skins). Aged papyrus became brittle, literally causing words to fall off the page. Furthermore, unlike papyrus, parchment could be "erased" and used again. The only biblical reference to papyrus paper is found in 2 John 12, where the Elder writes: "Though I have many things to write to you, I don't want to use paper and ink" (CSB).

New Testament manuscripts produced before the fourth century were written exclusively on papyrus; after the fourth century, almost all NT documents were preserved on parchment.

A modern variety of the ancient papyrus plant from whose stalks writing material was made

PAPHOS Town on the southwest side of Cyprus and capital of the island during NT times. Paul, Barnabas, and John Mark came to the city on their first missionary journey and possibly led the proconsul, Sergius Paulus, to Christ (Acts 13:6-12).

PAPS KJV term used for a woman's breasts (Ezek. 23:21; Luke 11:27) or a man's chest (Rev. 1:13).

PARABLES Stories, especially those of Jesus, told to provide a vision of life, especially life in God's kingdom. Parable means a putting alongside for purposes of comparison and new understanding. Parables use figures of speech such as metaphors and similes and frequently extend them into a brief story to make a point or disclosure. Parables are not allegories, although some parables bear close resemblance to allegories.

Common Theme of Jesus's Parables Jesus's great thesis centers on the kingdom of God (Mark 1:15). Jesus lifted the theme to new heights and through his parables portrayed the nature of the kingdom (Mark 4:26-29), the grace of the kingdom (Luke 18:9-17), the crisis of the kingdom (Luke 12:54-56), and the conditions of the kingdom such as commitment (Luke 14:28-30), forgiveness (Matt. 18:23-35), and compassion (Luke 10:25-37).

The parables further proclaim the kingdom as ethical, experiential or existential, eschatological, and evangelistic. Several parables accentuate ethical concerns such as attitude toward one's fellows (Luke 18:9-14; 15:25-32; Matt. 18:23-35). Jesus insisted on being religious through relationships. The rousing call to repentance embodied in many parables requires a moral and spiritual reorientation of life around the kingdom.

Many parables reach the water table of common experience and illumine existence or life. Jesus could expose a pale or petrified life. He could convey the moving experience of being lost in the far country and then to come to oneself and go home (Luke 15:17). His parables exposed the inauthentic life as aggressively self-centered and greedy (Luke 12:13-21; 16:19-31).

PARACLETE Transliteration of the Greek word literally meaning "called beside or alongside to help." John exclusively used the term in the NT. He described the Spirit as another "Paraclete" who teaches (John 14:16), reminds the disciples of what Jesus taught (John 14:26), testifies (John 15:26), and convicts of sin (John 16:7-8). John also described Jesus as the first "Paraclete" (John 14:16) or advocate (1 John 2:1).

PARADISE Old Persian term that means literally "enclosure" or "wooded park," used in the OT to speak of King Artaxerxes's forest (Neh. 2:8), and twice of orchards (Eccles. 2:5; Song 4:13). All three NT occurrences (Luke 23:43; 2 Cor. 12:4; Rev. 2:7) refer to the abode of the righteous dead (heaven).

PARAH Place-name meaning "heifer" or "young cow." Village in territory of Benjamin about five miles northeast of Jerusalem, identified with modern Khirbet el-Farah (Josh. 18:23). The Hebrew *parat*, often translated Euphrates (KJV, CSB, NASB, NRSV), may refer to the spring 'Ain Farah at Jer. 13:4-7 (cp. NASB, NRSV margin, "Parah"). NIV, REB simply transliterate the term.

PARAMOUR Illicit sexual partner (Ezek. 23:20 KJV, NASB, NRSV; Hos. 3:1 RSV). Other translations read: lovers (CSB, NIV); male prostitutes (REB); and oversexed men (TEV).

PARAN **1.** Wilderness area south of Judah, west of Edom, and north of Sinai. Israel camped there after leaving Sinai during the exodus and sent spies to scout out the promised land from Kadesh, a location in Paran (Num. 10:11-12; 13:3,26. **2.** Mount Paran appears as a poetic parallel to Mount Sinai (Deut. 33:2; cp. Hab. 3:3) as the place of revelation. If not the same place as Sinai, the location is unknown.

PARCHED GRAIN Common food prepared by roasting grains in a pan or by holding heads of grain over a fire (Lev. 23:14; Josh. 5:11; Ruth 2:14; 1 Sam. 17:17; 25:18; 2 Sam. 17:28).

Mosaic law prohibited the eating of parched grain before the first fruits of the grain had been offered to God.

South end of the Wilderness of Paran where Israel wandered (photo taken in sand storm)

PARDON Authoritative act reversing a sentence given under a guilty verdict. Prayer for God's pardon for sin is based on the greatness of God's covenant love and on the long history of God's acts of forgiveness (Num. 14:19; Mic. 7:18).

PARE To trim or shave off. The paring of nails served as a sign of mourning for lost parents (Deut. 21:12 KJV, REB, NRSV). An Israelite desiring to marry a female prisoner of war was required to allow her to cut her hair and pare her nails first. These actions perhaps symbolized purification on entering the covenant community.

PARMASHTA Personal name, probably of Persian origin, possibly meaning "strong-fisted" or "the very first." One of Haman's 10 sons (Esth. 9:9).

PARMENAS Personal name meaning "faithful" or "constant." One of the seven chosen by the Jerusalem congregation to distribute food to the Greek-speaking widows of that church (Acts 6:5).

PARNACH Persian personal name of uncertain meaning. Father of Elizaphan (Num. 34:25).

PAROSH Personal name meaning "flea." **1.** Ancestor of a postexilic family (Ezra 2:3; 8:3; KJV, Pharosh; 10:25; Neh. 7:8). **2.** One of the witnesses to Ezra's renewal of the covenant (Neh. 10:14), possibly the father of Pedaiah (Neh. 3:25). This Parosh was likely the chief member of the family above.

PAROUSIA Transliteration of Greek word which means "presence" or "coming." In NT theology, it encompasses the events surrounding the second coming of Christ.

PARSHANDATHA Personal name, probably of Persian origin, possibly meaning "inquisitive." One of Haman's 10 sons (Esther 9:7).

PARTHIANS Tribal people who migrated from Central Asia into what is now Iran. In 53 BC, the Romans invaded Parthia but were defeated on several occasions. They did not gain control of Parthia until AD 114. Some Parthians were among those in Jerusalem on the day of Pentecost who heard the gospel in their own language (Acts 2:9-11).

PARTRIDGE Stout-bodied, medium-size game bird with variegated plumage. David likened his life as a fugitive from Saul to a hunted partridge (1 Sam. 26:20).

PARUAH Personal name meaning "blossoming," "joyous," or "increase." Father of Jehoshaphat (1 Kgs. 4:17).

PARVAIM Source of gold for Solomon's decoration of the temple (2 Chron. 3:6). The place is perhaps el Farwaim (Farwa) in Yemen or a general term for the East.

PARZITES KJV alternate form of Perezites (Num. 26:20).

PASACH Personal name, perhaps meaning "divider." Member of the tribe of Asher (1 Chron. 7:33).

PASCHAL Adjective expressing relation to the Passover.

PASDAMMIN Place-name meaning "boundary of blood." Scene of David's victory over the Philistines (1 Chron. 11:13). The site is probably between Socoh and Azekah, the same as Ephesdammin (1 Sam. 17:1).

PASEAH Personal name meaning "lame." **1.** Member of the tribe of Judah (1 Chron. 4:12). **2.** Ancestor of a family of temple servants (Neh. 7:51; KJV "Phaseah"). **3.** Father of Joiada (Neh. 3:6).

PASHUR Personal name meaning "son of (the god) Horus." **1.** Chief officer in the Jerusalem temple in the last years before Nebuchadnezzar's victory over the city. He had Jeremiah beaten and imprisoned (Jer. 20:1-2). He or another Pashur was the father of Gedaliah (Jer. 38:1). **2.** Man in Zedekiah's court in Jerusalem (Jer. 21:1). As the Babylonian army approached, Pashur asked Jeremiah for a word from the Lord. Jeremiah prophesied the destruction of the city (21:1-7; cp. 38:1-3). **3.** Forebear of a priestly family (1

Chron. 9:12) who returned from the exile (Ezra 2:38) and who later gave up their foreign wives (Ezra 10:22; cp. Neh. 10:3; 11:12).

PASSION **1.** Any bodily desire that leads to sin (Rom. 6:12; Gal. 5:24; Eph. 2:3). Passion is especially used for strong sexual desire (Rom. 1:26-27; 1 Cor. 7:9; 1 Thess. 4:5). **2.** KJV twice used the phrase "like passions" (Acts 14:15; James 5:17) to mean "shared human nature." **3.** The suffering of Jesus during the last two days of his life. Luke uses a word translated "passion" only in Acts 1:3 (KJV, after his passion). The root is the Greek verb *pascho*, "to suffer." Acts 17:3 and 26:23 use *pathein* to speak specifically of Christ's suffering; Jesus foretold his sufferings a number of times and yet his disciples rejected this possibility (Matt. 16:21; Mark 9:12; Luke 17:25).

PASSOVER Hebrew feast, commemorating their deliverance from Egyptian bondage. See *Festivals*.

PASTOR Common translation of the Greek noun (Eph. 4:11) and its verb form; also the Hebrew *ra'ah* (Jer. 3:15; 10:21; 12:10; 22:22 KJV). Literally, a shepherd (or one who keeps animals, Gen. 4:2; 13:7; 46:32,34; Exod. 2:17; Isa. 13:20; Jer. 6:3; Luke 2:8,15,18,20), but used figuratively of those called by God to feed (Jer. 3:15; John 21:16), care for (Acts 20:28), and lead (1 Pet. 5:2) his people, who are his "flock." In the NT, pastor (shepherd) appears to depict aspects, or functions, of the responsibilities of the overseer/elder (1 Pet. 2:25, where the two are put together in Christ).

PASTORALS First and Second Timothy and Titus are called the Pastoral Epistles, a title first used by Anton in 1753.

PASTURE Open land surrounding towns and villages, regarded as common property to be freely used by village shepherds and herdsmen (Num. 35:2,7; Josh. 14:4; 21:11). The same Hebrew term designates open space around a city or the sanctuary (Ezek. 27:28; 45:2; 48:17).

PATH A walkway. Two contrasting paths are a common image for rival ways of life in Hebrew Wisdom literature. The path of the wicked (Prov. 4:14) who forget God (Job 8:13) is crooked (Prov. 2:15). This approach to life contrasts with the path of righteousness (Ps. 23:3; Prov. 2:13,20).

PATHROS Hebrew transliteration of Egyptian term for Upper (southern) Egypt. Upper Egypt included the territory between modern Cairo and Aswan. The NIV translates the term; other translations transliterate (Isa. 11:11; Jer. 44:1,15; Ezek. 29:14; 30:14).

PATHRUSIM Son of Mizraim (Egypt) and ancestor of the inhabitants of upper (southern) Egypt who bore his name (1 Chron. 1:12).

PATIENCE Active endurance of opposition, not a passive resignation. "Patience" and "patient" are used to translate several Hebrew and Greek words.

PATMOS Small island (10 miles by 6 miles) in the Aegean Sea located about 37 miles southwest of Miletus. The Romans used such places for political exiles. John's mention of the island in Rev. 1:9

probably means that he was such a prisoner, having been sent there for preaching the gospel. Eusebius (an early church father) wrote that John was sent to Patmos by Emperor Domitian in AD 95 and released after one and a half years.

The island of Patmos on which John was probably exiled by the Romans

PATRIARCHS Israel's founding fathers—Abraham, Isaac, Jacob, and the 12 sons of Jacob (Israel). The word "patriarch" comes from a combination of the Latin word *pater*, "father," and the Greek verb *archo*, "to rule." A patriarch is thus a ruling ancestor who may have been the founding father of a family, a clan, or a nation.

PATROBAS Personal name meaning "life of (or from) father." Member of a Roman house church whom Paul greeted (Rom.16:14).

PAU Edomite city meaning "they cry out." Hadar's (Hadad) capital (Gen. 36:39). The parallel in 1 Chron. 1:50 gives the name as Pai.

PAUL Outstanding missionary, theologian, and writer of the early church. Paul is a very important figure in the NT and in the history of Christianity. He wrote 13 epistles that comprise almost one-fourth of the NT. Approximately 16 chapters of the book of Acts (13–28) focus on his missionary labors. Thus Paul is the author or subject of nearly one-third of the NT and the most important interpreter of the teachings of Christ and of the significance of his life, death, and resurrection.

Early Life and Training (AD 1–35) Birth and Family Background Paul was born in a Jewish family in Tarsus of Cilicia (Acts 22:3), probably sometime during the first decade of the first century. Paul's family was of the tribe of Benjamin (Phil. 3:5), and he was named for the most prominent member of the tribe—King Saul. Paul probably came from a family of tentmakers or leatherworkers and, according to Jewish custom, was taught this trade by his father. Apparently the business thrived and Paul's family became moderately wealthy.

Paul was born a Roman citizen. Many speculate that Paul's father or grandfather was honored with citizenship because of some special service rendered to a military proconsul.

Rabbinic Training Acts 22:3 shows that Paul grew up in Jerusalem. Paul used this fact to prove that he was no Diaspora Jew who was more influenced by Gentile culture than Jewish ways. He was educated in Jerusalem in the Jewish religion according to the traditions of his ancestors (Acts 22:3). Acts 22 says that Paul was trained by Rabbi Gamaliel I, the member of the Sanhedrin mentioned in Acts 5:33-39. Gamaliel was a leading Jewish teacher in Paul's day. In Acts 26:5, Paul identifies himself with the sect of the Pharisees. His father had also been a Pharisee (Acts 23:6).

Persecution of Christians As an ideal Pharisee, Paul was probably active as a Jewish missionary winning Gentiles as proselytes. He may have been like the Pharisees Jesus described who traveled "over land and sea to make one convert" (Matt. 23:15 CSB).

Paul was probably in his thirties when he, with authorization from the chief priest, began to imprison believers first in the synagogues of Jerusalem and then later in Damascus. Paul's initial and adamant rejection of Jesus as the Messiah may largely have been motivated by Jesus's ignoble death. Death by crucifixion was indicative of divine curse (Deut. 21:23). Certainly the Messiah could not have died under the curse of God. But when Paul wrote his first epistle, this death curse was recognized as the grounds for substitutionary atonement (Gal. 3:10-14). In 1 Cor. 1, Paul explained that the idea of a crucified Messiah was a stumbling block to the Jews. Probably Paul was speaking from his own past experience.

Paul's Conversion (AD 35) While Saul was on his way to Damascus to arrest and imprison believers there, the resurrected and glorified Christ appeared to him with blinding radiance. Christ's words "It is hard for you to kick against the goads" (Acts 26:14 CSB) indicate that God had already begun his convicting work earlier. At the appearance of Christ, Saul immediately surrendered to his authority and went into the city to await further orders. There his blindness was healed, and he received the Holy Spirit and accepted believer's baptism.

Paul's Missionary Travels (AD 35–61) Early Travels Soon after his conversion, Paul traveled to Arabia where he began evangelization of the Nabatean Arabs (Gal. 1:17; 2 Cor. 11:32-33) and probably experienced his first opposition to the gospel from political authorities. He then returned to Damascus where he began to go into the synagogues to preach the message that had been revealed to him on the Damascus road: Jesus is the Son of God and the promised Messiah. The Jews in Damascus watched the city gates in

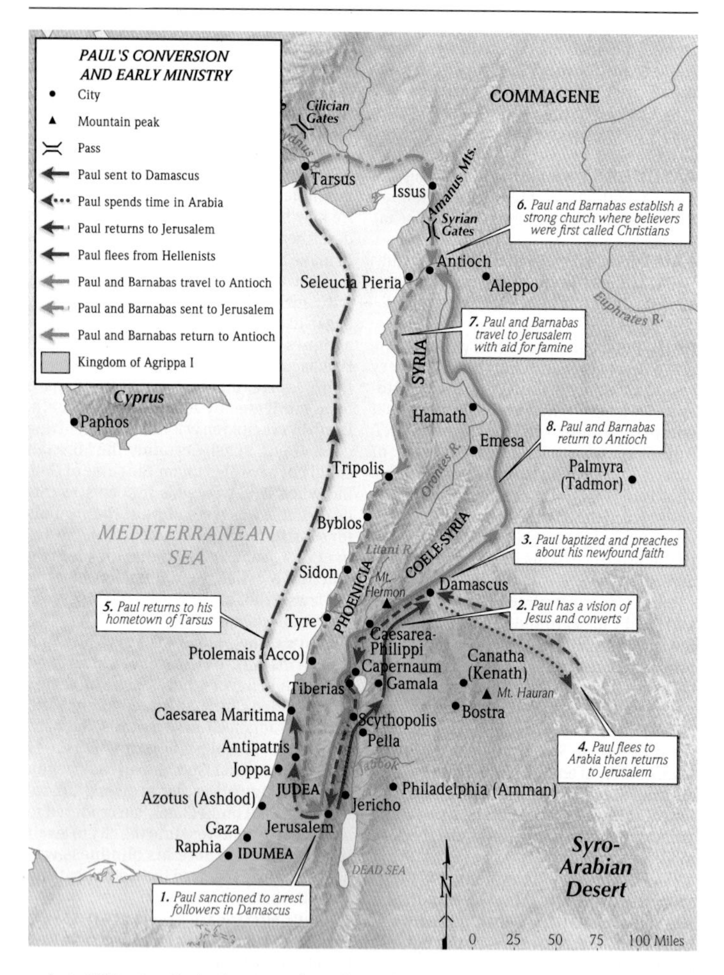

order to kill Paul, and he had to escape through a window in the wall by being lowered in a basket (Acts 9:22-25).

Paul then traveled to Jerusalem. Church leaders were initially suspicious of Paul but Barnabas intervened in his behalf (Acts 9:26-30 and Gal. 1:18). After 15 days in Jerusalem, visiting with Peter and James the Lord's brother, Paul returned to Tarsus, evangelizing Syria and Cilicia for several years. While in Syria, Barnabas contacted Paul and invited him to become involved in the Antioch church, where large numbers of Gentiles were responding to the gospel.

First Missionary Journey Paul and Barnabas soon began their first missionary journey, traveling through Cyprus and Anatolia probably during the years AD 47–48. The mis-

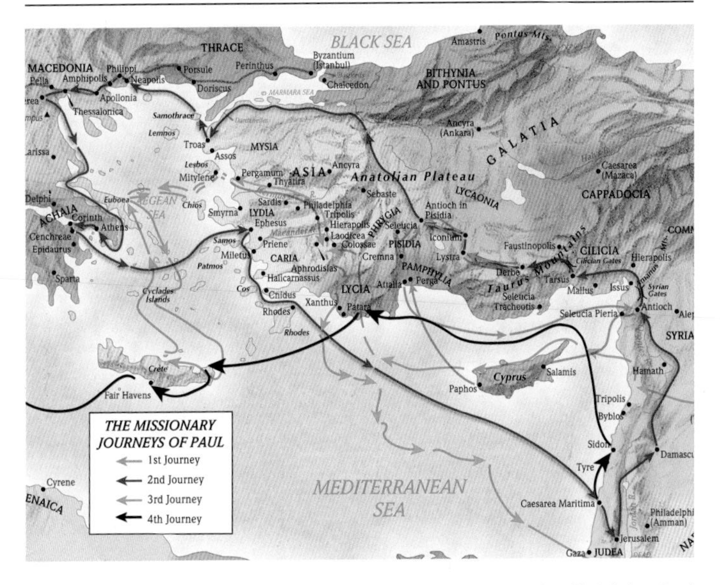

sionary team carried the gospel to the cities of Pisidian Antioch, Iconium, Lystra, and Derbe. These cities were located in the Roman province of Galatia, and it is probably these churches in south Galatia to which the epistle to the Galatians is addressed. Galatians was probably written during this journey.

Jerusalem Council When Paul returned to Antioch from the first missionary journey, he found himself embroiled in controversy over requirements for Gentile salvation. Peter and even Barnabas were vacillating on the issue of Jew-Gentile relationships. Even worse, some false teachers from the Jerusalem church had infiltrated congregations in Antioch and were teaching, "Unless you are circumcised according to the custom prescribed by Moses, you cannot be saved" (Acts 15:1 CSB). The church appointed Paul and Barnabas to go to Jerusalem and settle the matter. A council was convened in AD 49 that included the missionary team, those who insisted upon circumcision as a requirement for salvation, and the apostles. The apostle Peter and James the brother of Jesus spoke in defense of Paul's Law-free gospel and a letter was sent to the Gentile churches confirming the official view. Paul returned to Antioch and remained there from 49 to 51.

Second Missionary Journey The second missionary journey carried Paul through Macedonia and Achaia in AD 50–52. Paul and Barnabas parted company early in this journey in a disagreement about the participation of Barnabas's nephew John Mark. Mark had abandoned the team on the first journey (Acts 15:38). Paul took Silas and established churches in Philippi, Thessalonica, and Berea. Barnabas went with John Mark. Paul also spent 18 months in Corinth strengthening a fledgling church there. Four of Paul's letters are addressed to churches known from this second journey. Most scholars believe that 1 and 2 Thessalonians were written during this journey.

Third Missionary Journey Paul's third missionary journey (AD 53–57) focused on the city of Ephesus where Paul spent the better part of three years. Toward the end of this journey, Paul worked hard to collect another relief offering for Jerusalem believers. Paul wrote 1 and 2 Corinthians and Romans during this journey.

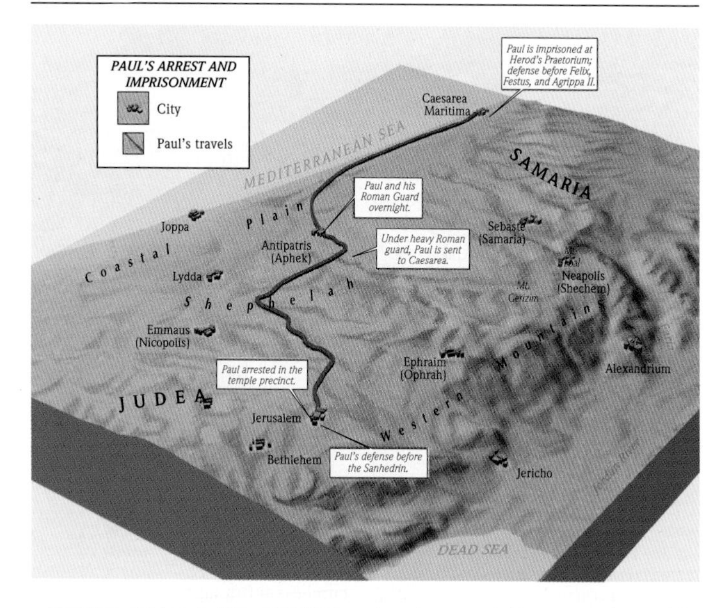

Final Years Paul carried the relief offering to Jerusalem. While he was in the temple performing a ritual to demonstrate his Jewish faithfulness to some of the Jerusalem believers, Jewish opponents incited a riot and Paul was arrested (AD 57). Paul was sent to Caesarea to stand trial before the procurator Felix. After two years of procrastination on the part of his detainers, Paul finally appealed to the Roman emperor for trial. After arriving in Rome, Paul spent two years under house arrest awaiting his trial. Paul wrote Philemon, Colossians, Ephesians, and Philippians during this first Roman imprisonment.

The record of Acts ends at this point, so information as to the outcome of the trial is sketchy. Early church tradition suggests that Paul was acquitted (ca. AD 63) or exiled and fulfilled the dream expressed in Rom. 15:23-29 of carrying the gospel to Spain (AD 63–67). Paul probably wrote 1 and 2 Timothy and Titus during the period between his acquittal and a second Roman imprisonment. According to church tradition, Paul was arrested again and subjected to a harsher imprisonment. He was condemned by Emperor Nero and beheaded with the sword at the third milestone on the Ostian Way, at a place called Aquae Salviae, and lies buried on the site covered by the basilica of St. Paul Outside the Walls. His execution probably occurred in AD 67.

Paul's Gospel Paul's gospel indicted all humanity for the crime of rejecting God and his rightful authority. Under the influence of Adam's sin, humankind plunged into the depths of depravity so that they were utterly unable to fulfill the righteous demands of God (Rom. 1:18-32; 3:9-20; 9:12-19) and deserved only the wrath of God (Rom. 1:18; 2:5-16). The sinner was alienated from God and at enmity with him (Col. 1:21). Consequently, the sinner's only hope was the gospel that embodied God's power to save those who had faith in Christ (Rom. 1:16). The focus of Paul's gospel was Jesus Christ (Rom. 1:3-4). Paul affirmed Jesus's humanity and his deity. Christ was a physical descendant from the line of David (Rom. 1:2), came in the likeness of sinful man (Rom. 8:3), and had assumed the form of a humble obedient servant (Phil.

2:7-8). Yet he was the visible form of the invisible God (Col. 1:15), all the fullness of deity living in bodily form (Col. 2:9), the very nature of God (Phil. 1:6), and possessed the title "Lord" (Greek title for the God of the OT), the name above all names (Phil. 2:9-11). Paul believed that by virtue of Jesus's sinlessness, Jesus was qualified to be the sacrifice which would make sinners right with God (2 Cor. 5:21). In his death on the cross, Jesus became the curse for sin (Gal. 3:10-14), and the righteous died for the unrighteous (Rom. 5:6-8). Salvation is a free gift granted to believers and grounded solely in God's grace. Salvation is not dependent upon human merit, activity, or effort, but only upon God's undeserved love (Eph. 2:8-10; Rom. 6:23). Those who trust Jesus for their salvation, confess him as Lord, and believe that God raised him from the dead (Rom. 10:9) will be saved from God's wrath, become righteous in God's sight (Rom. 5:9), be adopted as God's children (Rom. 8:15-17), and be transformed by the Spirit's power (Gal. 5:22-24). At the coming of Christ, believers will be resurrected (1 Cor. 15:12-57), will partake fully of the Son's righteous character (Phil. 3:20-21), and will live forever with their Lord (1 Thess. 4:17). By his union with Christ through faith, the believer participated spiritually in Christ's death, resurrection, and ascension (Rom. 6:1-7:6; Eph. 2:4-5). Consequently, the believer has been liberated from the power of sin, death, and the Law. He is a new, though imperfect, creation that is continually being made more Christlike (Col. 3:9-10; 2 Cor. 5:17). Although the believer is no longer under the authority of the written Law, the Holy Spirit functions as a new internal law that leads the believer to naturally and spontaneously fulfill the Law's righteous demands (Rom. 8:1-4). As a result, the Law-free gospel does not encourage unrighteous behavior in believers. Such behavior is contrary to their new identity in Christ. The union of believers with Christ brings them into union with other believers in the body of Christ, the church. Believers exercise their spiritual gifts in order to help each other mature, to serve Christ, and to glorify him, which is the church's highest purpose (Eph. 3:21; 4:11-13). Christ now rules over the church as its head, its highest authority (Eph. 1:22). When Christ comes again, his reign over the world will be consummated and all that exists will be placed under his absolute authority (Phil. 2:10-11; 4:20; Eph. 1:10). He will raise the dead: unbelievers for judgment and punishment; believers for glorification and reward (2 Thess. 1:5-10).

Reconstruction of Caesarea Maritima where Paul was imprisoned for two years (Acts 23:31-26:32)

PAVILION Large, often richly decorated tent.

PEACE OFFERING See *Sacrifice and Offering*.

PEACE A condition or sense of harmony, well-being, and prosperity. The biblical concept means more than the absence of hostility, and it is more than a psychological state.

Old Testament The Hebrew word *shalom* and its derivatives have been said to represent "one of the most prominent theological concepts in the OT." (The word group occurs about 180 times in the OT.) It was not a negative or passive concept but involved wholeness and completeness.

New Testament The term translated "peace" in the NT is *eirene*. It occurs in every NT book except 1 John (most frequently in Luke, 14 times; followed by Romans, 10; then Ephesians, 8). Outside the Bible, the Greek word was likely to mean the opposite of war, but its use to translate *shalom* in the Septuagint may have been what broadened its usage. Like *shalom*, the term in the NT could refer not only to the absence of hostility, strife, and disorder (1 Cor. 14:33), but also to the condition and sense of being safe and secure (Acts 9:31). Christ made peace between believing Jew and Gentile by making them into one new man in him (Eph. 2:14-15). The term could also describe a state of either physical or spiritual well-being.

PEACEMAKERS Those who actively work to bring about peace and reconciliation where there is hatred and enmity. God blesses peacemakers and declares them to be his children (Matt. 5:9). Those who work for peace share in Christ's ministry of bringing peace and reconciliation (2 Cor. 5:18-19; Eph. 2:14-15; Col. 1:20).

PEACOCK KJV translated two Hebrew words as "peacock." Modern translations replace "peacock" with "ostrich" at Job 39:13. NASB, NRSV read "peacock" with KJV at 1 Kgs. 10:22 and 2 Chron. 9:21. Other translations read "monkey" (REB, RSV) or "baboon" (CSB, NIV, NRSV margin).

PEDAHEL Personal name meaning "God delivers." Leader of the tribe of Naphtali whom Moses appointed to assist Joshua and Eliezer in the distribution of land to the tribes living west of the Jordan (Num. 34:28).

PEDAHZUR Personal name meaning "(the) Rock redeems." Father of Gamaliel (Num. 1:10; 2:20; 7:54,59; 10:23).

PEDAIAH Personal name meaning "Yah redeems." **1.** Maternal grandfather of King Jehoiakim (2 Kgs. 23:36). **2.** Father (1 Chron. 3:18-19) or uncle (Ezra 3:2,8; 5:2; Neh. 12:1; Hag. 1:1,12,14; 2:2,23) of Zerubbabel. First Chronicles presents Pedaiah and Shealtiel as brothers. **3.** Manassite father of Joel (1 Chron. 27:20). **4.** Son of Parosh assisting in Nehemiah's repair of the wall (Neh. 3:25). **5.** Witness to Ezra's renewal of the covenant (Neh. 8:4), perhaps identical with 4, above. **6.** Benjaminite father of Joed (Neh. 11:7). **7.** Levite whom Nehemiah appointed as temple treasurer (Neh. 13:13).

PEDDLER One who sells goods, usually on the street or door to door. Paul denied being a peddler of God's word (2 Cor. 2:17). Here Paul either emphasized that he did not preach for pay (1 Cor. 9:12,15) or that he did not use tricks to gain converts (2 Cor. 4:2; 12:16).

PEG Small, cylindrical, or tapered piece of wood (or some other material). Pegs were used: to secure tents (Judg. 4:21-22; 5:26); to hang articles (Isa. 22:23,25; Ezek. 15:3); to weave cloth (Judg. 16:14); even to dig latrines (Deut. 23:13).

PEKAH Personal name meaning "open-eyed." Officer in Israel's army who became king in a bloody coup by murdering King Pekahiah (2 Kgs. 15:25).

PEKAHIAH Personal name meaning "Yah has opened his eyes." King of Israel 742–740 BC. He succeeded his father, Menahem, as a vassal of the Assyrian throne (2 Kgs. 15:23).

PEKOD Hebrew for "punishment" or "judgment" that plays on the name Puqadu, an Aramean tribe inhabiting the area east of the mouth of the Tigris (Jer. 50:21; Ezek. 23:23).

PELAIAH Personal name meaning "Yahweh is wonderful (or performs wonders)." **1.** Descendant of David (1 Chron. 3:24). **2.** Levite assisting in Ezra's public reading of the Law (Neh. 8:7). **3.** Levite witnessing Nehemiah's covenant (Neh. 10:10), perhaps identical to 2, above.

PELALIAH Personal name meaning "Yahweh intercedes." Ancestor of a priest in Ezra's time (Neh. 11:12).

PELATIAH Personal name meaning "Yahweh delivers." **1.** Descendant of David (1 Chron. 3:21). **2.** One of the Simeonites destroying the remaining Amalekites at Mount Seir (1 Chron. 4:42). **3.** Judean prince who offered "wicked counsel," perhaps appealing to Egypt for help in a revolt against the Babylonians (Ezek. 11:1,13; cp. Jer. 27:1-3; 37:5,7,11). **4.** Witness to Nehemiah's covenant (Neh. 10:22).

PELEG Personal name meaning "division" or "watercourse." Descendant of Shem (Gen. 10:25), ancestor of Abraham (Gen. 11:16-19; 1 Chron. 1:19,25) and Jesus (Luke 3:35).

PELET Personal name derived from a root meaning "escape." **1.** Descendant of Caleb (1 Chron. 2:47). **2.** Benjaminite warrior who defected from Saul to David (1 Chron. 12:3).

PELETH Personal name meaning "swift." **1.** Father of On (Num. 16:1). The name is possibly a textual corruption of Pallu (Gen. 46:9; Num. 26:5,8), whose descendants are also associated with the Korah rebellion (Num. 26:9-10). **2.** A Jerahmeelite (1 Chron. 2:33).

PELETHITES Family name meaning "courier." Foreign mercenaries King David employed as bodyguards and special forces. Their leader was Benaiah (2 Sam. 8:18).

PELICAN Any member of a family of large, web-footed birds with gigantic bills having expandable pouches attached to the lower jaw. The Hebrew term translated "pelican" in Lev. 11:18; Deut. 14:17, however, suggests a bird that regurgitates its food to feed its young.

PELLA City just east of the Jordan River and southeast of the Sea of Galilee. It received a large part of the Jerusalem church when they fled there before the Roman destruction of the Holy City in AD 66.

PENINNAH Personal name, perhaps meaning "woman with rich hair," "coral," or "pearl." It may be an intentional wordplay meaning "fruitful." Elkanah's second wife and rival of barren Hannah (1 Sam. 1:2,4).

PENKNIFE Another name for a scribe's knife.

PENTAPOLIS League of five Philistine city-states that banded together to oppose the Israelite occupation of Canaan: Ashdod, Gaza, Ashkelon, Gath, and Ekron (1 Sam. 6:17).

PENTATEUCH The expression derives from two Greek words, *penta*, "five," and *teuchos*, "vessel, container," and refers to the first five books of the OT. This designation dates to the time of Tertullian (ca. AD 200), but Jewish canons label these books collectively as the Torah, which means "Teaching, Instruction." In English Bibles, these first five books are commonly called "Law." This designation is misleading because it misrepresents the content of the Pentateuch. Large portions are not law at all; they are actually inspiring narratives (virtually all of Genesis; Exod. 1–11; 14–20; 32–34; Lev. 8–10; Num. 1:1–3:4,7,9-14,16-17,20-28,31-33). Although *Deuteronomium* means "second law," the book presents itself as preaching, Moses's final pastoral addresses.

The Plot of the Pentateuch The pivotal event of the Pentateuch is God's revelation of himself at Sinai. Everything before is prologue, and all that comes after is epilogue. This is evident from the redundant highlighting of the place in Deut. 19:13, and also from the explicit anticipation of Exod. 3:12, where Yahweh told Moses that Israel's service to God at Mount Sinai would prove Yahweh had sent him. This is confirmed by Moses's demands to Pharaoh that he let Israel go to serve Yahweh in the desert (4:23; 5:1,3; 6:11; 7:16; 8:1,25-28; 9:13; 10:3,7,9,24-26). The patriarchal narratives also look forward to Sinai. In Gen. 12:2, God promises Abraham that he would be a blessing to the whole world. Later we learn that this would involve being the recipient of the divine revelation (cp. Deut. 4:5-8), being a kingdom of priests, a holy nation, a special treasure "out of all the peoples, although the whole earth is mine" (Exod. 19:5 CSB).

The narratives describing Israel's journey from Sinai to the Plains of Moab are told against the backdrop of Yahweh's covenant with Israel and Israel's promise to do all that the Lord had told them. Numbers 28:6 explicitly refers to the Sinai revelation. But the book of Deuteronomy, virtually in its entirety, represents Moses's exposition of the Sinai covenant. However, remember that the primary character is not human; this is a record of God's relationship with those he created in his own image, whom he elected, redeemed, and commissioned to be his agents on the earth.

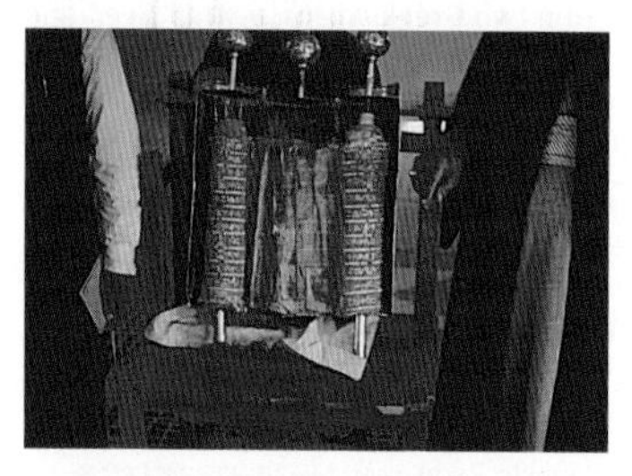

The Samaritan Pentateuch at Nablus. Samaritans consider only the Pentateuch as canonical.

PENTATEUCH, SAMARITAN See *Samaritan Pentateuch.*

PENTECOST See *Festivals (Feast of Weeks).*

PENUEL Name meaning "face of God." **1.** Descendant of Judah and founder (father) of Gedor (1 Chron. 4:4). **2.** A Benjaminite (1 Chron. 8:25). **3.** Site on Jabbok River northeast of Succoth where Jacob wrestled with the stranger (Gen. 32:24-32; cp. Hos. 12:4).

PEOPLE OF GOD Group elected by God and committed to be his covenant people. Scripture repeatedly defines who is included in the people of God. The history of revelation shows God electing Israel by grace.

PEOR Name, perhaps meaning "opening." **1.** Mountain in Moab opposite the wilderness of Judah. Balak brought Balaam there to curse the camp of the Israelites, which was visible from the site (Num. 23:28; 24:2). **2.** Abbreviated form of Baal-Peor (lord of Peor), a god whom the Israelites were led to worship (Num. 25:18; 31:16; Josh. 22:17). **3.** Site in Judah identified with modern Khirbet Faghur southwest of Bethlehem (Josh. 15:59 REB, following the earliest Greek translation).

PERDITION Describes the eternal state of death, destruction, annihilation, or ruin.

PEREA Roman district in Transjordan that became a part of Herod the Great's kingdom. The capital was Gadara where Jesus drove demons out of a man. Perea was the area through which the Jews traveled to avoid going through Samaria. Although not referred to by name in the NT, it is mentioned as "Judea beyond the Jordan" in several texts (Matt. 19:1; Mark 10:1 RSV).

PERESH Personal name meaning "separate." A Manassite (1 Chron. 7:16).

PEREZ Personal name meaning "breach." One of the twins born to the illicit affair between Judah and his daughter-in-law, Tamar (Gen. 38).

PEREZ-UZZA or **PEREZ-UZZAH** Place-name meaning "breach of Uzzah." Site of the threshing floor of Nacon (or Chidon) west of Jerusalem on the Kiriath-jearim road where the anger of the Lord "broke out" against Uzzah, who touched the ark to steady it (2 Sam. 6:8; 1 Chron. 13:11).

PERFECT To be whole or complete; also referred to as "mature." Throughout the Bible, especially in the OT, God is referred to as being "perfect" (Ps. 18:32). He is complete and lacks nothing. In the Sermon on the Mount, Jesus commanded, "Be perfect, therefore, as your heavenly Father is perfect"

(Matt. 5:48 CSB). The perfection demanded of Christians is a state of spiritual maturity or completeness.

PERFUME, PERFUMER Modern translation of a word translated as "apothecary" by the KJV (Exod. 30:25,35; 37:29; 2 Chron. 16:14; Neh. 3:8; Eccles. 10:1). Perfumes mentioned in the Bible include aloes, balsam (or balm), bdellium, calamus (or sweet or fragment cane), camel's thorn, cinnamon (or cassia), frankincense, galbanum, gum, henna, myrrh, nard (or spikenard), onycha, saffron, and stacte.

PERGA Ancient city in the province of Pamphylia, about eight miles from the Mediterranean Sea. Settlement at Perga dates to prehistory. Alexander the Great passed through the town during his campaigns and used guides from there. A temple to Artemis was one of the prominent buildings. Paul, Barnabas, and John Mark came to Perga from

Paphos (Acts 13:13). There young John Mark left the team to return home.

PERGAMOS (KJV, Rev. 1:11; 2:12) or **PERGAMUM** Place-name meaning "citadel." A wealthy ancient city in the district of Mysia in Asia Minor.

PERIDA Personal name meaning "unique" or "separated." Head of a family of Solomon's servants, some of whom returned from exile (Neh. 7:57; cp. Peruda, Ezra 2:55).

PERIZZITES Group name meaning "rustic." One of the groups of people who opposed the Israelite occupation of Canaan (Josh. 9:1-2). They dwelled in the land as early as Abraham's time (Gen. 13:7).

The temple of Athena at ancient Pergamum

The south Hellenistic gate of the ancient city of Perga in Pamphylia (modern Turkey)

PERJURY False statement given voluntarily under oath. Perjury involves either false witness to past facts or the neglect of what has been previously vowed. Mosaic law prohibited false swearing (Lev. 19:12; Exod. 20:7) and giving false witness (Exod. 20:16).

PERSECUTION Harassment and suffering that people and institutions inflict upon others for being different in their faith, worldview, culture, or race. Persecution seeks to intimidate, silence, punish, or even kill people. Jesus was persecuted and finally killed by the religious and political establishments of his day (Mark 3:6; Luke 4:29; John 5:16; Acts 3:13-15; 7:52; passion stories). Whole epistles and books like 1 Peter, Hebrews, and Revelation were written to encourage Christians in a situation of persecution (1 Pet. 3:13-18; 4:12-19; 5:6-14; Heb. 10:32-39; 12:3; Rev. 2–3). Something like a theology of persecution emerged, which emphasized patience, endurance, and steadfastness (Rom. 12:12; 1 Thess. 2:14-16; James 5:7-11); prayer (Matt. 5:44; Rom. 12:14; 1 Cor. 4:12); thanksgiving (2 Thess. 1:4); testing (Mark 4:17) and the strengthening of faith (1 Thess. 3:2-3); experiencing the grace of God (Rom. 8:35; 2 Cor. 4:9; 12:10); and being blessed through suffering (Matt. 5:10-12; 1 Pet. 3:14; 4:12-14).

PERSEVERANCE Maintaining Christian faith through the trying times of life. As a noun. the term "perseverance" occurs in the NT only at Eph. 6:18 (*proskarteresis*) and Heb. 12:1 (*hupomone*). The idea is inherent throughout the NT in the great interplay of the themes of assurance and warning.

PERSIA As a nation, Persia corresponds to the modern state of Iran. As an empire, Persia was a vast collection of states and kingdoms reaching from the shores of Asia Minor in the west to the Indus River valley in the east. It reached northward to southern Russia and in the south included Egypt and the regions bordering the Persian Gulf and the Gulf of Oman. In history the empire defeated the Babylonians and then fell finally to Alexander the Great.

Politically the Persian Empire was the best organized the world had ever seen. The Persian Empire had considerable influence on the Jews and biblical history. Babylon had conquered Jerusalem and destroyed the temple in 586 BC. When Cyrus conquered Babylon, he allowed the Jews to return to Judah and encouraged the rebuilding of the temple (Ezra 1:1-4). The work was begun but not completed. Then, under Darius I, Zerubbabel and the high priest, Joshua, led the restored community with the support and encouragement of the Persians. (Ezra 3–6 tells of some of the events while Haggai's and Zechariah's prophecies were made during the days of the restoration.) Despite some local opposition, Darius supported the rebuilding of the temple, which was rededicated in his sixth year (Ezra 6:15). In addition, both Ezra and Nehemiah were official representatives of the Persian government. Ezra was to teach and to appoint judges (Ezra 7). Nehemiah may have been the first governor

Column with inscription in Old Persian script ascribed to Cyrus the Great

of the province of Yehud (Judah). He undoubtedly had official support for his rebuilding of the walls of Jerusalem.

The Jews had trouble under Persian rule, too. Although Daniel was taken into exile by the Babylonians (Dan. 1), his ministry continued through the fall of the Babylonians (Dan. 5) into the time of the Persians (Dan. 6). His visions projected even further. Daniel 6 shows a stable government but one in which Jews could still be at risk. His visions in a time of tranquility remind readers that human kingdoms come and go. Esther is a story of God's rescue of his people during the rule of the Persian emperor Ahasuerus (also known as Xerxes I). The story shows an empire where law was used and misused. Jews were already, apparently, hated by some. Malachi, too, was probably from the Persian period. His book shows an awareness of the world at large and is positive toward the Gentiles and the government.

PERSIS Personal name meaning "Persian woman." Leader in the Roman church whom Paul greeted and commended for diligent service (Rom. 16:12).

PERVERSE Translation of one Greek and several Hebrew terms with the literal meaning "bent," "crooked," or "twisted," applied to persons involved in moral error.

PESHITTA Common Syriac version of the Scriptures. The OT was likely translated between AD 100 and 300. The NT translation dates from before AD 400. The Peshitta lacked those books rejected by the Syriac-speaking churches (2 Peter; 2 and 3 John; Jude; Revelation).

PESTILENCE Devastating epidemic that OT writers understood to be sent by God (Exod. 9:15; Jer. 15:2; Hab. 3:5; Amos 4:10), sometimes by means of a destroying angel (2 Sam. 24:16; 1 Chron. 21:15). God sent pestilence as punishment for persistent unbelief (Num. 14:12) and failure to fulfill covenant obligations (Deut. 28:21) as well as to encourage repentance (Amos 4:10).

PESTLE Small, club-shaped tool used to grind in a mortar (Prov. 27:22).

Church of St. Peter in Gallicantu that honors the traditional site of Peter's weeping after his denial of Jesus

PETER Derived from the Greek *petros*, meaning "rock." The name occurs 183 times in the NT. Simon was his personal name; Peter was given to him by Jesus (Matt. 16:18). Though Peter is dominant, there are three other names: the Hebrew Simeon (Acts 15:14), Simon, and Cephas (Aramaic for rock), used mostly by Paul (1 Cor. 1:12; 3:22; 9:5; 15:5; Gal. 1:18; 2:9,11,14) and one other time (John 1:42).

Peter's Family The Gospels provide information about Peter and his family. He was called Barjona (Aramaic for "son of Jona," Matt. 16:17) or son of John (Gk. for Barjona, Luke 1:42). Peter and his brother Andrew came from Bethsaida (John 1:44) and were Galilean fishermen (Mark 1:16; Luke 5:2-3; John 21:3) in business with James and John (Luke 5:10). Peter was married (Mark 1:30) and lived in Capernaum (Mark 1:21-31). Peter and Andrew were associated with John the Baptist prior to becoming disciples of Jesus (John 1:40).

Peter's Role among the Disciples Peter was leader and spokesman for the 12 disciples (Mark 8:29; Matt. 17:24). Peter often posed questions to Jesus representing concerns of the others (Matt. 15:15; 18:21; Mark 11:21; Luke 12:41). Sometimes he was spiritually perceptive (Matt. 16:16; John 6:68) and other times slow to understand spiritual matters (Matt. 15:15-16). Once he walked on water with Jesus, but his faith waned and he began to sink (Matt. 14:28-31). The greatest example of Peter's inconsistency was his confession "You are the Messiah" (Matt.

16:16 CSB) opposed to his denial "I don't know this man" (Mark 14:71). After Pentecost (Acts 2:1), Peter was bold when persecuted. On two occasions, Peter was arrested and warned to refrain from preaching about Jesus (Acts 4:1-22; 5:12-40). Herod imprisoned Peter with intent to execute him (Acts 12:3-5). Peter, however, was freed and delivered by an angel (Acts 12:6-11).

Peter's Role in the Early Church and His Legacy Though Peter led the disciples and took a prominent role in the early church (Acts 1–5), he did not emerge as the leader. Peter helped establish the Jerusalem church, but James the brother of Jesus assumed the leadership of the Jerusalem church (Acts 15). Though Peter was active in the spread of the gospel to the Gentiles (Acts 11–12), Paul became "the apostle to the Gentiles" (Acts 14; 16–28). Peter served as a bridge to hold together the diverse people of the early church (Acts 15). Peter became the "apostle to the Jews," preaching throughout Palestine. Peter died as a martyr in Rome under Nero, probably in AD 64 or 65 (1 Clement 5:1–6:1).

PETER, FIRST LETTER FROM First Peter is addressed to churches in Asia Minor experiencing persecution. Peter reminded them of their heavenly hope and eternal inheritance so that they would be strengthened to persevere in the midst of suffering. He emphasized that believers are called to holiness and a life of love. Believers are called upon to glorify God in their daily lives and to imitate Christ, who suffered on the cross for the sake of his people. Peter sketched what it means to live as a Christian, how believers relate to governing authorities, to cruel masters, and to unbelieving husbands. He warned believers that suffering may be intense, but believers should rely upon God's grace, knowing there is a heavenly reward.

If we accept Petrine authorship, the letter was likely written in the early 60s, before the composition of 2 Peter. The first verse of the letter indicates that the letter was written to various churches in the northern part of Asia Minor (present-day Turkey). The courier of the letter, presumably Silvanus, probably traveled in a circle in reading the letter to the various churches. The purpose of the letter was to fortify the churches and give them hope as they experienced persecution.

PETER, SECOND LETTER FROM In his second epistle, Peter wrote in response to false teachers who denied the second coming of the Lord Jesus Christ and advocated a libertine lifestyle. Peter maintained that God's grace is the foundation for a godly life and that living a life of godliness is necessary to obtain an eternal reward. Such a claim does not amount to works-righteousness, for such works do not merit salvation but are a result of God's transforming grace. Peter also vigorously defended the truth of Christ's second coming, which was anticipated in the transfiguration and promised in God's word. Those who reject Christ's coming deny God's sovereignty. They reject God's intervention in the world and remove any basis for ethical living. Peter urged his readers to grow in grace and knowledge until the day of salvation arrives.

The date of 2 Peter depends upon one's view of authorship. Probably Peter wrote the letter shortly before his death in the mid-60s. The letter was most likely written to the same readers who received 1 Peter (cp. 3:2), and hence it was probably sent to churches in Asia Minor.

PETHAHIAH Personal name meaning "Yahweh opens." **1.** Ancestor of a postexilic priestly family (1 Chron. 24:16). **2.** Royal adviser to the Persian king, either at his court or as his representative in Jerusalem (Neh. 11:24). **3.** Levite participating in Ezra's covenant renewal (Neh. 9:5). **4.** Levite with a foreign wife (Ezra 10:23), perhaps identical with 3, above.

PETHOR Place-name meaning "soothsayer." City in upper Mesopotamia identified with Tell Ahmar, 12 miles south of Carchemish near the confluence of the Sajur and Euphrates Rivers. Home of Balaam (Num. 22:5; Deut. 23:4).

PETHUEL Personal name meaning "vision of God" or "youth of God." Father of the prophet Joel (1:1).

PETRA Capital city of the Nabatean Arabs located about 60 miles north of the Gulf of Aqaba. Petra is sometimes identified with Sela (Judg. 1:36; 2 Kgs. 14:7; Isa. 16:1; 42:11) because both names mean "rock." Lack of archaeological evidence of Edomite settlement in the basin suggests that Sela is better identified with Um el Bayyarah on the mountain plateau overlooking Petra. The Nabatean king Aretas IV (2 Cor. 11:32-33) reigned from Petra.

A view from the front of the Treasury building of the narrow entryway into the Nabatean city of Petra

PEULLETHAI or **PEULTHAI** (KJV) Personal name meaning "recompense." A Levitical gatekeeper (1 Chron. 26:5).

PHANUEL Alternate form of the personal name Penuel meaning "face of God." Father of the prophetess Anna (Luke 2:36).

PHARAOH Title meaning "great house" for the ancient kings of Egypt. Egyptians applied "pharaoh" to the royal palace and grounds in the fourth dynasty (ca. 2500 BC). The title pharaoh came to be applied to the king from about 1500 BC until the Persian domination, about 550 BC.

References to 10 pharaohs can be clearly distinguished in the OT: the pharaoh of Abraham, Gen. 12:10-20; of Joseph, Gen. 39–50; of the Oppression, Exod. 1; of the exodus, Exod. 2:23–15:19; of 1 Chron. 4:18; of Solomon, 1 Kgs. 3–11; of Rehoboam, called Shishak, king of Egypt, 1 Kgs. 14:25; of Hezekiah and Isaiah, 2 Kgs. 18:21; Isa. 36; of Josiah, 2 Kgs. 23:29; of Jer. 44:30 and Ezek. 29:1-16.

PHARISEES Largest and most influential religious-political party during NT times. See *Jewish Parties in the New Testament.*

The funerary mask of King Tut (Pharaoh Tutankhamun) of Egypt

PHARPAR River associated with Damascus (2 Kgs. 5:12). The river is perhaps the Nahr el 'A'waj, which flows from Mount Hermon, passing about 10 miles south of Damascus, or else the Nahr Taura.

PHICHOL (KJV) or **PHICOL** Personal name meaning "mighty." The chief captain of the Philistine army under King Abimelech (Gen. 21:22). He witnessed covenants between his commander and Abraham (21:32) and Isaac (26:26-28).

PHILADELPHIA Place-name meaning "love of brother." A Hellenistic city in the province of Lydia in western Asia Minor. See *Asia Minor, Cities of; Revelation, Book of.*

Temple ruins at the site of the ancient city of Philadelphia in Asia Minor (modern Turkey)

PHILEMON, LETTER TO Personal name meaning "affectionate" and eighteenth book of the NT. Philemon owed his conversion to the Christian faith to the apostle Paul (v. 19). This conversion took place during Paul's extended ministry in Ephesus (Acts 19:10). There is no evidence that Paul ever visited Colossae where Philemon lived. Paul and Philemon became devoted friends. Paul referred to Philemon as a "dear friend and coworker" (v. 1 CSB).

Paul's only letter of a private and personal nature included in the NT was written to Philemon in AD 61. This letter concerned a runaway slave. The slave Onesimus had robbed Philemon and escaped to Rome. There Onesimus found the apostle Paul, who was imprisoned. Paul wrote to Philemon concerning Onesimus. Paul sent both the letter and Onesimus back to Colossae. The letter states that Onesimus was now a Christian. Paul requested that Philemon forgive and receive Onesimus not as a slave but as a brother (v. 16). This request was not made from Paul's apostolic authority but tenderly as a Christian friend: "welcome him as you would me" (v. 17 CSB).

PHILETUS Personal name meaning "beloved." Heretical teacher who asserted that the (general) resurrection had already occurred (2 Tim. 2:17-18), perhaps in a purely spiritual sense.

PHILIP Personal name meaning "fond of horses." **1.** A respected member of the church at Jerusalem who was chosen as one of the seven first deacons (Acts 6:5). Following Stephen's martyrdom, Philip took the gospel to Samaria, where his ministry was blessed (Acts 8:5-13). Subsequently he was led south to the Jerusalem-Gaza road where he introduced the Ethiopian eunuch to Christ and baptized him (Acts 8:26-38). He was then transported by the Spirit to Azotus (Ashdod) and from there conducted an itinerant ministry until he took up residence in Caesarea (Acts 8:39-40). Then, for nearly 20 years, we lose sight of him. He is last seen in Scripture when Paul lodged in his home on his last journey to Jerusalem (Acts 21:8). He had four unmarried daughters who were prophetesses (Acts 21:9). See *Deacon*. **2.** One of 12 apostles (Matt. 10:3). From Bethsaida. he called Nathanael to "come and see" Jesus (John 1:43-51). Jesus tested Philip concerning how to feed the multitude (John 6:5-7). He and Andrew took inquiring Gentiles to Jesus (John 12:21-22). Philip asked Jesus to show them the Father (John 14:8-9), opening the way for Jesus's teaching that to see him is to see the Father. See *Disciple*. **3.** Tetrarch of Ituraea and Trachonitis (Luke 3:1).

Philip's Martyrium at Hierapolis, built to commemorate the tradition that Philip the apostle was martyred here

PHILIPPI City in the Roman province of Macedonia. Paul did missionary work in Philippi (Acts 16:12) and later wrote a letter to the church there (Phil. 1:1).

Paul and Philippi Paul first visited Philippi on his second missionary journey in response to his Macedonian vision (Acts 16:9). They

Overlooking ruins of Philippi from atop the theater

and his companions sailed from Troas across the Aegean Sea to Neapolis, on the eastern shore of Macedonia (Acts 16:11). Then they journeyed a few miles inland to "Philippi, a Roman colony and a leading city of the district of Macedonia" (Acts 16:12 CSB).

On the Sabbath, Paul went to a prayer meeting on the riverbank. When Paul spoke, Lydia and others opened their hearts to the Lord (Acts 16:13-15).

The Roman character of the city is apparent from Paul's other experiences in Philippi. He healed a possessed slave girl whose owners charged that Jews troubled the city by teaching customs unlawful for Romans to observe (Acts 16:20-21). The city magistrates ordered Paul and Silas to be beaten and turned over to the jailer (Acts 16:20,22-23). After Paul's miraculous deliverance and the jailer's conversion, the magistrates sent the jailer word to release Paul (Acts 16:35-36). Paul informed the messengers that he was a Roman citizen. Since he had been beaten and imprisoned unlawfully, Paul insisted that the magistrates themselves come and release him (Acts 16:37). The very nervous magistrates went to the jail. They pled with Paul not only to leave the jail, but also to leave town (Acts 16:38-40).

PHILIPPIANS, LETTER TO THE

Eleventh book of the NT, written by Paul to the church at Philippi, the first church he established in Europe. It is one of the Prison Epistles (along with Ephesians, Colossians, and Philemon). The traditional date and place of writing is AD 61/62 from Rome.

Content of the Letter Philippians is structured much like a typical personal letter of that day. The introduction identifies the sender(s): Paul and Timothy, and the recipients: the saints, overseers, and deacons.

This typical letter form, however, is filled with Christian content. Paul expresses thanksgiving for the Philippian church's faithful participation in the work of the gospel (1:3-8), and a prayer that they may be blessed with an ever growing, enlightened, Christian love (1:9-11). The body of the letter begins with Paul explaining his current situation (1:12-26).

When Paul returned to Philippi, he hoped to find a church united in Christ. Philippians 1:27–4:9 is a multifaceted call for unity in the church. Those who follow Christ must follow him in selfless service to others (2:5-11).

Philippians 2:6-11 is known as the *kenosis* passage (from the Greek word translated "emptied" in 2:7 RSV). The language and structure of the passage have convinced most commentators that Paul was quoting a hymn that was already in use in the church. The purpose of the pre-Pauline hymn was probably to teach the believer about the nature and work of Christ. Preexistence, incarnation, passion, resurrection, and exaltation are all summarized in a masterful fashion.

General exhortations to rejoice and to remain faithful (4:4-9) led to Paul's expression of gratitude for the Philippians' faithful support of him and of the ministry (4:10-20). The letter closes in typical Pauline fashion, with an exchange of greetings and a prayer for grace.

PHILISTIA Coastal plain of southwestern Palestine that was under the control of the Philistines (Exod. 15:14; Pss. 60:8; 87:4; 108:9; Isa. 14:29-31). KJV sometimes referred to Philistia as Palestina (Exod. 15:14; Isa. 14:29-31). See *Gaza; Pentapolis.*

PHILISTIM (KJV, Gen. 10:14) or **PHILISTINES** One of the rival groups the Israelites encountered as they settled the land of Canaan. According to biblical references, the homeland of the Philistines was Caphtor (Amos 9:7; Jer. 47:4). See *Caphtor.*

Philistines are first mentioned in the patriarchal stories (Gen. 21:32,34). The most dramatic phase of Philistine history begins in the period of the Judges when the Philistines were the principal enemy of and the major political threat to Israel. This threat is first seen in the stories of Samson (Judg. 13–16). During the time of Samuel, the Israelites defeated the Philistines at times (1 Sam. 7:5-11; 14:16-23), but, generally speaking, their advance against the Israelites continued. Saul not only failed to check their intrusion into Israelite territory, but in the end lost his life fighting the Philistines at Mount Gilboa (1 Sam. 31:1-13). David finally checked the Philistine advance at Baal-perazim (2 Sam. 5:17-25).

PHILO JUDAEUS Early Jewish interpreter of Scripture known for use of allegory. Also known as Philo of Alexandria, he lived about the same time as Jesus (ca. 20 BC–AD 50).

PHILOLOGUS Personal name meaning "lover of words," either in the sense of "talkative" or of "lover of learning." Member, perhaps the head, of a Roman house church whom Paul greeted (Rom. 16:15). Philologus was perhaps the husband of Julia and father of Nereus and Olympas.

PHINEHAS Personal name meaning "dark-skinned" or "mouth of brass." **1.** Grandson of Aaron and high priest who, on several occasions, aided Moses and Joshua. **2.** One of Eli the priest's worthless sons. He engaged in religious prostitution (1 Sam. 2:22) and led the people to follow.

PHLEGON Personal name meaning "burning," perhaps in the sense of "zealous." Member of a Roman house church whom Paul greeted (Rom. 16:14).

PHOEBE Personal name meaning "bright." "Servant" (CSB), "minister" (REB), "deaconess" (NASB, NIV note), or "deacon" (NRSV) of the church at Cenchreae whom Paul recommended to the church at Rome (Rom. 16:1-2).

PHOENICIA Place-name meaning "purple" or "crimson," translation of Hebrew *Canaan*, "land of purple." The narrow land between the Mediterranean Sea and the Lebanon Mountains between Tyre in the south and Arvad in the north. New Testament Phoenicia reached south to Dor. Great forestland enabled the people to build ships and become the dominant seafaring nation. The forests also provided timber for export, Phoenician cedars being the featured material of Solomon's temple (1 Kgs. 5:8-10). The Phoenician princess Jezebel imported devotion to Baal to Israel.

Growth of Assyrian power about 750 BC led to Phoenicia's decline. The Persian Empire gave virtual independence to Phoenicia, using the Phoenician fleet against Egypt and Greece. Alexander the Great put an end to Phoenician political power, but the great cities retained economic power.

New Testament Jesus's ministry reached Tyre and Sidon (Matt. 15:21). Persecution, beginning with Stephen's death, led the church to spread into Phoenicia (Acts 11:19; cp. 15:3; 21:2-3).

Harbor at Tyre showing ancient Phoenician harbor (facing northwest).

PHOENIX Place-name, perhaps meaning "date palm." Port on the southeast coast of Crete that Paul and the ship's crew hoped to reach for winter harbor (Acts 27:12).

PHRYGIA Place-name meaning "parched." During Roman times, Phrygia was a subregion of Galatia, and her people often were slaves or servants. Some of the Phrygians were present in Jerusalem on the day of Pentecost and heard the gospel in their native language (Acts 2:10; cp. 16:6; 18:23).

PHYGELUS Personal name meaning "fugitive." Christian who deserted Paul (2 Tim. 1:15). The contrast with Onesiphorus, who was not ashamed of the imprisoned Paul (1:16-17), suggests that Phygelus abandoned Paul in prison.

PI-BESETH Egyptian city, name meaning "house of Bastet," located on the shore of the old Tanite branch of the Nile about 45 miles northeast of Cairo. Ezekiel mentions this city in his oracle against Egypt (Ezek. 30:17).

PICTURE KJV term in three passages where modern translations use a term better suited to the context. **1.** Carved stone figures (Num. 33:52). **2.** Settings (CSB, NASB, NIV, NRSV) or filigree (REB) (Prov. 25:11). **3.** Sailing craft or vessel (Isa. 2:16).

PIECE OF MONEY **1.** Translation of the Hebrew *qesitah*, a coin of uncertain weight and value (Gen. 33:19; Job 42:11 KJV, NASB, NRSV). CSB reads "piece of silver." **2.** KJV translation of the Greek term *stater* (Matt. 17:27). Modern translations read: stater (NASB); four drachma coin (NIV); shekel (RSV); coin (CSB, NRSV, REB).

PIETY Translation of a Hebrew expression and several Greek terms. **1.** CSB, NIV used "piety" to translate the Hebrew idiom "the fear [or reverence] of the Lord" (Job 4:6; 22:4; cp. REB). **2.** NRSV used piety to translate the Greek term meaning "righteousness" (Matt. 6:1), where the concern was with an external show of religion (Matt. 6:2-6). **3.** Piety translates two Greek terms for fear or reverence for God (Acts 3:12 NASB, NRSV; Heb. 5:7 NASB). **4.** Piety represents the religious duty of caring for the physical needs of elderly family members (1 Tim. 5:4 KJV, NASB).

PIGEON A general term referring to any of a widely distributed subfamily of fowl (*Columbinae*). The term "pigeon" basically is employed when referring to the use of these birds for sacrificial offerings.

PIHAHIROTH Hebrew place-name derived from the Egyptian, "house of Hathor," and interpreted in Hebrew as "mouth of canals."

The Israelites encamped at Pihahiroth in the early days of the exodus (Exod. 14:2,9; Num. 33:7).

PILATE, PONTIUS Roman governor of Judea remembered in history as a notorious anti-Semite and in Christian creeds as the magistrate under whom Jesus Christ "suffered" (1 Tim. 6:13). The NT refers to him as "governor," while other sources call him "procurator" or "prefect" (an inscription found in Caesarea in 1961).

The only known extrabiblical mention of Pilate's name is shown here in a Latin dedicatory inscription on a stone slab found at Caesarea Maritima.

PILDASH Personal and clan name, perhaps meaning "powerful." Sixth son of Nahor (Gen. 22:22), probably the ancestor of an otherwise unknown north Arabian tribe.

PILFER To steal secretly, usually little by little (John 12:6 NASB, REB; Titus 2:10 NASB, REB, NRSV).

PILHA Personal name meaning "millstone." Lay leader witnessing Ezra's covenant renewal (Neh. 10:24).

PILLAR Stone monuments (Hb. *matstsevah*) or standing architectural structures (Hb. *amudim*). **1.** Stones set up as memorials to persons. Jacob set up a pillar on Rachel's grave as a memorial to her (Gen. 35:20). Because Absalom had no son to carry on his name, he set up a pillar and carved his name in it (2 Sam. 18:18). **2.** Shrines both to the Lord and to false gods. Graven images often were pillars set up as gods. **3.** As structural supports, pillars were used extensively. The tabernacle used pillars for the veil (Exod. 26:31-32), the courts (27:9-15), and the gate (27:16). The temple in Jerusalem used pillars for its support (1 Kgs. 7:2-3), and the porch had pillars (7:6). Figuratively, pillars were believed to hold up heaven (Job 26:11) and earth (1 Sam. 2:8). **4.** God led Israel through the wilderness with a pillar of cloud by day and a pillar of fire by night (Exod. 13:21; cp. 14:19-20). These pillars were symbols of God's presence with Israel as much as signs of where they were to go. **5.** Solomon's temple had two freestanding brass pillars (1 Kgs. 7:15).

PILTAI Short form of personal name meaning "(Yah is) my deliverance." Head of a family of postexilic priests (Neh. 12:17).

PINNACLE Highest point of a structure. NRSV referred to the pinnacles of the temple or the city of Jerusalem (Isa. 54:12). The pinnacle (literally, "little wing") of the temple (Matt. 4:5; Luke 4:9) is not mentioned in the OT, intertestamental literature, or rabbinic sources.

The traditional "pinnacle of the temple"

PINON Edomite clan chief (Gen. 36:41; 1 Chron. 1:52), whose descendants perhaps settled Punon (Num. 33:42-43).

PIRAM Personal name, perhaps meaning "wild ass." King of Jarmuth southwest of Jerusalem and member of a coalition of five Amorite kings who battled Joshua unsuccessfully (Josh. 10:3,23).

PIRATHON, PIRATHONITE Place-name meaning "princely" or "height, summit" and its inhabitants. The town in the hill country of Ephraim was the home of the judge Abdon (Judg. 12:13,15) and of Benaiah, one of David's elite warriors (2 Sam. 23:30; 1 Chron. 11:31). The site is identified with Far'ata about five miles southwest of Shechem.

PISGAH Place-name, perhaps meaning "the divided one." Mountain in the Abarim range across the Jordan River from Jericho. Some Bible scholars believe it was part of Mount Nebo. God allowed Moses to view the promised land from the heights of Pisgah (Deut. 34:1) but would not let him cross into Canaan.

PISHON Name meaning "free-flowing," designating one of the rivers of Eden (Gen. 2:11). The identity of the river is unknown. Some suggest the "river" was a canal connecting the Tigris and Euphrates or another body of water, such as the Persian Gulf.

PISIDIA Small area in the province of Galatia in southern Asia Minor bounded by Pamphylia, Phrygia, and Lyconia. Only in 25 BC did the Romans gain control over the region through economic diplomacy. Antioch was made the capital, although some historians contend that the city was not actually in Pisidia. Paul and Barnabas came through Antioch (Acts 13:14) after John Mark left them in Perga (v. 13).

The snow-capped mountains of the ancient Roman province of Pisidia in Asia Minor (modern Turkey)

PISPA, PISPAH Personal name of unknown meaning. Member of the tribe of Asher (1 Chron. 7:38).

PITHOM AND RAMESES Egyptian cities located in northern Egypt (Nile Delta) in or near the Wadi Tumilat. They were built by the Israelites while in Egypt (Exod. 1:11) as supply hubs for royal, military, and religious purposes and were located near palaces, fortresses, and temples.

PITHON Personal name of unknown meaning. Descendant of Saul (1 Chron. 8:35; 9:41).

PITY Sympathetic sorrow toward one facing suffering or distress. Pity moved Jesus to heal (Matt. 20:34). Jesus used a compassionate Samaritan as an unexpected example of active pity (Luke 10:33). Such active concern for those in need serves as evidence that one is a child of God (1 John 3:17).

PLAGUES Disease interpreted as divine judgment, translation of several Hebrew words. The 10 plagues in the book of Exodus were the mighty works of God that gained Israel's release and demonstrated God's sovereignty and were called "plagues" (Exod. 9:14; 11:1), "signs" (Exod. 7:13), and "wonders" (Exod. 7:3; 11:9). They showed the God of Moses was sovereign over the gods of Egypt, including Pharaoh, who was considered a god by the Egyptians.

PLAISTER KJV variant form of plaster (Isa. 38:21). Here plaster refers to a fig poultice (cp. NIV, REB, NASB, NRSV).

PLAIT KJV term meaning "to braid" (1 Pet. 3:3). See *Hair*.

PLANKS Long, flat pieces of timber, thicker than boards, used in shipbuilding (Ezek. 27:5; Acts 27:44) and for the flooring of Solomon's temple (1 Kgs. 6:15 KJV). The "thick planks upon the face of the porch" in Ezekiel's vision of the renewed temple (Ezek. 41:25 KJV) likely refers to some type of canopy

(CSB, NRSV; overhang, NIV; covering, TEV; cornice, REB) or to a threshold (NASB).

PLANTATION KJV term (Ezek. 17:7) to designate a bed (NASB, REB, NRSV) or plot (CSB, NIV) where plants are planted.

PLASTER Pastelike mixture, usually of water, lime, and sand, that hardens on drying and is used for coating walls and ceilings. Mosaic law included regulations for treating homes in which mold or rot appeared in the plaster (Lev. 14:41-48). Writing was easy on a surface of wet plaster (Deut. 27:2-4).

PLATE **1.** Shallow vessel from which food is eaten or served. **2.** Sheet of metal (Exod. 28:36; Num. 16:38).

PLATTER Large plate. The platter bearing the head of John the Baptist was likely of gold or silver (Matt. 14:8,11 and parallels). Ceramic platters were in common use (Luke 11:39 NASB).

PLEDGE Something given as down payment on a debt. The OT regulated this practice. An outer garment given in pledge was to be returned before night since it was the only protection the poor had from the cold (Exod. 22:26; Deut. 24:12-13).

PLEIADES Brilliant grouping of six or seven visible stars located in the shoulder of the constellation Taurus (Job 9:9; 38:31; Amos 5:8).

PLUMB LINE Cord with a weight (usually metal or stone) attached to one end. The plumb line would be dangled beside a wall during its construction to assure vertical accuracy. Prophets spoke of the measurement God would use on the nation (Isa. 28:17; Amos 7:7-8). Israel had been built straight, but, because it was out of line, it would be destroyed.

POCHERETH-HAZZEBAIM Personal name signifying an official office, "binder (or hunter) of gazelles." Head of a family of Solomon's servants included in those returning from exile (Ezra 2:57; Neh. 7:59). KJV takes "Zebaim" as a place-name.

PODS Dry coverings split in the shelling of beans and similar plants. The pods of Luke 15:16 (CSB, NASB, NIV, REB, NRSV; husks, KJV; bean pods, TEV) were likely of the carob tree that served as a common feed for livestock. These sweet-tasting pods may reach one foot in length.

POETRY "Poetry" calls to mind a Western pattern of balanced lines, regular stress, and rhyme. Hebrew manuscripts do not distinguish poetry from prose in such a clear-cut way. Hebrew poetry has three primary characteristics—parallelism, meter, and the grouping of lines into larger units called stanzas. Each of the three elements mentioned may be found to a lesser extent in prose. One third of the OT is cast in poetry.

POLL **1.** KJV term for "to cut off" or "to trim" hair (2 Sam. 14:26; Ezek. 44:20; Mic. 1:16). Priests were permitted to "poll" their hair but not to shave their heads. Polling one's hair could be understood as a sign of mourning. **2.** KJV term for "the head," especially that part on which hair grows. To count every male "by their polls" (Num. 1:2; cp. 1 Chron. 23:3,24) is to count "heads."

POLLUX One of the twin brothers in the constellation Gemini (Acts 28:11).

POMEGRANATE Small tree, the fruit of which has a thick shell, many seeds, and a red pulp.

The pomegranate is one of the many fruits found in the Middle East.

POMMELS KJV term for the bowl-shaped capitals topping the temple pillars (2 Chron. 4:12-13).

POND At Exod. 7:19; 8:5, "pond" renders the Hebrew *'agam* meaning "marsh" or "muddy pool." The term is usually translated "pool."

PONTUS Province just south of the Black Sea in Asia Minor. Christianity spread to Pontus early. First Peter was addressed to the elect there (1:1-2). Citizens of Pontus were in Jerusalem on the day of Pentecost (Acts 2:9).

POOL Collection of water, natural or artificial. Small pools were commonly seen as a place to collect rainwater from the roof that was used for irrigation or drinking. These reservoirs were important sources of water supply in the arid climate of the Middle East.

POOR IN SPIRIT Not those who are spiritually poor, that is, lacking in faith or love, but those who have a humble spirit and thus depend on God (Matt. 5:3). Luke's parallel speaks simply of the poor (Luke 6:20). That God has chosen "the poor in this world to be rich in faith and heirs of the kingdom" was regarded as a well-established fact (James 2:5 CSB).

POOR, ORPHAN, WIDOW Three groups of people of the lower social classes in need of legal protection from the rich and powerful who sometimes abused them (Job 24:3-4). God's promise of care for the poor, the orphans, and the widows was a tremendous source of hope during times of severe difficulty.

PORATHA Persian personal name meaning "bounteous." One of Haman's 10 sons (Esth. 9:8).

PORCUPINE Large rodent, sometimes called a hedgehog, that has stiff, sharp bristles mixed with its hair. Disagreement exists about the translation of the Hebrew word. Some feel "porcupine" is the correct translation (Isa. 14:23; 34:11 NKJV, NLT). NASB uses "hedgehog" in Isaiah and Zeph. 2:14. Others have various translations (NIV, owl; KJV, bittern; NEB, bustard; CSB, heron).

PORPHYRY Rock composed of feldspar crystals embedded in a dark red or purple groundmass (Esth. 1:6; KJV, "red marble").

PORPOISE Any of several species of small-toothed whales. NASB uses porpoise skins for a covering over the tabernacle (Exod. 25:5; Num. 4:6; KJV, NKJV, badger; NIV, sea cow) and "sandals of porpoise skin" in Ezek. 16:10. See *Sea Cow*.

PORTER KJV term for a gatekeeper or doorkeeper. Such persons served at city gates (2 Sam. 18:26; 2 Kgs. 7:10), temple gates (1 Chron. 9:22,24,26), the doors of private homes (Mark 13:34), and even the gate of a sheepfold (John 10:3).

PORTION Allotment, allowance, ration, share. Portion is frequently used in the literal sense of a share in food, clothing, or property as well as in a variety of figurative senses. Wisdom writings often designate one's lot in life as one's portion (Job 20:29; 27:13; Eccles. 9:9).

POTENTATE KJV term in 1 Tim. 6:15 meaning "ruler" (NIV) or "sovereign" (CSB, NASB, NRSV, REB), used as a title for God.

POTIPHAR Personal name meaning "belonging to the sun." Egyptian captain of the guard who purchased Joseph from the Midianite traders (Gen. 37:36; 39:1).

POTIPHERA or **POTIPHERAH** Priest in the Egyptian city of On (Heliopolis) where the sun god, Re, was worshipped. Joseph married his daughter, Asenath, at the pharaoh's command (Gen. 41:45). Potipherah and Potiphar are the same in Egyptian, leading some to believe that one name was slightly changed in Hebrew to distinguish between the captain of the guard and the priest.

POTSHERD Fragment of a baked, clay vessel, "potsherd" (more commonly called a "sherd" by archaeologists) is used in the OT with both a literal and symbolic or figurative meaning. Job used a potsherd (2:8) to scrape the sores that covered his body; the underparts of the mythological monster Leviathan are said to be "jagged potsherds" (Job 41:30 CSB, NIV).

A modern Middle Eastern potter fashioning pottery in the same manner used in biblical times

POTTAGE Thick soup usually made from lentils and vegetables and spiced with various herbs. Jacob served pottage and bread to the famished Esau in return for the birthright (Gen. 25:29-34). Elisha added meal to a tainted recipe of pottage at Gilgal (2 Kgs. 4:38-41).

POTTER'S FIELD Tract of land in the Hinnom Valley outside Jerusalem used as a cemetery for pilgrims to the Holy City since the interbiblical era. The field was bought with the money paid for betraying Jesus (Acts 1:18). Matthew 27:3-10 records that the priests bought the field with the money Judas returned. Their reasoning was that the money had been used to bring about bloodshed and could not be returned to the temple treasury.

POUND See *Weights and Measures*.

POTTERY Everyday household utensils whose remains form the basis for modern dating of ancient archaeological remains. The few statements about the preparation of the clay, the potter "treads the clay" (Isa. 41:25 CSB), and the potter's failure and success on the wheel (Jer. 18:3-4) hardly hint at the

Pile of pottery sherds at Banias

importance and abundance in antiquity of "earthen vessels" (Lev. 6:21; Num. 5:17; Jer. 32:14), the common collective term for pottery in the Bible. However, the work of the potter in shaping the worthless clay provided the imagery the biblical writers and prophets used in describing God's creative relationship to human beings (Job 10:8-9; Isa. 45:9).

POWDERS, FRAGRANT Pulverized spices used as a fragrance (Song 3:6).

PRAETORIAN GUARD Roman military branch assigned to personal security for the imperial family and to represent and protect the emperor's interests in the imperial provinces. The term is used in Phil. 1:13 with regard to a unit of the Praetorian guard. Greetings from "those who belong to Caesar's household" (Phil. 4:22 CSB) do not prove Paul was in Rome when he wrote Philippians. The term "Caesar's household" was applied often to the Praetorian guard, and units were dispersed throughout the Roman Empire. *Praetorion* is used in Mark 15:16 in reference to the headquarters where Jesus was taken and subsequently mocked by Roman soldiers prior to his crucifixion. The NT locates the praetorium in Jerusalem as the palace of the Roman governor, the Tower of Antonia, located adjacent to the temple on the north-

The front of the praetorium at the palace of the Roman emperor Hadrian

western corner (Matt. 27:27; Mark 15:16; John 18:28,33; 19:9) of Temple Mount.

PRAISE One of humanity's many responses to God's revelation of himself. The Bible recognizes that men and women may also be the objects of praise, either from other people (Prov. 27:21; 31:30) or from God himself (Rom. 2:29), and that angels and the natural world are likewise capable of praising God (Ps. 148). Nevertheless, human praise of God is one of Scripture's major themes.

PRAYER Dialogue between God and people, especially his covenant partners.

Old Testament Israel is a nation born of prayer. Abraham heard God's call (Gen. 12:1-3), and God heard the cries of the Hebrew children (Exod. 3:7). Moses conversed with God (Exod. 3:1–4:17) and interceded for Israel (Exod. 32:11-13; Num. 11:11-15). God worked miracles through the prayers of Elijah and Elisha (1 Kgs. 17:19-22; 18:20-40).

The book of Psalms teaches that variety and honesty in prayer are permissible; the psalms proclaim praise, ask pardon, seek such things as communion (63), protection (57), vindication (107), and healing (6). Psalm 86 provides an excellent pattern for prayer. Daily patterned prayer becomes very important to exiles denied access to the temple (Dan. 6:10).

New Testament Jesus's example and teaching inspire prayer. Mark emphasized that Jesus prayed in crucial moments, including the disciples' appointment (3:13), their mission (6:30-32), and the transfiguration (9:2). The Lord's Prayer (Matt. 6:9-13; Luke 11:2-4) is taught to disciples who realize the kingdom is present but still to come in all its fullness. Significantly the disciples asked Jesus to teach them to pray after watching him pray (Luke 11:1). The prayer also provides a contrast to hypocritical prayers (Matt. 6:5). Although it is permissible to repeat this prayer, it may be well to remember Jesus was emphasizing how to pray, not what to pray.

Jesus's teaching on persistence in prayer is linked to the inbreaking kingdom (Luke 11:5-28; 18:18). God is not like the reluctant neighbor, even though Christians may have to wait for answers (Luke 11:13; 18:6-8). The ironies of prayer are evident: God knows our needs, yet we must ask; God is ready to answer, yet we must patiently persist. Children of the kingdom will have their requests heard

(Matt. 6:8; 7:7-11; 21:22; John 14:13; 15:7,16; 16:23; cp. 1 John 3:22; 5:14; James 1:5), particularly believers gathered in Jesus's name (Matt. 18:19).

Dialogue is what is essential to prayer. Prayer makes a difference in what happens (James 4:2). Our understanding of prayer will correspond to our understanding of God. When God is seen as desiring to bless (James 1:5) and sovereignly free to respond to persons (Jonah 3:9), then prayer will be seen as dialogue with God. God will respond when we faithfully pursue this dialogue. Prayer will lead to a greater communion with God and a greater understanding of his will.

PREEXILIC Period in Israel's history before the exile in Babylon (586–538 BC).

PREMARITAL SEX Engaging in sexual intercourse prior to marriage. The Song of Songs is an extended poem extolling the virtue of sexual fidelity between a king and his chosen bride. Sexual desire runs strong throughout the song as the king and his beloved anticipate their union together. At intervals, the poet repeats a refrain counseling sexual restraint: "Young women of Jerusalem, I charge you, by the gazelles and the wild does of the field, do not stir up or awaken love until the appropriate time" (Song 2:7 CSB; 3:5; 8:4).

PREPARATION DAY Sixth day of week in which Jews prepared life's necessities to avoid work on the Sabbath (cp. Exod. 20:8-11; Matt. 12:1-14; John 9:14-16). John explicitly identified the day of preparation as the day of Jesus's execution (John 19:14,31,42) and placed the Last Supper before Passover (John 13:1). The Synoptic Gospels, however, dated the Last Supper on the day of Passover (Matt. 26:17; Mark 14:12; Luke 22:7). This apparent contradiction in dating may depend on whether the Gospel writers were referring to the preparation day for the Sabbath or to the preparation day for the Passover.

PRESBYTER See *Elder*.

PRIDE Undue confidence in and attention to one's own skills, accomplishments, state, possessions, or position. It is the opposite of humility, the proper attitude one should have in relation to God. Pride is rebellion against God because it attributes to oneself the honor and glory due to God alone.

PRIESTHOOD OF BELIEVERS Christian belief that every believer has direct access to God through Jesus Christ and that the church is a fellowship of priests serving together under the lordship of Christ. The concept of priesthood is integral to both the OT and the NT and is fulfilled in Christ as mediator and great high priest.

PRIESTHOOD OF CHRIST That work of Christ in which he offers himself as the supreme sacrifice for the sins of humankind and continually intercedes on their behalf.

PRIESTS Persons who represent God to human beings and human beings to God. Priests performed numerous roles, the most important of which was officiating at sacrifices and offerings at worship places, particularly the tabernacle and temple. Aaron and his descendants of the tribe of Levi served in the tabernacle and temple as priests. Members of the tribe of Levi not related to Aaron assisted the priests but did not offer sacrifices. Priests were supported by offerings and Levites were supported by tithes (Num. 18:20-24).

PRINCE More frequently designates the position and authority of a ruler, not just the limited sense of a male heir of a sovereign or noble birth (cp. Zeph. 1:8, which distinguishes princes and king's sons).

PRINCESS Two Hebrew constructions are translated "princess." **1.** "Daughter of a king." Solomon's 700 wives were princesses married to seal political ties with their fathers (1 Kgs. 11:3). Lamentations 1:1 pictures the reversal of Jerusalem's fortune in the image of a princess turned servant. **2.** Feminine form of the common word for leader or ruler applied to a king's wife (Ps. 45:13 NIV, NRSV) and to the leading women of Judah (Jer. 43:6 NRSV). See *Prince*.

PRINCIPALITIES Supernatural spiritual powers, whether good or evil. Principalities were created by and are thus subject to Christ (Col. 1:16). Neither principalities nor any other force can separate a believer from God's love found in Christ (Rom. 8:38).

PRISCA or **PRISCILLA** See *Aquila and Priscilla*.

PRISON GATE KJV designation for a gate in Jerusalem (Neh. 12:39). Modern translations refer to the Gate of the Guard or Guardhouse Gate. The gate is perhaps identical with the Miphkad (Muster) Gate (Neh. 3:31).

PRISON, PRISONERS Any place where persons accused and/or convicted of criminal activity are confined and the persons so confined or captured in war.

PRIZE Award in an athletic competition. Paul used the image to illustrate the goal of the Christian life (Phil. 3:14; cp. 1 Cor. 9:24).

PROCHORUS Personal name meaning "leader of the chorus (or dance)." One of the seven selected to assist in distribution of food to the Greek-speaking widows of the Jerusalem church (Acts 6:5).

PROCONSUL Office in the Roman system of government. Proconsuls oversaw the administration of civil and military matters in a province. They were responsible to the senate in Rome. The NT refers to two proconsuls: Sergius Paulus in Cyprus (Acts 13:7) and Gallio in Achaia (Acts 18:12; cp. Acts 19:38).

PROCURATOR Roman military office that developed into a powerful position by NT times. Three procurators are named in the NT: Pilate (Matt. 27:2; some question whether Pilate was a procurator), Felix (Acts 23:24), and Festus (Acts 24:27).

PROMISE God's announcement of his plan of salvation and blessing to his people, one of the unifying themes integrating the message and the deeds of the OT and NT. God's promise begins with a declaration by God; it covers God's future plan for not just one race but all the nations of the earth. It focuses on the gifts and deeds that God will bestow on a few to benefit the many.

PROPHECY, PROPHETS Reception and declaration of a word from the Lord through a direct prompting of the Holy Spirit and the human instrument thereof.

Interior of the Mamertinum Prison in Rome, believed to be the place where Paul was held prior to his execution

Old Testament Moses, perhaps Israel's greatest leader, was a prophetic prototype (Acts 3:21-24). He appeared with Elijah in the transfiguration (Matt. 17:1-8). Israel looked for a prophet like Moses (Deut. 34:10).

Elijah and Elisha offered critique and advice for the kings. The prophets did more than predict the future; their messages called Israel to honor God. Their prophecies were not general principles but specific words corresponding to Israel's historical context.

Similarly the classical or writing prophets were joined to history. Israel's political turmoil provided the context for the writing prophets. The Assyrian rise to power after 750 BC furnished the focus of the ministries of Amos, Hosea, Isaiah, and Micah. The Babylonian threat was the background and motive for much of the ministry of Jeremiah and Ezekiel. The advent of the Persian Empire in the latter part of the sixth century set the stage for prophets such as Obadiah, Haggai, Zechariah, and Malachi. Thus the prophets spoke for God throughout Israel's history.

New Testament The word *prophetes* means "to speak before" or "to speak for." Thus it refers to one who speaks for God or Christ. Prophets were also called "pneumatics" (*pneumatikos*), "spiritual ones" (1 Cor. 14:37). The prophets played a foundational role in

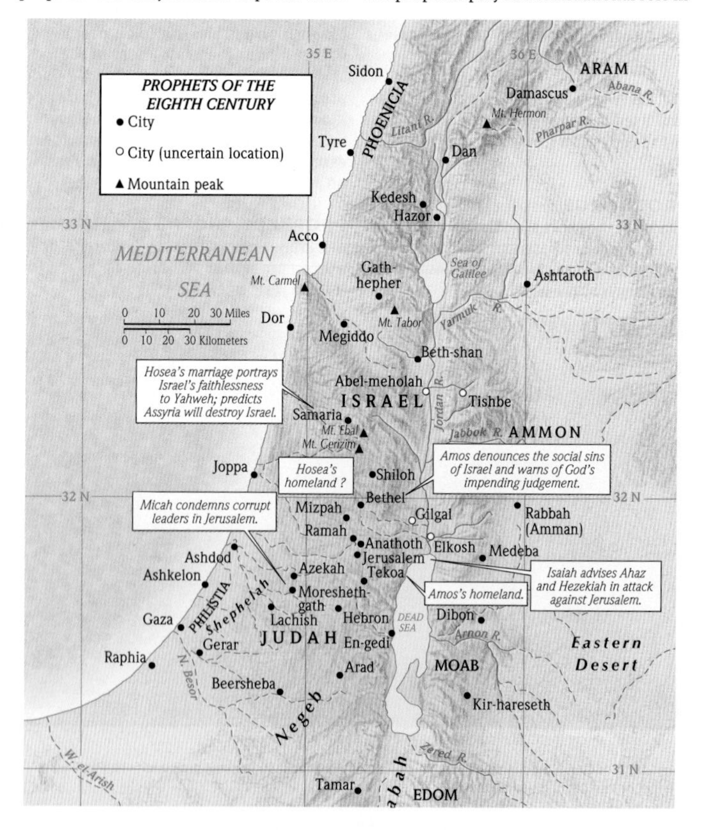

the early church (1 Cor. 12:28-31; Eph. 4:11; 2:20). Due to the presumed prophetic silence in the time between the Testaments, the coming of Jesus is seen as an inbreaking of the Spirit's work especially visible in prophecy. Jesus called himself a prophet (Luke 13:33). His miracles and discernment were rightly understood as prophetic (John 4:19). He taught not by citing expert rabbis but with his own prophetic authority (Mark 1:22; Luke 4:24).

The early believers saw the outpouring of the Spirit (Acts 2:17) as a fulfillment of Joel's prediction that all God's people, young and old, male and female, would prophesy. New Testament prophecy was limited (1 Cor. 13:9); it was to be evaluated by the congregation (1 Cor. 14:29; 1 Thess. 5:20-21). One may even respond inappropriately to prophecy (Acts 21:12). The supreme test for prophecy is loyalty to Christ (1 Cor. 12:3; Rev. 19:10).

PROPHETESS **1.** Female prophet; women serving as God's spokesperson. Five women are explicitly identified as prophetesses: Miriam (Exod. 15:20), Deborah (Judg. 4:4), Huldah (2 Kgs. 22:14), Noadiah, a "false" prophetess (Neh. 6:14), and Anna (Luke 2:36). **2.** The wife of a prophet (Isa. 8:3).

PROPITIATION See *Expiation, Propitiation.*

PROVENDER Grains and grasses used as animal feed (Isa. 30:24 KJV, RSV). Other translations use fodder or silage.

PROVERBS, BOOK OF The book of Proverbs contains the essence of Israel's wisdom. It provides a godly worldview and offers insight for living. Proverbs 1:7 provides the perspective for understanding all the proverbs: "The fear of the LORD is the beginning of knowledge; fools despise wisdom and discipline" (CSB). "Fear of the LORD" is biblical shorthand for an entire life in love, worship, and obedience to God.

Date and Composition Though the title of Proverbs (1:1) seems to ascribe the entire book to Solomon, closer inspection reveals that the book is composed of parts and that it was formed over a period of several hundred years. It is difficult to know precisely the role Solomon and his court may have had in starting the process that culminated in the book of Proverbs. This process may be compared to the way psalms of Davidic authorship eventually led to the book of Psalms.

Themes and Worldview In spite of being a collection of collections, Proverbs displays a unified, richly complex worldview. Proverbs 1–9 introduces this worldview and lays out its main themes. The short sayings of Proverbs 10–31 are to be understood in light of the first nine chapters. The beginning and end of wisdom is to fear God and avoid evil (1:7; 8:13; 9:10; 15:33). The world is a battleground between wisdom and folly, righteousness and wickedness, good and evil.

God has placed in creation a wise order that speaks to humankind of good and evil, urging humans toward good and away from evil. This is not just the "voice of experience," but God's general revelation, found throughout the Bible, that speaks to all people with authority. The world is not silent but speaks of the Creator and his will (Pss. 19:1-2; 97:6; 145:10; 148; Job 12:7-9; Acts 14:15-17;

PROVIDENCE God's benevolent and wise superintendence of his creation. God attends not only to apparently momentous events and people but also to those that seem both mundane and trivial. Thus, while he holds the lives of both kings and nations in his hand (cp. Isa. 40:21-26; Jer. 18:1-6), God also concerns himself with the welfare of the lowly and meek (cp. Pss. 104:10-30; 107:39-43). Indeed, so all-encompassing is God's attention to events within creation that nothing—not even the casting of lots—happens by chance (cp. Prov. 16:33).

With regard to God's role in the course of earthly events, one must avoid the error of deism on the one hand and that of fatalism on the other. Deism is the view that God created the universe as a sort of colossal machine, set it in motion according to various natural laws (which, perhaps, he himself established), and now simply sits back and watches events unfold in accordance with those laws. Fatalism is the view that every event that happens had to happen. Since Scripture clearly indicates that humans do face real choices and are in general responsible for their actions (cp. Deut. 30:11-20), fatalism is false.

PROVINCE Roman political region.

PSALMIST Writer of psalms or hymns. Second Samuel 23:1 calls David the "sweet psalmist of Israel." Superscriptions ascribe about half of the psalms to David.

PSALMS, BOOK OF The Hebrew title of the book means "praises." The English title (Psalms) comes from the Septuagint, the ancient Greek translation of the Hebrew Scriptures (OT). The Greek word *psalmoi* means "songs," from which comes the idea, "songs of praise" or "praise songs."

The individual psalms of the book came from several authors. David, the sweet psalmist of Israel (2 Sam. 23:1), wrote approximately half of the 150 psalms in the book. David's psalms became the standard followed by others, thereby imprinting a Davidic character to the entire book. Other authors include Asaph (12), the sons of Korah (10), Solomon (2), Moses (1), Heman (1), and Ethan (1). Approximately 48 psalms are anonymous.

The book of Psalms contains individual psalms covering a thousand-year period from the time of Moses (fifteenth century BC) to the postexilic period (fifth century BC). Most of the psalms were written in the time of David and Solomon (1010–930 BC). The final editor of the work was probably Ezra (450 BC).

PSALTER 1. Alternate name for the book of Psalms. **2.** Any collection of psalms used in worship.

PSEUDEPIGRAPHA Intertestamental literature not accepted into the Christian or Jewish canon of Scripture and often attributed to an ancient hero of faith. Ongoing discovery and research provide differing lists of contents. A recent publication listed 52 writings. They give much information about the development of Jewish religion and culture.

PSEUDONYMITY Text is pseudonymous when it is not authored by the person whose name it bears. Such works are written after the purported author's death by another person or during the attributed life by someone who is not commissioned to do so. Pseudonymous writings are not the same as anonymous texts. The former works make definite claims to authorship; the latter do not.

Many critical scholars believe that pseudonymity exists in the OT (e.g., Daniel) and the NT (e.g., the Pastoral Epistles). Some scholars argue that the early church was really only concerned about the content of works and not pseudonymity. But this theory does not explain the exclusion from the church's canon of several pseudonymous writings that were orthodox in their content (e.g., the Preaching of Peter, the Apocalypse of Peter, the Epistle of the Apostles, the Correspondence of Paul and Seneca, the extant Epistle to the Laodiceans, etc.).

Evidence is lacking to support pseudonymity in the Scriptures.

PTOLEMIES Dynastic powers that emerged in Egypt following the conquests of Alexander the Great.

PUAH 1. Personal name meaning "girl." Hebrew midwife who disobeyed Pharaoh's orders to kill male Hebrew infants (Exod. 1:15). **2.** Personal name meaning "red dye." Father of the judge Tola (Judg. 10:1) and an alternate form of Puvah (1 Chron. 7:1).

PUBLICAN Political office created by the Romans to help collect taxes in the provinces. The title "tax collector" is more correct than the older term "publican" in referring to the lowest rank in the structure.

PUBLIUS Personal name meaning "pertaining to the people." The highest official, either Roman or local, on Malta (Acts 28:7-8).

PUDENS Personal name meaning "modest." Roman Christian who greeted Timothy (2 Tim. 4:21). This Pudens is sometimes identified with the friend of the Roman poet Martial.

PUL 1. Alternate name of the Assyrian king Tiglath-pileser III (2 Kgs. 15:19; 1 Chron. 5:26). The name is perhaps a contraction of Pileser. See *Assyria*. **2.** The Hebrew Pul in Isa. 66:19 is likely a textual corruption of Put.

PULPIT KJV, RSV term for a raised platform on which a speaker stood (Neh. 8:4), not a lectern or high reading desk behind which a reader stands.

PULSE General term for peas, beans, and lentils (Dan. 1:12,16). Modern translations read "vegetables." The Hebrew is literally "things which have been sown," a designation including grains in addition to vegetables.

PUNITES Descendants of Puvah (Num. 26:23). Some manuscripts read "Puvanites" or "Puvites."

PUR or **PURIM** See *Festivals*.

PURAH Personal name meaning "beauty" or nickname meaning "metal container." Gideon's servant (Judg. 7:10-11). KJV used the form Phurah.

PURGE To cleanse from impurity, frequently in the figurative sense of cleansing from evil (Deut. 13:5), guilt (Deut. 19:13), idolatrous worship (2 Chron. 34:3), and sin (Ps. 51:7).

PURITY, PURIFICATION State of being or process of becoming free of inferior elements or ritual uncleanness. The primary Hebrew root word for pure (*tahar*) often refers to pure or flawless gold (1 Kgs. 10:21; Job 28:19; Ps. 12:6). *Tahar* and other Hebrew words for "pure" are used to describe other objects such as salt (Exod. 30:35), oil (Exod. 27:20), and incense (Exod. 37:29). A basic OT meaning is that of "refined, purified, without flaw, perfect, clean" (cp. Lam. 4:7). To be ritually pure means to be free of some flaw or uncleanness which would bar one from contact with holy objects or places, especially from contact with the holy presence of God in worship. God is the ideal of purity, and those who are to come in contact with God's presence are also to be pure. Habakkuk 1:13 indicates that God's eyes are too pure to look upon evil.

Most NT uses of words for purity relate to cleanness of some type. Old Testament meanings are often reflected. Perfection is the meaning in Mark 14:3; this is mixed with religious purity in Heb. 10:22; 1 John 3:3.

Ethical purity dominates in the NT. The person who is in right relationship with God is to live a life of purity (2 Tim. 2:21-22; Titus 1:15 and references to a pure heart—Matt. 5:8; 1 Tim. 1:5; Heb. 9:14; James 4:8; 1 Pet. 1:22). Purity is also listed among virtues (2 Cor. 6:6; Phil. 4:8; 1 Tim. 4:12; cp. Mark 7:15).

Purification through sacrifice is also mentioned in the NT and applied to the death of Christ, a purification which does not need repeating and thus is on a higher level than OT sacrifices (Heb. 9:13-14). The sacrifice of Christ brings purification; Christ cleansed as a part of the work of the high priest and his blood cleanses from sin (1 John 1:7).

PURLOIN KJV term meaning "to misappropriate" (Titus 2:10). Modern translations use "pilfer" or "steal."

PURPLE GARNET REB designation of a precious stone (Exod. 28:18; 39:11) that other translations identify as an emerald or turquoise.

PURSLANE Fleshy-leafed, trailing plant used as a potherb or in salads, which the RSV of Job 6:6 used as an illustration of tasteless food.

PUT Personal name and a geographic designation, perhaps derived from the Egyptian *pdty* meaning "foreign bowman." **1.** Son of Ham (Gen. 10:6; 1 Chron. 1:8) in the Table of Nations and ancestor of inhabitants of Put. **2.** Designation for a region of Africa bordering Egypt (Jer. 46:9; Ezek. 27:10; 30:5; 38:5; Nah. 3:9; and, by emendation, Isa. 66:19).

PUTHITES Family of Judahites (1 Chron. 2:53; KJV, Puhites).

PUTIEL Personal name meaning "he whom God gives" or "afflicted by God." Father-in-law of the priest Eleazar (Exod. 6:25).

PUVAH NASB (Num. 26:23) and CSB, NRSV (Gen. 46:13; Num. 26:23) form of the name of a son of Issachar. Other renderings include: Pua (KJV, REB); Puah (NIV, TEV); and Phuvah (KJV).

PYGARG KJV term for a white-rumped antelope (Deut. 14:5). Most modern translations identify the underlying Hebrew term with the ibex.

PYRE Pile of material to be burned, especially that used in burning a body as part of funeral rites (Isa. 30:33 NASB, NRSV; pile, KJV; fire pit, NIV, REB). God's preparation of a funeral pyre for the Assyrian king highlights the certainty of God's judgment.

PYRRHUS Personal name meaning "fiery red." Father of Paul's companion Sopater (Acts 20:4).

PYTHON **1.** Large constricting snake. **2.** A spirit of divination (*python*, Gk., Acts 16:16).

Q Abbreviation of the German *Quelle*, meaning "source," used to designate the hypothetical common source of more than 200 verses found in Matthew and Luke but not in Mark.

QOHELETH See *Koheleth*.

QUAIL The Hebrew term translated "quail" in the OT is found only in connection with God's provision of food for Israel in the wilderness (Exod. 16:13; Num. 11:31-32; Ps. 105:40).

QUARTERMASTER Officer charged with receipt and distribution of rations and supplies (Jer. 51:59 CSB, NASB, NRSV, REB).

QUARTUS Latin personal name meaning "fourth." Christian, most likely from Corinth, who sent greetings to the Roman church through Paul (Rom. 16:23). Quartus and Tertius, whose name means "third" (Rom. 16:22), were possibly the fourth and third sons of the same family.

QUATERNION KJV term for a squad composed of four soldiers (Acts 12:4; cp. John 19:23). By translating the underlying Greek as simply "squad," NASB and RSV failed to convey the size of the guard.

QUEEN Wife or widow of a monarch and the female monarch reigning in her own right. Queen mother refers to the mother of a reigning monarch.

Famous bust of Queen Nefertiti (from ca. 1356 BC), wife of Pharaoh Akhenaton of Egypt

QUEEN OF HEAVEN Goddess that women in Judah worshipped to ensure fertility and material stability (Jer. 7:18; 44:17). Forms of worship included making cakes (possibly in her image as in molds found at Mari), offering drink offerings, and burning incense (Jer. 44:25).

QUEEN OF SHEBA See *Sabean*.

QUICK, QUICKEN KJV terms meaning "living, alive" and "make alive, revive, refresh" (Pss. 55:15; 119:25; John 5:21; Acts 10:42).

QUICKSANDS KJV translation of the Greek *surtis* meaning "sandbar" (Acts 27:17). Modern translations take *surtis* as a proper name for the great sandbars off the west coast of Cyrene (modern Libya). NIV and REB paraphrase "sandbars of Syrtis," which conveys the sense.

QUILT NASB translation of a Hebrew term in 1 Sam. 19:13,16. Other possible translations include net (NRSV), pillow (KJV, RSV), and rug (REB).

QUIRINIUS Latin proper name which the KJV transliterated as Cyrenius. Modern versions prefer the Latin spelling. See *Cyrenius*.

QUIVER Leather case, hung over one's shoulder, for carrying arrows.

QUMRAN Archaeological site near the caves where Dead Sea Scrolls were discovered and center of Jewish Essene community.

QUOTATIONS IN THE NEW TESTAMENT See *Old Testament Quotations in the New Testament.*

The limestone cliffs of the Qumran region showing the caves in which the Dead Sea Scrolls were discovered

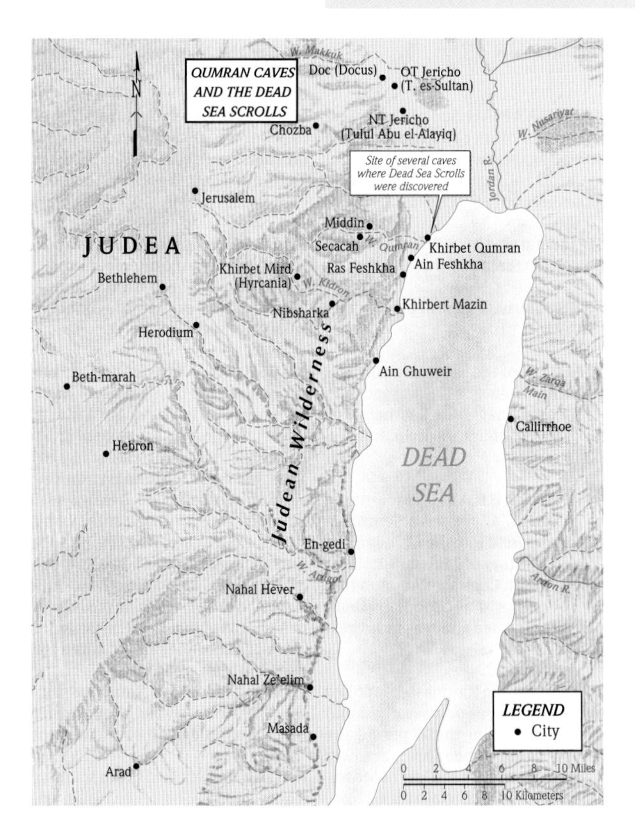

R

The traditional location of Rachel's tomb in Bethlehem

RAAMA or **RAAMAH** Son of Cush (Gen. 10:7) and ancestor of Sheba and Dedan. Arab tribes occupying southwest and west-central Arabia (1 Chron. 1:9). Raamah and Sheba were trading partners of Tyre (Ezek. 27:22).

RAAMIAH Returning exile (Neh. 7:7). Variant form of Reelaiah (Ezra 2:2).

RAAMSES Alternate form of place-name "Rameses" (Exod. 1:11).

RAB-MAG Title of the Babylonian official Nergal-sharezer (Jer. 39:3,13). If associated with the root for "magi," the Rab-mag was likely the officer in charge of divination (cp. Ezek. 21:21).

RABBAH or **RABBATH** Place-name meaning "greatness." **1.** Village near Jerusalem (Josh. 15:60) assigned to tribe of Judah but apparently in territory of Benjamin. Its location is uncertain. **2.** Capital of Ammon that Moses apparently did not conquer (Deut. 3:11; Josh. 13:25), located about 23 miles east of the Jordan River.

RABBI Title meaning "my master," applied to teachers and others of an exalted and revered position. During the NT period, the term "rabbi" came to be more narrowly applied to one learned in the law of Moses, without signifying an official office.

RABBIT (*Oractolagus cuniculus*) Small, long-eared furry mammal related to the hare but differing in giving birth to naked young. CSB, NASB, NIV, and TEV use "rabbit" for an unclean animal in Lev. 11:6; Deut. 14:7 where other English translations use "hare."

RABBITH Unidentified site in territory of Issachar (Josh. 19:20). Rabbith is possibly a corruption of Daberath, a site included in other lists of Issachar's territory (Josh. 21:28; 1 Chron. 6:72) but missing in Josh. 19.

RABBONI An Aramaic honorary title and variant spelling of "rabbi," meaning "teacher" that was used by blind Bartimaeus and Mary Magdalene to address Jesus (Mark 10:51; John 20:16). The term "Rabboni" possibly connotes heightened emphasis or greater honor than the almost synonymous expression "rabbi."

RABSARIS Assyrian court position with strong military and diplomatic powers. The OT records that the rabsaris was sent on two occasions to deal with the Israelite kings (2 Kgs. 18:17; Jer. 39:3).

RABSHAKEH Assyrian title, literally, "chief cupbearer." The position probably began as a mere butler but developed into a highly influential post by the time of its mention in the Bible. The official who dealt with Hezekiah spoke for the Assyrian king much as an ambassador would. He urged the people of Jerusalem to make peace with Assyria rather than believing King Hezekiah that God would protect Judah (2 Kgs. 18:17-32).

RACA Word of reproach, meaning "empty" or "ignorant," that the Hebrew writers borrowed from the Aramaic language. Jesus used it in Matt. 5:22 as a strong term of derision, second only to "fool." He placed it in the context of anger and strongly condemned one who would use it of another person.

RACAL Unidentified site in southern Judah (1 Sam. 30:29).

RACHEL Personal name meaning "ewe." Younger daughter of Laban, the second wife and cousin of Jacob, and the mother of Joseph and Benjamin. In flight from his brother Esau, Jacob met Rachel when she brought the sheep to water. She immediately became the object of his attention.

RADDAI Personal name meaning "Yahweh rules." Son of Jesse and brother of David (1 Chron. 2:14).

RAFT King Hiram's means of transporting timber for the temple by lashing logs together and floating them down the coast from Tyre to Joppa (1 Kgs. 5:9; 2 Chron. 2:16).

RAHAB Name meaning "arrogant, raging, turbulent, afflicter." **1.** Primeval sea monster representing the forces of chaos that God overcame in creation (Job 9:13; 26:12; Ps. 89:10; Isa. 51:9; cp. Ps. 74:12-17). **2.** Symbolic name for Egypt (Ps. 87:4). Isaiah 30:7 includes a compound name Rahab-hem-shebeth. Translations vary: "Rahab Who Just Sits " (CSB); "Rahab who has been exterminated" (NASB); "Rahab the Do-Nothing" (NIV); "Rahab the Subdued" (REB). **3.** The plural appears in Ps. 40:4 for the proud, arrogant enemies. **4.** Personal name meaning "broad." Harlot in Jericho who hid two Hebrew spies whom Joshua sent there to determine the strength of the city (Josh. 2:1). Matthew named Rahab as Boaz's mother (1:5) in his genealogy of Christ, making her one of the Lord's ancestors. Some interpreters think, however, that the Rahab in Matthew was a different woman. Hebrews 11:31 lists Rahab among the heroes of faith.

RAHAM Personal name meaning "mercy, love." Descendant of Judah (1 Chron. 2:44).

RAIL KJV term meaning "revile," "deride," "cast contempt upon," or "scold using harsh and abusive language" (1 Sam. 25:14; 2 Chron. 32:17; Mark 15:29; Luke 23:39).

RAIN Moisture from heaven providing nourishment for plant and animal life. Palestine was a land dependent upon the yearly rains to ensure an abundant harvest and an ample food supply for the coming year. Thus, the presence or absence of rain became a symbol of God's continued blessing or displeasure with the land and its inhabitants. See *Palestine*.

RAINBOW Caused by the reflection and refraction of sunlight by droplets of rain, a rainbow often appears after the passing of a thunderstorm, marking its end. The bow is colored by the division of sunlight into its primary colors. The rainbow served to remind Israel and her God of his covenant with Noah to never again destroy the earth by flooding (Gen. 9:8-17).

RAISIN CAKES Food prepared by pressing dried grapes together. David gave raisin cakes ("flagon," KJV) to those who accompanied the ark to Jerusalem (2 Sam. 6:19; 1 Chron. 16:3 NRSV). Hosea 3:1 (CSB, NRSV) links raisin cakes with the worship of pagan deities (cp. Jer. 7:18).

RAKEM Personal name meaning "variegated, multicolored." Grandson of Manasseh (1 Chron. 7:16).

RAKKATH Place-name meaning "spit," "narrow," or "swamp." Fortified town in the territory of Naphtali (Josh. 19:35).

RAKKON Place-name possibly meaning "swamp" or "narrow place." Village in the vicinity of Joppa allotted to Dan (Josh. 19:46).

RAM Personal name meaning "high, exalted." **1.** Ancestor of David (Ruth 4:19; 1 Chron. 2:9) and Jesus (Matt. 1:3-4). **2.** Jerahmeel's eldest son (1 Chron. 2:25,27), the nephew of 1, above. **3.** Head of the family to which Job's friend Elihu belonged (Job 32:2).

RAMA (KJV, Matt. 2:18) or **RAMAH** Place-name meaning "high," applied to several cities located on heights, especially military strongholds. **1.** Border town in tribal territory of Asher (Josh. 19:29). The precise location of the city is unknown, although most scholars would place it in the vicinity of Tyre. **2.** Fortified city of tribal territory of Naphtali (Josh. 19:36); this town is probably to be identified with present-day er-Rameh. **3.** Ramah of Gilead usually called Ramoth-gilead (cp. 2 Kgs. 8:28-29; 2 Chron. 22:6). See *Ramoth-gilead.* **4.** City in the inheritance of Benjamin listed along with Gibeon, Beeroth, Jerusalem, and others (Josh. 18:25). It is to be identified with modern er-Ram five miles north of Jerusalem. **5.** City of the Negev, the arid desert south of Judea, in the tribal inheritance of Simeon (Josh. 19:8). David once gave presents to this town following his successful battle with the Amalekites (1 Sam. 30:27). **6.** Birthplace, home, and burial place of Samuel (1 Sam. 1:19; 2:11; 7:17; 8:4; 15:34; 25:1).

RAMATH Place-name meaning "height, elevated place." An element of several names: Ramath-lehi meaning "height of the jawbone," site of Samson's victory over the Philistines (Judg. 15:17).

RAMATHAIM (NIV) or **RAMATHAIM-ZOPHIM** Birthplace of Samuel (1 Sam. 1:1). The first element in the name means "twin peaks." The final element distinguishes this Ramath from others. Zophim is perhaps a corruption of Zuph, the home district of Samuel (1 Sam. 9:5).

RAMATHITE Resident of Ramah (1 Chron. 27:27).

RAMESES Egyptian capital city and royal residence during the nineteenth and twentieth Dynasties (about 1320–1085 BC). See *Pithom and Rameses.*

RAMIAH Personal name meaning "Yahweh is exalted." Israelite having a foreign wife (Ezra 10:25).

RAMOTH-GILEAD Place-name meaning "heights of Gilead." One of the cities of refuge Moses appointed for unintentional killers (Deut. 4:43; cp. Josh. 20:8) and Levitical cities (Josh. 21:38). Solomon made Ramoth-gilead a district capital (1 Kgs. 4:13). After the division of the kingdom about 922 BC, the city fell to Syria (1 Kgs. 22:3) and remained there for almost 70 years. Ahab attempted to retake the city but was mortally wounded in the battle (1 Kgs. 22:29-40). Joram did recapture the city (2 Kgs. 9:14; cp. 8:28). In Ramoth-gilead, Elisha anointed Jehu as king over Israel (2 Kgs. 9:1-6). In 722 BC, the region was taken by Assyria.

The gateway to the city of Rameses (Tanis).

RAMPART Outer ring of fortifications, usually earthworks. The underlying Hebrew term is literally "encirclement" and can be applied to moats and walls as well as earthworks (2 Sam. 20:15; Ps. 122:7; Lam. 2:8). Because Jerusalem was ringed by steep valleys, only its north side had extensive ramparts.

RANGE KJV term for a rank or row of soldiers (2 Kgs. 11:8,15; 2 Chron. 23:14).

RAPE Crime of engaging in sexual intercourse with another without consent, by force and/or deception. Mosaic law required a man who had seduced a virgin to pay the bride price and offer to marry her (Exod. 22:16-17). The rape of an engaged woman was a capital offense (Deut. 22:25-27). The Mosaic code highlighted the victim's rights, both to monetary compensation and to recovery of dignity. This quest for dignity was a driving force behind acts of retaliatory violence recorded in the narrative texts. These texts, however, suggest the ease with which the victim is forgotten in the spiral of vengeful violence.

RAPHA Personal name meaning "he has healed." **1.** Fifth son of Benjamin (1 Chron. 8:2). The parallel in Gen. 46:21 gives the name "Naaman." **2.** KJV form of Raphah (1 Chron. 8:37), a descendant of Saul. Raphah is identified with Rephaiah of 1 Chron. 9:43.

RAPHU Personal name meaning "healed." Father of the Benjaminite representative among the 12 spies sent to survey Canaan (Num. 13:9).

RAPTURE God's taking the church out of the world instantaneously. The Latin term *rapio*, which means to "snatch away" or "carry off," is the source of the English word. While there are differing views of the millennium (Rev. 20:2-7) in relation to Christ's second coming (e.g., premillennial, postmillennial, and amillennial), nevertheless, all evangelicals affirm a literal return of Christ to the earth preceding the eternal state. In premillennialism, however, the distinct event of the rapture is often emphasized.

The main biblical passage for the rapture (Gk. *harpazo*) of the church is 1 Thess. 4:15-17. Other texts often used to support the doctrine of the rapture are John 14:1-3 and 1 Cor. 15:51-52.

There are three main approaches to understanding the rapture in premillennialism: (1) In the *pretribulational* view Christ raptures the church before any part of the seven-year tribulation begins (Dan. 9:24-27; Matt. 24:3-28; Rev. 11:2; 12:14). Upon Christ's coming in the air, which is distinct from and precedes his coming to the earth, believers will be "caught up together . . . in the clouds to meet the Lord in the air" (1 Thess. 4:17 CSB). In this view, believers are delivered "from the coming wrath" (1 Thess. 1:10) by being taken out of the world. (2) A *midtribulational* view also sees the rapture as a distinct event that precedes Christ's second coming and that delivers believers from the last half of the seven-year period, the "great tribulation" (Matt. 24:15-28; Rev. 16–18). (3) A *posttribulational* view holds that the rapture and the second coming occur at the same time. Therefore, the church remains on earth during "a time of trouble for Jacob" (Jer. 30:7 CSB). Unlike the world, however, believers who go through the tribulation will be protected from the devastating outpouring of God's wrath and judgment (1 Thess. 5:9).

RAT Large rodent listed among the unclean animals (Lev. 11:29), but they were eaten by a disobedient people (Isa. 66:17).

RAVEN The raven, conspicuous because of its black color (Song 5:11), is a member of the crow family. The raven acts as a scavenger and is listed among the unclean birds (Lev. 11:15; Deut. 14:14).

RAVEN, RAVIN KJV term for "prowl for food" or "feed greedily" (Ps. 22:13; Ezek. 22:25,27). KJV used "ravin" both as a verb meaning "to prowl for food" (Gen. 49:27) and as a noun meaning "something taken as prey" (Nah. 2:12).

REAIA (KJV, 1 Chron. 5:5) or **REAIAH** Personal name meaning "Yahweh has seen." **1.** Member of the tribe of Judah (1 Chron. 4:1-2). **2.** Member of the tribe of Reuben (1 Chron. 5:5). **3.** Head of a family of temple servants returning from exile (Ezra 2:47; Neh. 7:50).

REAP To harvest grain using a sickle (Ruth 2:3-9). Reaping is used as a symbol of recompense for good (Hos. 10:12; Gal. 6:7-10) and evil (Job 4:8; Prov. 22:8; Hos. 8:7; 10:13), of evangelism (Matt. 9:37-38; Luke 10:2; John 4:35-38), and of final judgment (Matt. 13:30,39; Rev. 14:14-16).

REBA Personal name from a root meaning "lie down." Midianite king whom Israel defeated in the time of Moses (Num. 31:8). Joshua 13:21 connects the defeat of the Midianite kings with that of the Amorite king Sihon (Num. 21:21-35).

REBECCA New Testament form of "Rebekah," Rom. 9:10; Greek transliteration used by KJV, NKJV, NRSV, RSV, REB, NJB, TEV.

REBEKAH Personal name, perhaps meaning "cow." Daughter of Bethuel, Abraham's nephew (Gen. 24:15); Isaac's wife (24:67) and mother of Jacob and Esau (25:25-26).

RECAB, RECABITES NIV form of Rechab, Rechabites.

RECAH Unidentified site in Judah (1 Chron. 4:12). Early Greek manuscript has Rechab in place of Recah.

RECHAB Personal name meaning "rider" or "charioteer." **1.** Leader, together with his brother, of a band of Benjaminite raiders. He and his brother murdered Saul's son Ish-bosheth, thinking to court David's favor. David's response was their execution (2 Sam. 4:1-12). **2.** Father or ancestor of Jehonadab, a supporter of Jehu's purge of the family of Ahab and other worshipers of Baal (2 Kgs. 10:15,23). **3.** Father or ancestor of Malchijah, who assisted in Nehemiah's repair of Jerusalem's walls (Neh. 3:14), possibly identical with 2, above.

RECHABITES Descendants of Jehonadab ben Rechab, who supported Jehu when he overthrew the house of Ahab (2 Kgs. 10:15-17). About 599 BC the Rechabites took refuge from Nebuchadnezzar in Jerusalem (Jer. 35).

RECONCILIATION Bringing together of two parties that are estranged or in dispute. Jesus Christ is the one who brings together God and humanity, with salvation as the result of the union. Several themes are essential to a biblical understanding of reconciliation. First is a recognition of the need for reconciliation (Rom. 5:10; Eph. 2:12; Col. 1:21). Sin has created the separation and alienation between God and man. Reconciliation assumes there is a need for separation to be bridged and for God and humanity to be restored in right relationship. Second, God is the Reconciler; reconciliation is his work. The incarnation is God's declaration that the initiative for reconciliation resides exclusively with him (2 Cor. 5:19). Third, the death of Jesus Christ is the means by which God accomplishes reconciliation (Rom. 5:10). Fourth, reconciliation is a completed work but is still being fulfilled. Although the substitutionary sacrifice of Christ has already procured reconciliation, human beings still receive God's reconciling work and gracious gift by grace through faith in Jesus Christ. Fifth, the divine-human act of reconciliation serves as the basis for authentic person-to-person reconciliation. Finally, God's reconciling work is in large measure the ministry of the church. Believers have been commissioned by the resurrected Lord to have a message and ministry of reconciliation. In this sense, reconciliation is not only a reality of life for believers, but it is also a purpose of their kingdom ministry.

RED KJV used "red" as the translation of several Hebrew terms where modern translations substitute another meaning: "foaming" or "blended" (Ps. 75:8); "pleasant" or "delight" (Isa. 27:2); and "porphyry" (Esth. 1:6).

RED HEIFER Function of the red heifer ceremony was production of ash for the water used to remove ritual impurity contracted through contact with a corpse, bones, or a grave (Num. 19). The rite involved: slaughter of a sacrificially acceptable heifer outside the camp; sprinkling blood toward the tent of meeting seven times; burning the entire heifer, including its blood and dung, together with cedarwood, hyssop, and scarlet thread (cp. Lev. 14:4); and storing the ash in a clean place outside the camp.

Hebrews 9:14 uses the image of the red heifer ceremony to picture Christ's cleansing believers of the effect of "dead works." Dead works refer either to acts that lead to death (NIV), "useless rituals" in view of salvation (TEV), or works produced prior to being made alive in Christ (cp. Heb. 6:1).

The Red Sea

RED SEA (REED SEA) Body of water God divided in the exodus. Red Sea is a common translation of two Hebrew words *yam suph*. *Yam* means "sea," but *suph* does not normally mean "red." *Suph* often means "reeds" (Exod. 2:3,5; Isa. 19:6) or "end," "hinder part" (Joel 2:20; 2 Chron. 20:16; Eccles. 3:11). *Yam suph* could be translated "Sea of Reeds" or "Sea at the end of the world."

No one knows the exact location of the place where Israel crossed the "Red Sea" on the way out of Egypt. Four primary theories have been suggested as to the place of the actual crossing of the isthmus of Suez: (1) the northern edge of the Gulf of Suez; (2) a site in the center of the isthmus near Lake Timsah; (3) a site at the northern edge of the isthmus and the southern edge of Lake Menzaleh; and (4) across a narrow stretch of sandy land that separates Lake Sirbonis from the Mediterranean Sea. Although no one knows the exact site of the crossing, the weight of the biblical evidence is on the side of suggested site number 2. See *Exodus*.

REDEEM, REDEMPTION, REDEEMER The first term means to pay a price in order to secure the release of something or someone. It connotes the idea of paying what is required in order to liberate from oppression, enslavement, or another type of binding obligation. The redemptive procedure may be legal, commercial, or religious.

In the OT, two word groups convey the idea of redemption. The verb *ga'al* and its cognates mean "to buy back" or "to redeem." When *ga'al* is used of God, the idea is redemption from bondage or oppression, typically from one's enemies. In the Exodus account, Yahweh declares to Moses: "I am the LORD, and . . . I will redeem you with an outstretched arm and great acts of judgment" (Exod. 6:6 CSB).

In the NT, two word groups convey the concept. The first consists of *lutron* and its cognates. They mean "to redeem," "to liberate," or "to ransom." The idea of ransom suggests the heart of Jesus's mission (Mark 10:45). His life and ministry culminated in his sacrificial death. His death served as the ransom to liberate sinners from their enslaved condition.

Another word family, *agorazein*, means "to buy at the market" or "to redeem." This group is used several times to express God's redemptive activity in Christ. For example, God's redemption of fallen humanity is costly (1 Cor. 6:20). Believers are liberated from the enslaving curse of the law (Gal. 3:13; 4:5). God's redemptive mission among the nations is cause for eschatological worship (Rev. 5:9; 14:3-4).

Paul provides the fullest explanation in the NT, connecting the redemptive work of Christ with the legal declaration of the sinner's pardon (justification) and the appeasement of God's wrath against sin (propitiation, Rom. 3:24; 1 Cor. 1:30).

REELAIAH Personal name meaning "Yahweh has caused trembling." Exile who returned with Zerubbabel (Ezra 2:2); identical to Raamiah (Neh. 7:7).

REFINE To reduce to a pure state; often used figuratively of moral cleansing.

REFORMATION Translation of the Greek *diorthosis* (Heb. 9:10). The term refers either to the new order for relating to God established by Christ (NIV) or to the process of establishing the new order (NRSV, TEV).

REGEM Personal name meaning "friend." Descendant of Caleb (1 Chron. 2:47).

REGEM-MELECH Personal name meaning "friend of the king." Delegate whom the people of Bethel sent to Jerusalem to inquire about continuing to fast in commemoration of the destruction of the Jerusalem temple (Zech. 7:2). The prophet repeated the word of previous prophets: God desires moral lives rather than fasts (7:9-10).

REGENERATION Special act of God in which the recipient is passive. God alone awakens the person spiritually through the power of his Holy Spirit. Both the OT and NT also speak of the renewing of the individual. In a technical sense, the act of regeneration takes place at the moment of conversion as the individual is spiritually awakened.

The term "regeneration" is a translation of the Greek word *palingenesia* (used only in Matt. 19:28 of creation and in Titus 3:5). The Titus text refers to the regeneration of the individual: "He saved us—not by works of righteousness that we had done, but according to his mercy, through the washing of regeneration and renewal by the Holy Spirit" (CSB). The Bible expresses the concept in numerous places with other terms like "born again," "renewed," "re-made," and "born of God." For instance, in John 3:3-8 Jesus tells Nicodemus that in order to enter the kingdom of God, he must be born again.

REGIMENT CSB, NIV term for "cohort," a tenth of a legion (Acts 10:1; 27:1).

REGISTER KJV term for a record of names, a genealogical registry (Ezra 2:62; Neh. 7:5,64). Modern translations use "register" more often in the verbal sense, to record in formal records (NASB: Num. 1:18; 11:26; 2 Sam. 24:2,4; Neh. 12:22-23; Ps. 87:6). See *Census.*

REHABIAH Personal name meaning "Yahweh has made wide." Son of Eliezer and ancestor of a group of Levites (1 Chron. 23:17; 24:21; 26:25).

REHOB Personal and place-name meaning "broad or open place." **1.** Father of a king of Zobah, an Aramean city north of Damascus (2 Sam. 8:3,12). **2.** Witness to Nehemiah's covenant (Neh. 10:11). **3.** Town in the vicinity of Laish in upper Galilee (Num. 13:21) See *Beth-rehob.* **4.** Town in the territory of Asher (Josh. 19:28,30). Asher was not able to drive out the Canaanite inhabitants (Judg. 1:31).

REHOBOAM Personal name meaning "he enlarges the people." One of Solomon's sons and his successor to the throne of the united monarchy (1 Kgs. 11:43). He reigned about 931–913 BC. While at Shechem for his crowning ceremony as king over Israel (1 Kgs. 12), the people asked Rehoboam if he would remove some of the tax burden and labor laws that his father had placed on them. Instead of taking the advice of the older men, he acted on the counsel of those who wanted to increase the burden further. The northern tribes revolted and made the rebel Jeroboam their king. Rehoboam was left with only the tribes of Judah and Benjamin. He continued the pagan ways that Solomon had allowed (14:21-24) and fought against Jeroboam and Shishak of Egypt. Some of his fortifications may be those at Lachish and Azekah.

REHOBOTH Place-name meaning "broad places." **1.** Rehoboth-Ir, "broad places of the city," likely denotes an open space within Nineveh or its suburbs (Gen. 10:11) rather than a separate city between Nineveh and Calah. **2.** Site of a well dug and retained by Isaac's men in the valley of Gerar (Gen. 26:22). The name affirms that God had made room for them following confrontations over rights to two previous wells. **3.** Unidentified Edomite city (Gen. 36:37; 1 Chron. 1:48).

REHUM Personal name meaning "merciful, compassionate." **1.** One returning from exile with Zerubbabel (Ezra 2:2); the parallel (Neh. 7:7) reads "Nehum." **2.** Persian official with oversight of the Trans-Euphrates territory, including Judah. His protest of the rebuilding of the Jerusalem temple and city walls resulted in suspension of the project (Ezra 4:8-24). **3.** Levite engaged in Nehemiah's repair of the wall (Neh. 3:17). **4.** Witness to Nehemiah's covenant (Neh. 10:25). **5.** Priest or priestly clan (Neh. 12:3), perhaps a corruption of Harim.

REI Personal name meaning "friendly." David's officer who sided with Solomon in his succession struggle with Adonijah (1 Kgs. 1:8).

REINS KJV term for kidneys, used both in a literal anatomical sense and in a figurative sense for the seat of the emotions. The substitutions made by the CSB are illustrative of those of other modern translations: literal sense as "kidneys" (Job 16:13), "inward parts" (Ps. 139:13), and "waist" (Isa. 11:5); figurative sense as "heart" (Job 19:27; Ps. 26:2; Jer. 11:20); "innermost being" (Ps. 73:21; Prov. 23:16), "thoughts" (Ps. 16:7), "emotions" (Ps. 7:9).

REKEM Personal and place-name meaning "maker of multicolored cloth." **1.** One of five Midianite kings whom Israel defeated in Moses's time (Num. 31:8; Josh. 13:21). Rekem was apparently the earlier name of Petra. See *Reba*. **2.** Descendant of Caleb (1 Chron. 2:43-44). **3.** Ancestor of a family living in Gilead (1 Chron. 7:16). **4.** Unidentified site in Benjamin (Josh. 18:27).

RELEASE, YEAR OF Hebrew expression that occurs only twice (Deut. 15:9; 31:10 KJV, RSV), both times in reference to the Sabbatical Year as a year of release from debt. Some confusion results from modern translations using the verb "release" in connection with both the Sabbatical Year and the Year of Jubilee.

REMALIAH Personal name meaning "may Yahweh be exalted" or "Yahweh adorned." Father of Pekah who murdered King Pekahiah of Israel and reigned in his stead (2 Kgs. 15:25; Isa. 7:1).

REMETH Place-name meaning "height." Town in Issachar's territory (Josh. 19:21), likely identical with Ramoth (1 Chron. 6:73) and Jarmuth (Josh. 21:29).

REMISSION Release, forgiveness. RSV used "remission" only in the sense of refraining from exacting a tax (Esth. 2:18). Other modern translations avoided the term. KJV frequently used the expression, "remission of sins," to mean release from the guilt or penalty of sins.

REMMON KJV variant of Rimmon (Josh. 19:7). RSV reads "En-rimmon." Other modern translations follow the KJV in understanding two cities: Ain and Rimmon.

REMMON-METHOAR KJV took Remmon-methoar as a proper name (Josh. 19:13).

REMNANT Something left over, especially the righteous people of God after divine judgment. Noah and his family may be understood as survivors, or a remnant, of a divine judgment in the flood (Gen. 6:5-8; 7:1-23). The same could be said of Lot when Sodom was destroyed (Gen. 18:17-33; 19:1-29), Jacob's family in Egypt (Gen. 45:7), Elijah and the 7,000 faithful followers of the Lord (1 Kgs. 19:17-18), and the Israelites going into captivity (Ezek. 12:1-16). They were survivors because the Lord chose to show mercy to those who had believed steadfastly in him and had been righteous in their lives.

The remnant doctrine was so important to Isaiah that he named one of his sons Shear-jashub, meaning "a remnant shall return" (7:3). The faithful would survive the onslaughts of the Assyrian army (4:2-6; 12:1-6) as illustrated by the remarkable deliverance of the few people in Jerusalem from the siege of the city by the Assyrians (chaps. 36–38).

In the NT, Paul quoted (Rom. 9:25-33) from Hosea and from Isaiah to demonstrate that the saving of a remnant from among the Jewish people was still part of the Lord's method of redeeming his people. There would always be a future for anyone among the covenant people who would truly turn to the Lord for salvation (chaps. 9–11).

REPENTANCE Change of mind; also can refer to regret or remorse accompanying a realization that wrong has been done or to any shift or reversal of thought.

Old Testament The concept of a whole-hearted turning to God is widespread in the preaching of the OT prophets. Terms such as "return," turn," and "seek" are used to express the idea of repentance.

New Testament Repentance was the keynote of the preaching of John the Baptist, referring to a complete turn from self to God. The emphasis upon a total life change continues in the ministry of Jesus. The message of repentance was at the heart of his preaching (Mark 1:15). When describing the focus of his mission, Jesus said, "I have not come to call the righteous, but sinners to repentance" (Luke 5:32 CSB).

REPENTANCE OF GOD Old Testament description of God's reaction to human situations. The Hebrew verb (*nacham*) expresses a strong emotional content, perhaps with a reference to deep breathing of distress or relief. It should be noted that "repent" is not always the best translation for *nacham* but was the translation used by the KJV. The scope of possible translations includes "repent" (Jer. 18:8,10 RSV), "grieve" (Gen. 6:7 NIV), "regret" (Gen. 6:7 CSB), "pity" (Judg. 2:18 NASB), "change of mind" (Ps. 110:4 REB), and "relent" (Ps. 106:45 CSB). God's repentance plays an important role in our understanding about the role of prayer and about certain attributes of God, such as immutability, timelessness, and impassability. The God who repents is free to answer prayer and to interact with people. This freedom is part of his being the same forever.

REPHAEL Personal name meaning "God heals." Temple gatekeeper (1 Chron. 26:7).

REPHAH Personal name meaning "overflow." An Ephraimite (1 Chron. 7:25).

REPHAIAH Personal name meaning "God healed." **1.** Descendant of David (1 Chron. 3:21). **2.** Simeonite living at Mount Seir (1 Chron. 4:42). **3.** Warrior from the tribe of Issachar (1 Chron. 7:2). **4.** Descendant of Saul (1 Chron. 9:43). **5.** One helping with Nehemiah's repair of the wall who had oversight of half of the administrative district embracing Jerusalem (Neh. 3:9).

REPHAIM **1.** Residents of Sheol, often translated "shades" or "the dead" (Job 26:5 NRSV; Ps. 88:10; Prov. 9:18; 21:16; Isa. 14:9; 26:14,19). See *Sheol*. **2.** Ethnic designation of the pre-Israelite inhabitants of Palestine, equivalent to the Anakim, the Moabite term *Emim* (Deut. 2:10-11), and the Ammonite term *Zanzummim* (2:20-21).

REPHAITES NIV alternate translation for the Hebrew *Rephaim* when applied to the pre-Israelite inhabitants of Canaan. See *Rephaim*.

REPHAN Term for a foreign, astral deity (Acts 7:43; NASB, Rompha). Acts 7 follows the earliest Greek OT translation reading at Amos 5:26. The Hebrew Masoretic text reads "Kaiwan," the Babylonian name for Saturn.

REPHIDIM Site in the wilderness where the Hebrews stopped on their way to Canaan just prior to reaching Sinai (Exod. 17:1; 19:2). There the people complained of thirst, and God commanded Moses to strike the rock out of which would come water. While the Hebrews were encamped at Rephidim, the Amalekites came against them and were defeated by Israel under Joshua's leadership. Moses's father-in-law, Jethro, came to Rephidim and helped the leader delegate his authority over the people (18:13-26). The exact location is unknown.

REPROACH Term used to indicate disgrace, dishonor, or to discredit someone or something.

REPROBATE KJV term used in two senses: that which fails to meet a test and is thus rejected as unworthy or unacceptable, as impure silver (Jer. 6:30) or persons (2 Cor. 13:5-7; Titus 1:16); and that which is depraved or without morals (Rom. 1:28; 2 Tim. 3:8). NASB and RSV used "reprobate" to mean "one rejected by God" (Ps. 15:4; cp. CSB, REB, TEV).

REPTILES Animals that crawl or move on the belly or on small short legs. This category of animals includes alligators, crocodiles, lizards, snakes, and turtles. It is generally agreed that in many instances the reptiles in the Bible cannot be specifically determined. Many times the same Hebrew word is translated in different ways.

RESEN Place-name meaning "fountain head." City that Nimrod founded between Nineveh and Calah (Gen. 10:12). Probably modern Salemijeh (in Iraq), 2.5 miles northwest of Nimrud.

RESERVOIR Place for catching and storing water for later use, either agricultural (2 Chron. 26:10; Eccles. 2:6) or as an urban supply in anticipation of a siege (2 Kgs. 20:20; Isa. 22:8b-11). Reservoirs were a necessity in most of Palestine where seasonal rains were the major water source.

RESH Twentieth letter in the Hebrew alphabet, which the KJV used as heading for the eight verses of Ps. 119:153-160 that all begin with this letter.

RESHEPH Personal name meaning "flame." An Ephraimite (1 Chron. 7:25).

RESIN NIV translation of "bdellium" (Gen. 2:12; cp. Num. 11:7).

RESTITUTION Act of returning what has wrongfully been taken or replacing what has been lost or damaged, and the divine restoration of all things to their original order.

RESURRECTION Future, bodily rising from the dead of all persons. Believers in Christ rise to eternal life and bliss with God; unbelievers to eternal torment and separation from God.

Resurrection is different from resuscitation. A resuscitation, like that of Lazarus, is a return to life, but eventually physical death comes again. Those resurrected will not die again.

RESURRECTION OF JESUS THE CHRIST Historical event whereby Jesus came back from physical death to newness of life with a glorified body, never to die again. The bodily resurrection of Jesus is one of the central tenets of the Christian faith. His bodily resurrection validates the claim that he is both Lord and Christ. It substantiates the proposition that his life and death were not just the life and death of a good man, but that he indeed was God incarnate, and that by his death we have forgiveness of sin.

The four Gospels are selective in the events they report surrounding the resurrection. Each emphasizes the empty tomb, but each is somewhat different in the post-resurrection appearances recounted.

The oldest account of the resurrection is found in 1 Cor. 15. In that passage, Paul recounted a number of post-resurrection appearances. He established that the believer's future resurrection is based on the historicity of Christ's bodily resurrection.

RETINUE NASB, REB, NRSV, REB term for the attendants of the queen of Sheba (1 Kgs. 10:2; KJV, train; NIV, caravan; CSB, entourage).

REU Personal name meaning "friend, companion." Descendant of Shem (Gen. 11:18-21; 1 Chron. 1:25), possibly the ancestor of a Semitic tribe associated with Ra'ilu, an island in the Euphrates below Anat.

REUBEN, REUBENITES Eldest son of Jacob, born to Leah (Gen. 29:32) while the couple was living with her father, Laban, in Paddan-aram, and the clan or tribe descended from him. Among his acts recorded in the Bible, Reuben found mandrakes (out of which a love potion probably was made for his mother to use with Jacob, 30:14,16-17) and had sexual relations with one of his father's concubines (35:22), for which he later was chastised (49:4). Reuben felt compassion for young Joseph when his brothers wanted to kill the brash dreamer (37:21-22) and was willing to be responsible to his father for Benjamin's welfare when the unrecognized Joseph commanded that the youngest brother be brought to Egypt (42:37).

The tribe named for Reuben held a place of honor among the other tribes. The territory the tribe inherited was just east of the Dead Sea and was the first parcel of land to be bestowed (Num. 32).

REUEL Personal name meaning "friend of God." **1.** Son of Esau and ancestor of several Edomite clans (Gen. 36:4,10,13,17; 1 Chron. 1:35,37). **2.** Exodus 2:18 identifies Reuel as the "father" of Zipporah, Moses's wife. Numbers 10:29 presents Reuel as the father of Hobab, Moses's father-in-law. Elsewhere Moses's father-in-law is called Jethro. The tradition is also divided regarding the background of Moses's father-in-law, either Midianite (Exod. 2:16; 3:1) or Kenite (Judg. 1:16; 4:11). **3.** A Gadite (Num. 2:14). **4.** A Benjaminite (1 Chron. 9:8).

REUMAH Personal name meaning "coral." Nahor's concubine, an ancestress of several Aramean tribes living northwest of Damascus (Gen. 22:24).

REVELATION OF GOD Content and process of God's making himself known to people. All knowledge of God comes by way of revelation. Human knowledge of God is revealed knowledge, since God, and he alone, gives it. He bridges the gap between himself and his creatures, disclosing himself and his will to them. By God alone can God be known.

Theologians make a distinction between general revelation and special revelation. General revelation is universal in the sense that it is God's self-disclosure of himself in a general way to all people at all times in all places. General revelation occurs (1) through nature, (2) in our experience and in our conscience, and (3) in history. God's general revelation is often misinterpreted because sinful and finite humans are trying to understand a perfect and infinite God. Men and women suppress God's truth because they do not like the truth about God. General revelation does not bring one into a saving relationship with God; it does reveal God to his creatures and they are, therefore, responsible for their response.

In contrast to God's general revelation, which is available to all people, God's special revelation is available to specific people at specific times in specific places. Special revelation is particular. God reveals himself to his people. These people of God are the children of Abraham, whether by natural (Gen. 12:1-3) or spiritual descent (Gal. 3:16,29). Special revelation is primarily redemptive and personal. In recognition of the human predicament, God chose at the very beginning to disclose himself in a more direct way. Within time and space, God has acted and spoken to redeem the human race from its own self-imposed evil. Through calling people, miracles, the exodus, covenant making, and ultimately through Jesus Christ, God has revealed himself in history.

REVELATION, BOOK OF Last book in the Bible. Its title is from its first word, *apokalupsis*, meaning to "unveil," "disclose," or "reveal." Revelation 1:1 gives the theme of the book: it is a revelation "of," "from," and "about" Jesus Christ.

Four times the author identifies himself as John (1:1,4,9; 22:8). Early Christian traditions attribute the Gospel of John, the three letters from John, and the book of Revelation. Revelation is the only one claiming to be written by someone named John. Though the author does not claim to be the apostle John, it seems unlikely that any other first-century Christian leader would have had the authority or was associated closely enough with the churches of Asia Minor to have referred to himself simply as John.

John's situation was one of suffering. He was a "brother and partner in the affliction" that is "in Jesus," and because of his testimony to Jesus, he was exiled to the island of Patmos (1:9 CSB).

Revelation was written late in the first century. Early tradition dated the book during the reign of the Roman emperor Domitian (AD 81–96). An alternative view dates it shortly after the reign of Nero (AD 54–68).

To encourage faithfulness, Revelation points to the glorious world to come, a world where "death will be no more; grief, crying, and pain will be no more" (21:4 CSB; cp. 7:16) at the reappearing of the crucified and risen Jesus. The enthroned Lord will return to conclude world history with the destruction of God's enemies, the final salvation of his people, and creation of a new heaven and a new earth (21–22). The intensity of John's experience is matched only by the richness of the apocalyptic symbolism employed to warn his readers of impending disasters and temptations that would require steadfast allegiance to the risen Lord. To be sure, the Lord will come in power and glory, but not before his enemies have exercised a terrible but limited (by divine mercy) attack on those who hold to the testimony of Jesus (cp. 1:9; 6:9; 12:11).

John concluded his prophecy by declaring the utter faithfulness of his words. Those who heed his prophecy will receive the blessings of God. Those who ignore the warnings will be left outside the gates of God's presence (22:6-15). Solemnly and hopefully praying for the Lord to come, John closed his book (22:17,20). The churches must have ears to hear what the Spirit has said (22:16). The people of God must, by his grace (22:21), persevere in the hour of tribulation, knowing their enthroned Lord will return in triumph.

REVERENCE Respect or honor paid to a worthy object. In Scripture, reverence is paid: to father and mother (Lev. 19:3; Heb. 12:9); to God (1 Kgs. 18:3,12; Heb. 12:28); to God's sanctuary (Lev. 19:30; 26:2); and to God's commandments (Ps. 119:48). The failure to revere God (Deut. 32:51) and the act of revering other gods (Judg. 6:10) have dire consequences. Reverence for Christ is expressed in mutual submission within the Christian community (Eph. 5:21). Christian persecution takes on new meaning as suffering becomes an opportunity for revering Christ (1 Pet. 3:14-15).

REZEPH Place-name meaning "glowing coal." Town the Assyrians conquered, most likely under Shalmaneser III (ca. 838 BC), and which the Assyrians used as a warning to King Hezekiah of Judah in 701 BC against relying on God to deliver him from them (2 Kgs. 19:12; Isa. 37:12).

REZIN King of Syria about 735 BC during the reigns of Pekah in Israel and Ahaz in Judah. When Ahaz refused to join Rezin and Pekah in fighting against Assyria, Rezin persuaded Pekah to ally with him against the Judean king (2 Kgs. 15:37; 16:5). Ahaz appealed for help to Tiglath-pileser of Assyria, who came against Rezin and Pekah and destroyed their kingdoms. Rezin died in 732 BC when Damascus fell to the Assyrians.

REZON Personal name meaning "prince." An Aramean leader who led a successful revolt against Solomon and established an independent state with its capital at Damascus (1 Kgs. 11:23-25).

RHEGIUM Place-name either derived from the Greek *rhegnumi* (rent, torn) or from the Latin *regium* (royal). Port located at the southwestern tip of the Italian boot about seven miles across the Strait of Messina from Sicily. Paul stopped there en route to Rome (Acts 28:13).

RHESA Ancestor of Jesus (Luke 3:27).

RHODA Personal name meaning "rose." Rhoda's relationship to the household of Mary, the mother of John Mark, is not clear. She was most likely a servant, though it is possible that she was a family member or a guest at the prayer service. In her great joy at finding Peter at the door, Rhoda failed to let him in. Her joy in rushing to tell the disciples and their response accusing her of madness recall details of Luke's resurrection narrative (Acts 12:13; cp. Luke 24:9-11).

RHODES Island off the southwest coast of Asia Minor in the Mediterranean Sea associated with the Dodanim (NASB, KJV; Gen. 10:4; Ezek. 27:15). When the apostle Paul stopped over on his voyage from Troas to Caesarea (Acts 21:1), Rhodes was only a minor provincial city.

The city and harbor area of the island of Rhodes

RIBAI Personal name meaning "Yahweh contends." Father of Ittai, one of David's 30 elite warriors (2 Sam. 23:29; 1 Chron. 11:31).

RIBBAND KJV form of ribbon (Num. 15:38). Modern translations read "cord" (CSB, NASB, NIV, NRSV) or "thread" (REB).

RIBLAH **1.** Syrian town located near Kadesh on the Orontes River near the border with Babylonia. There Pharaoh Neco imprisoned King Jehoahaz of Judah after the young monarch had reigned only three months (2 Kgs. 23:31-33). Later, when Zedekiah rebelled against

Nebuchadnezzar of Babylon, he was taken to Riblah as a prisoner and viewed the execution of his sons before having his eyes put out (25:4-7). **2.** Otherwise unknown town on eastern border of Canaan (Num. 34:11). Earliest translations read "Arbelah."

RIDDLE Enigmatic or puzzling statement, often based on the clever use of the ambiguities of language. The classic biblical example of a riddle is that posed by Samson to the Philistines (Judg. 14:12-14).

RIGHT MIND Sound mind, mentally healthy (Mark 5:15; Luke 8:35). Elsewhere, the underlying Greek term is rendered "with sober judgment" (Rom. 12:3 NRSV), "think sensibly" (CSB) or "be self-controlled" (Titus 2:6 CSB, NRSV).

RIGHTEOUSNESS Biblical terminology used to denote the term "righteousness" is from one basic word group. The Hebrew *tsadiq* is translated by the Greek *dikaiosune* and its various forms in both the Greek (Septuagint) OT and the NT. Psalms 111–112 provide a holistic picture of the righteousness of God and the righteous human. Righteousness itself is grounded in the character of God (Exod. 9:27; Deut. 32:4; Judg. 5:11; 1 Sam. 12:7; Mic. 6:4; cp. Ps. 103:6; Dan. 9:16; 2 Chron. 12:6; Ezra 9:15; Neh. 9:8; Pss. 119:137; 129:4). He is righteous; his law is righteous; and he alone credits righteousness to a person.

In the NT, like the OT, God and all that comes from him is righteous. His judgments are righteous (2 Thess. 1:5-6; Rev. 16:7; 19:2; 2 Tim. 4:8), as he himself is as a judge (John 17:23). All God's revealed will in Jesus's teachings is righteousness (Matt. 6:23; John 16:8-10).

Paul uses the idea of righteousness more than other writers in the NT. God demonstrates his righteousness perfectly in the propitiatory death of his Son (Rom. 3:21,25-26). Jesus's death on the cross was ordained by God, is in conformity with his character, and accomplishes God's righteous purposes with sinners (Rom. 5:16,18).

RIMMON Place-name and divine name meaning "pomegranate." **1.** Chief god of Syria, also called Hadad. Naaman worshipped Rimmon in Damascus (2 Kgs. 5:18). **2.** Town allotted to the tribe of Judah (Josh. 15:32) but then given to Simeon (19:7; cp. 1 Chron. 4:32). **3.** Levitical city in Zebulun (Josh. 19:13; 1 Chron. 6:77), probably the original reading for present Dimnah (Josh. 21:35). **4.** Rock near Gibeah to where the people of Benjamin fled from vengeful Israelites (Judg. 20:45-47), modern Rammun four miles east of Bethel. **5.** Father of Rechab and Baanah, who killed Saul's son Ish-bosheth (2 Sam. 4:2,9).

RIMMON-PAREZ (KJV) or **RIMMON-PEREZ** Place-name meaning "pomegranate of the pass." Campsite during Israel's wilderness wanderings (Num. 33:19-20).

RIMMONO Place-name meaning "his Rimmon." CSB, NIV, NASB, NRSV reading of Rimmon in 1 Chron. 6:77 (cp. Josh. 19:13; 21:25).

RINNAH Personal name meaning "ringing cry." Descendant of Judah (1 Chron. 4:20).

RIPHATH Personal name of foreign origin. Son of Gomer, likely the ancestor of an Anatolian tribe (Gen. 10:3). The name is likely a scribal corruption of Diphath (1 Chron. 1:6).

RISHATHAIM Mesopotamian king, Cushan-rishathaim, who conquered and oppressed Israel (Judg. 3:8). Cushan may relate to Guzana or Tell Halaf. KJV and CSB use Chushan-rishathaim.

RISSAH Place-name possibly meaning "dewdrop," "rain," or "ruins." Campsite during Israel's wilderness wanderings (Num. 33:21-22), modern Sharma, east of Gulf of Aqaba.

RITHMAH Place-name meaning "broom plant." Campsite during Israel's wilderness wanderings (Num. 33:18-19), possibly valley called er-Retame, east of Gulf of Aqaba.

RIZIA Personal name meaning "delight." Head of a family within the tribe of Asher who was a renowned warrior (1 Chron. 7:39-40).

RIZPAH Personal name meaning "glowing coals" or "bread heated over coals or ashes." Saul's concubine whom Abner took as wife in what amounted to a claim to the throne (2 Sam. 3:7; cp. 1 Kgs. 2:22). Rizpah is best known for her faithful vigil over the bodies of her executed sons (2 Sam. 21:10-14) until David commanded their burial.

ROCK Rocky sites used as places of refuge (Num. 24:21; Judg. 15:8; 20:47) led to the frequent image of God as a rock, that is, a source of protection. Titles of God include: the "Rock of Israel" (Gen. 49:24 CSB); the Rock (Deut. 32:4); the Rock of salvation (32:15); the Rock who begot Israel (32:18); "a rock that is high above me" (Ps. 61:2 CSB). Isaiah 8:14 pictures the Lord of hosts as a "rock to trip over" (CSB) to the unholy people of Israel and Judah. Paul identified Christ as the spiritual rock that nourished Israel in the wilderness (1 Cor. 10:4).

ROCK BADGER (NRSV) Maybe the hyrax, a mammal somewhat resembling a shrew (Lev. 11:5; Ps. 104:18; Prov. 30:26).

ROD, STAFF "Rod" designates a straight, slender stick growing on (Jer. 1:11) or cut from (Gen. 30:37-41) a tree. "Rod" is sometimes used interchangeably with "staff" (Isa. 10:5; Rev. 11:1). Elsewhere, rod designates a shorter, clublike stick (Ps. 23:4). Rods and staffs were used as walking sticks (Gen. 32:10), for defense (Ps. 23:4), for punishment (Exod. 21:20; Num. 22:27; Prov. 13:24; 1 Cor. 4:21), and for measurement (Rev. 11:1). Rods and staffs were also used as symbols of prophetic (Exod. 4:2-4; 7:8-24; Judg. 6:21), priestly (Num. 17:1-10), and royal (Gen. 49:10; Judg. 5:14; Jer. 48:17; Rev. 2:27) offices.

RODANIM Inhabitants of Rhodes (1 Chron. 1:7 CSB, NRSV). The parallel in Gen. 10:4 (KJV) reads "Dodanim" which should be preferred as the more difficult reading. Rhodians, however, fits well in the general geographic context.

ROE, ROEBUCK (*Capreolus capreolus*) One of the smallest species of deer, measuring about 26 inches at the shoulder (2 Sam. 2:18; Deut.12:15 KJV). Other translations use "gazelle" or "deer."

ROGELIM Place-name meaning "[place of] the fullers." City on the Jabbok River in Gilead (2 Sam. 17:27-29; 19:31). The site is perhaps Zaharet's Soq'ah. Tell Barsina lacks evidence of occupation in David's time.

ROHGAH Personal name, perhaps meaning "cry out." Leader of the tribe of Asher (1 Chron. 7:34).

ROLLER KJV term for something wrapped around the arm (Ezek. 30:21) as a bandage (CSB, NASB, REB, NRSV) or splint (NIV).

ROMAMTI-EZER Personal name meaning "I have exalted help." Temple musician (1 Chron. 25:4,31). Some scholars recognize a prayer of praise behind the names of the temple musicians Hananiah through Mahazioth (25:4).

ROMANS, LETTER TO THE Longest and most intensely theological of the 13 NT letters written by Paul. This letter is also the most significant in the history of the church. Martin Luther was studying Romans when he concluded that a person becomes righteous in the sight of God through faith alone. His discovery led to the Reformation battle cry, *sola fide*, "by faith alone."

Where and When Did Paul Write Romans? Romans 15:25-29 indicates Paul wrote Romans shortly before a trip to Jerusalem. He went to Jerusalem to present money collected by Gentile churches in Macedonia and Achaia for poor believers in Jerusalem (15:26). Paul hoped to travel from Jerusalem through Rome to Spain to "preach the gospel where Christ has not been named" (15:20 CSB). This fits well with Luke's description of Paul's travels at the close of the third missionary journey (Acts 19:21; 20:16).

What Is the Message of Romans? Romans 1:16-17 expresses the theme of the letter. Paul is not ashamed to proclaim the gospel because the gospel is God's saving power that accomplishes salvation for all who believe, whether they are Jews or Gentiles. The gospel reveals God's righteousness, both his justice and his activity of justifying sinners (Rom. 3:21-26). Salvation by faith was not new but was the message of the OT prophets (Rom. 1:17; Hab. 2:4).

Gentiles deserve God's wrath because their sins are not committed in ignorance but involve suppression of the truths about

God that are apparent to all. Jews as well as Gentiles deserve God's wrath. Though they preach and teach the law, they have failed to obey the law, thereby dishonoring God and blaspheming his name. Circumcision grants no protection against divine judgment.

Both the Law and the Prophets testify that God declares sinners who have failed to keep the law to be righteous in his sight if they believe in Jesus Christ. This righteous standing is granted freely by divine grace and based on the atoning sacrifice of Christ.

This righteousness was also credited to Abraham before the Mosaic law was given, further demonstrating that God grants this righteousness on the basis of faith and not law-keeping.

Because of justification, believers are at peace with God and joyfully anticipate full and final transformation. Through Jesus's sacrificial and substitutionary death, believers who were formerly God's enemies and deserved his wrath have been reconciled to God.

The impact of Adam's disobedience on the human race offers a negative parallel to the impact of Christ's obedience on believers. Just as the effects of Adam's disobedience were universal, the effects of Christ's obedience are also universal. The law did not introduce death into the world. It did offer Adam's descendants explicit commandments to defy just as Adam had done. This made sin more rampant and more heinous. This only served to magnify the abundance and greatness of God's grace.

One should not conclude from this that sin should be continued. The believer's union with Christ in his death, burial, and resurrection is inconsistent with a sinful lifestyle. The old person died with Christ. Now the believer has been liberated from sin's mastery. Eventually, the believer's union with Christ will result in the believer's resurrection and complete liberation from sin. Believers should live now in light of the fact that sin's mastery has been broken.

The law aggravates and arouses sin in unbelievers, but this does not mean the law is bad. The law is holy, righteous, and good, but the sinful nature uses the law to destroy sinners. The law still serves a positive function. It demonstrates humanity's utter corruption and slavery to sin. However, the law cannot liberate from that slavery. Paul illustrated this by describing his own frustration in trying to fulfill the law's demands. Paul had been caught in a tug-of-war between delighting in God's law and being dominated by sin. Paul confessed that this conflict would end only through the bodily resurrection. Yet the believer can enjoy victory over sin. The Spirit accomplishes for the believer what the law cannot. The Spirit liberates the believer from slavery to sin and moves the believer to fulfill naturally and spontaneously the law's righteous demands. The Spirit exercises the same power used to raise Jesus from the dead in order to produce new life in the believer. Those who live by God's Spirit are God's children and thus heirs who will share in God's glory. The whole creation longs for this glory. The believer longs for adoption through the redemption of the body.

God presently works through every circumstance for the spiritual good of the believer. God's eternal purpose will not be thwarted, and he will unfailingly make those whom he loved from eternity past become like his Son. The completion of the believer's salvation through justification at final judgment and the believer's glorification is certain because it is grounded in God's undying love.

The rejection of Christ by Israel, God's chosen people, might seem to contradict the infallibility of God's promises and shake the believer's hopes. However, God's promises to Israel have not failed. Not all physical descendants of Abraham are true Israelites. God's promises apply to those whom he has chosen. This choice is based not on human character or behavior but God's mysterious purpose.

Still, Israel is fully responsible for its spiritual condition. Gentiles obtained true righteousness by faith. Israel sought righteousness but attempted to establish her own righteousness through obedience to the law rather than faith in Christ. Israel did not find true righteousness despite all her efforts because the law is fulfilled only through faith in Christ. Salvation comes only through faith in Christ as the OT demonstrates.

Gentiles should not assume they have favored status with God. After all elect Gentiles have been saved, God will shift his focus to national Israel again. Great masses of Jews will be saved, because God's gifts and call are irrevocable. God has displayed his mysterious wisdom by using Gentiles and Jews to prompt one another to believe in Christ.

Believers respond to God's mercy by devoting themselves completely to him and by renewed minds that know God's will. The renewed mind recognizes the interdependency of the members of the church and does not establish a hierarchy based on spiritual gifts. The renewed mind is characterized by love. This love expresses itself through forgiveness, sympathy, harmony, humility, and kindness.

Believers should submit themselves to governing authorities. Governmental authority is appointed by God, preserves order, and thwarts lawlessness. For this reason, believers pay their taxes and show respect for political leaders.

Believers should fulfill the law by expressing love for others. Expressing love to others and living righteously are especially important since we are approaching Christ's return. Believers should accept one another in love even when they disagree over issues of conscience, even as they follow their own consciences. They should be careful not to allow their behavior to disturb other believers who hold different convictions. They should be especially careful not to encourage other believers to do something they do not believe is right. It is wrong to eat, drink, or do anything that disturbs one's conscience.

Jewish and Gentile believers, the weak and the strong, should live in unity and try to build up one another. They should learn to glorify God with one heart and one voice. Jesus himself came into the world as a servant to the Jews, fulfilling the promises to the Jews, and yet including Gentiles in God's plan so that they might glorify God as the OT foretold.

ROME AND THE ROMAN EMPIRE

International rule that the government in Rome, Italy, exercised after 27 BC when the Republic of Rome died and the Roman Empire was born. The first several emperors ruled at the time of the beginning of the Christian movement in the Roman Empire.

The famous Colosseum at Rome was built in the latter years of the first century AD.

Jesus was born during the reign of Augustus (27 BC–AD 14) and conducted his ministry during the reign of Augustus's successor, Tiberius (AD 14–37; cp. Luke 3:1). The latter's image was stamped on a silver denarius that Jesus referred to in a discussion about taxation (Luke 20:20-26). In about AD 18, Herod Antipas, the son of Herod the Great, built his capital on the western shore of the Sea of Galilee and named it Tiberias after the emperor. Tiberius was an extremely able military commander and a good administrator, leaving a large surplus in the treasury when he died. He followed Augustus's example of not expanding the borders of the empire and thus avoiding war. The *pax Romana* (peace of Rome) that Augustus had inaugurated was preserved, providing easy, safe travel throughout the empire. Paul undoubtedly referred to this in Gal. 4:4 when he wrote: "When the time came to completion, God sent his son" (CSB). Tiberius was never popular with the senate and chose to leave Rome at the first opportunity, choosing after AD 26 to rule the empire from his self-imposed seclusion on the Isle of Capri. In this year, Pontius Pilate was appointed governor of Judea, a post he held until AD 36, just prior to the death of Tiberius in AD 37.

Tiberius was succeeded by his mentally unbalanced grandnephew, Gaius (Caligula), who proved to be a disaster. During his reign

(AD 37–41) and that of his successor, his aging uncle Claudius (AD 41–54), most of the ministry of the apostle Paul took place. Claudius is reported to have expelled Jews from Rome who were creating disturbances because of Christ (cp. Acts 18:2). Initially, his contemporaries viewed Claudius as inept, but he proved to have considerable hidden talents of administration and turned out to be one of Rome's more proficient emperors. His fourth wife, Agrippina, is mentioned on a recently discovered sarcophagus in the Goliath family cemetery on the western edge of Jericho. She poisoned Claudius in AD 54 to speed up the succession of Nero, her son by a previous marriage.

Nero (AD 54–68) was in some respects worse than Caligula. He was a man without moral scruples or interest in the Roman populace except for exploitation of them. Both Paul and Peter seem to have been martyred during Nero's reign, perhaps in connection with the burning of Rome by Nero in AD 64, an event that he blamed on Christians. The Roman historian Tacitus wrote that when the fire subsided, only four of Rome's 14 districts remained intact. Yet Paul wrote, "All the saints send you greetings, especially those who belong to Caesar's household" (Phil. 4:22 CSB). Nero's hedonism and utter irresponsibility led inevitably to his death. The revolt of Galba, one of his generals, led to Nero's suicide.

Galba, Otho, and Vitellius, three successive emperor-generals, died within the year of civil war (AD 68–69) that followed Nero's death. Vitellius's successor was Vespasian, one of the commanders who had taken Britain for Claudius and who was in Judea squelching the first Jewish revolt. He was declared emperor by the Syrian and Danube legions and returned to Rome to assume the post, leaving his son Titus to finish the destruction of Jerusalem with its holy temple in the next year (AD 70). This event was prophesied by Jesus toward the end of his life when he said: "When you see Jerusalem surrounded by armies, then know that its desolation has come near" (Luke 21:20 CSB).

The Egnatian Way, shown here near Neapolis, was part of the extensive Roman road system.

The aristocratic Julio-Claudian dynasties that had reigned until the death of Nero were happily replaced by the Flavian dynasty, which issued from the rural middle class of Italy and reflected a more modest and responsible approach to the use of power. Vespasian's reign (AD 69–79) was succeeded by the brief tenure of his son Titus (AD 79–81), who at his death gave way to the rule of his brother Domitian (AD 81–96). The fourth-century historian Eusebius reported that the apostle John was exiled to Patmos (cp. Rev. 1:9) in the reign of Domitian. Eusebius also claimed that in Nerva's reign the senate took away Domitian's honors and freed exiles to return home, thus letting John return to Ephesus.

Nerva's reign was brief, lasting little more than a year (AD 96–98). He was succeeded by Trajan (AD 98–117), who bathed the empire red in the blood of Christians. His persecution was more severe than that instituted by Domitian. Irenaeus wrote in the second century that John died in Ephesus in the reign of Trajan. The persecution of the church, depicted in the book of Revelation, probably reflects the ones initiated by Trajan and Domitian. Trajan, the adopted son of Nerva, was the first emperor of provincial origin. His family roots were in the area of Seville, Spain. Marcus Aurelius, a later emperor of Spanish descent (AD 161–180), also persecuted the church.

ROOT Part of a plant buried in and gaining nourishment through the ground. In Scripture, "root" generally appears in a figurative sense. Root of Jesse (Isa. 11:10; Rom. 15:12) and root of David (Rev. 5:5; 22:16) serve as titles of the Messiah. In Paul's allegory of the grapevine,

Israel is the root of the plant, the church is the branches (Rom. 11:16-18).

ROSH Personal name meaning "head" or "chief." Seventh son of Benjamin (Gen. 46:21).

ROYAL CITY City having a monarchical government. Gibeon (Josh. 10:2) was compared in size and strength to cities with kings, such as Ai and Jericho. Gath (1 Sam. 27:5) was one of five Philistine cities ruled by kings or lords. Rabbah (2 Sam. 12:26) served as capital of the Ammonite kingdom.

RUDDY Having a healthy, reddish color (1 Sam. 16:12; 17:42; Song 5:10; Lam. 4:7; cp. Gen. 25:25).

RUE (*Ruta graveolens*) Strong-smelling shrub used as a condiment, in medicines, and in charms (Luke 11:42). Dill appears in the Matthean parallel (Matt. 23:23).

RUFUS Personal name meaning "red haired." **1.** Son of Simon of Cyrene and brother of Alexander (Mark 15:21). **2.** Recipient of Paul's greetings in Rom. 16:13. If Mark was written from Rome, both references likely refer to the same person.

RUHAMAH Personal name meaning "pitied." Name Hosea used to symbolize the change in Israel's status before God following God's judgment (2:1; cp. 1:6). First Peter 2:10 applies Hosea's image to Christians who have experienced God's mercy in Christ.

RUMAH Place-name meaning "elevated place." Home of Jehoiakim's mother (2 Kgs. 23:36), possibly identified with Khirbet Rumeh near Rimmon in Galilee or with Arumah.

RUSH, RUSHES English terms used to translate several types of reedlike plants.

RUST Coating produced by the corrosive effects of air and water on metal, especially iron. Rust on a copper cooking pot symbolized Jerusalem's persistent wickedness in Ezek. 24:6,12-13.

RUTH, BOOK OF OT book whose principal character is a Moabite woman named Ruth, an ancestor of David and Jesus. Given the nature of later Judaism with its denigration of women and its contempt for outsiders, it is remarkable that a biblical book was named for a Moabite woman. This is all the more striking since Ruth is not as important as Boaz and Naomi, and that the book's significance is linked directly to Boaz, as shown in the concluding genealogy.

After reading the book of Judges, which paints a dark and depressing picture of Israel, the reader is relieved to encounter Ruth. One learns that while Israel was in a state of severe moral and spiritual decline, Bethlehem represented an oasis of covenant loyalty in an otherwise barren landscape. Many have recognized in Ruth a supreme literary masterpiece, a delightful short story with a classical plot that moves from crisis (famine and death threaten the existence of a family), to complication (the introduction of a primary but less desirable candidate to resolve the crisis), to resolution (the desirable candidate rescues the family line). With great skill, the narrator draws the reader into the minds of the characters (successively Naomi, Ruth, and Boaz), inviting us to identify with their personal anxieties and joys and in the end to celebrate the movement from emptiness and frustration to fulfillment and joy. In the course of the narrative, each of the main characters proves to be a person of extraordinary courage and covenant love (*chesed*, "lovingkindness, faithfulness, loyalty," is the key word in the book: 1:8; 2:20; 3:10). These are people whose spiritual commitment is demonstrated clearly in godly living.

From the perspective of the author, the events of Ruth have significance, primarily because of the critical place these events have in the history of the Davidic line. One of the questions the book answers is, how can David, the man after God's own heart, emerge from the dark and demoralized period of the judges (cp. 1:1)? The answer is because of the providential hand of God on this family in Bethlehem.

Ultimately the book of Ruth is about the Messiah. Although the author may not have recognized the full significance of these events, when Matthew begins his Gospel with a long genealogy of Jesus the Messiah, the son of David and Abraham, the names of Boaz and Ruth appear (Matt. 1:5). Three other women in this genealogy (Tamar, v. 3; Rahab, v. 5; Bathsheba, v. 6) are also tainted. The theological significance of these women in this list of men is obvious: Jesus the Messiah represents all the peoples of the earth; if God can accept Gentiles like Ruth, and incorporate them into his plan of salvation, then there is hope for all (cp. Matt. 28:18-20).

RYE (*Secale cereale*) Hardy grass grown as a cereal (Exod. 9:32 KJV) and cover crop (Isa. 28:25 KJV, NASB). Other translations render the underlying Hebrew as "spelt."

Iron Age sacrificial altar located at the site of ancient Arad

SABAOTH An intensive title describing God as all-powerful. He is the God without equal (Ps. 89:8) who is present with his people (Ps. 46:7,11). See *Names of God.*

SABBATH Day of rest, considered holy to God because of his rest on the seventh day after creation and viewed as a sign of the covenant relation between God and his people. The day became a time for sacred assembly and worship (Lev. 23:1-3), a token of Israel's covenant with God (Exod. 31:1217). Jesus's failure to comply with the minute restrictions of the Pharisees about the Sabbath brought conflict (John 5:1-18). At first, Christians also met on the Sabbath with the Jews in the synagogues to proclaim Christ (Acts 13:14). Their holy day, the day that belonged especially to the Lord, was the first day of the week, the day of Jesus's resurrection (Rev. 1:10). They viewed the Sabbath and other matters of the law as a shadow of the reality that had now been revealed (Col. 2:16-23), and the Sabbath became a symbol of the heavenly rest to come (Heb. 4:1-11). See *Lord's Day.*

SABBATH DAY'S JOURNEY Distance a Jew in Jesus's day could walk on the Sabbath without violating its sanctity. The distance was probably just over one-half mile. This phrase appears only once in the Bible (Acts 1:12), describing the distance from the Mount of Olives to Jerusalem.

SABBATICAL YEAR Every seventh year when farmers rested their land from bearing crops to renew the soil (Lev. 25:1-7). Just as the law reserved the seventh day as holy to God, so was the seventh year set aside as a time of rest and renewal. This assured the continued fertility of the land by allowing it to lie fallow, and it also helped the poor. Peasants were allowed to eat from the natural abundance of the untended fields. It is possible that only a portion of the land was allowed to rest each Sabbath year, and the remainder was farmed as usual.

SABEAN Two Hebrew national names. **1.** Descendants of Seba, son of Cush (Gen. 10:7), who were expected to bring gifts signifying loyalty to Jerusalem (Isa. 45:14). God could use the Sabeans to "pay for" Israel's ransom from captivity (Isa. 43:3). **2.** Descendants of Sheba, the son of Raamah (Gen. 10:7b) or Joktan (Gen. 10:28). The rich queen of Sheba visited Solomon (1 Kgs. 10). Sabeans destroyed Job's flocks and herds and servants (Job 1:15).

SACKBUT A musical instrument (Dan. 3:5 KJV), identified in modern translations as zither (TEV), lyre (CSB, NIV), trigon (NASB, NRSV), or triangle (REB). It was apparently a triangular harp with four or more strings.

SACKCLOTH Garment of coarse material fashioned from goat or camel hair and worn as a sign of mourning or anguish (Isa. 58:5). See *Grief and Mourning.*

SACRAMENT Religious rite or ceremony regarded as an outward sign of an inward, spiritual grace. The Roman Catholic Church practices seven sacraments: confirmation, penance, ordination, marriage, last rites, baptism, and the Eucharist. Protestant churches recognize only two: baptism and the Lord's Supper, and these are generally referred to as ordinances rather than sacraments. Unlike sacraments, ordinances are not understood to convey some type of grace. They commemorate the death, burial, and resurrection of Christ. The ordinance of baptism is a believer's public profession of faith and serves as an initiatory rite of entrance into the community of faith. The Lord's Supper denotes a believer's continuing commitment to Christ. The idea that outward signs show spiritual realities is taught in the Bible, but the notion that sacraments convey grace is contrary to Scripture. Grace comes through faith, not works (Rom. 4:3).

SACRIFICE AND OFFERING Physical elements the worshiper brings to God to express devotion, thanksgiving, or the need for forgiveness. Sacrifice was practiced in early OT times. Cain and Abel brought offerings to the Lord from the produce of the land and from the firstborn of the flock (Gen. 4). Upon disembarking from the ark after the great flood, Noah built an altar and offered burnt sacrifices (Gen 8:20). The accounts of the patriarchs in Gen. 12–50 are filled with instances of sacrifice to God. But an organized system of sacrifice does not appear in the OT until after the exodus of Israel from Egypt. In the instructions given for the building of the tabernacle and the establishment of a priestly organization, sacrifices were to be used in the consecration or ordination of the priests (Exod. 29). Leviticus 1–7 gives the most detailed description of Israel's sacrificial system, including five types of sacrifices.

Burnt offering This sacrifice was offered in the morning and in the evening, as well as on special days such as the Sabbath, the new moon, and the yearly feasts (Ezra 3:3-6). Rituals performed after childbirth (Lev. 12:6-8), for an unclean discharge (Lev. 15:14-15) or hemorrhage (Lev. 15:29-30), or after a person who was keeping a Nazirite vow was defiled (Num. 6:10-11) required a burnt offering. The animal for this sacrifice could be a young bull, lamb, goat, turtledove, or young pigeon. The person bringing the offering was to lay a hand on the animal, indicating that the animal was taking the person's place, and then he was to kill it. Then the priest burned the animal as a sacrifice. The person who made this sacrifice did so to restore his relationship with God and to atone for his sin.

Grain offering ("meat offering," KJV) This sacrifice came from the harvest of the land, and it was the only offering that required no bloodshed. It was composed of fine flour mixed with oil and frankincense. Sometimes it was cooked into cakes before it was taken to the priest. Only a portion of this offering was burned on the altar, with the remainder going to the priests. While no reason is given for the grain offering, it may have recognized the blessings of God, who provided the harvest for the sustenance of life.

Peace offering This sacrifice consisted of a bull, cow, lamb, or goat that had no defect. As with the burnt offering, the worshiper killed the animal. The priests then sprinkled its blood around the altar. Only certain parts of the internal organs were burned. The priest received the breast and the right thigh (Lev. 7:28-36), but the person who offered the sacrifice was given much of the meat to prepare as a meal of celebration (Lev. 7:11-21). A peace offering was to be brought in response to an unexpected blessing (a "thank offering") or an answer to prayer (a "vow offering"), or for general thankfulness (a "freewill offering"). The idea of thanksgiving was associated with the peace offering. The "wave offerings" and the "heave offerings" were associated with the peace offerings. They were portions presented or lifted up before the Lord, mentioned first as part of the priestly ordination ceremony (Exod. 29:24-27).

Sin offering This sacrifice was made to purify the sanctuary from sin that had been committed unintentionally. If the priest or the congregation of Israel sinned, then a bull was required. A leader of the people had to bring a male goat, while anyone else sacrificed a female goat or a lamb. The poor were allowed to bring two turtledoves or two young pigeons. The same internal organs that were designated for burning in the peace offering were likewise designated in this sacrifice. The rest of the animal was taken outside the camp and burned.

Guilt offering This offering was concerned with restitution. It seems to overlap or relate to the sin offering (Lev. 4–5). In Lev. 5:6-7, the guilt offering is called a sin offering. A person who took another's property illegally was expected to repay it in full plus 20 percent of the value and then bring a ram for the guilt offering. Other instances in which the guilt offering was prescribed included the cleansing of a leper (Lev. 14), having sexual relations with the female slave of another person (Lev. 19:20-22), and the renewing of a Nazirite vow that had been broken (Num. 6:11-12).

The NT describes Christ's death in sacrificial terms. Christ is portrayed as the sinless high priest who offered himself up as a sacrifice for sinners (Heb. 7:27). Christ's sacrifice is superior to the Levitical system because his sacrifice—his death—had to be offered only once.

SADDUCEES See *Jewish Parties in the New Testament.*

SAINTS Holy people, a title for all God's people but applied in some contexts to a small group considered most dedicated to him. In the OT, to be holy is to separate oneself from evil and to dedicate oneself to God. This separation reflects God's character, since he is holy (Lev. 19:2). Holiness is portrayed as an encounter with the living God, which results in holiness of lifestyle (Isa. 6). Therefore, holiness is more than a one-time separating and uniting activity. It is a way of life (Dan. 7:18-28).

In the NT, saints are believers in Christ, or those who name Jesus as Lord. In the book of Revelation, however, where the word "saints" occurs 13 times, the meaning is further defined. Saints not only name Jesus as Lord, but they are faithful and true witnesses for Jesus. To believe in Jesus demands obedience and conformity to his will. A saint bears true and faithful witness to Christ in speech and lifestyle.

SALAMIS Most important city on the island of Cyprus where Barnabas and Paul preached during the first missionary journey (Acts 13:5). See *Cyprus.*

SALEM Abbreviated form of Jerusalem (Gen. 14:18). See *Jerusalem; Melchizedek.*

SALIM Place-name meaning "peace." Town near the site where John the Baptist baptized (John 3:23).

SALMON Personal and place-name meaning "coat." **1.** Father of Boaz and ancestor of David (Ruth 4:21; Matt. 1:5). **2.** KJV spelling of Zalmon (Ps. 68:14).

SALOME Personal name meaning "pacific." Wife of Zebedee and mother of James and John (if one combines Mark 16:1 and Matt. 27:56). She became a disciple of Jesus and was among the women at the crucifixion who helped prepare his body for burial.

SALUTATION Act of greeting, blessing, or welcoming by gestures or words, especially in the opening and closing of letters. The typical greeting in Greek letters was the infinitive "to rejoice." Paul fused the Greek word for the typical Hebrew blessing, "Peace," with the noun form of the Greek blessing, "Grace," to yield the distinctly Christian salutation, "Grace and peace." This salutation invoked mercy from God ("grace") and eternal well-being from God's presence ("peace").

SALVATION Rescue from sin and death. The need for salvation is demonstrated in the first three chapters of the Bible. Adam and Eve disobeyed God in the garden of Eden. Sin entered into God's created order, but God promised salvation through the seed of the woman (Gen. 3:15). Even though male and female were created in the image of God, now God's image was marred in all humankind. The results of sin included death and separation from God.

In the NT, salvation by grace alone through faith in the person and work of Jesus Christ is the dominant theme. Salvation begins with the initiating love of God (Eph. 1:3-6). God's eternal purpose is to save sinners through Jesus's atoning death on the cross. Thus, Christology is a vital component of the NT and relates directly to the doctrine of salvation. Jesus's nature as the God-man and his substitutionary death on the cross are the key elements of salvation.

The NT identifies several other key doctrines or elements as part of a complete concept of salvation. The Holy Spirit convicts a person of sin and brings about the new birth. "Conversion" is the term generally used to describe when a person actually receives salvation. This is the point when a person repents and believes. Faith and repentance are the conditions of salvation, according to the NT (Mark 1:15). Repentance means turning from self and sin to God and holiness while faith is believing the historic facts about Jesus and trusting him alone to forgive sin and to grant eternal life (Heb. 11:1-6).

At the moment of conversion, the sinner becomes a saint, not free from sin in this life but free from the death penalty brought on by sin. A lifelong process of growth in Christlikeness called "sanctification" through the work of the Holy Spirit now begins. Thus, salvation is a free gift from God that rescues the believer from sin and its consequences, renews the believer to a holy life, and restores the believer to a right relationship with God for all eternity. See *Conversion; Forgiveness; Grace; Justification; New Birth; Reconciliation; Redeem, Redemption, Redeemer; Repentance; Sanctification.*

Long colonnaded street built by the emperor Severus at New Testament Sebaste, which was the Old Testament city of Samaria

SAMARIA, SAMARITANS Place-name of a city and a region meaning "mountain of watching" and the residents of this region. The city of Samaria was founded by Omri, the sixth king of Israel (885–874 BC), when he purchased the hill of Samaria for his royal residence. The name of this city eventually became associated with the surrounding region, or the tribal territories of Manasseh and Ephraim. Finally, "Samaria" became synonymous with the entire northern kingdom (Jer. 31:5).

The name "Samaritans" originally was identified with the Israelites of the northern kingdom (2 Kgs. 17:29). When the Assyrians conquered Israel and exiled 27,290 Israelites, a "remnant of Israel" remained in the land. Assyrian captives from distant places also settled there (2 Kgs. 17:24). This led to the intermarriage of Jews of this region with Gentiles and to widespread worship of foreign gods. In the days of Christ, the relationship between the Jews and the Samaritans—whom the Jews considered half breeds and idol worshipers—was strained (John 8:48). The animosity was so great that the Jews bypassed Samaria as they traveled between Galilee and Judea.

Yet Jesus rebuked his disciples for their hostility to the Samaritans (Luke 9:55-56), healed a Samaritan leper (Luke 17:16), honored a Samaritan for his neighborliness (Luke 10:30-37), praised a Samaritan for his gratitude (Luke 17:11-18), asked for a drink of water from a Samaritan woman (John 4:7), and preached to the Samaritans (John 4:40-42). Then in Acts 1:8, Jesus challenged his disciples to witness in Samaria. Philip, a deacon, opened a mission in Samaria (Acts 8:5).

SAMARITAN PENTATEUCH Canon or "Bible" of the Samaritans, who revere the Torah as God's revelation to Moses on Mount Sinai and do not regard the rest of the Hebrew Bible as authoritative. Their Scripture includes Genesis through Deuteronomy with many variant readings from the Masoretic Text or Hebrew text currently used by scholars.

Samaritan priests with a copy of their Scripture—the Samaritan Pentateuch

SAMOS An island of Greece visited by the apostle Paul (Acts 20:15).

SAMOTHRACE or **SAMOTHRACIA** Place-name, perhaps meaning "height of Thrace." Mountainous island in the Aegean

Sea visited by the apostle Paul during his second missionary journey (Acts 16:11).

SAMSON Personal name meaning "of the sun." Last of the major judges of Israel about 1100 BC (Judg. 13:1–16:31). Before he was born Samson was dedicated by his parents to be a lifelong Nazirite (Judg. 13:3-7), a person especially consecrated to the Lord. Part of the vow included letting the hair grow and abstaining from wine and strong drink. Samson's legendary strength did not come from his long hair but from the "Spirit of the LORD," who enabled him to perform amazing feats of physical strength against the Philistines, enemies of Israel (Judg. 14:6,19; 15:14).

Samson was a headstrong young man with little self-control who failed to live up to his Nazirite vow. Every major crisis in his life was brought on by his relationships with Philistine women. Samson's fascination with Delilah finally brought his downfall. The Philistine leaders offered her money to find out the source of Samson's strength. She finally coaxed the truth from him, and Samson was captured by his enemies. In his death, Samson killed more Philistines than he had killed during his life (Judg. 16:30). He is listed with the heroes of faith in Heb. 11:32, because his strength came from God and he demonstrated his faith in his dying act.

SAMUEL Personal name meaning "name of God." Priest and prophet who linked the period of the judges with the monarchy (about 1066–1000 BC). Born in answer to his barren mother's prayer (1 Sam. 1:10), Samuel was dedicated to the Lord before his birth (1 Sam. 1:11). The priest Eli raised Samuel at the central sanctuary in Shiloh (1 Sam. 2:11). The sins of Eli's sons and the Philistine threat led the elders of Israel to appeal to Samuel to appoint a king for the nation (1 Sam. 8:3,5,20). Samuel warned Israel of the dangers of a monarchy before anointing Saul as Israel's first king (1 Sam. 10:1). Samuel's recording of the rights and duties of kingship (1 Sam. 10:25) set the stage for later prophets to call their monarchs to task for their disobedience of God's commands.

King Saul's stubbornness and disobedience brought Samuel's declaration of God's rejection of his kingship. At God's command, Samuel anointed David as the new king (1 Sam. 16:13). Samuel's death brought national mourning (1 Sam. 25:1; 28:3), and it also left Saul without access to God's word. In desperation, he acknowledged Samuel's power and influence by seeking to commune with Samuel's spirit (1 Sam. 28). Thus in life and death, Samuel cast a long shadow over Israel and its early experience with an earthly king.

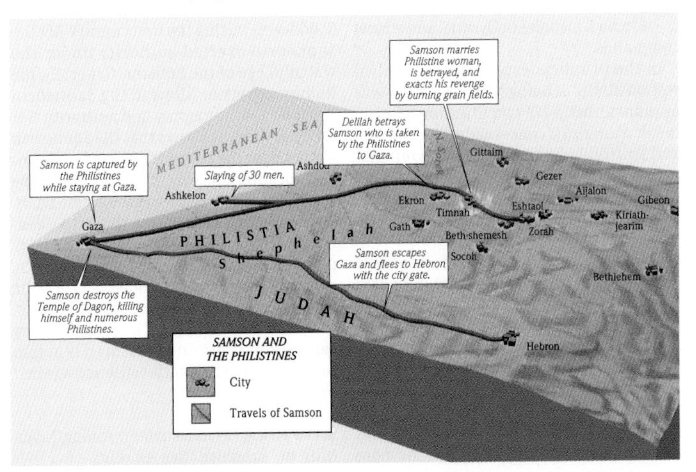

SAMUEL, BOOKS OF Two historical books of the OT named for the prophet Samuel, the major figure of its opening section. Samuel anointed King Saul as the first king of the nation of Israel and then later anointed David to the same position when Saul proved unworthy. Thus the books detail the transition of the nation from a loose confederation of tribes to a united kingdom under the leadership of a human king.

SANBALLAT Governor of Samaria around 407 BC who, along with Tobiah and Shemaiah, opposed Nehemiah's rebuilding of Jerusalem (Neh. 4:7-8; 6:1-4).

SANCTIFICATION Process of being made holy and growing into the likeness of Jesus Christ. The idea behind the word is to stand in awe of something or someone. God is separate, or holy, and people dedicated to him are also to be separate from the world and to reflect his holy nature. In the OT, the priests and Levites who functioned in the sanctuary were sanctified to the Lord by the anointing of oil (Exod. 40:12-15). Additionally, the Nazirite was consecrated to God (Num. 6:8), although only for a specified period of time. Finally, the nation of Israel was sanctified to the Lord as a holy people (Deut. 26:19). This holiness was closely identified with obedience to the law of holiness in Lev. 17–26, which includes both ritual and ethical commands.

In the prophets especially, the ethical responsibility of being holy in conduct was prominent. In the NT, sanctification is linked to salvation and is concerned with the moral and spiritual obligations assumed in that experience. Believers are set apart to God in conversion, and they live out this dedication to God in holiness (2 Thess. 2:13).

SANCTUARY Place set aside as sacred and holy, especially a place of worship. On sites where the patriarchs had erected altars, the people of Israel later built shrines and temples to commemorate their encounters with God. The tabernacle and the temple in Jerusalem were revered as sanctuaries.

SANDALS, SHOES Two types of shoes existed: slippers of soft leather and the more popular sandals with a hard leather sole. Thongs secured the sandal across the insole and between the toes. The removal of the sandals of guests and the washing of their dusty feet was the job of the lowliest servant. The prophet Isaiah walked barefooted to symbolize the impending poverty of Israel before the judgment of God (Isa. 20:2). See *Footwashing*.

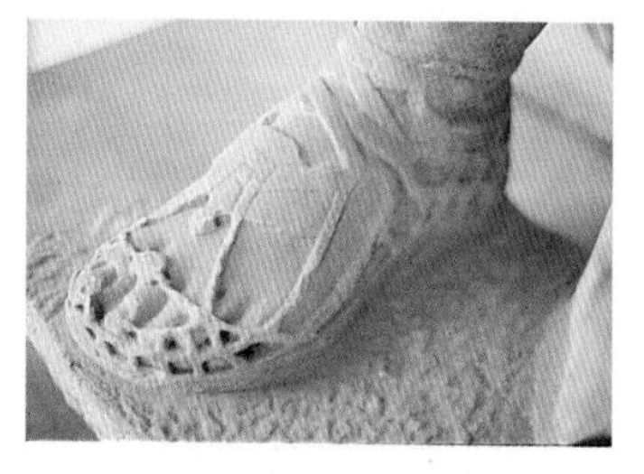

The sandaled foot on a Roman statue

SANHEDRIN Highest Jewish council in NT times. The word "Sanhedrin" is usually rendered "council" in English translations of the Bible. The council had 71 members and was presided over by the high priest. The Sanhedrin included representatives from the two main Jewish parties, Pharisees and Sadducees. During the first century AD, the Sanhedrin exerted authority under the watchful eye of the Romans. Generally, the Roman governor allowed the Sanhedrin considerable autonomy and authority. But the trial of Jesus shows that the Sanhedrin did not have the authority to condemn people to death (John 18:31). The Gospels describe the role of the Sanhedrin in the arrest, trials, and condemnation of Jesus. Under the leadership of Caiaphas the high priest, this body plotted to have Jesus killed (John 11:47-53). After his arrest, they brought Jesus into the council (Luke 22:66) and used false witnesses to condemn him (Mark 14:55-56). They sent him to Pilate and pressured him into pronouncing the death sentence against Jesus (Mark 15:1-15).

SAPPHIRA Personal name meaning "beautiful" or "sapphire." See *Ananias*.

SARA or **SARAH** Variant Hebrew form of the name Sarai. See *Sarai*.

SARAI Personal name meaning "princess." Wife of Abraham (Gen. 11:29–25:10) who was barren for many years before giving birth to Isaac. First called Sarai, she was Abraham's half sister, since she had the same father as Abraham. Marriages with half brothers were not uncommon in her time. Sarai traveled with Abraham from Ur to Haran. In her grief over her barrenness, Sarai gave her maid Hagar to Abraham in the hope of an heir; but she expressed resentment when Hagar conceived. When Sarai was almost 90 years old, God changed her name to Sarah and promised her a son. A year later, she bore Isaac. At the age of 127, Sarah died at Hebron, where she was buried in the cave in the field of Machpelah near Mamre.

SARDIS City of Asia Minor where one of the seven churches addressed in Rev. 3:1-6 was located. The church was condemned as being "dead," perhaps a reference to its ineffectiveness as a witness in the world.

SARGON King of Assyria who destroyed Samaria and deported the people of Israel to Media and other parts of the Middle East. He was succeeded by his son, Sennacherib.

SATAN Transliteration of Hebrew word meaning "adversary." The Hebrew term appears in Num. 22:22,32; 1 Sam. 29:4; 2 Sam. 19:22; 1 Kgs. 5:4; 11:14,23,25; Ps. 109:6, normally translated in English as adversary or accuser. In Job 1–2; Zech. 3:2; and 1 Chron. 21:1, the same term is translated as a proper name.

SATAN, SYNAGOGUE OF Term used in Revelation (2:9; 3:9) to describe Jewish worshipers who persecuted the church.

SATRAP, SATRAPY Political official who governed a province of the Persian Empire. A satrap's territory was called a satrapy (Ezra 8:36). These officials aided the people of Israel in rebuilding Jerusalem and the temple. See *Persia*.

SATYR Hairy, demonic figure with the appearance of a goat. The Israelites apparently sacrificed to such desert-dwelling demons, although they had a law forbidding such sacrifice (Lev. 17:7). King Jeroboam I of Israel (926–909 BC) appointed priests to serve these demons (2 Chron. 11:15).

Ruins of the Roman gymnasium at the ancient city of Sardis in Asia Minor (modern Turkey)

SAUL Personal name meaning "asked for." **1.** First king of Israel who reigned about 1020–1000 BC. Saul got off to a good start, but his presumptuous offering (1 Sam. 13:8-14) and violation of a holy war ban led to his break with Samuel and rejection by God (1 Sam. 15:7-23). The Spirit of the Lord left Saul and was replaced by an evil spirit that tormented him. David soothed the king by playing the lyre (1 Sam. 16:14-23). After David defeated the giant Goliath, Saul became jealous and fearful of David (1 Sam. 18:6-9,12), eventually making several attempts on his life (1 Sam. 18:10-11,25; 19:1,9-11). His final wretched condition is betrayed by his consultation of the witch at En-dor (28:7-8). The following day Saul and three sons were killed by the Philistines on Mount Gilboa (1 Sam. 31). **2.** King of Edom (Gen. 36:37-38). **3.** Son of Simeon (Gen. 46:10). **4.** Kohathite Levite (1 Chron. 6:24). **5.** Hebrew name of the apostle Paul. See *Paul.*

SAVIOR One who saves by delivering, preserving, healing, or providing (2 Sam. 22:2-7). God is the only true Savior (Isa. 45:15,21-22). Jesus is also the Savior because he is God incarnate, fully human and fully divine.

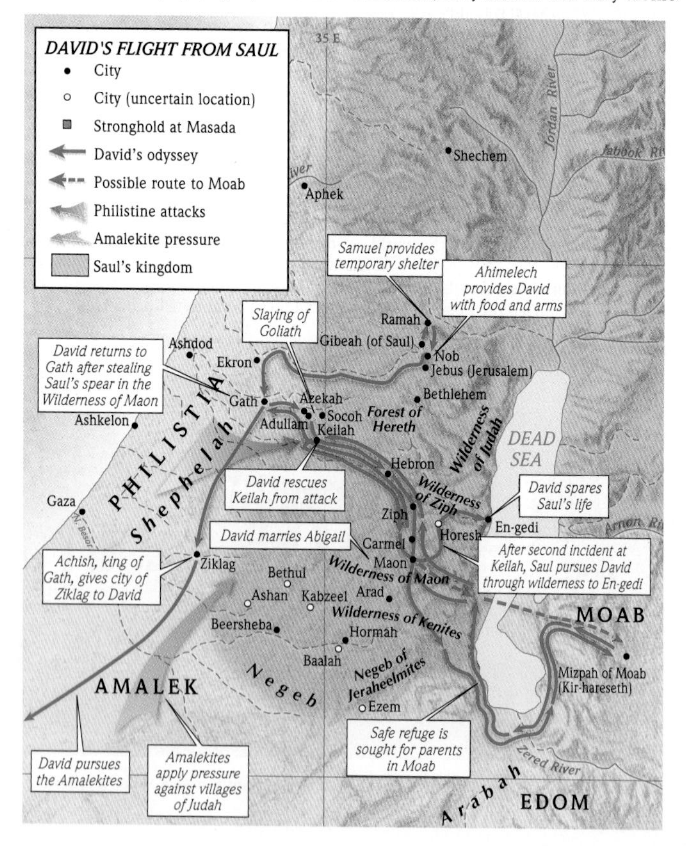

Sunset over the site of ancient Azekah near the location of a battle between Saul and the Philistines

Christianity is unique among world religions because it portrays salvation by the grace of a savior.

SCALL KJV term for a skin disease (Lev. 14:54). The disease caused head sores, itching, and hair thinning. Modern translations render this word as "scale" or "itch."

SCAPEGOAT Animal that carried away the sins of the people into the wilderness on the Day of Atonement (Lev. 16:8,10,26). On this one day of the year when the high priest went into the holy of holies to offer sacrifices for the sins of his family and for all the people, two goats were brought before him. One goat was killed as a sin offering, and the second was designated for "Azazel." This word is usually rendered as "scapegoat." By laying his hands on the goat's head, the priest transferred the sins of the people to it and then had the goat led away into the desert to symbolize the removal of their sins.

SCARLET Color used especially in clothing, often designating royal honor (Dan. 5:7,16,29).

SCEPTER Official staff or baton of a king that symbolized his authority. The scepter was extended to a visitor or dignitary (Esth. 5:2) to signal approval of the visit and allow the person to approach the throne.

SCEVA Jewish "high priest" in Ephesus with seven sons who tried unsuccessfully to exorcise demons in Jesus' sname as Paul had done (Acts 19:14). The evil spirit jumped on them instead.

SCHOOL Place and agency for education, particularly of children. Until the exile in Babylon (586 BC), the education of children was centered in the home. During their years of captivity, the exiles assembled on the Sabbath for prayer and worship. As time went by, buildings were erected where the people could meet. These little gatherings were the origin of the synagogue, which ultimately became the center of Jewish religious life after the exile. In the synagogue, the scribes taught the law to the people. By AD 200, a school specifically for the education of elementary-age children had become firmly established in the synagogue. Known as Beth-hasepher, the "house of the book," this school was devoted to study of the Jewish written law. Knowledge of the written word, in school as in the home, had the religious goal of bringing about obedience to the law.

SCORN, SCORNFUL Contempt and derision. Scorn is often expressed by laughter (2 Chron. 30:10). In deep trouble, psalmists often felt themselves scorned (Ps. 123:4). When his people are unfaithful to him, God can scorn them and their worship (Lam. 2:7).

SCORPION Small invertebrate animal known for the venom and sting in its tail. In the wilderness, God protected Israel from scorpions (Deut. 8:15).

SCOURGE Severe form of corporal punishment involving whipping and beating. The victim was usually tied to a post or bench, and the beating was administered by a servant of the synagogue (if for religious reasons) or by a slave or soldier. Jesus was scourged before his crucifixion (John 19:1).

SCRIBE Person trained in writing skills (1 Chron. 24:6). During the exile in Babylon, educated scribes apparently became the experts in God's written word, copying, preserving, and teaching the law. A professional group of such scribes developed by NT times (Mark 2:16). They interpreted the law, taught it to disciples, and were experts in cases where people were accused of breaking the law of Moses. They led in plans to kill Jesus (Luke 19:47). See *Jewish Parties in the New Testament.*

SCRIPTURE Sacred writings considered God's instruction for believers. New Testament writers often used formulas like "God says" to introduce OT passages. For the NT authors, Scripture was the record of God speaking and revealing himself to his people. Thus Scripture and God are so closely joined together that these writers could speak of Scripture doing what it records God as doing (Rom. 9:17). Because of their belief in the Scripture's divine origin and content, the NT writers described it as "strongly confirmed" (2 Pet. 1:19 CSB), "deserving of full acceptance" (1 Tim. 1:15), and "confirmed" (Heb. 2:3). The Bible was written for "instruction" and "encouragement" (Rom. 15:4), to guide people toward godliness (2 Tim. 3:16), and to equip believers for good works (2 Tim. 3:17).

Scripture, composed of 66 books, written by more than 40 authors spanning almost 1,500 years, reveals to God's people the unifying history of his redeeming words and acts. The ultimate focus of Scripture is the incarnation and redemptive work of Jesus Christ. He is the center to which everything in Scripture is united and bound together. See *Bible, Formation and Canon; Inspiration of Scripture.*

A Torah scroll being held in its wooden case at a celebration in Jerusalem

SCROLL Roll of papyrus (a paper-like material made of the papyrus plant) or parchment (specially treated leather) used as a writing material (Luke 4:17).

Dead Sea Scroll fragment

SCYTHIANS Nomadic, Indo-European people, referred to in the OT as Ashchenaz (Gen. 10:3).

SEA COW Aquatic herbivorous mammal related to the manatee whose skin is mentioned as a covering for the tabernacle (Exod. 25:5).

SEAL Signet containing a distinctive mark that represented the authority of the person who owned it. Joseph was given the Egyptian pharaoh's ring with his royal stamp of authority, or seal, when Joseph was placed in command of the country (Gen. 41:42). This showed that Joseph had the right to act for the king.

North Syrian and Hittite stamp-type seals

SECOND COMING Biblical teaching that Christ will return visibly and bodily to the earth to render judgment and complete his redemptive plan. The concept of the second coming originally derived from the OT teachings about a coming Messiah. The prophets foretold the Lord would send One from within the nation of Israel (Jer. 23:56) who would not only be God's anointed, but would in fact be God himself (Mic. 5:2). The NT clearly distinguishes between two comings of Jesus Christ, the Messiah: the first in the incarnation and the second at the end of this present age. The earliest instructions of this second coming are recounted in the Gospels where Christ himself explicitly claimed he would come again. He urged people to be prepared because he would come unexpectedly, like a thief (Luke 21:34-36). He also promised to return in order to claim his people and reward them (Matt. 25:31-46).

Later, other NT writers expanded Christ's teachings. They taught that he would come in glory to judge unbelievers, Satan, and even the earth itself (Rev. 19:20–20:3). Likewise, he would come in the heavens to gather all believers to himself by resurrecting the dead, catching them up along with the living into the air to meet him on his return, and then reward them for their faithfulness (1 Thess. 4:13-17). Because the second coming promised both vindication and salvation, it was a motivation for godly living and became the blessed hope of the early church (1 John 3:2-3).

SECOND DEATH Eternal separation from God. The concept is referred to in Rev. 2:11; 20:6,14; and 21:8. According to Rev. 20:15, it includes being "thrown into the lake of fire. See *Death; Resurrection*.

SECT Group having established their own identity and teachings over against the larger group to which they belong, especially the different parties making up Judaism in NT times.

SECUNDUS Personal name meaning "second." A believer who accompanied Paul when he carried the churches' contributions to the Jerusalem church (Acts 20:4).

SECURITY OF THE BELIEVER Teaching that God protects believers for the completion of their salvation. The Bible teaches that salvation does not depend upon human effort. God is the author of salvation (John 3:16). God justifies sinners who receive Christ in faith (Rom. 3:21-26). Security does not come by absolutions, church attendance, good works, reciting Scripture, or performances of penance. God who has begun the work of salvation in Christians also provides the necessary assurance to bring his work to its completion in the day of Christ (Phil. 1:6). God in Christ protects and keeps believers (2 Thess. 3:3). We do not have the strength to secure ourselves.

The biblical view of assurance or security is rooted in the conviction that when Jesus left the disciples, he did not leave them without support. He promised Christians that he would provide them with a companion Spirit (the Comforter or Paraclete) who would be within them—as much a part of them as their breath (John 14:16-18). The Spirit would be their sense of peace and security, their witness about Jesus, their attorney with the world, and their guide or teacher into all truth (John 14:25-30; 16:8-15).

In raising his Son Jesus, God provided Christians with the sign of the destinies and the basis for their security. As we identify with the power of Christ in the resurrection, we will experience the meaning of the security of the believer in the triumph of God (1 Cor. 15:20-28).

SEIR, MOUNT Place-name meaning "hairy" and thus "thicket." A mountain range that runs the length of biblical Edom. This region was home to Esau and his descendants (Josh. 24:4). Edom was sometimes referred to as Seir (Gen. 36:8). See *Edom*.

SELAH Term of unknown meaning appearing in psalms, outside the book of Psalms only in Hab. 3. The word probably called for a pause or an intensification of instruments or voices in worship.

SELEUCIA A city of Syria visited by Paul during his first missionary journey (Acts 13:4).

SELF-CONTROL Mastery of personal desires and passions. Believers are admonished to exercise self-control (2 Pet. 1:6). Freedom in Christ calls for a self-disciplined life, following Christ's example of being in the world but not of the world.

SELF-ESTEEM Acceptance of oneself as a person created in the divine image. Every person is of great value to God (1 Cor. 6:20) and supremely loved by him (1 John 4:10). Christians have a new nature that allows them to be self-confident, but only through Christ (2 Cor. 3:5). Paul taught that Christians should strive for a balanced self-esteem that enables them to minister to the needs of others (Rom. 12:3).

SELF-WILLED To do something arbitrarily without divine permission; to act on one's own decision rather than considering the needs of others and the purpose of God. Jacob rebuked Simeon and Levi for wanton, undisciplined actions (Gen. 49:6).

SEMITE A person who claims descent from Noah's son Shem (Gen. 5:32; 10:21-31). Genesis 10:21-31 lists the descendants of Shem. These people spread geographically from Lydia to Syria, to Assyria, to Persia. Armenia formed the northern boundary while the Red Sea and Persian Gulf formed the southern boundary. The Elamites, Assyrians, Lydians, Arameans, and numerous Arab tribes are said to have been descendants of Shem.

SENIR Mountain name meaning "pointed." Amorite name for Mount Hermon (Deut. 3:9). Song of Songs 4:8 may indicate that Senir was a different peak than Hermon in the Anti-Lebanon mountain range or that it indicated the entire range. See *Hermon, Mount*.

SENNACHERIB Assyrian royal name meaning "Sin (the god) has replaced my brother." King of Assyria (704–681 BC) who overran all the fortified cities of Judah except Jerusalem and then demanded tribute payments from King Hezekiah of Judah (2 Kgs. 18:13-16). See *Assyria*.

Ahab's palace in Samaria. Sennacherib conquered Samaria in 722 BC.

SENTRY Governmental official with responsibility for guarding a prison (Acts 5:23; 12:6) or possibly a captain over such a guard (Jer. 37:13).

SEPARATION Term used for the period when a woman is ritually unclean during menstruation (Lev. 12:2,5) or for a time of refraining from certain activities because of a vow (Num. 6). KJV term (water of separation) for water used to make a person ritually pure or clean (Num. 19).

SEPHARVAIM Racial name of foreign origin. Foreign peoples whom the Assyrians conquered and resettled in Israel to replace the Israelites they deported in 722 BC (2 Kgs. 17:24).

SEPTUAGINT Title meaning "the 70." Oldest Greek translation of the Hebrew OT. It also contains several apocryphal books. Most NT quotations of the OT are from the Septuagint, often abbreviated as LXX.

SEPULCHRE Tomb or grave (Gen. 23:6). Sepulchres usually were carved out of the walls in natural caves. Jesus was buried in such a cave (Mark 15:46).

SERAPHIM Literally "the burning ones," seraphim (a plural word) were winged beings who attended God's throne. Isaiah envisioned the seraphim as agents of God who prepared him to proclaim the Lord's message (Isa. 6:2).

SERGIUS PAULUS Proconsul of the island of Cyprus converted to Christ under the preaching of Paul during his first missionary journey (Acts 13:6-12).

SERMON ON THE MOUNT The first of five major discourses by Jesus in the Gospel of Matthew (Matt. 5–7). An exposition of the law and how it meshes with the new covenant in Christ, the sermon also offers a stinging indictment of Pharisaic legalism and cold, formal self-righteousness. Jesus emphasizes his demands for disciples and issues a call to demonstrate a righteousness of heart that the law cannot produce.

The sermon opens with the beatitudes (Matt. 5:3-12) and then moves to describe the witness Christ's disciples are to bear in the world (5:13-16). Jesus's relationship to and interpretation of the law follows (5:17-48); then he enumerates some specific acts of righteousness—including the model prayer (6:1-18). The heart attitudes Jesus requires of his disciples comes next (6:19–7:12), and the sermon closes with a challenge to live as true disciples (7:13-27). Jesus addressed his Sermon on the Mount primarily to his disciples, but the rest of the crowd heard it with interest. They marveled at his teaching because, unlike their teachers of the law, he spoke with authority (Matt. 7:28-29).

SERPENT English translation of several biblical words for "snake," a symbol of evil and Satan. God gave Moses a sign showing God's control of the feared serpents (Exod. 4:3; 7:9-10). Jesus accused the Pharisees of being as evil and deadly as serpents (Matt. 23:33).

SERVANT OF THE LORD Title Jesus took up from the OT, especially Isa. 40–55. The term is applied to many leaders of God's people: to Moses more than 30 times, to David more than 70 times, and to Israel as a nation a number of times. Isaiah 42 gives a remarkable picture of the ideal Servant of the Lord and the great work that God intends him to accomplish. He is to bring God's justice to all the nations (vv. 1,4). He will move forward with absolute confidence. He will

Sea of Galilee at Nof Ginnosar looking across the Sea to the Mount of Beatitudes, traditional site of the Sermon on the Mount

have such an understanding of his power that he can be meek and gentle as he does his work (vv. 2-4).

The Lord himself called attention to the inability of the nation of Israel to fulfill the picture of the ideal Servant. In Isa. 42:19, he says, "Who is blind but my servant, or deaf like my messenger I am sending?" (CSB). Israel had a responsibility to fulfill this ideal, but to do so was far beyond its power. Perhaps not all Israel could be meant, because some were blasphemers and idolaters. Could part of Israel be the real Servant? Or might it point to One who must come out of Israel—One who could represent Israel in accomplishing the task?

The NT pictures Jesus as the Suffering Servant fulfilling the glorious descriptions of Isaiah. In refusing to let disciples reveal his true identity, Jesus was the Servant who did not strive or cry out (Matt. 12:14-21). In the resurrection and ascension, God glorified Jesus the Servant (Acts 3:13). The apostles prayed that as God's servants they would speak with boldness and perform miracles through the name of "your holy servant Jesus" (Acts 4:29-30). See *Jesus Christ; Slave, Servant.*

SERVICE Work done for other people or for God and the worship of God. Jacob worked for Laban seven years for each of his wives (Gen. 29:15-30). Service could be slave labor (Exod. 5:11), farm work (1 Chron. 27:26), or daily labor on the job (Ps. 104:23). It could be service of earthly kingdoms (2 Chron. 12:8), of God's place of worship (Exod. 30:16), of God's ministers (Ezra 8:20), and of God (Josh. 22:27). Service at its best is worship. This involves the service of temple vessels (1 Chron. 9:28), of worship actions (2 Chron. 35:10), of bringing offerings (Josh. 22:27), and of priestly work (Num. 8:11). The NT speaks of forced service (Matt. 27:32), sacrificial living (Rom. 12:1), slave labor done for Christ's sake (Eph. 6:7), worship (Heb. 12:28), offerings (Rom. 15:31), and personal ministry (1 Tim. 1:12).

SETH Personal name meaning "he set or appointed" or "replacement." Third son of Adam and Eve, born after Cain murdered Abel (Gen. 4:25; 5:3). He was an ancestor of Jesus (Luke 3:38).

SEVEN CHURCHES OF ASIA Original recipients of book of Revelation (Rev. 1:4). See *Asia Minor, Cities of.*

SEVEN WORDS FROM THE CROSS Statements that Jesus made during the six agonizing hours of his crucifixion. (1) He asked forgiveness for those who crucified him (Luke 23:34). (2) He promised the penitent thief he would meet the Lord in paradise that very day (Luke 23:43). (3) He made provision for the care of his mother by the apostle John (John 19:26-27). (4) His fourth statement was a cry of isolation, quoting Ps. 22:1 (Mark 15:34). (5) His physical agony was expressed in the fifth statement, when he acknowledged his thirst (John 19:28). (6) "It is finished" (John 19:30) was a cry of victory, not defeat. (7) Jesus quoted Ps. 31:5 as he committed his spirit to God (Luke 23:46).

SEVEN, SEVENTH Number of completeness. See *Number Systems and Number Symbolism.*

SEVENTY WEEKS Time spoken of in Dan. 9:24-27, usually understood as 70 weeks of years or 490 years. A prophetic approach to this passage sees the 490 years as a reference to the future coming of Jesus Christ, the Messiah.

SEVENTY YEARS Prophetic and apocalyptic period pointing to the time of Israel's exile in Babylon and to the end of the nation's suffering in Daniel's vision. The prophet Jeremiah predicted that Judah would serve Babylon 70 years (Jer. 25:11). Second Chronicles 36:21 saw the completion of the 70 years in the coming of King Cyrus of Persia to power after his defeat of the Babylonians (538 BC). Daniel meditated on Jeremiah's prophecy (Dan. 9:2) and learned that 70 weeks of years were intended (v. 24).

SEX, BIBLICAL TEACHING ON God created human beings as male and female, both in his own image (Gen. 1:27). Thus gender is not a biological accident or social construction. The contrast and complementarity between the man and the woman reveal that gender is part of the goodness of God's creation. Modern efforts to redefine or redesign gender are contrary to the Bible's affirmation of maleness and femaleness as proper distinctions. Throughout the Bible, a complementary pattern of relation between man and woman, particularly within the institution of marriage, is presented as the divine intention. Both are equal in dignity and status, but a pattern of male leadership in the home and in the church is enforced by both descriptive and prescriptive passages (1 Tim. 2:8–3:7; 1 Cor. 14:34-38). The Bible places sex and sexual activity within the context of holiness and faithfulness, presenting an honest explanation of God's design for sex and its place in human life and happiness. The biblical writers affirm the goodness of sexuality as God's gift. The Song of Songs is an extended love poem with explicit erotic imagery and language. Sex is affirmed as a source of pleasure and shared intimacy between husband and wife. The Bible also places sexual activity within the context of the marital covenant. Sexual relations are limited to this covenant relationship. All forms of extramarital sexual activity are condemned, including premarital sex (fornication) and adultery (Exod. 20:14; 1 Cor. 6:9-10). At the same time, the husband and wife are ordered to fulfill their marital duties to each other and not to refrain from sexual union (1 Cor. 7:2-5). As human beings, we are sexual creatures, and as sexual creatures we are called to honor God with our bodies (1 Cor. 6:15-20). Within the context of the marital covenant, the husband and wife are free to express love for each other, to experience pleasure, and to join in the procreative act of sexual union. This is pleasing to God and is not to be a source of shame.

SHADDAI Transliteration of a Hebrew name for God, often translated "Almighty" (Exod. 6:3). See *Almighty; Names of God.*

SHADRACH Babylonian name of Hananiah, one of Daniel's three friends thrown into a fiery furnace for refusing to worship a graven image set up by King Nebuchadnezzar. The Lord miraculously delivered them (Dan. 3:30). See *Abednego; Daniel; Meshach.*

SHALLUM Personal name meaning "replacer" or "the replaced." **1.** King of Israel (752 BC). He assassinated Zechariah and was, in turn, assassinated by Menahem a month later (2 Kgs. 15:10-15). **2.** Another name for King Jehoahaz of Judah. **3.** Husband of Huldah (2 Kgs. 22:14). **4.** A temple gatekeeper (1 Chron. 9:17,19,31). This may be the same as Shelemiah (1 Chron. 26:14) and Meshelemiah (1 Chron. 26:1-14). **5.** A chief priest (Ezra 7:2). **6.** Descendant of Judah (1 Chron. 2:40). **7.** Jeremiah's uncle (Jer. 32:7). **8.** Temple doorkeeper (Jer. 35:4). **9.** Descendant of Simeon (1 Chron. 4:25). **10.** Descendant of Naphtali (1 Chron. 7:13). **11.** Father of Jehizkiah (2 Chron. 28:12). **12.** Porter who agreed to divorce his foreign wife (Ezra 10:24). **13.** Israelite with a foreign wife (Ezra 10:42). **14.** Supervisor of half of Jerusalem who helped Nehemiah rebuild the city walls (Neh. 3:12).

SHALMANESER Personal name meaning "Shalmanu (the god) is the highest ranking one." **1.** Assyrian king who ruled 1274–1245 BC. Records of his military exploits set a precedent that succeeding kings followed. **2.** Shalmaneser III ruled Assyria 858–824 BC. He fought a group of small kingdoms, including Israel, in the battle of Qarqar in 853 BC. Despite claiming victory, Shalmaneser proceeded no farther. **3.** Shalmaneser V ruled Assyria 726–722 BC. He completed the attack on Samaria begun by his predecessor, Tiglath-pileser III. In 722, Israel fell to Shalmaneser (2 Kgs. 17:6), thus ending the northern kingdom.

Replica of the Black Obelisk of Shalmaneser III (858-824 BC). The obelisk was found in 1846 during excavations at Nimrud, an ancient site south of Baghdad, Iraq.

SHAME AND HONOR Honor and shame were values that shaped everyday life in biblical times. Honor, the primary measure of social status, was based upon ascribed honor and acquired honor. *Ascribed* honor was social standing due to being part of a social unit, principally the family. *Acquired* honor was gained through meritorious deeds or public performance. The public forum provided challenges for gaining or losing honor. A challenge might show the superiority of one person or group over another. A challenge could be ignored if not worthy of response due to social distance between the parties, but a true honor challenge required response. The party recognized as winning gained honor and the other lost honor or social standing.

Shame was not simply the opposite of honor; both positive and negative shame existed. Shame could be handled positively by knowing how to keep matters out of public awareness. For example, a woman could bear shame well by remaining covered in public and by avoiding male dominated arenas. Shame could also designate dishonor or loss of honor. When people claimed an undeserved place of honor, shame resulted (Luke 14:7-11).

Perhaps the most vivid honor/shame text in the Bible is Phil. 2:5-11. Jesus had unquestionable ascribed honor; yet he gave it all up and took the most humble of all honor bases (a slave) and died the most shameful of all deaths, crucifixion. But God gave him the highest of all honor positions and a name above all names on the honor scale, causing everyone to bow before him. The honor code is thus defined by God instead of men.

SHAMGAR Judge of Israel who killed 600 Philistines with an ox goad, a metal-tipped pole (Judg. 3:31).

SHAPHAN Personal name meaning "coney." Scribe and treasurer under King Josiah of Judah who delivered the book of the law that had been discovered in the temple to the king's palace (2 Kgs. 22:14).

SHARD Pottery fragment found in archaeological excavations and used for dating.

SHARON, PLAIN OF Geographical name meaning "flat land" or "wetlands." **1.** Fertile coastal plain between Mount Hermon and the city of Joppa along the Mediterranean Sea (1 Chron. 27:29). **2.** Area of uncertain location east of the Jordan River inhabited by the tribe of Gad (1 Chron. 5:16).

SHEAF Harvested grain bound together into a bundle. Joseph's dream featured sheaves still in the field (Gen. 37:7). The prophets used sheaves as figures of judgment (Zech. 12:6).

SHEAR-JASHUB Symbolic personal name meaning "a remnant shall return." Name given by the prophet Isaiah to his first son, probably to show that a remnant would survive the fall of Judah to a foreign power (Isa. 7:3-4). See *Isaiah*.

SHEATH Protective holder for sword attached to a belt.

SHEBA, QUEEN OF Ruler of the Sabeans who visited King Solomon of Judah (1 Kgs. 10) to test his wisdom, learn about his God, and enhance trade relations.

SHECHEM Personal name and place-name meaning "shoulder" or "back." District and city in the hill country of Ephraim in north central Palestine. Shechem makes its earliest appearance in biblical history in connection with Abram's arrival in the land of Canaan (Gen. 12:6-7). When Jacob returned from Paddan-aram, he settled down at Shechem and purchased land from the sons of Hamor (33:18-19). In Gen. 33–34, Shechem was the name of the city and also of the prince of the city. When the Israelites conquered Canaan, Joshua built an altar on Mount Ebal (Josh. 8:30-35). Shechem was a city of refuge (Josh. 20:7) and a Levitical city (Josh. 21:21). Joshua led Israel to renew its covenant with God there (Josh. 24:1-17).

Rehoboam, successor to King Solomon, went to Shechem to be crowned king over all Israel (1 Kgs. 12:1). Later, when the nation divided into two kingdoms, Shechem became the first capital of the kingdom of Israel (1 Kgs. 12:25). Samaria eventually became the permanent political capital of the northern kingdom, but Shechem retained its religious

Shechem. Here between Mount Gerazim and Mount Ebal, Joshua led Israel to renew their commitment to the law of Moses.

importance. It apparently was a sanctuary for worship of God in the prophet Hosea's time about 750 BC (Hos. 6:9).

SHEEP A prominent animal in the sacrificial system of Israel. Sheep are first mentioned in Gen. 4:2 where Abel is identified as a keeper of sheep. The sheep of the Bible usually are the broad-tailed variety. The tail, weighing as much as 15 pounds, was sometimes offered as a sacrifice. Sheep were also a source for food and clothing. Symbolically, sheep portrayed people without leadership (1 Kgs. 22:17), innocent people not deserving of punishment (1 Chron. 21:17), and helpless people facing slaughter (Ps. 44:11,22). Straying sheep illustrate human sin (Isa. 53:6), but the silent lamb facing slaughter prepares the way for Christ's sacrifice (Isa. 53:7). The search for one lost sheep depicts God's love for his people (Luke 15).

SHEEPFOLD Place where sheep were kept (Gen. 49:14).

SHEET English translation of Greek word meaning "a linen cloth" and usually used for ships' sails. Such a cloth held all the clean and unclean animals in the vision that taught Peter that God offers salvation to all people, not just the Jews (Acts 10:11).

SHEKEL Hebrew weight of about four-tenths of an ounce. This became the name of a silver coin of that weight. See *Weights and Measures.*

SHEKINAH Transliteration of a Hebrew word that speaks of God's presence. The term means "that which dwells" and is implied throughout the Bible whenever it refers to God's nearness (Exod. 13:21).

SHEM Personal name meaning "name." Noah's oldest son and original ancestor of Semitic peoples, including the Israelites (Gen. 5:32). Through his line came Abraham and the covenant of blessing.

SHEMA Transliteration of a Hebrew imperative meaning "hear" (Deut. 6:4) and a name for the central statement of the Jewish law. The Shema became for the people of God a confession of faith by which they acknowledged the one true God and his commandments. Later worship practice combined Deut. 6:4-9; 11:13-21; and Num. 15:37-41 into the larger Shema as the summary of Jewish confession. When Jesus was asked about the "greatest commandment," he answered by quoting the Shema (Mark 12:29).

SHEMAIAH Personal name meaning "Yahweh heard." **1.** Prophet in the days of King Rehoboam of Judah whose message from God prevented war between Israel and Judah about 930 BC (1 Kgs. 12:22). His preaching humbled Rehoboam and the leaders of Judah, leading God not to permit Shishak of Egypt to destroy Jerusalem (2 Chron. 12). **2.** False prophet among Babylonian exiles who opposed Jeremiah (Jer. 29:24-32). **3.** Descendant of David and Zerubbabel (1 Chron. 3:22). **4.** Member of the tribe of Simeon (1 Chron. 4:37). **5.** Member of the tribe of Reuben (1 Chron. 5:4). **6.** A Levite (Neh. 11:15). **7.** A Levite (1 Chron. 9:16). **8.** Head of one of the six Levitical families under David (1 Chron. 15:8,11). **9.** Levitical scribe who recorded the priestly divisions under David (1 Chron. 24:6). **10.** Head of an important family of gatekeepers (1 Chron. 24:4-8). **11.** Levite in time of King Hezekiah of Judah. (2 Chron. 29:14). **12.** Head of a family that returned with Ezra from Babylonian exile (Ezra 8:13). **13.** Priest married to a foreign woman (Ezra 10:21). **14.** Man married to a foreign woman (Ezra 10:31). **15.** Keeper of east gate who helped Nehemiah repair Jerusalem's wall about 445 BC (Neh. 3:29).

16. Prophet whom Tobiah and Sanballat hired against Nehemiah (Neh. 6:10-12). **17.** Original ancestor of a priestly family (Neh. 10:8; 12:6,18). **18.** Leader of Judah who participated with Nehemiah in dedicating the rebuilt walls of Jerusalem (Neh. 12:34). **19.** Priest who helped Nehemiah dedicate the walls (Neh. 12:42). **20.** Priest whose grandson helped Nehemiah dedicate the walls (Neh. 12:35). **21.** Levitical musician who helped Nehemiah dedicate the walls (Neh. 12:36). **22.** Father of the prophet Urijah (Jer. 26:20). **23.** Father of an official at King Jehoiakim's court (Jer. 36:12). **24.** Levite in days of King Jehoshaphat who taught God's law to the people (2 Chron. 17:8). **25.** Levite in days of King Josiah (2 Chron. 35:9).

SHEMER Personal name meaning "protection, preservation." **1.** Head of clan from the tribe of Asher (1 Chron. 7:34). **2.** Original owner of the hill for whom the city of Samaria was named (1 Kgs. 16:24). See *Samaria, Samaritans.*

SHEMINITH Musical direction meaning "the eighth," used in titles of Pss. 6; 12; and in 1 Chron. 15:21. It may designate the instrument to be used in worship.

SHEOL Abode of the dead, both righteous and wicked, in Hebrew thought. It was thought to be deep within the earth (Amos 9:2) and was entered by crossing a river (Job 33:18). Sheol is pictured as a city with gates (Isa. 38:10), a place of ruins (Ezek. 26:20), or a trap (2 Sam. 22:6). It is sometimes personified as a hungry beast (Hab. 2:5) with an open mouth and an insatiable appetite. Sheol is described as a place of dust (Ps. 30:9) and of gloom and darkness (Job 10:21).

Though the overall picture of Sheol is grim, the OT nevertheless affirms that God is there (Ps. 139:8) and that it is impossible to hide from God in Sheol (Job 26:6). The OT also affirms that God has power over Sheol and is capable of ransoming souls from its depths (Job 33:18,28-30). In the majority of these passages, a restoration to physical life is clearly intended, though several (e.g., Ps. 49:15 with its image of God's receiving the one ransomed from Sheol) point the way toward the Christian understanding of afterlife with God.

SHEPHERD Keeper of sheep. The Hebrew word for shepherding is often translated "feeding." Shepherds led sheep to pasture and water (Ps. 23) and protected them from wild animals (1 Sam. 17:34-35). Shepherds took care of their sheep and even carried weak lambs in their arms (Isa. 40:11). The word *shepherd* came to designate not only persons who herded sheep but also kings (2 Sam. 5:2) and God himself (Ps. 23:1). The prophets referred to Israel's leaders as shepherds (Ezek. 34). Humble shepherds were the first people to visit Jesus at his birth (Luke 2:8-20). Jesus spoke of himself as "the good shepherd" who would lay down his life for his sheep (John 10:7-18).

SHESHBAZZAR Babylonian name probably meaning "may Shamash (sun god) protect the father." Jewish leader who accompanied the first group of exiles from Babylon to Jerusalem in 538 BC (Ezra 1:8). King Cyrus of Persia apparently appointed Sheshbazzar governor of restored Judah and supplied his company of people with provisions and many of the treasures that the Babylonians had taken from Jerusalem. He attempted to rebuild the temple (Ezra 5:16).

SHETHAR-BOZENAI or **SHETHAR-BOZNAI** (KJV) Persian name, perhaps meaning "Mithra is deliverer." Persian provincial official who questioned Zerubbabel's right to begin rebuilding the temple in Jerusalem (Ezra 5:3,6).

SHEWBREAD/SHOWBREAD Sacred bread that was set before the Lord in the tabernacle and temple as a continual sacrifice (Exod. 25:30). The old bread that it replaced was then eaten by the priests (Lev. 24:5-9).

SHIBBOLETH Hebrew password meaning "ears," "twigs" or "brook." People of Gilead east of the Jordan River used it to detect people of the tribe of Ephraim from west of the Jordan since the Ephraimite dialect evidently did not include the *sh* sound. The Ephraimites always said, "Sibboleth," a word not used elsewhere in Hebrew (Judg. 12:6).

SHIGGAION Technical term used in psalm titles (Ps. 7), possibly calling for an increased tempo in singing.

Ruins of an ancient synagogue at the site of the city of Shiloh

SHILOH Place-name, perhaps meaning "tranquil" or "secure." City about 30 miles north of Jerusalem that served as Israel's religious center for more than a century after the conquest of Canaan. At the tabernacle in Shiloh, Hannah vowed that if the Lord would give her a son she would give him back to God (1 Sam. 1). After the birth of Samuel, Hannah brought him to Shiloh in gratitude to God (1 Sam. 1:24-28). Shiloh became home for Samuel as he lived under the care of Eli, the high priest of Israel. Eventually Jerusalem became the capital city of Judah and the city where the ark was kept. The Bible gives no information on what happened to Shiloh. According to archaeological evidence, Shiloh apparently was destroyed about 1050 BC by the Philistines. Supporting this theory is the fact that when the Philistines returned the ark of the covenant to Israel, it was housed at Kiriath-jearim rather than Shiloh (1 Sam. 7:1). The prophet Jeremiah warned Jerusalem that it might suffer the same destruction as Shiloh (7:12).

SHIMEI Personal name meaning "my being heard." **1.** Grandson of Levi and head of a Levitical family (Num. 3:18). **2.** A Levite (1 Chron. 23:9). **3.** A relative of King Saul who cursed and opposed David as David fled from Absalom (2 Sam. 16). When David returned after Absalom's death, Shimei met him and pleaded for forgiveness and mercy, which David granted because of the festive occasion (2 Sam. 19). Solomon followed David's advice and had Shimei executed (1 Kgs. 2). **4.** Court personality who refused to support Adonijah against Solomon in the struggle for the kingship (1 Kgs. 1:8). **5.** District supervisor in territory of Benjamin responsible for supplying Solomon's court one month each year (1 Kgs. 4:18); he could be identical with 4, above. **6.** Ancestor of Mordecai, the cousin of Esther (Esth. 2:5). **7.** Brother of Zerubbabel (1 Chron. 3:19). **8.** Member of the tribe of Simeon (1 Chron. 4:26). **9.** Member of tribe of Reuben (1 Chron. 5:4). **10.** A Levite (1 Chron. 6:29). **11.** A Benjaminite (1 Chron. 8:21). **12.** Temple musician under David (1 Chron. 25:17). **13.** Supervisor of David's vineyards (1 Chron. 27:27). **14-15.** Two Levites under King Hezekiah (2 Chron. 31:12-13). **16.** Levite married to a foreign wife (Ezra 10:23). **17-18.** Two Jews married to foreign women (Ezra 10:33,38).

SHIN Next to last letter of Hebrew alphabet used as title for Ps. 119:161-168. Each verse of the section begins with this letter.

SHINAR, PLAIN OF Place-name of uncertain meaning. In the Bible it refers to Mesopotamia (Gen. 10:10). The tower of Babel was built in Shinar (Gen. 11:2-9).

SHIPHRAH Personal name meaning "beauty." Israelite midwife in Egypt who disobeyed Pharaoh and saved the baby Moses (Exod. 1:15-21).

SHIPMASTER Captain in charge of a ship (Jon. 1:6).

SHISHAK Egyptian royal name of unknown meaning. A pharaoh of Egypt who invaded Jerusalem and took away the temple treasures (1 Kgs. 14:25-26). Some equate him with the pharaoh whose daughter married King Solomon (1 Kgs. 3:1) and who later burned Gezer and gave it to his daughter (1 Kgs. 9:16). See *Egypt*.

SHITTIM Transliteration of a Hebrew word for acacia trees. **1.** Area in Moab where the Israelites camped before crossing into the promised land. **2.** In Joel 3:18 the symbolic meaning of acacias (note NASB) comes to the fore in the messianic picture of fertility for the Kidron Valley.

The yellow blooms of a modern variety of the acacia (shittim) tree in Israel

SHOA National name meaning "help!" A nation used by the Lord to punish his people (Ezek. 23:23).

SHOBACH Personal name of uncertain meaning. Commander of the Syrian army killed by David's troops (2 Sam. 10:16,18).

SHOPHAR Ceremonial ram's horn used to call the people of Israel together (Exod. 19:16). The shophar was to be blown on the Day of Atonement in the Jubilee Year to signal the release of slaves and of people from indebtedness. It was also used as a war trumpet.

SHOSHANNIM Transliteration of Hebrew word meaning "lotuses." Technical term used in titles of Pss. 45; 60; 69; 80, perhaps referring to the tune or melody to which these psalms were to be sung.

SHOVEL Instrument used to remove ashes from the altar in the tabernacle (Exod. 27:3).

SHRINE Small building devoted to the worship of a pagan god. Sometimes shrines were located in larger temples, set apart by a partition or niche in a wall. An Ephraimite, Micah, had a shrine in Israel during the days of the judges (Judg. 17:5).

SHROUD Long pieces of cloth wound around a body for burial. Spices were placed within the folds of the shroud. After his crucifixion, Jesus's body was buried in this manner by Joseph of Arimathea (Matt. 27:59-61).

SHULAMITE or **SHULAMMITE** Description of woman in Song 6:13, either as from Shunem or from Shulam, an otherwise unknown town; or Solomonite, referring to a relationship to Solomon; or a common noun meaning "the replaced one."

SHUNEM, SHUNAMMITES Place-name and clan name of uncertain meaning. The town of Shunem was located southeast of Mount Carmel in the territory of Issachar. The Israelites controlled it under Joshua (Josh. 19:18). As David lay dying, Abishag the Shunammite was hired to minister to the king (1 Kgs. 1:3). The prophet Elisha stayed often at the home of a Shunammite couple, prophesied that a son would be born to them, and raised the boy from the dead (2 Kgs. 4).

SHUR, WILDERNESS OF Place-name meaning "wall." Region on Egypt's north-

The Wilderness of Shur

eastern border where the Israelites made their first stop after crossing the Red Sea (Exod. 15:22).

SHUSHAN Persian place-name meaning "lily" or "lotus." The throne city of King Ahasuerus of Persia, generally referred to as Susa in modern translations. Shushan was the Persian king's winter residence (Esth. 1:2). See *Susa*.

SIBLING RIVALRY Tensions and fighting among brothers or sisters, including Cain and Abel (Gen. 4:1-16); Shem, Ham, and Japheth (Gen. 9:20-27); Jacob and Esau (Gen. 25:22–28:9); Leah and Rachel (Gen. 29:16–30:24); Joseph and his brothers (Gen. 37; 39–45); Er and Onan (Gen. 38:1-10); Moses, Aaron, and Miriam (Num. 12:1-15); Abimelech and Jotham (Judg. 9:1-57); David and Eliab (1 Sam. 17:28-30); Absalom and Amnon (2 Sam. 13:1-39); and Solomon and Adonijah (1 Kgs. 1:5-53). In each case one, or usually both, of the siblings attempted to gain status or favor over the other. The psalmist praised the goodness and pleasantness of brothers who are able to dwell together in unity (Ps. 133:1-3).

SICKLE Curved blade of flint or metal used to cut down stalks of grain. The sickle is often used symbolically to speak of coming judgment. Revelation 14 uses the analogy of Christ reaping the human harvest at the great judgment.

SIDON AND TYRE Phoenician cities located on the coastal plain between the mountains of Lebanon and the Mediterranean Sea (Gen. 10:15). Sidon and Tyre were ancient cities, having been founded long before the Israelites entered Canaan. Sidon seems to have been the more dominant of the two cities during the early part of their histories, but Tyre eventually surpassed Sidon. Both cities were known for their maritime exploits and as centers of trade. Israel had relations with the two cities, but especially with Tyre. David employed Tyrian stonemasons and carpenters and used cedars from that area in building his palace. (2 Sam. 5:11). The construction of the temple in Jerusalem during Solomon's reign depended heavily on the materials and craftsmen from Tyre.

The harbor at Sidon in the modern state of Lebanon

SIEGE Battle tactic in which an army surrounded a city and cut off all supplies so the enemy army was forced to surrender for lack of food and water. Judah suffered siege from King Sennacherib of Assyria (2 Kgs. 18–19) and from King Nebuchadnezzar of Babylon (2 Kgs. 24–25).

SIEGEWORKS Platforms or towers built by an army around and above the city walls of a city under siege. This allowed the besieging army to shoot arrows and throw missiles of war into the city.

SIEVE Instrument used to remove foreign matter from sand or grain. Pebbles or straw remained in the sieve, while the sand or grain passed through. God warned Israel that he would place them in a sieve of judgment from which no one would escape (Amos 9:9).

SIGN Symbol, action, or occurrence that points to something beyond itself. In the OT, signs often refer to miraculous intervention by God. They can point to knowledge of God, such as the events of the exodus (Deut. 4:34). Signs can reinforce faith through remembrance of his mighty deeds, such as memorial stones from the Jordan River (Josh. 4:6). Signs can also point to God's covenant with his people. These include the rainbow (Gen. 9:12), circumcision (Gen. 17:11), the Sabbath (Exod. 31:13), and the wearing of phylacteries on the wrist and forehead (Deut. 11:18).

In the NT, Luke records signs at the birth of Jesus. The "baby wrapped tightly in cloth" (CSB) was a sign to the shepherds that verified the angels' announcement (Luke 2:12), and Simeon prophesied that Jesus himself was a sign, one who would be opposed by many people (Luke 2:34). While signs can point to God's work, Jesus condemned the demand of the Pharisees for signs to prove that God was working through him (Matt. 12:39). The only sign they would be given was the sign of Jonah, a reference to his death and resurrection. In the Gospel of John, Jesus tells those following him after the feeding of the 5,000, "You are looking for me, not because you saw the signs, but because you ate the loaves and were filled" (John 6:26 CSB). They saw the signs Jesus performed but did not perceive their significance that he was the Son of God. While signs point to God and his Son Jesus, they are not enough by themselves to bring a person to saving faith.

SIHON Amorite personal name of unknown meaning. Amorite king who opposed Israel's passage through his country as they journeyed toward the promised land. He was defeated when he attacked the Israelites (Num. 21:21–30).

SILAS, SILVANUS A leader in the early Jerusalem church, Silas carried news of the Jerusalem conference to the believers at Antioch (Acts 15:22). He and Paul left Antioch together on a mission to Asia Minor (15:40-41) and later to Macedonia. In Philippi, they were imprisoned (16:19-24), but they later won the jailer and his family to the Lord after God delivered Paul and Silas from prison. Later in his ministry, Silas teamed with Peter on missions to Pontus and Cappadocia. He also served as Peter's scribe, writing the first letter from Peter and perhaps other letters.

SILENCE Silence is a sign of reverence to God (Hab. 2:20), a symbol of death (Ps. 94:17), a symbol of Sheol (Ps. 115:17), and an expression of despair (Lam. 2:10).

SILK Cloth made from thread that came from the Chinese silkworm. Some interpreters feel that the Hebrew word translated "silk" should be "fine linen" or "expensive material" (Ezek. 16:10), the Hebrew indicating something glistening white.

SILOAM Place-name possibly meaning "sending" or "sent." This place is easily confused with the waters of Shiloah men-

The Siloam Pool in Jerusalem

tioned in Isa. 8:6. Siloam was the pool created by King Hezekiah's tunnel that diverted the waters of Shiloah from the Siloam spring to a point inside the city walls of Jerusalem. John 9:7,11 uses the etymological significance of the term "Siloam" for a play on words to press the point that the blind man was "*sent*" to Siloah by one who was himself the One who was "*sent*." To gain his sight, the blind man obeyed the Sent One. The pool of Siloam is still in use today.

SILVANUS See *Silas, Silvanus.*

SILVER A precious metal. The Bible refers to the process of refining silver (Prov. 17:3). In most of the OT, it is given a priority over gold. Only in Chronicles and Daniel is gold considered to have more worth. Silver coins were first minted after 700 BC, but weight was the most common standard for determining their value. In the NT period, the drachma, a silver coin, was required for the temple tax. Figuratively, refining silver refers to the testing of human hearts (Isa. 48:10) and the purity of God's word (Ps. 12:6). Wisdom is declared to be of more value than silver (Job 28:10-15).

SILVERSMITH Person who works with silver, either refining silver from the ore or making refined silver into the finished product (Acts 19:23-41). Silver was used for making money and religious images (Judg. 17:4) and many of the utensils used in the tabernacle and temple (Num. 7:13).

SIMEON Personal name meaning "hearing" or possibly "little hyena beast." **1.** One of Jacob's 12 sons (Gen. 29:33). Joseph held his brother Simeon as a prisoner to ensure that the other brothers would bring Benjamin to Egypt (Gen. 42:24). **2.** Devout Jew who was promised by the Lord that he would not die before seeing the Christ (Luke 2:25). When Joseph and Mary brought Jesus to the temple for the purification rites, Simeon announced God's plan for the boy (2:34). **3.** Ancestor of Jesus (Luke 3:30). **4.** Prophet and teacher in church at Antioch (Acts 13:1). **5.** Alternate form in Greek for *Simon*, original Greek name of Peter.

SIMON Greek personal name meaning "flat-nosed." Used in NT as Greek alternative for the Hebrew "Simeon." **1.** The father of Judas Iscariot (John 6:71). **2.** One of Jesus's disciples; a son of Jonah and brother of Andrew. After he confessed Jesus as the Christ, the Lord changed his name to Peter (Matt. 16:17-18). See *Peter.* **3.** Pharisee who hosted Jesus at a dinner. Simon learned valuable lessons about love, courtesy, and forgiveness after a sinful woman anointed Jesus at this event (Luke 7:36-40). **4.** Native of Cyrene who was forced to carry Jesus's cross to Golgotha (Mark 15:21). **5.** Tanner of animal skins who lived in the seaport of Joppa. Peter stayed at his house (Acts 9:43), where he received a visionary message from God declaring all foods to be fit for consumption (10:9-16). **6.** Jesus's disciple, also called "the Canaanite" (Matt. 10:4) or the Zealot (Luke 6:15). **7.** Half brother of Jesus (Matt. 13:55). **8.** Leper who hosted Jesus and saw a woman anoint Jesus with costly ointment

The traditional area of the home of Simon the tanner in ancient Joppa (modern Jaffa near Tel Aviv).

(Matt. 26:6-13). **9.** Magician from Samaria who believed Philip's preaching, was baptized, and then tried to buy the power of the gospel (Acts 8:9-24).

SIN Actions by which humans rebel against God and miss his purpose for their lives. The cause of estrangement from God is sin, the root cause of humanity's problems. The Bible describes sin as rebellion against God. Rebellion was at the root of the problem for Adam and Eve (Gen. 3) and has been at the root of humanity's plight ever since.

The OT affirms that God established the law as a standard of righteousness, so any violation of this standard is defined as sin. Breach of the covenant between God and humanity is also caused by sin (Deut. 29:19-21). The OT also pictures sin as a violation of the righteous nature of God. As the righteous and holy God, he sets forth as a criterion for his people a righteousness like his own. (Lev. 11:45). Any deviation from God's righteousness is viewed as sin.

In the NT, sin is defined against the backdrop of Jesus as the standard for righteousness. His life exemplifies perfection. The exalted purity of his life creates the norm for judging what is sinful. Sin is also viewed as a lack of fellowship with God. Jesus taught that sin is a condition of the heart. He traced sin to inner motives, stating that the sinful thought leading to the overt act is the real sin. Anger in the heart is the same as murder (Matt. 5:21-22). The impure look is tantamount to adultery (Matt. 5:27-28). The real defilement in a person stems from the inner person (heart), which is sinful (Matt. 15:18-20). Sin, therefore, is understood as involving the essential being of a person— the essence of human nature.

The NT also interprets sin as unbelief—not just the rejection of a dogma or a creed but rejection of that spiritual light that has been revealed in Jesus Christ. The outcome of such rejection is judgment. The only criterion for judgment is whether a person has accepted or rejected the revelation of God as found in Jesus Christ (John 16:8-16). Death is a by-product of sin. Continual, consistent sin will bring spiritual death to any person who has not come under the lordship of Christ through repentance and faith (Rom. 6:23). Christ has negated the power of Satan and has freed people from slavery to sin and death (Heb. 2:14-15.)

SIN, WILDERNESS OF Barren region in the Sinai Peninsula where the Israelites stopped on their journey from Egypt to the promised land (Exod. 16:1). Here God provided manna and quail for them to eat.

The desolate country of the Wilderness of Sin

SINAI, MOUNT Mountain in northwestern Arabia where God made many revelations of himself and his purposes to Israel, including the giving of the Ten Commandments to Moses (Exod. 19:1-3). The Bible uses the term "Sinai" for both the mountain and the entire wilderness area where the Israelites settled for a time after the exodus from Egypt (Lev. 7:38). The term "Horeb" is often used to refer to Sinai. Since Horeb means "waste" or "wilderness area," it seems best to think of Horeb

Jebel Musa, the traditional site of Mount Sinai, in the southern Sinai Peninsula

A view of the surrounding rugged landscape around Jebel Musa

as the general term for the area and Sinai as the specific peak where God revealed himself to Moses. The modern name for the traditional site of Sinai is Jebel Musa (the mount of Moses). However, several other mountains in different locations have been suggested as the site of biblical Sinai.

SINEW Tendons and tissue that connect muscles to bone. Isaiah spoke of sinew in a figurative way to show rebellion against God (Isa. 48:4). The angel who wrestled with Jacob struck the sinew of his thigh. To commemorate this event, the Jews cut away this sinew from meat and did not eat it (Gen. 32:24-32).

SINNER Person who has missed God's mark for life, rebelling against him. The Bible considers every person a sinner (Rom. 3:23). In the OT, people who did not live by the law were considered sinners (Ps. 1). Paul spoke of sinners as those separated from God (Rom. 5:8). See *Law; Salvation; Sin.*

SIRION Sidonian name for Mount Hermon (Deut. 3:9). See *Hermon, Mount.*

SISERA Personal name meaning "mediation." **1.** Military leader of Jabin, king of Canaan (Judg. 4:2) who was killed by Heber's wife, Jael (v. 21). **2.** Nethinim descendant who returned to Judah with Zerubbabel (Neh. 7:55).

SISTER A general term for any close female relative, including a sister or stepsister (2 Sam. 13:2). The word *sister* was also used of people held in special esteem as a counterpart to brotherly affection (Song 4:9). See *Family; Woman.*

SITNAH Well dug by Isaac's servants near the city of Gerar (Gen. 26:21). The well was seized by the servants of Abimelech; therefore the name meaning "hatred" or "opponent."

SIVAN Third month (May–June) of the Hebrew calendar, the time of wheat harvest and Pentecost.

SKIN The human skin is often mentioned in relation to disease (Lev. 13). God made clothing from animal skin for Adam and Eve (Gen. 3:21). Animal skins were also used to make containers for liquids (Matt. 9:17). The skin is spoken of in several proverbial sayings: "Skin for skin" (Job 2:4), "the skin of my teeth" (Job 19:20), and "Can the Ethiopian (Cushite) change his skin?" (Jer. 13:23).

SLANDER To speak critically and maliciously of another person (Lev. 19:16). In a court of law, it means to accuse another person falsely (Deut. 5:20). Slander is a mark of the unregenerate world (1 Pet. 3:16). Jesus called Satan "a liar and the father of lies" (John 8:44 CSB).

SLAVE, SERVANT In the first Christian century, one out of three persons in Italy and one out of five elsewhere were slaves. Many were domestic and civil servants. Some slaves were highly intelligent and held responsible positions. A person could become a slave as a result of capture in war, default on a debt, being sold as a child by destitute parents, conviction of a crime, or kidnapping and piracy.

Slavery laws appear in Exod. 21:1-11; Lev. 25:39-55; and Deut. 15:12-18. A Hebrew sold to another Hebrew or a resident alien because of indebtedness was to be released after six years of service. A Hebrew who sold himself to another Hebrew or resident alien was to be released during the Jubilee Year. A slave could be redeemed at any time by a relative. A Hebrew girl sold by her father to another Hebrew to become his wife was to be released if that man or his son did not marry her. A slave permanently maimed by his or her master was to be freed (Exod. 21:26-27).

In the NT, Paul and Peter insisted that Christian slaves should be obedient to their masters (Eph. 6:5-8; 1 Pet. 2:18-21) and not seek freedom because of their conversion (1 Cor. 7:20-22). Masters were urged to be kind to their slaves (Col. 4:1). Neither Jesus nor the apostles condemned slavery. Slavery was so much a part of their society that to call for abolition would have resulted in violence and bloodshed. But Jesus and the apostles did set forth principles of human dignity and equality that eventually led to abolition of the practice.

Jesus adopted a servant's role (Mark 10:45) and indicated that his disciples should do the same (Luke 17:10). Paul referred to himself as a slave or servant of Jesus Christ (Phil. 1:1).

SLEEP Regenerative rest (Ps. 4:8). God causes "deep sleep," sometimes for revelation (Job 4:13) and sometimes to prevent prophetic vision (Isa. 29:10). Sleep is also spoken of metaphorically as a sign of laziness (Prov. 19:15) and physical death (1 Cor. 15:51). See *Death; Eternal Life.*

SLING, SLINGERS, SLINGSTONES Weapon consisting of two long straps with a piece between them at the end to hold a stone. Shepherds and professional soldiers used slings.

SLOTHFUL Loose, undisciplined. The slothful person becomes subjected to another's rule (Prov. 12:24). The wise, hardworking ant illustrates the opposite of sloth (Prov. 6:6). Jesus condemned an evil, lazy slave (Matt. 25:26) but praised and rewarded the "good and faithful slave" (Matt. 25:23 CSB).

SMYRNA Major city on the west coast of Asia Minor and site of one of the seven churches addressed in Rev. 2:8-11. See *Asia Minor, Cities of.*

Ruins of the forum at the site of the ancient city of Smyrna in Asia Minor (modern Turkey)

SNAIL Animal whose name apparently means "moist one." It illustrates the brevity of life (Ps. 58:8; CSB, "slug").

SNARE Trap for birds and animals. Figuratively, snares spoke of danger and destruction (Ps. 18:5). See *Fowler; Hunt, Hunter.*

SNOW Israel rarely has snow, although one snowfall is recorded in the Bible (2 Sam. 23:20). The word is used figuratively of whiteness (Isa. 1:18), cleanness (Job 9:30), and refreshing coolness (Prov. 25:13).

SNUFFERS Two different instruments—tongs and cutting tools—used to tend the lamps in the tabernacle and temple (Exod. 25:38).

SOAP Cleaner used to wash the body (Jer. 2:22) and to launder clothes (Mal. 3:2).

SOBER Characterized by self-control, seriousness, and sound moral judgment (1 Pet. 1:13). The KJV at 2 Cor. 5:13 used "sober" to mean in one's right mind.

SODOM AND GOMORRAH Place-names of uncertain meaning. Two cities in Canaan at the time of Abraham that were destroyed by the Lord because of their wickedness.

Bab Edh Dhra, believed by many archaeologists to be ancient Sodom and Gomorrah

Sodom and Gomorrah were probably situated in the Valley of Siddim (Gen. 14:3,8,10-11) near the Dead Sea. Abraham's nephew Lot settled in Sodom (Gen. 19:1). Despite Abraham's plea (18:22-32), not even 10 righteous men could be found in Sodom, and the cities were destroyed by the Lord (Gen. 19:24). The unnatural lusts of the men of Sodom (Gen. 19:4-8; Jude 7) have given us the modern term *sodomy*. The memory of the destruction of these two cities provided a picture of God's judgment (Jer. 49:18) and made them an example to be avoided (Deut. 29:23-25).

SODOMITE Originally a citizen of the town of Sodom, a city destroyed by the Lord because of its wickedness (Gen. 13:12). The term came to mean a male who has sexual relations with another male. The wickedness of Sodom became proverbial (Gen. 19:1-11). See *Homosexuality*.

SOLDIER In early Israelite history, every male was called on to fight when the tribes were threatened. David was the first to assemble a national army made up of professional soldiers. The NT warrior was usually the Roman soldier. See *Centurion*.

SOLOMON David's son and successor as king of Israel. He is remembered most for his wisdom, his building program—including the temple in Jerusalem—and his wealth generated through trade and administrative reorganization. In addition to building the temple (1 Kgs. 5–8), Solomon fortified a number of cities that helped provide protection to Jerusalem, built "store-cities" for stockpiling the materials required in his kingdom, and established military bases for charioteers (1 Kgs. 9:15-19). Solomon divided the country into administrative districts and had the districts provide provisions for the central government. This system made it possible for Solomon to accumulate vast wealth.

Solomon had faults as well as elements of greatness. His "seven hundred wives who were princesses and three hundred who were concubines" (CSB) came from many of the kingdoms with which Solomon had treaties (1 Kgs. 11:1,3). He apparently allowed his wives to worship their native gods and even had altars to these gods constructed in Jerusalem (1 Kgs. 11:7-8). Rebellions led by the king of Edom, Rezon of Damascus, and Jeroboam, one of Solomon's own officers, indicates that Solomon's reign was not without its turmoil. His oppressive taxation

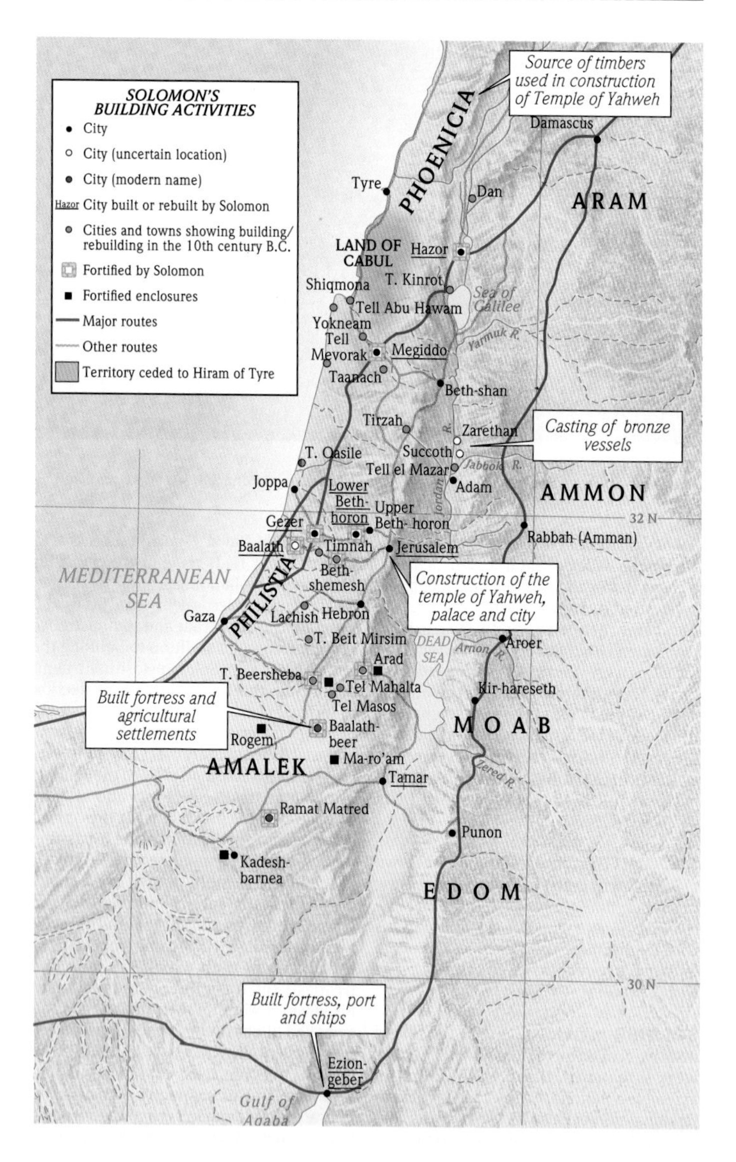
SOLOMON'S BUILDING ACTIVITIES
City
City (uncertain location)
City (modern name)
Hazor City built or rebuilt by Solomon
Cities and towns showing building/rebuilding in the 10th century B.C.
Fortified by Solomon
Fortified enclosures
Major routes
Other routes
Territory ceded to Hiram of Tyre
Source of timbers used in construction of Temple of Yahweh
PHOENICIA
Damascus
ARAM
Tyre
Dan
LAND OF CABUL
Hazor
Shiqmona
T. Kinrot
Tell Abu Hawam
Sea of Galilee
Yokneam
Tell Mevorak
Megiddo
Yarmuk R.
Taanach
Beth-shan
Tirzah
Zarethan
Casting of bronze vessels
T. Qasile
Succoth
Tell el Mazar
Jabbok R.
Adam
Joppa
Lower Beth-horon
Upper Beth-horon
AMMON
Gezer
32 N
Rabbah (Amman)
Baalath
Timnah
Jerusalem
Jordan R.
MEDITERRANEAN SEA
PHILISTIA
Beth-shemesh
Construction of the temple of Yahweh, palace and city
Gaza
Lachish
Hebron
T. Beit Mirsim
DEAD SEA
Arnon R.
Aroer
Arad
T. Beersheba
Tel Mahalta
Kir-hareseth
Tel Masos
Built fortress and agricultural settlements
Baalath-beer
MOAB
Rogem
AMALEK
Ma-ro'am
Zered R.
Tamar
Ramat Matred
Punon
Kadesh-barnea
EDOM
30 N
Built fortress, port and ships
Ezion-geber
Gulf of Aqaba

policies led the northern tribes to rebel and establish their own nation known as the northern kingdom of Israel (1 Kgs. 12:1–17).

SOLOMON'S PORCH The raised outermost part of the temple in Jerusalem during NT times (Acts 3:11). It is called "the portico of Solomon" (NASB, NRSV, REB) and "Solomon's Colonnade" (CSB, NIV), since Solomon's workers constructed at least the oldest portico on the east side. See *Temple of Jerusalem.*

SON OF GOD Term used to express the deity of Jesus as the one, unique Son of God. Jesus conceived of his divine sonship as unique, as indicated by such assertions as "the Father and I are one" (John 10:30 CSB) and "the Father is in me and I in the Father" (John 10:38). He frequently referred to God as "my Father" (John 15:15). At Jesus's baptism and transfiguration, God the Father identified Jesus as his Son. The term "Son of God" is closely associated with Jesus's royal position as Messiah. Paul emphasized the salvation that Jesus provided (Rom. 1:4), and the author of Hebrews focused on Jesus's priesthood (Heb. 5:5). All of these are related to his position as Son of God.

SON OF MAN Expression found in both the OT and the NT. "Son of Man" is used in these ways: (1) as a poetic synonym for "man" or "human," as in Pss. 8:4 and 80:17; (2) in Ezekiel as the title by which God regularly addresses the prophet (2:1,3: 3:1,3); and (3) in Dan. 7 as the identity of the glorious person whom the prophet sees coming with the clouds of heaven to approach the Ancient of Days. "The Son of Man" is a designation of Christ found frequently in the NT. It was Jesus's favorite designation of himself to imply both his messianic mission and his full humanity.

SONG OF SONGS, SONG OF SOLOMON Collection of romantic poetry that may have been written by King Solomon or on behalf of him. Solomon or "king" is mentioned in the book several times (1:1,4-5,12; 3:7,9,11; 7:5; 8:11-12), but scholars remain uncertain about its author. This book has been interpreted allegorically or symbolically in the past, but most modern scholars prefer a literal reading of the Song. Like Gen. 2:23-25, the Song celebrates God's gift of physical love between man and woman. Here the Creator's wisdom and bounty are displayed. The Song is an example of Israel's wisdom poetry (see Prov. 5:15-20; 6:24-29; 7:6-27; 30:18-20).

SONS OF THE PROPHETS Members of a band or guild of prophets. "Sons of" refers to membership in a group or class and does not imply a family relationship. This phrase occurs often in the book of 2 Kings, where the prophet Elisha is portrayed as the leader of the prophetic guild. The sons of the prophets functioned either as witnesses (2 Kgs. 2:3,5,7,15) or as agents of Elisha's ministry (2 Kgs. 9:1-3).

SOP A small piece of bread that could be dipped in a dish or wine (John 13:26-30 KJV). A host honored a guest by dipping a piece of bread into the sauce of the main dish and handing it to the guest. Most interpreters feel that Jesus was making his last appeal to Judas to change his mind about betraying him when he handed Judas a piece of bread at the Last Supper. See *Judas.*

SOPATER Personal name meaning "sound parentage." A believer who accompanied Paul on his final trip to Jerusalem (Acts 20:4). Some feel he is the same as "Sosipater" in Rom. 16:21.

SORCERER Person who practices sorcery or divination.

SORROW Emotional, mental, or physical pain or stress. Trouble and sorrow were not meant to be part of the human experience. Humanity's sin brought sorrow into the world (Gen. 3:16-19). Sorrow can lead a person to a deeper faith in God, or it can cause a person to live with regret, centered on the experience that caused the sorrow. Jesus gave believers words of hope to overcome trouble and sorrow: "You will have suffering in this world. Be courageous! I have conquered the world" (John 16:33 CSB).

SOSIPATER Personal name meaning "to save one's father." A kinsman of Paul who sent greetings to the Christians at Rome

(Rom. 16:21). "Sopater . . . from Berea" (Acts 20:4 CSB) may be the same person.

SOSTHENES Personal name meaning "of safe strength." A ruler of a synagogue in Corinth who was beaten by a mob when the apostle Paul was arrested (Acts 18:17).

SOUL The word *soul* has had a varied and complex constellation of meanings. Though it is often used to refer to the inner part of the person, or the nonphysical aspect of being, it is used in other ways in Scripture. In the OT, soul means primarily "life" or "possessing life." It is used of both animals (Ezek. 47:9) and humans (Gen. 2:7). The word sometimes indicates the whole person, as for instance in Gen. 2:7 where God breathes breath into the dust and thus makes a "soul." A similar usage is found in Gen. 12:5 where Abram takes all the "souls" (persons) who were with him in Haran and moves to Canaan. The word is also used in the OT to refer to the inner life, psychological or spiritual state of the human person (Ps. 42:12). The word also refers to the source of emotion in Job 30:25 (CSB): "Has my soul not grieved for the needy?"

In the NT, the soul is often equated with the total person (Rom. 13:1). Soul also indicates the emotions or passions (John 10:24). The soul is also referred to as something that is distinguishable from the physical existence of a person (Matt. 10:28). Scripture clearly teaches that persons continue to exist consciously after physical death. Jesus pointed out that as the God of Abraham, Isaac, and Jacob, he is the God of the living. These people still live, their souls having returned to God (Eccles. 12:7). In addition, Paul equated being absent from the body with being present with Christ. Whether it is the "immaterial" aspect of the soul that is consciously alive with God after death, awaiting resurrection completeness, or whether believers exist in some kind of physical form, uninterrupted existence is certain (2 Cor. 5:1-10).

SOVEREIGNTY OF GOD Biblical teaching that God possesses all power and is the ruler of all things (Dan. 4:34-35). God works according to his eternal purpose, even through events that seem to contradict his rule. Scripture testifies to God's rule over his creation (Rom. 8:20-21), including Christ's sustaining and governing of all things (Heb. 1:3). The Bible affirms also that God rules human history according to his purpose, from ordinary events in the lives of individuals (Prov. 16:9,33) to the rise and fall of nations (Acts 17:26). Scripture also depicts redemption as the work of God alone. God takes the initiative in the provision and application of salvation and in enabling one's willing acceptance (2 Tim. 1:9-10). See *God; Providence.*

SOWER Person who sowed seed, as in the parable of the sower told by Jesus (Matt. 13:3-9; Luke 8:4-8).

An Arab farmer near Bethlehem sowing seeds on his land

SPAIN Country still known by that name in the southwest corner of Europe. Paul wanted to go to Spain (Rom. 15:24,28). See *Tarshish.*

SPAN Half a cubit. A cubit is the length of the arm from the elbow to the tips of the fingers—about 18 inches. See *Weights and Measures.*

SPARROW A small bird. Jesus used sparrows (Luke 12:7) to show how God loves human beings. The God who cares for all of his creation, even the insignificant sparrow, certainly cares for people.

SPECK Modern translation of KJV "mote." See *Mote.*

SPELT Wheat of poor quality. Spelt had not sprouted when the plagues struck Egypt (Exod. 9:32). Spelt illustrates the farmer's planning, placing it on the outer edge of the field to retard the intrusion of weeds (Isa. 28:25).

SPICES Aromatic, pungent substances used in the preparation of foods, sacred oils for anointings, incense, perfumes, and ointments used for personal hygiene and for burial of the dead. Expensive and highly prized, spices were brought into Palestine from India, Arabia, Persia, Mesopotamia, and Egypt. Solomon had an extensive commercial venture with Hiram, king of Tyre, dealing in spices and other commodities. Some of the most important spices were:

Aloe Spice used to perfume garments and beds (Ps. 45:8). The extract from its leaves was mixed with water and other spices to make ointment for the anointing of the dead.

Balsam This product of Gilead was exported to Egypt and Tyre. The resin from this desert plant was used for medicinal and cosmetic purposes (Jer. 46:11). The "balm of Gilead" was likely a balsam product. See *Gilead*.

Cassia The dried bark or blooms of this plant were used in the preparation of the anointing oil; the pods and leaves were used as medicine (Exod. 30:24).

Cinnamon Highly prized plant, used as a condiment, in the preparation of perfumes (Prov. 7:17) and in the holy oil for anointing (Exod. 30:23).

Coriander Aromatic seed used as a spice in food; its oil was used in the manufacture of perfume. The Israelites compared the manna to the coriander seed (Num. 11:7).

Cumin This seed was used as a spice in bread. (Isa. 28:23-28).

Dill Seed and leaves of this plant were used to flavor foods and as medicine to wash skin wounds (Matt. 23:23; KJV, "anise").

Frankincense Resin of a tree that produced a strong aromatic scent. Frankincense was used in the preparation of the sacred oil for anointing of kings and priests and for the sacrifices in the temple. The wise men from the East presented frankincense to Jesus (Matt. 2:11).

Galbanum Fragrant resin that was one of the ingredients of the holy incense (Exod. 30:34).

Henna Plant used as a cosmetic; its leaves produced a dye (Song 4:13; KJV, "camphire").

Mint Leaves of the mint plant were used as a condiment (Luke 11:42).

Myrrh Resinous gum of a plant that was included in the preparation of the holy anointing oil (Exod. 30:23). It was also used for its aromatic properties (Ps. 45:8) and for female purification (Esth. 2:12). Myrrh was given to Jesus at his birth as a gift (Matt. 2:11) and as a drink when he was on the cross (Mark 15:23).

Onycha A type of cress used in holy incense (Exod. 30:34).

Rue Herb used as a condiment. Valued for its medicinal properties, its leaves were used to treat insect bites (Luke 11:42).

Saffron Substance of a plant that produced a yellow dye and was used to color foods. When mixed with oil, it was used as medicine and perfume (Song 4:14).

Spikenard Expensive fragrant oil used in perfumes and ointments. Also translated as "perfume" and "nard." A woman anointed Jesus with this expensive perfume (John 12:3).

Stacte Small tree which produced a resin used in the sacred incense (Exod. 30:34).

SPIDER Animal known for spinning a web. The spider's web is cited as a sign of frailty (Job 8:14).

SPINDLE In spinning, the stick around which spun thread was wrapped (Prov. 31:19, KJV). See *Cloth, Clothing*.

SPINNING AND WEAVING Making thread and cloth were familiar processes in biblical times. Thread was spun from raw fibers. Flax (Ezek. 40:3) and wool (Lev. 13:47) were the major fibers used. Raw fibers were pulled into a loose strand and twisted to form a continuous thread. A spindle (2 Sam. 3:29 CSB, NRSV) was a slender stick that could be twirled to twist drawn-out fibers caught in a hook or slot at the top. The finished product could then be used for weaving cloth (Exod. 35:25-26). Weaving was done on looms (Judg. 16:13-14). Weavers apparently were professionals who specialized in particular types of work. The OT differentiates between ordinary weavers, designers, and embroiderers (Exod. 35:35).

A Bedouin woman spinning wool into yarn

SPIRIT The word "spirit" is used of both God and human beings. In his conversation with Nicodemus (John 3), Jesus said that the Spirit is like the wind because a person cannot see it but can see its effects. This is true of both the Spirit of God and the spirit of a human being. At the beginning of creation, the Spirit of God hovered over the waters (Gen. 1:3). The Spirit of God is everywhere. The psalmist sensed that no matter where he was, God's Spirit was there (Ps. 139:7). Moses realized that the Spirit of God was on him, and he desired that God's Spirit be on all of his people (Num. 11:29). During the period of the Judges, the Spirit of the Lord came to people and empowered them to accomplish specific tasks (Judg. 11:29). Likewise, the Spirit came upon David when Samuel anointed him as king (1 Sam. 16:13).

Each of the four Gospels has numerous references to the Spirit of God or the Holy Spirit. The Spirit was the agent of Jesus's miraculous conception (Matt. 1:18,20), came down on Jesus at his baptism (Matt. 3:16), led him into the wilderness where he was tempted by the devil (Matt. 4:1), and enabled him to heal diseases and cast out demons (Matt. 12:28). Jesus promised the Spirit to his followers as he prepared to leave the world. The Spirit would serve as Comforter and Counselor, continuing to teach Jesus's followers and reminding them of what he had said to them (John 14:25-26). Not many days after Jesus's ascension, the promised Spirit came upon his followers during the Feast of Pentecost. The advent of the Spirit was accompanied by a sound that was like a mighty wind. The Holy Spirit empowered and guided the followers of Jesus in their mission to the world (Acts 11:12).

In both the OT and NT, spirit is associated with a wide range of human functions, including thinking and understanding, emotions, attitudes, and intentions. Elihu told Job it was "spirit in a person—the breath from the Almighty—that gives anyone understanding" (Job 32:8 CSB). Caleb had a different spirit than most of his contemporaries because he followed the Lord wholeheartedly (Num. 14:24). A person's spirit can be contrite (Ps. 34:18), steadfast (Ps. 51:10), willing (Ps. 51:12), broken (Ps. 51:17), and haughty (Prov. 16:18).

SPIRITS IN PRISON First Peter 3:19 declares that Christ "went and made proclamation to the spirits in prison" (CSB). Peter further says that they "in the past were disobedient, when God patiently waited in the days of Noah." These must have been people whom God destroyed in the flood and who were in hell or hades. Christ probably preached to these persons "in the spirit" through Noah while they were still alive.

SPIRITUAL GIFTS God-granted empowerment of believers for carrying out the work of ministry in the church. In the two lengthiest discussions of these gifts, Paul emphasizes the diversity that is to be found in the church, the body of Christ, as reflected in the various spiritual gifts (1 Cor. 12:1-31; Rom. 12:3-8).

Some gifts are spectacular in their manifestation. Gifts of miracles (1 Cor. 12:28-29) refer to the power by which the lordship of Christ over all of reality is demonstrated. "Message of wisdom" (1 Cor. 12:8 CSB) has to do with the ability to speak a word of wise counsel in any difficult situation. Many in the NT demonstrated remarkable gifts of healing, and these manifestations were among "the signs of an apostle" (2 Cor. 12:12). "Distinguishing between spirits" (1 Cor. 12:10) may refer to the ability to detect evil spirits (Acts 16:16-18) or the ability to have a discerning heart in dealing with spiritual needs (1 Cor. 2:14).

Other gifts are more "normal" and might not seem to come directly from God. These include teaching, service, administration, helping, and mercy. But Paul makes it clear in his analogy of the body that these "less honorable" (1 Cor. 12:23) gifts are just as important as the more visible and spectacular gifts. Though the gifts are many, the Spirit who grants them is one. God has given many different gifts to the church, since the needs of the Christian community are complex. Gifts entail ministry. All Christians have tasks to perform in the service of the Lord in the church.

SPIT, SPITTLE Spitting at or on someone is a sign of contempt. The soldiers who mocked Jesus before his crucifixion spat on him (Matt. 27:30). But Jesus used spittle to heal a blind man (John 9:6).

SPOIL Items taken from the enemy by a victorious army. In ancient warfare, a soldier could take anything he could carry that had belonged to a foe. Holy war laws dedicated all such booty to God (Deut. 20).

SPOON Shallow dish or bowl in which incense was burned in the tabernacle and temple (Num. 7:14 KJV).

SPORTS Several games of skill are alluded to in the Bible. Jacob's combat at Peniel may have been a wrestling match between two skilled fighters (Gen. 32:24-32). The fight at the pool of Gibeon between the soldiers of Abner and the soldiers of Joab may have begun as a show of strength through wrestling (2 Sam. 2:12-17). Foot races are alluded to in Ps. 19:5. Paul mentions Greco-Roman gladiatorial bouts, the most gruesome of all entertainment events (1 Cor. 15:32). The NT uses various games as figures of the Christian life. Paul often spoke of his work on behalf of the gospel as "running" (Gal. 2:2; 5:7) and compared the spiritual discipline required for successful living to that required for winning foot races and boxing matches (1 Cor. 9:24-27).

SPOT Skin blemish that made a person ceremonially unclean (Lev. 13:1-8). In the sacrificial system, only animals "without spot" (Num. 28:3 KJV) could be used for an offering to God. See *Sacrifice and Offering*.

STABLE Place where animals are sheltered. King Solomon kept large numbers of horses in stalls, or stables (1 Kgs. 4:26). Jesus was born in a stable, perhaps a cave where animals were kept (Luke 2:7). See *Manger*.

STACHYS Personal name meaning "head of grain." A fellow believer in Rome greeted by Paul (Rom. 16:9).

STACTE Gum of the storax tree which was combined with other elements to make the incense burned in the tabernacle (Exod. 30:34). See *Incense*.

STAG Modern translation of "hart," an adult male deer.

STAIRS Steps on which a person can climb to another level. Houses in Palestine usually had stairs to the roof on the outside. The steps in Jacob's dream about a ladder may have been stairs (Gen. 28:12).

STAKE Wooden peg used to anchor a tent. It was used figuratively of Jerusalem (Isa. 33:20).

STALL Place where animals were kept and fed.

STANDARD Flag or banner used to identify groups of soldiers or a central flag to rally all the soldiers at one time (Num. 1:52; 2:2). This word is also used figuratively of God (Isa. 59:19 KJV).

STARS Constellations, planets, and all heavenly bodies except the sun and the moon. God is acknowledged to be the Creator of the stars (Gen. 1:16) as well as the One who knows their names and numbers (Ps. 147:4).

Probably the most famous of all the stars mentioned in Scripture is the star of Bethlehem (Matt. 2). Scripture does not name the star. It is one of many miracles that attest to the power of God. In the final book of the Bible, the Lord Jesus is called "the bright morning star" (Rev. 22:16 CSB).

STATUTE Law or commandment. Different divine statutes were given by Moses to God's people (Exod. 15:25-26).

STEADFASTNESS Patient endurance. A steadfast person is reliable, faithful, and true to the end (Rom. 15:3-5). Trials that test our faith produce steadfastness (James 1:3 KJV).

STEEL KJV translation of a word that most modern versions translate as "bronze" (2 Sam. 22:35).

STEPHANAS Greek name meaning "crown." A believer in Corinth baptized by Paul (1 Cor. 1:16).

STEPHEN Personal name meaning "crown." The first Christian martyr. Stephen was so mighty in the Scriptures when he argued that Jesus was the Messiah that his Jewish opponents could not refute him (Acts 6:10). He accused the Jewish leaders of rejecting God's way as their forefathers had done (Acts 6:12–7:53). Saul of Tarsus heard Stephen's speech to the Jewish Sanhedrin and saw him die a victorious death. Stephen may have been the human agency that God used to transform Paul into the great Christian missionary.

St. Stephen's Gate (Lion's Gate) at Jerusalem

STEWARDSHIP Responsibility to manage all the resources of life for the glory of God. The biblical concept of stewardship, beginning with Adam and Eve and developed more fully in the NT, is that God is owner and provider of everything. Since all belongs to him, it should be used for his purposes. A collective responsibility was given to humankind to have dominion over the earth, care for it, and manage it for his glory. The believer is to seek the mind and will of God for every decision, whether financial resources, property, time, or influence. God not only expects us to return a portion of what he gives us as tithes and offerings; he expects us to use all that we have to his glory.

STOCKS Wooden frame which secured the feet and hands of prisoners (Job 33:11). The Romans often added chains along with the stocks.

STONE Hardened mineral matter comprising much of the earth. Israel is a stony country. Often it was necessary to clear a field of stones to prepare it for cultivation (Isa. 5:2). An enemy's fields were marred by throwing stones on them. Stones were used for construction, including city walls (Neh. 4:3), dwellings (Lev. 14:38-40), palaces (1 Kgs. 7:1,9), temples (1 Kgs. 6:7), in Persian Susa, pavement in courtyards, and columns (Esth. 1:6). The Israelites often heaped up stones to commemorate some great spiritual event or encounter with God (Gen. 31:46). Symbolically, a stone denotes hardness or insensibility (1 Sam. 25:37). The followers of Christ were called living stones that were built up into the spiritual temple of Christ. Christ himself became the chief cornerstone (1 Pet. 2:4-8).

STOREHOUSE, STORAGE CITY Storehouses were built early in human history to protect harvested crops. Special sections of Israelite towns were designated as storage areas, with several storehouses lining the streets. During the divided kingdom period, royal storage facilities were established in regional capitals to collect tax payments made in flour, oil, grain, or wine. A full storehouse was a symbol of God's blessing (Mal. 3:10).

Storage rooms, or storehouse, excavated at Tel Beer-sheba in the Negev

STORK Long-legged bird noted for its care of its young and for returning each year to the same nesting area. It was ceremonially unclean (Lev. 11:19). See *Birds*.

STRAIGHT STREET A street in Damascus where Paul stayed after his dramatic conversion (Acts 9:10-12).

STRANGER See *Alien*.

STRAW Stalks left after the grain has been stripped. Straw was usually used as bedding for animals. The Israelites were forced to make bricks without straw in Egypt (Exod. 5:6-13).

STREETS The layout of city streets was often determined by the shape of the defensive walls. In some cities a wide street followed the line of the wall. In other towns, streets radiated from a main plaza or thoroughfare. Streets were often paved with large, flat stones, although dirt paths were not uncommon. During the NT era, Roman engineers designed cities throughout the empire with wide, straight streets, usually leading to a central plaza or temple. Paul lodged in a house on Straight Street in Damascus after his conversion (Acts 9:11).

STRONG DRINK Intoxicating drink made from grain. It was denied to priests (Lev. 10:8-9) and those who took the Nazirite vow (Num. 6:3).

STUMBLING BLOCK Anything that causes a person to stumble or fall. The term is usually used metaphorically. Paul warned Christians not to let their freedom become

The street called Straight in Damascus, Syria

a stumbling block to other believers (1 Cor. 8:9). The disobedient are warned that Jesus himself could be a stumbling block (Rom. 9:32-33).

SUBMISSION, SUBORDINATION Voluntary placement of oneself under the authority and leadership of another. First Corinthians 11:3-10 teaches the headship of the husband in marriage and bases this instruction on the creation account. Ephesians 5:22-33 instructs wives to submit to the authority of their husbands, while husbands should love their wives. Peter also exhorts the wife to submit to her husband and cautions that the husband's authority should be exercised with understanding and honor toward his wife (1 Pet. 3:1-7). This structure, when balanced with Gen. 1:26-27, demonstrates that men and women are equal before God but different in their role and function.

The relationship between Christ and the church is a paradigm for submission and authority in marriage (Eph. 5:22-33). The church willingly submits herself to Christ, her designated head (Col. 1:18). Christ loves the church and gave himself for her (Eph. 5:25-27). All human beings are required to submit to God (Isa. 45:23). The Bible also teaches submission to God-appointed leaders (1 Pet. 5:1-5). Human beings are required to submit to governmental authorities (Rom. 13:1-7). Children should submit to their parents (Eph. 6:1-4).

SUBURBS Pastureland around cities that were used as common lands, or open range, for the grazing of livestock (Lev. 25:34 KJV).

SUCCOTH Place-name meaning "booths." **1.** A town whose leaders were punished by Gideon for not helping him in a campaign against the Midianites (Judg. 8:5-7,13-16). **2.** Place where the Israelites camped upon leaving Egypt (Num. 33:5-6).

SUFFERING The Bible asserts that suffering is inevitable in a fallen world (Acts 14:22). People have always asked, "Why does God allow suffering?" Scripture gives no comprehensive explanation. God's reasons and purposes transcend human knowledge, and we cannot always understand suffering. At times we must trust God without understanding (Job 42:2-3). We will not have complete answers until eternity (Rom. 8:18).

One cause of suffering is sinfulness (Hos. 8:7). Misuse of God's gift of freedom, beginning with the fall of Adam and Eve and continuing in all persons, brings devastating consequences (Rom. 3:23). However, the assumption that suffering is always the direct result of sin is wrong (John 9:1-3). Some evil and suffering transcend human depravity and are caused by Satan and demonic forces (Eph. 6:10-13). Another explanation for suffering is that God either sends or allows suffering to discipline and bring maturity to his people. Suffering reminds us of our finitude and teaches us to trust God (Job 1:9-12). Believers should not suffer with resignation but with hope (1 Pet. 5:8-11). Through hope in the resurrection, Christians can endure their suffering victoriously (Rom. 8:17-39). The ultimate solution to suffering comes in heaven (Rev. 21:4-5). Our suffering as believers is a shadow compared to the glory yet to come (Rom. 8:17-18).

SUICIDE The Bible records several instances of suicide (Abimelech—Judg. 9:54; Samson—Judg. 16:29-30; Saul—1 Sam. 31:4; Saul's armor-bearer—1 Sam. 31:5; Ahithophel—2 Sam. 17:23; Zimri—1 Kgs. 16:18; and Judas—Matt. 27:5). The deaths of Abimelech and Saul could be called "assisted" suicide. With the possible exception of Samson (whose death may be better termed a martyrdom), the Bible presents each person who committed suicide as an individual whose behavior is not to be emulated. While the Bible does not specifically prohibit suicide, it does proclaim the sanctity of life (Ps. 8:5) and declares that God's people should choose life over death (Deut. 30:15,19). The right to give life and to take it away belongs to God (Job 1:21).

SUMER A region between the Tigris and Euphrates Rivers referred to as Shinar (Gen. 10:10) or Chaldea (Jer. 50:10), now the southern part of modern Iraq. Archaeologists believe the inhabitants of ancient Sumer developed humanity's first high civilization about 3000 BC. Perhaps the most important Sumerian contribution to civilization was the invention of cuneiform writing, a wedge-shaped script formed by pressing a reed stylus into wet clay tablets. The Babylonians and other surrounding peoples adapted the cuneiform script to their own languages. For many centuries, cuneiform was the dominant mode of writing in ancient Mesopotamia. These tablets have given scholars information about life in this part of the world in Bible times.

SUN Ancient people often viewed the sun as a god, but the Bible views the sun as the "greater light" that God created to rule the day (Gen. 1:16). Thus God was superior to, and separate from, the sun. The Psalms compared the sun's brightness to God's glory by which it will one day be replaced (Ps. 84:11).

SUNDIAL Device used to measure time by the position of a shadow cast by the sun. The root of the Hebrew word translated "dial" (2 Kgs. 20:11) means "to go up" and usually refers to stairs. Most interpreters thus understand King Ahab's sundial to be a staircase on which a shadow went up as the day progressed (2 Kgs. 20:11).

SUPERSCRIPTION Usually the Romans identified a person's crime by writing it on a sign and nailing it to the person's cross. All four Gospels mention such a superscription in connection with Jesus's crucifixion (Matt. 27:37; Mark 15:26; Luke 23:38; John 19:19). The word "superscription" is also used for the titles of some psalms that give information about the writer and the context of the psalm.

SURETY Person who is legally responsible for the debt of another. Should default occur, the surety would have to pay the debt or even be enslaved until the debt was paid. Judah became surety for his brother Benjamin to Joseph (Gen. 43:9). Proverbs warns against being surety for a person you do not know well (11:15). In a positive sense, Jesus is surety for the faithful under the new covenant (Heb. 7:22). See *Loan; Pledge.*

SUSA Winter capital of the ancient Persian Empire. King Cyrus made Susa a capital city along with Ecbatana and Babylon. Some believe Susa to be the place where Queen Esther and King Ahasuerus ruled (Esth. 1:2 CSB). Also called Shushan (KJV). See *Esther, Book of; Persia.*

SUSANNA Personal name meaning "lily." A woman who followed Jesus and supported him financially (Luke 8:2-3).

SWADDLING CLOTHES A long piece of linen used to wrap babies (Luke 2:7,12) and broken limbs. The cloth or band of cloth was wrapped tightly around the body to prohibit movement.

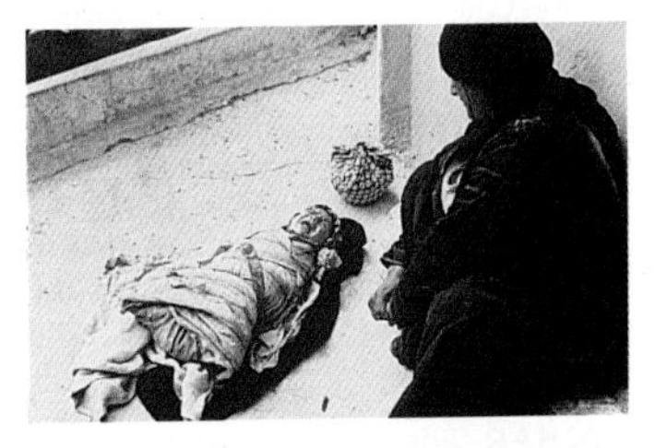

An Arab mother watches her baby who is wrapped in swaddling clothes

SWALLOW Bird that made nests in the temple (Ps. 84:3) and was often seen with the common sparrow. See *Birds.*

SWAN An unclean water bird (Deut. 14:16 KJV). Other versions translate as "desert owl" or "pelican" (NRSV) or "white owl" (NIV, NASB), or "barn owl" (CSB). See *Owl.*

SWIFT Bird similar to a swallow (Jer. 8:7 NASB, NIV). Other versions translate "swallow" (KJV, CSB, NRSV).

SWINE The swine of the Bible, in most instances, probably were wild pigs, still common in Palestine. The Mosaic law classified this animal as unclean and unfit for eating (Lev. 11:7). The fact that the prodigal son resorted to tending swine points to the extreme humiliation he experienced.

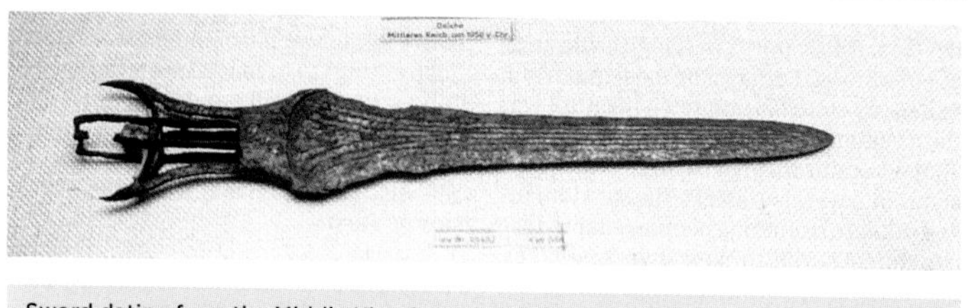

Sword dating from the Middle Kingdom of Egypt

SWORD Close-range offensive weapon. Symbolically, the sword represented war (Matt. 10:34), divine justice (Rev. 1:16), the tongue (Ps. 57:4), and the word of God (Heb. 4:12). The sword of the Spirit, which is the word of God, is part of the Christian's armament in the fight against evil (Eph. 6:17).

SYCAMORE Combination "fig" and "mulberry" tree; the fig tree in the Jordan Valley that had leaves like our mulberry tree. Its fruit was inferior to the fig tree and had to be punctured to make the fruit edible. The prophet Amos was employed as one "who took care of sycamore figs" (Amos 7:14 CSB).

SYCHAR Village in Samaria where Jesus talked with the Samaritan woman at Jacob's well (John 4:5-6).

SYMBOL Token or sign. The Bible is rich in symbolism and symbolic language. The universal and supreme symbol of Christian faith is the cross, an instrument of execution. For Christians, this hideous object is a sign of God's love for human beings. Baptism is a picture of the death, burial, and resurrection of Christ. In being baptized, one says to the world that one is identifying with the saving act being pictured, dying to sin and rising to walk in new life with God as the center of life. The Lord's Supper uses the ordinary elements of bread and wine to picture Christ's broken body and his blood shed for humanity's sin.

Several symbols in the OT are related to NT truths. For example, the sacrificial lamb in the OT points to the sacrificial death of Christ. The parables of Jesus are rich in symbols: grain, weeds, various kinds of soil, a lost sheep, a lost coin, and a lost son. Jesus used symbolic language in talking about himself and his relationship to persons: bread of life, light of the world, good shepherd, water of life, and the door.

SYNAGOGUE Local meeting place and assembly of the Jewish people during late intertestamental and NT times. The synagogue had its roots in the time after Solomon's temple was destroyed and the people of Judah went into Babylonian exile. Local worship and instruction became necessary. Even after Jews returned to Jerusalem and rebuilt the temple, places of local worship continued. By the first century these local meeting places were called synagogues.

A third-century synagogue at Capernaum

SYNOPTIC GOSPELS See *Gospels, Synoptic.*

SYNTYCHE Personal name meaning "pleasant acquaintance" or "good luck." Woman in the church at Philippi exhorted by Paul to settle her disagreement with another woman named Euodia (Phil. 4:2).

Reconstruction of a typical synagogue of the first century AD showing the large inner room where the men gathered and its loft above where the women gathered. This particular drawing is patterned after the synagogue at Capernaum.

SYRACUSE Major city on the island of Sicily where Paul stayed during his trip to Rome (Acts 28:12).

SYRIA Region or nation directly north of Palestine in the northwest corner of the Mediterranean Sea. The area covered by ancient Syria is roughly equal to the modern states of Syria and Lebanon with small portions of Turkey and Iraq. In most English versions of the OT, "Syria" and "Syrian" translate the Hebrew word *'Aram*, which refers to the nations or territories of the Arameans, a group akin to Israel (Deut. 26:5). The Arameans began to settle in Syria and northern Mesopotamia around the beginning of the Iron Age (about 1200 BC), establishing a number of independent states. The OT mentions the Aramean kingdoms of Beth-eden in north Syria, Zobah in south-central Syria, and Damascus in the south. In NT times, Judea was made part of a procuratorship within the larger Roman province of Syria (Matt. 4:24), the latter being ruled by a governor (Luke 2:2). Syria played an important role in the early spread of Christianity. Paul was converted on the road to Damascus (Acts 9:1-9) and subsequently evangelized in the province (Acts 15:41). Antioch, where believers were first called "Christians" (Acts 11:26), became the base for his missionary journeys (Acts 13:1-3).

SYROPHENICIAN (KJV) or **SYROPHOENICIAN** Combination of Syria and Phoenicia. The word reflects the joining of the two areas into one district under Roman rule. Jesus encountered in this district a woman whose daughter was possessed by a devil (Mark 7:26).

T

Reconstruction of the Israelite tabernacle and its court. The court was formed by curtains attached to erect poles. In front of the tent was placed the altar of burnt offerings and the laver. The tabernacle was always erected to face the east.

TAANACH Place-name of uncertain meaning. One of the sites along the northern slope of the Mount Carmel range protecting the accesses from the Plain of Esdraelon to the region of Samaria.

In the Bible, Taanach is mentioned only seven times, usually in lists such as tribal allotments (Josh. 17:11; 1 Chron. 7:29), administrative districts (1 Kgs. 4: 12), Levitical towns (Josh. 21:25), or conquered cities (Josh. 12:21; Judg. 1:27). The most famous biblical reference to Taanach is that of the battle fought at "Taanach by the waters of Megiddo" (CSB) where the Hebrew forces under Deborah and Barak defeated the Canaanites under Sisera (Judg. 5:19).

TAANATH-SHILOH Place-name likely meaning "approach to Shiloh." Village located about seven miles southeast of Shechem between Michmethath and Janoah (Josh. 16:6).

TABBAOTH Personal name meaning "signet ring." Head of a family of temple servants (Nethinim) returning from exile (Ezra 2:43; Neh. 7:46).

TABBATH Place-name, perhaps meaning "sunken." Site in the mountains of Gilead east of the Jordan where Gideon ended his pursuit of the Midianites (Judg. 7:22).

TABEEL Aramaic personal name meaning "God is good." **1.** Father of a man whom King Rezin of Damascus and King Pekah of Israel hoped to install as puppet king of Judah rather than Ahaz (Isa. 7:6). Alternately, Tabeel designates a region in northern Transjordan and home of the potential puppet. Spelling has been slightly changed in Hebrew to mean "good for nothing." **2.** Persian official in Samaria who joined in a letter protesting the reconstruction of the Jerusalem temple (Ezra 4:7).

TABERAH Place-name meaning "burning." Unidentified site in the wilderness wandering. The name commemorates God's "burning anger," which broke out in fire against the ever-complaining Israelites (Num. 11:3; Deut. 9:22). The name does not appear in the itinerary of Num. 33.

TABERING KJV term meaning "beating" (Nah. 2:7).

TABERNACLE, TENT OF MEETING Sacred tent, portable and provisional sanctuary, where God met his people (Exod. 33:7-10). Two compound phrases (*'ohel mo'ed* and *'ohel ha'eduth*) are used to designate this tent: "the tabernacle of the congregation" (Exod. 29:42,44), literally the "tent of meeting" (CSB, NRSV, NIV, NASB, REB) and "the tabernacle of witness" (Num. 17:7) or "tent of witness." In both cases, it was the place where the God of Israel revealed himself to and dwelled among his people. The basic Hebrew term (*mishkan*) translated as "tabernacle" (Exod. 25:9) comes from a verb that means "to dwell." In this sense, it is correctly translated in some instances as "dwelling," "dwelling place," "habitation," and "abode."

The OT mentions three tents or tabernacles. First, after the sin of the golden calf at Mount Sinai, the "provisional" tabernacle was established outside the camp and called the "tent of meeting" (Exod. 33:7). Second, the "Sinaitic" tabernacle was built in accordance with directions given to Moses by God (Exod. 25–40). Unlike the tent of meeting, it stood at the center of the camp (Num. 2). Third, the "Davidic" tabernacle was erected in Jerusalem for the reception of the ark (2 Sam. 6:17).

TABERNACLES, FEAST OF See *Festivals*.

TABITHA Aramaic personal name meaning "gazelle," which serves as the counterpart to the Greek name Dorcas (Acts 9:36). See *Dorcas*.

TABLE OF NATIONS Genesis 10 lists the descendants of Noah's sons to explain the origin of the nations and peoples of the known world. The account is unique for several reasons. First, a new chapter begins

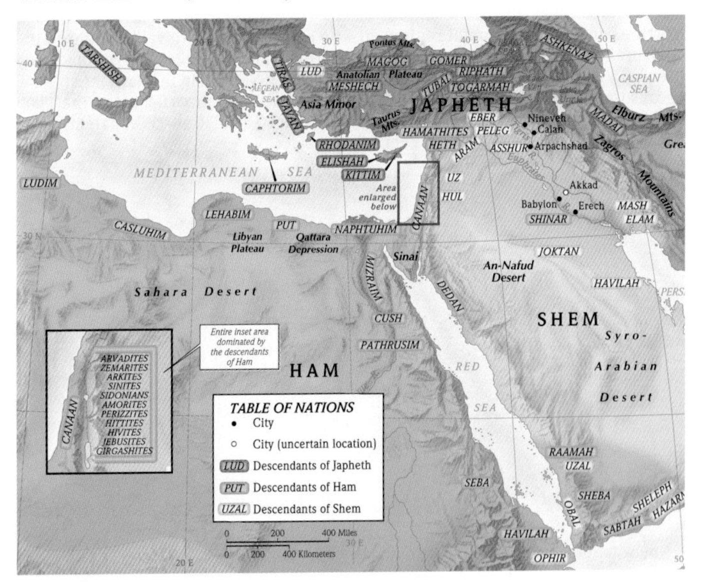

in biblical history at this point: humanity has a new beginning through Noah and his three sons. Second, the account highlights the ethnic makeup of the ancient world, listing some 70 different ethnic groups that formed the basis of the known world. Third, despite our lack of knowledge about many of the groups listed in the chapter, Gen. 10 underlines the fact that the Bible is based on historical events. Fourth, Gen. 10 provides the basis for understanding Abraham, introducing his world and his relationship to that world. The account of the Table of Nations, with a few variations, also appears in 1 Chron. 1:5-23.

The Table of Nations has three basic divisions. The people and lands of the known world fit into one of three families, the family of Shem, Ham, or Japheth. The names that appear in each of the families are names that come from several different categories: racial descent, geographical location, language differences, or political units.

Japheth's descendants (Gen. 10:2-5) inhabited the Aegean region and Anatolia or Asia Minor. The descendants of Ham (Gen. 10:6-20) were located especially in the regions of North Africa and the coastal regions of Canaan and Syria. The descendants of Shem (Gen. 10:21-31) are especially important because Abraham comes from the line of Shem. Thus Abraham is a Shemite or Semite. Because he is also a descendant of Eber, he is called a Hebrew (Gen. 11:14-32). The descendants of Shem were located generally in north Syria, that is, the region of the upper part of the Euphrates River, and Mesopotamia, especially the eastern part.

TABLET Usually a flat surface used for writing. **1.** *Law tablets.* Scripture names the stone objects bearing the Ten Commandments the tablets (or tables) of the law (Exod. 24:12), testimony (Exod. 31:18), and covenant (Deut. 9:9). These tablets were perhaps small steles such as those other nations used to publicize their laws. **2.** *Writing tablets.* Writing was often done on clay tablets (Ezek. 4:1) or wood tablets covered with wax (Luke 1:63). The heart is often described as a tablet upon which God writes his law (Prov. 3:3; Jer. 17:1; 2 Cor. 3:3).

TABOR Place-name of uncertain meaning, perhaps "height." **1.** Mountain in the valley of Jezreel. About six miles east of Nazareth, it has played an important role in Israel's history since the period of the conquest. Tradition holds that Tabor was the site of Jesus's transfiguration (Mark 9:2), although no evidence exists to validate the claim. **2.** Levitical city (1 Chron. 6:77), apparently replacing Nahalal in the earlier list (Josh. 21:35). It may be Khirbet Dabura. **3.** The "Plain of Tabor" (1 Sam. 10:3) was apparently near Gibea.

Mount Tabor located a few miles southeast of Nazareth

TABOR, OAK OF NASB, CSB, NRSV designation of a site between Rachel's tomb (near Bethlehem) and Gibeah of Saul (1 Sam. 10:3). Other translations read "plain" (KJV), "great tree" (NIV), or "terebinth" (REB) of Tabor.

TABRIMMON Personal name meaning "Rimmon is good." Father of King Ben-hadad of Damascus (1 Kgs. 15:18). Rimmon was the Akkadian god of thunder.

TACHES KJV term meaning "hooks" or "clasps" (Exod. 26:6,11,33) used to connect the individual curtains of the tabernacle into one tent.

TACKLING KJV form of tackle, that is, gear used to handle cargo and rigging to work a ship's sails (Isa. 33:23; Acts 27:19).

TADMOR Place-name of uncertain meaning. A city built by Solomon (2 Chron. 8:4), probably to control a caravan route. The site has been identified with Palmyra, a great Arabian city, located in modern Syria, about 120 miles northeast of Damascus.

TAHAN Personal name meaning "graciousness." **1.** Third son of Ephraim (Num. 26:35). The parallel list gives Tahath as Ephraim's third son (1 Chron. 7:20). **2.** Ephraimite ancestor of Joshua (1 Chron. 7:25).

TAHANITES Member of the Ephraimite clan descended from Tahan (Num. 26:35).

TAHASH Personal name meaning "porpoise" or "dugong." Third son of Nahor and Reumah (Gen. 22:24) and ancestor of an Arab tribe.

TAHATH Personal name and place-name meaning "beneath, low" or "substitute, compensation." **1.** A Levite (1 Chron. 6:24,37). **2.** Two descendants of Ephraim (1 Chron. 7:20). See *Tahan*. **3.** Stopping place during the wilderness wandering (Num. 33:26-27).

TAHCHEMONITE or **TAHKEMONITE** (NIV) Title of one of David's 30 elite warriors (2 Sam. 23:8), likely a scribal altering of the Hebrew *ha Hachmonite* (REB), which occurs in the parallel list (1 Chron. 11:11).

TAHPANHES Hebrew transliteration of an Egyptian place-name meaning "fortress of Penhase" or "house of the Nubian." City in the Nile Delta near the eastern border of Egypt (Jer. 2:16). Following the destruction of Jerusalem and continuing unrest in Judah, a large group of Jews took Jeremiah with them and fled to Tahpanhes (Jer. 43:7; 44:1). Jeremiah argued against the move (Jer. 42:19), warning that Nebuchadnezzar would again reach Tahpanhes (Jer. 46:14).

TAHPENES Egyptian royal consort; title for queen of Egypt in 1 Kgs. 11:19-20. Her sister was given in marriage to Hadad the Edomite, an enemy of David, and later of Solomon.

TAHREA Alternate form of Tarea (1 Chron. 9:41).

TAHTIM-HODSHI Site in northern Israel that David's census takers visited (2 Sam. 24:6).

TALENT Hebrew weight of about 76 pounds (about 3,000 shekels). In the NT, a talent was a large sum of money. See *Weights and Measures*.

TALITHA CUMI or **TALITHA KOUM** Transliteration of Aramaic phrase meaning "damsel, arise." Jesus's words to Jairus's daughter (Mark 5:41).

TALMAI Personal name meaning "plowman" or else derived from the Hurrian word for "big." **1.** One of three Anakim (giant, pre-Israelite inhabitants of Canaan) residing in Hebron (Num. 13:22). **2.** King of Geshur, father of David's wife Maacah and grandfather of Absalom (2 Sam. 3:3; 1 Chron. 3:2).

TALMON Personal name meaning "brightness." **1.** Levite whom David and Samuel appointed as a gatekeeper (1 Chron. 9:17), ancestor of a family of temple gatekeepers who returned from exile (Ezra 2:42; Neh. 7:45). **2.** Leader of the postexilic gatekeepers (Neh. 11:19; 12:25).

TALMUD Jewish commentaries. Talmud means "study" or "learning" and refers in rabbinic Judaism to the opinions and teachings that disciples learn from their predecessors particularly with regard to the development of oral legal teachings (halakah). The word "Talmud" is most commonly used in Judaism to refer specifically to the digest of commentary on the Mishnah. The Mishnah (a codification of oral legal teachings on the written law of Moses) was probably written down at Javneh in Galilee at about AD 220. Between AD 220 and 500 the rabbinic schools in Palestine and Babylonia amplified and applied the teachings of the Mishnah for their Jewish communities. Two documents came to embody a large part of this teaching: the Jerusalem Talmud and the Babylonian Talmud.

TAMAR Personal name meaning "date palm." **1.** Daughter-in-law of Judah, wife of his eldest son, Er (Gen. 38:6). **2.** Daughter of David raped by her half brother, Amnon (2 Sam. 13:14). **3.** Absalom named his only daughter Tamar. She is called "a beautiful woman" (2 Sam. 14:27). **4.** City built by Solomon "in the wilderness" (1 Kgs. 9:18). **5.** Fortified city at the southern end of the Dead Sea, marking the ideal limit of Israel (Ezek. 47:19; 48:28).

TAMARISK Shrublike tree (*Tamarix syriaca*) common to the Sinai and southern Palestine with small white or pink flowers. Abraham planted a tamarisk at Beer-sheba (Gen. 21:33), and Saul was buried beneath one at Jabesh-gilead (1 Sam. 31:13).

TAMMUZ Sumerian god of vegetation. The worship of Tammuz by women in Jerusalem was revealed as one of the abominations in Ezekiel (8:14-15).

TANHUMETH Personal name meaning "comforting." Father of Seraiah, a captain of forces remaining with Gedaliah in Judah following the deportation of Babylon (2 Kgs. 25:23; Jer. 40:8). A Lachish stamp witnesses to the name as does an Arad inscription.

TAPHATH Personal name meaning "droplet." Daughter of Solomon and wife of Ben-abinadab, a Solomonic official (1 Kgs. 4:11).

TAPPUAH Personal name meaning "apple" or "quince." **1.** A Calebite, likely a resident of a town near Hebron (1 Chron. 2:43). **2.** City in the Shephelah district of Judah (Josh. 15:34), possibly Beit Nettif about 12 miles west of Bethlehem. **3.** City of the north border of Ephraim (Josh. 16:8) whose environs were allotted to Manasseh (17:7-8), likely the Tappuah of Josh. 12:17 and 2 Kgs. 15:16.

TARAH KJV form of "Terah," the wilderness campsite (Num. 33:27-28).

TARALAH Place-name meaning "strength." Unidentified site in Benjamin, likely northwest of Jerusalem (Josh. 18:27).

TAREA Personal name of unknown derivation. Descendant of Saul (1 Chron. 8:35; "Tahrea" 1 Chron. 9:41).

TARES KJV term for grassy weeds resembling wheat, generally identified as darnel (*genus Lolium*) (Matt. 13:25-30,36-40).

TARGUM Early translations of the Bible into Aramaic, the native language of Palestine and Babylon in the first century AD. Targum, in its verbal Hebrew form, means "to explain, to translate."

TARPELITES KJV transliteration of an Aramaic title in Ezra 4:9. Most modern translations render the term "officials" (NIV, "men of Tripolis"; CSB, "magistrates from Tripolis").

TARSHISH Personal name and place-name of uncertain derivation, meaning "yellow jasper," as in the Hebrew of Exod. 28:20; Ezek. 28:13, or derived from an Akkadian term meaning "smelting plant." **1.** Son of Javan (Gen. 10:4; 1 Chron. 1:7) and ancestor of an Aegean people. **2.** Benjaminite warrior (1 Chron. 7:10). **3.** One of seven leading officials of King Ahasuerus of Persia (Esth. 1:14). This name possibly means "greedy one" in Old Persian. **4.** Geographic designation, most likely of Tartessus at the southern tip of Spain but possibly of Tarsus in Cilisia. Jonah sailed for Tarshish, the far limit of the Western world, from the Mediterranean port of Joppa in his futile attempt to escape God's call (Jon. 1:3). Tarshish traded in precious metals with Tyre, another Mediterranean port (Isa. 23:1;

Jer. 10:9; Ezek. 27:12). **5.** References to Tarshish in 1 Kings and 2 Chronicles suggest a nongeographic meaning. Solomon's (1 Kgs. 10:22; 2 Chron. 9:21) and Jehoshaphat's (1 Kgs. 22:48; 2 Chron. 20:36) fleets were based at Ezion-geber on the Red Sea. Solomon's cargo suggests east African trading partners. Thus "ships of Tarshish" may designate seagoing vessels like those of Tarshish or else ships bearing metal cargo like those of Tarshish (cp. Isa. 2:16, where "ships of Tarshish" parallels "beautiful crafts").

TARSUS Birthplace of Paul (Acts 9:11) and capital of Roman province of Cilicia.

TARTAK Deity worshipped by the Avvites, whom the Assyrians made to settle in Samaria after 722 BC (2 Kgs. 17:31).

TARTAN Title of the highest-ranking Assyrian officer under the king; commander in chief; supreme commander (2 Kgs. 18:17; Isa. 20:1).

The Cleopatra Gate at Tarsus commemorating Mark Antony's meeting of Cleopatra at this ancient city

TASKMASTER Oppressive overseers of forced labor gangs employed by monarchies for large public works projects (Egyptian: Exod. 1:11; 3:7; 5:6-14; Israelite: 2 Sam. 20:24; 1 Kgs. 4:6; 5:16; 12:18; 2 Chron. 10:18).

TATNAI (KJV) or **TATTENAI** Contemporary of Zerubbabel, governor of the Persian province "across the (Euphrates) River," which included Palestine (Ezra 5:3,6; 6:6,13).

TAU Twenty-second and final letter of the Hebrew alphabet, which the KJV used as a heading for Ps.119:169-176, each verse of which begins with the letter.

TAXES Regular payments to rulers. Early Israel paid taxes only to support the tabernacle and the priests. Terms in the OT that refer to taxes were "assessment," "forced labor," "tribute," and "toll." During David's reign, an army was maintained by tribute paid by conquered tribes. Taxes increased under Solomon's rule. Tradesmen and merchants paid duties; subject peoples paid tribute; farmers paid taxes in kind of oil and wine; and many Israelites did forced labor on the temple. The burden of taxation contributed to the rebellion following Solomon's death (1 Kgs. 12). Soon Israel became a vassal state, paying tribute—a compulsory tax—to Assyria and, eventually, to Rome.

In the NT era, Herod the Great levied a tax on the produce of the field and a tax on items bought and sold. Other duties owed to foreign powers were a land tax, a poll tax, a kind of progressive income tax (about which the Pharisees tested Jesus, Matt. 22:17), and a tax on personal property. In Jerusalem, a house tax was levied. These taxes were paid directly to Roman officials.

Export and import customs paid at seaports and city gates were farmed out to private contractors who paid a sum in advance for the right to collect taxes in a certain area. Such were Zacchaeus (Luke 19) and Matthew (Matt. 9).

The Israelites resented most deeply the duties paid to the occupying powers. Many zealous Jews considered it treason to God to pay taxes to Rome. When questioned about paying the poll tax, Jesus surprised his questioners by saying that the law should be obeyed (Mark 12:13).

TEBAH Personal name meaning "slaughter." Son of Nahor and ancestor of an Aramaean tribe (Gen. 22:24).

TEBALIAH Personal name meaning "Yahweh has dipped, that is, purified," or "loved by Yahweh," or "good for Yahweh." Postexilic Levitic gatekeeper (1 Chron. 26:11).

TEBETH Tenth month (December–January) of the Hebrew calendar (Esth. 2:16). The name derives from an Akkadian term meaning "sinking" and refers to the rainy month.

TEHAPHNEHES Alternate form of Tahpanhes (Ezek. 30:18).

TEHINNAH Personal name meaning "supplication" or "graciousness." Descendant of Judah responsible for founding Irnahash (1 Chron. 4:12).

TEIL TREE KJV term meaning "lime" or "linden tree," used to translate a Hebrew term generally rendered "oak" or "terebinth" (Isa. 6:13).

TEKOA Place-name meaning "place of setting up a tent." A city in the highlands of Judah six miles south of Bethlehem and 10 miles south of Jerusalem; home of the prophet Amos. God called Amos from among the shepherds of Tekoa to preach to the northern kingdom of Israel (Amos 1:1). The priest tried to send him back to Tekoa (7:12).

TEL-ABIB Place-name meaning "mound of the flood" or "mound of grain." Tel-abib on the Chebar River/Canal near Nippur in Babylon was home to Ezekiel and other exiles (Ezek. 3:15). The Babylonians may have thought it was the ruined site of the original flood.

TEL-ASSAR Place-name meaning "mound of Asshur." City in northern Mesopotamia that the Assyrians conquered (2 Kgs. 19:12 KJV, "Thelasar"; Isa. 37:12).

TEL-HARSA (KJV, Ezra 2:59) or **TEL-HARSHA** Place-name meaning "mound of the forest" or "mound of magic." Home of Babylonian Jews unable to demonstrate their lineage (Ezra 2:59; Neh. 7:61).

TEL-MELAH Place-name meaning "mound of salt." Babylonian home of a group of Jews unable to demonstrate their lineage (Ezra 2:59; Neh. 7:61).

TELAH Personal name meaning "breach" or "fracture." An ancestor of Joshua (1 Chron. 7:25).

TELAIM Place-name meaning "young speckled lambs." City in southern Judah where Saul gathered forces to battle the Amalekites (1 Sam. 15:4).

TELEM Personal name and place-name meaning "brightness" or "lamb." **1.** Levite with a foreign wife (Ezra 10:24). **2.** City in southern Judah (Josh. 15:24), a variant form of Telaim.

TELL Semitic term meaning "mound," applied to areas built up by successive settlements at a single site. "Tell" or "tel" is a common element in Near Eastern place-names.

TEMA Personal name and place-name meaning "south country." Tema, a son of Ishmael (Gen. 25:15; 1 Chron. 1:30), is associated with Tema (modern Teima), a strategic oasis located on the Arabian Peninsula 250 miles southeast of Aqaba and 200 miles north-northeast of Medina.

Modern Tekoa

TEMAH Family of temple servants (Nethinim) returning from exile (Ezra 2:53; Neh. 7:55).

TEMAN Personal name and place-name meaning "right side," that is, "southern." **1.** Edomite clan descended from Esau (Gen. 36:11,15; 1 Chron. 1:36). **2.** City of area associated with this clan (Jer. 49:7,20; Ezek. 25:13; Amos 1:12; Obad. 1:9; Hab. 3:3). Teman has often been identified with Tawilan, 50 miles south of the Dead Sea just east of Petra.

TEMANI (KJV) or **TEMANITES** Descendants of Teman or residents of Teman, the southern area of Edom. The land of the Temanites designates (southern) Edom (Gen. 36:34 KJV "Temani"; 1 Chron. 1:45). The Temanites were renowned for their wisdom (Job 2:11; cp. Jer. 49:7).

TEMENI Personal name, perhaps meaning "on the right hand," that is, "to the south." Descendant of Judah (1 Chron. 4:6).

TEMPLE OF JERUSALEM Place of worship, especially the temple of Solomon built in Jerusalem for national worship of Yahweh. When David built for himself a cedar palace, he thought it only proper he should build one for Yahweh, too (2 Sam. 7:1-2). Nathan at first approved his plan, but the Lord himself said he had been used to living in a tent since the exodus from Egypt. He would allow David's son to build him a house (temple), but he would build for David a house (dynasty, 2 Sam. 7:3-16). This covenant promise became exceedingly significant to the messianic hope fulfilled in the coming of the ideal king of the line of David.

There were three historical temples in succession, those of Solomon, Zerubbabel, and Herod in the preexilic, postexilic, and NT periods. Herod's temple was really a massive rebuilding of the Zerubbabel temple, so both are called the "second temple" by Judaism. All three were located on a prominent hill north of David's capital city, which

Reconstruction of Herod's temple (20 BC–AD 70) at Jerusalem as viewed from the southeast. The drawing reflects archaeological discoveries made since excavations began in 1967 along the south end of the Temple Mount platform.

he conquered from the Jebusites (2 Sam. 5:6-7). David had acquired the temple hill from Araunah the Jebusite at the advice of the prophet Gad to stay a pestilence from the Lord by building an altar and offering sacrifices on the threshing floor (2 Sam. 24:18-25). Chronicles identifies this hill with Mount Moriah, where Abraham had been willing to offer Isaac (2 Chron. 3:1; Gen. 22:1-14). So the Temple Mount today in Jerusalem is called Mount Moriah, and the threshing floor of Araunah is undoubtedly the large rock enshrined within the Dome of the Rock, center of the Muslim enclosure called Haram es-Sharif (the third holiest place in Islam, after Mecca and Medina). This enclosure is basically what is left of Herod's enlarged temple platform, the masonry of which may best be seen in its Western Wall, the holiest place within Judaism since the Roman destruction of Herod's temple.

A Christian monastery on the Mount of Temptation marks the traditional site of Jesus's temptation.

TEMPTATION Broadly defined, temptation is the enticement to do evil. Satan is the tempter (Matt. 4:3; 1 Thess. 3:5). Beginning with Eve, Satan successfully tempted Adam, Cain, Abraham, and David to sin. He was less successful with Job, and Jesus was "tempted in every way as we are, yet without sin" (Heb. 4:15 CSB). James explains that God cannot be tempted by evil, and he does not tempt anyone (James 1:13). Temptation may be for the purpose of destroying a person through sin leading to death and hell. This is Satan's intent. God may allow testing for the purpose of bringing forth faith and patience, which ultimately honor him, as in the case of Job. James further explains that a blessing awaits the one who endures temptation (James 1:12).

TEMPTATION OF JESUS Jesus was tempted by the devil in the wilderness subsequent to his baptism by John. Matthew and Luke describe in some detail three encounters between Jesus and Satan. The foremost difference between the accounts is the reversal of the order of the final two temptations. Matthew connects the first two with a connective particle that can have chronological implications. Luke's interest in Jerusalem and the temple (1:9; 2:22,25,37,41-50) make it more likely that he used the third temptation as a climax to the temptations.

Forty days in the wilderness is reminiscent of the fasts of Moses (Exod. 34:28; Deut. 9:9) and Elijah (1 Kgs. 9:8), and the 40 years of the Israelites in the desert (Num. 14:33; 32:13). The only parallel developed, however, is the wilderness wanderings of Israel. As God led Israel in the wilderness, likewise the Spirit led Jesus into the wilderness. God tested Israel in the wilderness and they failed. God allowed Jesus to be tempted by the devil, and he succeeded in resisting. Angels ministered to Jesus after the temptations. Luke is the only evangelist to note that Satan's departure was not the end of the conflict (4:13), but the intensity was not repeated until Gethsemane (22:40,46,53) and Golgotha (23:35-36,39).

Several significant features stand out as one contemplates Jesus's temptation in the wilderness. His encounter with the devil in the wilderness is a source of encouragement and instruction to believers as they battle temptation (Heb. 2:18; 4:15). His commitment

St. Catherine's Monastery as seen from atop Mount Sinai. The traditional site believed to be where Moses received the Ten Commandments.

to the Father's will, use of Scripture, and resolve to resist the devil (James 4:7) are helpful examples for battling temptation.

TEN COMMANDMENTS Although many people refer to the "Decalogue" as the Ten Commandments, this is unfortunate for several reasons. First, it obscures the fact that this is not what the OT calls them. Wherever it is referred to by title it is identified as *aseret haddebarim*, "the Ten Words" (Exod. 34:28; Deut. 4:13; 10:4). This sense is captured precisely in the Greek word *decalogos*. Second, in both the original context in which the Decalogue was given (Exod. 20:1) and Moses's remembrance of the event in Deut. 4:12 and 5:22, the Decalogue is presented as a set of spoken words rather than a written set of laws. Third, "Ten Commandments" obscures the fact that the Decalogue is a covenant document, whose form follows ancient Near Eastern treaty tradition. Fourth, as a code of laws, the Decalogue is virtually unenforceable. For all these reasons, although the 10 statements are in the form of commands, we should follow the lead of the biblical texts and refer to them as the "Ten Words/Declarations," the 10 fundamental principles of covenant relationship. The stipulations revealed in the "Book of the Covenant," the "Holiness Code," and other parts of the Pentateuch represent clarifications and applications of these principles. Presumably the stipulations of the covenant were reduced to 10 principles so they could be easily memorized.

Apart from Moses's citation of the Decalogue in Deut. 5, the OT gives little if any evidence of giving the Decalogue greater authority than any of the other laws revealed at Sinai. This does not mean that these tablets were not treated as special. On the contrary, Moses notes that the Decalogue contained the only revelation that was communicated by God directly to the people (Deut. 4:12-13; 5:22) and committed to writing on tablets of stone by God's own hand (Exod. 24:12; 31:18; 34:1; Deut. 4:13; 5:22; 10:1-4). All subsequent revelation at Sinai was communicated indirectly through Moses, the covenant mediator. The special status of the tablets is reflected in the fact that these tablets (and these alone) were deposited inside the ark of the covenant (Deut. 10:5; 1 Kgs. 8:9).

The Decalogue may legitimately be interpreted as a Bill of Rights, perhaps the world's first Bill of Rights. Yet unlike modern bills of rights, this document seeks not to secure my rights but to protect the rights of others. I am perceived as a potential violator of the other person's rights. Understood this way, the significance of the 10 declarations may be summarized as follows:

1. God's right to exclusive allegiance (Exod. 20:3; Deut. 5:7).
2. God's right to self-definition (Exod. 20:4-6; Deut. 5:8-10).
3. God's right to proper representation by his people (Exod. 20:7; Deut. 5:11).
4. God's right to his people's time (Exod. 20:8-11); a household's right to humane treatment by the head of the house (Deut. 5:12-15).
5. My parents' right to respect (Exod. 20:12; Deut. 5:16).
6. My neighbor's right to life (Exod. 20:13; Deut. 5:17).
7. My neighbor's right to a secure marriage (Exod. 20:14; Deut. 5:18).
8. My neighbor's right to personal property (Exod. 20:15; Deut. 5:19).
9. My neighbor's right to an honest hearing in court (Exod. 20:16; Deut. 5:20).
10. My neighbor's right to secure existence in the community (Exod. 20:17; Deut. 5:21).

The first four statements protect the rights of the covenant Lord; the last six protect the rights of the covenant community. The Decalogue calls on the redeemed to respond to the grace they have experienced in salvation with covenant commitment, first to God, and then to others. This is the essence of "love" (*'ahab*) as understood in both the OT and NT.

TENDERHEARTED KJV used "tenderhearted" in two senses: of timidity (2 Chron. 13:7) and of compassion (Eph. 4:32).

TENON KJV, NASB, REB, RSV translation of a Hebrew term meaning "hands," applied to projections designed to fit into a mortise or socket to form a joint (Exod. 26:17,19; 36:22,24). Other translations employ "projections" (NIV, TEV) or "pegs" (NRSV).

TERAH Personal name, perhaps meaning "ibex." **1.** The father of Abraham, Nahor, and Haran (Gen. 11:26). Along with a migration of people from Ur of the Chaldees, Terah moved his family, following the Euphrates River to Haran (11:31). He intended to continue from Haran into Canaan but died in Mesopotamia at the age of 205 (11:32). A debate has centered on Terah's religious practices, for Josh. 24:2 apparently points to his family when it claims records that the father worshipped gods other than Yahweh. **2.** Wilderness campsite (Num. 33:27-28).

TERAPHIM Transliteration of a Hebrew word for household idols of indeterminate size and shape. They were also referred to as "gods" (cp. Gen. 31: 19,30-35; 1 Sam. 19:13).

TEREBINTH Large, spreading tree whose species is uncertain so that translations vary in reading the Hebrew *'elah* into English (cp. 2 Sam. 18:9; Isa. 1:30; 6:13). The tree had religious connections as a place under which pagan gods were worshipped (Hos. 4:13; Ezek. 6:13) that were at times taken up in Israel's religion (Gen. 35:4; Josh. 24:26; Judg. 6:11; 1 Kgs. 13:14).

TERESH Personal name meaning "firm, solid," or derived from an Old Persian term meaning "desire." One of two royal eunuchs who plotted an unsuccessful assassination of the Persian king Ahasuerus. Following their exposure by Mordecai, the two were hung (Esth. 2:21-23).

TERTIUS Latin personal name meaning "third [son]." Paul's amanuensis (secretary) for the writing of Romans who included his own greeting at Rom. 16:22. Some suggest that Quartus, whose name means "fourth," is perhaps Tertius's younger brother (Rom. 16:23).

TERTULLUS Diminutive of the personal name Tertius, meaning "third" (Acts 24:1-8). Tertullus was the prosecutor opposing Paul before Felix, the Roman governor of Judea.

TETH Ninth letter of the Hebrew alphabet that KJV used as a heading for Ps. 119:65-72, each verse of which begins with this letter.

TETRARCH Political position in the early Roman Empire. It designated the size of the territory ruled (literally the "fourth part") and the amount of dependence on Roman authority. Luke 3:1 names one of the tetrarchs who served in the year of Jesus's birth.

TEXTUAL CRITICISM The art and science of reconstructing the text of a work that no longer exists in its original form. The word "criticism" is not a negative term in this context. It refers to methods of careful study and analysis whose aim is to determine the original text of each book with the greatest possible degree of detail and accuracy through the careful study and comparison of all extant manuscripts.

TEXTUS RECEPTUS Term that is generally applied to certain printed editions of the Greek NT, but sometimes extended to refer also to the ben Chayim edition of the Hebrew OT.

THADDAEUS Personal name, perhaps meaning "gift of God" in Greek but derived from Hebrew or Aramaic meaning "breast." An apostle of Jesus (Matt. 10:3; Mark 3:18), also called Lebbaeus Thaddaeus and Judas (not Iscariot).

THEBEZ Likely Tubas, 13 miles northeast of Shechem where the roads from Shechem and Dothan converge to lead down to the Jordan Valley. During the siege of Thebez, a woman of the city fatally wounded Abimelech by throwing an upper millstone on his head (Judg. 9:50-53; 2 Sam. 11:21).

THEOCRACY Form of government in which God directly rules. As the sovereign King, God may rule directly through unmediated means, or he may choose to use various mediators to manifest his rule. In either case, God himself is the sovereign Ruler.

The theocracy of God is revealed progressively in the Scripture. The giving of the Mosaic law by God to the Israelites gave the Hebrew people a unique theocratic structure. The next step in the development of the theocratic state was the taking of promised land (the conquest) and the period of the judges (conflict). Under Joshua's capable leadership, the Israelites were able to enter and conquer Canaan according to the promises of God. In this act, the people of God were provided a land in which to build a theocratic state.

The people soon asked for a king. The existence of a human king, however, did not ideally conflict with the theocracy. The king, as chosen by God, would not be a despotic, selfish dictator, but rather a man who would walk in the light of the Lord and seek God's guidance in all matters. Thus, the rule of the human monarch would glorify God and manifest the theocratic ideal.

The theocratic ideal experience declined among the Israelites following the division of the monarchy and the exilic/postexilic periods. There is a sense, however, in which the ideal of a theocracy is resumed in the NT. Christ, as the Messiah and the Davidic King, is the person in whom the kingdom of God resides. With his preaching and earthly ministry, he gave evidence that "the kingdom of God is in your midst" (Luke 17:20 CSB). Further, following his resurrection, he declared to his followers: "All authority has been given to me in heaven and on earth. Go, therefore, and make disciples of all nations" (Matt. 28:18-20 CSB). With this declaration, the risen King commissioned his followers to go and to proclaim the existence of his kingdom. As Christians individually and corporately submit and propagate the lordship of Christ, in a sense they experience and express the theocratic ideal of God's direct governance. Thus a NT church should endeavor to realize and appropriate the direct rule of the sovereign King in all areas.

THEOLOGY, BIBLICAL Discussion of what the Bible itself teaches about God and his dealings with human beings and the rest of creation. Biblical theology opens up the unity of the Bible by exposing and collecting its major themes. It demonstrates the many ways in which diverse books and material are united by the character of God the Father, Son, and Holy Spirit.

THEOPHANY Physical appearance or personal manifestation of God to a person. There are some five forms of theophanies: in human form (Gen. 32:30; Exod. 24:10), in visions (Isa. 6; Ezek. 1; Dan. 7:9), by the angel of the Lord (Gen. 16:7-13), not in human form (as at the burning bush, Exod. 3:2–4:17, and in the guidance through the wilderness, 13:21; cp. Acts 7:30), and as the name of the Lord (God's sacred name represented his presence, Deut. 12:5; Isa. 30:27; 59:19). The glory of the Lord appears to people in numerous passages. God's presence is in a cloud (Exod. 16:10; 33:9-10; Ezek. 10:4). God was also manifest in nature and history (Isa. 6:3; Ezek. 1:28; 43:2).

The incarnate Christ was not, and indeed is not, a theophany. The phenomena of theophanies were temporary, for the occasion that required them, and then disappeared. On the other hand, in the incarnate Christ his deity and humanity were joined, not for time alone, but for eternity.

THEOPHILUS Personal name meaning "friend of God;" the person to whom the books of Luke and Acts were written (Luke 1:3; Acts 1:1).

THESSALONIANS, FIRST LETTER TO THE Thessalonica was the largest city in first-century Macedonia and the capital of the province. It was a free city. Paul, Silas, and Timothy evangelized the city against the strong opposition of the Jews; though their stay was short, they were successful in establishing a church (Acts 17:4). There was not time to give much instruction to the new converts, so it is not surprising that questions arose as to the meaning of some aspects of the Christian faith and of the conduct demanded of believers.

Among the problems the Thessalonian church faced were persecution by pagans (2:14) and a temptation for believers to accept pagan sexual standards (4:4-8). Some of the Christians seem to have given up working and to have relied on the others to supply their needs (4:11-12). There was uncertainty about the fate of believers who had died, and some of the Thessalonians appear to have thought that Christ would come back soon and take them all to be with him. What would happen to those who had died before the great event (4:13-18)? Paul's reply to this gives us information about Christ's return that we find nowhere else. Again, some of the believers seem to have been concerned about the time of Jesus's return (5:1-11). So Paul wrote this pastoral letter to meet the needs of inexperienced Christians and to bring them closer to Christ.

THESSALONIANS, SECOND LETTER TO THE The exact date of Paul's mission to Thessalonica is not known, and the same is true of his letters to the very young church there. Most scholars agree that 2 Thessalonians must have been written not more than a year or two after Paul and Silas left the city. The church was apparently enthusiastic, but clearly the believers had not as yet matured in their faith. Paul wrote to committed Christians who had not progressed very far in the Christian life.

We see the enthusiasm and excitement of the Thessalonians expressed in the riots when the first Christian preachers visited them. Such a riot broke out in Thessalonica (Acts 17:5-8,13). Those who became Christians during this time did so with verve and enthusiasm. However, they had not yet had the time to come to grips with all that being a Christian means.

Second Thessalonians is not a long letter and does not give us a definitive outline of the whole Christian faith. Paul wrote to meet a present need, and the arrangement of his letter focuses on local circumstances. Perhaps we can say that there are four great teachings in this letter: (1) the greatness of God, (2) the wonder of salvation in Christ, (3) the second coming, and (4) the importance of life and work each day.

The Triumphal Arch of the Emperor Galerius built over the Egnatian Way in Thessalonica

THESSALONICA Name of modern-day Thessaloniki, given to the city about 315 BC by Cassander, a general of Alexander the Great. When the apostle Paul visited the city, it was larger than Philippi and reflected a predominantly Roman culture. Thessalonica was a free city, having no Roman garrison within its walls and maintaining the privilege of minting its own coins. Like Corinth, it had a cosmopolitan population due to the commercial prowess of the city. The recent discovery of a marble inscription, written partly in Greek and partly in a Samaritan form of Hebrew and Aramaic, testifies to the presence of Samaritans in Thessalonica. The book of Acts testifies to the presence of a Jewish synagogue there (17:1).

THEUDAS Personal name meaning "gift of God." Acts 5:36 refers to a Theudas who was slain after leading an unsuccessful rebellion of 400 men prior to the census (AD 6).

THIGH Side of the lower torso and the upper part of the leg. Sometimes the reference is simply physical (Judg. 3:16; Ps. 45:3; Song 3:8; 7:1). More often Scripture regards the thigh as the seat of vital functions, especially procreation. English translations often obscure this connection.

THOMAS Personal name from Hebrew meaning "a twin." One of the first 12 disciples of Jesus (Mark 3:18). His personality was complex, revealing a pessimism mixed with loyalty and faith (John 11:16). Thomas sought evidence of Jesus's resurrection (John 20:25) but, when convinced of the miracle, made a historic confession of faith (20:28).

THORN IN THE FLESH Greek word *skolops* occurred in classical Greek as a stake or sharp wooden shaft used to impale. Because false teachers in Corinth claimed receiving divine revelation, Paul shared his vision of the "third heaven" as miraculous evidence of his apostolic calling. Paul's revelation was balanced by a "thorn in the flesh" (2 Cor. 12:7). During this era, physical ailments were a constant problem. As a result, most patristic writers perceived Paul's affliction as either a painful, chronic physical problem or ongoing persecution.

In the Middle Ages, the "thorn" was taken as carnal temptation. The Vulgate encouraged the perception of the thorn as a sexual temptation. In the Reformation, Luther and Calvin rejected the idea of sexual temptation. Calvin interpreted the "thorn in the flesh" as a variety of physical and spiritual temptations. Luther interpreted the thorn as physical illness.

Four modern theories concern Paul's thorn in the flesh. The most common theory is some sort of recurring physical illness, possibly malaria, based on a perceived relationship to Paul's bodily illness of Gal. 4:13. Some hold that Paul suffered from an eye disease (*ophthalmia*), pointing to Gal. 4:13-15, where Paul confirmed that the Galatians would have given him, if possible, their eyes. Further, in Gal. 6:11, Paul indicates he wrote in large script, which is logical for a person with eye trouble. A third common theory was sorrow and pain because of Jewish unbelief (Rom. 9:1-3). A fourth theory is that of a "messenger of Satan," rather than a physical ailment, given as a redemptive judgment of God on Paul for the purpose of humility.

Other theories were hysteria, hypochondria, gallstones, gout, rheumatism, sciatica, gastritis, leprosy, lice, deafness, dental infection, neurasthenia, a speech impediment, and remorse for persecuting the Church.

THREE TAVERNS Rest stop on the Appian Way, 33 miles southeast of Rome and 10 miles northwest of the Forum of Appius, where Roman Christians met Paul on his trip to Rome (Acts 28:15).

THYATIRA City in the Lycus River valley. Thyatira was the center of a number of trade guilds that used the natural resources of

The ruins of Thyatira in ancient Asia Minor (modern Turkey)

the area to make it a very profitable site. Thyatira had a Jewish contingent out of which grew a NT church. One of Paul's first converts from the European continent, Lydia, was a native of Thyatira (Acts 16:14). She probably was a member of a guild there that dealt in purple dye. The church at Thyatira was praised for its works of charity, service, and faith (Rev. 2:19), but criticized for allowing the followers of Jezebel to prosper in its midst (2:20).

TIAMAT Sumerian-Akkadian goddess viewed by the Babylonians as one of the major gods of their pantheon.

TIBERIAS Mentioned only in John 6:23 (cp. 6:1; 21:1), Tiberias is a city located on the western shore of the Sea of Galilee encompassing today what in ancient times were two separate cities, Tiberias and Hammath, each surrounded by its own wall.

TIBERIUS CAESAR Person who had the unenviable task of following Augustus as Roman emperor. See *Rome and the Roman Empire.*

TIBHATH Place-name meaning "place of slaughter." City from which David took spoils (or received tribute) of bronze (1 Chron. 18:8). The site is likely in the vicinity of Zobah north of Damascus. The parallel in 2 Sam. 8:8 reads "Betah."

TIBNI Personal name meaning "intelligent" or "straw." Likely an army officer who struggled with Omri over succession to the throne of Israel following Zimri's suicide (1 Kgs. 16:21-22).

TIDAL One of four kings allied against five in Gen. 14:1,9. The name is similar to Tud'alia, the name of several Hittite kings, suggesting the king's origin in eastern Asia Minor. The king is perhaps Tudhalia I (about 1700–1650 BC).

TIGLATH-PILESER Personal name meaning "my trust is the son of Esarra (the temple of Asshur)." King of Assyria from 745 to 727 BC (2 Kgs. 16:7), also known as Tilgath-pilneser (1 Chron. 5:6; 2 Chron. 28:20) and Pul (2 Kgs. 15:19; 1 Chron. 5:26). See *Assyria.*

TIGRIS RIVER See *Euphrates and Tigris Rivers.*

TIKVAH Personal name meaning "hope, expectation." **1.** Father-in-law of Huldah, the prophetess (2 Kgs. 22:14; 2 Chron. 34:22). **2.** Father of Jahaziah who opposed Ezra's call for Israelites to divorce their foreign wives (Ezra 10:15).

Modern Tiberias, built over the ancient city of Tiberias, overlooks the Sea of Galilee

TIKVATH KJV alternate form of Tikvah (2 Chron. 34:22), perhaps representing original form of foreign name written in Hebrew as Tikvah.

The Tigris River flows through Iraq (ancient Mesopotamia).

TILON Personal name of uncertain meaning. Descendant of Judah (1 Chron. 4:20).

TIMAEUS Personal name meaning "highly prized" (Mark 10:46). Bartimaeus is Aramaic for "son of Timaeus."

TIMBREL KJV term for a tambourine.

TIME, MEANING OF God is Lord over time, because he created and ordained time (Gen. 1:45,14-19). God himself is timeless and eternal, not bound by space or time (Exod. 3:14-15; 1 Chron. 16:36; Pss. 41:13; 90:1-2; 93:2; 146:10; Isa. 9:6; John 1:1-18; 8:58; Heb. 13:8; 2 Pet. 3:8; Jude 1:25).

On the other hand, God is not removed from time. Through his providential care and especially in the incarnation of Jesus Christ, God enters into time without being limited by the constraints of time.

Because of his foreknowledge, only God knows and foreordains events in time (Dan. 2:20-22; Mark 13:31-32; Acts 1:7; 2:22-23). God sees all things in time from a perspective of eternity, sees the end from the beginning. Humans, however, are trapped in time, and sometimes cannot discern the meaning and significance of time in their own day (Eccles. 3:1-11; 9:12; Ps. 90:9-10; Luke 12:54-56; James 4:13-16). Being bound by the remorseless march of time is a telling reminder of human finitude and temporality.

TIMNA Personal name meaning "holding in check" or "she protects." **1.** Sister of the Horite clan chief Lotan (Gen. 36:22; 1 Chron. 1:39), concubine of Esau's son Eliphaz, and mother of Amalek (Gen. 36:12). **2.** Son of Eliphaz (1 Chron. 1:36; Gen. 36:16 "Teman") and Edomite clan chief (Gen. 36:40; 1 Chron. 1:51). Timna is associated with either Timna in southern Arabia or, following Gen. 36:16, Teman in southern Edom. It is the name of the capitol of Qataban. **3.** Modern name for an ancient copper-mining site 14 miles north of Elath.

The modern name Timna refers to a large copper-mining area north of the Gulf of Aqaba.

TIMNAH Place-name meaning "allotted portion." **1.** Town assigned to Dan (Josh. 19:43), located on the southern border with Judah (Josh. 15:10). **2.** Village in the hill country of Judah (Josh. 15:57). This Timnah was the likely scene of Judah's encounter with Tamar (Gen. 38:12-14).

Overview of Tell Batash (site of the ancient city of Timnah)

TIMNATH-HERES or **TIMNATH-SERAH** Place of Joshua's inheritance and burial (Judg. 2:9; Josh. 19:50; 24:30). Timnath-heres means "portion of the sun," suggesting a site dedicated to sun worship (Judg. 2:9). Timnath-serah means "remaining portion," pointing to land given to Joshua following distribution of land to the tribes (Josh. 19:50; 24:30).

TIMON Personal name meaning "honorable." One of seven chosen to supervise distribution of food to the Greek-speaking widows of the Jerusalem church (Acts 6:5).

TIMOTHY Personal name meaning "honoring God." Friend and trusted coworker of Paul. When Timothy was a child, his mother Eunice and his grandmother Lois taught him the Scriptures (2 Tim. 1:5; 3:15). A native of Lystra, he may have been converted on Paul's first missionary journey (Acts 14:6-23). Paul referred to Timothy as his child in the faith (1 Cor. 4:17; 1 Tim. 1:2; 2 Tim. 1:2). This probably means that Paul was instrumental in Timothy's conversion. When Paul came to Lystra on his second journey, Timothy was a disciple who was well respected by the believers (Acts 16:1-2). Paul asked Timothy to accompany him. Timothy not only accompanied Paul but also was sent on many crucial missions by Paul (Acts 17:14-15; 18:5; 19:22; 20:4; Rom. 16:21; 1 Cor. 16:10; 2 Cor. 1:19; 1 Thess. 3:2,6).

TIMOTHY, FIRST LETTER TO First of two letters Paul wrote to Timothy. The letter was written in approximately AD 63, following Paul's first imprisonment in Rome. It is likely that Paul left Rome and traveled to Ephesus. There is some debate concerning the place of writing. Rome and Macedonia have been offered as possibilities. Perhaps, in light of 1 Tim. 1:3, Macedonia could be the better choice. The letter was addressed to Timothy in Ephesus. Paul had urged Timothy to remain in Ephesus and lead this important church as its pastor (1:3).

Purpose Paul had hoped to visit Timothy in Ephesus but was fearful of a delay. If he were delayed, he wanted Timothy to "know how people ought to conduct themselves in God's household" (3:14-15 CSB). The epistle contains instructions concerning order and structure in the church and practical advice for the young pastor. One important theme in this and the other two Pastoral Epistles (2 Timothy and Titus) is sound teaching. Paul urged Timothy and Titus to confront the false teaching by sound or healthy teaching. This word occurs eight times in these three letters (1 Tim. 1:10; 6:3; 2 Tim. 1:13; 4:3; Titus 1:9,13; 2:1-2).

TIMOTHY, SECOND LETTER TO Second of Paul's letters to Timothy, pastor of the church in Ephesus. The letter was the last letter of which we have a record written by Paul. He wrote this letter from his jail cell during his second imprisonment in Rome. He was awaiting trial for his faith. It is clear that he felt he would not be released (4:6). If Nero executed Paul and if Nero was killed in AD 68, then Paul had to have been executed sometime before. The letter can be dated between AD 63 and 67. Timothy was the recipient of Paul's letter. He had been the apostle's representative in the city of Ephesus for some time.

Purpose The letter contains Paul's stirring words of encouragement and instruction to his young disciple. Paul longed to see Timothy (1:4) and asked him to come to Rome for a visit. It is generally believed that Timothy went. Paul asked him to come before winter (4:21) and bring the winter coat Paul had left in Troas (4:13). Timothy was also asked to bring the scrolls and the parchments so Paul could read and study (4:13).

TINKLING ORNAMENTS (KJV) Anklets making a tinkling noise as one walked. Part of the finery of the affluent women of Jerusalem (Isa. 3:16,18).

TIPHSAH Place-name meaning "passage, ford." **1.** City on the west bank of the Euphrates about 75 miles south of Carchemish, representing the northeastern limit of Solomon's kingdom (1 Kgs. 4:24). **2.** Site near Tirzah in Samaria (2 Kgs. 15:16), possibly a corruption of Tappuah, the reading of the earliest Greek translation that REB, RSV, TEV follow.

TIRAS Division of the descendants of Japheth who are all seagoing peoples (Gen. 10:2; 1 Chron. 1:5). Traditionally, they have been related to Turscha, part of the sea peoples Ramesses III (1198–1166 BC) fought. Some have identified them with the Etruscans of Italy.

TIRATHITES Family of Kenite scribes (1 Chron. 2:55).

TIRE KJV term meaning "turban" (Ezek. 24:17,23).

TIRHAKAH Egyptian pharaoh of the Twenty-fifth Dynasty (689–664 BC) who supported Hezekiah's revolt against the Assyrian king Sennacherib (2 Kgs. 19:8-9; Isa. 37:9).

TIRHANAH Personal name of uncertain meaning. Son of Caleb and Maacah (1 Chron. 2:48).

TIRIA Personal name meaning "fear." Descendant and family of Judah (1 Chron. 4:16).

TIRSHATHA Title of honor designating respect for an official, sometimes translated "your excellence" (Ezra 2:63; Neh. 7:65,70; 8:9; 10:1).

TIRZAH Personal name and place-name meaning "she is friendly." **1.** Daughter of Zelophehad who inherited part of tribal land allotment of Manasseh since her father had no sons. **2.** Originally a Canaanite city noted for its beauty (Song 6:4) but captured in the conquest of the promised land (Josh. 12:24).

TISHBITE Resident of Tishbe, used as a title of Elijah (1 Kgs. 17:1; 21:17,28; 2 Kgs. 1:3,8; 9:36). Tishbite is possibly a corruption of Jabeshite or a class designation (cp. the Hebrew *toshav,* which designates a resident alien, Lev. 25:6). See also *Elijah.*

TITHE Tenth part, especially as offered to God. Abraham presented a tithe of war booty to the priest-king of Jerusalem, Melchizedek (Gen. 14:18-20). Jacob pledged to offer God a tithe of all his possessions upon his safe return (Gen. 28:22). The tithe was subject to a variety of legislation. Some scholars think the differences in legislation reflect different uses of the tithe at various stages of Israel's history. Malachi 3:8 equates neglect of the tithe with robbing God. Jesus, however, warned that strict tithing must accompany concern for the more important demands of the law, namely, for just and merciful living (Matt. 23:23; Luke 11:42).

TITTLE A point (Matt. 5:18; Luke 16:17), the minute point or stroke added to some letters of the Hebrew alphabet to distinguish them from others that they resemble; hence, the very least point.

TITUS Gentile companion of Paul (Gal. 2:3) and recipient of the NT letter bearing his name. Titus may have been converted by Paul, who called him "my true child in our common faith" (Titus 1:4 CSB). As one of Paul's early associates, Titus accompanied the apostle and Barnabas to Jerusalem (Gal. 2:1), probably on the famine relief visit (Acts 11:28-30).

Though Acts does not mention Titus, he was quite involved in Paul's missionary activities as shown in the Pauline letters. He was evidently known to the Galatians (Gal. 2:1,3), possibly from the first missionary journey to that region. Titus also seems to have been a very capable person, called by Paul "my partner and coworker" (2 Cor. 8:23 CSB). He was entrusted with the delicate task of delivering Paul's severe letter (2 Cor. 2:1-4) to Corinth and correcting problems within the church there (2 Cor. 7:13-15). Titus's genuine concern for and evenhanded dealing with the Corinthians (2 Cor. 8:16-17; 12:18) no doubt contributed to his success which he reported in person to Paul, anxiously awaiting word in Macedonia (2 Cor. 2:13; 7:5-6,13-15). Paul responded by writing 2 Corinthians, which Titus probably delivered (2 Cor. 8:6,16-18,23).

Paul apparently was released after his first Roman imprisonment and made additional journeys, unrecorded in Acts. One of these took him and Titus to Crete, where Titus remained behind to oversee and administer the church (Titus 1:5). It was to Crete that Paul wrote his letter, asking Titus to join him in Nicopolis on the west coast of Greece (Titus 3:12). Following Paul's subsequent reimprisonment, Titus was sent to Dalmatia (2 Tim. 4:10). According to church tradition, Titus was the first bishop of Crete.

TITUS, CAESAR Roman emperor AD 79–81, eldest son of Vespasian. Titus, like his father, was a soldier. He served in Germany and Britain and later in the Middle East. When Vespasian left his Middle East command to become emperor in AD 69, he left Titus in charge of crushing the Jewish revolt. In AD 70 his troops captured the temple in Jerusalem. They took the last stronghold, Masada, in AD 73. His victory over the Jews was vividly depicted on the Triumphal Arch erected in Rome that still stands today.

Titus was deeply admired by his soldiers; when he later became emperor, the populace loved him. He was considered an honest ruler and an efficient administrator. An adherent of Stoic philosophy, he believed that the Roman emperor was the servant of the people. He and his father before him (the so-called Flavian emperors) struggled after the excesses of Nero to reestablish stability in the empire and in the government. They managed to return the empire to sound financial footing.

Titus was constantly plagued by the activities of his younger brother, Domitian. Even though he did not believe that Domitian was worthy to be his successor, he would not dispose of him. See *Rome and the Roman Empire*.

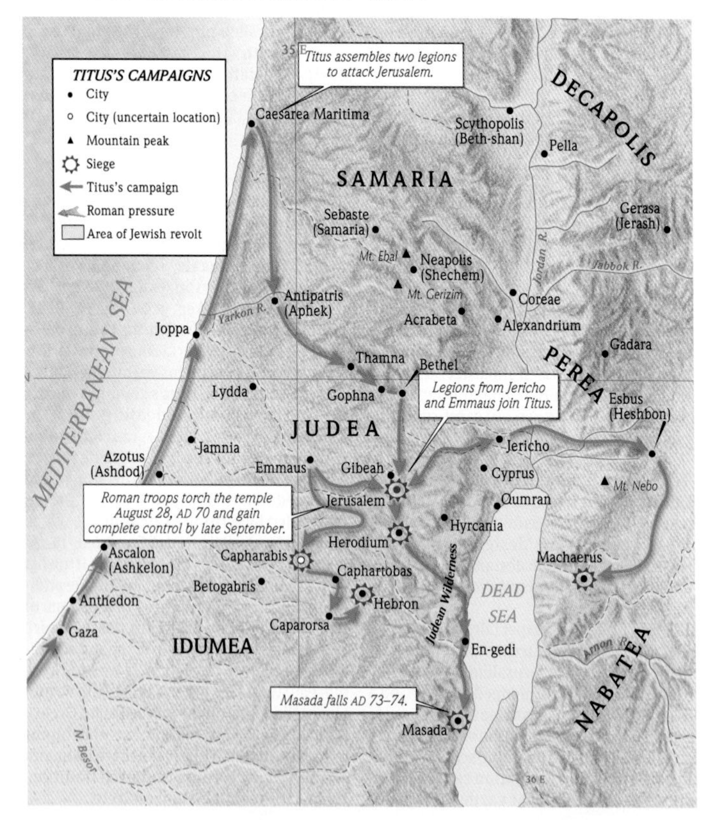

A close-up of the interior of the Arch of Titus in the Roman Forum showing the spoils of war taken during the First Jewish Revolt. The scene shows furnishings of the Jerusalem temple, including the seven-branch candlestick (the Menorah), plundered from the temple before it was destroyed.

TITUS, LETTER TO Paul the apostle wrote to Titus, a trusted Gentile coworker. See *Titus*. The circumstances of the writing of Titus are similar to those of the first letter to Timothy. After his first Roman imprisonment (AD 60–62), Paul returned to the east for missionary work. Apparently after Paul and Titus had evangelized Crete, Titus was left behind to set the churches in order, appointing elders in every city (Titus 1:5). Paul probably wrote this letter on the way to Nicopolis from Crete around AD 63–6**5.** Just as in the first letter to Timothy, Paul warned against false teachers and issued instructions to various groups regarding proper Christian behavior. Furthermore, he instructed Titus to join him in Nicopolis whenever a replacement arrived (3:12).

TIZITE Title of Joha, one of David's 30 elite warriors (1 Chron. 11:45), designating his hometown or home region, which is otherwise unknown.

TOAH Personal name, perhaps meaning "humility." A Kohathite Levite (1 Chron. 6:34). The parallel lists read Nahath (1 Chron. 6:26) and Tohu (1 Sam. 1:1).

TOB Place-name meaning "good." Syrian city in southern Hauran to which Jephthah fled from his brothers (Judg. 11:3-5). Tob contributed troops to an unsuccessful alliance against David (2 Sam. 10:6-13). Tob is perhaps identical with Tabeel (Isa. 7:6).

TOBADONIJAH Personal name meaning "Yah, my Lord, is good." Levite whom Jehoshaphat sent to teach the people of Judah (2 Chron. 17:8).

TOBIAH Personal name meaning "Yah is good." **1.** One of the major adversaries to Nehemiah's rebuilding efforts at Jerusalem, Tobiah was a practicing Jew who lived in a residence chamber in the temple (Neh. 2:10,19). **2.** Ancestor of clan who returned from exile but could not show they were Israelites (Ezra 2:60)

TOBIJAH Alternate form of Tobiah. **1.** Levite whom Jehoshaphat sent to teach the people (2 Chron. 17:8). **2.** Returned exile who apparently brought a gift of gold from Babylon for the Jerusalem community. Zechariah used him as a witness for his crowning of Joshua, the high priest, and to preserve the crowns in the temple (Zech. 6:9-14).

TOCHEN Place-name meaning "measure." An unidentified village in Simeon (1 Chron. 4:32). The parallel lists in Josh. 15:42; 19:7 have "Ether."

TOGARMAH Son of Gomer and name of a region of Asia Minor (Gen. 10:3; 1 Chron. 1:6; cp. Beth-togarmah, Ezek. 38:6) inhabited by his descendants. Togarmah was famed for its horses (Ezek. 27:14).

TOHU Ancestor of Samuel (1 Sam. 1:1). Parallel lists read "Nahath" (1 Chron. 6:26) and "Toah" (6:34) in the corresponding position.

TOI Personal name meaning "error." King of Hammath on the Orontes who sent tribute to David following his defeat of their mutual foe, Hadadezer of Zobah (2 Sam. 8:9-10; Tou, 1 Chron. 18:9-10).

TOKEN KJV term meaning "sign" (Gen. 9:12-17; Pss. 65:8; 135:9).

TOKHATH Alternate form of Tikvah (2 Chron. 34:22).

TOLA Personal name meaning "crimson worm." **1.** Issachar's firstborn son (Gen. 46:13; Num. 26:23; 1 Chron. 7:1-2). **2.** Judge who governed Israel for 23 years from Shamir, likely at or near Samaria (Judg. 10:1).

TOLAD Place-name. Alternate form of Eltolad (1 Chron. 4:29).

TOLAITE Division of Issachar descended from Tola (Num. 26:23-25).

TOMB OF JESUS According to the NT accounts, the tomb of Jesus was located in a garden in the place where Jesus was crucified (John 19:41) outside the city walls of Jerusalem (19:20). It was a "new tomb" that had been "cut into the rock" by Joseph of Arimathea (Matt. 27:60 CSB; cp. Luke 23:50-56), who had apparently prepared it for his own family's use.

TONGS Pinchers for holding coals (1 Kgs. 7:49; 2 Chron. 4:21; Isa. 6:6). KJV used "tongs" at Exod. 25:38; Num. 4:9 where modern translations read "snuffers" (CSB, NASB, NRSV) or "wick trimmers" (NIV).

TONGUES, GIFT OF The NT deals with the practice of speaking in tongues both by example and instruction in Acts and 1 Corinthians. There is also a brief mention of it in the long ending of Mark.

Tongues in the NT has three functions—to show the progress of the gift of the Spirit to the various people groups in the book of Acts in a salvation-history context, as a way of revealing the content of the NT revelation, and as a means of communicating cross-linguistically. The first two purposes would no longer be applicable, since the gospel has now gone out to the entire world and the NT revelation has been given. As regards the third purpose, no one would wish to limit God's ability to grant such a gift. There are stories of such events from the mission

The Garden Tomb is one site offered by tradition as the burial place of Jesus's body.

field, though undoubtedly some of them have been embellished. It is also the case that all Pentecostal groups that send missionaries send them for language training first.

TOPHEL Place near the site of Moses's farewell speech to Israel (Deut. 1:1), identified with et-Tafileh about 15 miles southeast of the Dead Sea between Kerak and Petra.

TOPHET or **TOPHETH** Name for a place in the Hinnom Valley outside Jerusalem derived from Aramaic or Hebrew meaning "fireplace" but altered by Hebrew scribes to mean "shameful thing" because of the illicit worship carried on there (Jer. 7:31-32; KJV, "Tophet"). Child sacrifice was practiced at Topheth, leading the prophet to declare a slaughter of people there when God would come in vengeance (Jer. 19:6-11).

TORAH Hebrew word normally translated "law," which eventually became a title for the Pentateuch, the first five books of the OT.

TORCH Long pole with cloths dipped in oil wrapped around one end used as a light. The Greek *lampas* is generally rendered "torch" (John 18:3; Rev. 4:5; 8:10), unless the context suggests the translation "lamp" (Acts 20:8). The lamps of the wise and foolish virgins (Matt. 25:1-8) were perhaps torches.

TOU Alternate form of Toi (1 Chron. 18:9-10).

TOW Short, broken fibers of flax, known to be easily broken and highly flammable, used as a figure for weakness and transience (Judg. 16:9; Isa. 1:31; 43:17).

TOWER Tall edifice erected so watchmen could guard pastures, vineyards, and cities. Towers ranged from small one-room structures to entire fortresses. Archaeological remains confirm the wide usage of towers from the earliest times. Most were made of stones, although some wooden towers have been unearthed. The word is used figuratively of God's salvation in 2 Sam. 22:51, indicating the strength of the Lord's action.

Watchtower overlooking grain fields near the valley of Lebonah

TRACHONITIS Place-name meaning "heap of stones." A political and geographic district in northern Palestine on the east side of the Jordan River (Luke 3:1).

TRADITION Teaching or ritual that is handed down. The term "tradition" has several usages. The term is often used to speak of denominations or distinct theological viewpoints, such as the Baptist tradition or the Reformed tradition. The term is also commonly used to refer to liturgical consistency or to historical practice, as in a tradition of the church. Tradition also is used to speak of legend material, such as the tradition of Peter asking to be crucified upside-down. From a technical standpoint, the term is used to describe two distinct groups of theological material: biblical material prior to its being written down as Scripture and writings that are not part of the Bible but are still esteemed by the church.

TRAIN Used to refer to the part of a robe that trails behind the wearer (Isa. 6:1 KJV, NASB, NIV).

TRANCE Translation of the Greek term that literally means a change of place. Trance is descriptive of an experience in which a person received a revelation by supernatural means (Acts 10:10; 11:5; 22:17). In these instances, the author of Acts, in reference to the experiences of Peter and Paul, seemed to be interested in showing that the trance was only a vehicle for a revelation from God. Luke illustrated that the trances that Peter and Paul experienced "happened" to them and were not self-induced. The distinctions between "trance," "dream," and "vision" are not always clear.

TRANSFIGURATION Transformation of Jesus in his appearance with Moses and Elijah before Peter, James, and John (Matt. 17:1-13; Mark 9:1-13; Luke 9:28-36; cp. 2 Pet. 1:16-18). This event took place shortly after the confession at Caesarea Philippi, the first passion prediction, and a discourse on the cost of discipleship. Jesus took Peter, James, and John to a mountain where the event took place. Jesus's personal appearance and that of his garments were changed. Moses and Elijah appeared and talked with Jesus.

The Place The traditional site is Mount Tabor in lower Galilee, but it is not a high mountain (only 1,850 feet) and was probably fortified and inaccessible in Jesus's day. Much more likely is Mount Hermon (9,100 feet) to the north of Caesarea Philippi.

Meaning A mountain in the Bible is often a place of revelation. Moses and Elijah represented the law and the prophets respectively, which testify to but must give way to Jesus. Clouds represent divine presence. The close connection of the transfiguration with the confession and passion prediction is significant. The Messiah must suffer, but glorification and enthronement, not suffering, is his ultimate fate. These involve resurrection, ascension, and return in glory. The disciples needed the reassurance of the transfiguration as they contemplated Jesus's death and their future sufferings.

Mount Hermon, one possible site of the transfiguration

TRANSGRESSION Image of sin as overstepping the limits of God's law.

TRANSJORDAN Area immediately east of the Jordan River settled by Reuben, Gad, half of Manasseh, Edom, Moab, and Amon. The most prominent topographical feature of Palestine is the Jordan River valley, referred to in the OT as the "Arabah" and called today, in Arabic, the *Ghor*.

Transjordan included the River Jabbok, scene of the account of Jacob's wrestling on his return from Aram (Gen. 32:22-32); the Plains of Moab, where the Israelites are said to have camped following their exodus from Egypt and where Balaam prophesied; and Mount Nebo, from which Moses viewed the promised land (Num. 22:1–24:25; Deut. 34). Three Transjordanian kingdoms (Ammon, Moab, and Edom) were contemporary with the two Hebrew kingdoms (Israel and Judah), sometimes as allies, sometimes as enemies (1 Sam. 11; 14:47; 2 Sam. 8:12; 10; 2 Kgs. 3; Amos 1:11–2:3). The prophet Elijah was from Tishbe, a town in the Transjordanian territory of Gilead (1 Kgs. 17:1). Other Israelite prophets and poets often referred to the territories and peoples of the Transjordan. See, for example, the allusions in Amos 4:1 and Ps. 22:12 to the cows and bulls of Bashan.

By NT times, a cluster of Greco-Roman-oriented cities with primarily Gentile populations (the so-called Decapolis cities) had emerged in the northern Transjordan (earlier Bashan, Gilead, and Ammon). The southern Transjordan (earlier Moab and Edom) was dominated by the Nabateans, a people of Arab origin who established a commercial empire along the desert fringe with its capital at Petra.

TRANSLATE **1.** KJV term meaning "to transfer," used of the transfer of Saul's kingdom to David (2 Sam. 3:10) and the transfer of believers from the power of darkness to the sphere of Christ's control (Col. 1:13). **2.** KJV term meaning "to take up," used of Enoch's being taken up into God's presence without experiencing death (Heb. 11:5). **3.** Converting text from one language to another, retaining the original meaning or putting words in simpler terms.

TREE OF KNOWLEDGE Plant in the midst of the garden of Eden whose fruit was forbidden to Adam and Eve (Gen. 2:17). The tree of knowledge was Adam and Eve's opportunity to demonstrate obedience and loyalty to God, but the serpent used it to tempt Eve to eat and to become like God, "knowing good and evil" (Gen. 3:5). When Adam joined Eve in eating the forbidden fruit, the result was shame, guilt, exclusion from the garden, and separation from the tree of life and from God. The result for humanity was disaster as they failed the test and fell to the temptation.

TREE OF LIFE Plant in the garden of Eden symbolizing access to eternal life. Also, a metaphor used in Proverbs. For the biblical writer, the tree of life was an important consideration only after Adam and Eve disobeyed. Their relationship to God changed radically when they disobeyed the command not to eat of the tree of knowledge. Chief among the radical changes was that they no longer had access to the tree of life (Gen. 3:22-24). The "tree of life" appears in Proverbs four times (Prov. 3:18; 11:30; 13:12; 15:4) and in Rev. 2:7; 22:2,14.

TRIAL OF JESUS Two systems of justice combined to produce a sentence of death for Jesus. Jewish religious leaders accused Jesus of blasphemy, a capital offense under Jewish law (Lev. 24:16). The Jewish leaders at Jesus's trial manipulated procedures to coerce Jesus into an admission that he was God's Son (Luke 22:66-71). For them this constituted blasphemy. Roman leaders allowed conquered people such as the Jews to follow their own legal system so long as they did not abuse their privileges. The Romans did not give the Jews the right of capital punishment for the accusation of blasphemy. The Jews had to convince a Roman judge that their demand for capital punishment was justified.

The Roman trial of Jesus also had three phases: first appearance before Pilate, appearance before Herod Antipas, and second appearance before Pilate. The Jewish leaders asked Pilate to accept their verdict against Jesus without investigation (John 18:29-31). Pilate refused this, but he offered to let them carry out the maximum punishment under their law, probably beating with rods or imprisonment. They insisted that they wanted death.

The Jews knew that Pilate would laugh at their charge of blasphemy. They fabricated three additional charges against Jesus that would be of concern to a Roman governor (Luke 23:2). Pilate concerned himself only with the charge that Jesus had claimed to be a king. This charge sounded like treason. The Romans knew no greater crime than treason.

Pilate interrogated Jesus long enough to be convinced that he was no political rival to Caesar (John 18:33-37). He returned to the Jews to announce that he found Jesus no threat to Rome and hence not deserving of death (John 18:38). The Jews responded with vehement accusations against Jesus's actions in Judea and Galilee (Luke 23:5). When Pilate learned that Jesus was from Galilee, he sent Jesus to Herod Antipas of Galilee who was then in Jerusalem (Luke 23:6-12). The king and his soldiers mocked and ridiculed Jesus, finally sending him back to Pilate.

When Herod returned Jesus to Pilate, the Roman governor announced that he still found Jesus innocent of charges of treason. Three times Pilate tried to release Jesus. First, Pilate offered to chastise or beat Jesus and then to release him (Luke 23:16). Second, he offered to release either Jesus or Barabbas, a radical revolutionary. To Pilate's surprise, the crowd chanted for Barabbas's release (Luke 23:17-19). Third, he scourged Jesus. Soldiers flailed at Jesus's bare back with a leather whip. The whip had pieces of iron or bone tied to the ends of the thongs. Pilate then presented the bleeding Jesus, who was wearing a crown of thorns and a mock purple robe, to the crowd as their king. He hoped that this spectacle would lead them to release Jesus out of pity. Again they chanted for crucifixion (John 19:4-6).

When Pilate seemed to waver one more time concerning crucifixion, the Jews threatened to report his conduct to Caesar (John 19:12). That threat triggered Pilate's action. After symbolically washing his hands of the entire affair (Matt. 27:24), he delivered Jesus for crucifixion (John 19:16).

TRIBES OF ISRAEL Social and political groups in Israel claiming descent from one of the 12 sons of Jacob. The tribal unit played an important role in the history of the formation of the nation of Israel.

The ancestral background of the "tribes of Israel" went back to the patriarch Jacob, whose name was changed to Israel. The nation of Israel was identified as the "children of Israel" or, more literally, the "sons of Israel." According to the biblical account, the family of Jacob, from which the tribes came, originated in north Syria during Jacob's stay at Haran with Laban his uncle. Eleven of the 12 sons were born at Haran, while the twelfth, Benjamin, was born after Jacob returned to Canaan. The birth of the sons came through Jacob's wives, Leah and Rachel, and their maids, Zilpah and Bilhah. The sons of Leah were Reuben, Simeon, Levi, Judah (Gen. 29:31-35), Issachar, and Zebulun, as well as one daughter named Dinah (Gen. 30:19-21). Rachel's sons were Joseph (Gen. 30:22-24), who became the father of Ephraim and Manasseh (Gen. 41:50-52), and Benjamin (Gen. 35:16-18). Jacob's sons through Zilpah, Leah's maid, were Gad and Asher (Gen. 30:9-13), while Bilhah, the maid of Rachel, bore Dan and Naphtali (Gen. 30:1-8).

This family of families or family of tribes occupied the focal point in the history of the development of Israel as a nation. While there are details of that history that we do not clearly understand and other groups simply referred to as "a mixed crowd" (Exod. 12:38 CSB) that were perhaps incorporated into the nation, the central focus is always on the "tribes of Israel," the descendants of Jacob.

THE 12 TRIBES OF ISRAEL

The 12 tribes of Israel descended from the 12 sons of the patriarch Jacob, whom God later renamed Israel. The land assignment and relative importance of each tribe reflected the birth order, birth mother, and individual actions of each son.

RECORD OF THE SONS' BIRTHS

Genesis 29:31–30:24; 35:16-20.

KEY HISTORICAL INCIDENTS IN THE SONS' LIVES

Genesis 34:25-31 Simeon and Levi kill the men of Shechem.

Genesis 35:21-22 Reuben sleeps with his father's concubine.

Genesis 37:2-11 Joseph is hated by his brothers but the favorite of his father.

Genesis 48:1-20 Jacob blesses Joseph's two children, Ephraim and Manasseh, and "adopts" them as his own.

Genesis 49:1-28 Jacob gives a prophetic blessing to each of his sons.

TRIBAL ALLOTMENTS IN THE LAND OF ISRAEL

Numbers 32:1-42 Allotment for Reuben, Gad, and one-half of Manasseh

Joshua 15:1-63 Allotment for Judah

Joshua 16:1–17:18 Allotment for Ephraim and one-half of Manasseh

Joshua 18:11-28 Allotment for Benjamin

Joshua 19:1-9 Allotment for Simeon

Joshua 19:10-16 Allotment for Zebulun

Joshua 19:17-23 Allotment for Issachar

Joshua 19:24-31 Allotment for Asher

Joshua 19:32-39 Allotment for Naphtali

Joshua 19:40-48 Allotment for Dan

Joshua 21:1-42 Allotment for Levi

TRIBULATION Generally refers to the suffering and anguish of the people of God. According to the NT, tribulations are an expected reality among the followers of Christ.

The Bible teaches several important truths concerning the tribulations of believers. First, the tribulations of Christ are the pattern for the sufferings of believers. As tribulation was inevitable and expected in the messianic ministry of Jesus, so tribulation will be present among his followers (Matt. 13:21; John 16:33; Acts 14:22; Rom. 8:35; 12:12; 1 Thess. 3:3; 2 Thess. 1:4; Rev. 1:9). Second, the tribulations of believers are in a sense participation in the sufferings of Christ (Col. 1:24; 2 Cor. 1:5; 4:10; Phil. 3:10; 1 Pet. 4:13). Third, the tribulations of believers promote transformation into the likeness of Christ (Rom. 5:3; 2 Cor. 3:18; 4:8-12,16). Tribulation teaches Christ's followers to comfort and encourage others in similar situations, enabling those suffering to persevere and persist (2 Cor. 1:4; 4:10; Col. 1:24; 1 Thess. 1:6).

Another biblical understanding of tribulation is eschatological. The expression "great tribulation" refers to the time of trouble that will usher in the second coming of Christ (Matt. 24:21; Rev. 2:22; 7:14). Jesus warned that the great tribulation will be so intense that its calamities will nearly decimate all of life (Matt. 24:15-22). Jesus's words in Matt. 24:29 may refer to Dan. 12:1, "a time of distress such as never has occurred since nations came into being until that time" (CSB). This allusion suggests an eschatological view of the great tribulation.

One's millennial view usually determines the interpretation of the time and nature of this period of intense tribulation. Postmillennialists and amillennialists consider the great tribulation as a brief, indefinite period at the end of this age, usually identifying it with the revolt of Gog and Magog in Rev. 20:8-9. Dispensational premillennialists identify the tribulation with the seventieth week of Daniel's prophecy (Dan. 9:27), a period of seven years whose latter half is the great tribulation. The rapture of the church precedes a literal, seven-year tribulation, which is followed by the second coming of Christ. Historical premillennialists (posttribulationalists) assert that the tribulation is a horrific period of trouble immediately preceding the millennium and typically teach that believers and unbelievers will both undergo this tribulation.

Although this event should rightly be regarded as a future occurrence, attempts to connect the time of tribulation with specific events or persons have proved futile. Believers are exhorted to watch for Christ and fix their hope on him, not upon events surrounding his coming (1 John 3:3).

TRIBUNE Commander of an ancient Roman cohort, a military unit ideally comprising 1,000 men.

TRIBUTE Any payment exacted by a superior power, usually a state, from an inferior one. The weaker state, called a vassal state, normally contributed a specified amount of gold, silver, or other commodities on a yearly basis.

TRIGON Small, three-cornered harp with four strings (Dan. 3:5,7,10; KJV "sackbut"; CSB, "lyre").

TRINITY Theological term used to define God as an undivided unity expressed in the threefold nature of God the Father, God the Son, and God the Holy Spirit. While the term "trinity" does not appear in Scripture, the trinitarian structure appears throughout the NT to affirm that God himself is manifested through Jesus Christ by means of the Spirit. The following four statements summarize the truths inherent in the Christian understanding of the Trinity.

God is One. The God of the OT is the same God of the NT. His offer of salvation in the OT receives a fuller revelation in the NT in a way that is not different but more complete. The doctrine of the Trinity does not abandon the monotheistic faith of Israel.

God has three distinct ways of being in the redemptive event, yet he remains an undivided unity. That God the Father imparts himself to humankind through Son and Spirit without ceasing to be himself is at the very heart of the Christian faith. A compromise in either the absolute sameness of the Godhead or the true diversity reduces the reality of salvation.

The primary way of grasping the concept of the Trinity is through the threefold participation in salvation. The approach of the NT is not to discuss the essence of the Godhead, but the particular aspects of the revelatory event that includes the definitive presence of the Father in the person of Jesus Christ through the Holy Spirit.

The doctrine of the Trinity is an absolute mystery. It is primarily known, not through speculation, but through experiencing the act of grace through personal faith. See *God; Holy Spirit; Jesus Christ.*

TRIUMPHAL ENTRY Term used for the entry of Jesus into the city of Jerusalem on the Sunday prior to his crucifixion. Because palm branches were placed before him, this day is often called "Palm Sunday." The event is recorded in Matt. 21:1-9; Mark 11:1-10; Luke 19:28-38; John 12:12-15. All accounts agree in substance with each adding certain detail.

TROAS City in northwest Asia Minor visited by Paul during his second and third missionary journeys (Acts 16:8,11; 20:5-6; 2 Cor. 2:12; 2 Tim. 4:13).

TROGYLLIUM Promontory on the west coast of Asia Minor less than one mile across the strait from Samos, a stopping place on Paul's return to Jerusalem according to the Western text of Acts 20:15.

TROPHIMUS Personal name meaning "nutritious." Gentile Christian from Ephesus who accompanied Paul to Jerusalem for the presentation of the collection (Acts 20:4; 21:29).

TRUTH Statements accurately reflecting facts, such as accurate and trustworthy witnesses (Prov. 12:17; cp. 1 John 2:21). Lying is the opposite of truth (Jer. 9:3; cp. Gen. 42:16). The people of God are to speak truth to one another (Zech. 8:16; Eph. 4:25). Jesus stresses the authority and certainty of his message in saying, "Truly I tell you" (Luke 9:27 CSB; cp. Luke 4:24; John 16:7). John stresses he is telling the truth about Jesus (John 19:35), and Paul emphasizes he is not lying (Rom. 9:1; cp. 2 Cor. 7:14; 1 Tim. 2:7; Acts 26:25).

For Moses, the covenant God abounds in truth (Exod. 34:6). His truth is eternal (Ps. 117:2). Human testimony can swear to truth by nothing higher than God (1 Kgs. 22:16; Isa. 65:16). Since God is true, so is his word (Ps. 119:160; cp. John 17:17; 2 Sam. 7:28; Pss. 43:3; 119:142,151). Scripture is this very word of truth and thus should be handled carefully (2 Tim. 2:15). The gospel is equated with the

A section of the ruins of the theater at Troas

truth (Gal. 2:5,14; Eph.1:13), and the truth is equated with the gospel (Gal. 5:7).

TRYPHAENA AND TRYPHOSA Personal names meaning "dainty" and "delicate." Two women whom Paul greeted as those "who have worked hard in the Lord" (Rom. 16:12 CSB). The two were perhaps deacons serving the Roman church (cp. Phoebe in Rom. 16:1) or else "marketplace" evangelists like Priscilla (Acts 18:26; Rom. 16:3). The similarity of their names suggests the two were perhaps (twin) sisters.

TUBAL Son of Japheth (Gen. 10:2; 1 Chron. 1:5) and ancestor of a people known for their metalworking ability, likely of Cappadocia or Cilicia in Asia Minor (Isa. 66:19; Ezek. 27:13; 32:26; 38:2-3; 39:1).

TUBAL-CAIN Son of Lamech, associated with the origin of metalworking (Gen. 4:22). The two elements in his name mean "producer" and "smith."

TUNIC Loose-fitting, knee-length garment worn next to the skin (Matt. 10:10; Mark 6:9).

Relief of two Roman men wearing tunics partially visible beneath their outer togas

TURBAN Headdress formed by wrapping long strips of cloth around the head. A distinctive headdress formed part of the garb of the high priest (Exod. 28:4,37,39; 29:6; 39:28,31; Lev. 8:9; 16:4). Removal of one's turban was a sign of mourning or shame (Isa. 3:18-23; Ezek. 24:17,23).

TURNING OF THE WALL Expression used in the KJV, elsewhere translated as "the corner buttress" (NASB), "the Angle" (CSB, NRSV), "the escarpment" (REB), and "the angle of the wall" (NIV). One segment of the Jerusalem ramparts probably located near the palace. It was fortified by Uzziah (2 Chron. 26:9) and rebuilt by Nehemiah (Neh. 3:19-20,24). Not to be confused with "the corner" (Neh. 3:31) or associated with the corner gate.

TYCHICUS Personal name meaning "fortunate." One of Paul's fellow workers in the ministry. A native of Asia Minor (Acts 20:4), he traveled with the apostle on the third missionary journey. Tychicus and Onesimus carried the Colossian letter from Paul (Col. 4:7-9) and were to relate to the church Paul's condition. Paul also sent Tychicus to Ephesus on one occasion (2 Tim. 4:12) and possibly to Crete on another (Titus 3:12). Tradition holds that he died a martyr.

TYPOLOGICAL INTERPRETATION Seeing persons, event, actions, and objects in the OT as foreshadowing persons, events, actions, and objects in the NT. Typological interpretation is different than allegorical interpretation. See *Allegory*.

TYRANNUS Latin form of the Greek term *turannos*, a ruler with absolute authority. After Paul withdrew from the synagogue in Ephesus, he preached for two years at the lecture hall of Tyrannus (Acts 19:9). Tyrannus was either the owner of the hall or a prominent philosopher associated with it.

TYRE See *Sidon and Tyre*.

TYROPOEON VALLEY Narrow depression between Jerusalem's Ophel (Hill of David) and the western or upper hill of the city. It was much deeper in ancient times but has been filled up with debris through the centuries, especially since the destruction of the city by the Romans in AD 70. When David captured the city, the valley served as one of the natural defensive barriers. During Hellenistic times, it was included within the city walls. During Herod's building campaign, he constructed bridges across the valley to connect the palace area with the temple complex.

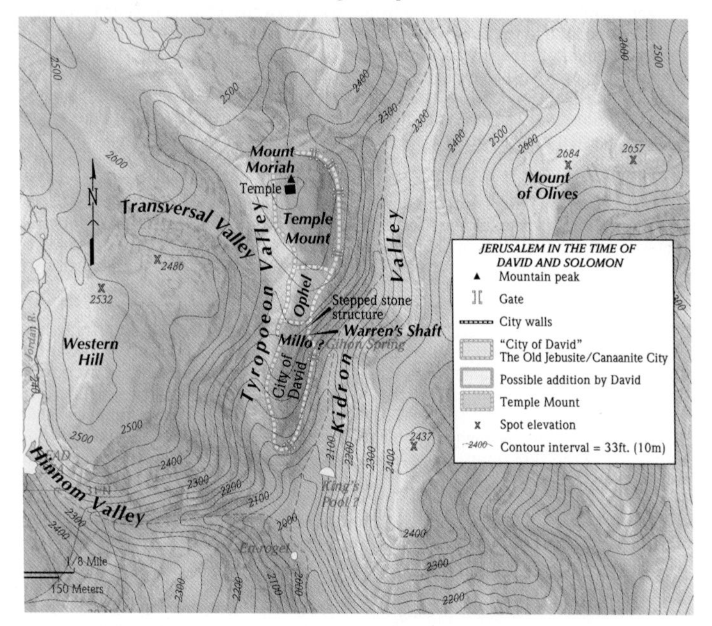

UV

The excavated areas of Ugarit which have yielded much material about Canaan and Canaanite religion

UCAL Personal name meaning "I am strong" or "I am consumed." Pupil of Agur, the wisdom teacher responsible for Prov. 30 (v. 1). REB followed the earliest Greek translation in rendering the proper names Ithiel and Ucal as "I am weary, God, I am weary and worn out" (cp. CSB, NRSV).

UEL Personal name meaning "will of God" or a contraction of Abiel meaning "God is father." Contemporary of Ezra with a foreign wife (Ezra 10:34; KJV, Juel).

UGARIT Important city in Syria whose excavation has provided tablets giving the closest primary evidence available for reconstructing the Canaanite religion Israel faced. Ruins of the ancient city of Ugarit lie on the Mediterranean coast about nine miles north of Latakia. The contemporary name is Ras Shamra, "head [land] of fennel."

ULAI Canal connecting the Kerkha and Abdizful Rivers just north of Susa (Dan. 8:2,16).

ULAM Personal name meaning "first" or "leader." **1.** Descendant of Manasseh (1 Chron. 7:16-17). **2.** Leader of a family of Benjaminite archers (1 Chron. 8:39-40).

ULLA Personal name meaning "burden" or "yoke." Descendant of Asher (1 Chron. 7:39). Scholars suggest a variety of emendations.

UMMAH Place-name meaning "kin." Town in Asher (Josh. 19:30). The name is perhaps a copyist's change from Acco as may be indicated by Greek manuscript evidence.

UNCTION KJV term meaning "anointing" (1 John 2:20,27).

UNDEFILED Ritually clean, frequently used for moral cleanness.

UNICORN KJV word for several related Hebrew terms that modern translations render as "wild ox" (Num. 23:22; 24:8; Deut. 33:17).

UNLEAVENED BREAD Bread baked without using leaven, a substance such as yeast that produces fermentation in dough. Unleavened bread was often served to guests (Gen. 19:3; Judg. 6:19; 1 Sam. 28:24). The eating of unleavened bread took on special significance through the Feast of Unleavened Bread celebrated in connection with Passover (Exod. 12:8,15,20; 13:3,6-7).

UNNI or **UNNO** Personal name, perhaps meaning "afflicted" or "answered." **1.** Levitical

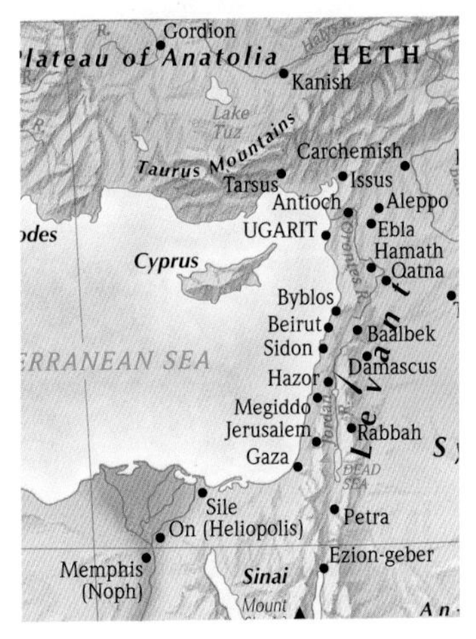

harpist in David's time (1 Chron. 15:18,20). **2.** Levite returning from exile with Zerubbabel (Neh. 12:9).

UNPARDONABLE SIN All three Synoptic Gospels (Matt. 12:31-32; Mark 3:28-29; Luke 12:10) refer to this concept. The context is identical in Matthew and Mark, following an exorcism by Jesus, including the accusation that Jesus casts out demons by Beelzebub's (Satan's) authority. The warning includes the statement that blasphemy against the Son of Man, while a sin, can be forgiven. This would be a rejection of the gospel, the good news of God's salvation in Jesus. In light of the context, the unpardonable sin can be defined as rejecting the power and authority of the Holy Spirit working in Jesus and crediting that authority to Satan.

The Pharisees' false accusation prompts the warning, but Jesus never explicitly says that they have crossed the line and committed the unpardonable sin. Perhaps this indicates that the unpardonable sin occurs when one knowingly credits the power and authority of the Holy Spirit to Satan. If so, some Pharisees may or may not have been guilty of making a charge against Jesus that they knew was false.

UPHAZ Unidentified source of fine gold (Jer. 10:9; Dan. 10:5) or else a term for fine gold. A related Hebrew term is translated "best gold" (1 Kgs. 10:18; Isa. 13:12). "Uphaz" is possibly a copyist's change for "Ophir" at Jer. 10:9 as indicated by early versions.

UPPER ROOM Upstairs room chosen by Jesus in which to hold a final meal with his disciples before his arrest (Mark 14:14-15).

The traditional site of the upper room, or Hall of the Coenaculum, in Jerusalem

UR Place-name meaning "fire oven." An ancient city in lower Mesopotamia that is mentioned as Abraham's birthplace. Ur was

The excavations at Ur showing the palace foundations in the foreground with the ziggurat in the distance

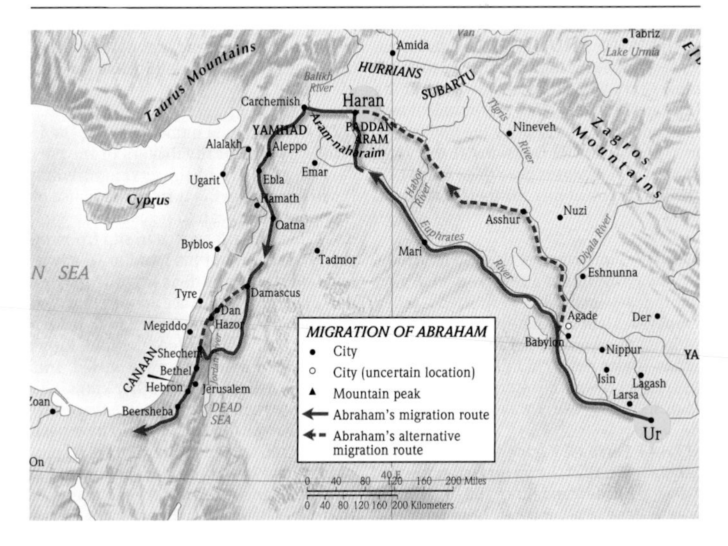

an important population center in Sumerian and Babylonian civilization. Abraham's family home is alluded to in Gen. 12:1 and Acts 7:2. The site associated with Ur is located in present-day Iraq, in the lower eastern portion of the Fertile Crescent.

URBANE (KJV) or **URBANUS** Personal name meaning "of the city," that is, "elegant, refined." Roman Christian whom Paul greeted as a "coworker in Christ" (Rom. 16:9 CSB).

URI Personal name meaning "fiery." **1.** Father of the tabernacle artisan Bezalel (Exod. 31:2; 35:30). **2.** Father of Geber, one of Solomon's officers charged with providing the royal household food for a month (1 Kgs. 4:19). **3.** Postexilic, Levitical singer with a foreign wife (Ezra 10:24).

URIAH Personal name meaning "fire of Yah." **1.** Hittite mercenary or native, perhaps noble, Israelite of Hittite ancestry, in David's army (2 Sam. 11), a member of David's elite warriors (23:39). He was the husband of Bathsheba, the woman with whom David committed adultery. The sin led to the eventual murder of Uriah after the king could cover the affair no longer. The Dead Sea Scrolls and Josephus report that Uriah was Joab's weapon-bearer. Uriah displayed more character and morality than did the king. **2.** High priest in Jerusalem temple under King Ahaz who followed the king's instructions in setting up an altar in the temple according to a Syrian pattern (2 Kgs. 16:10-16). He apparently served as a witness for Isaiah (8:2). **3.** Priest in time of Ezra and Nehemiah (Ezra 8:33; Neh. 3:4,21). **4.** Person who helped Ezra in informing the people of God's word (Neh. 8:4).

URIEL Personal name meaning "God is light" or "flame of God." **1.** Chief of the Levites assisting in David's transport of the ark to Jerusalem (1 Chron. 6:24; 15:5,11). **2.** Grandfather of King Abijah of Judah (2 Chron. 13:2).

URIJAH Personal name meaning "flame of Yahweh." Variant spelling of Uriah. **1.** Chief priest who complied with Ahab's order to build an Assyrian-style altar for the Jerusalem temple (2 Kgs. 16:10-16). **2.** Prophet who joined Jeremiah in preaching against Jerusalem. When King Jehoiakim ordered his execution, Urijah fled to Egypt. He was, however, captured, returned to Jerusalem, and executed (Jer. 26:20-23).

URIM AND THUMMIM Objects Israel, and especially the high priest, used to determine God's will. Little is known about the Urim and Thummim. They are first mentioned in Exodus as being kept by the high priest in a "breastplate for decisions" (Exod. 28:30 CSB). Later on, Moses gave the tribe of Levi special responsibility for their care (Deut. 33:8).

USURY Sum of money charged for a loan. OT laws prohibited a Jew from charging another Jew usury but permitted it when money was lent to a Gentile (Deut. 23:19-20). Although the word has negative connotations today, it was not so in biblical days when usury simply was the interest charged for a loan. Excessive usury was condemned.

UTHAI Personal name meaning "Yahweh is help" or "he has shown himself supreme." **1.** Postexilic descendant of Judah (1 Chron. 9:4). **2.** Head of a family of those returning from exile (Ezra 8:14).

UZ Personal name and place-name, perhaps meaning "replacement." **1.** Unspecified territory, most likely in Hauran south of Damascus (Jer. 25:20) or else between Edom and northern Arabia (Job 1:1; Lam. 4:21). **2.** Descendant of Shem's son Aram (Gen. 10:23; 1 Chron. 1:17) and progenitor of an Aramaean tribe. **3.** Descendant of Abraham's brother Nahor (Gen. 22:21). **4.** Descendant of Esau (Gen. 36:28) and member of the Horite branch of Edomites.

UZAI Personal name meaning "hoped for" or "he has heard." Father of one helping with Nehemiah's repair of the wall (Neh. 3:25).

UZAL Son of Joktan and ancestor of an Arabian tribe (Gen. 10:27; 1 Chron. 1:21). Scholars have linked the tribe with Izalla in northeastern Syria and Azalla near Medina. Ezekiel 27:19 includes them among Tyre's trading partners.

UZZA Personal name meaning "strength." **1.** Descendant of Benjamin (1 Chron. 8:7). **2.** Descendant of Levi (1 Chron. 6:29). **3.** Head of a family of postexilic temple servants or Nethinims (Ezra 2:49). **4.** Owner of the garden in which Manasseh and Amon were buried (2 Kgs. 21:18,26). **5.** Variant English spelling of "Uzzah."

UZZAH Personal name meaning "he is strong." **1.** One of the drivers of the cart carrying the ark of the covenant when David began moving it from the house of Abinadab in Gibeah to Jerusalem (2 Sam. 6:3). When the ark started to slip from the cart, Uzzah put out his hand to steady it, and God struck him dead for touching the holy object (6:6-7). **2.** Ancestor of exiles who returned to Jerusalem from Babylon (Ezra 2:49). **3.** Name of garden in which kings Manasseh and Ammon were buried. This distinguished them from other kings who "slept with their fathers," that is, were buried in the royal tomb. Uzzah may have been a noble who owned the garden burial plot or may have been a variant spelling of the Canaanite god Attar-melek. **4.** Member of the tribe of Benjamin (1 Chron. 8:7). **5.** Family of temple servants who returned from exile with Zerubbabel (Ezra 2:49). **6.** A Levite (1 Chron. 6:29).

UZZEN-SHEERAH Place-name meaning "ear of Sheerah." Village that Ephraim's daughter Sheerah founded (1 Chron. 7:24). The site is perhaps Beit Sira, three miles south of lower Beth-horon.

UZZI Personal name; an abbreviated form of "Yahweh is my strength." **1.** Aaronic priest (1 Chron. 6:5-6,51; Ezra 7:4). **2.** Family of the tribe of Issachar (1 Chron. 7:2-3). **3.** Descendant of Benjamin (1 Chron. 7:7; 9:8). **4.** Overseer of Jerusalem Levites after the exile (Neh. 11:22). **5.** Postexilic priest (Neh. 12:19). **6.** Musician involved in Nehemiah's dedication of Jerusalem's walls (Neh. 12:42).

UZZIA Personal name meaning "Yahweh is strong." One of 16 whom the Chronicler added to the list of David's 30 elite warriors (1 Chron. 11:44).

UZZIAH Personal name meaning "Yahweh is [my] strength." **1.** Descendant of Levi (1 Chron. 6:24). **2.** Father of one of David's treasurers (1 Chron. 27:25). **3.** Also known as Azariah (2 Kgs. 15:1,6-8,17,23,27); son and successor of King Amaziah of Judah. His death is famously cited in Isa. 6:1. **4.** Postexilic priest with a foreign wife (Ezra 10:21). **5.** Descendant of Judah and father of a postexilic resident of Jerusalem (Neh. 11:4).

UZZIEL Personal name meaning "God is strength." **1.** Descendant of Levi (Exod. 6:18; Num. 3:19; 1 Chron. 6:2,18) and ancestor of a subdivision of Levites, the Uzzielites (Num. 3:27; 1 Chron. 15:10; 26:23). **2.** One captain in the successful Simeonite attack on the Amalekites of Mount Seir (1 Chron. 4:42). **3.** Descendant of Benjamin (1 Chron. 7:7). **4.** Levitical musician (1 Chron. 25:4). **5.** Levite involved in Hezekiah's reform (2 Chron. 29:14). **6.** Goldsmith assisting in Nehemiah's repair of the Jerusalem walls (Neh. 3:8).

UZZIELITE Member of Levitical clan of Uzziel.

VAIZATHA or **VAJEZATHA** Persian personal name, perhaps meaning "the son of the atmosphere." One of Haman's 10 sons the Jews killed after Esther gained permission to retaliate against Haman's deadly plan (Esth. 9:9).

VALLEY Depression between mountains, a broad plain or plateau, a narrow ravine, or a low terrain. "Valleys" of varying shapes and sizes mark Palestine's landscape. "Valley" is often used symbolically to refer to the difficulties of life. The classic example of this is Ps. 23:4.

VANIAH Personal name possibly meaning "worthy of love." Man who married a foreign wife (Ezra 10:36).

VASHNI Personal name, perhaps meaning "weak." Samuel's son according to Hebrew text of 1 Chron. 6:28 (KJV).

VASHTI Personal name meaning "the once desired, the beloved." Wife of King Ahasuerus and queen of Persia and Media (Esth. 1:9). The king called for her to show off her beauty to a group he was entertaining, but she refused. Vashti was deposed as queen (1:19), and a beauty contest was arranged to select a new queen. Esther was chosen as the new queen (2:16).

VEIL (KJV "vail") Cloth covering. **1.** *Women's veils.* Rebekah veiled herself before meeting Isaac (Gen. 24:65). Her veil was perhaps the sign that she was a marriageable maiden. At Isa. 47:2, the removal of one's veil is again a sign of shamelessness. Paul regarded the wearing of veils as necessary for women praying or preaching ("prophesying") in public (1 Cor. 11:4-16). **2.** *Moses's veil.* Moses spoke to God with his face unveiled and then delivered God's message to the people with his face still unveiled. Afterward, Moses veiled his face (Exod. 34:33-35). **3.** *Imagery.* The "veil which is stretched over the nations" (Isa. 25:7 NASB) is likely an image for death, which is also swallowed up (25:8). The veil possibly includes reproach as well. **4.** *Temple veil.* This curtain separated the most holy place from the holy place (2 Chron. 3:14). Only the high priest was allowed to pass through the veil and then only on the Day of Atonement (Lev. 16:2). At Jesus's death, the temple veil was ripped from top to bottom, illustrating that in Christ God had abolished the barrier separating humanity from the presence of God (Matt. 27:51; Mark 15:38; cp. Luke 23:45). Hebrews 10:20 uses the tabernacle veil, not as the image of a barrier, but of access. Access to God is gained through the flesh of the historical Jesus (cp. John 10:7).

VENGEANCE The restoration of community integrity seems to have expected some deed(s) of retaliation or punishment by God. The range of meanings in this community motif goes beyond "vengeance" as punishment. They include the positive side as well, "vengeance" as "deliverance" for the people of God.

Human revenge against one's enemies is expressed in a variety of situations in the OT (Gen. 4:23-24; Jer. 20:10). Thus Samson's reaction to his enemies was described as "vengeance" in Judg. 15:7. Such "vengeance" was a just punishment directed at an adulterer (Prov. 6:32-34). It might also be directed against a whole ethnic group, such as the Philistines (1 Sam. 18:25). Sometimes this human "vengeance" is sought against Israel by her enemies (Ezek. 25:12,15,17).

In the context of loving one's neighbor, human revenge toward a fellow Hebrew was strictly forbidden (Lev. 19:17-18; Deut. 32:35). On occasion, however, the word *naqam* was used of legitimate punishment administered by humans on humans for wrongs having been done (Exod. 21:20,23-25; Lev. 24:19; Deut. 19:21). As an act of God on behalf of his people, the term is best understood as just retribution (Judg. 11:36) rather than emotion-driven vengeance.

New Testament The motif of "vengeance" in the NT occurs infrequently and is kept in perspective by a strong emphasis on "compassion" and "forgiveness."

Interestingly, Luke is the only Gospel writer who used both the verb and noun forms. He used them in Jesus's parable of the unjust judge/persistent widow. Vengeance against her enemies was reluctantly granted (Luke 18:1-8).

Paul forbade human "vengeance" much like Deut. 32:35 (cp. Lev. 19:18), asserting that God is the one who avenges wrong (Rom. 12:19; 1 Thess. 4:6-7). He used both the noun and verb forms in the Corinthian correspondence to speak of a "punishment" designed to bring about repentance (2 Cor. 7:10-11; 10:5-6). He also wrote of the eschatological wrath (vengeance/judgment) of God (2 Thess. 1:7-8; cp. Isa. 66:15; Ps. 79:6).

VENISON Flesh of a wild animal taken by hunting (Gen. 25:28; "game," NASB, NRSV; "wild game," NIV, CSB). The word is used only in the narrative of Jacob's stealing Esau's birthright. Isaac preferred Esau because of his love of wild game.

VENOM Poisonous secretion from an animal such as a snake, spider, or scorpion that is released into its victim by a bite or sting. Venom is a translation of *ro'sh* (Deut. 32:33; Job 20:16). The same Hebrew term is used for a dangerous, poisonous plant (Deut. 29:18; Hos. 10:4, among others).

VESPASIAN Emperor of Rome AD 69–79. He was born into a wealthy family and became a military hero as commander of a legion under Emperor Claudius. After becoming commander of three legions, he was ordered to quell the Jewish revolt in Palestine in AD 66. Three years into the war, he answered the call of the army to become emperor. Vespasian left his command to his son, Titus, and went to Rome. He sought to establish a dynasty, but it lasted only through his two sons, Titus and Domitian.

VIA DOLOROSA Literally, "way of suffering." Christian pilgrims from the time of the Crusaders have retraced the alleged path of Jesus from the Fortress of Antonia to the cross. This journey assumes the trial took place at the Antonian Fortress, which is debatable. Even if the fortress had been the location of Jesus's trial before Pilate, the centuries of remains have filled in and changed the streets from Jesus's time. Thus the 14 devotional "stations" of the cross are based on tradition.

One of the stations on the Via Dolorosa (the Way of Sorrow) in Jerusalem

VIAL Vessel that held oil, usually for anointing purposes (1 Sam. 10:1 KJV, NRSV; NASB, NIV, "flask").

The same word is used a number of times in the book of Revelation (5:8; 15:7; 16:1-4,8,10,12,17; 17:1; 21:9; CSB, NASB, NIV, NRSV, "bowls"). See *Anoint; Oil.*

VILLAGE OT distinguishes between city and village. The city was usually walled and much larger, while the village was characterized by no wall and usually homes consisting of one room (Lev. 25:29,31). The village had little or no organized government. Archaeology shows Israelite villages built around the circumference with house walls joining to form the only defense system and open community space left in the middle. Many villages had 20 to 30 houses. The cattle were kept in the inner open space where grain was stored. The main job in the villages was farming. Small craft manufacturing was practiced. Usually a common threshing floor was available. Shepherds often gathered around villages. The pastureland was seen as the possession of the village (1 Chron. 6:54-60).

VINE Any plant having a flexible stem supported by creeping along a surface or by climbing a natural or artificial support. While ancient Israel grew different types of plants that produced vines, such as cucumbers and melons (Num. 11:5; Isa. 1:8), the word "vine" almost always refers to the grapevine or vineyard. The climate of Palestine was well suited for growing vineyards. Along with the olive and fig trees, the grapevine is used throughout the OT to symbolize the fertility of the land (Deut. 6:11; Josh. 24:13; 1 Sam. 8:14; 2 Kgs. 5:26; Jer. 5:17; 40:10; Hos. 2:12).

Grapes growing on the vine

The Bible frequently uses "vine" and "vineyard" as symbols. Vine is often used in speaking of Israel. Thus Israel is said to have been brought out of Egypt and planted as a vine on the land but was forsaken (Ps. 80:8-13; cp. Isa. 5:1-7). Israel was planted a "choice vine" but became a "wild vine" (Jer. 2:21; cp. Hos. 10:1). As the dead wood of a vine is good for nothing but fuel, so the inhabitants of Jerusalem would be consumed (Ezek. 15:1-8; 19:10-14).

On the other hand, the abundance of vines and vineyards was seen as an expression of God's favor. The fruit of the vine gladdens the heart of humankind (Ps. 104:15; Eccles. 10:19) and suppresses pain and misery (Prov. 31:6-7). Israel was "like grapes in the wilderness" when God found them (Hos. 9:10), and the remnant surviving the exile is compared to a cluster of grapes (Isa. 65:8). Finally, an abundance of the vine symbolizes the glorious age to come when the treader of the grapes will overtake the one who sows the seed (Amos 9:13-15; cp. Gen. 49:10-12).

In the NT, Jesus often used the vineyard as an analogy for the kingdom of God (Matt. 20:1-16). Those who hope to enter the kingdom must be like the son who at first refused to work in his father's vineyard but later repented and went (Matt. 21:28-32 and parallels). Ultimately, Jesus himself is described as the "true vine" and his disciples (Christians) as the branches (John 15:1-11).

VINEGAR Literally, "that which is soured," related to Hebrew term for "that which is leavened" and referring to a drink that has soured, either wine or beer from barley (Num. 6:3). In biblical times, vinegar was most commonly produced by pouring water over the skins and stalks of grapes after the juice had been pressed out and allowing the whole to ferment. However, any fruit could be used for making wine or vinegar. In the NT, it is mentioned only in connection with the crucifixion. The first instance, which Jesus refused, was a mixture used to deaden the sense of the victim and nullify the pain. Possibly the vinegar mentioned in the second instance, which Christ accepted, was the customary drink of a peasant or soldier called *posca*, a mixture of vinegar, water, and eggs. Vinegar was most commonly used as a seasoning for food or as a condiment on bread (Ruth 2:14). Solomon figuratively used vinegar to describe the irritation caused by a lazy man's attitude.

VIOLENCE Use of force to injure or wrong. The OT affirms that God hates violence (Mal. 2:16). The flood was God's response to a world filled and corrupted by violence (Gen. 6:11,13). The exile was likewise God's response to a Jerusalem filled with violence (Ezek. 7:23).

The Wisdom literature often warns that those who live lives of violence will meet violent ends (Ps. 7:16; Prov. 1:18-19; 21:7; cp. Matt. 26:52). Through the prophets God demanded an end to violence (Jer. 22:3; Ezek. 45:9). Such violence was especially evidenced in the oppression of the poor by the rich (Pss. 55:9,11; 73:6; Jer. 22:17; Mic. 6:12; James 5:1-6). The servant of the Lord models a nonviolent response to violence (Isa. 53:9; cp. 1 Pet. 2:23; James 5:6). Isaiah anticipated the end of violence in the Messianic Age (60:18).

Matthew 11:12 is one of the most difficult texts in the NT. Does the kingdom of heaven suffer violence (CSB, KJV, NASB, REB, NRSV), or does the kingdom come "forcefully" (NIV)? The violence which John the Baptist (Matt. 14:3-10) and believers (Matt. 5:10-11; 10:17; 23:34) suffer argues for the former.

Candidates for church leadership should be nonviolent persons (1 Tim. 3:3; Titus 1:7).

VIPER Poisonous snake. Several species of snakes are called vipers, and the various words used in the Bible for them probably do not designate specific types. Jesus spoke of the wicked religious leaders as vipers (Matt. 3:7) because of their venomous attacks on him and their evil character in leading the people astray. Paul was bitten by a viper (Acts 28:3) but suffered no ill effect.

A viper partially hidden in the surrounding grass and wildflowers

VIRGIN, VIRGINAL CONCEPTION (OR VIRGIN BIRTH) The event that initiated the incarnation of Christ whereby he was supernaturally conceived in the womb of a virgin without the participation of a human father. The NT texts that deal with the virgin birth are Matt. 1:18-25 and Luke 1:26-35.

Theological Relevance The virginal conception affects two major areas of theology. First, it relates to the truthfulness of Scripture. The NT clearly states that Jesus was born of a virgin, and to deny this is to question the veracity and authenticity of the text. Second, the virgin conception is linked to the deity of Christ, for through this event he simultaneously retained his divine nature and received a sinless human nature. Scripture reveals it as a critical aspect of the incarnation.

VISION Experience in the life of a person whereby a special revelation from God was received. The revelation from God had two purposes. First, a vision was given for immediate direction, as with Abram in Gen. 12:1-3; Lot, Gen. 19:15; Balaam, Num. 22:22-40; and Peter, Acts 12:7. Second, a vision was given to develop the kingdom of God by revealing the moral and spiritual deficiencies of the people of God in light of God's requirements for maintaining a proper relationship with him. The visions of prophets such as Isaiah, Amos, Hosea, Micah, Ezekiel, Daniel, and John are representative of this aspect of revelation.

VOPHSI Personal name of uncertain meaning. Father of Nahbi of the tribe of Naphtali (Num. 13:14). Nahbi was one of the spies Moses sent into Canaan.

VOWS Voluntary expressions of devotion usually fulfilled after some condition had been met. Vows in the OT usually were conditional. A common formula for vows was the "if . . . then" phrase (Gen. 28:20; Num. 21:2; Judg. 11:30). The one making the religious vow proposed that if God did something (such as give protection or victory), then he or she in return would make some act of devotion. Not all vows, however, were conditional. Some, such as the Nazirite vow

(Num. 6), were made out of devotion to God with no request placed upon God. Whether conditional or not, the emphasis in the Bible is on keeping the vow. A vow unfulfilled is worse than a vow never made. While vows do not appear often in the NT, Paul made one that involved shaving his head (Acts 18:18).

VULGATE Latin translation of the Bible by Jerome about AD 400.

VULTURE Both carrion vulture and vulture are listed separately in the unclean bird lists (Lev. 11:13-19; Deut. 14:12-18 RSV).

A mosaic in the chapel of Jerome's Room, the traditional site where Jerome translated the Latin Vulgate, located under the Church of the Nativity in Bethlehem

The wadi through the limestone cliffs at Qumran near the Dead Sea

WADI Transliteration of Arabic word for a rocky watercourse that is dry except during rainy seasons. These creek beds can become raging torrents when especially heavy rains fall. Wadis are numerous in the Middle East.

WAGES Terms of employment or compensation for services rendered encompass the meaning of the Hebrew and Greek words. Their usage in the text applies to commercial activities and labor service, as well as judgmental recompense for one's actions in life.

WAGON Vehicle of transportation with two or four wooden wheels. The two-wheeler was usually called a cart. Wagons were used to transport people and goods (Gen. 45:17-21). Sometimes wagons were used as instruments of war (Ezek. 23:24). Wagons were usually pulled by oxen.

WALK Slower pace contrasted with running. It is used literally (Exod. 2:5; Matt. 4:18) and figuratively to mean a person's conduct or way of life (Gen. 5:24; Rom. 8:4; 1 John 1:6-7).

WALLS Outside vertical structures of houses and the fortifications surrounding cities. In ancient times, the walls of cities and houses were constructed of bricks made of clay mixed with reed and hardened in the sun. Archaeologists estimate that the walls of Nineveh were wide enough to drive three chariots abreast and the walls of Babylon were wide enough to drive six chariots abreast on the top.

In scriptural language, a wall is a symbol of salvation (Isa. 26:1; 60:18), of the protection of God (Zech. 2:5), of those who afford protection (1 Sam. 25:16; Isa. 2:15), and of wealth of the rich in their own conceit (Prov. 18:11). A "fortified wall of bronze" (CSB) is symbolic of prophets and their testimony against the wicked (Jer. 15:20). The "wall of partition" (Eph. 2:14 KJV; CSB, "dividing wall of hostility") represented temple worship and Jewish practice separating Jew from Gentile.

WANDERINGS IN THE WILDERNESS Israel's movements from Egypt to the promised land under Moses, including the place-names along the routes. A reconstruction of the Israelites' wilderness wanderings is more complex than a casual reading of the biblical account at first would seem to indicate.

WATCH Division of time in which soldiers or others were on duty to guard something. They are listed as "evening," "midnight," "crowing of the rooster," and "morning" (Mark 13:35 CSB). Nehemiah set watches that may mean armed persons or just citizens on guard (4:9; 7:3). The OT seems to have had three watches rather than four. There was the "first watch of the night" (Lam. 2:19), the "middle watch" (Judg. 7:19), and the "morning watch" (Exod. 14:24 CSB).

WATCHMAN One who stands guard. Ancient cities had watchmen stationed on the walls. Their responsibility was to sound a warning if an enemy approached (2 Kgs. 9:17; Ezek. 33:2-3). Israel's prophets saw themselves as watchmen warning the nation of God's approaching judgment if the people did not repent. Vineyards and fields also had watchmen, especially during harvest. Their responsibility was to guard the produce from animals and thieves.

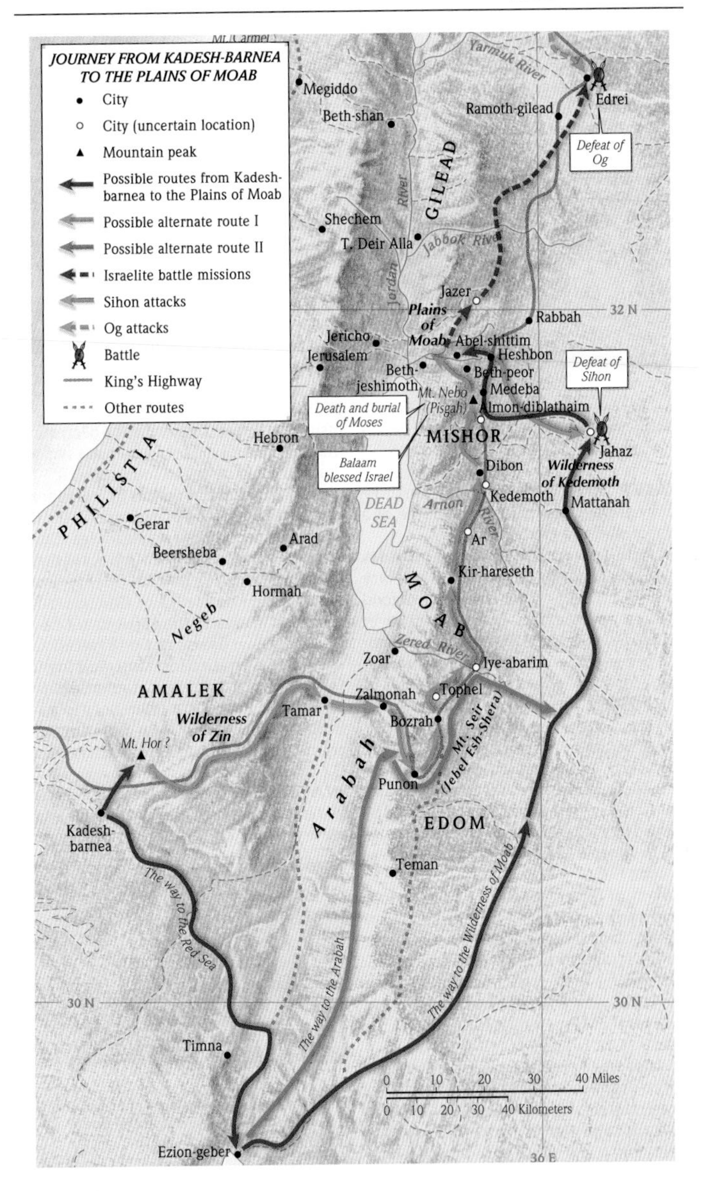
JOURNEY FROM KADESH-BARNEA TO THE PLAINS OF MOAB
City
City (uncertain location)
Mountain peak
Possible routes from Kadesh-barnea to the Plains of Moab
Possible alternate route I
Possible alternate route II
Israelite battle missions
Sihon attacks
Og attacks
Battle
King's Highway
Other routes
Megiddo
Beth-shan
Ramoth-gilead
Edrei
Yarmuk River
Defeat of Og
GILEAD
Shechem
T. Deir Alla
Jabbok River
Jordan River
Jazer
Plains of Moab
Rabbah
32 N
Jericho
Jerusalem
Abel-shittim
Heshbon
Beth-jeshimoth
Beth-peor
Medeba
Mt. Nebo (Pisgah)
Almon-diblathaim
Defeat of Sihon
Death and burial of Moses
Balaam blessed Israel
Hebron
MISHOR
Jahaz
Dibon
Wilderness of Kedemoth
Kedemoth
Mattanah
PHILISTIA
Gerar
DEAD SEA
Arnon River
Arad
Ar
Beersheba
Kir-hareseth
Hormah
MOAB
Negeb
Zered River
Zoar
Iye-abarim
AMALEK
Tophel
Zalmonah
Tamar
Wilderness of Zin
Bozrah
Mt. Seir (Jebel Esh-Shera)
Mt. Hor ?
Arabah
Punon
Kadesh-barnea
EDOM
Teman
The way to the Red Sea
The way to the Wilderness of Moab
The way to the Arabah
30 N
Timna
0 10 20 30 40 Miles
0 10 20 30 40 Kilometers
Ezion-geber
36 E

WATCHTOWER Tower on a high place or built high enough to afford a person to be able to see for some distance. The person doing the watching might be a soldier or a servant (2 Kgs. 9:17; Isa. 5:2; Mark 12:1). See *Tower*.

An ancient watchtower remains relatively unchanged in an open field in Israel.

WATER The Bible speaks of water in three different ways: as a material resource, as a symbol, and as a metaphor.

A Material Necessity That God Provides Water as a material resource is necessary for life. God made water a part of his good creation, and he exercises sovereignty over it (Gen. 1–2; Isa. 40:12). He controls the natural processes of precipitation and evaporation, as well as the courses of bodies of water (Job 5:10; 36:27; 37:10; Pss. 33:7; 107:33; Prov. 8:29). God normally assures the provision of water for human needs (Deut. 11:14). However, water is sometimes used in punishment for sin, as with the flood of Noah's day (Gen. 6:17) or the drought proclaimed by Elijah (1 Kgs. 17:1). The divine control of water teaches people obedience to and dependency upon God.

Many of the great acts of God in history have involved water, such as the parting of the sea (Exod. 14:21), the provision of water for the Israelites in the wilderness (Exod. 15:25; 17:6), and the crossing of the Jordan River (Josh. 3:14-17). Water was also involved in several of Jesus's miracles (Matt. 14:25; Luke 8:24-25; John 2:1-11).

Water was a crucial element in God's gift of the promised land to Israel (Deut. 8:7). Israel, and the surrounding area, contains several natural sources of water: rain, springs, wells, and a few short, perennial streams. The average annual rainfall in this region is about 25 inches, all of which normally falls between November and April. The dry months of May to October made necessary the use of cisterns and pools for water storage. Several famous biblical cities had pools, such as Gibeon (2 Sam. 2:13), Hebron (2 Sam. 4:12), Samaria (1 Kgs. 22:38), and Jerusalem (2 Kgs. 20:20). See *Palestine*.

A Theological Symbol and Metaphor The OT contains laws for the use of water in rituals as a symbol of purification. Priests, sacrificial meat, and ritual utensils were washed before involvement in rituals (Lev. 1:9; 6:28; 8:6). Unclean people and things were also washed as a symbol of ritual cleansing (Lev. 11:32-38; 14:1-9; 15:1-30; Num. 31:23). The book of Genesis uses water as a symbol of instability before the completion of creation (1:2), and Ezekiel spoke of water as a symbol of renewal in the age to come (47:1-12).

The Bible contains dozens of metaphorical usages of water. For example, in the OT, water is a metaphor or simile for fear (Josh. 7:5), death (2 Sam. 14:14), sin (Job 15:16), God's presence (Ps. 72:6), marital fidelity (Prov. 5:15-16), the knowledge of God (Isa. 11:9), salvation (Isa. 12:3), the Spirit (Isa. 44:3-4), God's blessings (Isa. 58:11), God's voice (Ezek. 43:2), God's wrath (Hos. 5:10), and justice (Amos 5:24). Among the metaphorical uses of water in the NT are references to birth (John 3:5), the Spirit (John 4:10), spiritual training (1 Cor. 3:6), and life (Rev. 7:17).

WATERPOT Vessel made for carrying water, usually made of clay although some were made of stone (John 2:6). Large pots

An Arab man drinks from the spout of a multispouted waterpot as he would have done in biblical times.

stored water (1 Kgs. 18:33; John 2:6); a woman could carry smaller pots on her shoulder (John 4:28). Small pitchers were used for pouring water (Luke 22:10; Jer. 19). Water was also carried in animal skins. See *Pottery; Skin.*

WAVE OFFERING See *Sacrifice and Offering.*

WAW Sixth letter in the Hebrew alphabet. Heading of Ps. 119:41-48 (KJV, Vau) in which each verse begins with the letter.

WEALTH AND MATERIALISM Physical possessions having significant value, such as land, livestock, money, and precious metals, and the practice of valuing such possessions more highly than they ought to be valued, especially when this results in the misalignment of ones' priorities and undermines one's devotion to God.

Wealth To understand the biblical view of wealth, one must understand the biblical account of creation. On that account, God created the universe—and everything therein—out of nothing (Gen. 1:1-27). Thus, in virtue of being the absolute Creator, God's claim on the universe and everything therein is absolute—everything ultimately belongs to him and to him alone (cp. Ps. 50:10-12).

Since everything belongs ultimately to God, whatever one possesses—and thus owns—comes as a trust from him; for this reason, one's right of ownership is never absolute—one's property always belongs first and foremost to God himself. Second, since it comes as a trust from God, ownership of property carries with it significant responsibilities. For instance, God holds those to whom he has entrusted wealth responsible for giving to his work (cp. Num. 18:20-32; Deut. 14:28-29; Mal. 3:8-10; 2 Cor. 9:6-14) and for caring for the poor among them (cp. Prov. 29:7; Amos 5:11-12; Matt. 19:21; 1 Tim. 5:3-5). In addition, they are accountable to God for how they use the rest of their resources.

God has blessed some with abundant wealth. Abram, Isaac, Solomon, and Job were each blessed with great riches (cp. Gen. 13:2; 26:12-14; 1 Kgs. 3:13; Job 42:12). This does not mean, however, that poverty is a sign of God's disfavor. According to Scripture, God takes special interest in the poor (Ps. 72:12-15). Moreover, Job was righteous when God allowed him to become impoverished (Job 1:1,13-19).

Materialism Scripture warns against valuing one's wealth too highly. Riches can prevent one from bearing spiritual fruit (cp. Luke 8:14). Perhaps awareness of this lay behind Agur's plea that he not be given riches lest he deny God (Prov. 30:8-9). A generous spirit accompanies righteousness. Zacchaeus responded to Jesus not only by restoring fourfold what he had gained dishonestly, but also by giving freely to the poor (Luke 19:8), and the members of the church in Jerusalem shared their possessions with one another (Acts 2:44-45; 4:32-35). Such generosity characterizes those who have been freed from love of money and have sought to store up for themselves treasure in heaven rather than on earth (Matt. 6:19-21).

WEAPONS Since mankind's beginnings, the desire to impose one's will upon another person(s) or being has led to active conflict using many types of weapons. Human

Reconstruction of a Roman siege tower with battering ram (first century AD)

history shows marked means by which the implements were advanced technologically through the past six millennia.

The implements of warfare and defense are known from three sources: excavations; pictorial representations in murals, reliefs, and models; and written documents. Tombs of Egypt contained actual weapons and models. Assyrian reliefs depicted great battles in detail. Excavations have uncovered numerous examples of stone and metal weapons; and biblical and inscriptional sources provide names of objects, strategy and tactics, and methods of construction.

Military action has been defined in terms of ability to achieve supremacy over the enemy in three fields: mobility, firepower, and security. Mobility is exemplified by the chariot and cavalry; firepower by bow, sling, spear, ax, and sword; and security by shield, armor, and helmet.

Reconstruction of a Roman battering ram (first century AD)

WEASEL Unclean animal (Lev. 11:29); a small mammal related to the mink.

WEB 1. A fabric usually woven on a loom (Judg. 16:13-14). See *Loom*. **2.** The weaving of a spider that looks like thread. The spider's web is used figuratively for that which is impermanent and untrustworthy (Job 8:14).

WEDDINGS In biblical times, the father selected the bride for his son. Abraham sent his servant to Haran to find a wife for his son Isaac (Gen. 24). In arranging a marriage, the bridegroom's family paid a price (Hb. *mohar*) for the bride (cp. Gen. 34:12; Exod. 22:16; 1 Sam. 28:25). When the marriage had been arranged, the couple entered the betrothal period, usually lasting a year and much more binding than the engagement of today.

The wedding was largely a social event during which a blessing was pronounced on the bride: "Our sister, may you become thousands upon ten thousands. May your offspring possess the city gates their enemies" (Gen. 24:60 CSB). The blessing reflected the concept of God's blessing, namely, a large family and victory over one's enemies. The marriage itself was secured by the formalizing of a marriage contract.

The parable of the 10 virgins is rich with explanation of the Jewish wedding (Matt. 25:1-13). The wedding ceremony began with the bridegroom bringing home the bride from her parents' house to his parental home. The bridegroom, accompanied by his friends and amid singing and music, led a procession through the streets of the town to the bride's home (cp. Jer. 16:9). Along the way, friends who were ready and waiting with their lamps lit would join in the procession (Matt. 25:7-10). Veiled and dressed in beautifully embroidered clothes and adorned with jewels, the bride, accompanied by her attendants joined the bridegroom for the procession to his father's house (Ps. 45:13-15). Isaiah 61:10 describes the bridegroom decked out with a garland and the bride adorned with jewels. The bride's beauty would be forever remembered (Jer. 2:32). The bride and groom were considered king and queen for the week. Sometimes the groom even wore a gold crown.

Once at the home, the bridal couple sat under a canopy amid the festivities of games and dancing which lasted an entire week—sometimes longer (Song 2:4). Guests praised the newly married couple; songs of love for the couple graced the festival. Sumptuous meals and wine filled the home or banquet hall (John 2:1-11). Ample provision for an elaborate feast was essential—failure could bring a lawsuit (John 2:3). The bridal couple wore their wedding clothes throughout the week; guests also wore their finery, which was sometimes supplied by wealthy families (Matt. 22:12).

WEEK For the Jews, any seven consecutive days ending with the Sabbath (Gen. 2:1-3). The Sabbath began at sunset Friday and lasted until sunset Saturday. The Christians moved their day of worship to Sunday, the first day of the week. In this way, they called attention to the resurrection of their Lord Jesus Christ (Luke 24:1-7). The week is of ancient Semitic origin. It was shared with the ancient world through the Bible and the religious practice of both Jews and Christians.

WEIGHTS AND MEASURES Systems of measurement. In the ancient Near East, weights and measures varied. The prophets spoke against merchants who used deceitful weights (Mic. 6:11).Weights and measures in biblical times are seldom precise enough to enable one to calculate exact metric equivalents, but the Lord set forth an ideal for "just" balances, weights, and measures. Different standards in surrounding Near Eastern countries affected biblical standards. Sometimes there were two standards operating at the same time, such as short and long, light and heavy, common and royal. There is enough evidence to figure approximate metrological values for the biblical weights and measures.

WELL Source of water created by digging in the earth to find available water. In the semiarid climate of ancient Israel, the availability of water was a constant concern, and the Bible contains many references to the sources used for obtaining it.

A chaduf for raising well water near ancient Lystra in south central Asia Minor (modern Turkey)

"Well" is also used figuratively of a "wayward woman" (Prov. 23:27 CSB) and of a wicked city (Jer. 6:7). Elsewhere it is used as a metaphor for sexual pleasure (Prov. 5:15; Song 4:15).

WHALE Large aquatic mammal that resembles a large fish (Ezek. 32:2; Jon. 1:17; Matt. 12:40). The Greek word translated "whale" in Matt. 12:40 (KJV) is also called "a great fish" (Jon. 1:17), "great creature" (Gen. 1:21; Ps. 148:7 NIV), "monster" (Job 7;12; Ezek. 32:2 CSB, NIV). The exact identification of the animal is impossible with present knowledge.

WHEAT Staple grain of the ancient Near East (Num. 18:12). Wheat has been raised in this region since at least Neolithic times (8300–4500 BC). Many species exist, and exact types cannot be determined from the biblical words. It became the major crop after the nomads began settling into agrarian societies. It is used as an analogy to speak of God's judgment (Matt. 3:12) and his care (Ps. 81:16). Wheat was used to make bread and was also parched (Lev. 23:14). KJV often translated "wheat" by the word "corn" (Mark 4:28). Wheat harvest was an ancient time reference (Exod. 34:22) and was celebrated by the Feast of Weeks. Wheat is said to have been harvested (1 Sam. 6:13), threshed (Judg. 6:11), and winnowed (Matt. 3:12).

WHEEL Disk or circular object capable of turning on a central axis. Archaeologists and historians believe that the wheel was probably invented in Mesopotamia before 3000 BC.

The Bible describes both a functional use and symbolic meaning for the wheel. The wheel was indispensable for transportation. It was used on wagons, carts, and chariots, and the word "wheel" could be a synonym for any of these vehicles (Ezek. 23:24; 26:10; Nah. 3:2). In Solomon's temple there were 10 stands upon which rested 10 lavers. Each of the stands was adorned with four wheels (1 Kgs. 7:30-33).

Ezekiel's vision of the great wheel in the sky (1:4-28; 10) was a symbol of God's pres-

A burned Roman wagon wheel

A small whirlwind in the desert of the Wadi Arabah

ence. There were four cherubim around the throne. Beside each there was a wheel which had a "gleam like beryl" (1:16 CSB). Ezekiel described the rims of the wheel as "tall and awe-inspiring" and "full of eyes" (v. 18 CSB). The exact meaning of these mysterious images is unknown. Perhaps they represented the wheels of God's invisible chariot moving across the sky ("chariots of the sun," 2 Kgs. 23:11) or the wheels of God's throne (Dan. 7:9).

Other symbolic uses of the wheel are a whirlwind (Ps. 77:18 CSB, NIV, NRSV, NASB) and God's judgment, as a wheel is driven over the wicked (Prov. 20:26). Jeremiah 18:13 describes God's redemption as the reshaping of marred clay on a potter's wheel.

WHELP Lion's cub, used figuratively in the OT (Gen. 49:9; Jer. 51:38; Nah. 2:11). See *Lion*.

WHIRLWIND English translation of four Hebrew words that designate any windstorm that is destructive. Only Ps. 77:18 uses a term indicating circular motion. True whirlwinds and tornadoes are rare in Israel. They usually occur near the coast where the cool breezes of the Mediterranean Sea collide with the hot wind from the desert. Lesser whirlwinds are seen as whirling dust is thrown up into the air. The Lord used the raging wind to take Elijah to heaven (2 Kgs. 2:1,11) and to talk with Job (38:1; 40:6). The prophets used the "storm wind" as a figure for judgment (Isa. 5:28; Jer. 4:13; Hos. 8:7; Amos 1:14; Zech. 7:14). God comes to deliver his people riding the stormy winds (Zech. 9:14).

WILD BEASTS Designation of any wild animal in contrast to domesticated animals, translating different Hebrew words. Most often the Hebrew is *chayyah* indicating living creatures (Gen. 1:24) including wild animals (Gen. 1:25). The same Hebrew form indicates humans as "living" beings (Gen. 2:7). The context shows the precise type of creature meant.

WILD GOURD Poisonous plant, probably *Citrillus colocynths* (2 Kgs. 4:39).

WILDERNESS Holy Land areas, particularly in the southern part, with little rainfall and few people. The words for "wilderness" in the OT come close to our word "desert," because they usually mean a rocky, dry wasteland.

Geographically the wilderness lay south, east, and southwest of the inhabited land of Israel in the Negev, Transjordan, and the Sinai. A particular wilderness, closer to home, lay on the eastern slopes of the Judean mountains in the rain shadow leading down to the Dead Sea.

Historically the wilderness was particularly connected with the wandering of the Hebrews after their miraculous escape from Egypt and just prior to the conquest of Transjordan. This was remembered in their retelling of the story as "the great and terrible wilderness" (Deut. 1:19; 8:15 CSB).

The prophets felt that most of Israel's religious troubles began with the settlement of Canaan and apostasy to Canaanite idolatry, but they also looked forward to a renewed

Arabs winnowing grain in the ancient way with wooden winnowing forks

grain fall back to the ground (Isa. 30:24). John the Baptist used winnowing as an analogy of God's judgment, when the Lord would separate the sinful from the righteous (Matt. 3:12).

WINTER Season between fall and spring, usually short and mild in Israel. Winter is also the rainy season for that land (Song 2:11).

WINTER HOUSE Part of a palace or a separate home of the rich that is heated and thus warmer than the rest of the house (Jer. 36:22) or built in a warmer part of the country. Amos spoke of the destruction of the winter house because of Israel's sin against God (3:15).

WISDOM LITERATURE A genre of writing featuring wise sayings and astute observations. These writings teach how to live according to such principles as intelligence, understanding, common sense, statecraft, and practical skills. With regard to the Bible, the term refers to the books of Job, Proverbs, and Ecclesiastes. Portions of other biblical books—such as Esther, Psalms, Song of Songs, and Daniel—can also be classified as Wisdom literature, as can the apocryphal books Sirach (Ecclesiasticus) and the Wisdom of Solomon. Ancient Egypt and Babylon also produced Wisdom literature, but biblical Wisdom literature is unique, teaching that the fear of God is the foundation of true wisdom (Prov. 9:10) and ultimate success (Ps. 25:12-13; Eccles. 8:12-13).

WITCH Female whose work was in divination and magic.

WITNESS, MARTYR Refers generally to something or someone who bears testimony to things seen, heard, transacted, or experienced.

Old Testament The words translated "witness" and "testimony" derive from three Hebrew words: *'ed*, a legal witness, and *mo'ed*, or sometimes *'edah*, meaning agreement or appointment.

Legal The chief usage of "witness" is in the legal sphere, referring to facts or personal experiences (Lev. 5:1; Num. 23:18; Isa. 8:2). It also denotes the proof or evidence presented in a court case, primarily by the prosecution (Num. 5:13; 35:30; Deut. 17:6-7; 19:15). False, unrighteous, and overhasty witnesses are disdained and subject to reprisals (Deut. 19:16-21; Exod. 23:1; Pss. 26:12; 34:11; Prov. 6:19; 12:17; 19:5; 21:28). Examples of a witness to an agreement are found in Ruth 4:9-10 and Jer. 39:10,25,44. God may be invoked as a witness to one's integrity (Job 16:19). In an accusatory sense, the Israelites stand self-accused if they return to idolatry (Josh. 24:22). Israel is also a witness to the uniqueness, reality, and deity of God on the basis of their experience of election by God (Isa. 43–44).

Memorial Inanimate objects sometimes served as witnesses to promises, pacts, and covenants. Altars (Josh. 22), piles of stones (Gen. 31:44; Josh. 24:27), and even God's law (Exod. 25:22) are examples. *Mo'ed* is used over 100 times for "witness" in the phrase "Tent of Witness" (*'ohel mo'ed*), meaning the appointed place where God met Moses (Exod. 25:22).

Moral This ideological nuance of witness involves the proclamation of certain truths, views, and internal convictions one holds by faith, and for which one would willingly die. This sense is not as distinct in the OT as it later became in the NT and early church. A firm case cannot be made for any kind of martyr theology in the OT.

New Testament Legal In the judicial sense, "witness" refers to a person who gives testimony and/or to the content of that testimony (John 1:7; 3:28; 1 Pet. 5:12; Matt. 18:16; cp. Deut. 19:15), whether true or false (Matt. 26:60-68). Jesus tells the scribes and Pharisees they are self-accusing witnesses (Matt. 23:31).

Personal Witness is used to mean "reputation" (Luke 4:22, Acts 6:3; 1 Tim. 3:7; Rev. 3:1) and may also refer to one's own life or person (as John the Baptist; John 1:6-7). Jesus, throughout John's Gospel, was a witness to God's love and gift of eternal life to believers and was an accusing witness to nonbelievers (John 20:30-31; 21:24).

Evangelistic Especially in the Lukan material, "witness" is used in an active, evangelistic sense. Christians proclaim the gospel (*kerugma*) in an active, insistent way, encouraging listeners to receive and respond to their message (Acts 2:40; 18:5; 1 Thess. 2:11-12).

Mortal The word *martus* refers to a martyr, one who is deprived of life as a result of one's testimony for Jesus Christ. This term is used only three times in the NT (Acts 22:20; Rev. 2:13; 17:6). See *Martyr*.

WOLF Largest of wild carnivorous canines (*Canis lupus*; *Canis pallipes*) that include dogs, foxes, and jackals. It is thought to be the primary ancestor of the domestic dog. The wolf is known for its boldness and fierceness of attack (Luke 10:3). It often killed more than it could eat because the taste of blood put it into a frenzy. Shepherds knew the wolf as the greatest enemy of sheep. The wolf was well known in biblical days (John 10:12), yet nearly every reference to wolves is in a figurative sense. Its name is used symbolically to describe deceitful and greedy people (Gen. 49:27; Jer. 5:6; Ezek. 22:27; Zeph. 3:3; Acts 20:29). Jesus used the figure of the false prophet as a wolf in sheep's clothing (Matt. 7:15). One of the signs of the Messianic Age is that the "wolf and the lamb will feed together" (Isa. 65:25 CSB).

WOMAN The Bible's paradigm for womanhood, while allowing for diversity and uniqueness, is nevertheless entirely consistent in its presentation of the Creator's plan for the nature and purposes of womanhood.

The Origin of the Woman The woman came after the man as his acknowledged offshoot, having a nature like his but her own unique existence. She is the only creature said to be "built" by God (Hb. *banah*, "made" in 2:22, literally "built"). God "built" the woman from raw resources derived from the man (Gen. 2:22).

Man and woman are created "in the image of God" and their position in Christ eliminates any possibility of inferiority of either to the other. Yet, because they are complementary, they cannot be identified one as the other. Equal dignity prohibits the despising of one by the other; complementary interaction of one with the other requires that differences be honored. Together man and woman are equipped to continue the generations and to exercise dominion over the earth and its resources.

Old Testament Israelite women managed the household and performed the duties of wives and mothers (Prov. 31:10-31). They had a measure of anonymity in life and were subordinate to their husbands. Beauty is associated with women in the Bible but without detail as to what makes them beautiful (Gen. 12:11; 26:7; 29:17; 2 Sam. 11:2; Song 4:2-3). Inner beauty, defined as "the fear of the Lord" and a "gentle and quiet spirit," is elevated over an attractive countenance (Prov. 31:30; 1 Tim. 2:9-10; 1 Pet. 3:3-4).

The husband was the patriarch of his family or clan, and the wife became part of her husband's family. Women were an integral part of the community and were to be protected therein. Marriage was the ideal (Gen. 2:24); a good wife was usually praised and honored (Prov. 31:10-31); godly women were admired and their contributions greatly valued (e.g., Deborah, Hannah, Abigail, Naomi, Ruth, Esther); widows were to be protected (Deut. 24:19-22; 26:12).

A woman's legal position in Israel was weaker than a man's. Though a husband could divorce his wife for "something indecent about her," no law is given suggesting that a wife could divorce her husband (Deut. 24:1-4 CSB). Wives could be required to take a jealousy test if they were suspected of unfaithfulness to their husbands, but no law is given permitting a wife to require the same of her husband (Num. 5:11-31). If a man and a woman were caught in the act of adultery, both were to be stoned (Deut. 22:22).

Hebrew laws did offer protection for women. If a husband added a second wife, he was not allowed to ignore the needs of his first wife (Exod. 21:10). Even a woman taken captive in war had rights (Deut. 21:14), and a man found guilty of raping a woman was stoned to death (Deut. 22:23-27). Although men usually owned property, daughters could receive the inheritance from their fathers if there were no sons in the family (Num. 27:8-11). Often the importance of the dowry to women is overlooked. Since theoretically the dowry belonged to the bride, some have suggested that this gift represented the daughter's share of her father's estate. She received her "inheritance" upon marriage, while her brothers had to wait to receive their shares until the father's death.

The Bible identifies women who were active in ancient society: Deborah, a prophetess and judge; Esther, a queen whose skills in diplomacy saved the Jews from extinction; Lydia, a tradeswoman with a thriving business. Just because the placement of women in civil and business pursuits is the exception rather than the rule does not lessen the valuable role of women in society. From the ancient world until now, society stands or falls according to its infrastructure, that is, the family, over which the wife and mother plays an irreplaceable role.

Children were to respect both mother and father equally (Exod. 20:12), even though they were the mother's special charge (Exod. 21:15; Prov. 1:8; 6:20; 20:20). The names of mothers appeared in biographies of successive kings (2 Chron. 24:7; 27:6). To disobey or curse either parent was punishable by stoning (Deut. 21:18-21).

The husband exercised his spiritual leadership by presenting the sacrifices and offerings for the family (Lev. 1:2), but only women offered a sacrifice after the birth of a child (Lev. 12:6). Women also participated in worship, but they were not required, as the men, to appear before the Lord (Deut. 29:10; Neh. 8:2; Joel 2:16). This optional participation may have been because of their responsibilities as wives and mothers (1 Sam. 1:3-5,21-22).

New Testament Jesus offered women new roles and equal status in his kingdom. A woman was the first to bear witness of his resurrection (Matt. 28:8-10). Women followed Jesus with the multitudes (Matt. 14:21), and Jesus featured women and used things associated with them in his parables and illustrations (Matt. 13:33; 25:1-13; Luke 13:18-21; 15:8-10; 18:1-5).

In the NT the birth and infancy narratives note a remarkable number of women. Matthew includes four—Tamar, Rahab, Ruth, and Bathsheba—in his genealogy of Christ (Matt. 1:3,5-6). Through these women to whom God extended his forgiveness, Messiah would come. Jesus spoke to women (John 4) and taught them individually and privately (Luke 10:38-42). A company of women often traveled with him (Luke 8:1-3), and he spoke highly of women (Matt. 9:20-22; Luke 21:1-4). He safeguarded the rights of women, especially in his teachings on marriage and divorce (Matt. 5:27-32; 19:3-9). For Jesus to expend time and energy in teaching women indicates that he saw in them not only intellectual acumen but also spiritual sensitivity.

The Kingdom of Christ Scripture affirms that women functioned in the early church with service, influence, leadership, and teaching. Mark's mother Mary and Lydia of Thyatira opened their homes for meetings of believers and practiced hospitality (Acts

12:12; 16:14-15). Paul mentioned Phoebe with favor (Rom. 16:1-2), and he employed women in kingdom service (Phil. 4:3). Priscilla, with her husband Aquila, instructed Apollos in individual ministry (Acts 18:26). Women offered themselves in special ministries to Jesus (John 12:1-11).

Some women are identified as prophetesses: Miriam, who led the women of Israel (Exod. 15:20); Huldah, whose only prophecy in Scripture was to a man who consulted her at home (2 Kgs. 22:14-20); Anna, who prophesied in the temple (Luke 2:36-40); and the daughters of Philip (Acts 21:9). God also reserves the right to interdict history with the unexpected or extraordinary by his own divine fiat, such as calling Deborah to be a judge of Israel (Judg. 4–5).

Paul commended learning for women (1 Tim. 2:11). He exhorted spiritually mature women to instruct the younger women and outlined what they were to teach (Titus 2:3-5). Women are admonished to share the gospel (1 Pet. 3:15), and mothers and fathers are to do lifestyle teaching to their children (Deut. 6:7-9).

WOODWORKER Person who worked with wood in some sense—cutting trees in a forest (1 Kgs. 5:6), bringing the logs to where they were needed (v. 9), building the house and the furniture needed for it (2 Kgs. 22:6), and making beautiful objects of art from wood.

WOOL Thick hair, forming the coat of sheep and some other animals. It was made into thread and used to make clothing, blankets, and other articles. It was one of the major economic factors in Israel and the surrounding countries. Gideon used a piece of wool to determine God's will for his life (Judg. 6:35-40). Wool was also used as a symbol of whiteness and purity (Isa. 1:18).

WORD Utterance or saying that may refer to a single expression, the entire law, the gospel message, or even Christ.

Old Testament *Davar* is the primary Hebrew expression for "word." It has various meanings and can refer to a spoken utterance, a saying, a command, a speech, or a story—linguistic communication in general. *Davar* can also mean a thing, event, or action (Gen. 18:14).

New Testament *Logos* and *rhema* are the two primary Greek words meaning "word." They are used interchangeably and variously as with the OT *davar*. The NT can use these words to apply to Jesus's message, the message about Jesus, and Jesus himself.

Jesus's message of the coming kingdom can be called a "word" (Mark 2:2; 4:33; Luke 5:1), as can his individual sayings (Matt. 26:75; Luke 22:61; John 7:36). Significantly, Jesus avoided citing rabbinic authorities or using the traditional language of a prophet who would claim "that the word of the Lord came to me" or declare "thus says the Lord." Perhaps these phrases did not significantly honor his special relationship with the Father and his own authority (Matt. 11:27; cp. 5:21-26; Mark 3:28-29). As in the OT, so also Jesus's word demanded decision on the part of the hearers (John 8:51; 12:47).

The message concerning Jesus can also be called "a word." Paul spoke of "the word of God that you heard from us" that is mediated by his human words (1 Thess. 2:13 CSB). Jesus himself is the Word—the living Word. The preexistent Word who was with God "in the beginning" has now become flesh (John 1:1-18). Scholars have frequently claimed that John used *logos* in a philosophical sense to refer to the world's controlling rational principle (Stoicism) or to the created intermediary between God and his world (*Philo*). However, John's word is not a principle or divine characteristic. It is a preexistent, life-giving person. John opposed Greek philosophy by arguing that salvation comes not by humankind's escape from this world but by God entering and redeeming creation. More probably *logos* was chosen because of its meaning in the OT, its Greek translation, and contemporary Hebrew literature, where the concepts of "wisdom" and "word" were being spoken of as a distinct manifestation of God. John saw that the same agent of God who gave life in the first creation was also giving life in the new creation inaugurated by Jesus's coming. The creative Word of God became flesh; being divine he embodied divine communication. Now the Word dwells among us revealing the glory of God (John 1:14).

Power of the Word It is often assumed that in Hebrew thought words had a mysterious binding authority. For example, when Isaac discovered he had been deceived and had wrongly given his blessing to Jacob, he declared that his blessing had been given and Jacob would be blessed (Gen. 27:33). Isaac's word seems conclusive—like an arrow once shot, it could not be recalled. Caution must be exercised here. Actually, only God's word has this type of irresistible potency (Isa. 55:11) and absolute creative power (Gen. 1:3-31; Luke 1:32-35; cp. Isa. 9:8; 31:2; 45:23). Most occurrences like Isaac's may be explained in terms of their social custom. Following a prescribed social custom, a person could form a bond, or a will, by speaking a word. Even today a couple can make or create a marriage by saying "I do." We must also note that Scripture teaches that a person's word is often powerless (1 Cor. 2:4; 4:19-20) and frequently fails (Matt. 21:28-32).

Words are capable of great good and great evil (Matt. 12:36; James 3:5-6,8). Words can deeply injure (Prov. 12:18; 18:14) or revive (Prov. 12:18,25; 16:24). Words can have a widespread influence: words from the wicked are like "a scorching fire" (Prov. 16:27-28 CSB); words from the righteous can be "a fountain of life" (Prov. 10:11; 12:14).

WORK, THEOLOGY OF Refers to the significance of work in light of the nature of God. God is a personal being whose manifold activities and works not only bestow blessings upon his creatures, but even infuse the act of work with meaning and divine significance, enjoining upon humans an obligation to engage in work even as God works.

Genesis opens with the image of a working, collaborative Creator, whose primal work constitutes an investment of his creativity, intelligence, words, breath, and "hands" (the image of the Son and Spirit as the two "hands of God" is a later second-century theological development).

God's purpose for humans, who are the pinnacle of his creation, was to work, specifically in Eden, to till the soil (Gen. 2:15) and to manage the garden as good stewards. Despite the perfection of God's creation, human disobedience marred the image of God in them, resulting in a curse on the ground (Gen. 3:17-19). Henceforth, the cooperative relationship between humans and the rest of creation turned work from a pleasant task into toil and hardship. This state will continue until that eschatological time when the curse is lifted and all creation is redeemed (Rom. 8:19-23). In the intervening time, both the OT and NT teach that work (no longer restricted to agriculture but expanded to include business dealings, household obligations, and any employment in which people find themselves) brings to humans a sense of joy, satisfaction, dignity and respect (Eccles. 3–4). God's people are not only to put forth their best efforts to accomplish their tasks; they are also called upon to maintain the highest moral and ethical standards. Transacting business with integrity, working with all diligence, and treating one's employees well are admired and praised (Boaz in Ruth 2:4), while dishonesty, laziness, and slothfulness are abhorred (Prov. 6).

In the NT, creaturely labor is somehow sanctified because the Son of God also worked. Jesus and his disciples exemplified a life of working in various occupations (fishing, carpentry), and through many of his parables Jesus taught kingdom principles by using illustrations involving work (fairness and generosity in dealing with employees: Matt. 18:23-35; 20:1-16; resourcefulness in investing: Matt. 25:14-30; shrewdness and prudence: Luke 16:1-13). In general, the Gospels and the Pauline literature portray work positively and exhort God's people to labor faithfully, honestly, fruitfully and with a view to pleasing God more than earthly masters. Diligence receives praise while idleness draws censure (Eph. 6:5-9; 1 Thess. 2:9; 4:11-12; 2 Thess. 3:6-12).

WORKS Refers to acts, deeds, or accomplishments of both God and human beings. The Gospels asserted that believers demonstrate by good works that God is active in their lives (Matt. 5:16; John 6:28-29; 14:12).

Much debate exists concerning the relationship of faith and works in the salvation process. Paul stated that justification comes from faith alone apart from works (Rom.

4:2-3,9-10; Gal. 3:9-11; Eph. 2:8-9; Phil. 3:7-9). James, however, seems to affirm a closer relationship (James 2:14-24). This apparent contradiction has troubled many, especially Luther, who called James "an epistle of straw" and declared its message to be "flatly against St. Paul and all the rest of Scripture in ascribing justification to works."

There is a credible solution to the apparent contradiction. Paul, often dealing with Jewish legalists, used the term to describe "works of the law," which legalists believed would earn salvation. Paul rejects these "works" as insufficient. However, he freely acknowledged the inevitability of good works by those genuinely converted by faith (Eph. 2:10). Conversely, James's argument is that any "faith" that cannot be seen by the evidence of "works" is not true saving faith (2:14). The definite article in the text (*ha pistis*) indicates James is not speaking of genuine saving faith, but rather of a particular fictitious faith, proven to be such by a lack of good deeds. Paul and James are speaking from two sides of the same coin. Works of the law are insufficient to earn one's salvation, while good works are a natural consequence of saving faith. As Calvin put it: "Faith alone saves, but the faith that saves is not alone!"

WORLD A term that has a number of different meanings in the Bible.

"World" often refers to the universe or the cosmos. Biblical writers often use "world" when talking about the planet earth and more specifically dry land, as opposed to the sea and other bodies of water (notice the three categories: heavens, earth, and sea—Neh. 9:6 and Exod. 20:11).

Humankind was often referred to in Scripture as the "world" or "earth," because humankind is the most important part of God's creation. John 3:16, "God loved the world in this way: He gave his one and only Son" (CSB), that is, the world of human habitation. Sin entered the world of humankind through one man's transgression and brought death with it (Rom. 5:12).

The Scriptures use the term "world" to describe that environment or spirit of evil and enmity toward God and the things of God. It may also refer to those people who manifest this attitude because they do not know Christ. Particularly in John, "world" takes on this sinister meaning.

Scriptures often use "world" as an equivalent to the word "age" denoting a distinction between the temporality of this present evil world (Gal. 1:4; 1 John 2:17; Ps. 102:25-26; 1 Cor. 7:31) and the world to come.

WORM Small, slender, soft-bodied animal without a backbone, legs, or eyes. *Worm* is also used in the Bible as a figure of lowliness or weakness (Ps. 22:6; Job 17:14; Isa. 41:14). Both the OT and the NT speak of the place of the ungodly and unbeliever as being where the worm is always alive and working (Isa. 66:24; Mark 9:44,48).

WORMWOOD Nonpoisonous but bitter plant common to the Middle East. Wormwood often is used in analogy to speak of bitterness and sorrow. OT prophets pictured wormwood as the opposite of justice and righteousness (Amos 5:7; Jer. 23:15). Revelation 8:10-11 describes as wormwood one of the blazing stars that brings destruction.

WORSHIP Term used to refer to the act or action associated with attributing honor, reverence, or worth to that which is considered to be divine by religious adherents. Christian worship is often defined as the ascription of worth or honor to the triune God. Worship is more fully understood as an interrelation between divine action and human response: worship is the human response to the self-revelation of the triune God. This includes (1) divine initiation in which God reveals himself, his purposes, and his will; (2) a spiritual and personal relationship with God through Jesus Christ on the part of the worshiper; and (3) a response by the worshiper of adoration, humility, submission, and obedience to God.

Two central features of Christian worship are the ordinances of baptism (Matt. 28:19; Acts 2:38,41) and the Lord's Supper (Luke 22:19; 1 Cor. 11:17-34). Since there is no order of worship prescribed in the NT, it seems best to conclude that Christian worship should draw from the several models of worship in the Bible while employing the various elements of worship that are more clearly defined in Scripture.

WRATH, WRATH OF GOD Used to express several emotions, including anger, indignation, vexation, grief, bitterness, and fury. It is the emotional response to perceived wrong and injustice. Both humans and God express wrath. When used of God, wrath refers to his absolute opposition to sin and evil. When used of humans, however, wrath is one of those evils that is to be avoided.

God is a personal moral being who is unalterably opposed to evil and takes personal actions against it. Wrath is the punitive righteousness of God by which he maintains his moral order, which demands justice and retribution for injustice. Moreover, God's wrath is inextricably related to the doctrine of salvation. If there is no wrath, there is no salvation. If God does not take action against evil and sinners, there is no danger from which sinners are to be saved. The good news of the gospel is that sinners who justly deserve the wrath of God may be delivered from it. Through the atoning death of Christ, God is propitiated, and his anger is turned away from all those who receive Christ (Rom. 3:24-25). Therefore, those who have faith in Christ's blood are no longer appointed to wrath but are delivered from it and appointed "to obtain salvation" (1 Thess. 1:10; 5:9).

WRITING Human ability to record and communicate information through etching signs on stone or drawing them on skins or papyrus. Present knowledge shows that writing began in the ancient Near East about 3500 BC.

Several writing systems were in use in Syria-Palestine by the time of Moses and Joshua. Many Bible texts refer to Moses being directed to write down accounts of historical events (Exod. 17:14), laws and statutes (Exod. 34:1-9), and the words of the Lord (Exod. 24:4). Joshua wrote on stones a copy of the law of Moses (Josh. 8:32) and later wrote down statutes and ordinances in the book of the law of God (Josh. 24:26). Gideon had a young man of Succoth to write down the names of the 77 officials and elders of that town (Judg. 8:14). Samuel wrote down the rights and duties of kinship (1 Sam. 10:25). David could write his own letter to his general (2 Sam. 11:14). Kings engaged in international correspondence (2 Chron. 2:11). Many references to the chronicles of the kings of Israel and Judah perhaps indicate court diaries or annals (1 Kgs. 14:19). The prophets wrote, or dictated, their oracles (Isa. 8:1,16; 30:8; Jer. 30:1-2; 36:27-28). By at least 800 BC, court scribes were tallying the payment of taxes (cp. the *Samaria Ostraca*). Commemorative and memorial inscriptions were in use (cp. the Siloam inscription and the Siloam tomb inscription). Nehemiah as an official under Persian appointment wrote down the covenant to keep the law of God (Neh. 9:38), to which several men set their seals as witnesses (Neh. 10:1-27).

Similarly, in the NT period literacy was widespread. Jesus could both read (Luke 4:16-21) and write (John 8:6). The writers of the Gospels and Paul wrote in excellent Greek, with Paul regularly using an amanuensis or scribe.

The various kinds of documents and writings mentioned in the Bible were letters (personal and official), decrees (religious and civil), legal documents, deeds of sale, certificates of divorce, family registers, topographical descriptions, and books of scrolls containing laws, court records, and poetic works.

XYZ

The tomb of Xerxes located in the modern state of Iran

XERXES Persian king who reigned 486–464 BC, known in the book of Esther as Ahasuerus. He was the son of Darius the Great and grandson of Cyrus the Great. He campaigned militarily against the Greeks, avenging the loss at Marathon in 490. However, his armada suffered a crippling defeat in the Bay of Salamis in 480.

YAH Shortened form of *Yahweh*, the Hebrew name for the God of the covenant. See *God; Jehovah; Lord; YHWH.*

YEAR OF JUBILEE See *Festivals.*

YELLOW Two Hebrew words are translated "yellow." *Cheruts* (Ps. 68:13) refers to gold strongly alloyed with silver or the sallow color of sick skin (Lev. 13:49). *Tsahov* (Lev. 13:30,32,36) refers to the color of hair in a patch of skin that lets the priest know it is leprous. The basic meaning of *tsahov* is "shining" and represents bright red or gold.

YHWH Known by the technical term *Tetragrammaton* (Gk., meaning "four letters"), these are the four consonants that make up the divine name (Exod. 3:15; found more than 6,000 times in the OT). The written Hebrew language did not include vowels; only the consonants were used; thus readers supplied the vowels as they read (this is true even today in Hebrew newspapers). Reverence for the divine name led to the practice of avoiding its use, lest one run afoul of commandments such as Exod. 20:7 or Lev. 24:16. In time, it was thought that the divine name was too holy to pronounce at all. Thus the practice arose of using the word *Adonai:* "Lord." Many translations of the Bible followed this practice. In most English translations, YHWH is recognizable where the word LORD appears in caps.

A Latinized form of this was pronounced "Jehovah," but it was actually not a real word at all. From the study of the structure of the Hebrew language, most scholars today believe that YHWH was probably pronounced Yahweh (Yah´ weh). See *God.*

YOD Tenth letter of the Hebrew alphabet used as title of Ps. 119:73-80 (KJV, "Jod"), in which all verses begin with this letter.

YOKE Wooden frame placed on the backs of draft animals to make them pull in tandem. The simple yokes consisted of a bar with two loops either of rope or wood that went around the animals' necks. More elaborate yokes had shafts connected to the middle with which the animals pulled plows or other implements. The word is used most often to speak of slavery, bondage, and hardship (1 Kgs. 12:4; Jer. 27:8). Positive usages include the yoke of Christ (Matt. 11:29-30) and the joint nature of the church's work (Phil. 4:3).

An ox and a donkey yoked together and pulling a wooden plow

ZAANAN Place-name, possibly meaning "sheep country" or "outback." Unidentified city in southernmost Judah (Mic. 1:11), probably identical with Zenan (Josh. 15:37).

ZAANANNIM Place-name of uncertain meaning. Town on northeastern corner of tribal allotment of Naphtali near Kadesh (Josh. 19:33; Judg. 4:11). The "plain of Zaanaim" (Judg. 4:11 KJV) is literally translated "great tree in Zaanannim" (NIV) or "oak in Zaanannim" (NASB; note transliterations of REB, NRSV). This probably indicates a "sacred tree" associated with a worship center.

ZAAVAN Personal name meaning "tremble or quake." Son of Ezer (Gen. 36:27).

ZABAD Place-name meaning "he has given" or "gift." **1.** Member of the tribe of Judah (1 Chron. 2:36-37). **2.** An Ephraimite (1 Chron. 7:21). **3.** One of David's 30 elite warriors (1 Chron. 11:41); the first of 21 names the Chronicler appended to a list paralleling that of 2 Sam. 23:24-39. **4.** Assassin of King Joash (2 Chron. 24:26), called Jozacar in 2 Kgs. 12:21. **5.** Three postexilic laymen ordered to divorce their foreign wives (Ezra 10:27,33,43).

ZABBAI Abbreviated personal name, perhaps meaning "pure." **1.** Son of Bebai who promised Ezra he would put away his foreign wife (Ezra 10:28). **2.** Father of Baruch who worked on the wall of Jerusalem with Nehemiah (3:20). 1 and 2, above, may be the same person. The early scribal note (*qere*) in Nehemiah writes the name Zaccai.

ZABBUD Personal name meaning "gift." Descendant of Bigvai who returned to Jerusalem with Ezra after the exile (Ezra 8:14) according to written Hebrew text. Scribal note (*qere*) has Zaccur.

ZABDI Personal name meaning "my gift" or short form of "Yah gives." **1.** Son of Zerah of the tribe of Judah (Josh. 7:1). **2.** Man of the tribe of Benjamin (1 Chron. 8:19). **3.** Man in charge of the wine cellars of David (1 Chron. 27:27). **4.** Son of Asaph who led in thanksgiving and prayer (Neh. 11:17).

ZABDIEL Personal name meaning "God gives gifts" or "my gift is God." **1.** Descendant of David (1 Chron. 27:2). **2.** Overseer in Jerusalem during the time of Nehemiah (Neh. 11:14).

ZABUD Personal name meaning "endowed." Son of Nathan, a priest and Solomon's friend (1 Kgs. 4:5).

ZACCAI Personal name meaning "pure" or "innocent." One whose descendants returned to Jerusalem with Zerubbabel (Ezra 2:9; Neh. 7:14).

ZACCHAEUS or **ZACCHEUS** Greek form of Hebrew name meaning "innocent." A corrupt tax collector in first-century Jericho (Luke 19:2-9). Out of curiosity, he went to hear Jesus. Because of his short stature, he had to climb a tree to catch a glimpse of the Lord. To his surprise, Jesus called him by name to come down and Jesus went home with Zacchaeus. There the official believed and was converted. As a result of his newfound faith, he restored with interest the money he had taken illegally.

ZACCHUR or **ZACCUR** Personal name meaning "well remembered." **1.** Father of Shammua of the tribe of Reuben (Num. 13:4). **2.** Descendant of Mishma of the tribe of Simeon (1 Chron. 4:26). **3.** Descendant of Merari among the Levites (1 Chron. 24:27). **4.** Son of Asaph (1 Chron. 25:2; Neh. 12:35). **5.** Son of Imri who helped Nehemiah rebuild the walls of Jerusalem (3:2). **6.** One who sealed the covenant of reform during the time of Ezra and Nehemiah (10:12). Father of Hanan, one of the treasurers appointed by Nehemiah (13:13).

ZADOK, ZADOKITES Personal name meaning "righteous," a short form of Zedekiah, "the Lord is righteous." See *Zedekiah*. **1.** Son of Ahitub and father of Ahimaaz, descended from Aaron through Eleazar and was a priest in the time of David (2 Sam. 8:17; 1 Chron. 6:3-8). As a reward for Zadok's loyalty to Solomon and as punishment for the sins of Eli's sons, Zadok's descendants (the line of Eliezer) replaced the descendants of Ithamar as the leading priests. The developing role of Jerusalem as the exclusive center of Israel's worship furthered the position of the Zadokites. In later days, Ezekiel declared that the priests who were sons of Zadok were the only faithful ones at the time of the exile, and that they only would be allowed to serve in the ideal future temple. This statement agrees with the genealogies of Chronicles that list only two families as far as the captivity—David of Judah and Zadok the descendant of Aaron through Eleazar. **2.** Grandfather of Jotham, king of Judah (2 Kgs. 15:33). **3-4.** Men who helped Nehemiah rebuild the Jerusalem wall (Neh. 3:4,29). **5.** Leader who signed Nehemiah's covenant (Neh. 10:21). **6.** A faithful scribe whom Nehemiah appointed as a treasurer (Neh. 13:13).

ZAHAM Personal name meaning "fatness" or "loathing." Son of King Rehoboam by Abihail (2 Chron. 11:18-19).

ZAHAR Source of wool traded with Tyre (Ezek. 27:18 NIV; "Sahar," TEV; "Suhar," REB). KJV, CSB, NASB, and RSV translate the Hebrew as "white wool."

ZAIR Place-name that means "small." Place where Joram, king of Judah (853–841 BC), fought with Edom (2 Kgs. 8:20-21). The location of Zair is still in dispute. Some place it south of the Dead Sea near Edom. Others equate it with Zoar (Gen. 13:10) or Zior (Josh. 15:54; cp. 2 Chron. 21:9).

ZALAPH A personal name meaning "caper plant." Father of Hanun, who helped Nehemiah repair the walls of Jerusalem (3:30).

ZALMON Personal name and place-name meaning "little dark one" or "small image." **1.** Mountain near Shechem where Abimelech and his men cut brush with which to burn the tower of Shechem (Judg. 9:48-49). **2.** One of David's 30 mighty men (2 Sam. 23:28). He is also known as Ilai (1 Chron. 11:29). **3.** Psalm 68:14 mentions a "hill of Bashan" named Zalmon (KJV, "Salmon). This may refer to the Golan Heights.

ZALMONAH Place-name meaning "dark" or "shady." Israel's first stop after leaving Mount Hor (Num. 33:41-42). The place cannot be identified.

ZALMUNNA Personal name meaning "protection is withdrawn" or "Zelem (god) rules." King of Midian captured and killed by Gideon (Judg. 8:1-21; Ps. 83:11).

ZAMZUMMIM or **ZAMZUMMITES** (NIV) Name the Ammonites gave to the Rephaim. They lived east of the Jordan River until the Ammonites drove them out (Deut. 2:20).

ZANOAH Place-name meaning "broken district" or "stinking." **1.** Village in Judah identified with Khirbet Zanu about three miles south-southeast of Beth-shemesh (Josh. 15:34). **2.** City in the highlands of Judah (Josh. 15:56), whose identification with Khirbet Zanuta, 10 miles southwest of Hebron or Khirbet Beit Amra, is disputed.

ZAPHENATH-PANEAH or **ZAPHNATH-PAANEAH (KJV)** Personal name meaning "The god has said, he will live." Pharaoh's name for Joseph when he made Joseph second only to himself in Egypt (Gen. 41:45). See *Joseph*.

ZAPHON Place-name meaning "north." **1.** City east of the Jordan River in Gad's territory (Josh. 13:27). **2.** Mountain viewed as home of the gods in Canaanite thought, perhaps referred to in Ps. 48:2 (NIV), Isa. 14:13 (NRSV), and Job 26:7 (NRSV), showing Yahweh controls what Canaan thought their gods possessed.

ZAREPHATH Place-name possibly meaning "smelting, refining." A town on the Mediterranean seacoast just south of Sidon. At God's command, Elijah fled there after prophesying a drought in Israel (1 Kgs. 17:2-9). While in Zarephath, he was hosted by a widow and her son. Although the drought affected the widow's income, too, her supply of meal and oil were miraculously sustained (17:12-16). Elijah also restored her son to life and health (17:17-23).

ZARETH-SHAHAR (KJV) See *Zereth-shahar*.

ZARETHAN or **ZARETAN** (KJV) Place-name, perhaps meaning "cooling." The Jordan River backed up and Israel passed over into Canaan on dry ground near there (Josh. 3:16).

ZARHITE KJV form of Zerahite, descendants of Zerah, one of the twins born to Judah by Tamar (Num. 26:20; cp. 1 Chron. 9:6; Neh. 11:24).

ZATTHU (KJV) or **ZATTU** Head of family who returned to Jerusalem after the exile (Ezra 2:8; Neh. 7:13). Some of the sons of Zattu put away their foreign wives (Ezra 10:27). He seems to be the same as the "Zatthu" who signed the covenant in Nehemiah's time (Neh. 10:14).

ZAYIN Seventh letter of the Hebrew alphabet. Title of Ps. 119:49-56, where each verse begins with this letter.

ZEALOT One who had a "zeal" for a particular cause. The term came to refer to a Jewish segment that sought to overthrow foreign control over Palestine, particularly Roman control. See *Jewish Parties in the New Testament.*

ZEBADIAH Personal name meaning "Yahweh has given." **1.** Son of Beriah (1 Chron. 8:15). **2.** Son of Elpaal (1 Chron. 8:17). **3.** Son of Jehoram of Gedor (1 Chron. 12:7). **4.** A gatekeeper (1 Chron. 26:2). **5.** Fourth captain in David's army (1 Chron. 27:7). **6.** One of nine Levites sent by Jehoshaphat to teach the law in the towns of Judah (2 Chron. 17:8). **7.** Son of Ishmael who ruled civil cases in a court system Jehoshaphat set up (2 Chron. 19:11). **8.** Son of Shephatiah who returned to Jerusalem from Babylon (Ezra 8:8). **9.** Priest who put away his foreign wife in Ezra's time (10:20).

ZEBAH Personal name meaning "slaughter" or "sacrifice." He and Zalmunna were Midianite kings whom Gideon captured and killed because they had killed Gideon's brothers (Judg. 8:4-21; Ps. 83:11; Isa. 9:4; 10:26). This account shows the act of blood revenge that often prevailed in that day and marks a turning point in Israel's struggles against Midian.

ZEBAIM Home of the children of Pochereth (Ezra 2:57) who returned to Jerusalem from Babylonian captivity (KJV).

ZEBEDEE Greek form of Hebrew personal name meaning "gift." A fisherman on the Sea of Galilee and father of James and John, two of Jesus's first disciples (Mark 1:19-20). Based at Capernaum on the north shore of the sea, Zebedee ran a fishing business that included several hired servants, Simon Peter, and Andrew (Luke 5:10). His wife also followed Jesus and ministered to him (Matt. 27:56). The Bible does not say if Zebedee ever became a believer, but he did not stand in the way of his sons or wife becoming Jesus's disciples.

ZEBIDAH Personal name meaning "gift." Daughter of Pedaiah of Rumah and the mother of King Jehoiakim (2 Kgs. 23:36; KJV "Zebudah").

ZEBINA Personal name meaning "purchased." One who had a foreign wife during Ezra's time (Ezra 10:43).

ZEBOIIM Place-name, possibly meaning "hyenas." One of the cities in the Valley of Siddim (Gen. 14:2-3) at the southern end of the Dead Sea. The site probably is under water now. Although the text is not clear, it appears the city was delivered when Abram defeated Chedorlaomer (14:16-17). Zeboiim was destroyed when God sent fire and brimstone on Sodom and Gomorrah (Deut. 29:23; cp. Hos. 11:8). Recent attempts to identify Zeboiim in the Ebla tablets have been hotly debated.

ZEBOIM Place-name meaning "hyenas" or "a wild place." Not to be confused with Zeboiim. **1.** One of the towns the Benjaminites occupied upon returning to Palestine from exile (Neh. 11:34). It may be Khirbet Sabije. **2.** Valley in Benjamin between Michmash and the wilderness overlooking the Jordan River (1 Sam. 13:17-18). It may be Wadi el-Oelt or Wadi Fara.

ZEBUL Personal name meaning "prince" or "captain." Resident of Shechem who was a follower of Abimelech, son of Gideon. When Gaal plotted against Abimelech in Shechem,

Zebul sent word to Abimelech who came to Shechem and defeated Gaal (Judg. 9:30-41).

ZEBULUN Personal and tribal name, probably meaning "elevated dwelling." Jacob's tenth son and sixth by Leah (Gen. 30:20). The tribe named for him settled in the area between the Sea of Galilee and Mount Carmel (Josh. 19:10-16). The tribe hosted the other tribes with religious festivals at Mount Tabor (Deut. 33:18-19). Their menu included the delicacies fished from the Sea of Galilee. Militarily, the tribe distinguished itself in the struggles to possess the land, fighting faithfully in the armies of Deborah and Barak, and Gideon (Judg. 4:6; 6:35).

ZECHARIAH Personal name meaning "Yah (Yahweh) remembered." **1.** Son of Jeroboam II, who reigned over Israel for six months in the year 746 BC until he was assassinated by Shallum (2 Kgs. 15:8-12). See *Israel.* **2.** The prophet Zechariah, who flourished immediately after the exile in 520–518 BC and urged the people of Judah to rebuild the temple. **3.** Grandfather of Hezekiah (2 Kgs. 18:2). **4.** Priest and prophet whom the people stoned and Joash, the king, killed (2 Chron. 24:20-22). **5.** Postexilic gatekeeper of temple (1 Chron. 9:21). **6.** Member of family who lived in Gibeon (1 Chron. 9:37); spelled Zecher in 8:31. **7.** Temple musician (1 Chron. 15:20). **8.** Community leader Jehoshaphat the king sent to teach in the cities of Judah (2 Chron. 17:7). **9.** One of Josiah's overseers in repairing the temple (2 Chron. 34:12). **10–11.** Men who accompanied Ezra on return from Babylon (Ezra 8:3,11). **12.** Man whom Ezra sent to get Levites to return from Babylon (Ezra 8:16). **13.** Israelite with foreign wife (Ezra 10:26). **14.** Man who helped Ezra as he taught the law (Neh. 8:4), perhaps identical with 12 or other one, above. **15.** Ancestor of postexilic resident of Jerusalem (Neh. 11:4). **16.** Ancestor of postexilic resident of Jerusalem (Neh. 11:5). **17.** Ancestor of priest in Nehemiah's day (Neh. 11:12). **18.** Leading priest in time of Joiakim's high priesthood, possibly the same as the prophet (Neh. 12:16). **19–20.** Priestly musicians who helped Nehemiah celebrate (Neh. 12:35,41). **21.** High official Isaiah used as witness, perhaps the same as 3, above. **22.** Son of Jehoshaphat the king whom his brother Jehoram killed upon becoming king (2 Chron. 21:2-4). **23.** Godly adviser of King Uzziah (2 Chron. 26:5). **24.** Descendant of tribe of Reuben (1 Chron. 5:7). **25.** Father of leader of eastern half of tribe of Manasseh

A tomb in Jerusalem which is said by local tradition to be Zechariah's tomb

(1 Chron. 27:21). **26–34.** Levites (1 Chron. 15:18,24; 24:25; 26:2,14; 26:11; 2 Chron. 20:14; 29:13; 35:8). **35.** A priest in Jerusalem and the father of John the Baptist (Luke 1:5-64); also called Zacharias, KJV.

ZECHARIAH, BOOK OF Eleventh of the so-called Minor Prophets. In 538, Cyrus the Great, emperor of the Persian Empire, issued an edict (Ezra 1:2-4; 6:3-5) allowing the Jews in exile in Babylon to return to Jerusalem. Over the next two decades, many exiles took advantage of Persian leniency, returned home, and began to reestablish life in Jerusalem or Judah. Apparently an effort was made to begin rebuilding the temple under an official named Sheshbazzar (Ezra 5:14-16) and perhaps Zerubbabel (Ezra 3:1-13; Zech. 4:9), but the work stopped due to opposition from persons who had not been in exile and from the local officials. Cyrus was succeeded by his son Cambysees, who died in 521 BC with no heir, so the empire was thrown into disarray as two men, Darius I and Gautama, fought for the crown. In the midst of that turmoil, God raised up two prophets, Haggai and Zechariah, to urge the people to finish the temple.

The message of Zechariah may be summarized under two headings: prosperity and purification. Simply put, God promised the people of Judah and Jerusalem prosperity if they purified themselves from sin. This message is found in the first six chapters of the book of Zechariah. Those chapters are written in the form of eight visions, with two messages of exhortation. The structure of the book anticipates the structure of later books called apocalypses, books like Revelation; the book of Zechariah itself is not, however, an apocalypse.

ZEDAD Place-name meaning "a sloping place" or "mountainous." It is Sadad, 62 miles north of Damascus, the northern border of Canaan (Num. 34:8; Ezek. 47:15).

ZEDEKIAH Personal name meaning "Yahweh is my righteousness" or "Yahweh is my salvation." **1.** False prophet who advised King Ahab to fight against Ramoth-gilead, assuring the king of victory (1 Kgs. 22). His prophecy conflicted with that of Micaiah, who predicted defeat. **2.** Last king of Judah (596–586 BC). Zedekiah was made king in Jerusalem by Nebuchadnezzar of Babylon (2 Kgs. 24:17). When he rebelled, the Babylonian army besieged Jerusalem and destroyed it. Zedekiah was taken to Riblah along with his family. At Riblah, he witnessed the executions of his sons before his own eyes were blinded (25:7). Then Zedekiah was taken to Babylon. He apparently died in captivity. **3.** Son either of Jehoiakim or Jeconiah (1 Chron. 3:16), the Hebrew text being unclear at this point. **4.** Signer of Nehemiah's covenant (10:1; spelled Zidkijah by KJV). **5.** Prophet who promised quick hope to exiles in Babylon (Jer. 29:21). Jeremiah pronounced God's judgment on him. **6.** Royal official in Jeremiah's day (36:12).

ZELA or **ZELAH** Place-name meaning "rib, side, slope." Town allotted to Benjamin (Josh. 18:28) in which the bones of Saul and Jonathan were buried (2 Sam. 21:14). The site is probably Khirbet Salah between Jerusalem and Gibeon or else another site in the hills north and west of Jerusalem.

ZELEK Personal name meaning "cleft, fissure." One of David's 30 elite warriors (2 Sam. 23:37; 1 Chron. 11:39).

ZELOPHEHAD Personal name meaning "protection from terror" or "the kinsman is my protector." A Hebrew who wandered in the wilderness with Moses. He had no sons to receive his property and carry on his name, so his daughters pled with Moses to receive a share of inheritance following his death (Num. 26:33; 27:1-4). Despite the inheritance customs that allowed only men to own property, God led Moses to declare the daughters eligible (27:6-7). The only stipulation was that the women had to marry within their own tribe (36:5-9).

ZELOTES KJV transliteration of name for Simon, Jesus' disciple. Modern translations translate as "Zealot."

ZELZAH Unidentified site near Rachel's tomb in the territory of Benjamin, site of the first of three signs that Samuel promised Saul as confirmation of his kingship (1 Sam. 10:1-2).

ZEMARAIM Place-name meaning "twin peaks." **1.** Town allotted to the tribe of Benjamin (Josh. 18:22), likely Ras ex-Zeimara about five miles northeast of Bethel. **2.** Mountain in the territory of Ephraim where Abijah rebuked Jeroboam (2 Chron. 13:4).

ZEMARITES Canaanites inhabiting the area north of Lebanon between Arvad and Tripolis (Gen. 10:18; 1 Chron. 1:16). The Zemarites possibly gave their name to the town Sumra in this region. The town figures in the Tell Amarna letters and in Assyrian records. NRSV emended the text of Ezek. 27:8 to read "men of Zemer" (KJV, "thy wise men, O Tyrus").

ZEMER Place-name meaning "wool." See *Zemarites*.

ZEMIRA or **ZEMIRAH** Personal name meaning "song." Descendant of Benjamin (1 Chron. 7:8).

ZENAN Place-name meaning "flocks." Village in the Shephelah (wilderness) district of Judah (Josh. 15:37), likely identified with 'Araq el-Kharba. Zenan is perhaps identical to Zaanan (Mic. 1:11).

ZENAS Abbreviated form of the personal name Zenodoros meaning "gift of Zeus." Christian lawyer whom Paul asked Titus to send, together with Apollos, on his way, lacking nothing (Titus 3:13). Paul had in mind, no doubt, material provisions for itinerant evangelistic work. Zenas and Apollos perhaps delivered Paul's letter to Titus.

ZEPHANIAH Personal name meaning "Yahweh sheltered or stored up" or "Zaphon (god) is Yahweh." **1.** Prophet whose preaching produced the thirty-sixth book of the OT. **2.** Priest whom King Zedekiah sent asking Jeremiah to pray for the nation threatened by Nebuchadnezzar of Babylon (Jer. 21:1-7; 37:3). He reported false prophecy from Babylon to Jeremiah (29:24-32). When Jerusalem fell, the priest was executed (52:24-27). **3.** Father of Josiah and Hen (Zech. 6:10,14), possibly identical with 2, above. **4.** A Levite (1 Chron. 6:36), perhaps the same as Uriel (1 Chron. 6:24).

ZEPHANIAH, BOOK OF Only three chapters in length, this book looks toward the punishment of all sinful nations, including Judah, followed by the restoration of Judah and the nations as well.

The Prophet Zephaniah The first verse tells all we really know about the prophet. His ancestry is traced back four generations to a man named Hezekiah. Some scholars think Hezekiah was the king of Judah by that name who reigned in the late eighth century during the ministry of Isaiah (2 Kgs. 18–20). If so, Zephaniah would have belonged to the royal line. According to 1:1, Zephaniah's ministry occurred during the reign of Josiah (640–609 BC). Most scholars date the book in 630 or between 630 and 621.

Contents of the Book Zephaniah looked toward a future punishment. In 1:2-6, he predicted punishment upon the whole world, including Jerusalem. The second chapter contains a series of threats against the Philistines (vv. 4-7), the Moabites and Ammonites (vv. 8-11), the Ethiopians (v. 12), and the Assyrians (vv. 13-15). Zephaniah called all nations to repent and become righteous and meek. The third chapter is marked by a change in perspective between verses 7 and 8. God's purpose is expressed in vv. 9–13 to purify from the nations a people united to worship him. Their speech will be cleansed of sinful pride and idolatry (Isa. 2:17–18; 6:5; Hos. 2:17). Terms used of the remnant in v. 13 are used of the Lord in v. 5. It will be a time of right, of truth, and of security (cf. Jer. 50:19; Ezek. 34:14; Mic. 4:4; 7:14).

ZEPHATH Place-name meaning "watchtower." City in southwestern Judah in the vicinity of Arvad. Following their destruction of the city, the tribes of Judah and Simeon renamed the site Hormah (Judg. 1:17).

ZEPHATHAH Place-name meaning "watchtower." Asa met Zerah, the Ethiopian king, in battle "in Zephathah Valley at Mareshah" (2 Chron. 14:10 CSB). The earliest Greek translation translated *Zaphon* as "north" instead of Zephathah. If Zephathah is identified with Safiyah, less than two miles northeast of Beit Jibrin, the valley of Zephathah is the Wadi Safiyah.

ZEPHI or **ZEPHO** Short form of personal name meaning "purity" or "good fortune." Descendant of Esau (1 Chron. 1:36) called Zepho in the parallel passage (Gen. 36:11,15).

ZEPHON Personal name, perhaps meaning "north." Eldest son of Gad and ancestor of the Zephonites (Num. 26:15). The Samaritan Pentateuch and the earliest Greek translation support the identification with Ziphion, son of Gad cited in Gen. 46:16.

ZEPHONITE Member of clan of Zephon.

ZER Place-name meaning "narrow" or "enemy." Fortified town in the territory of Naphtali (Josh. 19:35), possibly identified with Madon, which is conspicuously absent from this list. Commentators often take "Zer" as a copyist's modification, repeating the Hebrew for "fenced cities."

ZERAH Personal name meaning "sunrise." **1.** A twin born to Tamar and her father-in-law, Judah (Gen. 38:30; Zarah, KJV). One of his descendants was Achan, who was executed for taking forbidden war-time spoils (Josh. 7:1,25). Zerah is included in Matthew's genealogy of Christ, although his twin, Perez, was the direct ancestor (1:3). **2.** Descendant of Esau and thus clan leader of Edomites (Gen. 36:13,17). **3.** Ancestor of Edomite ruler (Gen. 36:33). **4.** Clan leader in the tribe of Simeon (Num. 26:13), apparently same as Zohar (Gen. 46:10). **5.** Levite (1 Chron. 6:21,41). **6.** Cushite general God defeated in answer to Asa's prayer about 900 BC (2 Chron. 14:8-13).

ZERAHIAH Personal name meaning "Yahweh has dawned." **1.** Priest descended from Phinehas (1 Chron. 6:6,51; Ezra 7:4). **2.** Descendant of Pahath-Moab ("governor of Moab") and father of Eliehoenai (Ezra 8:4).

ZERAHITES Name of two families, one from the tribe of Simeon (Num. 26:13), the other from the tribe of Judah (Num. 26:20; Josh. 7:17), descended from men named Zerah. Two of David's 30 elite warriors, Sibbecai and Maharai, were Zerahites (1 Chron. 27:11,13).

ZERED River name, perhaps meaning "white thorn." A stream that empties into the southern end of the Dead Sea. Its entire length is only about 38 miles, but it drains a large area of land. Israel crossed the Zered after wandering in the wilderness for 38 years (Deut. 2:13-14).

ZEREDA or **ZEREDAH** Place-name of uncertain meaning. **1.** Site in Ephraim of the home of Jeroboam (1 Kgs. 11:26), possibly identified as Ain Seridah in the Wadi Deir Ballut in western Samaria. **2.** City in the Jordan Valley (2 Chron. 4:17). The parallel text in 1 Kgs. 7:46 reads Zerethan.

ZEREDATHAH (KJV, 2 Chron. 4:17) See *Zereda*.

ZERERAH or **ZERERATH** (KJV) Site on the route by which the defeated Midianites fled from Gideon (Judg. 7:22; KJV, Zererath); possibly a variant rendering of Zarethan (Josh. 3:16; 1 Kgs. 4:12; 7:46) or Zeredah (2 Chron. 4:17).

ZERESH Personal name meaning "shaggy head, disheveled." Haman's wife and counselor (Esth. 5:10,14; 6:13).

ZERETH Personal name, perhaps meaning "splendor." Descendant of Judah (1 Chron. 4:7).

ZERETH-SHAHAR Place-name meaning "splendor of the dawn." The city located "on the hill of the [Dead Sea] valley" was allotted to Reuben (Josh. 13:19).

ZERI Personal name meaning "balsam." Levitical harpist (1 Chron. 25:3). Zeri is possibly a copying variant of Izri (25:11).

ZEROR Personal name meaning "bundle, pouch" or "particle of stone." Ancestor of Saul (1 Sam. 9:1).

ZERUAH Personal name meaning "stricken" or "leprous." Mother of King Jeroboam (1 Kgs. 11:26).

ZERUBBABEL Personal name meaning "descendant of Babel." The grandson of King

Jehoiachin (taken to Babylon in the first exile in 597 BC by Nebuchadnezzar; 2 Kgs. 24:10-17) and the son of Shealtiel (Ezra 3:2), second son of Jehoiachin (1 Chron. 3:16-17). He is named in Ezra 2:2 among the leaders of those who returned from exile. The list in Ezra 2:1-67 (cp. Neh. 7:6-73a) probably names people who returned in 539, the first year of the reign of Cyrus the Great, ruler of the Persian Empire (Ezra 1:1), or between 539 and 529, despite the contention of many American scholars that the list belongs to an unmentioned second return led by Zerubbabel in 521/520.

According to Ezra 3, Zerubbabel and Jeshua (Joshua, the high priest) rebuilt the altar and in their second year (538?) laid the foundation of the temple, but their work was halted by opposition from persons who had remained in Judah during the exile (4:1-6,24). Darius (Persian emperor, 522–486 BC) granted the Jews permission to continue rebuilding the temple (6:1-12). Under the urging of Haggai (Hag. 1:1,12-15; 2:1,20) and Zechariah (Zech. 4:6-10a), Zerubbabel, now governor (Hag. 1:1) in place of Sheshbazzar (Ezra 5:14), resumed the task (Ezra 5:1-2), completed in 515 BC.

Zerubbabel is not mentioned in subsequent narratives.. He was a Davidic prince, so it is possible that the Jews tried to crown him king during the civil war surrounding the rise of Darius as emperor (522/521). Zechariah 6:9-14 may reflect the wish to crown Zerubbabel, but his fate remains unknown.

ZERUIAH Personal name meaning "perfumed with mastix" or "bleed." Sister of David and mother of three of David's generals who were known as the "sons of Zeruiah": Joab, Abishai, and Asahel (2 Sam. 2:18).

ZETHAM Personal name meaning "olive tree." Levite who served as a temple treasurer (1 Chron. 23:8; 26:22).

ZETHAN Personal name meaning "olive tree" or "olive merchant." Member of the tribe of Benjamin (1 Chron. 7:10).

ZETHAR Personal name, perhaps meaning "slayer," "kingdom," or "victor." One of seven eunuchs who served King Ahasuerus of Persia (Esth. 1:10).

ZEUS Greek god of the sky and chief of the pantheon; ruler over all the gods. His devotees believed all the elements of weather were under his control. The worship of Zeus was very prevalent throughout the Roman Empire during the first century. Barnabas was mistaken for Zeus (equivalent of the Roman god Jupiter) by the people of Lystra after Paul healed a crippled man (Acts 14:8-12).

ZIA Personal name meaning "trembling." Head of a family of the tribe of Gad (1 Chron. 5:13).

ZIBA Personal name, perhaps Aramaic for "branch." Servant of Saul. When David desired to show kindness to surviving members of Jonathan's family, Ziba directed David to Mephibosheth (2 Sam. 9:1-8). David placed Ziba in charge of Mephibosheth's restored property (9:9-13). During Absalom's rebellion, Ziba assisted David with supplies and (falsely) accused Mephibosheth of treason (2 Sam. 16:1-4).

ZIBEON Personal name meaning "little hyena." Horite chieftain (Gen. 36:29) and ancestor of one of Esau's wives (Gen. 36:2). Zibeon established kinship between the Horites and Edomites (Gen. 36:20,24,29; 1 Chron. 1:38,40).

ZIBIA Personal name meaning "gazelle." Head of a family of Benjaminites (1 Chron. 8:9).

ZIBIAH Personal name meaning "female gazelle." Mother of King Jehoash (Joash) of Judah (2 Kgs. 12:1; 2 Chron. 24:1).

ZICHRI or **ZICRI** (NIV) Personal name meaning "remembrance, mindful." **1.** Levite in Moses's time (Exod. 6:21). **2.** Heads of three families of Benjaminites (1 Chron. 8:19,23,27). **3.** Levite (1 Chron. 9:15), perhaps identical to Zaccur (1 Chron. 25:2,10; Neh. 12:35) and Zabdi (Neh. 11:17). **4.** Descendant of Moses assisting with David's treasury (1 Chron. 26:25). **5.** Reubenite (1 Chron. 27:16). **6.** Father of one of Jehoshaphat's army commanders (2 Chron. 17:16). **7.** Father of one of Jehoiada's generals (2 Chron. 23:1). **8.** Ephraimite warrior assisting Pekah in the elimination of Ahaz's family and advisers (2 Chron. 28:7). **9.** Father of the leading Benjaminite in postexilic Jerusalem (Neh. 11:9). **10.** Postexilic priest (Neh. 12:17).

A reconstruction of a ziggurat dating (to the Babylonian period (605–550 BC)

ZIDDIM Place-name meaning "sides." Fortified town in Naphtali (Josh. 19:35), perhaps identical with Hattin el-Qadim about eight miles west-northwest of Tiberias. Some commentators see it as copyist's repetition of "fenced cities."

ZIDKIJAH (KJV, Neh. 10:1) See *Zedekiah*.

ZIDON, ZIDONIANS KJV alternate forms of Sidon and Sidonians.

ZIGGURAT Stepped building, usually capped by a temple. The architecture was made popular by the Babylonians. The design consisted of placing smaller levels of brick on top of larger layers. Those so far excavated reveal advanced building techniques used by ancient civilizations. Most biblical scholars believe the tower of Babel was a ziggurat (Gen. 11:3-9).

The ziggurat, or temple tower, located at Ur in ancient Mesopotamia (modern Iraq)

ZIHA Egyptian personal name meaning "the face of Horus (god) has spoken." **1.** Family of temple servants (*nethinim*) (Ezra 2:43; Neh. 7:4,6). **2.** Overseer of postexilic temple servants (Neh. 11:21).

ZIKLAG City in tribal inheritance of Judah given to Simeon (Josh. 15:31; 19:5). Ziklag appears to have belonged to the Philistines and was taken by Israel during the time of Israel's judges (1 Sam. 27:6). The town was given to David by Achish, king of Gath, during David's "outlaw" period. The gift may have been a means of shortening Philistia's over-extended borders. Ziklag appears never to have been a part of Philistia proper.

ZILLAH Personal name meaning "shadow." Second wife of Lamech and mother of Tubal-Cain and Naamah (Gen. 4:19,22-23).

ZILLETHAI Personal name; an abbreviated form of "Yahweh is a shadow," that is, a protector. **1.** Family of Benjaminites (1 Chron. 8:20). **2.** Manassite supporter of David at Ziklag (1 Chron. 12:20).

ZILPAH Personal name, perhaps meaning "short-nosed." Leah's maid (Gen. 29:24; 46:18), given to Jacob as a concubine (30:9; 37:2); mother of Gad and Asher, who were regarded as Leah's sons (30:10,12; 35:26).

ZILTHAI (KJV) See *Zillethai*.

ZIMMAH, ZIMNAH (TEV) Personal name; perhaps an abbreviation of "Yahweh has considered or resolved." A Levite (1 Chron. 6:20,42; 2 Chron. 29:12).

ZIMRAN Personal name meaning "celebrated in song, famous" or "mountain goat." Son of Abraham and Keturah and ancestor of an Arabian tribe (Gen. 25:2; 1 Chron. 1:32), possibly identified with Zabram, located somewhere west of Mecca on the Red Sea, and with Zimri (Jer. 25:25).

ZIMRI Short form of personal name meaning "Yah helped," "Yah is my protection," or "Yah is my praise." **1.** Son of Zerah and grandson of Judah (1 Chron. 2:6). **2.** Chariot captain in Israel who usurped the throne by killing Elah (1 Kgs. 16:9-10). **3.** Leader of tribe of Simeon slain by Phinehas for bringing Midianite woman into the wilderness camp (Num. 25). **4.** Descendant of Saul (1 Chron. 8:36). **5.** A difficult name of a nation God judged (Jer. 25:25), often taken as a copying change from the Hebrew for Cimmerians or a coded designation for Elam clarified by the immediate mention of Elam. Nothing is known of a nation of Zimri.

ZIN, WILDERNESS OF Rocky desert area through which Israel passed en route from Egypt to Canaan (Num. 20:1; 27:14; 33:36). The Wilderness of Zin, stretching from Kadesh-barnea to the Dead Sea, formed part of the southern border of Canaan and later Judah (Num. 34:3-4; Josh. 15:1,3). The Wilderness of Zin should be distinguished from the Wilderness of Sin, which embraces the western Sinai plateau.

ZION Transliteration of the Hebrew and Greek words that originally referred to the fortified hill of pre-Israelite Jerusalem between the Kedron and Tyropean Valleys. Scholars disagree as to the root meaning of the term. Some authorities have suggested that the word was related to the Hebrew word that meant "dry place" or "parched ground." Others relate the word to an Arabic term that is interpreted as "hillcrest" or "mountainous ridge."

The name "Zion" was mentioned first in the account of David's conquest of Jerusalem

An overview of the Canaanite/Jebusite Jerusalem. Notice the "stepped-stone structure" in the center of the photograph. One view is that this is "the stronghold of Zion."

(2 Sam. 5:6-10; 1 Chron. 11:4-9). The most common usage of "Zion" was to refer to the city of God in the new age (Isa. 1:27; 28:16; 33:5).

Zion was understood, also, to refer to the heavenly Jerusalem (Isa. 60:14; Heb. 12:22; Rev. 14:1), the place where the Messiah would appear at the end of time. The glorification of the messianic community will take place on the holy mountain of "Zion."

ZIOR Place-name meaning "smallness." Village allotted to Judah, located in the hill country near Hebron (Josh. 15:54). Archaeological research indicates that the frequently suggested site Si'ir about five miles north-northeast of Hebron was uninhabited before AD 400.

ZIPH Personal name and place-name, perhaps meaning "flowing." **1.** Son of Mareshah and grandson of Caleb (1 Chron. 2:42). The text perhaps means Mareshah was the founder of Ziph near Hebron. **2.** Family of the tribe of Judah (1 Chron. 4:16). **3.** Town in the Judean hill country (Josh. 15:24), likely Tell Zif about three miles southeast of Hebron. **4.** Town in the Negev (Josh. 15:24), likely Khirbet ez-Zeifeh, southwest of Kurnub.

ZIPHAH Clan name, perhaps meaning "flowing." Family of the tribe of Judah (1 Chron. 4:16).

ZIPHIMS KJV alternate form of Ziphites (superscription of Ps. 54). See *Ziph*.

ZIPHRON Place-name, perhaps meaning "fragrance." Site on the northern border of Canaan, near Hazar-enan (Num. 34:9). It may be modern Zapherani, southeast of Restan between Hamath and Homs.

ZIPPOR Personal name meaning "(little) bird." Father of King Balak of Moab (Num. 22:2,4,10).

ZIPPORAH Personal name meaning "small bird" or "sparrow." Moses's first wife (some believe the woman named in Num. 12:1 may be a reference to Zipporah, too) and mother of his children, Gershom and Eliezer (Exod. 2:21-22; 18:4). She was one of the daughters of Reuel, a priest of Midian. By circumcising Gershom, she saved Moses's life when the Lord sought to kill him (4:24-25). It appears that Zipporah stayed with her father until Moses had led the people out of Egypt (18:2-6).

ZITHER Stringed instrument composed of 30 to 40 strings placed over a shallow soundboard and played with a pick and fingers (Dan. 3:5,7,10,15 NASB margin).

ZIV Second month of calendar (1 Kgs. 6:1).

ZIZ Place-name meaning "blossom." Site involved in Judah's battle plans with Ammon and Moab (2 Chron. 20:16). A pass through a steep place where the people of Ammon, Moab, and Mount Seir were going to enter Judah to attack King Jehoshaphat. It is often located at Wadi Hasasa, southeast of Tekoa near the Dead Sea. The Lord won this battle for his people without their fighting (vv. 22-30), causing surrounding nations to fear God.

ZIZA or **ZIZAH** Personal name meaning "shining" or "brightness." **1.** Son of Shiphi who was a part of the expansion of the tribe of Simeon into Gedor (1 Chron. 4:37). **2.** Son of Shimei, a Levite from Gershon, following some manuscript and early translation evidence (1 Chron. 23:10). "Zina" is the reading of KJV, NASB, REB following Hebrew text. **3.** One of Rehoboam's sons by Maachah (2 Chron. 11:20).

ZOAN Hebrew name for Egyptian city of Tanis located at San el-Hagar on the Tanitic arm of the Nile. Zoan became capital of Egypt about 1070 BC under Smendes I and remained so until 655 BC. Numbers 13:22 notes that Hebron was seven years older than Zoan, but the exact date when either was built is not known. The prophets used Zoan to refer to the Egyptian government and its activities (Isa. 19:11,13; 30:4; Ezek. 30:14). The psalmist praised God for exodus miracles near there (Ps. 78:12,43).

ZOAR Place-name meaning "small." One of the cities in the Valley of Siddim, also known as Bela (Gen. 14:2). It was attacked by Chedolaomer but apparently delivered by

Abraham (14:17). Lot fled to Zoar with his family just before God destroyed Sodom and Gomorrah (19:23-24).

ZOBA(H) City-state name, perhaps meaning "battle." First Saul (1 Sam. 14:47), then David (2 Sam. 8:3) fought the kings of Zobah (cp. title of Ps. 60). Zobah seems to be roughly where Syria later became a nation, northeast of Damascus.

ZOBEBAH Personal name of uncertain meaning. Descendant of Judah (1 Chron. 4:8; NIV "Hazzobebah").

ZOHAR Personal name, perhaps meaning "witness." **1.** Hittite (Gen. 23:8; 25:9). **2.** Son of Simeon (Gen. 46:10; Exod. 6:15), also called Zerah (Num. 26:13; 1 Chron. 4:24). **3.** Descendant of Judah according to the traditional marginal correction (*Qere*) at 1 Chron. 4:24. The Hebrew text reads *Izhar*.

ZOHELETH Place-name meaning "creeping one," "sliding," or "serpent stone." Stone of sacrifice where Adonijah offered sacrifices in light of his coming coronation as king (1 Kgs. 1:9). This place was near En-rogel, a spring or well near Jerusalem where the Kidron Valley and the Valley of Hinnom meet. Adonijah's bid for the throne was short lived. David named Solomon to follow him on the throne (vv. 29-30).

ZOHETH Personal name of uncertain meaning. Son of Ishi (1 Chron. 4:20) and the head of one of the families in Judah.

ZOPHAH Personal name, perhaps meaning "jug." Family in the tribe of Asher (1 Chron. 7:35-36).

ZOPHAI Personal name, perhaps meaning "honeycomb." Son of Elkanah (1 Chron. 6:26).

ZOPHAR Personal name of uncertain meaning. One of Job's three friends who came to sit with him in his misery (2:11). Zophar probably was the youngest of the three since he is mentioned last. He was the sharpest critic of the three men and was more philosophical in his criticism of Job. His words were more coarse and his dogmatism more emphatic. Although there was a place called Naamah in Judah (Josh. 15:41), doubt remains that it was Zophar's home.

ZOPHIM Place-name meaning "watchers" or common noun meaning "the Field of the Watchers" (REB) or lookout post. It was a high place at the top of Pisgah, near the northeastern end of the Dead Sea. Balak took Balaam there to curse the Israelites (Num. 23:14).

ZORAH Place-name meaning "wasps" or "hornets." City of Dan (Josh. 19:41) about 13 miles west of Jerusalem on the border with Judah (Josh. 15:33; KJV, "Zoreah"). It was the home of Manoah, Samson's father (Judg. 13:2). Rehoboam, king of Judah, strengthened Zorah in case of war (2 Chron. 11:5-12). It is modern Sarah.

ZORATHITES Descendants of Shobal who lived in Zorah (1 Chron. 2:52-53).

ZOROASTER Ancient Iranian prophet after whom a religion called Zoroastrianism was named. See *Persia*.

ZOROBABEL (KJV, Matt. 1:12-13; Luke 3:27) See *Zerubbabel*.

ZUAR Personal name meaning "young" or "small." Member of the tribe of Issachar (Num. 1:8; 2:5; 7:18,23; 10:15).

ZUPH Personal name and place-name meaning "honeycomb." **1.** Levitic ancestor of Elkanah and Samuel (1 Sam. 1:1; 1 Chron. 6:16,26,35) from Ephraim. He is called a Levite in another passage (1 Chron. 6:16,26,35). **2.** "Land of Zuph" where Saul was looking for some donkeys (1 Sam. 9:5). Its exact location is not known.

ZUR Personal name meaning "rock." **1.** Midianite tribal chief (Num. 25:15 CSB, NIV) whose daughter, Cozbi, was killed along with an Israelite man by Phinehas. Zur was later killed in a battle Moses led (Num. 31:7-8). **2.** King Saul's uncle (1 Chron. 8:30; 9:36).

ZURIEL Personal name that may mean "God is a rock." Son of Abihail and head of the Merari family of Levites (Num. 3:35).

ZURISHADDAI Personal name meaning "Shaddai is a rock." The father of Shelumiel, a leader of the tribe of Simeon, in the wilderness wanderings (Num. 1:6).

ZUZIM or **ZUZITE** (NIV) National name of uncertain meaning. People who lived in Ham and were defeated by Chedorlaomer (Gen. 14:5). They are apparently called the Zamzummin in Deut. 2:20.

ART CREDITS

Holman Bible Publishers expresses deep gratitude to the following persons and institutions for use of the graphics in this book. Where we have inadvertently failed to give proper credit for any graphic used in this book, please contact us (bhcustomerservice@lifeway.com) and we will make the required correction on the next printing.

PHOTOGRAPHS

Museum Abbreviations

JAC = Joseph A. Calloway Archaeological Museum, The Southern Baptist Theological Seminary, Louisville, Kentucky
MGV = Museum of Giula Villa, Rome Italy
NMN = Naples Museum, Naples, Italy
TLP = The Louvre, Paris, France

Photographers

Arnold, Nancy, Freelance Photographer, Nashville, Tennessee: pages 233, 291, 310, 360 lower right, 470.

Biblical Illustrator: page 357.

Biblical Illustrator **(James McLemore, photographer), Nashville, Tennessee:** pages 49, 56, 96, 133, 236 top, 276, 272, 290 middle left, 332 lower, 359.

Biblical Illustrator **(David Rogers, photographer), Nashville, Tennessee:** pages 18, 27, 39, 62, 194, 196 top, 196 bottom, 208 (TLP), 248 lower left, 265, 267 left, 283, 308 middle right, 270 lower right, 356 middle right, 284 lower right, 366, 400, 411 (JAC), 415, 416, 420, 441, 480.

Biblical Illustrator **(Bob Schatz, photographer), Nashville, Tennessee:** pages 4, 8, 26 middle right, 42, 87, 104, 148 right, 164 right, 171, 172, 182, 183, 192, 195, 209, 246, 253, 292, 311 upper left, 406 upper left, 417.

Biblical Illustrator **(Ken Touchton, photographer), Nashville, Tennessee:** pages 22 lower left, 66, 70, 99, 93, 96, 145, 140, 148 left, 149, 155 left, 156, 128, 170, 175, 187, 194 left, 197, 235, 241, 279, 287, 248, 320, 359, 365 upper right, 393, 405, 406 lower left, 426, 444,

Brisco, Thomas V., Dean and Professor of Biblical Backgrounds and Archaeology, Logsdon School of Theology, Hardin-Simmons University, Abilene, Texas: pages 28, 47, 108, 121, 100, 155, 255, 289, 311 lower right, 321, 312, 317, 336, 337, 338 upper, 338 lower, 451 upper left, 456, 457, 500.

Corel Images: page 239.

Couch, Ernie, Graphics Consultant, Nashville, Tennessee: page 344.

Ellis, C. Randolph, M.D., General Practice, Surgery, and Anesthesiology, Malvern, Arkansas: pages 346, 389.

Illustrated World of the Bible: page 306.

Langston, Scott, Associate Professor of Biblical Studies, Southwest Baptist University, Bolivar, Missouri: pages 65, 248 lower right, 229, 280 lower left, 330 middle right, 451, 476 upper left, 481 left.

Scofield Collection, E.C. Dargan Research Library, LifeWay Christian Resources, Nashville, Tennessee: pages 4, 35, 62, 53, 72, 92, 94 upper, 104, 129, 130, 142, 145, 146, 154, 158, 170 bottom, 214, 217, 228, 270 lower, 293, 308 lower left, 309 upper, 360 upper left, 361 upper left, 369, 393, 400, 417, 433 upper right, 472, 473, 476 lower right, 483, 490 upper, 490 lower, 494.

Southwestern Baptist Theological Seminary, A. Webb Roberts Library, Fort Worth, Texas: page 1.

Stephens, Bill, Retired Senior Curriculum Coordinator, LifeWay Christian Resources, Nashville, Tennessee: pages 243, 257, 267 right, 270 upper, 288, 299, 304, 316 (MGV), 331 (MGV), 334, 338, 339, 342, 343, 371, 376, 407 (NMN—The Farnese Collection), 418, 434 upper, 445, 462, 474 lower.

Tolar, William B., Retired Distinguished Professor of Biblical Backgrounds, Southwestern Baptist Theological Seminary, Fort Worth, Texas: pages 91, 123, 151, 190, 248 top, 262, 277, 259, 279, 297 lower left, 422, 423, 449 upper, 450 middle, 465, 499 upper.

ILLUSTRATIONS AND RECONSTRUCTIONS

***Biblical Illustrator*, Linden Artist, London, England:** page 12.

Latta, Bill, Latta Art Services, Mt. Juliet, Tennessee: pages 24, 234, 299 upper, 236, 351, 435 lower, 436, 443, 477, 478, 482, 499 lower.